WILLIAM WILBERFORCE

WILLIAM WILBERFORCE

The Life of
the Great Anti-Slave Trade
Campaigner

—◦◉◦—

WILLIAM HAGUE

HARCOURT, INC.

Orlando   Austin   New York   San Diego   London

www.HarcourtBooks.com

First published in Great Britain by HarperCollins*Publishers*

Library of Congress Cataloging-in-Publication Data
Hague, William, 1961–
William Wilberforce : the life of the great anti-slave trade
campaigner / William Hague. — 1st U.S. ed.
p. cm.
"First published in Great Britain by
HarperCollinsPublishers"—T.p. verso.
Includes bibliographical references and index.
1. Wilberforce, William, 1759–1833. 2. Legislators—Great Britain
—Biography. 3. Abolitionists—Great Britain—Biography.
4. Philanthropists—Great Britain—Biography.
5. Great Britain—Politics and government—1760–1820.
6. Great Britain—Politics and government—1820–1830. I. Title.
DA522.W6H34 2008
326.092—dc22
[B]   2007045981
ISBN 978-0-15-101267-1

Text set in PostScript Linotype Minion

Printed in the United States of America
First U.S. edition
A C E G I K J H F D B

For Ffion

CONTENTS

ILLUSTRATIONS

(*The Slave Ship*) by J.M.W. Turner, 1840. *(Museum of Fine Arts, Boston, Henry Lillie Pierce Fund (99.22). © 2007 Museum of Fine Arts, Boston/ Bridgeman Art Library)*

The 'Wilberforce Oak' at Holwood, Kent. *(Wilberforce House, Hull City Museums and Art Galleries)*

The Old Palace Yard by Thomas Malton. *(The British Museum, Prints and Drawings – 1958,0712.357)*

Wilberforce's daily assessments of how he had spent his time were mercilessly accurate and self-critical. *(Bodleian Library, Oxford – Mss Wilberforce b.2 f.10)*

Wilberforce, aged twenty-nine, by John Rising. *(Wilberforce House, Hull City Museums and Art Galleries/Bridgeman Art Library)*

The diagram of the *Brookes*, showing how 482 slaves could be crammed into a small ship. *(Library of Congress, Washington D.C., USA/Bridgeman Art Library)*

Thomas Clarkson. Portrait by A.E. Chalons. *(Wilberforce House, Hull City Museums and Art Galleries/Bridgeman Art Library)*

Illustration from Thomas Clarkson's *The History of the African Slave Trade by Parliament*, Vol. I, 1808.

Josiah Wedgwood's classic medallion showing a kneeling slave in chains became the emblem of the abolitionists. *(The Wedgwood Museum, Barlaston)*

Granville Sharp. Engraving, 1806, by Charles Turner after a portrait by Lemuel Francis Abbott. *(Guildhall Art Gallery, City of London/Bridgeman Art Library)*

James Stephen, painted and engraved by John Linnell. *(National Portrait Gallery, London)*

Zachary Macaulay, c.1800, founder of the Anti-Slavery Society. *(Hulton Archive/Getty Images)*

The Clapham group, gathered in the library at Battersea Rise. *(Private collection. Photograph: Photographic Survey, Courtauld Institute of Art)*

The Abolition of the Slave Trade by Isaac Cruikshank. *(Library of Congress, Prints and Photographs Division. Reproduction number LC-USZC4–6204)*

Barbarities in the West Indias, by Gillray, 1791. *(Courtesy of the Warden and Scholars of New College, Oxford/Bridgeman Art Library)*

Charles James Fox. Portrait by by Sir Thomas Lawrence. *(Private collection/Bridgeman Art Library)*

William Pitt the Younger. Portrait by John Hoppner. *(Private Collection/ Bridgeman Art Library)*

The storming of the Bastille in Paris on 14 July 1789. Artist unknown. *(The Art Archive/Musée Historique Lorrain Nancy/Dagli Orti)*

The town of Cap-Français, Saint-Domingue, in flames, 22 August 1791. French School, 1795. *(Private collection/Bridgeman Art Library)*

A living slave suspended by the ribs in Surinam in 1796. Illustration by William Blake from *Narrative of a Five Years' Expedition against the Revolted Negroes of Surinam* by John Gabriel Stedman (London, 1796). *(The British Library/HIP/Topfoto)*

After years of bloody warfare French troops were never able to regain control of Saint-Domingue, leading to the creation of independent Hayti. *(Bettmann/Corbis)*

Barbara Wilberforce. Portrait by John Russell. *(Private collection)*

Gore House, Kensington. *(Photograph by John Rogers © the Royal Borough of Kensington & Chelsea Libraries and Arts Service)*

Philanthropic Consolations after the loss of the Slave Bill by Gillray, 1796. *(Library of Congress, Prints and Photographs Division. Reproduction number LC-USZC4–8775)*

The Weather Cock of St Stephen's, 1795, by James Sayers. *(Private collection/ Bridgeman Art Library)*

A procession at Wootton Bassett in Wiltshire celebrates the end of the British slave trade. *(The Art Archive/Eileen Tweedy)*

William Wyndham Grenville. Portrait by John Hoppner, c. 1800. *(National Portrait Gallery, London)*

The *Antonio* takes on slaves in the Bonny River, West Africa. Coloured lithograph by T.C. Dutton after N.M. Condy. *(National Maritime Museum, Greenwich)*

Gillray's *Sketch of the Interior of St Stephen's, as it now stands*, 1802. *(National Portrait Gallery, London)*

The 'trial' of Queen Caroline in the House of Lords, by Sir George Hayter. *(National Portrait Gallery, London)*

Henry Brougham. Portrait (replica) by James Lonsdale, 1821. *(National Portrait Gallery, London)*

Wilberforce in 1820. Mezzotint by William Say, after Joseph Slater. *(National Portrait Gallery, London)*

William Wilberforce Junior, Wilberforce's first son, whose disastrous venture into farming destroyed the family fortune. *(Hulton Archive/Getty Images)*

Wilberforce in the last year of his life, painted by George Richmond, 1833. *(National Portrait Gallery, London)*

ACKNOWLEDGEMENTS

I had already embarked upon the writing of this book when I returned to front-line politics in December 2005, and the challenge represented by the completion of it has made me particularly grateful for all the assistance I have received. The work of my indefatigable researcher, Elana Cheah, has been indispensable to me. She has bravely combined working for me part-time as one of my parliamentary researchers with working for me privately on this book. No event or document has proved too obscure for her to find, and she has unfailingly made helpful and perceptive suggestions about each chapter as it has emerged.

We have received expert help and advice from many libraries and record offices, including the House of Commons Library – especially Corie Chambers, Catherine Blair and Andrew Parker; the British Library; the Bodleian Library, Oxford; Cambridge University Library; the North Yorkshire Record Office; Sheffield Archives; Hampshire Record Office; Northamptonshire Record Office; the Centre for Kentish Studies; Lambeth Palace Library; Liverpool Record Office; Bury Record Office; the East Riding of Yorkshire Archives Service and the National Archives of Scotland.

I am grateful, as ever, for the encouragement of my literary agent, Michael Sissons, and of the excellent team I have worked with at HarperCollins, most particularly Richard Johnson, Robert Lacey, Caroline Hotblack and Helen Ellis. Two authors of earlier biographies of Wilberforce, the Reverend John Pollock and Kevin Belmonte, have been generous with their time and advice, showing a solidarity among Wilberforcean authors of which our subject would have strongly approved. Historical expertise has also been available to me in the form of James Walvin, who read and commented on the text, and Brian

Edwards, who, with a specialist knowledge of Evangelical history, cast his eye over Chapter 4.

Further assistance has come from Vanessa Salter at the Wilberforce House Museum in Hull; Marylynn Rouse of the John Newton Society, who supplied copies of the correspondence between Wilberforce and Newton; Viscount Sidmouth, who arranged for me to have a copy of a letter from Wilberforce to his distinguished ancestor; Sebastian Wilberforce, who enthusiastically offered many suggestions; and Jean Wrangham, my constituent and friend, who supplied a number of books and documents in her possession. To me, one of the pleasures of writing a book is the excuse it provides to acquire a large number of old and unloved volumes, whose value to a writer of history is nonetheless very great indeed, and for some years I have been able to rely on Robert and Agnes Ronald at A&R Booksearch to track down somewhere in the world any book that I have wished to buy.

My wife Ffion has tolerated with good humour my complete preoccupation either with events of the present day or with those of two hundred years ago, which has sometimes left very little space for anything else. More than that, she has shown a lively interest in what I have been writing, and made valuable comments on the text.

Finally, while I am indebted to all of the above, the responsibility for any mistakes, misunderstandings or omissions very much rests with me.

William Hague
February 2007

PROLOGUE

An observer of the House of Commons that Monday afternoon, 23 February 1807, might have thought it a day like any other: the Members walking in and out in the middle of predictable speeches, others sitting facing each other on the tiered green benches, all giving off the hubbub of gossip which was a sure sign that they were waiting for something important and were not enthused by the proceedings before it.

There was, after all, no shortage of subjects for the Members to discuss as they watched and waited. The government of Lord Grenville was at such an impasse in its relations with King George III that its fall from power could be imminent, and the war with France, which over fourteen years had cost tens of thousands of lives and added £350 million to the national debt, seemed deadlocked. If national crisis and European conflict were not enough for them there was plenty of drama closer to home: that morning, at the hanging at Newgate of three convicted murderers, Messrs Holloway and Haggerty and Elizabeth Godfrey, the attendant crowd of twenty thousand had become so tightly packed that thirty spectators had died in the crush. No wonder the MPs that afternoon seemed to pay little attention to the tedious routine of their chamber: a complaint against the Sandwich Road Bill, a committee seeking to take evidence in Ireland, a short debate on the Poor Laws Bill, an alteration of the general election result in Chippenham, all typical of the daily fare of the House of Commons at the beginning of the nineteenth century. Only after all these matters had been considered did the Speaker call for the business that was keenly awaited on the floor of the House and in the public gallery, and ask the Secretary of State for Foreign Affairs, Lord Howick, to move the second reading of the Slave Trade Abolition Bill.

The slave trade had been debated in the same chamber and by many of the same people for nearly two decades. Year after year the evils of the trade, 'founded in robbery, kidnapping and murder, and affording an incentive to the worst passions and crimes',[1] as Lord Howick was soon to refer to it, had been brought before the attention of MPs. Year after year the Bills proposed had been rebuffed, delayed, abandoned amidst the lengthy taking of interminable evidence or brusquely thrown out in the House of Lords. Once again that Monday afternoon the arguments were deployed. The abolition of the trade would lead to the better treatment of slaves already in the West Indies; the great ports of Liverpool and Bristol were not remotely dependent on it; and most of all, the House of Commons could no longer accept the principle 'that British subjects are allowed to tear by violence from their home their fellow creatures, to take them from their family, and from their friends, to convert them from free men into slaves, and to subject them for the remainder of their lives to the arbitrary will and wanton caprice of others'.[2] Once again, as afternoon wore on into evening and the candles were lit around the chamber for a sitting long into the night, the House had to endure the arguments to the contrary. There was General Gascoyne, the Member for Liverpool and 'conservative to the backbone', drawing attention to the capital invested in forty thousand tons of shipping and the employment of four thousand seamen. He warned of mass insurrection among the slaves if the Bill were carried. There was Mr Bathurst of Bristol calling for a tax on the importation of Negroes rather than total abolition, for 'sufficient notification had not been given'.[3] There was George Hibbert of London, who had twenty-five years' experience of investments in Jamaica, arguing that Africa had 'invited' the slave trade rather than 'the slave trade seduced Africa'.[4] For those who had longed for Britain to take the lead in removing 'one of the greatest sources of crimes and sufferings ever recorded in the annals of mankind',[5] the arguments deployed were a heartrending reminder of the defeats and disappointments of the past.

Yet on this night there was one crucial difference, and everyone present knew it. The Bill would be passed, not merely by a small margin but by a huge one; not then passed into oblivion but this time enacted within a few weeks as the law of His Majesty's Kingdom and all of his Islands, Colonies, Dominions, and Territories. A nation which had transported over three million Africans across the Atlantic and invested vast sums in doing so would, from 1 May that year, outlaw such a trade and declare any vessel fitted out for it to be forfeit. The Royal Navy, the most powerful on earth, which had henceforth protected that trade, would from that day enforce its annihilation.

This Bill would finally succeed in abolishing the practices of decades and changing the behaviour of an Empire, and the MPs, still in their seats as midnight came on, now knew it. For unlike its predecessors, it came with the full force of a united ministry behind it and had already been passed by the House of Lords, for all the fulminations of the future King, the Duke of Clarence. Its passage would be hailed by the Prime Minister himself as the 'most glorious measure that had ever been adopted by any legislative body in the world',[6] while the veteran campaigner Granville Sharp would drop to his knees in prayer and thanksgiving: the dam which had held back twenty years of anger, revulsion, education, petitioning, campaigning and parliamentary struggle had finally burst.

When four o'clock in the morning came the Members were still there in force, and in voting 283 for the Ayes and only sixteen for the Noes they would render the close or negative votes of earlier years hard to believe. Yet before they did so, speaker after speaker would single out one of their number as the architect of the victory to come; one who had found twenty years before that the trade was 'so enormous, so dreadful, so irremediable' that he had 'from this time determined that I would never rest till I had effected its abolition';[7] one whose speech against the trade in 1789 was, according to the great Edmund Burke, 'not excelled by anything to be met with in Demosthenes';[8] and one who through all the dark years of war and revolution since then had persisted in the face of heavy defeats, gnawing and nagging his way to an objective he believed had been set before him by God.

Sir John Doyle referred to 'the unwearied industry' of this man, and 'his indefatigable zeal . . . which washed out this foul stain from the pure ermine of the national character'. Lord Mahon said his 'name will descend to the latest posterity, with never fading honour', and Mr Walter Fawkes said he looked 'with reverence and respect' to a man who has 'raised a monument to his fame, founded on the basis of universal benevolence'.[9] As the debate approached its climax, it was Sir Samuel Romilly, the Attorney General, who compared the same individual with the tyrant Napoleon across the Channel. The Emperor might seem 'when he sat upon his throne to have reached the summit of human ambition and the pinnacle of earthly happiness', but in his bed 'his solitude must be tortured and his repose banished by the recollection of the blood he had spilled and the oppressions he had committed'. By contrast, a certain Member of the House of Commons would that night 'retire into the bosom of his happy and delighted family' and lie down on his bed 'reflecting on the innumerable voices that would be raised in every quarter of the world to bless him; how much more pure and permanent felicity must he enjoy, in the consciousness of having preserved so many millions of his fellow creatures, than the man with whom he had compared him, on the thrones of which he had waded through slaughter and oppression'.[10] As Romilly closed, he was followed by an almost unheard-of event: the House of Commons rose as a body, cheering to the echo a man whom many of them had once ignored, opposed or abused. The object of their adulation found that the scene, as he later wrote, left him 'completely overpowered by my feelings',[11] and the tears streamed down his face. A slight and hunched figure amidst a sea of tributes, he would indeed attain that night one of 'the two great objects' which he had long believed should be the work of his life. To some a 'sacred relic', yet to others the 'epitome of the devil', he was one of the finest debaters in Parliament, even in its greatest age of eloquence. While he never held ministerial office, his extraordinary combination of humanity, evangelism, philanthropy and political skill made him one of the most influential Britons in history. For the man saluted by the Commons that night, tearful, emotional, but triumphant as the hated slave trade was voted into history, bore the name of William Wilberforce.

WILLIAM WILBERFORCE

I

One Boy, Two Paths

My Mother hearing I had become a Methodist, came up to London
to ascertain the fact and finding it true took me down to Hull almost
heartbroken.

WILLIAM WILBERFORCE, *Autobiographical Notes*[1]

No pious parent ever laboured more to impress a beloved child with
sentiments of piety, than they did to give me a taste of the world and
its diversions.

WILLIAM WILBERFORCE, *Recollections*[2]

THE PEDIGREE OF William Wilberforce was impeccably Yorkshire. His grandfather, another William Wilberforce, had come to
Hull to make his fortune early in the eighteenth century, but he had
not come far: for centuries the family known as Wilberfoss had lived
and prospered around the Yorkshire Wolds. A William Wilberfoss had
been Mayor of Beverley at the time of the Civil War. The family could
trace its ancestral line with certainty back to the small town of Wilberfoss* near York in the reign of Henry II (1154–89), and with some imagination and a hint of legend to the great conflicts of 1066, in which a
Wilberfoss was said to have fought at Hastings and to have slain the
would-be king, Harold Hardrada, at the Battle of Stamford Bridge.

This was a family proud of its traditions: among them civic leadership, commercial acumen and the prominence of the names William

---

* Wilberfoss was at the edge of what was once the forest of Galtres, from whose herds of
wild boar it took the name of 'Wild-Boar-Foss', and hence Wilberfoss.

and Robert, both of which had featured in most of their generations since the fourteenth century. When grandfather William Wilberforce came to Hull he was soon elected as Mayor, and his two sons were duly named William and Robert, products of a marriage with Sarah Thornton, daughter of another successful trading family. William Wilberforce the future politician was the third child of the second son, Robert, and he was to owe his great inheritance to the lack of competing male progeny in his generation: he was an only son, two of whose three sisters died at an early age, while his uncle William – who confusingly married his cousin Hannah Thornton – was childless. The Wilberforce family would thus provide in full to its most famous descendant one of the most powerful formative influences of his early years: wealth.

The source of the family wealth was the Baltic trade. As a port on the east coast of England, Hull was well positioned to take advantage of the eighteenth-century boom in trade with northern Europe. Acquired by King Edward I in the thirteenth century,* it had long been 'a good trading town by means of the great river Humber that ebbs and flows like the sea'.[3] Its population of 7,500 in 1700 would almost quadruple in the following hundred years, with the town bursting out from medieval fortifications which were then erased, and a mass of warehouses, offices and fine homes being erected by the prospering merchants. London excepted, Hull became by far the busiest port on the east coast of England, with customs receipts over four times those of Newcastle. It was outstripped only by the great west coast ports of Bristol and Liverpool, with their access to the rich transatlantic trade, which included the trade in slaves. In the absence of any general quay, each merchant family needed its own private staiths for the loading and unloading of ships on the river Hull, just before its confluence with the great estuary of the Humber. The result was that the merchants' houses nestled alongside each other on the High Street, which ran parallel to the river, with their gardens at the rear opening out

---

* Hence it was called the King's town, producing its correct modern name of Kingston upon Hull.

directly onto the busy and sometimes chaotic scene of their private docks. Business and family life were thus conducted from a single site. An idea of the complexity of this arrangement was furnished in due course by Robert Wilberforce's will: 'My house in the High Street in Kingston upon Hull wherein I now dwell with all the Outhouses, Warehouses, Cellars, Staiths, Staith Chambers, Granaries, Scales, Scale beams, Scale weights, Gardens, Pumps, Pipes of Wood or Lead and other appurtenances thereto.'[4]

One such property, no. 25 High Street, was inherited by Alderman Wilberforce on the death of his father-in-law in 1732. A smart and spacious red-brick house, built in the 1660s but substantially altered by the Wilberforce family, it was to be the headquarters for the management of further additions to the Wilberforce fortune in subsequent decades. It must have been a bustling and noisy place, with many powerful and lingering smells. The congestion caused by carts, wagons and carriages crowding into the narrow streets required the authorities to bring in new regulations in the 1750s to ensure 'THAT no cart, waggon, truck or other wheel carriage, with or without horses or other cattle, shall be permitted to remain in any of the public streets, squares, lanes or passages in the said town, longer than is or shall be necessary for loading or unloading the same . . .'[5] Such a scene outside the front door of the house was only a hint of what would be happening at the bottom of the garden to the rear: ships were moored to each other as they waited, sometimes for weeks, for customs officers to give permission to unload; when they did so the staiths would groan beneath the weight of imported goods – timber, iron ore, yarn, hemp, flax and animal hides from Scandinavia, manufactured goods and dyes from Germany and Holland, and, as the century wore on and a growing population took to importing its food, large quantities of wheat, rye, barley, beans, peas, beef, pork and butter, all to be washed down with thousands of gallons of Rheinish Hoch. While goods for export, such as lead, and in later years a growing weight of cotton, tools, and cutlery, piled up waiting to be loaded, the whole atmosphere would hang heavily with the stench of the whale blubber refineries, joining with the smells of oilseed mills and tar yards in a particularly foul combination.

It was into this crowded scene that William Wilberforce was born, in the family home on the High Street, on 24 August 1759. His father had taken over the house four years before, when old Alderman Wilberforce retired to the quieter atmosphere of a country home at Ferriby, seven miles upstream on the Humber. Robert Wilberforce had married Elizabeth Bird and had taken over the management of the family business in the absence of his elder brother, who had evidently decided to make the most of the family's prosperity and move to London. Robert and Elizabeth were to have four children. The first and the fourth, Elizabeth and Anne, would die at the ages of fourteen and eight respectively: even in a well-to-do household childhood mortality in the eighteenth century was high. The second daughter, Sarah, was eighteen months old when the baby William was born. He was a discouragingly small and fragile child, with weak eyesight to compound the gloom, and he is said to have expressed thankfulness in later life 'that I was not born in less civilised times, when it would have been thought impossible to rear so delicate a child',[6] and such a frail little thing could have been abandoned. Very little is recorded of his earliest years, but it was soon obvious that despite his physical infirmities he was intelligent and personable. The Wilberforce family presumably hoped that if he lived he would become the latest in their line of successful merchants, part of the 'property, trade and profits' which were the 'dominant terms' of eighteenth-century England.[7] Those looking for clues to his later choices in life will not find them in his infant years. While his great future friend William Pitt, born only twelve weeks before him, was already resolved at the age of seven to serve in the House of Commons, the young William Wilberforce spent his first eight years in a household dominated by the business world. His immediate family had no strong connection with national politics, and showed no special zeal for religion. For all the fact that their son was born in the great 'year of victories', in which Canada and India were falling under British dominion, and Horace Walpole was writing, 'One is forced to ask every morning what victory there is, for fear of missing one,'[8] it seems that the horizons of Robert and Elizabeth Wilberforce were predominantly local and financial.

If family wealth was a first crucial ingredient in the later career of William Wilberforce, then the experience of learning from a teacher he liked and respected was a second. While the Wilberforces were rich, they did not adopt the practice of the nobility and landed gentry by sending their son to a private school such as Eton. It is fair to assume that the bustling nature of their household and the family's strong participation in local affairs turned them against the other educational option for the wealthy of the eighteenth century, educating a child at home. Consequently, William joined the sons of other Hull merchants in attending Hull Grammar School, a short walk from 25 High Street down the cobbled Bishop Lane, through the teeming marketplace and past the Holy Trinity church. He later recalled walking there 'with satchel on my shoulder'[9] and having his meals at home.

Eighteenth-century grammar schools varied enormously in the quality of education they provided. Often dependent on a single teacher, their fortunes thereby fluctuated along with the standards of that teacher. The subjects taught could amount to anything from a strict classical curriculum to the inclusion of more 'practical' subjects such as arithmetic, navigation, science or French. William was lucky, because the departure of the incumbent headmaster within a few months of the new pupil's arrival brought onto the scene a new teacher, Joseph Milner, with whom he would enjoy a lifelong friendship.

Joseph Milner was brought up in Leeds, the son of a journeyman weaver who placed a high priority on his sons' education despite his poverty, and who recalled that 'Once, on a Saturday evening, I surprised my wife, by sending home a Greek book for my son Joseph, instead of a joint of meat for the succeeding Sunday's dinner. It was too true that I could not send home both.'[10] Sent to Leeds Grammar School despite his father's lack of formal education, he rapidly emerged as a prodigy, with verses published in the local newspaper and his teacher declaring that 'Milner is more easily consulted than the dictionaries ... and he is quite as much to be relied on.'[11] Having been dispatched to Cambridge with the financial support of 'several liberal gentlemen' of Leeds, he was twenty-three years old when he was interviewed for the job of headmaster at Hull, and duly appointed with the influential support of Alderman Wilberforce. With him he brought his younger brother Isaac, who had been taken out of school when he was twelve because of his father's death. Isaac too showed exceptional intelligence, and now briefly performed the role of school usher, helping to teach the younger boys.

Under Milner's leadership, it was not long before Hull Grammar School had become a popular and educational success. One of his pupils later recalled: 'He appeared as if he knew all the different authors by heart; entered at once into their meaning, genius, taste, history . . . His mind shone every day with the utmost brightness and splendour . . . His whole school loved, revered, adored him for his wonderful abilities, for his simplicity, and for his easiness and readiness in communicating knowledge.'[12] Others recollected that 'he rarely latterly inflicted corporal punishment', and remembered 'the caustic yet temperate ridicule with which he remarked on the custom of getting by heart the Latin syntax before some progress was made in the language . . . When some proficiency in the Latin language was obtained, he directed us simply to read a book, so as to be able to answer questions on the substance of it.'[13] Milner thus brought an innovative touch to the teaching of the traditional curriculum, and his pupils also loved mathematics and algebra, and had the benefit of the town having spent seven guineas on a pair of globes, the first recorded in the school. A large and apparently ungainly man, Milner 'generally came in about nine in the morning: at eleven the school was dismissed: the scholars went to learn writing and arithmetic elsewhere. The afternoon school hours are from two til five in the summer, and until four in the winter months.'[14] Within two years the schoolroom was 'crowded', with plentiful fees bringing Milner's income to 'upwards of two-hundred pounds per annum'[15] rather than the salary of thirty guineas which had originally been envisaged.

While William might easily have been bullied or lacking in confidence on account of his fragility, his experiences at Hull Grammar School evidently fortified his natural abilities. He was bright, engaging and confident; Isaac Milner would later recall that William's elocution 'was so remarkable that we used to set him upon a table, and make him read aloud as an example to the other boys'.[16] It must have been a happy time for a seven-year-old boy: a good teacher, many friends, a caring family, and a large house enjoying an endless procession of visitors, traders and activities. In the summer months he was able to go out to his grandfather's house at Ferriby and enjoy the sights and sounds of the English countryside. Then tragedy struck. In the late spring of 1768, when William was almost nine, his family was torn apart. Only months after celebrating the birth of his fourth child, Anne, and around the same time as the death of the eldest daughter, Elizabeth, Robert Wilberforce died at the age of thirty-nine. This tragic sequence was to bring about the first of two wrenching upheavals in William's early life.

Elizabeth Wilberforce struggled to cope after the death of her husband. Wilberforce would later write, 'Some months after [his father's death] my Mother had a most long and dangerous fever.'[17] It was decided that he would be moved to London, into the care of his father's elder brother William and his wife Hannah. Arriving in London in the autumn of 1768 after a week's stay with his cousins in Nottingham, William made his first acquaintance with what would become very familiar territory: his aunt and uncle owned a spacious villa in Wimbledon, then a village of just under a thousand residents separated by several miles of countryside from the capital, as well as a house in St James's Place, yards from London's fashionable clubs. For all their resources, his aunt and uncle did not find for him a school to measure up to the education he had been used to at Hull. He was sent to a boarding school at Putney, which he later remembered as 'one of those little schools where a little of everything reading, writing, arithmetic etc is taught: a most wretched little place. I remember to this day the Scotch usher we had: a dirty disagreeable man.'[18] Charity boys were crammed into the upstairs; William and other pupils from better-off families, including a number of sons of West Indian plantation-owners, lived downstairs. He considered it 'a very indifferent school', a rather generous judgement given the mediocre education it gave him and the necessity of coping with 'the things which we had for breakfast, which were so nasty, that I could not swallow them without sickening'.[19]

The consolation was spending his vacations at Wimbledon, described by Jonathan Swift in 1713 as 'much the finest place' near London. He grew fond of his aunt and uncle, and settled in happily at their tranquil villa, Lauriston House. This would be an eight- or nine-bedroom house once its garrets were converted into bedrooms a few years later, with its own extensive grounds. Lauriston House was on the south side of Wimbledon Common, where the mansions were described in a guide book as 'an assemblage of gentleman's houses, most delightfully situated', with 'good gardens from whence is a pleasant prospect over the luxuriant vale beneath'.[20] William must have felt at home here; years later this would be the place where he would entertain his closest friends, and what would in later life become an insatiable appetite for rural air may well have been fostered in the fields and woods around Wimbledon. Before long, the move to London had turned into a happy one after all. Despite the miseries of attending school, William had a new home he liked and a loving relationship with his relatives. And of far greater significance to his later beliefs, he was about to acquire something else; something which his mother had certainly not intended for him when she sent him away, but which would become another vital ingredient in the personality of the young William Wilberforce. That something was religion; and not merely religion, but religion with enthusiasm.

The Christianity which William had encountered with his immediate family in Hull had been of the classic Church of England variety: a necessary and formal requirement for active and respectable citizens, but not usually intrusive or demanding. His mother 'always went to church prayers on Wednesdays and Fridays, but at this time had no true conception of the spiritual nature and aim of Christianity'.[21] He would later write that 'her piety was rather of that standard to which the Church of England had then so generally declined . . . She had a better opinion of the world than she should have had and was not aware of its wickedness.'[22] The approach of his uncle William and aunt Hannah was wholly different, for they were adherents of a relatively new movement which asked much more of its followers and challenged the complacency of the established Church. This was Methodism, a view of Christianity which John Wesley and George Whitefield were preaching energetically to vast and growing crowds. Their challenge to the Church was stark, and the controversy and passions they aroused were intense.

Methodism was one of a number of movements which had arisen early in the eighteenth century in reaction to the diluted nature of the Christianity preached by the Church of England and the hypocritical and lacklustre way in which it was practised. It had begun with a group of students clustered around John and Charles Wesley at Oxford in 1729. Rising early each morning to practise their devotions, and spending several evenings a week reading the New Testament to each other, they regarded religion seriously, and adopted a programme of charitable work, self-examination and fixed times for the study of the scriptures reinforced by mutual oversight. Variously described as 'Methodists', 'Enthusiasts', 'Bible Moths' or the 'Holy Club', their determination 'to observe with strict formality the method of study and practice laid down in the statutes of the University'[23] was the crucial characteristic which allowed the term 'Methodism' to stick.

The desire of these men to reform the Church, reinforced by the preachings of Whitefield from the late 1730s, found a ready audience in England and in the American colonies. It is not surprising that many people were willing to hear the message that Christianity should be practised with a stronger sense of purpose, stricter rules and more pressing obligations. The abuse of ecclesiastical offices and the neglect of religious purpose in the Church of the eighteenth century had fully invited such a reaction, for it was mired in a period of place-seeking, money-grabbing and moral irrelevance. It was not just the Methodists who denounced the state of the Church. Jonathan Swift would make harsh and terrible claims about the deans and bishops he knew, while other observers spoke of the eighteenth-century Church as 'one of the most corrupt in its administration', or as 'the biggest den of thieves in the whole world'.[24] As Voltaire put it, 'There is only just enough religion in England to distinguish Tories who have a little from Whigs who have none.'[25]

Many observers considered that Christianity was largely absent from much of the Church's preaching. The renowned lawyer Sir William Blackstone did the rounds of the best preachers in London before declaring that 'Not one of the sermons contained more Christianity than the writings of Cicero.'[26] The vicar Henry Venn considered, after listening to sermons in York, that 'excepting a single phrase or two, they might be preached in a synagogue or mosque without offence'.[27] It was common for apathetic clergy simply to buy sermons from each other, saving themselves the thought or effort required to come up with their own words. William's Hull Grammar School teacher Joseph Milner would assert in the 1780s, 'That sermons should be sold to them by a person advertising the newspapers, is a flaming proof of the low state of their religious views and studies.'[28] This was not surprising in an age when many of the clergy ceased to perform religious duties at all. Having been appointed to a lucrative parish, it was common practice for clergymen to become absentees, keeping the living obtained from the parish and delegating curates to carry out their duties at a much lower rate of pay. In 1771 the Reverend Dr John Trustler started a business 'abridging the Sermons of eminent divines, and printing them in the form of manuscripts, so as not only to save clergymen the trouble of composing their discourses, but even of transcribing them'.[29] One commentator wrote that 'Country towns abound with curates who never see the parishes they serve but when they are absolutely forced to it by duty: that several parishes are often served by the same person, who, in order to double or treble his curacy, hurries through the service in a manner perfectly indecent; strides from the pulpit to his horse and gallops away as if pursuing a fox.'[30] Indeed, the hunting parson became the caricature of the eighteenth-century Church. One clergyman in Suffolk 'kept an excellent hunter, rode well up to the hounds, drank very hard ... he sang an excellent song, danced remarkably well, so that the young ladies considered no party complete without him'.[31] Hard drinking was common, Wesley writing from St Ives in 1747 that two clergymen 'were led home at one or two in the morning in such a condition as I care not to describe'.[32]

Above all, it was the ruthless competition for the most lucrative parishes and dioceses that made the eighteenth-century Church a place of touting and toadying ambition, and caused understandable anger amongst a general population whose tithe payments funded the generous livings and evident abuses. There seemed no end to the number of positions a bishop might occupy: 'The bishops are frequently archdeacons and deans, rectors, vicars and curates, besides holding professorships, Clerkships, prebends, precentorships, and other offices in cathedrals.'[33] One observer recorded that 'the late Bishop of Salisbury is said to have died worth upwards of £150,000 . . . I can hardly think it probable that he could amass so much wealth . . . I never heard him accused of avarice: nor did I ever hear that he had any great fortune with any of his four wives.'[34] Nepotism only made matters worse. It was said of one family alone, the Beresfords, that one of them had cumulatively received over £350,000 from his Church living, another just under £300,000, a third £250,000 and a fourth, with four livings simultaneously, earned £58,000. In total, through eight clerics this family obtained £1.5 million from the Irish Church. Families with political connections were proud of their ability to obtain Church livings. The tombstone of one lady of the Stanhope family proudly declared: 'She had the merit to obtain for her husband and children, twelve several appointments in Church and State.'[35] Lord Hugh Percy, Bishop of Carlisle, received over £250,000 from the Church, and ensured a steady supply of canonries, prebends and rectories for his sons and sons-in-law.

With such rewards available, the Church was converted into a branch of the aristocracy. To cap it all, political patronage was decisive in most of the senior appointments. 'No man,' complained Dr Johnson, 'can now be made a Bishop for his learning and piety: his only chance of promotion is his being connected with someone who has parliamentary interest.'[36] One relative of Lord North, Prime Minister in the 1770s, became a bishop at thirty, was later promoted to the highly lucrative see of Winchester, and is said to have gained around £1,500,000 from Church funds over his life, while additionally securing thirty livings for other members of his family. Such sums are the equivalent of many tens of millions of pounds in today's money. Meanwhile, low-paid curates struggled to do the work for which the clergy were paid, often receiving only a shilling a day and turning to farming or weaving for part of the week in order to supplement their income. Neglected Anglican congregations declined sharply during the eighteenth century, and the Church failed to establish itself in the new industrial towns. By 1750 Manchester had a population of twenty thousand, but only one parish church.

Of course there were still bishops and vicars who lived more frugally or honestly, but it was not difficult to make the case that parts of the English Church in the eighteenth century were in a state of virtual paganism, and that a radical new approach was required. To John Wesley, it was not necessary to change the doctrines or liturgy of the Church, but it was essential for both its clergy and its followers to adopt a purer and more devout approach in their public and private conduct. Since the Church appeared so uncontrollably corrupt and licentious, and set such a poor example to the population at large, Methodists believed that strict rules should be adopted for the regulation of daily life. Methodists were required to attend weekly class meetings and permit probing enquiries into their daily conduct. Their General Rules forbade 'the profaning of the day of the Lord by either doing ordinary work thereon, or by buying or selling', as well as 'drunkenness, buying or selling spirituous liquors, or drinking them, less in cases of extreme necessity', along with 'uncharitable or unprofitable conversation' and 'the putting on of gold or costly apparel'.[37] They were also told to avoid 'the singing of songs, or reading those books, which do not tend to the knowledge or love of God; softness or needless self-indulgence'.[38] Wesley told them too that they should 'take no more food than nature required', to 'sleep early and rise early', and to wear cheap and plain dress.[39] The adoption of such a lifestyle was meant to follow the conversion of the individual, in which a period of despair about his or her sins would be followed by a sense of forgiveness, and it would ultimately bring its reward in salvation in the eyes of God. Those who did not seek it would have much to fear from 'the wrath to come'.[40]

The Methodist message, and the bold and emotional style in which it was preached, soon came up against the hostility of the Church. By 1740 Whitefield found churches closed to his preaching, but this simply caused him to take up the still more adventurous initiative of preaching to huge numbers of people in the open air. Crowds of fifty thousand at a time were known at such events: vast, silent gatherings which gave way after the preaching to dramatic conversions amidst much crying and emotion. Horace Walpole commented in 1749, 'This sect increases as fast as almost ever any religious nonsense did.'[41] Whitefield became such a celebrated figure that David Garrick, the best-known actor of the time, was reputed to have said that he would give £100 to be able to say 'Oh' in the way Whitefield said it.[42] By the late 1760s Wesley and Whitefield had travelled hundreds of thousands of miles, claiming twenty-five thousand people as strict Methodists but influencing the opinions of far more.

Among Whitefield's converts in the 1750s was John Thornton, a rich man 'in great credit and esteem',[43] known for his charity and generosity, who owned a country estate at Clapham, a village to the south of London and only a few miles from the Wimbledon of his half-sister Hannah, William's aunt. She, apparently, 'was a great admirer of Whitefield's preaching, and kept up a friendly connection with the early Methodists'.[44] Now she took her nine-year-old charge to church to hear Evangelical preachers, including the great John Newton. Newton was in his mid-forties at the time, and had led a dramatic and extraordinary life: press-ganged into the navy in his teens, shipwrecked off Africa, abandoned as a slave to a planter's black mistress, he eventually returned home to marry his sweetheart and become master of a slaving ship, writing in the 1750s diaries which were among the most intimate and detailed accounts of the purchasing of slaves off the coast of Africa. By the 1760s he had turned to religion, started writing hymns and become curate at the village of Olney in Buckinghamshire. He was a man of great presence, and his preaching made a deep impact on the young Wilberforce, who remembered 'reverencing him as a parent when I was a child'.[45]

Not every child of nine or ten would have responded to such preaching, but for whatever reason of personality or inclination, the ear of the young William Wilberforce was sensitive from the outset to the beat of a religious drum. 'Under these influences,' he later wrote, 'my mind was interested by religious subjects. How far these impressions were genuine I can hardly determine, but at least I may venture to say that I was sincere.'[46] Listening to Newton and admiring the devotion and sincerity of his aunt and uncle, he adopted Methodism as his creed. In his own words, 'My uncle and aunt were truly good people, and were in fact disciples of Mr Whitefield. At that time when the church of England had so much declined I really believe that Mr Whitefield and Wesley were the restorers of genuine religion.'[47]

What happened next would, thirty years later, be ascribed by Wilberforce to the intervention of Providence. Whatever the truth of that, the event took the physical form of the arrival of a very insistent and angry mother who removed him from London forthwith. For however strong the convictions of Hannah and Uncle William, they were not shared by most members of church-going society, or by the rest of the Wilberforce family at Hull. 'When my poor mother heard that I was disposed to join the Methodists,' Wilberforce recalled, 'she was perfectly shocked.'[48] In 1771 a determined Elizabeth Wilberforce took a coach to London and descended on Wimbledon. William would later recall that 'After consultation with my grandfather [she] determined to remove me from my uncle's, fearful lest I should imbibe what she considered as little less than poison which indeed I at that time had done.'[49] He was torn from Wimbledon and put on a coach to Hull amidst much emotion and unhappiness: 'being thus removed from my uncle and aunt affected me most seriously. It almost broke my heart.'[50] Once returned to Hull he would write to his uncle, 'I can never forget you as long as I live.' The confrontation between mother and aunt had evidently been quite a spectacle, with Elizabeth Wilberforce making neat use of the Methodist belief that God was present in the smallest action: 'If it be the work of grace you know it cannot fail.'[51] Uncle and aunt were apparently 'also inconsolable for the loss of me'.[52]

William's grandfather was adamant that he should be detached from Methodist influence, saying, 'If Billy turns Methodist he shall not have a sixpence of mine.'[53] The family must have felt under siege, since to the astonishment of the local community the previously respected Joseph Milner had turned Methodist as well. William could not, in the light of this, even be returned to his former school. In the more ecumenical climate of the twenty-first century it is difficult to imagine the horror and suspicion occasioned in the late eighteenth century by flirtation with Methodist teaching. It is a measure of such suspicion that for all Milner's effectiveness and popularity, the effect of his adherence to Methodism was to cause an exodus from the school, a sharp reduction in his income, and virtual ostracism in the town: 'Few persons who wore a tolerably good coat would take notice of him when they met him in the street.'[54]

Wesley and Whitefield could attract and rouse huge crowds, but they seemed threatening, intrusive or ridiculous to many others. The Anglican hierarchy attacked their claims to superiority as well as their doctrines of salvation by faith and the idea of conversion or new birth. In particular, Methodists' earnestness and enthusiasm came in for much mockery. The Cornish actor, dramatist and theatre manager Samuel Foote wrote of Whitefield: 'If he is bit by Fleas, he is buffeted by *Satan*. If he has the good Fortune to catch them, God will subdue his Enemies under his Feet.'[55] Sydney Smith attacked the Methodists because they 'hate pleasure and amusements; no theatre, no cards, no dancing, no punchinello, no dancing dogs, no blind fiddlers – all the amusements of the rich and of the poor must disappear wherever these gloomy people get a footing'.[56] Accusations of hypocrisy on the part of Methodist preachers were mingled with suspicion of their hostility to alcohol, as in this verse from *She Stoops to Conquer* (1773) by the popular playwright Oliver Goldsmith:

> When Methodist preachers come down,
> A preaching that drinking is sinful,
> I'll wager the rascals a crown,
> They always preach best with a skinful.[57]

More seriously, there were occasional riots against Methodist preachers, whose appeal to the poor and conversion of women and young people could disrupt family life and cause divisions in a parish. Their classes and so-called 'love feasts' were sometimes viewed as a cover for suspicious or even obscene practices. Others simply objected to being lectured by them. As the Duchess of Buckingham put it, 'It is monstrous to be told that you have a heart as sinful as the common wretches that crawl on the earth. This is highly offensive and insulting and at variance with high rank and good breeding.'[58]Such scorn would not succeed: there would be over seventy thousand practising Methodists by the 1790s, and perhaps over 400,000 by 1830.

Cut off from the age of twelve from the aunt and uncle he adored, and not even returned to the teacher he had liked, William was now sent to board at Pocklington School, his grandfather's old school thirteen miles from York. This kept him safely within reach of his family and entirely separated from Methodist teaching under the watchful eye of the master, the Reverend Kingsman Baskett. Pocklington, an endowed grammar school, could accommodate about fifty pupils, but was going through a difficult patch in 1771, with only about thirty in attendance. Baskett did not require his pupils to work hard; Wilberforce remembered him as 'an elegant though not deep scholar and of gentlemanly mind and manners'.[59] The school was paid the generous sum of £400 a year to take William and to give him certain privileges – considerable ones, in view of the fact that a normal fee at most schools for a year's boarding was a mere £10. These included 'a very good room to myself',[60] dining with the headmaster and being specially tutored by him. Here he stayed for five years, 'going in the holydays to my Mother's at Hull and occasionally going to visit my grandfather'.[61]

Even in this sanitised environment, it would take several years for William's attachment to Methodist teaching and to his distant aunt and uncle to fade. A letter to his uncle in November 1771 ends:

> May the blessing of the living God keep you and preserve you in this world and may he bring you unto his Kingdom of bliss and joy. I am your, dearest, dearest son, W Wilberforce
> ps. I cannot write more because it is seen where the letter is to.[62]

Later in the same month he wrote: 'I own I would give anything in the world to be with you again yet I trust that everything is ordered for the best and if we put our whole trust and confidence in Him we shall never be confounded.'[63] In August 1772 he complained to his aunt that 'one of the greatest misfortunes I had whilst at Hull was not being able to hear the blessed word of God, as my mama would not let me go to High Church on a Sunday afternoon'.[64] And the following month, he took the opportunity of writing 'by the maid who goes away tomorrow; thinking it a better way than sending it to my uncle, since grandpa might perhaps see the letter'.[65] Yet in his essays, overseen by Baskett, Methodist sentiments were absent. Those that have survived suggest a serious, thoughtful young man who could express himself clearly. Too much should not be made of the significance of school essays, which then, as now, were principally written with the reader and marker in mind, but it is striking how many of Wilberforce's opinions in later life seem to have already been formed before the age of fifteen. 'Since there is so much to be begot by the society of a good companion and as much to be lost by that of a bad one we ought to take the greatest care not to form any improper connections,' he wrote in March 1772. 'We never ought to admit anyone into that class till we are perfectly acquainted both with his Morals and Abilities.'[66] In 1773 he ventured the opinion that 'Those who bend their thoughts upon gaining popularity, will find themselves most egregiously mistaken, if they expect to find it so desirable as is represented by some . . . When a man once aims at popular applause he must part with everything though ever so near and dear to him at the least nod of a giddy multitude.'[67] In 1774 he produced this: 'Life is a very uncertain thing at best, therefore we ought not to rely upon any good Fortune, since perhaps this moment we may enjoy the greatest Worldly Happiness; the next be plunged into the Deepest Abyss of unutterable Misery.'[68]

Whether or not William felt he had been 'plunged into the deepest abyss' when uprooted from Wimbledon, he now showed a teenager's resilience in recovering from it. His own feelings about this period of his life would change over the years. Twenty-five years later he wrote in his journal that 'My mother's taking me from my uncle's when about twelve or thirteen and then completely a Methodist, probably has been the means of my becoming useful in life, connected with political men. If I had staid with my uncle I should probably have become a bigoted, despised Methodist.'[69] As he would later see it, he had been rescued from a life devoted wholly to religion and given the opportunity to put his beliefs into practice. For if wealth, an early glimpse of knowledge and a temporary immersion in religion were the governing influences of Wilberforce's early years, a final and crucial factor was his busy social life as a teenager, which amplified the ease, grace and charm he would always show in society, and make it possible for him to succeed in public life.

Nothing could have been more antithetical to Methodist attitudes than the social life of the Hull merchant class into which his family now ensured that William was plunged. Methodists thoroughly dis-approved of theatres, and a local preacher would say in 1792 that 'Everyone who entered a playhouse was, with the players, equally cer-tain of *eternal* damnation,'[70] but Hull's new Theatre Royal, completed in 1770, was central to the social life of the town. Proceedings would commence as early as six in the evening with a play, followed by a musical or a comic opera, and then by dancers, jugglers, and sometimes performing dogs. Tate Wilkinson, actor-manager of the Theatre Royal, called Hull 'the Dublin of England' on account of its hearty welcome, and reported 'the many acts of kindness I received in that friendly seat, occasions my being oftener in bad health in Hull than at any other place in my yearly round'.[71] Balls were held which 'continued with unremitting gaiety to a late hour . . . and gave such a zest to hilarity, that numbers were left at four o'clock in the morning enjoying the united pleasures of the enlivening dance'.[72] Residents reported that 'We have a very Gay Town with diversions of some or other kind.'[73]

William at first resisted these pleasures; when he was first taken to a play it was almost by force. As he wrote himself, Hull 'was then as gay a place as could be found out of London. The theatre, balls, great suppers, and card parties, were the delight of the principal families in the town. The usual dinner hour was two o'clock, and at six they met at sumptuous suppers. This mode of life was at first distressing to me, but by degrees I acquired a relish for it, and became as thoughtless as the rest. As grandson to one of the principal inhabitants, I was everywhere invited and caressed: my voice and love of music made me still more acceptable. The religious impressions which I had gained at Wimbledon continued for a considerable time after my return to Hull, but my friends spared no pains to stifle them. I might almost say, that no pious parent ever laboured more to impress a beloved child with sentiments of piety, than they did to give me a taste of the world and its diversions.'[74] His vacations were therefore an endless round of social events; every self-respecting family in Hull would have wanted to meet the young man with a lively mind, a kind disposition, a melodious voice and a fortune in the offing. His growing enjoyment of gambling, card parties, theatre-going and socialising long into the night would have outraged his aunt and uncle: 'After tea we played cards till nine; then there was a great supper, game, turkey etc . . . In this idle way did they make me live; giving me a taste for cards, introducing me to pretty young women etc.'[75] In later years he would similarly report 'utter idleness and dissipation . . . cards, assemblies, concerts, plays; and for two last years with the girls all the morning – religion gradually wearing away till quite gone'.[76] He was now 'about 14 or 15 a boy of very high spirits',[77] and his circumstances 'did not dispose me for exertion when I returned to school'.[78]

The Methodism had been drawn out of him. In 1774, with his mind no longer on his aunt and uncle, the religious sentiments expressed in his letters to them ceased. As he contemplated his next move, to Cambridge University, his many attributes and advantages in life were clear: sociability, wealth, thoughtfulness and an easy command of language. No one, including him, yet had any idea how he would use them.

2

Ambition and Election

As much pains were taken to make me idle as were ever taken to make any one else studious.

WILLIAM WILBERFORCE, *Recollections*[1]

Some time before when an uncle of mine had got into parliament, I recollect thinking it a very great thing.

WILLIAM WILBERFORCE, *Recollections*[2]

IN HIS OWN WORDS, Wilberforce was armed upon his arrival as an undergraduate at Cambridge with 'a perfect command of money'.[3] The death of both the other living William Wilberforces, his grandfather in 1776 and his uncle in 1777, left him as the sole male heir of the Wilberforce line. This meant that he was now in possession of a considerable fortune, and without the distraction of having to run the family business from which that fortune had been derived. Since his father's death eight years earlier it had been Abel Smith, a scion of the rising Nottingham banking family who had married his mother's sister, who had presided over the enterprise at Hull, now renamed Wilberforce and Smith.

The precise dimensions of Wilberforce's fortune are unclear. He was not one of the super-rich of those days, the great landed families like the Fitzwilliams who owned colossal mansions and tens of thousands of acres, or the 'nabobs' who had returned from India with the wealth to set themselves up with land and pocket boroughs. It seems likely, given what is known about his assets and what can be calculated from the size of the losses which dissipated his family's wealth half a century later, that he could lay claim to a personal fortune in the low hundreds of thousands of pounds, with £100,000 at that time roughly corresponding to £10 million today. He was, therefore, by no means able to set up a great country house, even had he wished to, but he easily had enough to live comfortably as a gentleman for the rest of his life.

This was a dangerous position for a seventeen-year-old arriving at Cambridge to be in. It was at St John's College, alma mater of Kingsman Baskett, that his name was entered in the admissions book on 31 May 1776 (with 'Wilberfoss' crossed out and replaced with 'Wilberforce' as the college authorities belatedly caught up with the development of the family name), and he arrived there in October of that year. 'I was introduced on the very first night of my arrival,' he wrote, 'to as licentious a set of men as can well be conceived. They drank hard, and their conversation was even worse than their lives . . . often indeed I was horror-struck at their conduct.'[4]

This might be thought, by anyone who has attended Oxford or Cambridge at any point in history, to be the entirely normal reaction of a provincial innocent on his first night in college. Yet Cambridge does seem to have been particularly open to a dissolute lifestyle at that time. A sermon preached in the university church a few years later bemoaned 'the scandalous neglect of order and discipline throughout the University', and one observer complained that 'It disgusts me to go through Cambridge . . . where one meets nothing academic or like a place of study, regularity or example.'[5] In the very year of Wilberforce's arrival, Dr Ewin, a local Justice of the Peace, was hoping, forlornly it seems, that 'young men see the folly of intemperance . . . vice and disorderly conduct . . . we never were at a greater pitch of extravagance in living, not dining in the halls, neglect of chapel . . . and not without women are our present misfortunes'.[6] Even by the normal standards of a boisterous university, rioting and the breaking down of other students' doors were particularly prevalent. One St John's freshman wrote to his father about a series of riots, complaining that 'they had broke my door to pieces before I could get hold of my trusty poker',[7] and the Master of the College felt it necessary in 1782 to denounce 'scandalous outrages' and to make clear that 'Whoever shall be detected in breaking down the door of any person in college . . . shall be rusticated without hope of ever being recalled.'[8] Wilberforce considered he had been introduced to 'some, I think of the very worse men that I ever met with in my life'.[9]

To any teenager of a purely pleasure-loving or disruptive disposition, then, there was much to look forward to alongside several years of academic indolence. Neither Oxford nor Cambridge was a great centre of intellectual ferment at this point: the numbers of students had declined mid-century, and the dons were 'decent easy men' who 'from the toil of reading, or thinking, or writing . . . had absolved their conscience'.[10] Medical students preferred to study in Holland; religious dissenters went to Edinburgh; the old English universities had become sleepy, conservative, and 'the starting line in the race for Church livings'.[11]

A further temptation to academic inactivity for Wilberforce arose from his being a Fellow Commoner, less exalted than a nobleman in the class-conscious eyes of those times, but enjoying many privileges over the pensioners and sizars, who paid lower fees and were generally on their way to a career in the Church. Fellow Commoners paid extra fees to 'common' (i.e. dine) at the Fellows' table, and were exempt from many lectures and studies, although St John's had recently introduced new rules requiring them to be publicly examined twice a year. Even so, the tutors told Wilberforce he really need not bother with work: 'Their object seemed to be, to make and keep me idle. If ever I appeared studious, they would say to me, "Why in the world should a man of your fortune trouble himself with fagging?"'[12] The result was that he did a certain amount to get through the exams, but, while shaking off within a year or so his initial and shocking companions, spent the rest of the time socialising: 'I used to play at cards a great deal and do nothing else and my tutor who ought to have repressed this disposition, if not by his authority at least by his advice, rather encouraged it: he never urged me to attend lectures and I never did. And I should have had nothing, all the time I was at college but for a natural love of classical learning and that it was necessary for a man who was to be publicly examined to prevent his being disgraced.'[13]

The resulting academic record was undistinguished: in the college exams of December 1776, his performance 'would have been mentioned sooner if he had prepared himself in the whole of Stanyan' (Greek history); in 1777 he was said to be due 'some praise', and later in the year 'was good in the Classic' and in 1778 'did well in Butler' (Analogy of Religion).[14] But as to mathematics, which he later thought his mind 'greatly needed', he was 'told that I was too clever to require them'.[15]

Undeniably, however, he had a good time, without the truly excessive drinking, womanising and violence of some of his contemporaries, but falling happily into the category of 'sober dissipation',[16] as he described it himself. He was already 'so far from what the world calls licentious, that I was rather complimented on being better than young men in general',[17] but he was very quickly a popular figure, showing to full effect all the abilities of singing, conversation and hospitality which the years of Hull society had honed in him. Unprepossessing as he must have been in appearance, only five feet four inches tall, with an eyeglass on a ribbon, his life at Cambridge soon became a foretaste of his future residence at Westminster, with people always clustering around him and filling his rooms. Thomas Gisborne, who was to become a renowned writer, poet, moralist and natural philosopher, had the rooms next door to Wilberforce but was much more studious, remembering him in the streets 'encircled by young men of talent'. Wilberforce apparently kept a great Yorkshire pie in his rooms (an unlikely journey for a pie before the days of refrigeration), and 'whatever else the good things was, to console the hungry visitor'.[18] He lived, according to Gisborne, 'far too much for self-indulgence in habits of idleness and amusement. By his talents, his wit, his kindness, his social powers, his universal accessibility, and his love of society, he speedily became the centre of attraction to all the clever and the idle of his own college and of other colleges. He soon swarmed with them from the time when he arose, generally very late, like he went to bed. He talked and he laughed and he sang, and he amused and interested everyone.'[19]

In later life Wilberforce would deeply regret the waste of time.

When he ought to have been 'under a strict and wholesome regimen',[20] he found that 'As much pains were taken to make me idle as were ever taken to make any one else studious.'[21] If he gained anything specific from his Cambridge years it was certain friendships which further broadened his horizons: William Cookson, the uncle of Wordsworth, who took him during vacations to the Lake District and gave him a lifelong adoration of that part of England, soon to become his regular fresh-air retreat; Gerard Edwards, an entertaining young landowner who would one day make one of the most important introductions of Wilberforce's life; and Edward Christian, whose brother Fletcher would soon enjoy the lasting fame of leading the mutiny on the *Bounty*. Three whole years of card parties and late-night drinking went by until, as these friends began to leave Cambridge in 1779, Wilberforce turned his mind to what to do with the rest of his life.

Many of the options available were presumably fairly easily dismissed. He had no wish to go into the family business, now in the capable hands of Abel Smith, and in any case probably was not attracted to spending the rest of his life in Hull. While others in search of a career would have gone into practising law, he had no record of the necessary studious application and no need of the money either. The majority of his fellow Cambridge graduates would have gone into the Church, but at this stage in his life this would not have offered a remotely desirable lifestyle, and his early Methodism had left him with serious doubts about the established Church – his sons reported in their biography of him that while at Cambridge he briefly refused to declare his assent to the Articles of the Church. He could, of course, have been a gentleman of pure leisure, but to a man of twenty who so much enjoyed being a centre of attention and part of a lively community that would have been an unlikely and premature retirement.

Instead, he had resolved to be a Member of Parliament. There is no record of how he arrived at this ambition, or of the reaction of his friends and family to the news that he wished to enter politics, except his own statement that 'At this time I knew there was a general election coming on and at Hull the conversation often turned to politics and rooted me to ambition.'[22] His family may well have been surprised:

they had a tradition of civic, but not parliamentary, leadership; and his friends did not at this stage include the great swathe of would-be rulers of Britain with whom he would soon be acquainted. Yet there were present in his personality many of the essential components of a young political aspirant: ability to perform for an audience, an easy popularity, and an interest in the world beyond his own town or college. As for paying the expenses of an election, that was what that inheritance was for.

On top of these factors was something else which may have been decisive: the time through which the young Wilberforce was living was one of the most arresting for decades in demanding the attention of those remotely interested in national affairs. A critical ingredient of youthful commitment to politics was present: that great events and dramatic change were in the offing. For Britain was at war, a war that was rapidly widening, and the increasingly ill-tempered debates of the House of Commons were testimony to the fact that at present the country was not winning it.

It was in 1775, while Wilberforce was still partying in Hull and studying at Pocklington School, that the gunfire at Lexington signalled the start of the American War of Independence. In 1776, while he was falling in with the gamblers at St John's College, Britain had waved farewell to an armada of hundreds of ships and a force of thirty-two thousand troops which, it was widely assumed, would soon bring the recalcitrant colonies to heel. Yet the war in America was never as simple as a conflict between Americans and Britons.

Just as there were many loyalist 'Tories' in the colonies who wished to remain under the rule of their mother country, so there was no shortage of spokesmen among the opposition in Britain who had favoured a policy of conciliation rather than confrontation, and now opposed the war. Among them were some of the greatest orators of the age, or indeed of any age, including the foremost opponents of the government of Lord North: Charles James Fox and Edmund Burke. As the colonies declared themselves independent in 1776, Fox was arguing that it would be better to abandon America than to oppress it, and denouncing the 'diabolical measures' of the government: 'How cruel and intolerable a thing it is to sacrifice thousands of lives almost without prospect of advantage.'[23] He attacked the 'boasts, blunders, and disgraces of the Administration', and the following year was launching onslaughts on the Secretary of State for the Colonies, Lord George Germain, as 'that ill-auspicious and ill-omened character' who was guilty of 'arrogance and presumption . . . ignorance and inability'.[24] To add to the drama, the Elder Pitt, first Earl of Chatham, thundered out of retirement to rock the House of Lords with denunciations of the war. Most dramatically of all, Chatham's final onslaught on the mismanagement of the war in April 1778 was cut short by his own collapse and subsequent death, ending for good speculation that he would again be called upon to rescue his country. 'We shall be forced,' he told the government at the beginning of the American War, 'ultimately to retract: let us retract while we can not when we must.'[25] By 1778 these critics of the entire notion of fighting a war in the American colonies were being proved right, with the army of General Burgoyne capitulating at Saratoga and France and Spain gleefully joining in the war to make the most of their chance of crippling the British Empire. 1779 saw the Royal Navy stretched to breaking point as French and Spanish warships cruised unmolested in the English Channel. The assumption of four years earlier that British forces could soon compel the colonists to pay their taxes and accept continued rule from London had been shattered.

By any standards, therefore, the late 1770s were a time of intensifying partisanship, stridency and bitterness in domestic politics. As the government of Lord North looked steadily shakier and as Germain came under increasingly furious attack, the morale of the political opposition rose correspondingly. In February 1779 there was exultation among the opposition following the acquittal of Admiral Keppel, whose court martial after a badly-managed encounter with the French fleet resulted in the revelation that the inadequate arming of the Royal Navy was the direct result of the government's own incompetence. Crowds took to the streets and broke the windows of government ministers in celebration of the huge embarrassment. For there was more to the political atmosphere of the time than arguments over a war that had gone wrong: there was also a feeling that the mismanagement and lack of coordination of the war effort pointed to systemic failings in the British state, and that the absence of any responsiveness to hostile public opinion on such a vital issue was a sign of corruption and excessive place-seeking. It was thus not just the ministry but the entire system of government which came under attack, and not just the ministers but the powers of King George III himself. Almost a third of the House of Commons and much of the House of Lords held titles, sinecures or pensions in the gift of the King and his ministers; almost half of the House of Commons sat for 'pocket boroughs' which were controlled by a small number of men, and sometimes literally bought by the Treasury itself. Failure in war opened the way for these practices to be attacked. The Whig aristocracy feared that the powers of the Crown had grown to the extent that the balance of the constitutional settlement arrived at in the aftermath of the Glorious Revolution of 1688 had been upset, and now Edmund Burke led their calls for 'economical reform', involving the abolition of swathes of sinecures and of the expensive additions to the royal household.

Outside Parliament, movements such as the Yorkshire Association of the Reverend Christopher Wyvill arose, campaigning for the reform of parliamentary representation and the holding of elections every three years instead of seven. There was a feeling that great change was in the air, and would soon be conceded. In April 1780 the opposition MP John Dunning succeeded in carrying his famous motion 'That the powers of the Crown have increased, are increasing, and ought to be diminished' on the floor of the House of Commons. In London there was a feeling of political crisis; overseas the war went on unabated. If any time in the eighteenth century was likely to draw a thoughtful and ambitious young man into politics, then this was it.

It was in the highly charged political atmosphere of the winter of 1779–80 that Wilberforce, finding little need to stay in permanent residence in Cambridge when so few academic demands were made of him, began paying regular visits to London and venturing into the public gallery of the House of Commons. At that time the public gallery was only fifteen feet above the floor of the Commons, supported by pillars reaching down among the benches. The entire chamber measured only fifty-seven feet by thirty-three, and had been uncomfortably crowded on busy days ever since the Act of Union with Scotland in 1707 had swelled the number of MPs to 558. A visitor to the gallery was thus readily enveloped in an often hot and boisterous atmosphere, all the more so as the debates about the American War and the nature of the constitution raged only yards from where he was sitting. As he looked beneath him, Wilberforce would have seen the great figures of late-eighteenth-century British politics locked in oratorical combat. But it was alongside him in the gallery that winter that he was to find a friend who, for the next five years at least, would be one of the greatest influences on his life. For also sitting in the gallery, with an attitude of earnest studiousness which Wilberforce would have found hard to match, was William Pitt, son of the great Chatham, and ultimately known to history as William Pitt the Younger.

Pitt and Wilberforce must have looked and seemed a strange couple as they sat observing the debates. For one thing, Pitt must have been nearly a foot taller than Wilberforce. He also had, even at that age, an aloof manner towards people he did not know well, suggestive of his always being conscious of being his father's son, but also the product of his natural diffidence: 'I am the shyest man alive,'[26] he would say to Wilberforce once their friendship had developed. Such shyness evidently soon evaporated in the warmth of Wilberforce's friendly disposition. They had been barely acquainted at Cambridge, Pitt having been largely confined within the walls of Pembroke College by a more demanding tutor and an eagerness for classics and mathematics. Yet soon Wilberforce, the unknown son of a Hull merchant, and Pitt, the son of the most revered British statesman of the eighteenth century, were firm friends.

It would be obvious from the events of later years that there was a genuine warmth in the friendship between Pitt and Wilberforce. As it happened, there was also a happily complementary nature to the advantages each of them possessed if they wished to become active in politics: Pitt had plentiful connections, widespread recognition and a famous name, but no money; Wilberforce had exactly the opposite. In years to come, Pitt would enjoy Wilberforce's generous hospitality. For now, it was Wilberforce who found in Pitt an additional enticement to the world of politics. Pitt had firm views, being strongly in favour of the prevailing fashions of economical and parliamentary reform, and he followed his deceased father in his opposition to the American War. He had an appreciation of great oratory, being thrilled to hear a formidable speech by Burke that winter – 'I had no idea until now of his excellence'[27] – but critical of some speakers in the House of Lords – 'Paltry matter and a whiney delivery'.[28] He also had impressive and immediate connections, with Fox himself coming into the gallery to join this young observer in analysing the debates – 'But surely, Mr Fox, that might be met thus . . .'[29] The extent to which this friendship and such conversations persuaded Wilberforce of the attractions of entering Parliament cannot be known, but it is clear that by the time he went down from Cambridge in the spring of 1780 he was resolved, like his friend, to enter Parliament at the forthcoming general election if he could.

Neither Pitt nor Wilberforce could countenance delay. Great events were at hand. The outcome of the war was in the balance, the House of Commons was becoming harder to control, and a general election was due by 1781 at the latest – one in which the North administration might lose a significant number of seats. Pitt was training at the Bar because he needed a source of income; Wilberforce had no need of such trifles. Both of them wanted to get into Parliament, and fast. Where and how could two young men approaching twenty-one years of age go about it?

Their age, which would seem precocious for a political career in later centuries, was no barrier. In the House of Commons about to be elected there would be fully a hundred Members under the age of thirty.* Since MPs were entirely unpaid and were generally able to live on a private income, most of them had no need of an alternative career beforehand, and since most electorates were small and buyable there was no need to spend many years building up support and recognition,

---

* Compared to only three MPs under the age of thirty elected in 2005.

as would become necessary in the days of a universal franchise. Two individuals as famous as Pitt and as wealthy as Wilberforce were highly likely to be able to get into the Commons, but that still required the careful selection and handling of an appropriate constituency; since neither of them belonged to the main parties of government or opposition, nor to the great landed families that controlled many of the seats, the exercise would require a certain amount of ingenuity or personal expense.

Unable to incur great expense, Pitt went for ingenuity. Neither he nor Wilberforce was able to contemplate standing for one of the great county seats at this stage. These supplied the eighty Members who represented forty counties, among which the most prestigious were Yorkshire and Middlesex. They were generally under the control of the aristocracy and country gentry, often divided by agreement between government and opposition, and their size and relatively large electorates meant that they were inordinately expensive to fight if they were contested: one candidate had spent £40,000 (the equivalent of more than £5 million today) contesting Oxfordshire in 1754, but had still not been successful. It would not have been too difficult for Pitt, with his many connections, to obtain a pocket borough, but, fired by an idealistic belief in rooting out corruption and pursuing parliamentary reform, he wished to be elected in his own right, and in a more open contest. He therefore decided to stand for the one place he knew well, Cambridge University, which elected two MPs and which also had a relatively democratic electorate of several hundred members of the University Senate. As it turned out he was heavily defeated there, and ended up temporarily accepting a pocket borough after all, albeit on a '*liberal, Independent* footing',[30] from the northern borough-monger Sir James Lowther.

Wilberforce, by contrast, could indulge in simple expense. Although he could have bought an average pocket borough for about £4,000 and never needed to visit it in his life, his continuing affection for Hull, and a possible affinity with Pitt's belief that it was better to arrive at the House of Commons through at least the semblance of a real election, led him in an obvious direction. Hull was a respected and ancient borough, with two Members of Parliament, but with approaching 1,500 voters it was certainly not a rotten one, nor permanently residing in anyone's pocket. As things stood, the two seats were divided, as was so often the case, between government and opposition. The government's supporter was Lord Robert Manners, a General who backed Lord North and had now been an MP for thirty-three years. The opposition representative was David Hartley, who was a distinguished opponent of the American War and a talented inventor of fireproofing for buildings and ships, but who suffered from giving such boring speeches that in the Commons 'his rising always operated like a dinner-bell'.[31] Wilberforce decided, with good reason, that his local popularity, myriad family connections and abundant funds would allow him to break the long-established grip of the main political groupings and become Member of Parliament for Hull without being dependent on anyone.

All of these factors were important in Wilberforce's election campaign. In some constituencies only the members of the corporation (the local council) or owners of certain properties or burgages possessed the vote, with the result that there were sometimes only a handful of voters; in others, like the city of Westminster and the counties, the franchise extended to all forty-shilling freeholders, and would generally include a good few thousand males with property above that rental value. In the case of Hull, it was the freemen of the town (those formally honoured by being given its 'freedom') who possessed the franchise, with the interesting complication that they did so by hereditary descent, and were therefore neither necessarily the richest inhabitants of the town, or even inhabitants at all. Several hundred of them were to be found living in London, and Wilberforce entertained them 'at suppers in the different public houses of Wapping'.[32] In common with voters throughout the rest of the country, the Hull freemen regarded their votes as financially precious, and expected to be paid for using them, the going rate being two guineas in return for one of their two votes, and four guineas in return for a 'plumper', a vote for that candidate and no one else. Those who needed to travel to Hull would expect to be paid their expenses, which might average £10.

A few decades later the freemen of Hull would be described as 'generally persons in a low station of life, and the manner in which they are bribed shows how little worthy they are of being entrusted with a privilege from which so many of the respectable inhabitants of the town are excluded'.[33] The intervention of Wilberforce would have been hugely welcome to the freemen in 1780, because it meant that there would be three candidates for the two seats, and therefore a contested election with expenses to be paid. Few things were more unwelcome to them than an uncontested election, as demonstrated by this account of the withdrawal of a candidate for Hull ten years later:

> The plump jocund risibility, that an hour before enlightened all countenances, was gradually drawn down into a longitudinal dejection, which pervaded every face, even the friends of the opposition, shrunk with the consciousness of their own approaching unimportance, sensible that their consequence was then (for want of a protracted canvass) sunk to nought, and that nothing could restore it but a THIRD MAN; the cry of which resounded in all parts, while scoured through the streets of HULL the disappointed crowds; and a Bell was sent forth to the adjacent towns, to ring out an invitation to a third CANDIDATE FOR HULL.[34]

While the freemen happily sold their votes, this did not mean they auctioned them to the highest bidder. They simply expected any candidate they voted for to pay the going rate, and since there was no secret ballot at that time, and the vote of every freeman could be observed, each candidate was duly able to pay for the votes he received, and generally did so two weeks after the close of the poll – since allegations of bribery had to be brought forward before that time. Possession of money did not of itself, therefore, guarantee success, although it certainly inspired confidence that the appropriate payments would be made in due course. It also enabled a candidate to treat his potential supporters in other ways, most commonly through the provision of alcohol, food and accommodation. In some campaigns, tickets were issued to proven or promised supporters entitling them to claim a certain amount of drink and food, and even a bed at a particular supportive inn. The quantities consumed could be enormous: the £8,500 spent by the Grosvenor family at Chester towards inn-keepers' bills in one election paid for 1,187 barrels of ale, 3,756 gallons of rum and brandy, and over twenty-seven thousand bottles of wine.[35] This was in a city of a similar size to Hull, with 1,500 electors. To refuse to treat the voters was regarded as an insult, and in a freeman borough such as Hull would certainly have led to electoral disaster, and quite possibly disorder. Everyone understood that the best way to avoid chaos at election times was properly conducted treating 'to humour the voters and to reward the faithful'.[36]

On top of all this, a good deal of money was spent on ancillary trades. Groceries, linen and meat purchased for use in the election were carefully and locally sourced, bands were employed at considerable expense, and carpenters and rosette-makers made a good profit. Yet since such employment could be had from more than one candidate, and payments for votes were made at a standard rate, it was still necessary to bring other means of persuasion to bear on the electorate. It was common for a Hull candidate or his agent to write to every inland merchant and manufacturer with any connection to Hull, to add to the pressure on local merchants to vote the right way. A candidate who had good connections with the government of the day could also dispense jobs in the customs service, obviously a major source of employment in a port.

What was very much unnecessary, astonishingly so by the standards of later centuries, was for a candidate to have policy positions, a manifesto or any kind of programme for government. National political organisations had not been developed. Since national newspapers were also in their infancy, there was usually little sense of the voters taking part in a single election along with their compatriots elsewhere in the country. A general election was more normally a multitude of disparate contests, and was not generally expected to lead to any change of government: when governments did change it was because of a shift in coalitions or royal favour rather than any discernible 'swing' among the voters. National issues could intrude into a constituency, and the opposition of David Hartley to the American War led to him being disowned by the Hull corporation, and very probably cost him votes in this particular election since the town, with a wartime garrison and a large customs service, had many loyal instincts. Such matters, however, did not predominate. The freemen were more interested in electing a candidate who would pay them a great deal of attention and ably handle their interests in Parliament. The Members for Hull were expected to speak up for the interest of the merchants and keep in touch with the local corporation – or bench, as it was called locally – and to present to ministers the various letters and grievances sent their way. A former Member for Hull, William Weddell, an associate of the main opposition party, the Rockingham Whigs, had lost his seat at the previous election as a result of his 'want of activity'.[37] A good candidate would engage in a comprehensive canvass of the freemen – one in 1790 canvassed every single one of them – and show them considerable deference. As the Earl of Sefton was told when he contested Liverpool some years later, 'You have no conception how great a personage every Freeman conceives himself to be on the eve of a contest.'[38]

Wilberforce was well equipped for such a contest. He already knew all the principal families of Hull, and they knew that his pockets were deep. From May 1780, although still not twenty-one, he set about canvassing and writing to the freemen in expectation of an election within the following year. One surviving response of a freeman living in Reading said that he would not come to Hull unless his expenses were paid, and hoped that Wilberforce would support 'the rights, liberties, and commercial interests of the people'. Another insisted that he would persist 'in voting as Lord Rockingham shall direct'.[39] Throughout the energetic canvassing there was little record of Wilberforce expressing decided opinions. One of his opponents, David Hartley, was an early opponent of slavery, and Wilberforce would later recall that 'I expressed my hope to him that the time would come when I should be able to do something on behalf of the slaves,'[40] the first recorded instance of his interest in this subject, which had yet to come to the attention of the public at large. The only positions Wilberforce had to take up in this first campaign were rather more local and personal: a stone was thrown at him during the hustings on election day, following which he was approached by the local butcher, Johnny Bell, who said, 'I have found out who threw the stone at you, and I'll kill him tonight.'[41] This brought forth Wilberforce's first appeal for patience and restraint in politics. He told the no doubt disappointed butcher that 'You must only frighten him,'[42] but it was an illustration that violence was never far beneath the surface of eighteenth-century politics.

June 1780 brought the Gordon Riots, the most serious outbreak of disorder in London for many decades, which illustrated the immense power of religion in general, and the fear of Catholic and thereby foreign influence in particular, among the general population of eighteenth-century Britain. A gathering of tens of thousands of members of the Protestant Association marched to Westminster under the leadership of Lord George Gordon to demand the repeal of the Catholic Relief Act, an attempt to recruit more soldiers by removing the practice of requiring recruits to take an oath denying the supremacy of the Pope. In a country where the Stuart kings of the seventeenth century had plotted with Catholic powers against their own subjects until they were driven out once and for all in 1688, and which had seen Jacobite attempts to seize the throne in 1715 and 1745, anti-Catholic feeling could still very easily reach boiling point. When Gordon lost control of the crowds, there were five days and nights of rioting in which dozens of buildings were burnt down and hundreds of people were killed, until the King himself took to the streets with troops to disperse the mob. In Hull, a smaller mob joined in the frenzy by burning down a new Roman Catholic chapel. As a friend to Catholic relief, as well as an opponent of the war, David Hartley was a doubly wounded candidate, quite apart from being up against the undoubted local popularity of both Lord Robert Manners and Wilberforce.

All that remained was for Wilberforce to conduct a vigorous campaign and for the election itself to be called. The first reached a climax with a famous ox-roast on his twenty-first birthday, accompanied by many hogsheads of ale for the electors and merchants of Hull. The second obligingly followed within days, although had it been a little earlier he would have been too young to take his seat. On 1 September

1780 a general election was called. The polling took place in Hull on the eleventh, with a truly dramatic result. David Hartley had received 453 votes and had lost his seat, with Lord Robert Manners polling 673. But William Wilberforce, at the age of twenty-one years and eighteen days, had received exactly as many votes as the two of them put together, 1,126. In an election where each voter could cast two votes, this meant that the vast majority must have cast one of their votes for him. It also meant a very large bill. Wilberforce noted 'the election cost me 8 or 9,000 £* – great riot – D. Hartley and Sir G. Savilles lodgings broke open in the night and they escaping over the roof'.[43] His charm, sociability, obvious intelligence and wealth had won through decisively. Now he would take these advantages into the far bigger world of Westminster.

Wilberforce took the oath as a Member of Parliament in the House of Commons on 31 October 1780, and took his seat on the backbenches opposite Lord North and the other ministers. One of his first impressions was: 'When I first came into parliament you could not go to the opposition side of the house without hearing the most shocking swearing &c. It was not so bad on the ministerial side tho' not I'm afraid from their being much better than their opponents.'[44] North's ministry had survived the general election, having taken the opposition by surprise with its timing, and could expect a reasonable majority in the House provided it retained the support of the 'King's friends', who would support whoever George III wished to have as First Lord of the Treasury, and a reasonable proportion of the independent Members. Wilberforce, elected at Hull entirely as his own man, certainly regarded himself as one of the latter. He resolved within hours of his election 'to be no party man',[45] indicating from the outset an absence of appetite for ministerial office and a detachment from the main political groupings which would resurface much more strongly in his later years. As

---

* The equivalent of more than £1 million today. The highest expenditure by a single candidate in the 2005 election was £13,212.

such, he was in good company. Probably around a third of the House at that time regarded themselves as independent to some degree, at a time when British political parties were rather weaker than they had been fifty years earlier, and dramatically weaker than they would become fifty years later.

Wilberforce's own election was a good illustration of why many seats were not within the control of any one faction. The terms 'Whig' and 'Tory' had lost much of the meaning which, decades earlier, divisions over the Glorious Revolution and the Hanoverian succession had given them; 'Tory' had become a pejorative and generally rejected label, while the label 'Whig' had been so widely adopted by the successful politicians of the mid-eighteenth century that it had become a commonplace. As William Pitt put it at this time, the name Whig 'in words is hardly a distinction, as everyone alike pretends to it'.[46] At the beginning of the Parliament of 1780 it was thought that Lord North's government could rely on the votes of at least 220 MPs, some of whom could be termed Tories, but who could more specifically be categorised as around eighty supporters of North and around 140 'King's friends'. About a hundred MPs could be identified as firmly in the opposition camp, most of them in the 'Whig' opposition led by Fox and Burke in the Commons and Rockingham in the Lords, but others in a smaller grouping loyal to the memory of Chatham and led from the House of Lords by the Earl of Shelburne. The whole notion of faction or 'party' was thought by many to be wrong and unpatriotic: for an independent MP to arrive at the House of Commons, speak up for his constituency, vary his vote and mix with all of the parties was therefore perfectly normal. Wilberforce set out on his Westminster career as just such an MP.

Wilberforce's beginnings as a parliamentary debater were relatively slow and undistinguished. From what can be discerned from the far from comprehensive records of the debates at the time, he first spoke on 17 May 1781 on a Bill for the Prevention of Smuggling, arguing that 'It would not only be severe, but unjust to confiscate the vessel: a master of a ship might take in the necessary quantity of spirits for three months' voyage; and by fortunately having a fair and brisk wind, perform the voyage in six weeks; the custom house visit his ship and finding in it a greater quantity of spirits etc. than the law allows, insist that the vessel should be confiscated.'[47] His dutiful spokesmanship on behalf of the interests of Hull continued with what appears to be a second speech on 5 December 1781, in which he expressed both patriotism – it made 'every Englishman's breast glow with the noblest ardour whenever he heard of Great Britain being involved in a contest with France and Spain' – and a request for government contracts for Hull: 'A ship of the line called the *Temple* had been built some years since at the town he had the honour to represent, Kingston-upon-Hull; and ships might be procured from the same yard regularly if encouragement was given.'[48] Unfortunately this brought forth a rather withering retort from the minister, Lord Mulgrave, who reported that 'The *Temple*, after having been at sea only three years, on a fine Summer's day, in weather perfectly calm, went down and was lost,'[49] but the young Member was nevertheless doing his best for his constituents.

While he was assiduous in attending the House of Commons, Wilberforce found himself welcomed with open arms into wider London society. He took rooms in the St James's area, placing him only a few hundred yards from the House of Commons and squarely in the middle of London's thriving clubland. The late eighteenth century was the heyday of the gentlemen's clubs: White's, which was exclusive and aristocratic; Boodle's, full of the hunting and country squire set; and Brooks's, founded only two years before Wilberforce's arrival in London but rapidly becoming the playground of the opposition Whigs. These and other clubs were descended from the chocolate and coffee houses of earlier decades. Such places had steadily turned into centres for drinking and gambling, and eventually they were turned by wealthy people into private clubs so that such activities could be enjoyed in seclusion from the lower orders. It is testimony to Wilberforce's social popularity and political independence that it was not long before he was a member of all three of the most celebrated clubs, along with a string of others such as Goostree's, and Miles and Evans.

It was in the clubs of St James's Street and Pall Mall that Wilberforce would witness at first hand one of the most licentious and decadent times in London's social history. The extravagance, immorality and sheer abandon of that era would do much to contribute to the stricter morals of Victorian times which were a natural reaction to them. Wilberforce's own later views would be partly shaped by his experiences in London in the early 1780s, as he joined in with activities which he enjoyed at the time but which would later appal him. Gambling and heavy drinking could be pursued around the clock, notwithstanding the seniority and responsibilities of those involved. Horace Walpole's description of three days in the life of Charles James Fox in 1772 give a flavour of the habits of the time:

> He had sat up at playing at hazard at Almack's from Tuesday evening 4th, till five in the afternoon of Wednesday, 5th. An hour before he had recovered £12,000 that he had lost, and by dinner, which was at five o'clock, he had ended losing £11,000. On the Thursday, he spoke in [a Commons debate]; went to dinner at past eleven that night; from thence to White's, where he drank till seven the next morning; thence to Almack's, where he won £6,000; and between three and four in the afternoon he set out for Newmarket. His brother Stephen lost £11,000 two nights after, and Charles £10,000 more on 13th; so that in three nights, the two brothers, the eldest not twenty-five, lost £32,000.[50]

By this age Fox is thought to have lost £140,000, approximately comprising his whole fortune. Young aristocrats lost their entire estates, with White's described as 'the bane of half the English nobility'[51] because of the terrible consequences of 'that destructive fury, the spirit of play'.[52] Huge sums of money were bet at hazard, faro, piquet, backgammon and even whist. Walpole wrote: 'The young men lose five, ten, fifteen thousand pounds in an evening. Lord Stavordale, not one-and-twenty, lost eleven thousand last Tuesday, but recovered it by one great hand at Hazard. He swore a great oath – "Now, if I had been playing deep, I might have won millions!"'[53] When games were not available, there was much betting on events. Each club had a betting book in which its members would wager against each other as to who would be Prime Minister by the end of the year, or even when the King would die. When George II had gone off to the European war in

1743, the going rate against his being killed was 4:1. On another occasion 'A man dropped down at the door of White's; he was carried into the house. Was he dead or not? The odds were immediately given and taken for and against. It was proposed to bleed him. Those who had taken the odds the man was dead, protested that the use of a lancet would affect the fairness of the bet.'[54]

The addiction to gambling was not confined to the aristocracy. A state-run lottery had been established in 1709 which collected a good deal of money from the poor and helped fund a whole range of fine projects, from the British Museum to Westminster Bridge, as well as helping to finance the American War. As he ventured to the gaming tables of St James's in the winter of 1780–81, Wilberforce could easily have lost most or all of his inheritance. He had the encouragement of winning money from the Duke of Norfolk in Boodle's at an early stage, and knew that, as he later wrote, 'They considered me a fine, fat pigeon whom they might pluck.'[55] When he first played faro at Brooks's and a friend tried to interrupt, the well-known wit and rake George Selwyn responded greedily, 'Oh sir, don't interrupt him, he is very well employed.'[56] But Wilberforce was careful not to play for ruinous stakes. His diary records the occasional loss of £100, yet it seems to be his winnings rather than his losses which began to give him an aversion to gambling. Asked to play the part of the bank one night at Goostree's he 'rose the winner of £600. Much of this was lost by those who were only heirs to future fortunes, and could not therefore meet such a call without inconvenience.'[57] Such experiences nurtured in him a feeling of guilt which would be a powerful influence on his future, very different, behaviour.

Gambling was only one aspect of this time of excess. It was fashionable to drink heavily, particularly claret and port wine, and to eat greedily, with huge steaks and scores of turtles being the favourite dinners of the London clubs. Prince George, Prince of Wales, who was rapidly becoming the despair of King George III and Queen Charlotte through his disloyalty, decadence, extravagance and indebtedness, fully represented in his own person the barely controlled behaviour of the time. Holding fêtes and balls which would carry on from noon of one day into the morning of the next, and becoming so drunk that at one party he fell over while dancing and was sick in front of his guests, he also made the most of a string of mistresses, and was sometimes happy to share them with Charles James Fox. His brother, the Duke of Clarence and future King William IV, kept a mistress to whom he paid two hundred guineas every quarter for twenty years, and was so open about it that the first negotiations about her terms were actually reported in the press.

In such society, the possession by a married man of a mistress was regarded not only as a necessity, but her position was little short of official, understood and acknowledged by the rest of the establishment. In addition, the gentlemen walking from their gambling in one club to drinking in another could easily avail themselves of some of more than ten thousand prostitutes who plied their trade on the streets of London, who were 'more numerous than at Paris, and have more liberty and effrontery than at Rome itself. About nightfall they arrange themselves in a file in the footpaths of all the great streets.'[58] In Pall Mall itself, nestling among the gentlemen's clubs was Mrs Hazer's Establishment of Pleasure, where there was 'naked dancing, and the floorshow included a Tahitian love feast' involving twelve nymphs and twelve youths. Whether Wilberforce yielded to such temptations is not known. Years after his death, his son Samuel told the Bishop of Oxford that 'his father when young used to drink tea every evening in a brothel', although this was said to be 'not ... from any licentious purpose – his health alone would then have prevented that'.[59] On the contrary, his ill health appeared to be no barrier to any social activity at this time: he was gambling, drinking, eating heartily, and singing beautifully – the Prince of Wales is meant to have told the Duchess of Devonshire that he would go anywhere to hear Wilberforce sing. But it does seem that, even at this stage, Wilberforce lived with more care and thoughtfulness than most of his social companions. He readily took advice from wise old birds such as the former Lord Chancellor, Lord Camden, who told him to desist from using his wonderful powers of mimicry because 'It is but a vulgar accomplishment.'[60] This did not quite put paid to the habit, particularly since he was in much demand for his impression of Lord North, but the relationship illustrated his need for genuine discussion rather than mere social frivolity: Camden 'took a great fancy to me because, I believe, when all the others were wasting their time at cards or piquet we would come and talk with him and hear his stories of the old Lord Chatham'.[61]

Wilberforce was already displaying an extraordinary facility, which he would maintain throughout his life, of being careful about his own behaviour yet simultaneously sought-after for his good company and humour. As his Cambridge friend Gerard Edwards, who remained a close companion in London, put it even at this time, 'I thank the Gods that I live in the age of Wilberforce and that I know one man at least who is both moral and entertaining.'[62] His circle of friends naturally widened, now including many young politicians such as Pitt, Lord Euston, Edward Eliot and Henry Bankes, but still encompassing his old companions from Hull. To one of the latter, a B.B. Thompson, he wrote from London on 9 June 1781:

> My Dear Thompson,
> We have a blessed prospect of sitting till the end of next month. Judge how agreeable this must be to me, who was in the hope ere now to be indulging myself amongst the lakes of Westmoreland. As soon as ever I am released from my parliamentary attendance I mean to betake myself thither . . . Between business in the morning and pleasure at night my time is pretty well filled up. Whatever you . . . used to say of my idleness, one is, I assure you, as much attended to as the other.
> The papers will have informed you how Mr William Pitt, second son of the late Lord Chatham, has distinguished himself; he comes out as his father did a ready-made orator, and I doubt not but that I shall one day or other see him the first man in the country. His famous speech, however, delivered the other night, did not convince me, and I staid in with the old fat fellow: by the way he grows every day fatter, so where he will end I know not.
> My business requires to be transacted at places very distant from each other, and I am now going to call on Lord R.M. [Robert Manners] thence to Hoxton, and next to Tower Hill; so you may judge how much leisure I have left for letter writing . . .[63]

This single letter sums up Wilberforce's predilections and personality as a young MP approaching the age of twenty-two. His eagerness to spend the summer in Windermere – he had rented a house, Rayrigg, with views over the lake – illustrates his determination to enjoy the hills and countryside; his assiduousness in attending Parliament and constant travelling around London to meetings demonstrate his seriousness amidst the continuing enjoyment of London nightlife; his political independence is displayed, since staying in with 'the old fat fellow' is a reference to voting with Lord North against the opposition; but his simultaneous and growing admiration for his friend and vocal member of the opposition, William Pitt, shines through.

Such admiration would soon draw him into more serious participation in national affairs. For as Wilberforce dreamt of rural pleasures that summer, on the other side of the Atlantic the armies of Washington and Lafayette were manoeuvring to bring the final hopes of British victory to ashes. British politics was on the edge of a series of convulsions which would bring the youthful William Pitt to power and place Wilberforce in the thick of parliamentary and electoral battle.

3

The Devoted Acolyte

Who but madmen would enter a contest for such a county, or indeed
for any county?

PHILIP FRANCIS TO CHRISTOPHER WYVILL,
on the subject of an election for the county of Yorkshire, 1794[1]

Tear the enemy to pieces.

WILLIAM PITT TO WILLIAM WILBERFORCE, 24 March 1784[2]

HOWEVER QUIET the scene when a tired messenger rode his
horse up to Lord George Germain's house in Pall Mall on the
morning of Sunday, 25 November 1781, the contents of the message he
carried would lead to two and a half years of upheaval and crisis in
the government and politics of Britain. All night long the relays of
horses from the port of Falmouth in Cornwall had borne towards
London the news that Lord North and his embattled ministers must
have dreaded: at Yorktown in Virginia, an entire British army under
General Cornwallis had capitulated. While military commanders might
calculate that the war could be continued from the British stronghold
of New York, others knew that this disaster would 'occasion the loss of
all the Southern colonies very speedily',[3] and that British possessions
in the West Indies, including Jamaica, could be 'in imminent danger'.[4]
Germain, the dogged but hapless Secretary of State, would soon produce a plan for struggling on with the war, trying to hold New York,
Charleston and Savannah while mounting amphibious raids and court-
ing American loyalists. But Lord North, possessed as usual with a sure

feel for parliamentary opinion, knew that in domestic politics the game was up. 'Oh God it is all over!'[5] he exclaimed when the news of Yorktown reached Downing Street that fateful Sunday morning.

Caught between the implacable George III on the one side and the growing view among MPs that further fighting would bring ruin at the hands of France and Spain in addition to the now inevitable loss of the American colonies, the North administration staggered uncertainly on through the winter of 1781–82, sacrificing Germain that January but still failing to win the confidence of Parliament or the nation. The attacks mounted on the enfeebled administration by Fox, Burke, Pitt and other opposition Members were merciless and scathing, while at the same time a growing number of independent MPs concluded that North must be ousted and the war ended. Wilberforce was among them, delivering a speech on 22 February 1782 which was his first major display of political partisanship in the Commons. While the year before he might have 'staid in with the old fat fellow', Wilberforce now turned on the same portly figure of Lord North. He declared that 'while the present Ministry existed there were no prospects of either peace or happiness to this Kingdom'. It was clear that the government intended to pursue the ruinous war in a cruel, bloody and impracticable manner; the actions of ministers more 'resembled the career of furious madmen than the necessarily vigorous and prudent exertions of able statesmen'.[6] He voted solidly with the opposition in the close-fought divisions of late February and early March 1782. On 20 March he would have witnessed the resignation of North after twelve years in office, the snow falling outside the House of Commons as British politicians turned their minds to how to construct a fresh government while rescuing a tottering Empire. Nominally still an independent Member, Wilberforce had clearly aligned himself with the opposition, and was invited to their meetings. That he should have taken such a strong stand against the North government and the American War is not surprising. He had befriended Pitt, for whom opposition to the war was second nature; he admired Fox, whom he found 'very pleasant and unaffected'[7] at a number of dinners and who had masterminded the tactics of the opposition; he was also alert to the political mood and alive to the simple reality of the time, namely that the only way in which the British could mitigate their defeat was to turf out the ministers who could be blamed for it.

While 'no party man', Wilberforce would find himself for the next four years very much categorised as belonging to a party. The common thread which would run through all his political dispositions until 1786 was loyalty to his great friend Pitt. Pitt was not a member of the new government formed from among the opposition groupings in March 1782, having rather haughtily declared in advance that he could 'never accept a subordinate situation',[8] and not having been offered a senior one. Nevertheless, he and Wilberforce were firm supporters of this new Whig-led government, headed by the Marquis of Rockingham, who was as munificent in his wealth and aristocratic grandeur as he was inadequate as a political leader or manager. Fox, the new Secretary of State and ministerial leader in the Commons, seethed with indignation that the King had seen fit only to conduct negotiations with the lesser of the opposition groupings, that led by Shelburne. Wilberforce was included in the discussions held about the formation of the government, and remembered 'Fox awkwardly bringing out that Lord Shelburne only had seen the King, in short jealousy between Foxites and Shelburneites manifested, tho' for a long time suppressed'.[9] The wily George III, in a 'masterpiece of Royal skill',[10] had ensured that the Rockingham administration would be poisoned from the outset with a rich dose of resentment and suspicion. He did not intend that those who had opposed the American War would stay in office for long.

The Rockingham administration did indeed turn out to be one of the most ill-fated in British history. Within weeks Fox and Shelburne were at furious loggerheads over the terms of the peace treaty being negotiated in Paris, and within three months of entering office Rockingham was dead. Wilberforce had been much courted by Rockingham during his final months. The formerly unknown Member for Hull was by now identified as an active MP who could think more clearly and speak more forcefully than most of his colleagues. With Rockingham keen to secure the loyalty of an able Yorkshireman, and the Whigs looking forward to creating new peers who could strengthen their position in the House of Lords, there were even rumours that Wilber-force would soon be ennobled. Eager suppliers of ermine robes were in touch with him to try to secure his business in the event of this happy elevation taking place.

It seems unlikely that Wilberforce would have accepted a peerage at the age of twenty-two, even though peerages in the eighteenth century were far scarcer than they have since become, and at that time carried the automatic guarantee of being passed on through the generations. Like Pitt, he saw the Commons as the only place for a young man of ambition and energy. At this stage of his life Wilberforce certainly harboured some ambitions for office, but in July 1782 he could only watch loyally as yet another new government took office, this time with Shelburne as First Lord of the Treasury and the twenty-three-year-old Pitt as Chancellor of the Exchequer.

There is no trace of jealousy in Wilberforce's attitude towards the spectacular promotion of his friend. Indeed, it was in the summer of 1782 that these two young men began to form a bond of companionship sufficiently strong that it could never be completely ruptured even by the sharpest of disagreements in later years. They were both key members of the group of twenty-five Cambridge graduates who formed Goostree's club in Pall Mall, dining, drinking and gambling there every night when Parliament was sitting. There, with Lord Euston, Pepper Arden, Henry Bankes and Edward Eliot, 'all youngsters just entering into life',[11] they enjoyed themselves to the full, going on to the House of Commons where George Selwyn could find them 'singing and laughing à gorge déployée', making him 'wish for one day to be twenty'.[12] Some evenings or in the recess Pitt would ride out to Wimbledon to spend the night at Lauriston House, which Wilberforce had now inherited, and 'for near three month slept almost every night there'.[13] Despite the political responsibilities they now enjoyed, their letters and diary entries of this period suggest an atmosphere of almost carefree youth. Pitt would write to Wilberforce from the Commons in the afternoon, 'Eliot, Arden and I will be with you before curfew and expect an early meal of peas and strawberries.'[14] Wilberforce's diary entries in the summers of 1782 and 1783 include: 'Delicious day – lounged morning at Wimbledon with friends, foyning* at night, and run about the garden for an hour or two,' or 'To Wimbledon with Pitt and Eliot, at their persuasion,' or 'Fine hot day, went on water with Pitt and Eliot fishing, came back, dined, walked evening. Eliot went home, Pitt stayed.'[15] There was evidently much boisterous activity, with reports of neighbours being 'alarmed with noises at their door'[16] and of Pitt having cut up the silk hat of another visitor, a future Foreign Secretary, one night and strewn the remnants around the flowerbeds. Not only did Wilberforce admire Pitt's political abilities, he also loved his company, thinking him 'the most truly witty man he had ever met',[17] and later recording, 'Mr Pitt was systematically witty . . . the others were often run away with by their wit. Mr Pitt was always master of his. He could turn it to any end or object he desired.'[18] Pitt, in turn, cherished Wilberforce's good humour and political support.

At Easter 1782, the two Williams had holidayed together in Bath and Brighthelmstone (modern-day Brighton). But with Pitt in office as Chancellor, Wilberforce was unable to take his friend with him later that year on the extended summer tour that would become his perennial habit over the next few years. Abandoning plans for a trip to the Continent because of a sudden by-election in Hull (Lord Robert Manners had died and was in due course succeeded, unopposed, by the previously defeated David Hartley), Wilberforce made once again for Rayrigg on Windermere before visiting Weymouth in the autumn. He simply could not do without country air, explaining to his sister in the summer of 1783 that the House of Commons was unable 'to compensate to me for the loss of air, pleasant walks, and what Milton calls "each rural sight, each rural sound"'.[19] 'I never leave this poor villa,' he wrote from Wimbledon, 'without feeling my virtuous affections confirmed and strengthened; and I'm afraid it would be to some degree true if I were to add that I never remain long in London without their being somewhat injured and diminished.'[20] To Rayrigg he would take an assortment of books,

---

* Fencing with a weapon designed for thrusting or lunging – but in this context meaning verbal fencing.

including 'classics, statutes at large and history',[21] and welcome a succession of friends.

In the Lakes he found solitude through riding, walking and boating, but also lifelong friendship, in particular with Colonel John Pennington, more than a quarter of a century older than Wilberforce and another admirer of Pitt, who as Lord Muncaster would become the recipient of a vast proportion of Wilberforce's letters on public affairs. Other visitors included Pitt's future political hostess the Duchess of Gordon, and a procession of Hull family friends, one of whom found Wilberforce to be 'riotous and noisy'.[22] Once ensconced at Weymouth in the middle of October, he was writing to Edward Eliot to say that 'So mild is the climate and so calm and clear is the sea that on this very fifteenth day of October I am sitting with my window open on its side and am every moment wishing myself up to the chin in it.'[23] It was an abiding characteristic that he would seek out the long summer periods of rest and contemplation which his wealth permitted and his inclination and constitution required. Where Pitt was happy to spend many of his summers dealing with the grind of dispatches and correspondence and darting a short distance out of London for a brief respite, Wilberforce drew strength and inspiration from a more balanced existence. It was a difference of temperament which helped to make one of them suitable for high office, and the other designed for high ideals.

Pitt's aptitude for high office was soon tested. His boss, the Earl of Shelburne, proved unable or unwilling to broaden the political base of his ministry during the long summer recess, leaving Pitt as a principal spokesman in the House of Commons for a government which had only minority support. By the time the preliminaries of the peace agreement with France, Spain and the new United States of America were ready to be put to Parliament for approval in February 1783, the Shelburne ministry was vulnerable to parliamentary ambush. The proposed peace treaties represented a reasonable settlement under all the circumstances, with Britain's negotiating position having been strengthened by a crucial naval victory in the West Indies in April 1782. Britain would give up the Floridas and Minorca to Spain, St Lucia and some other islands to France, and the huge tracts of territory between the Appalachians and the Mississippi were awarded to America at the same time as her independence was recognised. Shelburne had simultaneously taken great care to negotiate an extensive commercial treaty with America. While these proposals were wholly realistic, and even far-sighted, Fox took the opportunity to attack them as a means of removing his hated rival from power. In one of the great unholy alliances of British political history, the supporters of Fox, who had always opposed the war, and the party of North, which had prosecuted it, now came together to drive Shelburne from office, and Pitt with him.

Pitt asked Wilberforce to give one of the leading speeches in a crucial debate on the peace treaty on 17 February 1783. Clearly he believed that the voice of Wilberforce was already influential and eloquent; for his part Wilberforce was ready to do anything for his friend. Wilberforce was tense as he prepared for his most important speech to that date. He spent a weekend with 'his sleep disturbed at the thoughts of a full House of Commons',[24] walked for several hours on the Sunday afternoon, and made a plea for the necessity of peace in his speech on the Monday afternoon, arguing that if the Fox–North coalition defeated the ministry on this issue, 'no Minister would in future dare to make such a peace as the necessity of the country might require'.[25] Wilberforce's speech was well regarded, although he recorded the events of that day in his diary in a very matter-of-fact way:

> 17th. Walked down morning to House to get Milner into gallery. Seconded the address. Lost the motion by 16. Did not leave House till about eight in the morning, and bed about nine.[26]

It must have been a deflating experience. Pitt's own speech was regarded indifferently, and the government defeat by sixteen votes meant that the Shelburne ministry was virtually finished. In the climactic debate of four days later, Pitt pulled himself together to deliver a stirring defence of his colleague's policy and his own conduct which established him as a major political force. Wilberforce again spoke up for his friend, and wrote down what has become a celebrated note of Pitt's physical sickness at the time: 'Pitt's famous speech on second day's debate – first day's not so good. Spoke three hours, till four in the morning. Stomach disordered, and actually holding Solomon's porch door opened with one hand, while vomiting during Fox's speech to whom he was to reply.'[27]

The combination of Pitt's oratorical performances, the shortage of weighty figures in the Commons and the desperation of George III to find a parliamentary figure who could prevent the Fox–North coalition from coming to power catapulted William Pitt into the front rank of political life as a potential Prime Minister. Shelburne resigned on 24 February, but for the whole of March Pitt remained in office as Chancellor of the Exchequer in a government without a leader while the King thrashed about in an increasingly desperate search for a Prime Minister he did not hate. Twice during the five-week crisis Pitt came close to accepting office as Prime Minister while still only twenty-three years old, but twice he had the good sense to recognise that he would have had no defence against a hostile House of Commons moving quickly to vote him out. The irascible King varied for five weeks between trying to insist that Pitt take office, begging other ex-ministers to do so, sending for Pitt's uncle, Thomas Pitt, as a desperate resort – 'Mr Thomas Pitt or Mr Thomas anybody',[28] threatening to abdicate and finally, in late March, accepting the Fox–North coalition into power with the Duke of Portland as its nominal head. He did this with the worst possible grace, accompanied by a fixed resolution to create no peerages or honours at their request and a secret determination to eject them from office whenever a convenient pretext arose: 'I trust the eyes of the Nation will soon be opened as my sorrow may prove fatal to my health if I remain long in this thraldom.'[29]

Throughout the chaos Wilberforce remained closely connected to Pitt, both socially and politically. If he felt any jealousy about the spectacular rise to prominence of his friend he was good at hiding it, although on the day Pitt was first offered the premiership he noted: '24th. Dined Pitt's – heard of the very surprising propositions.'[30] When Pitt resigned at the end of March, he gravitated immediately to the happy society of Goostree's and Wilberforce's villa: '31st. Pitt resigned today. Dined Pitt's then Goostree's where supped. Bed almost three o'clock. April 3rd. Wimbledon, where Pitt &c. dined and slept. Evening walk – bed a little past two.'[31] Released from the cares of office, Pitt started to plan a summer of travel, including a visit to France, involving Wilberforce and their close mutual friend Edward Eliot. Knowing that conspiratorial meetings were taking place between George III, Earl Temple, and the former Lord Chancellor, Lord Thurlow, with the intention of putting Pitt into office in more favourable circumstances than those available in March, they kept an eye on political events, but when Parliament rose in July Fox and North were still in office, while the King chafed. Pitt wrote to Wilberforce from Brighton on 6 August: 'I have only to tell you that I have *no news*, which I consider as making it pretty certain that there will be none now before the meeting of Parliament [in November]. The party to Rheims holds of course, at least as far as depends upon me.'[32]

Most of Pitt's letters to Wilberforce from this time reveal two principal concerns about his friend: the first that he was having serious trouble with his eyesight, and the second that his punctuality and travel plans could not be relied upon. Pitt would end letters with: 'I am very glad to see you write without the assistance of a secretary. Perhaps, however, you will not be able to read without the assistance of a decypherer. At least in compassion to your eyesight it is as well for me to try it no further,'[33] and Wilberforce's diaries in 1783 have many entries such as 'My eyes bad. Bed early,'[34] and 'Bad day. Eyes indifferent.'[35] In Pitt's concern about Wilberforce's timekeeping there is a friendly hint of a more widespread opinion which had taken shape about him, that, as the first Lord Carrington was later to put it, 'As to his fitting office his careless and inaccurate method of doing business rendered him wholly unfit for it.'[36] Pitt's letter of 6 August enjoins Wilberforce to 'recollect that you have to deal with punctual men, who would not risk their characters by being an hour too late for any appointment'.[37] By 22 August, with the trip to France imminent, Pitt was writing to Wilberforce:

Dear Wilberforce,

I hope you have found benefit enough from your inland rambling, to be in perfect order now for crossing the seas. Eliot and
I meet punctually at Bankes's the 1st September, and in two days
after shall be in London. Pray let us see you, or hear from you by
that time, and do not verify my prophecy of detaining us a fortnight and jilting us at the end of it. We shall really not have a day
to lose, which makes me pursue you with this hasty admonition.
Adieu ever yours, W Pitt.[38]

Pitt need not have worried on this occasion about Wilberforce's
reliability, for he duly turned up at Bankes's house in Dorset in early
September after a visit to his family and constituency in Hull. Pitt
should, however, have been even more concerned about Wilberforce's
eyesight, because he nearly shot him while taking aim at a partridge.
Wilberforce was sceptical about whether he had come so close to
wiping out the nation's political future, but, 'So at least,' he later
recorded, 'my companions affirmed, with a roguish wish, to make the
most of my short-sightedness and inexperience in field sports.'[39]

With the naïvety of young men who had never set foot outside
their own country before, Wilberforce, Pitt and Eliot sailed for Calais
in early September without the preparation and documents which
were necessary for comfortable travel overseas in the eighteenth century. Having arrived in France with only a letter of introduction to a
M. Coustier of Rheims, who was assumed to be a senior businessman
or banker, Wilberforce described what happened next in a letter to
Henry Bankes:

> From Calais we made directly for Rheims, and the day after our
> arrival dressed ourselves unusually well, and proceeded to the
> house of Mons. Coustier to present, with not a little awe, our only
> letters of recommendation. It was with some surprise that we
> found Mons. Coustier behind a counter distributing figs and
> raisins. I had heard that it was very usual for gentlemen on the
> continent to practise some handicraft trade or other for their
> amusement, and therefore for my own part I concluded that his
> taste was in the fig way, and that he was only playing at grocer

for his diversion; and viewing the matter in this light, I could not help admiring the excellence of his imitation; but we soon found that Mons. Coustier was a 'véritable epicier,' and that not a very eminent one.[40]

Not only was M. Coustier not one of the local gentry, he could not even effect an introduction to them. The disorganised trio spent over a week at an inn, 'without making any great progress in the French language, which could not indeed be expected of us, as we spoke to no human being but each other and our Irish courier'.[41] But eventually they persuaded their grocer 'to put on a bag and sword and carry us to the intendant of the police, whom he supplied with groceries'.[42] The astonished police officer initially found their story incredible, and told the Abbé de Lageard, who under the Archbishop of Rheims wielded civic as well as religious authority, that 'There are three Englishmen here of very suspicious character. They are in a wretched lodging, they have no attendants, yet their courier says that they are "*grands seigneurs*" and that one of them is the son of the great Chatham; but it must be impossible, they must be "*des intrigants*".[43] Having thus come close to being arrested for spying, the three now found their luck changed dramatically: the Abbé was a generous man who provided huge meals, long conversations and 'the best wine the country can afford'.[44] After a week of such indulgence they were presented to the Archbishop, whose accessibility and normality made a very positive impression on Wilberforce: 'N.B. Archbishops in England are not like Archevêques in France; these last are jolly fellows of about forty years of age, who play at billiards, &c. like other people.'[45]

Having turned themselves from suspicious strangers into local celebrities in Rheims, the travellers were able to proceed to Paris, where even the Queen, Marie Antoinette, had heard about their time with the grocer and teased them about it. Joining the French court at its hunting retreat of Fontainebleau, they embarked on a whirlwind of meals, opera, cards, backgammon and billiards, and were often in the company of Marie Antoinette, whom Wilberforce found 'a monarch of most engaging manners and appearance'.[46] He wrote on his return that 'they all, men and women, crowded round Pitt in shoals'.[47] Such scenes must have been an enduring reminder to Wilberforce and Eliot that their friend already carried with him immense fame and prestige. The world of European politics was thrown open to them; they met Lafayette and Benjamin Franklin, and while Pitt was stag-hunting, Eliot and Wilberforce were taken to see Louis XVI himself, a 'clumsy, strange figure in immense boots'.[48] Eating, drinking and gambling were their vices for the trip, and there are no accounts of the three young men becoming intimate with the local women. Pitt had no hesitation in refusing the offer of marriage to the daughter of the vastly wealthy and powerful Jacques Necker – she would subsequently almost rival him as an antagonist of Napoleon as Madame de Staël. At this stage of their lives, none of the three had marriage in mind. Wilberforce had already rejected one overture himself, saying that he preferred to remain 'that isolated unproductive and stigmatised thing, a Bachelor'.[49]

They just had time to see the sights of Paris, 'going every night to a play, of which we were not able to make out a syllable',[50] before their six-week visit to France was ended abruptly. On 22 October 1783 a special messenger arrived for Pitt, summoning him back to England with all possible speed. By the twenty-fourth they were on the road from Dover to London. One of the greatest constitutional crises of British history was imminent. However great their attachment and friendship, Pitt, Wilberforce and Eliot would never enjoy such carefree travels together again.

Wilberforce noted that he returned 'to England . . . and secret plottings – the King groaning under the Ministry that had been imposed on him'.[51] He was back to the familiar life of Wimbledon, Goostree's and late-night dinners. Pitt, Eliot and Pitt's elder brother, Lord Chatham, were his most frequent dining companions, but he was still sufficient of an independent, at least nominally, to be invited to dinner at Downing Street by the Duchess of Portland with Charles James Fox in attendance. Even so, there could be little doubt where Wilberforce would stand in the great confrontation between Pitt and Fox which was about to grip the nation.

After seven months in government, Fox, the inveterate gambler, decided to risk all on his East India Bill in the House of Commons. More than two centuries later, it is sometimes difficult to grasp the huge importance of India in eighteenth-century British politics. British business in India was conducted under the auspices of the East India Company, but the scale of the fortunes to be made and the importance of the decisions taken within the Company, which could affect the lives of millions of people and determine the course of a war or the duration of peace, meant that East India business was increasingly the business of the British government. In the 1770s Lord North had attempted to put the affairs of the East India Company on an acceptable political footing, introducing a Governor General, a Council and a Supreme Court. These reforms were now seen as failing, partly because of the intense loathing for each other evidenced by the Governor General, Warren Hastings, on the one hand and the members of the Council, such as Philip Francis, on the other. In the early 1780s Fox's great ally Edmund Burke had led the denunciations of Hastings and the parliamentary assault on the alleged mismanagement of Indian affairs. Now they were in power, Fox and Burke intended to bring true political accountability to the Company's decisions. Their Bill, presented to Parliament on 18 November 1783, included a proposal to create a Board of seven Commissioners, appointed by Parliament and with extensive powers over the officers and business of the East India Company, thus providing political authority over the Company's management.

This was no innocent proposal. So extensive were the riches to be acquired in India that the power of the seven Commissioners to make key appointments within the East India Company would make them very powerful men. Furthermore, their appointment for fixed terms by parliamentary vote meant that the Fox–North majority would be able to determine all seven Commissioners to begin with, that they could not be immediately dismissed by a new administration, and that the King was shut out of a vital area of patronage and influence. Such would be the patronage accruing to the Fox–North coalition once they carried the Bill that it would materially consolidate their hold on power at Westminster. Well-intentioned as it may also have been, the East

India Bill was therefore a direct challenge to the opposition and to George III to do their worst.

Fox intended to rush the Bill through within weeks as Pitt sought frantically to bring MPs to Westminster and denounced it as 'one of the most boldest, most unprecedented, most desperate and alarming attempts at the exercise of tyranny that ever disgraced the annals of this or any other country'.[52] Wilberforce was there to help his friend. In a debate on 20 November he spoke 'with humour and ability' and said that 'If the present Bill passed we might see the government of Great Britain set up in India, instead of that of India in Great Britain.'[53] That Wilberforce was speaking at Pitt's behest rather than in any way representing the wider views of the independent MPs became clear when Fox carried the Bill through the Commons with three-figure majorities and, in early December, proudly carried it to the House of Lords for approval.

It was a gamble too far. Earl Temple warned the King that the Bill was 'a plan to take more than half the royal power, and by that means to disable His Majesty for the rest of the reign'.[54] After quietly consulting Pitt through an intermediary, George III took the unprecedented step of secretly asking members of the House of Lords to vote against the Bill, and then dismissed the Fox–North coalition from office on the grounds that their measure had been defeated in Parliament. On 19 December 1783, George III appointed Pitt as Prime Minister, even though Fox and North clearly continued to command majority support in the House of Commons. Few events in the entire history of the British constitution have roused such intense passions as this brutal exercise of royal power. To supporters of the King, he had been justified in ridding himself of ministers 'who held him in bondage, and who meditated to render that bondage perpetual'.[55] But to opponents, the dismissal by the King of a government with a clear majority in the House of Commons, and the handing out of royal instructions to members of the House of Lords on how to vote, were utterly unconstitutional and a total violation of the constitutional settlement of 1688. As an enraged Charles James Fox put it to the House of Commons, it was an issue which would decide 'whether we are henceforward free men or slaves; whether this House is the palladium of liberty or the engine of despotism'.[56] Pitt, at twenty-four by far the youngest Prime Minister in British history, would take office in the most difficult conceivable circumstances, on the back of a constitutional manoeuvre which was dubious at best and with a majority of MPs determined to remove him.

Seasoned observers believed Pitt to have little chance of surviving in office. Wilberforce himself recorded one of the most famous descriptions of the fledgling government in his diary on 22 December as Earl Temple, one of the few senior politicians prepared to join Pitt in the cabinet, resigned after only three days in office:

> 22nd. Lord Temple Resigned. No dissolution. Drove about for Pitt. Sat at home. Then Goostrees. 'So your friend Mr Pitt means to come in,' said Mrs Crewe;* 'Well, he may do what he likes during the holidays, but it will only be a mince-pie administration depend on it.'[57]

The mince-pie administration, it was believed, would not last far into January 1784, but Pitt spent the period forming his government and winning over some MPs as best he could. Wilberforce was present throughout many key decisions – '23rd. Morning Pitt's . . . Pitt nobly firm. Evening Pitt's. Cabinet formed.'[58] Pitt managed to bring in the relatively undistinguished Lord Sydney as Home Secretary and Earl Carmarthen as Foreign Secretary, but it was scornfully noted in many quarters that the only distinguishing feature of his government was their collective capacity for drink. For junior ministerial positions Pitt was able to look to some of his friends and personal allies, but at no stage does he appear to have contemplated asking Wilberforce, perhaps his closest friend and companion, to join the ranks of the ministers. Wilberforce could have been forgiven for having been puzzled by this. Leaving Downing Street on the evening of 23 December he said to Tom Steele, another MP and close friend of Pitt, 'Pitt must take care whom he makes Secretary of the Treasury,' only to receive the reply, 'Mind

---

* Frances Crewe was a highly fashionable hostess and was regarded as one of the greatest beauties of her time, much admired by Fox, Burke and Sheridan.

what you say, for I am Secretary of the Treasury.'[59] There is no record of Pitt offering office to Wilberforce and him refusing it. The subject seems simply not to have come up, either then or on any subsequent occasion.

Why would Pitt not offer a position to a friend he particularly trusted and liked, and who had already proved his parliamentary ability? Wilberforce was still only a junior MP, but so were several of the new ministers, including the Prime Minister himself. He needed more experience in debate, but so did many others, including Steele. He was popular, and could have held some sway over the Independent MPs whose votes would be desperately needed in the weeks ahead. The answer may be that Wilberforce was determined, even at this stage, to retain his nominal independence and to resist taking on a ministerial office which would have put an end to his travels to his beloved Lake District and elsewhere. He may even have made this clear to Pitt during their many long evenings at Wimbledon or in France, without making any record of it. Perhaps more likely, Pitt knew Wilberforce well enough, or thought he did, not to offer him a position which required skills of management and administration. His friends clearly thought of him as often being disorganised or late, not much of a recommendation in the days when ministers did most of their own work, with very few officials to assist them. And could a man who wrote to Henry Bankes earlier that year to say that his eyes had been so weak that he had been unable to write a letter for two or three weeks, carry out any function which involved the reading and writing of scores of letters each day? It would not have been difficult for Pitt to come to the conclusion that Wilberforce, however valuable as a personal friend and political ally, was neither physically nor temperamentally suited to ministerial office. If he had thought otherwise, Wilberforce's life could well have run a very different course.

The passionate Commons debates of January to March 1784, as Fox inflicted one defeat after another on the infant administration while Pitt stoically refused to resign, were exhausting to many of the participants. Wilberforce was continually active on Pitt's behalf, keeping in touch with the Independents, who at one stage made a serious move

to bring about a grand coalition as a mediated solution to the constitutional impasse, voting regularly in the Commons and giving Pitt
moral support. On the night of 28 February he called at White's to see
Pitt after he had been rescued from a violent affray in St James's Street,
and stayed up as so often until three in the morning. Two days later
he spoke in the debate which became the climactic confrontation of
the crisis, asserting that the conduct of Pitt 'was dictated by a laudable
ambition, which he would always be proud to cherish, as it tended to
the salvation of the country'.[60] He noted that night that he was
'extremely tired'.[61] As it happened, the debate of 1 March 1784 opened
the way to Pitt's triumph. Two months previously, Fox had been
defeating him by majorities of more than fifty on the floor of the
House of Commons. That night the majority against Pitt fell to only
one. In the meantime loyal addresses had poured in from all over the
nation acclaiming the appointment of Pitt and the actions of the
King. Pitt now had the necessary support and the justification for a
dissolution of Parliament. The most tumultuous general election of
the eighteenth century was about to take place. It was a contest for
which Wilberforce harboured a private hope, one so secret he had
shared it with no one else.

The events of late March 1784 would lead Wilberforce to display to the
full his ability to combine clear support for a cause with a mastery of
the practical minutiae of politics. They would prove that his eloquence
and determination were major forces to be reckoned with, and they
would elevate him, against all expectations except his own, into being
one of the most prestigious Members of Parliament in the land.

   With a general election imminent, Wilberforce set out initially not
to Hull, where he would be expected to run for re-election, but to the
city of York, where a major meeting of freeholders from across Yorkshire was due to take place on 25 March. He did this even though 'he
knew ... nobody in York but Mr Mason the poet'.[62] Such a meeting,
in this case called to consider a loyal address to the King approving his
recent actions, was of sufficient importance to carry national weight,

for Yorkshire was generally considered to be a county of the highest political importance. This was partly on account of its size, in terms of both geography and electorate, with over twenty thousand freeholders eligible to vote: these were residents in towns and villages from all over Yorkshire, except those who returned MPs from their own boroughs. A successful election for the county of Yorkshire required a candidate to have recourse to either great popularity or enormous expense. Furthermore, the politics of the county in 1784 provided a major test for some of the principal political interests of the nation. It was in Yorkshire that some of the great Whig families particularly expected to hold sway, including the Fitzwilliams (Earl Fitzwilliam had succeeded his uncle, the Marquis of Rockingham, as one of the great landed magnates of the north) and Cavendishes. It was also the domain of the Yorkshire Association, formed by the Reverend Christopher Wyvill five years earlier to campaign for parliamentary reform, and now using its established organisation to campaign against the Fox–North coalition. The scene was thus set for a major confrontation at York, with both sides striving to bring their supporters to the city for 25 March in order to carry or defeat the address to the King, with the added expectation of this being immediately followed by a trial of strength as to who would be returned as the county's two MPs.

The influence of the Whig Lords was so great in the county that Wilberforce doubted that it would be possible to 'get up an opposition in Yorkshire'.[63] He arrived in York on 22 March, met Wyvill, helped to draw up the address to the King, and prepared for the meeting on the twenty-fifth, which was a 'cold hailing day'[64] with a huge crowd assembled in the Castle Yard from ten o'clock in the morning to half-past four in the afternoon. There, in a 'wonderful meeting for order and fair hearing',[65] the proposers of the address came up against the full firepower of the Yorkshire Whigs: Lord Fitzwilliam, Lord John Cavendish (the former Chancellor of the Exchequer), Lord Carlisle and Lord Surrey (the future Duke of Norfolk) were assembled to denounce the Pitt ministry. As Wilberforce prepared to speak late into the meeting he had two powerful forces working in his favour: the first was that a national tide of opinion was running in Pitt's favour, creating, perhaps uniquely in the eighteenth century, a countrywide 'swing' of opinion in favour of the new government, irrespective of local factors. Across the country, county meetings had voted loyal addresses, and in the coming days would voice such vociferous hostility to candidates representing Fox and North that many would stand down rather than meet the expense of a doomed contest. The combined impact of the unprincipled nature of the coalition, affection for the King, support for the apparently incorruptible nature of Pitt and the distribution by a burgeoning newspaper industry of far more political information and caricature than had ever been seen before, was about to unseat scores of opposition MPs and give Pitt a huge majority.

The second factor working in Wilberforce's favour was his own native ability to command a huge meeting despite his tiny physical stature. Many of the crowd of four thousand had been unable to hear properly, amidst bad weather and weak speeches. An eyewitness thought, as Wilberforce mounted the platform, that the weather was so bad 'that it seemed as if his slight frame would be unable to make head against its violence'.[66] As it turned out, other observers would consider it 'impossible, though at the distance of so many years to forget his speech, or the effect which it produced'.[67] James Boswell told Henry Dundas that 'I saw what seemed a mere shrimp mount upon the table; but, as I listened, he grew and grew until the shrimp became a whale.'[68] Newspapers considered that his speech showed 'such an exquisite choice of expression, and pronounced with such rapidity, that we are unable to do it justice in any account we can give of it',[69] that it included both an effective answering of the arguments of the Whigs and the successful spreading of fear among the suddenly attentive audience: 'He dwelt long on the odious East India Bill; read several clauses of it . . . he alarmed the Freeholders, by shewing that it might have been a Precedent for exercising the same tyranny over the property of every Man in the Kingdom.'[70]

This was a masterly politician and orator at work. To complete the effect, his speech was interrupted after an hour by the arrival of a King's messenger, who pushed through the crowd and handed up to him a letter from Pitt himself. As the first sentence of the letter gave him the information that Parliament would be dissolved that very day, he was able to announce this immediately to the steadily more supportive crowd, drawing attention to his own powerful connections and provoking a new wave of enthusiasm. He took care not to read out a later section of the letter which had instructed him to 'tear the enemy to pieces', and certainly did not reveal Pitt's comment that 'I am told Sir Robert Hildyard is the right candidate for the county.'[71] That was a matter on which Wilberforce had other ideas.

As Wilberforce would later confide in a letter to a friend: 'I had formed within my own heart the project of standing for the county. To anyone besides myself I was aware that it must appear so mad a scheme that I never mentioned it to Mr Pitt, or any of my political connexions. It was undoubtedly a bold idea but I was then very ambitious.'[72] He knew that since he was not acquainted with the nobility and gentry of the county he would be considered, as the son of a merchant rather than an aristocrat, to be rather unsuitable for county representation. Having never previously been thought of as the candidate, with the general election already announced, he knew it would be thought an 'utterly improbable' proposition.[73] He considered that 'It was very unlikely that the son of a merchant and with only my property could come in to represent Yorkshire, where the Members had always been persons of the oldest family, and the largest fortune. However I knew that such things had some times happened but I thought it foolish to talk about what was so unlikely and therefore I did not mention it to anyone.'[74] Yet he now supplied the burst of intense activity and skill which was necessary to bring it to fruition.

The county's two incumbent Members, Foljambe and Duncombe, were both ready to take the field again, Foljambe being the candidate of the Whigs, and Duncombe the choice of the Yorkshire Association. In any normal contest, these two candidates would probably have been returned again without the need for an actual poll; such was the expense and difficulty of fighting a contested election in Yorkshire that only twice that century had the voters needed to go to the ballot box, and not at all for the previous forty-three years. But there was nothing normal about 1784, and Wilberforce knew it. Such was the strength of the pro-Pitt mood, and so strong was the impression that Wilberforce had made in the Castle Yard, that by the time the rival camps retired to their respective taverns for many hours of dinner and drinking Wilberforce was being openly touted as a running mate for Duncombe in a fight to unseat Foljambe and the Whigs altogether. As squabbling and drunkenness broke out, it was Wilberforce who helped Wyvill to restore order and secure a united front 'by showing them the folly of giving up our common object . . . and by reminding them of the great constitutional principles which we all maintained. This confirmed the disposition to propose me for the county, an idea which had begun to be buzzed about at dinner, among all ranks.'[75] By midnight, the cry from the York Tavern was 'Wilberforce and Liberty!' It had taken him precisely eight hours to move from being the shrimp on the table to the joint candidate to represent the great county of Yorkshire.

The next morning, 26 March, the Yorkshire Whigs tried to salvage what they could from the situation by suggesting the agreed election of their nominee, Foljambe, and whoever was preferred by the anti-coalition forces. This would inevitably have meant Duncombe. But Wilberforce had succeeded in giving the Yorkshire Association and its allies the confidence to try for both seats. Although there were two factions, Associators and non-Associators, 'they determined that every-one should go into his own neighbourhood and see whether he had sufficient strength to encounter the great body of the aristocracy that was arrayed against us . . . I appeared to be so Independent and to observe so strict a neutrality that they both joined in asking me.'[76] Thus was the gauntlet flung down for a full-scale election. An immense organisational effort was immediately set in train, with the Association mounting a canvassing operation with the efficiency and thoroughness of any modern political party, but with the added burden of securing the necessities of an eighteenth-century election campaign. The full-time clerk of the Association, William Gray, appointed agents for every wapentake* with the intention of canvassing over thirteen thousand

---

* The counties of Yorkshire, Derbyshire, Leicestershire, Northamptonshire, Nottingham-shire, Rutland and Lincolnshire were divided into wapentakes, just as most of the remainder of England was divided into hundreds.

freeholders spread all over the county in just ten days. He engaged horses, chaises and inns on the road to York so that freeholders could be assured of the necessary free transportation and lodging, and secured in advance two-thirds of all the public houses and stables in the city of York for the likely duration of the poll. Plans were made to bring up to 1,300 supportive freeholders into the city each day, organised into 'companies' and taken to vote according to a schedule, since 'At the last election most of them were eating and drinking whilst they should have been waiting on the road and their number helped to swell the public house bills considerably.'[77] The instructions to agents give some flavour of the effort that was expected to be involved when polling itself took place. They were enjoined to 'poll all such voters as are in the enemy's strong country and all dubious ones as early as possible'; to ensure that freeholders arrived 'under the lead and direction of some principal gentleman within the district'; to provide for 'some strong active and zealous persons' to 'facilitate the approach of the free-holders'; to bring freeholders into the polling booths as early as possible in the day in order to 'excite a spirit of emulation and exertion'; and 'to have a confidential *corps de reserve* always ready to poll in case of exigency'.[78]

Such organisation was a great advantage for the Association, it being noted at the same time that 'The hurry and eagerness commonly attendant upon the opening of canvass are great hindrances to its regular arrangement.'[79] With the Whigs struggling to match either the organisational scope of the Association or the popularity of Pittite candidates, there was now every chance that Wilberforce would be elected as one of the two Members for the county. Nevertheless, it was still a good way from being a certainty, and it was therefore necessary for him to do what was perfectly common in an uncertain electoral situation in the eighteenth century: to ensure that he was elected elsewhere. In the very same election, for instance, Charles James Fox was fighting an intense battle to retain his seat in the City of West-minster – so closely fought that the poll was kept open for nearly six weeks – but had already ensured that he would be returned by a tiny electorate in the Orkney Islands. Once elected in a prestigious but risky contest, an MP would simply abandon the less distinguished of his constituencies, with the result that eighteenth-century elections were invariably followed by a swathe of by-elections to fill seats immediately vacated. To treat a rotten borough in this manner was easy enough, but to risk insulting the pride of the freemen of Hull was a more perilous proposition; Wilberforce therefore set out from York to Hull on the evening of 26 March to carry out an energetic canvass in his existing constituency. After arriving there at 2 a.m. he embarked on a tour next day, and found 'people not pleased at my not canvassing'[80] earlier. By the thirtieth he was noting: 'Canvass all day – extremely hard work – till night – tired to death,'[81] and two days later snowballs and other projectiles were thrown at him. Some effective speaking and his local popularity pulled him through, and he once again came top of the poll, although with fewer votes than in his 1780 triumph: he polled 807 votes compared to 751 for Samuel Thornton, son of John Thornton, and only 357 for a defeated and dejected David Hartley.

Duly elected for Hull on 1 April, Wilberforce was back on the road to York that same evening to resume his battle for the bigger prize. If by now he lacked energy, having considered himself thoroughly tired for at least a month, and having spent the previous two weeks continually travelling or campaigning well into the night, the ambitious twenty-four-year-old candidate certainly did not want for determination. With the canvassing of Yorkshire at fever pitch before the opening of the poll on 7 April, Wilberforce and Duncombe embarked on a tour of the West Riding towns, illustrated by his diary notes of these hectic few days:

> To Rotherham – drawn into town – public dinner. At night to Sheffield – vast support – meeting at Cutler's Hall . . . off to Barnsley . . . then to Wakefield . . . then off to Halifax. Drawn into town . . . after dinner (drunken postboy) to Bradford. Drawn into town – vast support. Then on to Leeds . . .[82]

As he travelled, express letters were being sent from Westminster by Pitt, who had been triumphantly returned for Cambridge University and could now abandon his own tame constituency of Appleby, with lists of the requests he had sent out for votes and money for Wilber-force. As things turned out, Pitt need not have worried: while his re-election for Hull had cost Wilberforce £8,807, nearly all of which had to be drawn from his own fortune, the county campaign had already brought in subscriptions and donations exceeding £18,000, along with the expectation of a great deal more. And although Wilber-force and Duncombe had 'passed many great houses', and 'not one did we see that was friendly to us', the canvass returns coming in from the freeholders of Yorkshire were truly crushing. With towns such as Wakefield and Halifax reporting margins up to thirty votes to one, Gray's canvass reported 10,812 freeholders supporting Duncombe and Wilberforce, with only 2,758 opposed or undecided. Lord Fitzwilliam and the Whigs, moaning they had been 'beat by the ragamuffins', had no better option remaining than to avert both the humiliation and the expense of going to the polls. Wilberforce and Duncombe had returned to York on the evening of 6 April when, at 8 p.m. at the York Tavern, a message was received from their opponents conceding defeat without a single vote having to be cast.

It was a moment for exultation. The 'utterly improbable' project that Wilberforce had kept to himself until only twelve days earlier had come to fruition, and he was now to be the Member for one of the most sought-after seats in Parliament. He sat down immediately to write several letters of delight, telling Edward Eliot:

> I am or at least shall be tomorrow (our enemies having this evening declared their intentions of declining a Poll)
> Knight of the Shire for the
> County of York.[83]

The celebrations were busy and varied: '7th. Up early – breakfasted tavern – rode frisky horse to castle – elected – chaired – dined . . . 8th. Walked – called – air balloon – dined . . .'[84] When news reached London two days later, Pitt would write: 'I can never enough congratulate you on such glorious success.'[85] Across the country Pitt had won a decisive victory, remarkable for both its quality and quantity: not only did the new government have a three-figure majority in the House of

Commons, but they had also won a huge proportion of those constituencies where there had been serious electoral competition, with the victory of Wilberforce as one of the jewels in Pitt's electoral crown.

Cynical observers thought that Pitt would now be certain to include Wilberforce in the ministerial ranks. It was even thought that Wilberforce had switched constituencies with this uppermost in his mind, with Richard Sykes, from a prominent family in Hull, writing: 'He has always lived above his income and it is certain he is now in expectation of a lucrative post from Government of which he is in the utmost need.'[86] He went on to say that this would entail a by-election for the county, and 'The accuracy of this intelligence may be depended upon,'[87] showing that political gossip in the eighteenth century could be as wildly inaccurate as in any other age. Yet, however careless Wilberforce may have become about money, his election for Yorkshire made it even less likely than before that he would embark on a ministerial career. Pitt, preoccupied in the summer of 1784 with his own India Bill and his first budget, did not in any event carry out a major reshuffle of his government that year. Nor is there any reason to suppose that he had changed his opinion of Wilberforce's suitability for high office. And from Wilberforce's point of view, the burdens of representing and attending to his constituents had just been made vastly greater. He would now be expected to make tours of the county during the summer recess, and to represent all year round a vast range of interests, from the clothiers of Halifax to the manufacturers of Sheffield and the merchants of many small towns. An eighteenth-century county constituency did not fit well with a ministerial career: not only did it require a good deal of attention and representation, but the compulsory requirement to fight a by-election when accepting appointment as a minister could have been ruinously expensive. Contrary to the suspicions of Mr Sykes, it is likely therefore that, in Wilberforce's own mind, his decision to stand for Yorkshire was consistent with political ambitions which were parliamentary rather than governmental. He had indeed sought greater power and prestige, but it was the prestige of an MP with elevated status and an independent power base, rather than as a minister rising in the ranks of the government of his friend.

Wilberforce was conscious from the beginning of the need to look after his new constituency. His first speech in the new Parliament, on 16 June 1784, was in favour of the principle of parliamentary reform, the much-cherished objective of the Yorkshire Association that had ensured his election. Once Parliament rose for the summer, he headed north to commune with his new constituents, becoming the 'joy of York races' and learning in detail about his new constituents – even years later he was still asking for lists of influential persons, graded according to their influence, '"Li" for little, – "Mi" for middling, – "Gr" for great, – and "V.Gr" for very great',[88] together with useful observations such as, 'Whether he likes the leg or wing of a fowl best, that when one dines with him one may win his heart by helping him, and not be taken in by his "just which you please, sir." '[89]

After all the trials of the political season Wilberforce's mind was once again set on travel, this time on a full-scale Continental tour. The old friend he initially asked to accompany him was unable to go, but holidaying at Scarborough later that summer Wilberforce found himself in the agreeable company of Isaac Milner, his school usher of sixteen years earlier and younger brother of Joseph. Wilberforce decided to ask Isaac to accompany him on a tour of several months with all expenses paid. It would turn out to be one of the most important decisions of his life.

4

Agony and Purpose

I must awake to my dangerous state, and never be at rest till I have made my peace with God.

WILLIAM WILBERFORCE, 27 November 1785[1]

Surely the principles as well as the practice of Christianity are simple, and lead not to meditation only but to action.

WILLIAM PITT TO WILLIAM WILBERFORCE, 2 December 1785[2]

AFTER SUMMERING in York and Scarborough, Wilberforce set out over the Pennines in the early autumn of 1784 to visit his beloved Rayrigg, and 'looked over all the old scenes again with vast pleasure'.[3] His visit there had many frustrations: his eyes were in too poor a state for reading, no visitor of any interest passed through, and he failed to find a spot on which he could locate his 'future residence'.[4] By 20 October, after brief stops in London and Brighton, he had set out on his Continental tour and, in spite of the calm conditions, suffered from seasickness while sailing from Dover to Calais. His party travelled in two coaches. The first contained his mother, his sister and 'a couple of sick cousins, very good girls, whose health we hope to re-establish by the change of air'.[5] In the other were Wilberforce himself, a small mountain of neglected correspondence – 'which, to my sore annoyance and discomfort, I have brought in my chaise to the heart of France'[6] – and the even larger bulk of Isaac Milner.

Feeling threatened by the prospect of several months with only women of his own family for company, Wilberforce had resorted to inviting on the tour a man he did not then know very well. Yet soon he would be describing Milner as 'a most intelligent and excellent friend of mine'.[7] Milner had a broad Yorkshire accent and was physically enormous, being described in later years by Marianne Thornton as 'a rough loud and rather coarse man', and 'the most enormous man it was ever my fate to see in a drawing-room',[8] but he had a gentle nature and a ready wit which Wilberforce found highly congenial. He also happened to be intellectually brilliant: shortly after Wilberforce had known him as a school usher, having been plucked away from being a Leeds weaver by his elder brother Joseph, he had entered Queen's College Cambridge, where he revealed an extraordinary intelligence. Many years later, Cambridge dons were still discussing his triumphant progress: by 1774 his academic performance was considered 'incomparabilis', and two years later he was a Fellow of his college, going on to become a tutor, rector and, at the age of thirty-two, the first Jacksonian Professor of Natural Philosophy. Some observers were even moved to believe that 'The university, perhaps, never produced a man of more eminent abilities.'[9]

It says a lot for Wilberforce's charm and reputation that such a man was happy to ask for leave of absence from his college and set off on a journey expected to last several months with the Wilberforce family in tow. Fortunately, Milner had always thought well of Wilberforce, and he presumably had the additional incentive of being able to visit foreign parts which, having never been wealthy himself, he did not expect to be able to visit on his own. Wilberforce found him 'lively and dashing in his conversation',[10] and they were soon covering many subjects in the days and weeks they spent travelling south across France. On the journey they had much to enjoy: 'the wines, Côte Rotie, Hermitage, &c. all strong'; along the Rhône to Avignon in a barge 'without a cloud (in October)'; the Frenchmen 'who always make you a bow where an Englishman would give you an oath'; the 'large, quiet, sleepy' town of Aix; Marseilles, 'the most entertaining place I ever saw, all bustle and business'; and then the final journey towards Nice with 'astonishing rocks hewn through, and ready to close over you'.[11] Inside the carriage, religion was only an occasional talking point, although if it came up Milner always gave a hint of holding powerful convictions. Even back in Scarborough early that year, when Wilberforce had described an Evangelical rector as one who took things too far, Milner had replied, 'No, how does he carry them too far?' and continued the argument. Similarly in France, as Wilberforce ridiculed the Methodist views of his aunt and John Thornton, having 'quite forgotten the beliefs I had when a child',[12] Milner eventually said to him, 'Wilberforce, I don't pretend to be a match for you in this sort of running fire. But if you really wish to discuss these topics in a serious and argumentative manner I should be most happy to enter on them with you.'[13]

Such a considered discussion did not take place immediately. Their arrival in Nice brought the usual round of dinners, card parties and gambling in the company of a fair slice of London society. They even experienced one of the intriguing fads of the time when an operator of animal magnetisers* 'tried his skill upon Milner and myself but neither of us felt anything, owing perhaps to our incredulity'.[14] While Mrs Wilberforce refused Sunday invitations, Milner had no such scruples: 'he appeared in all respects like an ordinary man of the world, mixing like myself in all companies, and joining as readily as others in the prevalent Sunday parties. Indeed, when I engaged him as a companion in my tour I knew not that he had any deeper principles.'[15]

Yet those deeper principles would shortly emerge. It is unclear how long Wilberforce intended to stay in Nice, and even though the new session of Parliament was to begin on 25 January 1785, the happy party remained on the Riviera throughout that month. Wilberforce later remembered that 'Many times during the month of January we carried our cold meat into some of the beautiful recesses of the mountains and rocks by which the place is surrounded on the land side and dined in the open air as we should here, in the summer.'[16] Sometime that month, however, he would have received from Pitt a letter written on 19 December 1784 explaining that 'as much as I wish you to bask on, under an Italian sun, I am perhaps likely to be the instrument of

---

* 'Animal magnetism' was meant to have great healing powers, released by powerful magnets or other devices. For a time it was taken seriously by the French Academy of Science.

snatching you from your present paradise ... A variety of circumstances concur to make it necessary to give notice immediately on the meeting of Parliament of the day on which I shall move the question of the Reform.'[17] If Pitt as Prime Minister was making a major push for parliamentary reform, it was unthinkable for Wilberforce to be absent. Pitt had worked with Wyvill on a scheme which would abolish seventy-two seats in rotten boroughs and allocate them to newly populous towns and cities. Loyalty to Pitt and to Yorkshire demanded that Wilberforce be present to argue for such a proposal. As a result, it was decided that he and Milner would return to England, leaving the ladies where they were and coming back to join them in the summer. Just before leaving Nice on 5 February, Wilberforce asked Milner if a book he had happened to pick up, Doddridge's *The Rise and Progress of Religion in the Soul*, was worth reading. Milner responded: 'It is one of the best books ever written. Let us take it with us and read it on our journey.'[18]

In the whole course of Wilberforce's life, no volume would be more influential in determining his conduct than the book he so casually selected from among the possessions of his cousin, Bessy Smith. He would write thirty-two years later to his daughter, 'You cannot read a better book. I hope it was one of the means of turning my heart to God.'[19] Philip Doddridge had published the book in 1745, six years before his death at the age of forty-nine. Doddridge's version of 'vital Christianity' was itself built on the seventeenth-century work of Richard Baxter, an English Puritan minister who had become a leading Presbyterian non-conformist. Baxter had urged Christians to concentrate on the fundamental points on which the wide spread of Christian denominations should be able to reach a consensus. In his turn, Doddridge advocated Christian unity and religious toleration, along with a practical faith and a powerful vision of heaven. It was thus in the course of an uncomfortable midwinter journey across France that Wilberforce sat in his carriage absorbing many of the essentials of English Puritanism. For Doddridge set out in his book a complete framework for religious observation, and a philosophy of how to live, which initially merely caused Wilberforce to think, but which would eventually provide the framework for his whole life. *The Rise and Progress of Religion in the Soul* emphasised the importance of daily self-examination, prayer, early-morning devotions, diligence in business, prudence in recreation, the careful observation of Providence, the importance of solitude, and the value of time. It stressed the certainty of death and judgement, and the need for humankind to show its usefulness throughout a lifetime. The message of the book was designed first to be worrying: 'Thousands are, no doubt, already in hell, whose guilt never equalled thine; and it is astonishing, that God hath spared thee to read this representation of thy case;'[20] and then to be uplifting: 'You will wish to commence a hero in the cause of Christ; opposing with a rigorous resolution the strongest efforts of the powers of darkness, the inward corruption of your own heart, and all the outward difficulties you may meet with in the way of your duty, while in the cause and in the strength of Christ you go on conquering and to conquer.'[21] Doddridge's enjoinders would subsequently become Wilberforce's prescription for life: 'Be an advocate for truth; be a counsellor of peace; be an example of candour; and do all you can to reconcile the hearts of men, especially of good men, to each other, however they may differ in their opinions about matters which it is impossible for good men to dispute.'[22]

The immediate effect on Wilberforce, no doubt encouraged by Milner, was that 'he determined at some future season to examine the Scriptures for himself and see if things were stated there in the same manner'.[23] For the moment, more immediate events would break back into his mind, for both the journey home and the political situation on his return were more difficult than he might have anticipated. The return journey involved bad roads, filthy inns and terrible food, without any of 'those things which in England we should deem indispensable for our comfort and even our health'.[24] In heavy snow in Burgundy, when Milner and Wilberforce were walking behind their chaise it slipped on the ice, and looked like toppling over a precipice with the horses, had Milner not used all his strength to hold it. The weight of Milner's luggage might not have helped, since he was 'invariably carrying about with him an assortment which, to most persons, appeared uselessly large, of implements of a heavy kind – such as scissors of various sizes, pincers, files, penknives, razors and even hammers'.[25] After these adventures, it was 22 February before they arrived in London and Wilberforce 'took up my quarters for a short time under the roof of Mr Pitt',[26] which literally meant lodging in 10 Downing Street, where the maid accidentally burned about fifty of his letters, many unopened: 'I dreaded the effects on my reputation in Yorkshire but happily no bad consequence ensued.'[27]

Wilberforce showed no resentment that the haste of his return proved unnecessary when the great debate on Reform was put off until late March, and then again until 18 April. He threw himself back into London's political and social whirl, and was soon noting in his diary that he was 'sitting up all night singing', and had 'danced till five in the morning'.[28] When the Reform debate finally took place Wilberforce was in his place to support Pitt and to speak up for Yorkshire, but his speech, however much it accorded with his own views and ideals, was not calculated to win over sceptical MPs. Showing his disdain for political parties, he argued that the abolition of rotten boroughs would 'tend to diminish the progress of party and cohesion in this country from which . . . our greatest misfortunes arose . . . By destroying them the freedom of opinion would be restored, and party connexions in a great measure vanish.'[29] MPs with less secure parliamentary seats than Wilberforce might well have considered as they listened to him that if party connections vanished, they might well vanish themselves. Even this modest measure of reform was thrown out, by 248 votes to 174, and one of Pitt's most cherished projects among 'his good hopes of the country, and noble, patriotic heart',[30] in Wilberforce's words of that time, went down to defeat. Wilberforce's diary for that day said it all: 'To town – Pitt's – house – Parliamentary Reform – terribly disappointed and beat – extremely fatigued – spoke extremely ill, but commended. – Called at Pitt's – met poor Wyvill.'[31]

The following month he was again on his feet in the House of Commons supporting Pitt, this time even against the wishes of some of his constituents. Pitt's so-called 'Irish Propositions' were designed to create freer trade between Ireland and England, with the object of reducing discontent in Ireland and strengthening England's security. They were opposed, however, by many manufacturers, including the woollen businesses of the Yorkshire West Riding. It was either his efforts to reconcile these conflicting views or his general lifestyle which caused Wilberforce physical discomfort and even disorientation in the debate of 12 May. He noted that he 'cannot preserve the train as some could do, and too hot and violent',[32] and it was reported that 'overcome with sensibility, the fatigue of having sat in the House so many hours, and with the pressure of infirmity, he sunk upon his seat'.[33] It was not an easy session for him. As he wrote to one dissatisfied constituent, 'The situation of a Representative disagreeing with his constituents on a matter of importance must ever be a situation of pain and embarrassment,'[34] but he continued to admire Pitt, who he thought 'spoke wonderfully' on the same subject, and to be loyal to his old friend. Yet there were also the first signs of a developing dissatisfaction with the political and social scene. A letter from Pitt later in the year refers to Wilberforce's 'constant call for *Something out of the Common Way*'.[35] At the same time, his disapproval of a variety of public habits was becoming evident in his diary. He found the laughing at a christening 'very indecent', considered a dance at the opera 'shocking', and after talking with one wealthy friend thought it 'strange that the most generous men and religious, do not see that their duties increase with their fortune, and that they will be punished for spending it in eating, etc'.[36]

The change in his sentiments was to gather pace when he and Milner resumed their travels once Parliament had risen at the end of June. Heading first for Genoa for a reunion with the ladies, they then travelled to Switzerland, where Wilberforce was overcome by the beauty of the mountains: 'I have never since ceased to recur with peculiar delight to its enchanting scenery, especially to that of Interlaken, which is a vast garden of the loveliest fertility and beauty stretched out at the base of the giant Alps.'[37] He wrote to Muncaster on 14 August that 'I have never been in any other part of the world, for which I could quit a residence in England with so little regret,' but while retaining his normal good humour – 'If you read on thus far, I am sure your patience will hold out no longer, and my letter goes into the fire, which in your cold part of the world you will certainly be sitting over when my packet arrives' – he said he was in despair at 'the universal corruption and profligacy of the times', which had now 'extended its baneful influence and spread its destructive poison through the whole body of the people. When the mass of blood is corrupt, there is no remedy but amputation.'[38] While in Geneva he happily entertained the many contacts and friends, such as de Lageard, Wyvill and Earl Spencer, who turned up there; but others were evidently noticing a distinct change in his behaviour. When they reached Spa in the Austrian Netherlands (present-day Belgium), he noted: 'Mrs Crewe cannot believe that I think it wrong to go to the play. – Surprised at hearing that halting on the Sunday was my wish and not my mother's.'[39] When he wrote to congratulate Eliot on his marriage to Pitt's sister Harriot, he expressed his growing contempt for the pursuit of money, saying that if a man had enough, then 'to torment himself for fresh acquisitions as delusive in this enjoyment and uncertain in their possession as these are, seems to me a perfect madness'.[40]

Closeted in his carriage with Milner and the Greek version of the New Testament, to the point that the ladies complained of him paying them insufficient attention, Wilberforce was becoming gradually convinced of the Evangelical Christian case. He always liked to examine a question before pronouncing his view on it; now Milner's arguments left him intellectually convinced by, but not yet emotionally committed to, the need for a new approach to life. Much later he would recall: 'I got a clear idea of the doctrines of Religion, perhaps clearer than I have had since, but it was quite in my head. Well, I now fully believed the Gospel and was persuaded that if I died at any time I should perish everlastingly. And yet, such is man, I went on cheerful and gay.'[41] Very soon, however, he was to be overwhelmed by the force of what he now believed to be true. 'What madness is all this,' he began to think, 'to continue easy in a state in which a sudden call out of the world would consign me to everlasting misery, and that, when eternal happiness is within my grasp!!' By the time he was preparing to return to England in late October 1785, 'the deep guilt and black ingratitude of my past life forced itself upon me in the strongest colours, and I condemned myself for having wasted my precious time, and opportunities, and talents'.[42] The 'great change' was upon him.

In the autumn of 1785 Wilberforce experienced a classic conversion to Christian evangelicalism, a mental and spiritual experience of enormous power. When it came, the climax of his conversion was neither as dramatic nor as seemingly supernatural as in many other documented cases of the eighteenth century. Charles Wesley had experienced his conversion in 1738 when his sleep was interrupted by someone entering his room and saying, 'In the name of Jesus of Nazareth, arise, and believe . . .', the speaker turning out to be a friend's sister who had dreamt that Christ had knocked at her door and told her to do this.[43] The celebrated Colonel James Gardiner, who was killed in battle with the Jacobites in 1745 but immortalised in a biography written by Doddridge, experienced his conversion when a 'blaze of light'[44] fell upon a book he was reading and he lifted up his eyes to see a vision of Christ on the Cross, causing him 'unutterable astonishment and agony of heart',[45] with the result that 'the whole frame and disposition of his soul was new-modelled and changed; so that he became, and continued to the last day of his exemplary and truly Christian life, the very reverse of what he had been before'.[46]

Many other famous conversions can be pinpointed to a single day. John Wesley could trace his own such moment to 8.45 p.m. on 14 May 1738, when 'I felt my heart strangely warmed. I felt I did trust in Christ, Christ alone, for salvation; and an assurance was given me, that he had taken *my* sins, even *mine*, and saved *me* from the law of sin and death.'[47] John Newton's conversion followed a near shipwreck in which he 'dreaded death now, and my heart foreboded the worst, if the Scriptures which I had long since opposed, were indeed true'.[48] His survival and recovery from a subsequent fever led him 'from that time' to be 'delivered from the power and dominion of sin . . . I now began to wait upon the Lord.'[49] William Huntington, whose conversion led to him building his own chapel in London after a dissolute youth, also had a sudden conversion – one day, he became intensely conscious of sin: 'I leapt up, with my eyes ready to start out of my head, my hair standing erect, and my countenance stained with all the horrible gloom and dismay of the damned. I cried out to my wife, and said, "Molly, I am undone for ever; I am lost and gone; there is no hope or mercy for me; you know not what a sinner I am; you know not where I am, nor what I feel!"' He later saw a vision of the Holy Ghost and 'heard a voice from Heaven, saying unto me in plain words, "Lay by your forms of prayers, and go pray to Jesus Christ; do you not see how pitifully he speaks to Sinners."'[50]

It is not possible to pinpoint Wilberforce's own conversion to a single day, nor did he report the intervention of an other-worldly vision or voice. Yet the time which elapsed between him going about his normal business in the late spring of 1785 and the adoption of an entirely new and rigorous approach to life that December was unusually short. Many such conversions followed years of intellectual doubt and agonising. Gardiner had kept his religious side subordinate for eleven years before his conversion burst through; the 'awakening' of the Wesleys also took place over many years; Newton endured periods of internal conflict spread over twelve years; and the great George White-field experienced his conversion crisis six years after being deeply affected by listening to a sermon. In another documented case, that of William Grimshaw, the son of a poor farmer from Lancashire who became second only to the Wesleys in Methodist authority, his final conversion took place eight years after he had first been 'powerfully awakened and alarmed'.[51] Wilberforce was clear in later life that true religious conviction could only emerge after a period of self-examination, doubt, and often agony. Writing of his son Samuel's expectation of his own 'great change', he said: 'I come again and again to look to see if it really be begun, just as a gardener walks up again and again to his fruit trees to see if his peaches are set; if they are swelling and becoming larger, finally they are becoming ripe and rosy.'[52] Away from the daily cares of Westminster that summer, and with a companion in Milner who had 'doctrines of religion in his head though not then I think in his heart',[53] Wilberforce found that his own period of doubt and awakening was relatively short.

A role model of the kind Isaac Milner provided for Wilberforce could be crucial in providing reassurance that conversion was both attainable and desirable. Wilberforce had always been struck by Milner's intellect, coherence and equanimity; he had a quiet strength to which it is not surprising that the sometimes erratic and overheated young Member of Parliament aspired. There are clear parallels with the cases of others: the conversion of the great Scottish preacher Ebenezer Erskine followed on from 'his realisation that others have found an experience which he lacked',[54] and that of Lady Huntingdon, founder of a radical Calvinistic movement within Methodism, apparently came about because 'the happiness of her sister-in-law induced a longing for the same condition'.[55] Wilberforce had this factor and many others in common with those who underwent a similar religious experience. For instance, many of them had been exposed to strong religious influences in childhood. Gardiner, Whitefield, the Wesleys and Newton all had mothers with strong personalities who managed to give their children a religious inclination even if it did not become apparent until much later in life. Wilberforce's own acceptance of religious teaching from his aunt and uncle at the age of nine is a different but comparable case. Yet it is also true that those who experienced conversion were not 'weak-minded' or 'over-suggestible',[56] but tended to be particularly thoughtful, as well as eloquent, individuals: John Berridge, vicar of Everton, was a prolific hymn-writer; William Cowper became one of the most popular poets of his time; John Fletcher became a foremost theologian and Methodist leader; Thomas Halyburton was a Professor of Divinity; the Countess of Huntingdon was a formidable figure who founded sixty-four chapels and a training college for Methodist ministers; Legh Richmond was a curate, later influenced by Wilberforce, who became a prolific author, with works translated into nineteen languages;* Thomas Scott was a biblical scholar who wrote widely read books such as *The Force of Truth*; and Henry Venn was a highly active vicar who wrote *The Complete Duty of Man*. Isaac Milner was, of

---

* Richmond is credited with the idea of using boards with movable numbers to inform congregations about which hymns they would be singing. He was the author of *The Dairyman's Daughter*.

course, an outstanding academic who was to become Master of Queen's College Cambridge.

Since Wilberforce's life followed or overlapped with those of these and comparable figures, he knew at the time of his conversion that he was in good company. Those who had embraced varying forms of Methodism and evangelicalism and experienced a crisis of religious conversion were often persuasive, well connected and, as in the case of his kinsman John Thornton, a leading figure in the Evangelical revival of the time, comfortingly rich. Nevertheless, they were a small minority, still open to the strong suspicions and hostility which Wilberforce had witnessed in his mother in earlier years, and in most cases they saw their newly crystallised religious duty as being to spread the word of God through preaching and missions rather than to try to pursue Christian principles through the political world. The tumult going on in Wilberforce's mind that summer would therefore have embraced serious doubts about the viability of the political career he had recently done so much to advance.

In spite of these considerations, Wilberforce clearly felt an ineluctable pull towards an enthusiasm for Christianity which would guide and dictate all his future actions in every aspect of life. While he attributed his new feelings to the intervention of Providence, in common with the experience across faiths of nearly all kinds of religious conversion, with a sense of being controlled from above and accepting Divine Grace, there were many personal factors which could have affected him. His effortless possession of great wealth, and the long period of relative leisure which it had permitted, may have helped to create in him a feeling of guilt towards other people. Certainly, one of his early resolutions as he adopted a new regimen of life was to live more frugally. His diary for 25 November recorded, 'Walked, and stagecoach, to save the expense of a chaise,'[57] and he would become increasingly generous towards a wide range of charitable causes. In addition, there are signs that he was suffering a twinge of disillusionment with conventional politics by the middle of 1785. His call to Pitt for 'something out of the common way' almost certainly reflects his disappointment that Pitt's triumph of the earlier year had failed to elevate the conduct of politics as a whole. Reform had been defeated, rotten boroughs remained, idealism on Ireland had been frustrated, the culture of place-seeking, patronage and parties remained. As time and travel separated him from the intense partisanship of the 1784 election, his disdain for fixed party loyalties may already have been resurfacing. He had always idealised the exercising of independent judgement, and a fresh philosophical framework for such judgement must have had its appeal.

It is impossible to know what other subconscious forces pushed William Wilberforce that November into the agony of his conversion crisis. Such was the effect, he later wrote, of the 'sense of my great sinfulness in having so long neglected the unspeakable mercies of my God and Saviour ... that for months I was in a state of the deepest depression ... nothing which I have ever read in the accounts of others exceeded what I then felt'.[58] Having attained the great heights of becoming a Member for Yorkshire, but having no expectation of becoming a minister, did he reflect, at the age of twenty-six, that his personal ambitions had already reached their limit? Was it that the excesses of the London clubland he inhabited, with its gambling, womanising, gluttony and prostitution, had finally revolted him? Had the enormous amount of time he had spent travelling, and the futility of his recent efforts in the Commons, given him a stronger than usual sense of waste and lack of purpose? Or was it that having discovered that attaining his ambitions and satisfying all his material needs did not lead to satisfaction, he was predisposed to search for something which could represent for him the highest ambition of them all? By November 1785 some mixture of these influences, added to his early receptiveness towards religion, the guidance of Doddridge's writing, and the force of Milner's arguments, produced in William Wilberforce a true conversion crisis.

In his book *The Psychology of Religion*, published at the end of the nineteenth century, E.D. Starbuck identified the mental attributes of a full-blown conversion crisis: 'struggle after the new-life: prayer, calling on God; sense of estrangement from God; doubts and questioning: tendency to resist conviction; depression and sadness; restlessness, anxiety, and uncertainty; helplessness and humility; earnestness and seriousness . . . The central fact in it all is the sense of sin.'[59] For a time, such a crisis could produce a state of deep dissatisfaction and a divided personality, the individual concerned oscillating between aiming for new ideals and believing that he cannot attain them. The more the prospective convert struggled to be free of sin, the more he would become conscious of his past sins and his unworthiness. The stricter he tried to become about religious devotion, observances and prayer, the more likely he was to be tempted away by the various attractions of human society, and to feel that he was trying to adopt a standard which could not be maintained. Such internal conflict, well documented by John Wesley, Whitefield, Fletcher and Henry Venn, eventually produces a mental breaking point, resulting in conversion, retreat or collapse. The honesty and thoroughness of Wilberforce's diary-keeping meant that he left behind him a clear and revealing account of this agony:

> 25th. Up at six – private devotions half an hour – Pascal three quarters* – to town on business. I feel quite giddy and distracted by the tumult, except when in situations of which I am rather ashamed, as in the stage coach: the shame, pride; but a useful lesson . . .
>
> Sunday 27th. Up at six – devotions half an hour – Pascal three quarters – Butler** three quarters – church – read the Bible, too ramblingly, for an hour – heard Butler, but not attentively, two hours – meditated twenty minutes – hope I was more attentive at church than usual, but serious thoughts vanished the moment I went out of it, and very insensible and cold in the evening service – some very strong feelings when I went to bed; God turn them to account, and in any way bring me to himself. I have been thinking I have been doing well by living alone, and reading generally on religious subjects; I must awake to my dangerous state, and never be at rest till I have made my peace with God.

---

* Blaise Pascal was a seventeenth-century French philosopher whose book *Pensées* included a section on 'The Misery of Man Without God'.
** Joseph Butler was famous for his *Analogy of Religion, Natural and Revealed* (1736).

My heart is so hard, my blindness so great, that I cannot get a
due hatred of sin, though I see I am all corrupt, and blinded to
the perception of spiritual things.

28th. I hope as long as I live to be the better for the meditation
of this evening; it was on the sinfulness of my own heart, and its
blindness and weakness. True, Lord, I am wretched, and miserable
and naked. What infinite love, that Christ should die to save such
a sinner and how necessary is it He should save us altogether that
we may appear before God with nothing of our own! God grant
I may not deceive myself, in thinking I feel the beginnings of
gospel comfort. Began this night constantly family prayer, and
resolved to have it every morning and evening, and to read a
chapter when time.

Tuesday 29th. I bless God I enjoyed comfort in prayer this evening.
I must keep my own unworthiness ever in view. Pride is my
greatest stumbling block; and there is danger in it in two ways –
lest it should make me desist from a Christian life, through fear
of the world, my friends, &c.; or if I persevere, lest it should
make me vain of so doing. In all disputes on religion, I must be
particularly on my guard to distinguish it from a zeal for God
and his cause. I must consider and set down the marks whereby
they may be known from each other. I will form a plan of my
particular duty, praying God to enable me to do it properly, and
set it before me as a chart of the country, and map of the road
I must travel . . .

November 30th. Was very fervent in prayer this morning, and
thought these warm impressions would never go off. Yet in vain
endeavoured in the evening to rouse myself. God grant it may not
all prove vain; oh if it does, how will my punishment be deservedly
increased! The only way I find of moving myself, is by thinking
of my great transgressions, weakness, blindness, and of God's
having promised to supply these defects. But though I firmly
believe them, yet I read of future judgement, and think of God's
wrath against sinners with no great emotions . . .[60]

It was all there: doubt, shame, and sometimes near despair, all in an
atmosphere of agonising introspection. He would always regard this as
the most difficult experience of his life: 'I was filled with sorrow. I am

sure that no human creature could suffer more than I did for some months. It seems indeed it quite affected my reason; not so as others would observe, for all this time I kept out of company. They might see I was out of spirits.'[61]

Astonishingly, when he did appear in public he gave no sign of his inner torment, Pitt's sister writing on 10 November that she had been 'agreeably surprised by a visit from Mr Wilberforce who has come home remarkably well'.[62] But although he complained to his diary that 'all religious thoughts go off in London',[63] he was finding that he could no longer see the great men of the political world in the same light as before. Dining with the cabinet at Downing Street, he 'was often thinking that pompous Thurlow [the Lord Chancellor] and elegant Carmarthen would soon appear in the same row with the poor fellow who waited behind their chairs'.[64] By the end of November he felt he had to explain to his closest friends what was happening to him, but on a confidential basis so as to avoid any public reaction. The letter in which he explained himself to Pitt has not survived, but he later recalled that 'I told him that though I should ever feel a strong affection for him, and had every reason to feel that I should be in general able to support him, yet I could no more be so much a Party man as I had been before.'[65] Pitt's reply, written from Downing Street on 2 December 1785, suggests that Wilberforce had raised the idea of withdrawing from general society and possibly from the political world. His immediate response was to affirm his friendship, begin to argue, and seek a discussion, in a letter which was all the more remarkable for having been written by a busy Prime Minister. He began by saying that he was 'too deeply interested in whatever concerns you not to be very sensibly affected by what has the appearance of a new era in your life, and so important in its consequences for yourself and your friends. As to any public conduct which your opinions may ever lead you to, I will not disguise to you that few things could go nearer my heart than to find myself differing from you essentially on any great principle.'[66] He went on to say that whatever happened, 'it is impossible that it should shake the sentiments of affection and friendship which I bear towards you ... They are sentiments engraved in my heart and will never be effaced or weakened.'[67] But he followed this up with the first gentle advice to Wilberforce from any quarter to use his religious convictions for wider purposes:

> ... but forgive me if I cannot help expressing my fear that you are nevertheless deluding yourself into principles which have but too much tendency to counteract your own object, and to render your virtues and your talents useless both to yourself and mankind. I am not, however, without hopes that my anxiety paints this too strongly. For you confess that the character of religion is not a gloomy one, and that it is not that of an enthusiast. But why then this preparation of solitude, which can hardly avoid tincturing the mind either with melancholy or superstition? If a Christian may act in the several relations in life, must he seclude himself from them all to become so? Surely the principles as well as the practice of Christianity are simple, and lead not to meditation only but to action.[68]

Concerned that Wilberforce was about to isolate himself and make an irrevocable breach with public life, Pitt went on to ask for an urgent discussion:

> What I would ask of you, as a mark both of your friendship and of the candour which belongs to your mind, is to open yourself fully and without reserve to one, who, believe me, does not know how to separate your happiness from his own. You do not explain either the degree or the duration of the retirement which you have prescribed to yourself; you do not tell me how the future course of your life is to be directed, when you think the same privacy no longer necessary; nor, in short, what idea you have formed of the duties which you are from this time to practise ... I will not importune you with fruitless discussion on any opinion which you have deliberately formed ... name any hour at which I can call upon you tomorrow. I am going to Kent, and can take Wimbledon in my way. Reflect, I beg of you, that no principles are the worse for being discussed, and believe me that at all events the full knowledge of the nature and extent of your opinions and intentions will be to me a lasting satisfaction.

Believe me, affectionately and unalterably yours,
W. Pitt.[69]

The next day Pitt did indeed call at Wimbledon. In the same house in which they had eaten, drunk and played so much, the two friends engaged in two hours of earnest discussion. Wilberforce recalled that 'he tried to reason me out of my convictions but soon found himself unable to combat their correctness, if Christianity was true. The fact is, he was so absorbed with politics, that he had never given himself time for due reflection on religion.'[70] Yet Pitt's plea to Wilberforce that a Christian life should produce action rather than mere meditation was well considered, and may have made its mark. Wilberforce had clearly toyed with the idea of at least a period of retreat and isolation, and many other cases of religious conversion had led the individual concerned towards a life of preaching, concentration on religion, and often a lack of interest in worldly affairs. Whether Pitt influenced Wilberforce away from such a path cannot be known, but fortunately for history the next person to whom he turned in his agony was able to influence his future life with every advantage of long experience and deep religious conviction.

It was on 30 November that Wilberforce first 'thought seriously this evening with going to converse with Mr Newton – waked in the night – obliged to compel myself to think of God'. With Milner experiencing his own conversion crisis, Wilberforce needed to draw on the strength of someone with long-established beliefs. By 2 December, the day before his conversation with Pitt, Wilberforce noted: 'resolved again about Mr Newton. It may do good; he will pray for me his experience may enable him to direct me to new grounds of humiliation . . . It can do no harm . . . Kept debating in that unsettled way to which I have used myself, whether to go to London or not, and then how – wishing to save expense, I hope with a good motive, went at last in the stage to town – inquired for old Newton; but found he lived too far off for me to see him . . .'[71] Now possessed of sufficient courage to discuss his beliefs with the great John Newton, the very man he had 'reverenced as a parent' in his youthful days at Clapham, he made his way into London from Wimbledon again on Sunday, 4 December, and delivered a letter to Newton's church asking for a meeting. The letter showed his dread of his evangelicalism being publicly revealed before he was ready for it: 'I am sure you will hold yourself bound to let no-one living know of this application, or of my visit till I release you from the obligation. p.s. Remember that I must be secret, and that the gallery of the House is now so universally attended, that the face of a Member of Parliament is pretty well-known.'[72]

Newton, the former slave trader, was now sixty years old, rector of St Mary Woolnoth in the City of London and the author of many hymns, including 'Amazing Grace'. He had wise counsel for Wilberforce, such as telling him not to become cut off from his friends. Meeting Wilberforce three days after the delivery of the letter, 'he told me he always had entertained hopes and confidence that God would sometime bring me to him', and produced 'a calm, tranquil state' in Wilberforce's tortured mind.[73] It was Newton who not only calmed and soothed Wilberforce but, from that time and for a good decade afterwards, fortified him in combining his religious beliefs with a continued political career. In 1786 he would write of Wilberforce to the poet William Cowper: 'I hope the Lord will make him a blessing both as a Christian and a statesman. How seldom do these characters coincide!! But they are not incompatible.'[74] Two years later he wrote to Wilberforce: 'It is hoped and believed that the Lord has raised you up for the good of his Church, and for the good of the nation,'[75] and in 1796: 'I believe you are the Lord's servant, and are in the post which He has assigned you; and though it appears to me more arduous, and requiring more self-denial than my own, I know that He who has called you to it can afford you strength according to your day.'[76] And it was Newton who gradually widened the circle of friends in the Evangelical community to whom he could turn for advice. By Christmas Eve 1785 John Thornton was writing to Wilberforce: 'you may easier conceive than I can express the satisfaction I had from a few minutes' converse with Mr Newton yesterday afternoon. As in nature, so in Grace, what comes very quickly forward rarely abides long: I am aware of your difficulties which call for great prudence and caution.

Those that believe, must not make haste, but be content to go God's pace and watch the leadings of his providence.'[77]

Thornton advised Wilberforce not to make haste, and to accept that such a change took time. Through December and into the new year Wilberforce's many doubts about his own worthiness and ability to uphold his new beliefs did indeed continue. His diary is peppered with such statements as: 'I am colder and more insensible than I was – I ramble – oh God, protect me from myself'; 'colder than ever – very unhappy – called at Newton's and bitterly moved; he comforted me'; and 'was strengthened in prayer, and first I shall be able to live more to God, which determined to do – much affected by Doddridge's directions for spending time, and hoped to conform to them in some degree: it must be by force at first, for I find I perpetually wander from serious thoughts when I am off my guard'.[78] Steadily, as the weeks went by, his willpower and new convictions prevailed. He resigned from the clubs at which he had passed so many happy evenings, spent many hours each day studying the Bible, and took new lodgings in London 'at one of the Adelphi hotels',[79] which gave him easier access to Evangelical preaching. He wrote earnestly to his sister about his beliefs, and reassuringly to his mother about his continuance in public life: he would not 'fly from the post where Providence has placed me'.[80] He continued to visit Downing Street and attend the House of Commons, his mind more at peace as he realised he could live up to the standards he had set himself without forsaking the world he had always known.

One study of religious conversion contends that once conversion is complete 'there is the sensation of liberation and victory, which the convert displays by a powerful and integral joy of the spirit'. The convert also has a 'sense more or less like the sense of vision or touch of nearness to God', and of 'an answering touch which thrills and recreates him'.[81] By Easter 1786 Wilberforce was writing to his sister from Stock in Essex on a beautiful day: 'the day has been delightful. I was out before six . . . I think my own devotions become more fervent when offered in this way amidst the general chorus with which all nature seems to be swelling the song of praise and thanksgiving; and accept the time which has been spent at church and at dinner . . . and neither in the sanctuary nor at table I trust, had I a heart unwarmed with gratitude to the giver of all good things.'[82] William Wilberforce had found his faith.

Wilberforce would later describe his emergence as an Evangelical convert as being akin to wakening from a dream and recovering 'the use of my reason after a delirium'.[83] His governing motives had been 'emulation, and a desire of distinction . . . ardent after the applause of my fellow creatures, I quite forgot that I was an accountable being; that I was hereafter to appear at the bar of God'.[84] Now he believed 'that if Christianity were not a fable, it was infinitely important to study its precepts, and when known to obey them',[85] and resolved to regulate his political conduct according to a new golden rule, 'to do as I would be done by'.[86] He was clear that he would stay in politics, but from now on his political activity would be directed and armed by the philosophy of Christian evangelicalism, of which he was now an adherent and would eventually become a leader.

Most people found it hard to distinguish between the Evangelicals and Methodists. As Sydney Smith wrote in 1808: 'Arminian and Calvinistic Methodists and the Evangelical clergymen of the Church of England . . . We shall use the general term of Methodism to designate those three classes of fanatics, not troubling ourselves to point out the finer shades and nicer discriminations of lunacy, but treating them all as in one general conspiracy against common sense and rational ortho-dox Christianity.'[87] Another observer had written in 1772: 'As soon as a person begins to show any symptoms of seriousness and strictness more than the fashion of the age allows he is called a Methodist, though he may happen to have no sort of connection with them; and when once this stigma is fixed upon him, he becomes like a deer whom the sportsmen have marked out for a chase.'[88] Evangelicals such as Newton also blurred matters by insisting that religious experience was more important than 'nice distinctions' between different categories of Christians. Methodism and evangelicalism were indeed part of the same religious movement. They both had their intellectual origins in German Pietism and English Puritanism, which had stressed 'a reformation or purification in worship as well in life'. They both contended that every person was lost in sin and could only be rescued and achieve personal salvation through faith in Christ. They had both moved on from the seventeenth-century Puritans of Civil War times by determinedly staying within the Church of England (although the Methodists broke away in 1795), and giving complete loyalty to the Crown. The general themes of Methodists and Evangelicals were indistinguishable, and Methodists would generally have regarded themselves as Evangelicals: it was not sufficient merely to observe the forms of being a Christian; eternal damnation could only be avoided by allowing Christian beliefs to guide all the habits and actions of daily life. Their theology was no different from that of the established Church, but the seriousness with which they practised it most certainly was.

Any doctrinal differences between Methodists and Evangelicals were blurred by the cross-currents of beliefs within each grouping: some Evangelicals, such as Newton, held to the Calvinistic concept of predestination favoured by some Methodists; others were in accord with Wesley himself in believing in unlimited atonement and the free will of human beings. The crucial differences between Methodists and Evangelicals were therefore largely of nuance and organisation, but these led to important differences in the type of person likely to join each group. Methodists were organised around their own Societies and Conferences, with a national and eventually international network and hierarchy, while Evangelicals were entirely outside such machinery. Evangelicals tended to be more in tune with prevailing English culture, less likely to separate themselves from society, less austere in their attitudes to simple sports and leisure, more likely to encourage a broad education, and readier to involve themselves in public life. Such differences of view partly stemmed from, and in turn strengthened, the general tendency for leading Evangelicals to be drawn from the more highly educated and business-orientated classes, while the tens of thousands of converts to Methodism were drawn heavily from lower income groups. Wilberforce was therefore a natural Evangelical, and would in due course find no shortage of people with a similar background to his own who could share his habits and thinking.

If Evangelicalism was more an attitude towards Christianity than a separate branch of the faith, what were its defining attributes, as now adopted by Wilberforce? One was certainly a belief in the all-encompassing role of Providence: God's hand could be detected in events great and small. It was Providence, he believed, that had enabled him to win his seat in Parliament by methods he would later have found unacceptable, thus launching him on a political life when an earlier conversion would have kept him away from it. If he escaped without injury from an accident, as he did when the linchpin on his coach fell out, he saw Providence at work; when Napoleon dominated Europe, Wilberforce considered him 'manifestly an instrument in the hands of Providence', and 'When God has done with him he will probably show how easily he can get rid of him.'[89] That anything would happen entirely accidentally was now alien to Wilberforce's thinking: 'How I abhor that word, fortunate; as if things happen by chance!'[90]

A second fundamental aspect of Evangelical beliefs was that Christian principles should be applied to all areas of life. They should guide every aspect of human life, not merely be added on to other beliefs or conflicting activities. As a result, drunkenness, gambling, duelling, the unfairness of the penal system, every form of immorality and the lack of observation of the Sabbath were all targets of Evangelical attack. Evangelicals considered themselves as ambassadors of God on earth, and to be at all times, an example of his godliness, holiness and compassion. Such activities as card-playing, public dancing and horse-racing were a distraction from devotion to God. Worldly indulgence was to be avoided, and leisure was seen as an opportunity for renewal rather than an end in itself. By contrast, prayer and devotion were essential: 'There is nothing more fatal to the life and power of religion; nothing which makes God more certainly withdraw his grace', than neglect of prayer.[91] And it was not sufficient for that prayer to be calculating, or to signify mere intellectual acceptance of Christian truth: an Evangelical needed to show that his 'whole heart is engaged',[92] as Wilberforce approvingly noted of Newton.

Above all, the Evangelicals felt an overpowering sense of account-ability, and a responsibility to God, for their actions. As one commen-tator would later note of them: 'I recall an abiding sense of religious responsibility, a self-sacrificing energy and works of mercy, an Evangel-istic zeal, an aloofness from the world, and a level of saintliness in daily life such as I do not expect again to see realised on earth. Every-thing down to the minutest detail of action and speech were considered with reference to eternity.'[93] Although he had always been good at documenting his actions, Wilberforce would now do so with all the more rigour, as humble preparation for a day of judgement. His money, abilities and power had been given to him by God, and he considered himself accountable in the smallest detail for how he would now use them. His mission now was to apply Christian principles as he understood them to the world as he saw it around him. He would say later that 'I was strongly impressed with a sense of it being incumbent on me to perform my Parliamentary duties with increased diligence and conscientiousness.'[94] As Newton wrote to him in March 1786, they had 'great subjects to discuss, great plans to promote, great prospects to contemplate'.[95] Now Wilberforce would turn his own mind to what those subjects and plans would be.

<h1>5</h1>

<h1>Diligence and New Causes</h1>

———————=:O:=———————

What madness I said to myself, is this! Here have I been throwing
away my time all my life past!

WILLIAM WILBERFORCE, autumn 1786[1]

There is a prospect of his being a very useful member of society if his
life is preserved.

CATHERINE KING TO GEORGE KING, 1 November 1786[2]

THE WILLIAM WILBERFORCE who resumed his attendance at
the House of Commons in the spring of 1786 was a changed man,
yet this would not have been immediately apparent to an observer in
the public gallery who happened to study his parliamentary behaviour.
In time, his conversion to Evangelical Christianity would give him
the moral force and unshakeable will to become one of the greatest
campaigners, and liberators, in the whole course of British history. In
old age, Wilberforce would write to his son Samuel, 'The best preparation for being a good politician, as well as a superior man in every
other line, is to be a truly religious man. For this includes in it all
those qualities which fit men to pass through life with benefit to others
and with reputation to ourselves.'[3] Yet the immediate impact on his
performance as a Member of Parliament was subtle rather than sharp,
underlining the fact that his conversion reinforced many of his existing
traits more than it created in him a new personality. Determined to
apply himself with diligence to the post in which Providence had placed
him, and writing to Wyvill that he now had a 'higher sense of the

94

duties of my station, and a firmer resolution to discharge them with fidelity and zeal',[4] Wilberforce had always been an assiduous MP by the standards of the eighteenth century, in attending both to the chamber of the House of Commons and to the needs of his Yorkshire constituents. Resolved now, as he had told Pitt, 'to be no Party man', he had always remained nominally an Independent, and had from his first election to the Commons styled himself as a man who would pursue his own views. For some years his theoretical profession of independence but practical loyalty to Pitt had given him an ambiguous political stance; his new approach to life led to a shift of emphasis within that ambiguity rather than a departure from it. And while he would now take up a variety of well-intentioned causes, many of them were, at least initially, taken up at the behest of his constituents, as they might have been before, with his speeches on the main issues of the day indicating no change in his wider political philosophy.

April 1786 saw the beginning of a series of highly charged debates on the floor of the House of Commons about the conduct of Warren Hastings as Governor General of India. When Hastings had returned to Britain the previous year, he had expected the plaudits of the nation for a period of rule which had seen him use every military and economic means to extend and confirm British power in India; he had been a victor in war, and a guarantor of great profits. In the process, however, he had created two powerful groups of enemies within the British body politic. The first consisted of those who had been his political rivals in India, such as Philip Francis, who also returned to Britain and entered the House of Commons to pursue him. The second group was led by Edmund Burke, for whom the ruthless and arbitrary nature of Hastings' governing of India was in conflict with their sense of British justice and law, and who, perhaps significantly for Wilberforce's future work, demonstrated a new level of concern about the colonial mistreatment of native peoples.

As Burke thundered out his accusations of tyrannical conduct against Hastings that April, Wilberforce had no problem as a back-bencher in joining in with Pitt's official line: he accused Burke of an excess of passion, and in a speech on 1 June argued that it was too late now to blame Hastings for actions taken many years earlier under the government of Lord North: 'To punish Mr Hastings now was like eating the mutton of the sheep which we have previously shorn of its fleece. Certainly we ought to have recalled him when he committed the fault; but having suffered him to wear out his constitution in our service, it was wrong to try him when he could be of no farther use.'[5] Wilberforce therefore joined Pitt in voting down the initial charges against Hastings. When he did turn against Hastings, it was once again in conjunction with Pitt, and seemingly at his behest. Pitt's celebrated *volte face* followed him beckoning to Wilberforce to join him behind the Speaker's chair and saying, 'Does not this look very ill to you?', with Wilberforce replying, 'Very bad indeed.'[6] Pitt then went to the dispatch box to declare that the latest charge against Hastings did indeed concern behaviour which was 'beyond all proportion exorbitant, unjust, and tyrannical',[7] and that it could merit his impeachment. This bombshell paved the way for a dramatic but undistinguished chapter in British history: the trial of Warren Hastings would eventually commence amidst huge excitement in Westminster Hall in 1788, consume great political energy and substantial resources, and after seven long years of proceedings would end in his acquittal in 1795, a ruined and embittered man. Wilberforce would always maintain that Pitt's judgement on Hastings was based on nothing other than the evidence: 'He paid as much impartial attention as if were a jury-man,'[8] yet in thinking this Wilberforce may have been a little naïve, since Pitt was probably looking for a reason to abandon Hastings as a means of disarming his own opponents.

Wilberforce was still essentially loyal to Pitt, and recorded that 'I was surprised to find how generally we agreed.'[9] The following session would see him giving energetic support to one of Pitt's earliest achievements, the concluding of a commercial treaty with France. This treaty, which opened up many domestic markets to trade, did not create the alarm occasioned by the ill-fated Irish Propositions two years earlier, and Wilberforce could support it without any qualms whatsoever: it accorded with his previous views, was championed by his friend, and 'It gave him a particular pleasure to be able to say that whilst he was acting in conformity with the dictates of his own conscience, he was voting agreeably to the general wishes of his constituents.'[10]

Such support for the Pitt ministry, coming from a man with such close personal connections with the Prime Minister, would have gone unremarked at Westminster. It confirmed Wilberforce as an active and valued debater of the great questions of the day. But ironically it was when he struck out on his own in this period that he ran not only into greater political obstacles, but into a degree of self-doubt; and not only adopted worthwhile measures of reform, but supported others which appeared rather bizarre. The first measure he attempted to take through the Commons in 1786 was a Registration Bill, a cherished project of parliamentary reformers such as Wyvill and Lord Mahon, Pitt's brother-in-law. Introduced into the Commons by the two Yorkshire Members, Wilberforce and Duncombe, on 15 May, it was an attempt to bring about some positive change in the electoral system after the heavy defeat of wider reform the previous month. The plan was to improve the conduct of county elections by requiring voters to be registered in advance, the polling to take place in a single day but at a variety of locations. It was, therefore, a precursor of modern electoral arrangements, but it was opposed by many of Wilberforce's own constituents, leading him to think that he had made a mistake in introducing it, that it had been a 'very ill-advised measure', and that it would be better that it were defeated in the House of Lords in case 'the odium we have incurred by it will . . . be quite decisive of our fate at the next general election'.[11] The Bill was indeed too much for their Lordships, and was never passed; this was possibly the last time in his life that Wilberforce had cause to be grateful for the entrenched and unyielding conservatism of the House of Lords.

The next proposal Wilberforce adopted was again at the instigation of a Yorkshire constituent, in this case, a prominent surgeon and devout Methodist from Leeds who was to be a lifelong correspondent, William Hey. Hey persuaded Wilberforce that the rule by which only the bodies of executed murderers could be made available for dissection was encouraging body-snatching and inhibiting anatomical research. Wilberforce therefore found himself coming forward with a proposal that the bodies of executed criminals who had not committed murder but were guilty of other capital offences, should be sold for dissection in the same way as those of murderers. This would have greatly enlarged the number of such bodies: a typical issue of the *Gentleman's Magazine* in 1787 would list a sizeable number of people executed on a single day for crimes other than murder:

> Wednesday 14 March. The following malefactors convicted in December were executed according to their sentence: Frederic Daniel Lucas for robbing Wm Pawlett on the highway on the Edgeware road, of a watch and a few shillings; Samuel Phipps, for robbing his master's house of a gold watch and many other valuables; James Brown for robbing James Williamson, of his money; Dennis Sullivan, for breaking into the house of Henry Ringing, and stealing goods; William Adams, for robbing the house of William Briggs and stealing goods; Wm. Jones, Henry Staples, and John Innrer, for robbing James Pollard on Constitution hill; Robert Horsley, for robbing Jane Bearblock of her watch; and James Dubson, the letter carrier, for feloniously secreting a certain packet containing notes to the amount of £1000 . . .[12]

As Hey put it: 'Such bodies are the most fit for anatomical investigation, as the subjects generally die in health, the bodies are sound and the parts are distinct. Why should not those be made to serve a valuable purpose when dead, who were a universal nuisance when living?'[13] While the legislative proposal which resulted may seem strange in later centuries, it was nevertheless a sound and well-argued case. Wilberforce prepared thoroughly, putting the drawing-up of the Bill into the hands of senior lawyers and working for the first time with Samuel Romilly, a lawyer with humanitarian concerns. Romilly persuaded him of the merits of another proposal, which Wilberforce incorporated into his Bill: the abolition of the law that a woman committed of high and petty treason (which in those days included murdering her husband) be sentenced to be burnt as well as hanged. In practice the hanging was carried out first in such cases, as this account of an execution in 1769 demonstrates:

A post about seven feet high, was fixed in the ground; it had a peg near the top, to which Mrs Lott, standing on a stool, was fastened by the neck. When the stool was taken away, she hung about a quarter of an hour, till she was quite dead; a chain was then turned round her body, and properly fastened by staples to the post, when a large quantity of faggots being placed round her, and set on fire, the body was consumed to ashes . . . It is computed there were 5,000 persons attending the execution.[14]

Wilberforce's Bill for 'Regulating the Disposal after Execution of the Bodies of Criminals Executed for Certain Offences, and for Changing the Sentence pronounced upon Female Convicts in certain cases of High and Petty Treason'[15] did indeed pass through the House of Commons without much discussion, but once again the House of Lords was far more sceptical of change of any kind. There, the leading Whig lawyer Lord Loughborough was able to gain the satisfaction of not only venting his views but of obstructing the projects of young MPs associated with Pitt. He denounced these 'raw, jejune, ill-advised and impracticable' ideas,[16] argued that the incorporation of burning into a death sentence made it more severe 'than mere hanging', and that dissection was such a strong deterrent, given the prevailing belief that it prevented the resurrection of the deceased, that unless it was reserved for capital crimes, burglars would be more likely to commit murders. Wilberforce's first attempt at humanitarian reform therefore ended rather ignominiously and with another defeat in the House of Lords, a result with which he would one day become even more horribly familiar. For a great reformer, it had not been an auspicious start.

As soon as the session of 1786 was over in early July, Wilberforce set off to the north to see his family, taking several days to travel through Grantham and Hull to Scarborough. Soon afterwards he was established, with his mother and sister, at the country home of his cousin, Samuel Smith, at Wilford near Nottingham. If his mother had been worried by reports of his new religious enthusiasm she soon discovered she need not have been, for in personality as in politics, much of the effect of Wilberforce's conversion was the reinforcement of some of his better habits rather than a complete change in their nature. He wished, as he recorded in his notes that summer, to 'be cheerful without being dissipated',[17] and in advance of joining his mother he made a note to be 'more kind and affectionate than ever ... show respect for her judgement, and manifest rather humility in myself than dissatisfaction concerning others'.[18] Allied to his natural cheerfulness and interest in all subjects, the result was a most acceptable combination when it came to conversation, inducing Mrs Sykes to remark as he left Scarborough: 'If this is madness, I hope that he will bite us all.'[19] Now, and for the rest of his life, religion was never to make Wilberforce dreary, melancholy or intolerant. Years later he was to write to Bob Smith: 'My grand objection to the religious system still held by many who declare them orthodox Churchmen ... is, that it tends to render Xtianity so much a system of prohibitions rather than of privilege and hopes, and thus the injunction to rejoice so strongly enforced in the New Testament is practically neglected, and Religion is made to wear a forbidding and gloomy air and not one of peace and hope and joy.'[20] It was an attitude which meant that he was never shunned, socially or politically, but could combine what had always been an appealing personality with the force of steadfast belief.

Even so, he struggled a great deal behind the scenes throughout 1786, constantly setting targets and resolutions for himself in line with his new beliefs, and then disapproving of his inadequacies when he failed to live up to them. Evangelicals followed Puritans and Methodists in keeping a diary 'not as a means of recording events, but of self-examination of the recent past and adjustment to the future; it was the Evangelical equivalent of the confessional'.[21] The Wesleys and Whitefield had kept such journals, and Doddridge, whose writings had such influence on Wilberforce, had recommended serious reflection each day on such topics as 'What temptations am I likely to be assaulted with? ... In what instances have I lately failed? ...'[22] Wilberforce had always been a keen diarist and note-taker, and his scribbles now became the means by which he recorded and fortified his intentions and tested his performance against them. He became steadily more systematic in doing so as the years went by. Thus on 21 June he was noting, 'to endeavour from this moment to amend my plan for time, and to take account of it – to begin to-morrow'.[23] On 22 June it was, 'did not think enough of God. Did not actually waste much time, but too dissipated when I should have had my thoughts secretly bent on God.'[24] 'June 25th . . . I do not think I have a sufficiently strong conviction of sin: yet I see plainly that I am an ungrateful, stupid, guilty creature . . . July 2nd I take up my pen because it is my rule; but I have not been examining myself with that seriousness with which we ought to look into ourselves from time to time. That wandering spirit and indolent way of doing business are little if at all defeated, and my rules, resolved on with thought and prayer, are forgotten.'[25] Sometimes, as in one case that November after he had dined with Pitt at Downing Street, he reproached himself for falling victim to 'temptations of the table', which he thought 'disqualified me for every useful purpose in life, waste my time, impair my health, fill my mind with thoughts of resistance before and self-condemnation afterwards'. As a result he created fresh rules for himself about dining: 'No dessert, no tastings, one thing in first, one in second course. Simplicity. In quantity moderate . . . Never more than six glasses of wine; my common allowance two or three . . . To be in bed always if possible by eleven and be up by six o'clock. In general to reform in accordance with my so often repeated resolutions . . . I will every night note down whether have been so or not . . .'[26]

Wilberforce's determination not to waste time, and his conviction that he had frittered away most of his time hitherto – 'What madness I said to myself, is this! Here have I been throwing away my time all my life past!'[27] – led him to make a huge effort that summer to catch up on the education he thought he should have received in his youth. Lamenting his 'idleness at college', he now made it his object 'to improve my faculties and add to my slender stock of knowledge. Acting on this principle for many subsequent years, I spent the greater part of my Parliamentary recess at the House of one friend or another, where I could have the command of my time and enjoy just as much society as would be desirable for maintaining my spirits and enabling

me to continue my labours with cheerfulness and comfort.'[28] He spent
nine or ten hours a day studying by himself, very often reading the
Bible, but also devouring recent works of literature, philosophy and
economics: Locke, Pope, Montesquieu, Adam Smith, Rousseau,
Voltaire and Dr Johnson, committing to memory many verses by
Shakespeare and Cowper. Continuing with this through the whole of
August and September afforded few breaks to visit his constituents and
meant he avoided the traditional summer progress around Yorkshire,
but with both the country and the county in a state of reasonable
political contentment, he was able to get away with just a brief trip to
the great annual Cutlers' feast at Sheffield on 7 September, that city
having become the centre of cutlery-making in the seventeenth century.
His comparative abstinence certainly altered his appearance, with one
Hull resident writing that autumn: 'I was much shocked to see him,
he looks so emaciated and altered,' although she also thought that 'he
spoke in a very pretty and feeling manner. There is a prospect of
his being a very useful member of society if his life is preserved.'[29]
Wilberforce's main complaint was that his eyes seemed even worse, a
situation all the more frustrating to him now that he had become keen
on so many daily hours of reading. In a letter to Muncaster in late
October he refers to himself as 'half-blind', and reports that he had
been to see William Hey about his eyes and general health.[30] On Hey's
advice, he dawdled only briefly in London when he returned that
November, and set off instead to take the waters of Bath.

Since Wilberforce did not bore his friends with his beliefs, he was
able to retain the wide circle of friendships he had already developed,
and was always welcome in the houses of MPs and other acquaintances
as he travelled. He made lists of friends who he thought needed help
or prayer, but tended to try to nudge them towards religion rather
than impose it on them. He expressed great concern that autumn
about the state in which he might find 'poor Eliot and Pitt'[31] – the first
having lost his wife and the second his sister when she died suddenly
that September, five days after giving birth. Eliot would indeed shortly
become a close companion in evangelicalism, while remaining a strong
link between Wilberforce and Pitt. In future years they would pray for

each other and attend chapel together: 'We can render each other no more effectual service.'[32] If friends seemed open to religion, then Wilberforce would indeed set about persuading them, urging regular prayer or even reading Doddridge aloud to them. Some, like Lord Belgrave and Matthew Montagu MP, would succumb to him, but others gave playful rebuffs. His long-standing friend and fellow parliamentarian Pepper Arden explained to Wilberforce, 'I hope things are not quite as bad as you say. I think a little whipping would do for me, not with any severity, I assure you.'[33] Above all, Wilberforce would always regret that he could never persuade Pitt to treat religion with the seriousness he thought it deserved. Prevailing upon Pitt eventually to join him in listening to a sermon from a noted Evangelical preacher, Richard Cecil, he was deeply disappointed when on the way out of the church Pitt said, 'You know, Wilberforce, I have not the slightest idea what that man has been talking about.'[34]

Wilberforce had never been very materialistic. When he visited his Yorkshire estate in 1786 he remarked only on 'my land, just like anyone else's land'.[35] And although he had stayed at Wimbledon a good deal in 1786, albeit in a quieter way than during the boisterous summers a few years before, he now decided to sell Lauriston House, since travelling there wasted his time and owning it consumed money he thought he could spend to better effect. Instead, he would shortly set himself up in 4 Old Palace Yard, directly opposite the House of Commons and Westminster Hall, and as near to the centre of political action as a private residence could ever be.* For in Wilberforce's mind, the learning and opinions he was accumulating from his books and his travels had a clear and overriding purpose: to turn Christian principles into political action.

The voracious reading on which Wilberforce had embarked soon brought him into contact with the writings of Dr Josiah Woodward,

---

* The site of this house is now a grassed area with a statue of George V opposite St Stephen's entrance to the Houses of Parliament.

who in 1701 had written *An Account of the Progress of the Reformation of Manners*. Woodward had written about the 'very great success' of efforts made towards 'the suppressing of profane swearing and cursing, drunkenness and prophanation of the Lord's Day, and the giving a great check to the open lewdness that was acted in many of our streets' in the late seventeenth century, following a Proclamation by William and Mary in 1692 issued 'for the encouragement of piety and virtue; and for the preventing of vice, prophaneness and immorality'.[36] Such Proclamations were issued routinely on the accession of a new sovereign, but the difference in this case was that it had actually been followed up: local 'Societies for the Reformation of Manners' had been formed to assist in the detection of crime and to ensure that prosecutions were brought in circumstances when a lone individual would hesitate to act. The work of such societies continued into the early eighteenth century: a summary of the action they had taken in the year 1718, for instance, included 1,253 prosecutions for lewd and disorderly practices, 492 for exercising trades or callings on the Lord's Day, 228 for profane swearing and cursing, thirty-one for the keeping of bawdy and disorderly houses, seventeen for drunkenness and eight for keeping common gaming houses. Nevertheless, as the eighteenth century wore on, the efforts of such societies were overwhelmed by the riot of gambling, drunkenness, prostitution and petty crime which became commonplace in Hanoverian England. By 1759, the London Society was reduced to thanking a donor for a gift of ten guineas and giving 'notice to all grocers, chandlers, butchers, publicans, pastry-cooks, and others whom it may concern' that they were resolved to launch indictments concerning the 'great and growing evil' of trading on the Lord's Day, but such threats appear no longer to have been taken seriously.

In a remarkably short space of time, and with an energy which illustrated the idealism and determination to act with which he was now possessed, Wilberforce became the driving force behind the issuing of a fresh Royal Proclamation and the attempted mobilisation of the country's moral and social leaders in a nationwide struggle against vice. His vision was straightforward: 'In my opinion the strength of a country is most increased by its moral improvement, and by the moral and religious instruction of its people. Only think what a country that would be, where every one acted upon Xtian principles.'[37] He was convinced that crimes and misdemeanours could not be combated successfully in a piecemeal fashion; what was necessary was the transformation of the moral climate of the times. As he wrote to Wyvill, 'the barbarous custom of hanging has been tried too long, and with the success which might have been expected from it. The most effectual way of preventing the greater crimes is by punishing the smaller, and by endeavouring to repress that general spirit of licentiousness, which is the parent of every species of vice. I know that by regulating the external conduct we do not at first change the hearts of men, but even they are ultimately to be wrought upon by these means, and we should at least so far remove the obtrusiveness of the temptation, that it may not provoke the appetite, which might otherwise be dormant and inactive.'[38]

In the spring of 1787 Wilberforce took up this plan according to another new friend, the Right Reverend Beilby Porteus, recently appointed Bishop of London, 'with indefatigability and perseverance' and 'made private application to such of his friends of the Nobility and other men of consequence'.[39] In Wilberforce's mind, the reforming of the entire moral framework of society was the perfect as well as the ultimate issue. If carried out successfully, it would make more difference to daily life and save more souls when they came to account for their lives before God than any number of well-intentioned Acts of Parliament. 'God has set before me as my object,' he wrote in his journal, 'the reformation of manners.'[40] To William Hey he wrote that this cause 'is of the utmost consequence, and worthy of the labours of a whole life'.[41]

Such an all-encompassing campaign was certainly likely to require the labours of a whole life. England in the eighteenth and early nineteenth centuries was rife with every activity of which Wilberforce now disapproved. In London, brothels had become fashionable and acceptable, and 'prostitution is so profitable a business, and conducted so openly, that hundreds of persons keep houses of ill-fame, for the reception of girls not more than twelve or thirteen years of age, without a blush upon their integrity'.[42] According to Sydney Smith, 'Everyone is drunk. Those who are not singing are sprawling. The sovereign people are in a beastly state.'[43] In the Gordon Riots of 1780, many deaths had been caused when a distillery had been broken into and people had drunk unrefined gin from the gutters. A commentator earlier in the century had written:

> What an intolerable Pitch that Vice is arriv'd at in this Kingdom, together with the astonishing NUMBER OF TAVERNS, COFFEE-HOUSES, ALEHOUSES, BRANDY-SHOPS, &c. now extant in London, the like not to be paralleled by any other City in the Christian world . . . If this DRINKING SPIRIT does not soon abate, all our Arts, Sciences, Trade, and Manufacturers will be entirely lost, and the Island become nothing but a Brewery or Distillery, and the Inhabitants all Drunkards.[44]

A House of Lords debate in the 1740s had heard that 'You can hardly pass along any street in this great city, at any hour of the day, but you may see some poor creatures, mad drunk with this liquor [gin], and committing outrages in the street, or lying dead asleep upon bulks, or at the doors of empty houses.'[45] Ministers and Members of Parliament seemed to be as bad as anyone, with George Rose, the Secretary to the Treasury, writing to Wilberforce on one occasion: 'I have actually been drunk ever since ten o'clock this morning, and have not yet quite the use of my reason, but I am, Yours most faithfully and cordially, George Rose.'[46]

As to crime, 'The most barefaced villains, swindlers, and thieves walk about the streets in the day-time, committing their various depredations, with as much confidence as men of unblemished reputation and honesty.'[47] A comprehensive analysis of crime in London in 1796 produced 'a shocking catalogue of human depravity', along with the calculation that 115,000 (out of a population of little more than a million) supported themselves 'in and near the metropolis by pursuits either criminal, illegal, or immoral'. Nearly half of these were thought to be 'unfortunate females of all descriptions, who support themselves chiefly or wholly by prostitution', but the other categories mentioned in the remarkably detailed and oddly precise calculations included eight thousand 'Thieves, Pilferers, and Embezzlers', 7,440 'Swindlers, Cheats, and low Gamblers' who lived 'chiefly by fraudulent transactions in the Lottery', three thousand 'Spendthrifts, Rakes, Giddy Young Men, inexperienced and in the pursuit of criminal pleasures', two thousand 'Professed Thieves, Burglars, Highway Robbers, Pick-pockets and River Pirates', a thousand 'Fraudulent, and dissolute Publicans who are connected with Criminal People' and 'allow their houses to be rendezvous for Thieves, Swindlers and Dealers in Base Money' – all the way down to sixty 'Professed and known Receivers of Stolen Goods of whom 8 or 10 are opulent'.[48]

It was against this daunting background that Wilberforce unfolded his plan to Porteus, who considered that 'the design appeared to me in the highest degree laudable, and the object of the greatest importance and necessity; but I foresaw great difficulties in the execution of it unless conducted with great judgement and discretion . . . My advice therefore was to proceed in the beginning cautiously and privately, to mention the Plan in confidence, first of all to the leading men in Church and State, the Archbishop of Canterbury and Mr Pitt to engage their concurrence . . . and then by degrees to . . . obtain if possible the assistance of the principal and most respectable characters among the nobility, clergy and gentry in and about London and afterwards throughout the Kingdom.'[49] Wilberforce proceeded precisely along these lines, winning the 'entire approbation' of the Prime Minister and the Archbishop,[50] and, via the Archbishop, the approval of the King and Queen. By the end of May, he could hope that 'The persons with whom I have concerted my measures, are so trusty, temperate, and unobnoxious, that I think I am not indulging a vain expectation in persuading myself that something considerable may be done.'[51] It was thus largely at Wilberforce's behest that on 1 June 1787 King George III issued a new Proclamation, observing 'with inexpressible concern, the rapid progress of impiety and licentiousness and that deluge of prophaneness, immorality, and every kind of vice which, to the scandal of our holy religion, and to the evil example of our loving subjects, have broken in upon this nation', and commanding the 'Judges, Mayors,

Sheriffs, Justices of the Peace and all our other subjects' to set about the prosecution of all persons guilty of 'excessive drinking, Blasphemy, profane Swearing and Cursing lewdness, Profanation of the Lord's Day, or other dissolute, immoral, or disorderly Practices; and that they take Care also effectually to suppress all publick Gaming Houses and other loose and disorderly Houses, and also all unlicensed Publick Shews, Interludes, and Places of Entertainment'.[52]

While the population at large greeted the Proclamation with the customary indifference, Wilberforce's objective was to mobilise leading figures to pursue the aims expressed in it over time rather than to achieve instant results. Throughout the late spring and summer of 1787 he was to be found circulating his plan to people of influence, persuading the Duke of Montagu to become President of the 'Society for Giving Effect to His Majesty's Proclamation against Vice and Immorality' and visiting Bishops as far afield as Worcester, Hereford, Norwich, Lincoln, York and Lichfield. He met with much approval and sympathy, some of the aristocracy seeing his plan, as he did, as something which could ultimately lead to more humane and proportionate punishments; the Duke of Manchester wrote, 'if you and other young men who are rising in the political sphere would undertake the arduous task of revising our code of criminal law ... I mean largely the number of capital punishments, I am satisfied it would go far towards bettering the people of this country'.[53] But others were more cynical or mistrustful. When Wilberforce was bold enough to visit Earl Fitzwilliam, who had tried to prevent his election for Yorkshire in 1784, Fitzwilliam laughed in his face and argued that the only way to avoid immorality was to become poor – 'I promised him a speedy return of purity of morals in our own homes, if none of us had a shilling to spend in debauchery out of doors.'[54] Involving outwardly respectable people in pressing on with such ideas, according to Fitzwilliam, would only expose their hypocrisy in due course. Another nobleman apparently expressed similar scepticism, responding to Wilberforce's proposals by pointing to a painting of the crucifixion as an example of how idealistic young reformers met their end.

Nevertheless, when the names of the forty-nine founding members of the Society were published, they included four Members of Parliament (including the Prime Minister), ten peers, six Dukes and a Marquis, along with seventeen Bishops and the Archbishops of both Canterbury and York. While such impressive leadership had the advantage of showing that this was a powerful movement in which leading figures in society intended to display both activity and example, the disadvantage was that critics could easily point out that it was mainly poorer people who would have to change their behaviour if the great swathe of restrictions mentioned in the Proclamation were enforced. In the words of Hannah More: 'Will not the common people think it a little inequitable that they are abridged of the diversions of the public-house and the gaming-yard on Sunday evening, when they shall hear that many houses of the first nobility are on that evening crowded with company, and such amusements carried on as are prohibited by human laws even on common days?'[55] Years later, when the work of the Proclamation Society had been overtaken by the Society for the Suppression of Vice, Sydney Smith would characterise them as having the aim of 'suppressing the vices of persons whose income does not exceed £500 per annum'.[56]

It is certainly true that, while Wilberforce had by now withdrawn himself from the pleasures and gaming tables of gentlemen's clubs, he avoided making a direct assault on their members' habits, writing to Dudley Ryder in September 1789, 'Don't imagine I am about to run amuck and tilt at all I meet. You know that on many grounds I am a sworn foe to the Clubs, but I don't think of opening my trenches against them and commencing open war on such potent adversaries. But then I honestly confess to you that I am restrained only by the conviction that by such desperate measure I should injure rather than serve the cause I have in view; and when ever prudential motives do not repress my "noble rage" I would willingly hunt down vice whether at St James's or St Giles's.'[57] In making this judgement, Wilberforce was demonstrating what would become an obvious attribute: his idealistic objectives were always pursued by means which took into account practical and political constraints. Rather than denounce the activities of the better-off, but conscious of the possible charge of hypocrisy, he set out to involve senior national figures in order to change the prevailing fashion and habits of the times, at all social levels including their own. He believed that those who could set an example had adopted an inverted pride in which they claimed their behaviour to be worse than it actually was: 'We have now an hypocrisy of an opposite sort, and I believe many affect to be worse in principle [than] they really are, out of deference to the licentious moral [sic] of the fashionable world.'[58]

The founding of the Proclamation Society was thus a forerunner of the many projects and causes Wilberforce would pursue throughout his life: in his methods, objectives and weaknesses, the same pattern would emerge again and again. His method was to win over leading figures in politics and society by the force of persuasion and the power of example, never failing to show due respect to their rank and to take enormous trouble over assuaging their doubts and fortifying their consciences. His objectives would always centre on using spiritual improvement to ameliorate the human condition by practical steps rather than dramatic transformation; in this case he was seeking a higher moral climate for the betterment of rich and poor, law-abiding and law-breaking alike, but not the social and political revolution which others would soon be advocating. He wanted to improve society rather than render it unrecognisable. Such methods and objectives would always have the weakness of being open to charges of excessive caution or conservatism, and be easily subject to mockery. In his book The Spirit of the Age (1825), William Hazlitt would write: 'Mr Wilberforce's humanity will go to all lengths that it can with safety and discretion, but it is not to be supposed that it should lose him his seat for Yorkshire, the smile of Majesty, or the countenance of the loyal and pious.'[59] His proposals were easily seen as being either puritanical or hypocritical. When the great playwright and opposition MP Richard Brinsley Sheridan was found years later lying drunk in a gutter and was asked to give his name, he famously replied, 'Wilberforce!'[60]

Yet Wilberforce would also display, in his efforts to reform the nation's manners, other attributes which would become lifelong characteristics of a great campaigner: steady persistence and a step-by-step accumulation of small additions towards his goal. The Proclamation Society duly succeeded in broadening its membership and support among the magistracy and gentry, and disseminating a great deal of instruction and guidance on enforcement – as in this attempt to help judge the state of intoxication:

> Particularly as to drunkenness to use caution and prudence in judging whether a man is drunk. Though a man that cannot stand upon his legs, or that reels or staggers when he goes along the streets and is heard to falter remarkably in speech, unless in the cause of some known infirmity or defeat, may ordinarily be presumed to be drunk.[61]

In the later view of Sidney and Beatrice Webb, the Proclamation Society 'set going a national movement' which actually produced a marked lull in rioting, disorderly conduct and brutal amusements, and became 'an important contributory cause of the remarkable advance of "respectability" made by the English working man during the first two decades of the nineteenth century'.[62] Such a 'lull' is difficult to validate statistically, although it appears from the records of convictions for murder in London throughout the eighteenth century that violent crime was certainly on a downward trend which continued through this period. It may well be that British society was becoming less drunk, less violent and less disrespectful after a bout of mid-century excess, but it is also hard to deny that the Proclamation Society achieved practical results: convening conferences of magistrates to try to improve prison government and the regulation of vagrancy, and obtaining court judgements or Acts of Parliament which allowed brothels to be closed or the special nature of Sundays to be observed. As Britain began to move from Hanoverian excess to Victorian self-discipline, Wilberforce's Proclamation Society would become one of the many forces propelling it on its way.

Busy as Wilberforce had been in conceiving of and launching the Proclamation Society, it was by no means his sole preoccupation in late 1786 and throughout 1787. For most of the rest of his life he would simultaneously pursue several issues in parallel, flitting between the mountains of correspondence and long lines of visitors which each issue aroused. Continually finding outlets for his public philanthropy, he was often also busily attending to the spiritual or financial condition of friends and relatives. Still close to Pitt, he became an intermediary to Robert Smith, later Lord Carrington, who had offered to sort out Pitt's chaotic domestic finances. This would prove to be an impossible task at any stage in the next two decades, and would often call for Wilberforce's intervention. 'Indifferently as I thought of our friend's domestic management,' Smith wrote to him in 1786, 'I was not prepared for such an account as the box contained . . . the necessity, however, of bringing his affairs into some better order is now so apparent, that no man who is attached to his person, or values his reputation, can be easy while he knows it is undone.'[63]

The following year Wilberforce received a series of entreaties from his sister in Hull, usually demanding an answer by return of post, requesting advice on Christian conversion or his judgement about what entertainments she was permitted to be involved in. Asked to determine whether his family should attend the theatre, he confessed in his reply to agonising over the pain he would cause his mother, a consciousness that he would have to 'account for my answer to it at the bar of the great Judge of quick and dead', and concluded: 'in one word, then, I think the tendency of the theatre most pernicious . . . You talk of going only to one or two plays, and of not staying the farce . . . how will the generality of those who see you there know your motives for not being as frequent an attendant as formerly, and for not remaining during the whole performance? . . . Will not, then, your presence at the amusements of the theatre sanction them in the minds of all who see you there?'[64] The need to combine political action, Evangelical principles and personal example meant that Wilberforce always had to fight on many fronts. And even as he wrote such letters, the greatest concern and most central campaign of his life was opening up.

While Wilberforce was with his family in Yorkshire in 1786 he had received a letter from Sir Charles Middleton MP which led him to promise to visit the Middleton family home, Barham Court at Teston in Kent, that autumn. He had many reasons for going. He already knew Middleton well, and had a high regard for him: Middleton was the father-in-law of Wilberforce's friend Gerard Edwards, and was at that stage one of the few other Evangelical Members of Parliament. He was also serving as the highly effective Comptroller of the Navy and Head of the Navy Board, implementing the much-needed reforms demanded by Pitt to strengthen the Royal Navy and root out corruption in the dockyards after the failures of the American War. Furthermore, Middleton's indomitable wife Margaret was an early Evangelical, a friend of Hannah More, Dr Johnson and Garrick, whose mind was 'so constantly on the stretch in seeking out opportunities of promoting in every possible way the ease, the comfort, the prosperity, the happiness temporal and eternal, of all within her reach that she seems to have no time left for anything else and scarce ever appeared to bestow a single thought upon herself'.[65] Their combination of naval experience and Evangelical beliefs had given the Middletons emphatic views about what they considered to be the greatest outrage of the eighteenth-century world. Those views were fully shared by another man who Wilberforce would have seen when he stayed at Teston, and who he had met before, James Ramsay, who had served in the navy, become a rector, and was now serving as vicar of the local parish. Two years earlier, Ramsay had written his seminal *Essay on the Treatment and Conversion of African Slaves in the British Sugar Colonies*. Wilberforce knew from Middleton's letter that this would be the subject of the discussion when he stayed at Teston. For his hosts had in mind for him a simply stated but vastly complicated task: to lead in Parliament a campaign to abolish the slave trade.

6

The Trade in Flesh and Blood

From the hour of their birth, some are marked out for subjection, others for rule.

ARISTOTLE, *Politics* (350BC)[1]

The *Negro-Trade* and the natural Consequences resulting from it, may be justly esteemed an inexhaustible Fund of Wealth and Naval Power to this Nation.

MALACHY POSTLETHWAYT, 1746[2]

S LAVERY HAS NEVER BEEN ABSENT from the record of human civilisation.* The ancient Egyptians owned and traded in black slaves; the armies of Persia's great king Xerxes contained slaves from Ethiopia; and Greek and Roman civilisations were characterised by the ownership of slaves on a vast scale. Athens boasted sixty thousand slaves in its prime; Rome perhaps two million at the end of the Republic: these included black slaves such as the one depicted serving at a banquet in a mosaic at Pompeii, but also Celts and Saxons from the northern fringes of the Empire. For the whole of the first millennium AD slavery was an accepted part of northern European life, with the slave markets at Verdun and elsewhere doing a busy trade in the empire of Charlemagne, and only the arrival of an effective system of serfdom putting an end to slavery around the eleventh century.

It was in the countries of southern Europe and northern Africa

---

* Shockingly, it still is not absent. In the year 2004 it was estimated that twenty-seven million people were enslaved in some form of forced or bonded labour.

that slavery continued to flourish in the Middle Ages. While the Christians held Spain they used Muslim slaves; after the conquest of Spain by the Moors tens of thousands of Christians were in turn enslaved, with as many as thirty thousand Christian slaves working in the kingdom of Granada as late as the fourteenth century. At the same time, slavery remained common in the Arab world, fed largely by the trans-Saharan trade in black slaves taken from West Africa. There, African kings collected slaves for the lucrative export market but also employed thousands of their own as palace servants or soldiers.

Against such a background, it is not surprising that as the Portuguese ventured down the west coast of Africa and Columbus made his celebrated voyages across the Atlantic in the fifteenth century, a new form of slave trade sprang up simultaneously. By 1444, slaves from West Africa were on sale in the Algarve. Slaves joined gold and ivory among the rich pickings that could be obtained on voyages to the south, the leader of one early expedition reporting: 'I herded them as if they had been cattle towards the boats. And we all did the same, and we captured on that day . . . nearly 650 people, and we went back to Portugal, to Lagos in the Algarve, where the Prince was, and he rejoiced with us.'[3] The first transatlantic slave voyage was sent on its way by none other than Columbus himself, although, strangely in view of what would later transpire, it was in a west-to-east direction, and consisted of Caribbean natives sent for sale in Europe. It was evident almost immediately that such a trade would not be a success. Half of the second consignment died when they entered Spanish waters due to 'the unaccustomed cold', and a Genoese observer reported: 'They are not people suited to hard work, they suffer from the cold, and they do not have a long life.'[4] Not only did South Americans turn out to be unsuitable for export to Europe, but their numbers in their own lands were about to be devastated by the diseases which the Spanish and Portuguese brought with them across the Atlantic.

By 1510, King Ferdinand II of Spain was giving permission for four hundred slaves to be taken from Africa to the New World: he could not have known it was to be the beginning of one of the greatest involuntary migrations in human history. Goldmines soon created a demand for tough and expendable labourers, but it was the discovery in the early sixteenth century that sugarcane could be grown as easily in the Caribbean as any indigenous crop that would create, over time, an insatiable demand for African slaves. With Europeans unwilling to perform the backbreaking drudgery involved in tending and growing sugarcane, and the native population still reeling from disease and in any case less physically strong than their African counterparts, the solution was obvious. In the first half of the sixteenth century, what was to become the familiar triangular slave trade thus began: ships from Portugal would carry manufactured goods to the Guinea coast or the Congo, sell them in return for slaves, and carry their new captive cargo across the Atlantic. The third leg of the journey was completed with a cargo of hides, ginger, pearls and, increasingly, sugar for the home market.

It was not long before buccaneering Englishmen wanted to try their hand at the same game. In 1562 Captain John Hawkins, 'being, among other particulars, assured that Negroes were very good merchandise in Hispaniola, and that [a] store of Negroes might easily be had upon the Coast of Guinea', decided 'to make trial thereof'.[5] Although Queen Elizabeth I combined her approval for the expedition with the hope that slaves would not be taken against their will – something 'which would be detestable and call down the vengeance of Heaven upon the undertakers'[6] – it was certainly not possible to take them in any other way, although the three hundred slaves taken on board by Hawkins on his first voyage had already been rounded up by the Portuguese. Hawkins 'made a good profit' for his investors on this and later voyages,[7] despite a series of bloody encounters with the Spanish. And behind the English came the Dutch, who, having decided that it was morally unacceptable to sell slaves in Rotterdam or Amsterdam, nevertheless also sent expeditions to buy slaves in West Africa and sell them in the Caribbean. This was to become the hallmark of British and European attitudes to slavery for the following two hundred years: while it could not be sanctioned at home, it was an acceptable institution overseas, out of sight of governments and the general population alike.

In the early seventeenth century, Portuguese ships were still the main carriers of slaves, but with British colonies being developed in the Americas the British slave trade developed steadily alongside them. In the 1620s, black slaves were taken by British ships to North America, where they were 'bartered in Virginia for tobacco'.[8] With African slaves costing up to £20 a head, they seemed a better investment than the £10–15 cost of an indentured labourer from Europe, since they were capable of harder work and more tolerant of tropical diseases. Even so, the Atlantic slave trade in the first half of the seventeenth century was still small in scale, involving the transporting of about eight thousand slaves a year across the Atlantic. It was the surge in European demand for sugar which transformed slavery and the slave trade from the scale of small enterprise to that of a massive industry. In Barbados between 1645 and 1667, land prices increased nearly thirty times over as small tobacco farms were replaced by large sugar plantations, and the number of slaves on the island was increased from six thousand to over eighty thousand. As coffee, tea and chocolate became part of the staple diet in London, Paris and Madrid, so the plantations boomed. For the owners this meant profits akin to finding goldmines, but for the slaves it meant that whatever trace of normality or family life they had previously been allowed disappeared into barrack-style accommodation and the endless grind of mass production. Even at the beginning of this period, in 1645, the Reverend George Downing,* chaplain of a merchant ship, had written: 'If you go to Barbados, you shall see a flourishing island, [with] many able men. I believe that they are bought this year no less than a thousand Negroes and, the more they buy, the better able are they to buy for, in a year and a half, they will earn (with God's blessing) as much as they cost.'[9] The slave trade was becoming an integral part of the growth in British trade and wealth. In 1672 King Charles II granted a charter to the Royal African Company:

> We hereby for us, our heirs and successors grant unto the same Royal African Company of England ... that it shall and may be lawful to ... set to sea such as many ships, pinnaces and barks as

---

* Downing Street is named after this man, despite the fact that he served under Cromwell and then betrayed some of his colleagues to the Royalists.

should be thought fitting . . . for the buying, selling, bartering and
exchanging of, for or with any gold, silver, Negroes, slaves, goods,
wares and manufactures . . .[10]

With the escalating demand for sugar, combined with the gold rush
which began in Brazil in the late 1690s, the beginning of the eighteenth
century saw the slave trade growing rapidly: perhaps 150,000 slaves
were carried to Brazil alone in the first decade of the century. Furthermore, under the terms of the Treaty of Utrecht, signed at the conclusion
of the War of the Spanish Succession in 1713, Spain ceded to Britain
not only the strategic possessions of Gibraltar and Minorca, but also
the much-prized *Asiento* – the contract to import slaves and other
goods to the Spanish Indies. The fact that this contract was sold on by
the British government to the South Sea Company for the truly vast
sum of £7.5 million is evidence of the commercial excitement it generated, and the confidence that enormous profits were at hand. Such
confidence was somewhat misplaced, since many slaving voyages made
losses and the trade would become less profitable later in the century,
but there was no doubt that lucky or skilful traders could make a
spectacular return. In the 1720s British ships carried well over 100,000
slaves to the Americas, mainly to Jamaica and Barbados, with 150 ships,
principally based in Bristol and London, fully engaged in the trade. In
the 1730s British ships carried around 170,000 slaves, overtaking the
Portuguese for the first time. This was the decade that saw a great
increase in slave traffic to North America: in 1732 South Carolina
became the first English colony on the American mainland to register
a black majority. It was also the decade that saw the rise of Liverpool
as Britain's foremost slaving port. Well positioned on England's west
coast for Atlantic traffic, Liverpool also had the advantages of being
well away from the French navy in time of war, paying crews lower
rates than competing ports and being able to evade duty on the goods
carried on the homeward voyage by landing them on the Isle of Man
(which became 'a vast warehouse of smuggled goods'[11]). Several
Liverpool families who plunged heavily into the trade were able to
fund commercial dynasties partly as a result, ploughing their profits

into banking and manufacturing as the slave trade continued to grow.

In the 1740s, British ships transported no fewer than 200,000 African slaves. Furthermore, the triangular trade this facilitated was fuelling the rapid growth of domestic manufacturing. Some 85 per cent of English textile exports went to Africa at this stage, helping the export trade of cities such as Manchester to soar, while the demand for slaving ships in Liverpool made it a world leader in shipbuilding. With the vast profits coming back from the sugar plantations, cotton exports soaring, and the slave trade itself usually yielding a profit, it is no wonder that it could be written in 1772 that the African slave trade was 'the foundation of our commerce, the support of our colonies, the life of our navigation, and first cause of our national industry and riches'.[12] On taking office in 1783, William Pitt would estimate that profits from the trade with the West Indies accounted for 80 per cent of the income reaching Britain from across the seas. And such was the expansion of colonial production and demand for slaves that in the 1780s, as Wilberforce and Pitt began their political careers, slave traders would carry the truly colossal total of three-quarters of a million people across the Atlantic against their will, with around 325,000 being carried in British ships. Massive in its scale and long-established in its habits, the Atlantic slave trade seemed to many to be crucial to Britain's prosperity and an indispensable component of her Caribbean empire.

While the statistical record of the slave trade is impressive or horrifying enough, reaching a cumulative total of eleven million people imprisoned and transported across the ocean between the seventeenth and nineteenth centuries, few people in Europe at the time could have made an accurate guess as to the scale of the trade their nations fostered. More importantly, they would have been entirely unaware of the nature of the human tragedy which every single one of those millions represented. Each one was a child torn from a family, a sister separated from a brother, a husband from a wife or a family removed from the only place in the world they knew or loved. It is only when the slave trade is examined in its individual human consequences that it moves from a study in economic history to a tale of indefensible barbarity.

A glimpse of the heartrending circumstances in which slaves were taken is afforded by the autobiographical writings of Olaudah Equiano (c.1745–97), a slave who was captured as a child in the 1740s in what is now Nigeria, but who subsequently earned his freedom and wrote his story in the English language. His first-hand account of the brutalities of the slave trade played a major role in informing and influencing popular opinion and became a roaring success, with nine editions printed during his lifetime alone.*

> One day, when all our people were gone out to their work as usual, and only I and my dear sister were left to mind the house, two men and a woman got over our walls, and in a moment seized us both; and without giving us time to cry out, or make resistance, they stopped our mouths, and ran off with us to the nearest wood. Here they tied our hands, and continued to carry us as far as they could, till night came on, when we reached a small house, where the robbers halted for refreshment and spent the night ... The next morning we left the house, and continued travelling all the day. For a long time we had kept to the woods, but at last we came into a road which I believed I knew. I had now some hopes of being delivered; for we had advanced but a little way before I discovered some people at a distance, on which I began to cry out for their assistance: but my cries had no other effect than to make them tie me faster and stop my mouth; they then put me into a large sack. They also stopped my sister's mouth, and tied her hands; and in this manner we proceeded till we were out of the sight of those people ... The next day proved a day of greater sorrow than I had yet experienced; for my sister and I were then separated, while we lay clasped in each other's arms. It was in vain that we besought them not to part us; she was torn

---

* Written first-hand accounts of slavery were rare, although a further such work would emerge in 1782 with the publication of *The Letters of the Late Ignatius Sancho, An African*. Sancho was born on a slave ship in 1729, but ran away when he was twenty. By the 1770s he was a freeholder in the City of Westminster, and was the first black person of African origin to be able to vote in British elections.

from me, and immediately carried away, while I was left in a state
of distraction not to be described.[13]

Such kidnapping was common. A nineteenth-century study of the
origins of subsequently freed slaves suggested that 30 per cent of them
had been kidnapped (by other Africans), while 11 per cent had been
sold after being condemned by a judicial process (for adultery, for
example), 7 per cent had been sold to pay debts and a further 7 per
cent had been sold by relations or friends.[14] The largest proportion of
all, 34 per cent, had been taken in war, but John Newton was probably
being too sanguine when he argued that 'I verily believe, that the far
greater part of the wars, in Africa, would cease, if the Europeans would
cease to tempt them, by offering goods for slaves.'[15] African kingdoms
fought wars against each other and enslaved each other's people long
before the Europeans arrived to make matters worse, but there seems
little doubt that the lure of the slave trade sometimes contributed to
the outbreak of conflict. One observer of the time wrote: 'The wars
which the inhabitants of the interior part of the country . . . carry on
with each other are chiefly of a predatory nature, and owe their origin
to the yearly number of slaves which [they] . . . suppose will be wanted
by the vessels which arrive on the coast.'[16] On the other hand, a Royal
Navy captain, John Matthews, argued that 'the nations which inhabit
the interior parts of Africa . . . profess the Mahometan religion; and,
following the means prescribed by their prophet, are perpetually at
war with the surrounding nations who refuse to embrace their religious
doctrines . . . The prisoners made in these religious wars furnish a
great part of the slaves which are sold to the Europeans; and would
. . . be put to death if they had not the means of disposing of them.'[17]

At minimum, the feeding of the slave trade became a way of life
for tens of thousands of Africans and a source of power and wealth
for trading networks which stretched deep into the interior of the
continent, such as that of the Aro traders, and kingdoms which supplied huge numbers of slaves, such as the Lunda empire. It was the
supplying of slaves which gave such people access to large quantities
of copper, iron and, perhaps above all, guns. One cargo list of a ship

setting out to purchase 250 slaves in 1733 included a certain amount of textile products, but showed that the vessel carried most of its estimated value in metals and arms, including four hundred 'musquets', forty pairs of 'Common large Pistols' and forty 'blunderbuses', along with fourteen tons of iron, one thousand copper rods and eighty bottles of brandy.[18] Whatever benefit the African tribes derived from the sale of slaves, it was most unlikely to make them more peaceable.

Since most slaves originated far from the coast, perhaps hundreds of miles inland, the first part of their journey involved a long trek on foot, usually yoked together and underfed, with a consequently high rate of mortality. The original kidnappers might have received only a small fraction of the final price of the slave by the time they had paid tolls and duties in the course of a journey and sold on their captives to intermediary traders, at large fairs held specifically for that purpose. In the words of Alexander Falconbridge, a surgeon aboard slave ships who would later give evidence to Parliament:

> The unhappy wretches thus disposed of are bought by the black traders at fairs, which are held for that purpose, at the distance of upwards of two hundred miles from the sea coast; and these fairs are said to be supplied from an interior part of the country. Many Negroes, upon being questioned relative to the places of their nativity, have asserted that they have travelled during the revolution of several moons (their usual method of calculating time) before they have reached the places where they were purchased by the black traders . . . From forty to two hundred Negroes are generally purchased at a time by the black traders, according to the opulence of the buyer, and consist of all ages, from a month to sixty years and upwards. Scarcely any age or situation is deemed an exception, the price being proportionable. Women sometimes form a part of them, who happen to be so far advanced in their pregnancy as to be delivered during their journey from the fairs to the coast; and I have frequently seen instances of deliveries on board ship.[19]

Despite the constant supply of slaves thus proceeding to the coast, such was the competition among European traders that they often had to anchor for many weeks while slowly filling their decks with slaves amidst much haggling. John Newton's diary for the year 1750 gives some flavour of what was involved.

> Wednesday 9th January ... the traders came onboard with the owner of the slave; paid the excessive price of 86 bars which is near 12£ sterling, or must have let him gone on shoar again, which I was unwilling to do, as being the first that was brought on board the ship, and had I not bought him should have hardly seen another. But a fine man slave, now there are so many competitors, is near double the price it was formerly. There are such numbers of french vessels and most of them determined to give any price they are asked, rather than trade should fall into our hands, that it seems as if they are fitted out not so much for their own advantage, as with a view of ruining our purchases. This day buried a fine woman slave, number eleven, having been ailing sometime, but never thought her in danger till within these two days; she was taken with a lethargick disorder, which they seldom recover from ...
>
> Thursday 17th January ... William Freeman came onboard with a woman girl slave. Having acquitted himself tolerably, entrusted him with goods for 2 more. Yellow Will sent me word he had bought me a man, but wanted another musquet to compleat the bargain, which sent him.
>
> Wednesday 23rd January ... Yellow Will brought me off a boy slave, 3 foot 10 inches which I was obliged to take or get nothing.
>
> Fryday 25th January ... Yellow Will brought me a woman slave, but being long breasted and ill-made refused her, and made him take her onshoar ...[20]

Sometimes the traders resorted to simple trickery to fill their cargoes, as in this eyewitness account of Falconbridge:

> A black trader invited a negroe, who resided a little way up the country, to come and see him. After the entertainment was over, the trader proposed to his guest, to treat him with a sight of one of the ships lying in the river. The unsuspicious countryman readily consented, and accompanied the trader in a canoe to the side of the ship, which he viewed with pleasure and astonishment.

> While he was thus employed, some black traders on board, who
> appeared to be in the secret, leaped into the canoe, seized the
> unfortunate man, and dragging him into the ship, immediately
> sold him.[21]

For most slaves, the moment of being taken on board a ship was one
of utter terror. Very often they were convinced they were to be eaten –
Equiano recalled that when he saw 'a large furnace of copper boiling
and a multitude of black people, of every description, chained together,
every one of their countenances expressing dejection and sorrow, I no
longer doubted of my fate'.[22] Newton remembered how the women
and girls were taken on board 'naked, trembling terrified, perhaps
almost exhausted with cold, fatigue and hunger', only to be exposed
to 'the wanton rudeness of White savages'. Before long they would
be raped: 'The prey is divided upon the spot, and only reserved till
opportunity offers.'[23] It was said that a slave ship was usually 'part
bedlam and part brothel'. Newton recorded that while he was on shore
one afternoon one of his crew 'seduced a women slave down into the
room and lay with her brute like in view of the whole quarterdeck, for
which I put him in irons. If anything happens to the woman I shall
impute it to him, for she was big with child. Her number is 83.'[24] Not
surprisingly, it was at this point that many slaves made desperate
attempts to escape or to kill themselves, something which their captors
were unable to comprehend. As another British captain recorded:

> the men were all put in irons, two and two shackled together, to
> prevent their mutiny or swimming ashore. The Negroes are so
> wilful and loth to leave their own country, that they have often
> leap'd out of canoes, boat and ship into the sea, and kept under
> water until they were drowned to avoid being taken up and saved
> ... they having a more dreadful apprehension of Barbados than
> we have of hell though, in reality they live much better there than
> in their own country; but home is home.[25]

If the slaves did indeed have a premonition of hell, then they were not
far wide of the mark, for, unbelievably, the worst part of their ordeal
was yet to come. The economics of the slave trade required the

maximum number of slaves to be carried in the smallest possible space, with the result that they were forced into a hold, usually shackled together and often without space to turn round, in which some of their number would have already resided for several weeks. Equiano recalled that:

> the stench of the hold, while we were on the coast, was so intolerably loathsome, that it was dangerous to remain there for any time . . . now that the whole ship's cargo were confined together, it became absolutely pestilential. The closeness of the place, and the heat of the climate, added to the number of the ship, being so crowded that each had scarcely room to turn himself, almost suffocated us. This produced copious perspirations, so that the air soon became unfit for respiration, from a variety of loathsome smells, and brought on a sickness among the slaves, of which many died . . . The shrieks of the women, and the groans of the dying, rendered it a scene of horror almost inconceivable.[26]

Of course, it was in the interests of slave traders to keep their slaves in some degree of health, and during the day they would be taken up above decks and encouraged to 'dance', which generally meant jumping up and down with the encouragement of a whip. But in rough weather they would be confined below decks, with the portholes closed, in a scene of sometimes unimaginable horror. Falconbridge explained that the movement of the ship would cause the wooden planks to rub the skin off shoulders, elbows and hips, 'so as to render the bones in those parts quite bare'.[27] The result was that they not only suffered from excessive heat and the rapid spread of fevers, but that 'the deck, that is the floor of their rooms, was so covered with the blood and mucus which had proceeded from them in consequence of the flux, that it resembled a slaughter-house. It is not in the power of the human imagination, to picture a situation to itself more dreadful or disgusting.'[28]

At this stage only the Portuguese had made any effort to regulate the conditions in which slaves could be carried. Amidst the terrible overcrowding and putrid stenches of the slave ships, an average of around one in ten of all the slaves carried on the 'middle passage' across the Atlantic during the eighteenth century died before reaching the Americas, but on ships which were hit by bad weather or severe fevers the death toll was far higher. The journey across the ocean normally took at least five weeks, but it could take many months, with disastrous consequences: the captain of one French ship which lost 496 of its 594 slaves in 1717 blamed his appalling rate of loss on the 'length of the voyage' as well as 'the badness of the weather'.[29] It is not surprising that many of those confined in these circumstances lost the will to live: 'Some throw themselves into the sea, others hit their heads against the ship, others hold their breath to try and smother themselves, others still try to die of hunger from not eating . . .'[30] Consequently, force-feeding was added to the list of brutal treatments. Falconbridge reported that 'upon the negroes refusing to take sustenance, I have seen coals of fire, glowing hot put on a shovel and placed near to their lips, as to scorch and burn them. And this has been accompanied with threats of forcing them to swallow the coals, if they any longer persisted in refusing to eat.'[31] While there were certainly slaving captains who tried to be humane, others behaved brutally and lost their temper with the slaves in their charge, as in this eyewitness account of a ship's captain trying to force a child of less than a year old to eat:

> the last time he took the child up and flogged it, and let it drop out of his hands, 'Damn you (says he) I will make you eat, or I will be death of you;' and in three quarters of an hour after that the child died. He would not suffer any of the people that were on the quarterdeck to heave the child overboard, but he called the mother of the child to heave it overboard. She was not willing to do so, and I think he flogged her; but I am sure that he beat her in some way for refusing to throw the child overboard; at last he made her take the child up, and she took it in her hand and went to the ship's side, holding her head on one side, because she would not see the child go out of her hand and she dropped the child overboard. She seemed to be very sorry, and cried for several hours.[32]

There were many instances of the slaves fighting back and rising against their captors if the opportunity arose, particularly if they were still within sight of Africa. On rare occasions such mutinies were successful, and led to the murder of the entire crew; more usually they were brutally put down and the ringleaders treated with pitiless harshness. Newton recalled seeing rebellious slaves 'sentenced to unmerciful whippings, continued till the poor creatures have not had power to groan under their misery', and others 'agonising for hours, I believe for days together, under the torture of the thumbscrews'.[33]

Those who survived the grotesque horrors of the middle passage were by no means at the end of their torment. They still had to experience the process of being sold in the markets of Jamaica, Barbados or Rio de Janeiro. A visitor to Rio described how 'There are Shops full of these Wretches, who are exposed there stark naked, and bought like Cattle.'[34] Others were sold by 'scramble', with several hundred of them placed in a yard together and available at an equal price to whoever could get to them first when the gates were opened. Falconbridge noted: 'It is scarcely possible to describe the confusion of which this mode of selling is productive,'[35] and Equiano, who was himself sold by this method in Barbados, recalled that 'the noise and clamour with which this is attended, and the eagerness visible in the countenances of the buyers serve not a little to increase the apprehensions of the terrified Africans . . . In this manner, without scruple, are relations and friends separated, most of them never to see one another again.'[36]

This was the Atlantic slave trade: brutal, mercenary and inhumane from its beginning to its end. Yet in British politics the assumption had always been that its abolition was inconceivable. Even Edmund Burke, as he thundered out his denunciations of colonial misrule in India and called for the radical reform of the British state, concluded in 1780 that a rough plan for the immediate mitigation and ultimate suppression of the trade could not succeed, as the West Indian lobby would prove too powerful in Parliament. Three years earlier, another MP, Thomas Temple Luttrell, had given voice to the received wisdom of the times when he said, 'Some gentleman may . . . object to the slave trade as inhuman and impious; let us consider that, if our colonies are to be maintained and cultivated, which can only be done by African

Negroes, it is surely better to supply ourselves . . . in British bottoms.'[37]
This, until the mid-1780s, was the general and settled presumption.
But no MP of that time could fully perceive the power of the new ideas
that were beginning to take hold in many minds, or that those ideas
would shortly become the inspiration of some remarkable and brilliant
individuals.

Even while the slaves were being forced into ships on the African coast
in record numbers in the second half of the eighteenth century, a major
shift was taking place in moral and political philosophy which would
open the door to the slave trade being questioned and attacked. For
the eighteenth century saw the arrival of what has subsequently been
termed the 'Age of Enlightenment': a rapid growth in human knowledge and capabilities, accompanied by new beliefs concerning the
relationship of individuals to the state and to each other, coming
together to create a sense of progress and modernity which in turn
allowed traditional views and hierarchies to be challenged. The scien-
tific and mathematical revolution precipitated by Sir Isaac Newton
earlier in the century gave huge momentum to the development of
new thinking based on rational deductions and 'natural law'. Soon,
political philosophers would be arguing for a rational new basis to the
understanding of ethics, aesthetics and knowledge, setting out the
concept of a free individual, denouncing the alleged superstition and
tyranny of medieval times, and paving the way for modern notions of
liberalism, freedom and democracy. This gathering change in philosophical outlook came alongside a quickening pace of economic and
social change: the dawn of the Industrial Revolution saw the arrival of
new manufacturing techniques, such as the 'spinning jenny', which
revolutionised the production of cotton goods in Britain from the 1760s
onwards, and allowed newly prosperous merchants and industrialists to
compete with the aristocracy for political power; a rapid growth in
population in urban settings, comprising people who were less willing than their rural predecessors to accept old notions of class and
authority; a huge expansion in the availability of newspapers and

pamphlets, which allowed political ideas to be communicated to a vastly greater number of people than ever before; and a maturing of imperial possessions and conquests which brought greater debate about the appropriate treatment of native peoples who had become colonial subjects.

It was changes such as these that would release intellectual movements which would underpin some of the epoch-changing events of the late eighteenth century, including the French and American Revolutions and the independence movement in Latin America; but an important offshoot of Enlightenment thinking was the belief that in a rational world, institutionalised slavery could not be defended. In his celebrated *L'Esprit des lois*, published in 1748, Montesquieu brilliantly summed up what would become the Enlightenment case against slavery:

> Slavery in its proper sense is the establishment of a right which makes one man so much the owner of another man that he is the absolute master of his life and of his goods. It is not good by its nature; it is useful neither to the master nor to the slave: not to the slave, because he can do nothing from virtue; not to the master, because he contracts all sorts of bad habits from his slaves, because he imperceptibly grows accustomed to failing in all the moral virtues, because he grows proud, curt, harsh, angry, voluptuous, and cruel.[38]

It was not long before other French thinkers, whose work would be fundamental to the upheavals of the subsequent Revolution, would go further, with Rousseau arguing in 1762 in *Le Contrat social* that men were born with the right to be free and equal, and that 'The words *slave* and *right* contradict each other, and are mutually exclusive.'[39] It was not only the view of radical and revolutionary writers that slavery stood condemned. The Scottish philosopher Adam Ferguson argued in 1769 that 'No one is born a slave; because everyone is born with all his original rights ... no one can become a slave; because no one, from being a person, can ... become a thing or subject of property.'[40] He was following in the tradition of a previous professor of philosophy in Scotland, the Irishman Francis Hutcheson (1694–1746), who had argued in *A System of Moral Philosophy* that 'All men ... have strong desires of liberty and property,' and that 'No damage done or crime committed can change a rational creature into a piece of goods void of all right.'[41] Yet another Glaswegian professor who would subsequently add massively to the intellectual case against slavery was Adam Smith, whose words carried all the more significance because they were part of his general justification for capitalism and market economics. He argued that slavery was inefficient economically because it was an artificial constraint on individuals acting in their own self-interest, and was thus an obstruction to maximum economic efficiency. In *The Wealth of Nations* (1776) he argued that

> the experience of all ages and nations, I believe, demonstrates that the work done by slaves, though it appears to cost only their maintenance, is in the end the dearest of any. A person who can acquire no property, can have no other interest but to eat as much, and to labour as little as possible. Whatever work he does beyond what is sufficient to purchase his own maintenance can be squeezed out of him by violence only and not be any interest of his own.[42]

Other hugely influential British writers followed in Smith's wake, with William Paley mocking slavery in *Moral Philosophy* (1785), which was widely circulated as a textbook:

> But necessity is pretended; the name under which every enormity is attempted to be justified. And after all, what is the necessity? It has never been proved that the land could not be cultivated there, as it is here, by hired servants. It is said, that it could not be cultivated with quite the same conveniency and cheapness, as by the labour of slaves; by which means, a pound of sugar, which the planter now sells for sixpence could not be afforded under sixpence halfpenny; – and this is the necessity![43]

The views of such figures as Smith and Paley are of huge significance since they meant, in more modern terms, that the intellectual attack on slavery came from the right as well as the left; it was not necessary to believe in an entirely new social order or in inalienable rights of man in order to accept that slavery could not be economically justified or pragmatically accepted. For young, conservative-minded British politicians such as Pitt and Wilberforce, the works of Adam Smith and William Paley were high on their list of reading materials.

The changing intellectual climate of the late eighteenth century helped to awaken a Christian concern about slavery which had occasionally surfaced in earlier centuries, to little effect. Vatican rulings against the keeping of slaves in the seventeenth century had been understood to refer to natives of the Americas rather than to African Negroes, and the call for 'an end to slavery' by Pope Clement XI early in the eighteenth century was greeted with total indifference in Lisbon and Madrid. Yet while established Churches, whether in Rome or Canterbury, were too politically constrained and philosophically complacent to mount a serious challenge to such a widely accepted institution as slavery, the subject was a natural one for Christians of a more reforming or Evangelical disposition. As early as 1671 George Fox, the founder of the Quakers, had called on slave-owners not to use cruelty towards Negroes, and 'that after certain years of servitude they should set them free'.[44] By the late eighteenth century, as the scale and growth of slavery became more widely acknowledged and the moral climate of the times moved against it, it became a natural target for Evangelicals and Methodists. Moreover, their beliefs in applying Christian principles to the whole of life, in the importance of Providence and their accountability to God, gave many of them a sense of unavoidable responsibility to combat slavery, rather than a choice of whether or not to do so. By 1774 John Wesley was railing against the slave trade and all who took part in it, threatening slave traders with a worse fate than Sodom and Gomorrah and reminding them that '*He shall have Judgment without mercy that hath showed no mercy.*' He told plantation-owners that '*Men-buyers* are exactly on a level with *Men-stealers,*' and merchants that their money was being used 'to steal, rob, murder men, women and children without number'; 'Liberty is the right of every human creature, as soon as he breathes the vital air. And no human law can deprive him of that right, which he derives from the law of nature.'[45]

It was on the basis of such thinking that in due course British Evangelicals would eventually become an indispensable component of the campaign against the slave trade.

It was, however, the Quakers who would lead the way in setting out the Christian case against slavery and the slave trade, bringing to bear an influence far beyond their numbers, partly because they included highly active and respected individuals, and partly because they constituted a genuinely transatlantic community. The Quakers included many influential traders and merchants, and when the annual meeting of the Society of Friends in Philadelphia in 1754 came to the conclusion that 'to live in ease and plenty by the toil of those who violence and cruelty have put in our power' was incompatible with Christianity, it was a decision of more than token significance.[46] The decisions of the Philadelphia Society of Friends led within a short time to their London counterparts coming to the same conclusion. Similarly, when the Quaker Anthony Benezet's anti-slave-trade tract *Observations on the Enslaving, Importing, and Purchasing of Negroes* was published in America in the 1760s the London Quakers responded by ordering 1,500 copies and distributing them to every member of both Houses of Parliament. Benezet's powerful arguments against slavery not only rested on Christian principles but were wholly in tune with Enlightenment ideas: 'Nothing,' he wrote in 1767, 'can more clearly and positively militate against the slavery of the Negroes than the several declarations lately published that "all men are created equal, that they are endowed by their creator with certain unalienable rights." '[47]

The arguments of the Quakers were one of several powerful forces at work in North America in the 1760s and 1770s which would contribute to opening up the debate over the slave trade in Britain. A second factor was the growing fear in some of the North American colonies that the continued importation of large numbers of slaves would create an uncontrollable population prone to revolution in the future. In the words of Benjamin Franklin, 'Slaves rather weaken than strengthen the State, and there is therefore some difference between them and sheep; sheep will never make insurrections.'[48] This concern led some states, such as New Jersey in 1769, to impose a prohibitive level of duty on the import of slaves. Once the American Revolution was underway, the second Continental Congress passed a resolution opposing slave imports in 1776, and many of the northern states went on to act against slavery itself – Pennsylvania, for instance, passed a law in 1780 ensuring that all future born slaves would become free at the age of twenty-eight. Within a year of the end of the American War of Independence, all of the New England states had made legal provision for the abolition of slavery on their territory.

The British reaction to the American Revolution was a third factor which may have helped to inculcate the idea that the institution of slavery was no longer immutable. While Samuel Johnson taunted the Americans with the question, 'How is it that we hear the loudest *yelps* for liberty among the drivers of Negroes?',[49] British generals seeking every possible weapon to use against the colonists made extensive promises of freedom to slaves held in North America. In 1775 the Governor of Virginia, the Earl of Dunmore, offered freedom to all slaves who would bear arms against the rebellion: the subsequent years of war saw tens of thousands of slaves desert their owners, and some of them did indeed serve alongside the British Army. Sometimes the population of entire plantations managed to run away, with some states losing over half their slaves. At the end of the war, these desertions would leave the defeated British with the problem of what to do with large numbers of former slaves who had come under their protection, many of them congregated in still-loyal New York, with the eventual result that thousands of them would be unsatisfactorily resettled in Nova Scotia.

One of the effects of the American Revolution was, therefore, to create a significant free black population in the nascent United States, but it also left behind it a sharp political disagreement over the future of slavery and the slave trade, which would divide the United States and influence debate in the rest of the English-speaking world. While northern states responded to American Independence by emancipating slaves, southern states, which were much more heavily economically dependent on slave labour, responded to the end of the war with a surge of slave imports to make up for the large numbers of deserters. Within a remarkably short time the future battle lines of the American

Civil War of eighty years later were drawn, facilitated by the historic compromise at the constitutional convention which declared that: 'The importation of such persons as any of the States now existing shall think proper to admit, shall not be prohibited prior to the year eighteen hundred and eight.'[50] The future President James Madison would defend the compromise as 'a great point gained in favour of humanity, that a period of twenty years may terminate forever within these States a traffic which is so long and so loudly upbraided as the barbarism of modern policy',[51] but the result was that the period from 1787 to 1807 saw more slaves sold into the United States than any other two decades in history. By the end of the century, opinion in the southern states had turned firmly against the anti-slavery assumptions of the Founding Fathers, and abolitionist sentiment was once again largely confined to the ranks of the valiant Quakers.

In the meantime, Quaker campaigners such as Anthony Benezet had been discovering useful allies across the Atlantic. In his work specifically directed at a British audience *A Caution and Warning to Great Britain and her Colonies* (1766), Benezet asked British Christians:

> Do we indeed believe the truths declared in the Gospel? Are we persuaded that the threatenings, as well as the promises therein contained, will have their accomplishment? If indeed we do, must we not tremble to think what a load of guilt lies upon our Nation generally, and individually so far as we in any degree abet or countenance this aggravated inequity?[52]

1773 saw Benezet bring his arguments to London, followed soon afterwards by his pupil William Dillwyn, whose declared purpose was to help the English Quakers organise a campaign for the abolition of the slave trade. There they were introduced to another figure who shared their steadfast persistence and beliefs, and who would come to occupy a central role in the forthcoming campaign against the trade: Granville Sharp.

The grandson of an Archbishop of York, Sharp had become involved in the issue of slavery in 1765, when he had befriended a slave in London and tried to rescue him from being re-sold and returned to the West Indies. His views were reinforced by his contact with Benezet, and were similarly based on strong religious convictions. He was the first in a series of extraordinarily determined and talented individuals in Britain who were to give their time and energy to the anti-slavery cause over the following decades. He was said to have 'a settled conviction of the wickedness of our race . . . tempered by an infantile credulity in the virtue in each separate member of it',[53] but his chief quality was indefatigable perseverance in any cause he adopted. Told when he was working as an apprentice to a linen draper that his ignorance of Greek made it impossible for him to understand a theological argument, he went on to gain such a mastery of Greek that he was able to correct previously unnoticed errors in the translation of the New Testament. When a tradesman whom he knew found that his claim to be the rightful heir to a peerage was scornfully dismissed, Sharp pursued the matter until his friend was duly seated in the House of Lords. For seven years from 1765 he applied this quality of determination to trying to prevent plantation-owners from forcibly removing their slaves from England. This work culminated in 1772 with the case of James Somerset, an escaped slave who had been recaptured and was being held on board a ship in London preparing to sail for Jamaica. Since there was no dispute that a Virginia slave-owner held legal title to Somerset, Sharp now had the test case he had been looking for, which could show that slave-ownership was incompatible with the laws of England, irrespective of any legal claim valid elsewhere.

It was a legal point which the Lord Chief Justice, Lord Mansfield, had struggled for years to avoid. Now, despite a series of adjournments and efforts to settle the matter out of court, Sharp pursued the case until Mansfield was forced to give a definitive judgement. That judgement was that a slave-owner had no right to compel a slave to leave England for a foreign country. Slavery, Mansfield found, was not provided for in English law, and was something 'so odious that nothing can be suffered to support it but positive law'. Such a ruling was, partly inadvertently, a death blow to slavery within the British Isles themselves, where it is thought some thousands of slaves were being held or maintained at the time. Sharp would be disappointed if he thought the ruling would have legal ramifications in British colonies, but he had chalked up an important victory which had the practical effect of ending slavery on British soil. Working with Benezet, he continued his opposition to slavery. In *The Just Limitation of Slavery in the Laws of God* (1776) he presented his argument in biblical terms, arguing that the Israelites were 'reminded of their *Bondage in Egypt*: for so the almighty *Deliverer* from *Slavery* warned his people to limit and moderate the *bondage* . . . by the remembrance of *their own former bondage* in a foreign land, and by a remembrance also of his great mercy in *delivering them* from that *bondage*'.[54]

As he did so, the circle of committed Christians who agreed with him and were prepared to act was quietly growing.

It is an irony of history that David Hartley, one of the very few MPs to attack the slave trade in the House of Commons in the course of the 1770s, was the very man unseated by William Wilberforce when he stormed to victory at Hull in 1780. In defeating him, Wilberforce later recalled that 'I expressed my hope to him that the time would come when I should be able to do something on behalf of slaves.'[55] In the same year he apparently asked a friend travelling to Antigua to collect information for him, and again expressed 'my hope, that some time or other I should redress the wrongs of those wretched and degraded beings'.[56]* While there is no reason to doubt that his interest was genuine, the slave trade did not become a topic of parliamentary debate in the early 1780s, and Wilberforce did not attempt to raise it. Yet as Wilberforce turned to devouring books in the summer of 1786, he would have found among many of his chosen authors – Montesquieu, Adam Smith, William Paley – a universal condemnation of slavery. And in the preceding two or three years he would certainly have read a number of new publications which stated the case against the slave trade more effectively and authoritatively than ever before.

---

* There is no record of Wilberforce having written to a York newspaper at the age of fourteen in opposition to the slave trade, as asserted by his sons in their biography of him.

One such publication was likely to have been the record of the court proceedings in 1783 concerning the slave ship *Zong*, circulated by Granville Sharp. The *Zong*, owned by Liverpool merchants, had sailed from São Tomé in the Gulf of Guinea in 1781 with more than four hundred slaves on board. Poor navigation by the captain, Luke Collingwood, led to them overshooting their destination and water on board becoming scarce, with many of the slaves dying or falling ill. Calculating that if the slaves died on board the loss would be borne by the owners, but that should there be a sufficiently sound pretext of the crew being in danger, 'If the drowned were to be paid for by the insurers, they still constituted a part of the value of the cargo, and the master retained his whole profits,'[57] Collingwood decided to throw 133 slaves overboard. They were thrown over the side in three groups. The third group of twenty-six, realising what was happening to them, fought back and were consequently thrown into the sea with their arms still in shackles. Only one of the 133 survived, climbing back on board when no one was looking and stowing himself away.

The efforts of the owners to sue the underwriters were a failure, since the shortage of water was not satisfactorily proved, but Lord Mansfield made clear at the time that in legal terms 'the case of slaves was the same as if horses had been thrown overboard'.[58] Equally, the efforts of Granville Sharp to launch a prosecution against the owners met with no success: there was no law against a master drowning slaves if he wished to do so. While Sharp suffered a legal defeat, the effect was a moral victory: the terrible story of the *Zong* became widely known in Britain, and fed a growing sense of outrage.

The same year that the case of the *Zong* came to court saw the creation of the London Quaker Abolition Committee, and the publication of a flurry of poems and pamphlets denouncing the slave trade. The following year, 1784, the Reverend James Ramsay published two powerful pamphlets – *An Essay on the Treatment and Conversion of African Slaves in the British Sugar Colonies* and *An Inquiry into the Effects of the Abolition of the Slave Trade*. The importance of Ramsay's work was that it was based on twenty-two years' actual experience of living in the West Indies, at a time when hard facts about slavery and the slave trade were difficult to establish and British people with first-hand knowledge were unwilling to speak out. Brought up in Aberdeen, Ramsay had been a surgeon during the Seven Years' War on the British warship *Arundel*, captained by Sir Charles Middleton. Ordered by Middleton to go aboard a slave ship recaptured from the French, Ramsay would never forget the desperate scenes he found there, with diseased and plague-ridden slaves dying in the hold. Going on to become a clergyman on the island of St Kitts, where he stayed until 1781, he developed a revulsion for the slave markets and the punishment meted out to slaves which made him into an enemy of the entire system. Unpopular with the whites of the West Indies as a result, but always held in high esteem by the Middletons, he was given the living of Teston in Kent by a wealthy friend of Lady Middleton, and settled down to live alongside his old friends in a more peaceful setting.

Ramsay's publications developed many of the arguments which would be used by the abolitionists in the years ahead, reasoning that slavery could be dispensed with gradually, and be replaced by the immigration of free people, with a beneficial effect on the businesses and profits of the plantations. In particular, he called for an immediate end to the slave trade, since this would force slave-owners to treat their existing slaves better, and to refrain from the brutalities he had witnessed on St Kitts. Africa too would benefit from the end of the slave trade, perhaps able to develop sugar plantations itself, and 'The improvement of Africa is a compensation which we owe for the horrid barbarities we have been instrumental in procuring to be exercised on her sons.'[59]

Ramsay performed two great services for the abolitionist cause, providing information and ammunition to be used against the slave trade, and also attracting the attention of like-minded people so that a nucleus of future campaigners could be formed. In 1786 he and the Middletons were visited at Teston by a young would-be clergyman from Cambridge whose importance to the future campaign against the slave trade would rival that of Wilberforce himself: Thomas Clarkson. Like Wilberforce, Clarkson was a graduate of St John's College. Entering a competition in Latin Essays in 1785, he was set the subject 'Is it right to make slaves of others against their will?' Little could the Vice Chancellor, Dr Peckard, who chose this subject, have guessed at the dramatic results his choice would produce. Clarkson worked furiously at his project, particularly consulting the work of Anthony Benezet, and produced an essay which won first prize and also left him with a deep hostility to slavery: 'but if Kings then, to whom their own people have granted dominion and power, are unable to invade the liberties of their harmless subjects, without the highest injustice; how can those private persons be justified, who treacherously lie in wait for their fellow creatures, and sell them into slavery? What arguments can they possibly bring in their defence?'[60]

The essay was translated into English and published the following year by Ramsay's Quaker publisher. Clarkson would later write a celebrated account of how he came to the conclusion, while riding from Cambridge to London, that he should set aside everything else in life to take up the cause of the slaves:

> I stopped my horse occasionally, and dismounted and walked. I frequently tried to persuade myself in these intervals that the contents of my Essay could not be true ... Coming in sight of Wades Mill in Hertfordshire, I sat down disconsolate on the turf by the roadside and held my horse. Here a thought came into my mind, that if the contents of the Essay were true, it was time some person should see these calamities to their end.[61]

With Clarkson staying at Teston for a month in the summer of 1786, and deciding after discussion with Ramsay and the Middletons to give up his ecclesiastical ambitions in favour of fighting against the slave trade, the 'Testonites' were becoming a small but purposeful group. When Lady Middleton tried to persuade Sir Charles to champion their cause in Parliament, he had sufficient self-knowledge to know that his skills were in administration rather than campaigning, and recommended looking for an alternative Member. Few MPs were suited to such a task. Whichever one of them was to lead this campaign needed to be an eloquent and experienced parliamentary performer, to have strong convictions consistent with denouncing the slave trade and slavery, to be sufficiently free of ministerial ambition and party affiliations as to be able to win support from all parts of the Commons, and yet be sufficiently well connected in ministerial circles to have a chance of influencing the government. It must have been clear very quickly, as the Middletons discussed whom to approach, that William Wilberforce was uniquely fitted for the role. His credentials as an Independent, his closeness to Pitt, his recent adoption of evangelism and his outstanding qualities as an orator meant that he must be their man.

As Wilberforce sought to educate himself about slavery in late 1786, the Testonites – now including Bishop Porteus and a leading member of the Moravian sect,* Ignatius La Trobe – gently increased the pressure on him to accept the challenge. His initial response to the letter he received in Hull from Middleton assured them 'that he felt the great importance of the subject, and thought himself unequal to the task allotted to him, but yet would not positively decline it'.[62] He read a copy of the African Code drafted by Burke some years before and deposited in 10 Downing Street, and read, then or earlier, Ramsay's writings of two years before, which, according to Porteus 'particularly made a strong impression on Mr Wilberforce, who told me (if I recollect right) that it gave him the first idea, or at least confirmed him in the resolution of bringing the question of the slave trade before Parliament'.[63] Decades later Wilberforce would write that 'It was the condition of the West Indian slaves which first drew my attention, and it was in the course of my enquiry that I was led to Africa and the abolition.'[64] He discussed the matter thoroughly with the Middletons, Ramsay and La Trobe, and was probably also influenced by John Newton, of whom he saw a lot around this time.

Early in 1787, Thomas Clarkson called at 4 Old Palace Yard with a copy of his essay on slavery. It was the first meeting between the two men, who would spend most of the rest of their lives pursuing the

---

* The Moravians were a Protestant sect who had rebelled against the Roman Catholic Church a century before Martin Luther. During a major revival in the eighteenth century they were influential in the conversion of John Wesley.

William Wilberforce aged eleven,
painted in his aunt's house in
Wimbledon. A bright and
engaging boy, he was soon taken
back to Yorkshire to remove him
from Methodist influence.

The house in the High Street,
Hull, where Wilberforce was
born. At the back of the house
were the staiths where the
imports of the booming
Baltic trade were unloaded.

Lauriston House, Wimbledon,
the place which helped to
give Wilberforce a taste for
rural sights and sounds. By
the early 1780s a coterie of
young MPs were to be found
relaxing in its gardens.

Isaac Milner, whose conversations with Wilberforce while journeying across France were crucial to the latter's Evangelical conversion. Cambridge University 'perhaps never produced a man of more eminent abilities'.

John Newton, the reformed slave trader and author of 'Amazing Grace'. He told Wilberforce, 'You are the Lord's servant, and are in the post He has assigned you.'

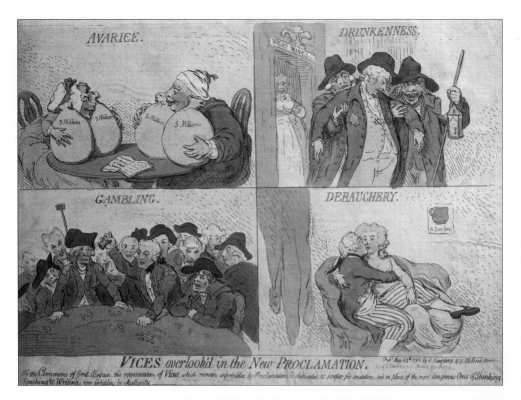

Vices overlooked in the New Proclamation, by James Gillray, 1792. Wilberforce's campaign for moral reform is mocked by scenes showing the royal family enjoying every species of vice.

Making decent!! Wilberforce is shown trying to hide the figleaf on the great statue of Achilles in Hyde Park, caricaturing his disapproval of public lewdness.

Olaudah Equiano.
His heart-rending account of being kidnapped and sold into slavery became a best-selling book which fuelled the abolitionist campaign.

TO BE SOLD on board the Ship *Bance-Island*, on tuesday the 6th of *May* next, at *Aſhley-Ferry*; a choice cargo of about 250 fine healthy

NEGROES,

juſt arrived from the Windward & Rice Coaſt. —The utmoſt care has already been taken, and ſhall be continued, to keep them free from the leaſt danger of being infected with the SMALL-POX, no boat having been on board, and all other communication with people from *Charles-Town* prevented.

Auſtin, Laurens, & Appleby.

N. B. Full one Half of the above Negroes have had the SMALL-POX in their own Country..

A notice of a slave sale in South Carolina, 1766. The purchasing of black slaves was a routine event throughout much of the Americas.

The slave trade. After journeys of hundreds of miles on foot, slaves were taken in small boats to the trading ships waiting offshore.

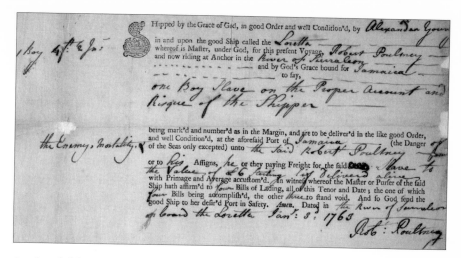

A printed shipping bill for a slave boy 'to be deliver'd in the like good Order, and well Condition'd' at the port of Jamaica.

While defenders of the slave trade testified that slaves were so happy that they danced onboard ships, Wilberforce revealed the truth to the Commons: that they did so under the threat of the lash.

Slavers Throwing Overboard the Dead and Dying – Typhoon Coming On (The Slave Ship) by J.M.W. Turner, 1840. The terrible story of the slave ship the *Zong*, from which slaves were thrown overboard so that insurance could be claimed, became a classic instance of the horrors of the trade.

The 'Wilberforce Oak' at Holwood, Kent. Sitting beneath it on a spring day in 1787 with William Pitt and William Grenville, Wilberforce resolved to destroy the slave trade. The stone bench was erected by Earl Stanhope in 1862.

Old Palace Yard. Next to Westminster Abbey and opposite the entrance to the House of Commons, Wilberforce's house was usually thronged with MPs, abolitionist campaigners and Yorkshire constituents.

Wilberforce's daily assessments of how he had spent his time were mercilessly accurate and self-critical. 'Serious reading and meditation' could reach eleven hours on a Sunday, but on other days up to four hours were considered 'squandered'.

William Wilberforce, aged twenty-nine, by John Rising. 'God has set before me two great objects: the Reformation of Manners and the Abolition of the Slave Trade.'

issues they now discussed. Clarkson remembered that, 'On my first interview with him, he stated frankly, that the subject had often employed his thoughts, and that it was near his heart. He seemed earnest about it, and also very desirous of taking the trouble of inquiring further into it.'[65] Clarkson thereafter became a regular visitor, although on the first occasion on which he intended to ask Wilberforce squarely to lead the parliamentary campaign, his courage temporarily deserted him. Instead he arranged a dinner on 13 March 1787 at the house of Bennet Langton, a wealthy landowner, at which the other guests included Charles Middleton, Isaac Hawkins Brown MP, Sir Joshua Reynolds, James Boswell and William Windham MP. The subject of Africa was delicately brought up, and, after a discussion Wilberforce was asked to spearhead the campaign. His reply was highly significant: 'He had no objection to bring forward the measure in Parliament, when he was better prepared for it, and provided no person more proper could be found.'[66] In the early months of 1787, and in parallel with preparing his campaign to reform the nation's behaviour, Wilberforce had indeed become convinced with all his heart that he should take up the cause of abolishing the slave trade. In October of that year he would write, 'God Almighty has sent before me two great objects, the suppression of the slave trade and the reformation of manners.'[67] Armed with the evidence of Ramsay, the arguments of Clarkson and Sharp, and the urging of the Middletons and their friends, he decided that the destruction of the slave trade would become one of the central purposes of his life. The reports he had heard of the high death rate among slaves during the Atlantic crossing clinched the issue in his mind. It was something that 'speaks for itself . . . As soon as I had arrived thus far in my investigation of the slave trade, I confess to you, so enormous, so dreadful, so irremediable did its wickedness appear that my own mind was completely made up for the abolition . . . Let the consequences be what they would, I from this time determined that I would never rest until I had effected its Abolition.'[68]

7

Early Optimism

———❖ΙΟΙ❖———

The cause of our poor Africans goes on most prosperously.

WILBERFORCE TO WYVILL, 25 January 1788[1]

Let free-born hands attend the sultry toil,
And fairer harvests shall adorn the soil;
The teeming earth shall mightier stores disclose.
And Trade and Virtue be no longer foes.

Letter in favour of the abolition of the slave trade
from the Isle of Wight, March 1788[2]

WHEN WILLIAM WILBERFORCE DECIDED IN 1787 to take up the cause of the slaves he was already embarking on a parallel effort to reform the nation's manners which he thought 'worthy of the labours of a whole life'.[3] He could not have known that in committing himself to fight for the abolition of the slave trade he was taking on a task which would consume most of the remaining active years of his life, and become one of the most protracted and demanding political and parliamentary struggles in the whole of British history.

It must have been obvious to even the most optimistic observer that a campaign to abolish the slave trade would be the work of several years at the very least, certainly not of months, and that it would require the defeat of powerful interests and a successful outcome to the most extensive inquiries. Yet it is possible that Wilberforce underestimated the enormous scale of the task he was about to take on. His early assurance 'that there is no doubt of our success'[4] may partly have been a show of confidence that was necessary to encourage others, but there was also about him an initial optimism that bordered on naïvety – in the words of one historian, he seemed 'strangely unaware of the real power of the interests he opposed'.[5] It was as well that he did not foresee the length and intensity of the contest he was about to take on – knowledge of it would have daunted the most determined of men. As it was, a powerful combination of forces now pushed him towards the most important commitment he had yet made in his life: the persuasiveness and strong opinions of his friends, his urgent desire to pursue Christian principles through political action, his natural horror at what he had so far discovered about the trade, his need to account to God for the use of each day and hour, and his belief that Providence had given him the power and opportunity to act, all came together to give him an unambiguous resolve.

As Wilberforce's reaction at Bennet Langton's dinner table had shown, his mind had been moving for some time towards an acceptance of the parliamentary leadership of the future campaign. Two months later, in May 1787, he made his final decision. He was a regular visitor to Holwood in Kent, where Pitt had bought a modest country home with woods and gardens which provided him with a respite from the smell and noise of London. It was where Pitt loved to retire with his closest friends, cutting and planting in the gardens while assessing the political world and framing a fresh bout of reforms. Here, on a spring day, Wilberforce sat beneath an oak tree with Pitt and William Grenville, another rising star who was Pitt's cousin and future Foreign Secretary. 'I distinctly remember,' he recalled in old age, 'the very knoll upon which I was sitting near Pitt and Grenville.'[6]* In Pitt's mind, Wilberforce's interest in slave-trade abolition would have appeared as both a personal and a political opportunity: Wilberforce would make a less troubled friend, and a less troubling colleague, if occupied by a campaign which was in any case worthwhile. His advice was clear: 'Wilberforce, why don't you give notice of a motion on the subject of

---

* Only a remnant of the tree exists today. The spot is commemorated by a stone bench erected in 1862 by Earl Stanhope.

the slave trade? You have already taken great pains to collect evidence, and are therefore fully entitled to the credit which doing so will ensure you. Do not lose time, or the ground may be occupied by another.'[7]

Prime ministerial support tipped Wilberforce over the edge. 'Pitt recommended me to undertake its conduct, as a subject suited to my character and talents. At length, I well remember, after a conversation in the open air at the root of an old tree at Holwood just above the steep descent into the Vale of Keston, I resolved to give notice on a fit occasion in the House of Commons of my intention to bring the subject forward.'[8] From that moment, William Wilberforce adopted his cause, busied himself in its prosecution, and set out on a struggle which would be the main preoccupation of his life for decades to come.

In later centuries, such a meeting, constituting an agreement between a powerful Prime Minister with a large parliamentary majority and two other influential young politicians to outlaw a particular trade as soon as possible, would have been regarded as the death knell of the trade in question. Pitt had triumphed in the election of 1784, his position was secure and his reputation high. Why did the backing of a Prime Minister nearing the peak of his powers not guarantee rapid success for the campaigners against the slave trade?

The answer is that political parties were not remotely as well developed in the late eighteenth century as they were to become only a few decades later. The ability of a late-nineteenth- or twentieth-century Prime Minister to bludgeon most or all of his party into voting for the measures that he wanted, by virtue of control over the party's membership and most of the key positions in the state, simply had not yet arisen. And if parties were discernible at election time at all, which indeed they had been in the pitched battle between the Pittites and the Foxites in 1784, they certainly did not produce an election manifesto or programme of legislation which each member of the party had an obligation to support. A Prime Minister would rely for his support on a mixture of groupings and individuals, some of whom would owe their positions and sinecures to the King rather than to him, and others of whom would give their prime loyalty to a factional leader, a borough-monger, or simply their own opinions. The fact that they could be relied on to support the government's existence in office could in no way be taken to mean that they would support any particular piece of legislation which the Prime Minister happened to favour. Furthermore, if his usual supporters refused to back his legislation, there was almost nothing the Prime Minister could do about it, as Pitt had already discovered to his cost when he had seen his Irish Propositions emasculated and his reform proposals defeated in earlier years.

To win a majority in Parliament for slave-trade abolition it would be necessary to secure the votes of country gentlemen whose attendance was erratic, friends of the King who took their cue from Windsor rather than Downing Street, and members of the House of Lords whose first instinct was to be suspicious of change. Wilberforce himself was at pains to explain this point in his autobiographical notes:

> Mr Pitt's enemies having called in question his sincerity as a friend of the abolition but certainly without any just ground tho' not without plausibility especially in the instance of those who are unacquainted with the actual practice of Parliament . . . the Minister is not considered as being entitled to require the votes of the inferior members of government except on political questions or those in which the credit or stability of the government be fairly supposed to be in some measure at stake (implicated) for instance when Mr Pitt brought forward his measure for improving the Poor Laws, many of his warmest political adherents opposed this measure without its being supposed by any one that they were less attached to him than before – in short what shall and what shall not be a government question is not an arbitrary arrangement nor is it dependent on the Minister's will, it turns in fact on the answer to the question, is the credit or stability of an administration at stake – in the instance therefore of my motion for abolishing the slave trade every one was perfectly at liberty to vote as he should see fit – it was in no sense a party question.[9]

An added obstacle was that the Enlightenment values which motivated the trio of twenty-seven-year-olds who had sat beneath the oak tree at

Holwood were by no means the governing influences in the minds of older members of the political establishment, whether in the cabinet or the royal family itself. King George III was noted for rigid adherence to whatever upheld the constitution and the Empire, while one of his sons, the Duke of Clarence, was moved by his time in the navy to become an ardent defender of the slave trade. In the cabinet itself, the Home Secretary, Lord Sydney, was no friend of abolition, while the Lord Chancellor, Lord Thurlow, saw it as his business to puncture and obstruct almost all of Pitt's progressive ideas. More ominously, Pitt's most able lieutenant in the government ranks who sat in the Commons itself, Henry Dundas, was an enthusiastic proponent of the rights and importance of the colonies – no small consideration, given the vice-like grip he was developing on virtually the entire parliamentary represen-tation of Scotland. The hostility to abolition of such powerful establish-ment figures would be a huge barrier for Wilberforce to overcome, and one that he underestimated at his peril.

Later analysis would show that only a small number of MPs became partisan supporters of either the pro- or anti-abolition forces, and that the vast majority of them formed an impressionable and persuadable group in the middle. This meant there was a second considerable hurdle in the path of Wilberforce and his fellow abolitionists: the emerging facts about the slave trade which might persuade such an impressionable majority were not widely known or discussed. The writings of Thomas Clarkson and the accounts of the abominable events aboard the *Zong* had been noticed, but were not at the forefront of public debate. Wilberforce himself was persuaded that the facts demonstrated the iniquity of the slave trade, but he had spent months in discussions to which his colleagues in Parliament had not been party. Despite the burgeoning of the newspaper industry, only a handful of items relating to the abolition of the slave trade appeared in leading newspapers in the whole of the thirty months prior to September 1787. Even for most parliamentarians, therefore, the trade remained as it always had been: something which did not intrude into daily thoughts or conversation.

A third major difficulty was that many of the facts that would be necessary to convince parliamentary sceptics of the merits of abolition had not yet been clearly established, and would certainly not go undisputed. Eighteenth-century debate took place without the plethora of independently audited statistics to which politicians of a later age are accustomed. As a result, vitally important issues – whether Liverpool and Bristol were dependent on the slave trade or could prosper without it; what amount of capital was committed to the trade and what profits were derived from it; whether the birth rate among slaves would be such that fresh imports might be rendered unnecessary; how slaves were treated and how many died on the voyage – could be argued from either perspective and without any agreed statistical basis.

Taken together, these factors meant that abolishing the slave trade was not simply a matter of drawing up a Bill and asking a reliable parliamentary majority to pass it. It would be necessary to establish facts which had never been nailed down, to inform people who had never been interested in the subject, and to persuade key individuals who were highly reluctant to act: three requirements which would make the abolitionist campaign exhausting in its length, painstaking in its detail and, for its time, unique in its scope. The ascertaining of the facts would require hundreds of hours of evidence to be given and scores of witnesses to be marshalled before a series of inquiries and committees. It would involve Thomas Clarkson in an extraordinary feat of travel as detective, confessor and campaigner. The efforts to inform would necessitate the formation of the first pressure group of the modern age, using every written, verbal and visual means to publicise their case to Parliament and the people. Finally, the need to persuade would call forth some of the most impassioned debates of parliamentary history; debates in which William Wilberforce would not be alone in scaling the highest peaks of parliamentary oratory.

On 22 May 1787, later in the same month that Wilberforce had sat beneath the oak tree with Pitt, a meeting was held in a London bookstore and printing shop 'for the purpose of taking the slave trade into consideration'.[10] Round the table were twelve men, including Thomas

Clarkson, Granville Sharp and the Pennsylvanian Quaker William Dillwyn, who formed the 'Committee of the Society for the purpose of effecting the abolition of the Slave Trade', and immediately 'Resolved that the said Trade was both impolitick and unjust'.[11] That they met in the printing shop of one of their number, James Phillips, was significant: two days later they met again to hear Clarkson's 'enumeration of facts relative to the Inhumanity and Impolicy of the Slave Trade', and resolved there and then that two thousand copies of his words be printed.[12]

Equally significant was the title they had chosen for themselves, for it showed that a group of men largely driven together by their hatred of slavery had decided that the destruction of slavery itself was beyond their immediate reach, but that the abolition of the trade ought to be within it. Their chairman, Granville Sharp, who had already spent twenty-two years working for the complete emancipation of slaves, wanted nothing less than that to be their objective. But in the minds of the others there was no real choice: the prospect of the rapid freeing of several million slaves would conjure up fears they could not possibly overcome, and would be seen as a fundamental attack on the 'property' rights of the plantation-owners which, along with an intrusion into the legislative rights of the colonies, would take the Westminster Parliament beyond the range of its established power.

Given the indisputable right of Parliament to regulate a trade carried on in British ships, it was the cutting-off of the supply which would be 'laying the axe at the very root',[13] as Clarkson put it, of the institution of slavery, and would in the meantime force the planters to treat their existing slaves with less cruelty. In Clarkson's words, 'It appeared soon to be the sense of the Committee, that to aim at the removal of both would be to aim at too much, that by doing this we might lose all.'[14] Decades later, Wilberforce would insist that the abolition of the trade was always seen by him and his fellow campaigners as a step towards the eventual destruction of slavery. The slaves, he said, would be 'GRADUALLY *transmuted* into a free Peasantry; but this, the ULTIMATE object, was to produce progressively by the operation of multiplied, chiefly moral causes; and to appear at last to have been the almost insensible result of the various improvements: not to have been an object all along in view, and gradually but slowly advanced upon'.[15]

Wilberforce was not at this stage a member of the abolitionist Committee, preferring to keep his independence, and not to alarm his parliamentary colleagues by being a signed-up member of an agitating extra-parliamentary campaign. It was a reflection of his instinct to persuade from the inside rather than threaten from the outside. Yet he was in close touch with the members of the Committee as they met weekly or fortnightly through the rest of 1787, steadily accumulating their funds and distributing their facts. In their first year of operation they raised £2,760.2*s*.7*d* (the equivalent of about £290,000 today), and spent over £1,000 of this on the distribution of more than eighty thousand pamphlets and books, ranging from 11,500 accounts of debates in Parliament to 3,580 copies of 'Newton's Thoughts' and one copy of *The History of Jamaica*.

They were not wasting their time. The winter of 1787–88 would later be judged by historians as a 'decisive moment of advance' in stirring the conscience of the wider public.[16] In the thirty-three months prior to October 1787, only fifteen items regarding the slave trade appeared in *The Times*, and only four of those related to abolition. But in the fifteen months beginning with October 1787, 140 items on the slave trade appeared, of which 136 related to the arguments over abolition.[17] The use of newspaper reports to whip up public support was a new tactic in eighteenth-century politics, made possible by the booming circulation of a rapidly expanding range of titles. The *Morning Herald*, the *Daily Universal Register* (which became *The Times*), the *Star and Evening Advertiser*, the *Sunday Chronicle* and the *Observer* were all founded between 1780 and 1791. The abolitionist Committee further exploited the developing habits of their time with their next tactic: the production of medallions which could be worn or displayed in order to indicate sympathy with their cause. This was an idea pioneered by John Wilkes in his successful election campaigns of the early 1760s. In July 1787 the Committee enlisted the help of no less a figure than the great pottery-maker Josiah Wedgwood, who, happily combining a commercial opportunity with a cause in which he believed, produced what was to become the celebrated seal of the Committee, showing a kneeling slave 'in chains in supplicating posture', beneath the motto: 'Am I not a man and a brother?'[18] Simply but brilliantly conceived, this image appealed to Christian compassion and Enlightenment ideas of equality while giving fashionable ladies and gentlemen the opportunity to demonstrate that they shared in these virtuous notions. It was not long before gentlemen were having Wedgwood's slave medallion 'inlaid in gold on the lid of their snuff boxes', and many ladies 'wore them in bracelets, and others had them fitted up in an ornamental manner of pins for their hair'.[19] The thousands of copies of Wedgwood's seal were the start of a small flood of medallions and tokens which would characterise the abolitionist campaign for the next two decades, culminating in commemorative medals when victory was finally secured.

The persuasive power of a visual impression did not stop at medallions, for the late eighteenth century saw an enormous expansion in the circulation of printed cartoons and images. When a schematic representation of a slave ship, the *Brookes*, originated in the Plymouth abolitionist committee in late 1788, the London Committee soon saw its potential and printed more than eight thousand copies in poster form. Showing how 482 slaves could be crammed into a small ship, the diagram appeared in books, magazines and newspapers, and made 'an instantaneous impression of horror upon all who saw it'.[20] While the diagram of the *Brookes* was deliberately exploited by the abolitionists, there began in 1788 a simultaneous surge in the expression of abolitionist sentiment through paintings, poems and caricatures. The celebrated artist George Morland exhibited his painting *Execrable Human Traffic* at the Royal Academy that year. Vicious caricatures were produced by the pioneering cartoonists of the time, including works by Gillray which showed the Duke of Clarence with a black mistress or which, several years later, attacked the slave trade directly in *Barbarities in the West Indias*, showing a black slave being tormented in a huge vat of sugar juice while black body parts are nailed to the wall.

The classic example of abolitionist poetry came from William Cowper, in 'The Negro's Complaint' (1788):

> Deem our nation brutes no longer,
> Till some reason ye shall find
> Worthier of regard and stronger
> Than the colour of our kind.
> Slaves of gold, whose sordid dealings
> Tarnish all your boasted powers,
> Prove that you have human feelings,
> Ere you proudly question ours!

One of the objectives of the Committee's early activities was to mobilise public support for a large number of petitions to be sent to Parliament from all over the kingdom. This tactic was not new, but it had only recently been heavily exploited in an organised way – Pitt's supporters had employed it with overwhelming effect in the run-up to the election of 1784. In early 1788 Wilberforce was writing that he and Pitt were anxious that 'Petitions for the abolition of the trade in flesh and blood should flow in from every quarter of the Kingdom'.[21] On the same day, 25 January, he wrote to Wyvill asking for similar action in Yorkshire:

> I think there is little reason to doubt of the motion for the aboli-
> tion of this horrid traffic in flesh and blood being carried in
> parliament. But yet for many reasons which I have not either
> leisure or eyesight to state . . . it is highly desirable that the public
> voice should be exerted in our support as loudly and as universally
> as possible; many places and some counties have already deter-
> mined our petitions to parliament. I should be sorry that our
> little kingdom should be backward in its endeavours to rescue our
> fellow creatures from mercy and rescue our national character
> from the foulest dishonour.[22]

While the people of Liverpool were stirred to petition against abolition, their compatriots in Manchester led the way, with thousands of signa-tures: in early 1788 petitions were sent to Parliament calling for aboli-tion with a total of between sixty thousand and 100,000 signatures, a very large number by the standards of the time. It was significant, though, that at this stage the weight of signatures came from the newly expanding industrial towns, which had little representation in Parliament; Wyvill wrote back to Wilberforce apologetically from Yorkshire to explain 'that no assistance can be procured for your unfortunate Africans', but more because of apathy concerning the calling of the appropriate meetings rather than because of 'any positive disapprobation of your virtuous efforts'.[23]

Central to the mobilisation of public opinion was the organisation of lectures and meetings. Speakers fanned out across the country, finding large audiences in 'town halls, guild halls, music halls, Leeds coloured cloth hall, chapels, churches',[24] with Thomas Clarkson as the most energetic and most sought-after speaker of them all. Between 1787 and 1794 he would cover thirty-five thousand miles on lecture tours around Britain, carrying with him a diagram of the *Brookes*, shackles and other instruments from slave ships, and samples of African cloths to show that an alternative and civilised trade could be substituted for slavery. From the formation of the London Committee, Clarkson worked full-time on abolition, with much of the first year's expenses of £618 allocated to 'collecting information and evidence' and 'travelling charges' being spent in his support. In the early days of his travels, research was his highest priority, particularly in Bristol and Liverpool. He managed to examine and measure slave ships, finding one only thirty feet long which had carried seventy slaves. But most of all he dug deep into the facts of what was to become a key part of the abolitionists' argument: that not only were the slaves themselves appallingly mistreated, but so were the British sailors on board the same ships. Through personal interviews in the taverns, he collected stories of the deaths and mistreatment of sailors, and through copying down ships' rolls he was able to calculate how many sailors had died on each trip. Eventually he could claim that 'In London, Bristol and Liverpool, I had already obtained the names of more than twenty thousand seamen . . . knowing what had become of each.'[25]

In Bristol, Clarkson witnessed how the sailors were forced into the trade, seeing that 'music, dancing, rioting, drunkenness, profane swearing, were kept up from night to night',[26] and that 'Seamen . . .

were boarded in these houses, who, when the slave-ships were going out, but at no other time, were encouraged to spend more than they had money to pay for; and to these, when they had thus exceeded, but one alternative was given, namely, a slave-vessel, or a gaol.'[27] He found that the sailors were 'not only personally ill-treated . . . but that they were robbed by artifice of those wages which had been held up to them as so superior in this service',[28] since half the wages were paid to them in the currency of the country where they landed, and 'by means of this iniquitous practice the wages in the Slave-trade, though nominally higher to induce seamen to engage in it, were actually lower than in other trades'.[29] It was Clarkson who linked up with the former slave-ship surgeon Alexander Falconbridge, who led him to still more seamen who were 'in a very crippled and deplorable state',[30] and urged him to enquire into the murder of one of their colleagues by their chief mate. With the stories of deaths, disease and floggings mounting up, Clarkson, who on first seeing Bristol had begun 'to tremble . . . at the arduous task I had undertaken, of attempting to subvert one of the branches of the commerce of the great place which was then before me',[31] now concluded that he had seen 'nothing but misery in the place',[32] and hastened away from it. By the time he arrived in Liverpool he found people saying that 'they had heard of a person turned mad, who had conceived the thought of destroying Liverpool, and all its glory',[33] and then realised they were talking about him. Generating lively controversy night after night in the King's Arms tavern where he stayed and dined, Clarkson found his enquiries were increasingly resented: he 'received anonymous letters, entreating me to leave it [Liverpool], or I should otherwise never leave it alive',[34] and on one occasion he narrowly escaped being thrown off a pier head, but 'not without blows'.[35]

Clarkson's research was of fundamental importance to the abolitionist campaign, both in the information gathered directly and in the discovery of witnesses who could appear before subsequent inquiries. Yet fifty years later an unseemly dispute would arise between him and Wilberforce's sons, Robert and Samuel, who published the first biography of their father in 1838. The sons reacted against Clarkson's assertions that it was he who had first introduced Pitt to the subject of the slave trade and introduced Wilberforce to Newton, all of which was obviously untrue. They also resented the fact that Clarkson's *History of the Rise, Progress and Accomplishment of the Abolition of the Slave-Trade* (1808) skated over the twelve-year period after 1794, in which he was absent from the campaign, and depicted Wilberforce more as 'a sort of parliamentary agent'[36] than as the leader of the campaign. There is indeed evidence that Wilberforce himself considered that 'Clarkson's conduct . . . is certainly very far from the simple plain proceeding of a fair mind: though I would hope that vanity has more to do with it than any more deeply laid . . . plot,'[37] but his sons overreacted by claiming that Wilberforce had 'from the first'[38] directed the endeavours of the Committee, and by unfairly playing down the key role played by Clarkson. When their account of their father's life was published in 1838, Clarkson was so incensed by what he believed were its inaccuracies that he came out of retirement to write *Strictures on a Life of William Wilberforce*. He was seventy-nine years old, 'An age,' as one reviewer put it, 'when quietude is especially needed.'[39]

Even two hundred years later, the dispute about who was the more important to the abolition campaign, Clarkson or Wilberforce, continues as a proxy for contending that either popular pressure or parliamentary debate was the most important element of the campaign. The truth was, of course, that neither could have done without the other; that both Clarkson and the Wilberforce sons were sometimes at fault in their depiction of events; and that to see Wilberforce as the mere parliamentary mouthpiece of the campaign, or Clarkson solely as a collector of facts, is unfair. Equally, to try to choose between popular will and parliamentary persuasion as the decisive component in the eventual achievement of abolition would be futile: success could not have been achieved in the absence of either. In their own lifetimes, Wilberforce and Clarkson worked closely and highly productively together, a case in point being Clarkson's discoveries about the high death rate of seamen, which were used very effectively by Wilberforce on the floor of the House of Commons. Wilberforce was always clear that Clarkson 'took up the cause before him', and Clarkson probably gave as correct an account as anyone when he said: 'I certainly do think that Mr Wilberforce could not have got on, as he did, without my aid and that of the Committee; but neither could the Committee have got on without Mr Wilberforce and myself; nor could I have worked to the effect attributed to me, without Mr Wilberforce and the Committee.'[40]

As Wilberforce began to shape his parliamentary tactics in the summer of 1787, such disputes were half a century away. Yet he was looking for a route to rapid abolition, and as Pitt humiliated France in the autumn of 1787, he thought he had found it.

There was no doubting that Wilberforce, a Member of Parliament of still only seven years' experience and only twenty-eight years of age, brought great weight to the abolitionists' campaign. In the words of Granville Sharp, 'The respectability of his position as Member for the largest county, the great influence of his personal connexions added to an amiable and unblemished character, secure every advantage to the cause.'[41] Despite his declared independence, Wilberforce remained close to Pitt in the winter of 1787–88, his diary entries being littered with notes such as: 'Called in at Pitt's at 7, for a short time; and staid supper'; 'Pitt's before House – dined'; 'After House to Pitt's – supped.'[42] The slave trade was frequently a topic of their conversation, for while Pitt as yet refrained from any public statements, he had made the Treasury's files available for the researches of the abolitionists, and continued to encourage Wilberforce with plans and ideas.

The spring of 1787 had seen the formal concluding of Pitt's commercial treaty with France; the summer saw a tense confrontation between London and Paris over French involvement in the affairs of Holland. With Pitt preparing for war, Louis XVI and his ministers backed down, revealing for the first time in foreign affairs the dire weakness of a French state that was already tottering to its terrible fall. In October, William Grenville, who had been sent to Paris at the height of the crisis, returned with the news that the French Foreign Minister, de Montmorin, could be sympathetic to the abolition of the slave trade.

Pitt and Wilberforce decided to make use of the continued presence in Paris of William Eden, later Lord Auckland, the special envoy who had shown enormous skill in negotiating the commercial treaty and who enjoyed excellent contacts with the French government. They knew that one of the main arguments against abolition was that the French would carry on with the trade anyway, and, even worse, pick up the lion's share of the trade the British would deny to themselves. Suddenly there was the alluring possibility of a bilateral agreement even before the opposition could mobilise: both countries would strike down the trade together.

Both Wilberforce and Pitt wrote to Eden asking him to pursue the matter urgently with the French. Wilberforce offered to travel to Paris to assist. On 23 November 1787 he sent Eden a long letter setting out the case against the trade, as he currently saw it: 'This trade instead of being like others, a nursery of seamen, may be rather termed their grave; it consumes annually about a ¼ of those engaged in it,'[43] and, writing again on 7 December, he urged on Eden the attractions for the French government of acting quickly: 'The less the measure is made the subject of common town talk the more likely it is to be adopted by your Kings and Ministers and gentry of that description . . . If in this case the splendour of the measure dazzles one, would not this effect be diminished and its operation proportionately weakened if the Court seems rather to follow the general opinion than to lead it?' He assured Eden that there was 'no doubt' of success in Britain: 'The evident, the glaring justice of the proposition itself; Mr Pitt's support of the measure and the temper of the House'[44] were all pointing in the same direction. Eden did his best, and the French were not averse to abolition in principle, but he had to report that de Montmorin had told him 'that there were great doubts here, respecting the possibility of stopping the slave trade, without utter and sudden ruin to the French Islands'.[45] A further problem was that French ministers did not necessarily believe that Britain would indeed act: while Louis XVI could abolish the French slave trade literally at the stroke of his pen, Pitt would have to fight his way through the procedures of both Houses of Parliament. It is likely that the French government, which faced a mounting financial crisis, was too weak to launch such a bold initiative. By early 1788, Wilberforce's flickering hopes for what would have been a stunning solution to the whole issue had been snuffed out. His diary for 24 January reads: 'Called at Pitt's at night – he firm about African trade, though we begin to perceive more difficulties in the way than we had hoped there would be.'[46] Ahead of him lay the long, tortuous road of securing British abolition unilaterally, without international agreement of any kind.

As the pamphlets and medallions circulated and the petitions began to roll in, Pitt and Wilberforce pencilled in February 1788 for the first public political moves against the slave trade. Pitt's move, on 11 February, was easily enough accomplished, since it was something which, as First Lord of the Treasury, he could set in train without reference to Parliament: an inquiry by the Privy Council into 'the present State of the Trade to AFRICA, and particularly the Trade in SLAVES'.[47] For the first time, a branch of British government would seek to establish objective facts concerning the slave trade, and require those for and against abolition to state their case in detail.

The second prong of the attack that February was to involve Wilber-force in moving a motion in the House of Commons which would give notice of his intention to seek the abolition of the slave trade in the next session of Parliament, that is in 1789. He busied himself furiously in preparation for the impending debate, conferring with Pitt, writing off for petitions, planning with the London Committee, preparing witnesses and counsel to appeal before the Privy Council inquiry, seeking allies in the Commons, while all the time attending to his other causes, including a new Register Bill, the launching of the Proclamation Society on 12 February, and the weight of constituency business which flowed in without interruption. It was perhaps because of this that he began to feel 'very unwell' at the end of January.[48] When Clarkson came to see him to take his leave before travelling to Bristol, 'He was then very ill, and in bed ... After conversing as much as he well could in his weak state, he held out his hand to me, and wished me success. When I left him, I felt much dejected. It appeared to me as if it would be in this case, as it is often in that of other earthly things, that we scarcely possess what we repute a treasure, when it is taken from us.'[49]

Clarkson was not exaggerating, for Wilberforce was suddenly and seriously ill. By 19 February he was noting that he suffered 'great languor, total loss of appetite, flushings &c',[50] seemingly with the debilitating condition which would later become known as ulcerative colitis. For over two weeks he was unable to attend the Commons, but struggled on with small amounts of work. He wrote on 29 February: 'I . . . am still a close prisoner, wholly unequal even to such little business as I am now engaged in: add to which my eyes are so bad that I can scarce see how to direct my pen.'[51]

On 4 March he went to stay with John Thornton at Clapham, Pitt having urged him to take some country air; by the eighth he thought he was 'now recovering', and that relaxation and the waters of Bath 'will restore me again to the duties of my station';[52] later the same day he fell into a worse condition than ever, which brought his mother and sister down to London to his bedside, and caused his friends intense concern. They called in one of the most prominent physicians of the time, Dr Richard Warren, whose gloomy forecast was: 'That little fellow, with his calico guts, cannot possibly survive a twelve-month.'[53] Other experts thought 'that he had not stamina to last a fortnight'.[54]

After a fortnight had gone by, Wilberforce was actually making a good recovery, a secretary writing to Wyvill on 27 March: 'Mr Wilberforce being still under Injunctions not to write or do any business, I have undertaken with great pleasure the office of thanking you for two letters with which you have lately favoured him . . . It is with infinite satisfaction I am able to add that there is the greatest reason to hope that his valuable life will long be preserved to his friends and the public . . . Within the last fortnight . . . his strength has been restored . . . Little now is wanting for his recovery, but repose of body and mind.'[55] By 25 April he was in Bath, 'a banished man from London and business', as he wrote to Wyvill. 'As to the slave question,' he went on, 'I do not like to touch on it, it is so big a one it frightens me in my weak state . . . To you in *strict confidence* I will entrust that Pitt, with a warmth of principle and friendship that have made me love him better than I ever did before has taken on himself the management of the business, and promises to do *all* for me if I desire it, that, if I were an efficient man, it would be proper for me to do myself. This is all I can now say; I might add more were we side by side on my sofa.'[56]

It was evident that Wilberforce would be out of action for months, if not forever. This caused huge consternation among the abolitionists, who had now managed to stir up over a hundred petitions to Parliament, and were eagerly awaiting the forthcoming debate. Yet Pitt was as good as his word, summoning Granville Sharp to see him, ensuring that the giving of evidence to the Privy Council was properly supervised, and undertaking himself the introduction of a motion in the Commons, 'That the House will, early in the next session, proceed to take into consideration the circumstances of the slave trade.' Introducing this motion on 9 May 1788, Pitt studiously avoided giving his own opinion, and confined himself to arguing that the matter should be discussed, a tactic which has been criticised subsequently as showing a lack of sincerity. But Pitt would have been conscious of the dangers of mobilising the opposition at too early a stage, both in his own cabinet and elsewhere: his approach allowed him to avoid cabinet discussion while setting in train a process which would permit him to come down on the abolitionists' side at a later stage, with, hopefully, a decisive effect.

For all Pitt's cautious tactics, the debate of 9 May proved to be one of two important parliamentary skirmishes that session which showed that the abolition of the slave trade would be no easy matter. While Pitt's motion was carried without a vote, and with the strong support of the most eloquent and powerful spokesmen of the opposition in the form of Charles James Fox and Edmund Burke, it also brought forth the first parliamentary speeches in defence of the trade, with Bamber Gascoyne of Liverpool asserting that his constituents involved in the trade 'were men of such respectable characters, that they were above the reach of calumny',[57] and Lord Penrhyn dismissing the argument that captains mistreated their slaves 'because the whole profits of the voyage of the Captains employed in the slave trade arose from the numbers of Negroes they could bring to the West Indian market in good health'.[58]

The second skirmish was on a matter of real substance, and by revealing the split in the cabinet it forced Pitt prematurely off the fence. An MP for Oxford University, Sir William Dolben, had managed to inspect an empty slave ship at anchor in the Thames. He had been so outraged by seeing the tiny spaces into which the slaves were confined that on 1 May he introduced a Bill to limit the number of slaves that could be carried on a ship to one for each ton of the vessel. Although the Bill passed the Commons easily in a thin House, the opposition expressed to even this modest measure led Pitt to lose his cool. Liverpool MPs argued that 'The proposed limitations on the number of slaves to be carried in a given space . . . would infallibly produce the utter ruin of the traffic.'[59] Pitt declared that if such a regulation could not be accepted 'he would retract what he had said on a former day' and 'give his vote for the utter abolition of a Trade which was shocking to humanity, abominable to be carried on by any country, and which reflected the greatest dishonour on . . . the British nation'.[60]

In spite of this threat, the Bill encountered fierce opposition in the Lords, from veteran admirals and from Pitt's own cabinet colleague Lord Thurlow, who denounced the passage of legislation in 'five days' fit of philanthropy'.[61] Pitt felt so strongly about the Bill that he told Grenville that if it was defeated in the Lords, 'the opposers of it and myself cannot continue members of the same Government'.[62] It went through by fourteen votes to twelve: the cabinet stayed uneasily together, a minimal amount of regulation was passed, and the difficulty of passing a measure as radical as the complete abolition of the trade had been amply demonstrated.

Wilberforce was nowhere to be seen in the summer of 1788 as the opening shots were fired in the most important battle of his life. For him personally, the question had been whether his life would be preserved at all, since his illness had at one stage seemed to affect all his vital functions. Yet in Bath that April he had begun to convalesce, noting in his journal in early May, 'my head was much weakened during my illness. I mended exceedingly during my stay. Much out airing. Never visited but saw good deal of company at home. Too dissipated a place, except the waters are necessary.'[63] His 'habits of idleness'[64] assisted his recovery from what the jottings in a stray red notebook, likely to have been written by him since he kept such a book for personal notes, suggest had been a traumatic time for him psychologically as well as physically. At one stage he complained that 'corrupt imaginations are perpetually rising in my mind', and 'innumerable fears close me in on every side',[65] and he prayed to God for 'succour and support, O Lord let it come speedily . . . I am in great troubles, insurmountable by me; but to thee slight and inconsiderable; look upon me O Lord with compassion and mercy, and restore me to rest, quietness, and comfort, in the world, or in another by removing me hence into a state of peace and happiness. Amen.'[66] Prayers, rest and a little company evidently all had a beneficial effect, but it seems that a crucial ingredient of the treatments that returned him to health was one which would have been surprising in a later age: opium.

Although obviously addictive, opium was a commonly used medicine in the eighteenth century. It was deployed to combat a wide variety of ailments: 'to mitigate pain, to allay spasm, to promote sleep, to relieve nervous restlessness, to produce perspiration and to check profuse mucous discharges from the bronchial tubes and gastro-intestinal canal'.[67] It was particularly well known for preventing digestive disorders: Isaac Milner, who took far heavier doses than Wilberforce, wrote to him a few years later, 'However be not afraid of the *habit* of such medicine, the *habit* of growling guts is infinitely worse.'[68] Earlier in the century, Clive of India had used opium because of a painful bowel disease, although the taking of a double dose at the age of forty-nine might have been what killed him. One of the hazards of opium consumption was that the age and quality of the grains could vary widely, so that the same quantity of the drug might be much stronger or weaker one day compared to the next.

Wilberforce remained dependent on opium for the rest of his life, although he managed to avoid increasing the dose over time, and claimed that it had no noticeable effect on his mind: 'If I take but a single glass of wine, I can feel its effect, but I never know when I have taken my dose of opium by my feelings.'[69] Scientists and doctors of the time were still battling to understand the effects of opium consumption, although a document of 1700 had pointed to the dangers of sudden withdrawal: 'Great, and even intolerable distresses, anxieties and depression of spirit', but also referred to agreeable effects of regular use: 'pleasant dreams, freedom from anxiety, indolence, or exemption from pain'.[70] There was still much dispute over whether it had a stimulating or sedative effect, although a clue might have been taken from the fate of a distinguished Edinburgh doctor who took a larger dose than usual before a crucial speech at his medical society, and promptly fell fast asleep.

The stigma attached to the habit of taking such a drug in the twentieth century simply did not exist in the eighteenth, and since there were no steroids or similar drugs to control internal inflammations, there was little alternative. Throughout his life, Wilberforce never hesitated to recommend the use of opium to other people, and thirty years later he would note that his dose was 'still as it has long been', four grains three times a day, and that if he forgot to take the last dose of the day he would be forced next day 'to lie in bed, great sneezing and other signs of spasm'.[71] It was not until the publication of Thomas de Quincey's *Confessions of an English Opium-Eater* in 1822, amidst the growing evidence of the dangers of addiction, that opium use began to be questioned, although Gladstone took laudanum, based on tincture of opium, in his coffee. With the benefit of hindsight in the nineteenth century, Wilberforce's friend Bob Smith (the first Lord Carrington) would comment: 'It is extraordinary that his health was restored by that which to all appearances would have ruined it, namely the constant use of opium in large quantities,'[72] but Wilberforce was certainly confident that this was so.

Thus fortified, he left Bath on 5 May, and took three days to travel to Cambridge, having sent instructions to his college to avoid giving him 'a damp bed and rather let me have one that has been slept in, sheets and all, for a month together'.[73] Once there, he 'lived more regularly and quietly than I had done for a long time',[74] and spent his evenings with Milner, while finding the academics in general disappointing: 'They had neither the solidity of judgement possessed by ordinary men of business, nor the refined feelings and elevated principles which become a studious and sequestered life.'[75] Early June saw him travel all the way to the Lake District, staying in the familiar house, his beloved Rayrigg, and collecting his mother and sister on the way.

Being at Rayrigg that summer was intended to bring several benefits: the company of his friends, Milner and Muncaster, as well as his immediate family; a visit from Pitt, who was intending to travel to the north of England and Scotland for the first time in his life; and the peace and quiet he could obtain by rowing his boat out onto Lake Windermere and finding a shady spot near an island to read and rest. To his mounting irritation, this happy plan was largely frustrated. Pitt was prevented from travelling so far by the pressure of government business, while an ever-growing army of other visitors arrived, leading to 'a scene of great temptation, – a perpetual round of dissipation and my house overflowing with guests'.[76] It did not help that one of the visitors was the Duchess of Gordon, a bold, flirtatious and generally indomitable woman who had become a patron and hostess for Pitt in London, and expected his friends to treat her as a figure of great importance. Having bumped into the Duchess and her daughter one day in early July, Wilberforce forlornly recorded that 'their tapping at our low window announced that they had discovered our retreat and would take no denial. I went to them and told the Duchess, "I cannot see you here, I have with me my old mother, who being too infirm to make new acquaintances, is no more in your way than you are in hers." '[77] Nevertheless, the Duchess and other guests were soon filling Wilberforce's days, until he was concluding by the end of July that 'The life I am now leading is unfavourable in all respects both to mind and body, as little suitable to me considered as an invalid ... as it is becoming my character and profession as a Christian.' He found it hard to adhere to his plans for reading and study, and continually succumbed to the temptations of the table.

By the time he left the Lake District to return to Bath in the early

autumn he had decided not to renew the lease on Rayrigg, writing
to Newton, 'I shall lay my plans in future with more foresight and
circumspection. At this moment my cottage overflows with guests.'[78]
But this experience, which so obviously challenged his sense of discipline and devotion, aroused in him a new bout of resolutions as he
fought once again to master his own habits and mind. Whilst still at
Rayrigg he was noting that 'I must still strive to loose myself from this
bondage of sin and Satan, calling on the name of the Lord,'[79] and
urging himself to 'guard against habits of idleness, luxury, selfishness,
and forgetfulness of God'.[80] The renewed struggle with himself would
continue through that winter, documented in increasingly detailed
note-taking. He was determined to 'live by rule', to use his mind
productively at all times of day: 'Remember Red Book rules and hints,
respecting the employment of odd half hours, and of thoughts and
company or alone,'[81] all accompanied by fresh warnings to himself of
his unworthiness: 'How little have I availed myself of the opportunities
of usefulness, which have been so abundantly afforded me! Be more
diligent and watchful for the future – the night cometh when no man
can work. Let this consideration quicken my exertions.'[82]

Wilberforce had been worried that his Yorkshire constituents would
think that he was now permanently out of action, and wrote to
Wyvill: 'I am informed on all hands that a report prevails and is very
industriously circulated by our political adversaries, that my state of
health is such as to have induced me to resolve not to propose myself
a candidate in the event of any future election for the county of
York. This impression it is easy to see may operate greatly to my
disadvantage.'[83] To counter this, he published an address to his constituents in August:

> Having heard from various quarters that a report prevails
> throughout the county that on account of the infirm state of my
> health I do not intend to offer myself at the next election as a
> candidate ... I think it right thus publicly to assure you that
> the progress of my recovery affords me reason to hope that my
> constitution will be equal to the labours of a parliamentary life
> and as long as my constituents shall be disposed to continue to

me the important charge with which they have intrusted me, I
feel too highly gratified by such a mark of their confidence not to
be desirous of retaining it, however conscious I may be of the
little right I have to so flattering a distinction.[84]

Yet as he took the Bath waters that October, he had passed eight
months while taking no visible part in the political world. By early
November 1788 the pleas both of his constituents and his friend in
Downing Street could no longer be resisted. He had not communed
with his constituents at any time that year. Wyvill now advised him that
his attendance in York on 5 November for the centennial celebrations of
the Glorious Revolution was imperative: 'Your appearance at so great
a meeting of your friends as will then be held at York is absolutely
necessary, so that nothing short of inability to move ... without
endangering your health ought to prevent it.'[85] It was this letter which
brought forth from Wilberforce in his reply the words which have
always been taken to define his approach to the mixing of Christian
principles with practical politics: 'My walk I am sensible is a public
one; my business is in the world; and I must mix in assemblies with
men, or quit the post which Providence seems to have assigned me.'[86]

Wilberforce accordingly left Bath on 27 October, arrived in London
the following evening, visited Pitt at Holwood two days later, left
London on the thirty-first and arrived in York four days after that.
Despite his physical fragility, he was never daunted by the many days
he spent on the road, travelling much further and more frequently
than most of his contemporaries. In the space of just over a month,
and at a time when he was meant to be resting, he had now travelled
from the Lake District in north-west England, to Hull on the east
coast of Yorkshire, down to Bath in the south-west, then eastwards to
London, before returning to Yorkshire along the two-hundred-mile
journey to York. This was at a time when travelling by coach was a
jolting and uncomfortable experience, and to cover fifty miles in a day
was considered fairly good going. Most Members of Parliament would
have thought an annual journey to London and back as much as they
could stand; Pitt never ventured more than eighty miles north of
London in his life; yet Wilberforce enjoyed having the resources to

travel as comfortably as possible, as well as a blend of patience and curiosity which meant that travel seemed never to bore him.

Having duly made his appearance in York, Wilberforce was soon back on the road south again, initially unaware that on the very day he had been celebrating the anniversary of the constitutional settlement and the Protestant succession to the Crown, the living symbol of this fundamental basis of eighteenth-century politics, George III, had apparently taken leave of his senses. When Wilberforce reached Birmingham on 11 November he 'stopped all day for intelligence',[87] having heard confused accounts of the serious illness of the King. In the politics of that time, the incapacity or death of the King, both of which were now strongly rumoured, was more than just an interesting piece of news: it presaged a political and constitutional crisis of the first order. The death of the King would cause the succession to the throne of George, Prince of Wales, whose loathing of his father and all associated with him, and well-known habit of spending dissolute evenings with key figures in the opposition, left no room for doubt that this would spell the end of Pitt's premiership and a wholesale change of government. Alternatively, if the King's behaviour, which had become bizarre, irrational and sometimes violent, rendered him incapable of exercising his responsibilities, the Prince would have to be declared Regent, presumably with an identical result.

It was small wonder that in these circumstances all politicians raced for Westminster, with Thomas Steele, one of Pitt's key lieutenants, writing to Wilberforce, 'It is very desirable that you should be in town . . . unless it materially interferes with your health.'[88] Wilberforce thus arrived in Bath in mid-November only to set off for London again, but arriving there to find that Pitt had succeeded in adjourning Parliament for two weeks, he returned to Bath for another ten days before returning yet again to the capital. From then on, frail or not, he was plunged into the frenetic parliamentary manoeuvres over whether a Regency should be declared, and on what terms.

It says much for Wilberforce's standing as an MP that he was appointed to all the key committees which deliberated at crucial moments of a crisis that now continued for nearly three months: his combination of professed independence with closeness to Pitt meant that he was seen in Downing Street as an indispensable parliamentary ally at a time when the prospect of a change in administration caused less reliable or less principled supporters to defect. He was happy to sit on committees which Pitt invented to use up time, including the Committee on Precedents in December 1788, and the Committee to examine the evidence of the physicians in January 1789. With Pitt doggedly holding his own against the odds, Wilberforce's political independence seemed to desert him: he wrote to Wyvill that 'My friend is every day matter of fresh and growing admiration. I wish you were as constantly as I am witness to that simple and earnest regard for the public welfare, by which he is so uniformly actuated; great as I know is your attachment to him, you would love him more and more.'[89] Regularly to be found in Downing Street with Pitt and Dundas in the small hours – 'late hours bring many evils with them'[90] – Wilberforce was in the thick of the crisis, arguing with Pitt only over the plan to place severe restrictions on the powers Prince George would enjoy as Regent over the royal household. Yet even though Wilberforce baulked at this in private, he was happy to defend his friend's policy in public, getting to his feet in the Commons on 19 January to argue that 'The Prince might be declared Regent, but it behove the House to take a special care, that during the lifetime of his father, he was not placed upon the Throne.'[91]

Wilberforce was distracted by the continuing crisis well into the new year: his diary notes refer to him being 'very much shattered', 'weak in the morning' and at best indifferent in health.[92] The long hours and late nights of the crisis made him complain anew that he was 'too dissipated', and was wasting too much time.[93] He had earlier complained to Wyvill that 'The least irregularity in point of hours, diet, &c reminds me that I am a valetudinarian yet I think by care I shall be tolerably equal to my work.'[94] By late January he was forcing himself to focus once again on the business of the slave trade, conscious that the debate which had been proposed the preceding year would soon be due. His deliberations brought him into contact for the first time with James Stephen, a brilliant Scottish lawyer working in St Kitts at the West Indian bar. Stephen could not admit publicly that he was opposed to the slave trade without losing his income, but he had formed on his first arrival in the West Indies an enduring hatred of slavery, having witnessed an unfair trial in a court in Barbados which resulted in two slaves being condemned to be burnt alive. Evangelical in disposition and hugely knowledgeable in legal and commercial matters, Stephen was a natural soulmate for Wilberforce, although neither of them would have guessed how close they would become as they break-fasted together for the first time in Old Palace Yard on 31 January 1789.

By mid-February, the way was opening for Wilberforce to make his great push for abolition. The drawn-out giving of evidence to the Privy Council inquiry was coming to a close, and with the convalescence of the King, the political crisis ended with the routing of the opposition and the triumph of Pitt. The private celebrations brought yet further trials for Wilberforce's attempts to live abstemiously – 'Went to Hol-wood with Pitt, and there exceeded rules . . . yet will I struggle and not give up the combat.'[95] But the return to normality in Parliament meant that a full-scale debate on the slave trade was now in view. By April Wilberforce was spending eight or nine hours a day with his collaborators, particularly Clarkson and Ramsay. He missed the great national celebration of the King's return to health on 23 April, St George's Day, to be at Teston, going over the evidence and the arguments yet again. Yet at the same time, around Westminster, prep-arations were being made by MPs who took a very different view. The Privy Council inquiry, the abolitionist campaign and the feverish preparations of Wilberforce had persuaded the defenders of the slave trade that this was not a threat that would simply melt away. As Wilberforce considered his tactics for the debate now set for 12 May 1789, his enemies were doing the same.

8

Eloquence Without Victory

———————— ◆ ————————

The nature and all the circumstance of this trade are now laid open
to us: we can no longer plead ignorance, we cannot evade it . . . we
cannot turn aside.

Wilberforce's speech to the House of Commons,

12 May 1789[1]

You, Sir, will stand in the British Parliament . . . with the whole force
of truth, with every rational argument, and with all the powers of
moving eloquence upon your side, and all to no purpose.

DR PECKARD, 1791[2]

WHATEVER THE MORAL and practical arguments in favour of
the abolition of the slave trade, there was no doubting that a
wide range of vested interests was certain to defend it: ship-owners
and traders in Liverpool and Bristol, manufacturers of goods exported
to Africa from growing industrial towns, and above all the owners of
plantations in the West Indies, for whom slavery was fundamental to
their wealth. Wide-ranging though these interests were, they did not
automatically command a powerful bloc of parliamentary support: the
West Indian colonies had their own legislatures, and were not directly
represented in the British Parliament; Liverpool and Bristol mustered
only two Members of Parliament apiece; and manufacturers of the
relevant exports were not sufficiently concentrated or numerous to
have serious political clout outside Lancashire. There were only around
twenty MPs with direct interests in the West Indies as merchants or

planters in the Parliament who had been elected in 1784, and historians would later calculate that the number of MPs who could be absolutely relied upon to oppose abolition was somewhere in the thirties in a Parliament of 558 Members – and roughly the same number could be relied upon to support it. There was therefore an initial symmetry to the pro- and anti-abolition forces as they squared up to each other at Westminster, with both sides only able to secure victory if they won over uncommitted MPs and made maximum use of the support of powerful individuals in the political system.

On the face of it, the disposition of the most powerful individuals in Parliament favoured the abolitionists. Pitt himself, the Prime Minister, along with the dominant figures in the Whig opposition, Charles James Fox and Edmund Burke, were on their side. But the defenders of the trade were not slow to make contact with their own sympathisers at senior levels, and since these included several men who sat in either the cabinet or the House of Lords, and in many cases both, they inhibited Pitt's freedom of manoeuvre and maintained a powerful backstop in the upper House ready to veto any rash decision made by the MPs in the Commons.

Foremost among those organising the anti-abolition activities was Stephen Fuller, the agent for Jamaica based in London. As the abolitionist campaign gathered pace early in 1788, he urged caution on his own side – 'We have nothing as yet but a Phantom to contend with'[3] – and sought at first a way of quietly strangling the campaign at birth rather than confronting it with public arguments which would only inflame the debate. On 29 January 1788 Fuller wrote to the Home Secretary, Lord Sydney, to express the fear that even discussion of abolition would bring revolt and violence in the West Indies: 'Your Lordship may depend upon it, that during the time this business is agitated in Parliament, the slaves will be minutely acquainted with all the proceedings ... It becomes my indispensable duty to call upon your Lordship for your interference with his Majesty, graciously and in good time, to lay such commands upon his Governors as may prevent it.'[4] Sydney was one of several leading members of the cabinet who opposed abolition; when he duly lobbied Pitt he received a response which showed that, for a time at least, Pitt played a double game, trying to allow the abolitionist campaign to gather force while keeping the cabinet quiet. He assured Sydney that 'it would be well if it [abolition] could be brought about; but that there were so many points of the greatest consequence to this country involved in the question that he should never think of supporting any plan until after the fullest investigation'.[5]

Fuller was not an unthinking opponent of abolition. He repeatedly urged his clients in Jamaica to take action to improve the rights and living conditions of slaves, and to encourage them to marry and have children, both to reduce the need for imports and to take away some of the arguments of those opposed to slavery. But he was clear that slavery could not be carried on without the slave trade, and therefore that unilateral abolition spelt disaster: 'The more I look into it the more I am convinced of the absurdity and impossibility of abolishing Slavery; and if we do not avail ourselves of the labour of slaves, our enemies will to our certain undoing.'[6]

The Privy Council inquiry of 1788 to 1789 forced the defenders of the trade to come forward with their arguments and evidence, as Pitt and Wilberforce had intended it would. Fuller himself gave evidence on fifty-three different issues, and his response to the question as to whether the plantations could be cultivated by Europeans or by free blacks gives a flavour of his position:

> We think it impossible with Europeans: So far as Experience can determine we find that the same Exposure to the Sun, which cheers the African, is mortal to the European; Nine in Ten of them would die in Three Years.
>
> As to free Negroes; – in Jamaica no Free Negro has ever yet known to hire himself, or be employed in Agriculture upon the Sugar Plantations: The Men are averse to labour the Ground even for themselves; and whenever they do it, it is only to supply their immediate Wants: They have all the Vices of Slaves, and no Planter could controul them.[7]

This argument, that the plantations would be impossible to operate without a regular supply of slaves, was a crucial one for the anti-abolitionists, almost as much as their fundamental argument that only Britain's rivals would benefit. As Admiral Edwards told the Privy Council: 'The French and Dutch would immediately get Possession of this Trade. He does not believe that the Natives of Africa would be much pleased with such a Resolution, as they would be equally Slaves in their own Country; and when once they have quitted it, they do not show any Desire to return to it.'[8] Even less convincingly, other witnesses sought to persuade the Privy Council that the slave trade maintained high standards of care, and that the slaves themselves were often happy with their lot. The same Admiral Edwards reported that he 'has frequently seen Guineamen arrive in the West Indies and the Negroes usually appeared cheerful and singing – That you are apprized of the Arrival of the Guineamen by the Dancing and Singing of the Negroes on Board';[9] and a Captain Robert Heatley argued 'that a Slave on Board a Guineaman, in respect of Food and Attention, is as well, perhaps better situated, than many Kings and Princes in their own Country'.[10] Captain Robert Norris maintained that 'The Men play and sing, whilst the Boys dance for their Amusement – the Women and Girls divert themselves in the same Way';[11] another witness said that 'Nine out of Ten rejoice at falling into our Hands. They seem they are aware they are bought for Labour, and by their Gestures wish to convince the Purchasers that they are fit for it';[12] while Mr James Penney maintained that 'he has shewn to the principal People of the Country in Africa the Accommodations on Board his Ship, and they have held up their Hands, and said, The Slaves here will sleep better than the Gentlemen do on Shore . . . they are comfortably lodged in Rooms fitted up for them, which are washed and fumigated with Vinegar or Lime Juice every Day . . . They lie on the bare Boards, but the greatest Princes in their own Country lie on their Mats, with a Log of Wood for their Pillow.'[13]

Such assertions may seem ridiculous, but there were certainly people sitting in London disposed to believe them, and in a world with no photographic or recording devices it was difficult to prove to universal satisfaction that they were false. And while the traders defended themselves before the Privy Council, pro-slavery writers took up their pens to do battle with the burgeoning flow of abolitionist pamphlets. In his *Scriptural Researches on the Licitness of the Slave Trade*, published in Liverpool in 1788, the Reverend Raymund Harris argued that slavery had 'the sanction of divine authority'. If slavery were not authorised by God, he wrote, why did the Bible say in Leviticus, 'both thy bond-men and bond-maids, says the supreme law-giver, which thou shalt have, shall be of the heathen that are round about you; of them shall ye buy bond-men and bond-maids'?[14] And in his *Remarks Upon the Situation of Negroes in Jamaica* the wealthy socialite and plantation-owner William Beckford first advanced the argument later employed by William Cobbett, that compassion should begin at home:

> If Great Britain be seriously bent upon humanity, let it enlarge the scale of benevolence, and take in ... all colours, and all conditions of men; and reform at home before it venture to make romantic trials of compassion abroad! Let it look into itself, into its own internal system! Let it look into the situation of the peasantry; let it look into the state of the parochial, and canvass that of the extra-parochial poor; let it look into prisons where people from misfortunes only ... are confined for life ... Let the legislature look if there be not slaves of their own religion, and colour in England.[15]

Arguments that would later be considered as pure racism were freely advanced by some anti-abolitionists: 'A cordial and unalterable attachment is not to be expected from a Negro; and, were he possessed of a power over his own species, nothing would exceed his tyranny.'[16] By the summer of 1789 feelings were running high, with letters to the *Gentleman's Magazine* denouncing the abolitionists' 'mistaken notion of humanity'[17] or saying, 'The publick will judge of the fitness of men to conduct the concern of a great, a powerful, and wise nation who would sacrifice its most important interest, and rob 58,000 of our fellow-subjects of the means of existence to humour *the cant of hypocrites* ... or to serve a temporary selfish political purpose.'[18]

It was not without feeling, therefore, that pro-slavery MPs prepared for the coming struggle. They included some, like Richard Pennant, later Lord Penrhyn, who had inherited the largest estate in Jamaica, or Sir Francis Baring, who provided credit essential to the slave trade, who had a direct interest in the trade's continuation. Others were MPs for affected constituencies, such as Bamber Gascoyne, one of the Members for Liverpool, soon to be joined at the 1790 election by the colourful figure of Colonel Banastre Tarleton, who had cut a bloody and womanising dash through the American War of Independence, had an affair with the celebrated Mary Robinson, former mistress of the Prince of Wales, and was a staunch defender of the slave trade. His supporters at the election would chant:

> If our slave trade had gone, there's an end to our lives,
> Beggars all we must be, our children and wives,
> No ships from our ports their proud sails e'er would spread,
> And our streets grown with grass, where the cows might be fed.[19]

As for the House of Lords, it numbered anti-abolitionists far weightier than those in the Commons, including cabinet ministers like Sydney, Hawkesbury and Thurlow, who were motivated by their instinctive conservatism, and others like the naval Admiral Lord Rodney and the distinctly less heroic Duke of Clarence, influenced mainly by their experiences in the West Indies. Clarence's endless philandering did not disqualify him from active naval command, but his quarrelsome nature and inability to work with others did. Unfortunately, such defects of character would provide no impediment to his trenchant defence of the slave trade in the House of Lords.

As Wilberforce busied himself with preparations for the great debate, resolving 'to live with a view to health – Slave business . . . no waste of eye-sight; and may God bless the work',[20] these were some of the forces ranged against him. Yet most difficult of all for him to counter would be the petitions presented to Parliament on the very day of the debate, which presented the case against abolition to which MPs would most naturally respond. From Bristol it was declared that abolition would be 'to the very great loss of the petitioners, and to the

Ruin of Thousands of Individuals who are maintained thereby, but who are not sensible of the impending Danger . . . that the Petitioners have large capitals, expensive works, docks, ships, buildings, and warehouses, together with a great number of people, employed in their several trades and manufactures, and their chief support and dependence for carrying on their different occupations, are the Trade to Africa, and the Exports and Imports to and from the West India islands, which have been found . . . to constitute full three-fifths of the Port of Bristol'.[21]

From Liverpool came the plea that should the trade be abolished, 'Thousands of industrious honest Artificers, will thereby be reduced to a most distressing situation, perhaps be sent forth solitary Wanderers into the World, to seek Employment in Foreign Climes.'[22] From Birmingham came the petition of the manufacturers of goods exported to Africa, asserting 'that a very considerable part of the various manufactures in which the petitioners are engaged, are adapted to and disposed of for the African trade, and are not saleable at any other market; and that several thousands are employed in, and maintained by, such manufactures'; and from the merchants and ship-owners of London came the argument that abolition 'would tend greatly to the Aggrandizement of the French, Spaniards, Dutch, Portuguese, Danes, and others, who are giving every Encouragement for the Promotion and Improvement of that Branch of Commerce'.

Such were the concerns and fears that would inevitably weigh heavily on the minds of Members of Parliament. As Wilberforce rose from his seat on the afternoon of Tuesday, 12 May 1789, he knew he had to prove them wrong. One of the great parliamentary struggles of British history was about to begin.

Distinctly frail after his illness of the previous year and his recent exertions, Wilberforce arrived at the House of Commons on 12 May feeling unwell: 'Tuesday very indifferent. Came to town, sadly unfit for work, but by Divine grace was enabled to make my motion so as to give satisfaction – three hours and a half – I had not prepared my language, or even gone over all my matter, but being well acquainted with the whole subject I got on.'[23]

He was no doubt cheered by receiving both moral and practical support from his friend the Prime Minister, for Pitt allowed him to make his speech from the government front bench, with the dispatch box in front of him, giving him something on which to rest his notes and his hands, as well as letting him perform from the true centre-stage of the House. Yet Wilberforce had other and greater advantages when it came to making such a speech. For one thing, he was a naturally fluent and attractive speaker: the man who had wrested the political control of the whole of Yorkshire in a single speech in the Castle Yard at York was now becoming known as 'the nightingale of the House of Commons', a tribute both to his melodious voice and his regular, nightly attendance. Even more importantly, his assiduous attendance at parliamentary committees and debates until his enforced absence of the previous year had incubated in him a perfect command of the techniques of parliamentary oratory. In old age he explained what advice he would give to a young Member about developing these talents:

> He would particularly caution him against courting applause at the outset of his career, by ambitiously aiming to make what is called a fine speech. Should the attempt prove successful, such an undue estimate might probably be formed of the speaker's abilities as would render his subsequent and less studied efforts failures. Or should he unfortunately break down – a case by no means uncommon under such circumstances – vexation and disappointment might possibly seal his lips for ever. There was no better preparation, he added, for the style of speaking most adapted to the House, than a diligent attendance on committees, and a careful attention to the details of business and evidence which come before them ... By frequently taking a part in these, a man of any ability for speaking would soon acquire the habit of reasoning and expressing himself correctly and with parliamentary tact ... To aim at a logical arrangement of the ideas, and to cultivate the habit of elegant and correct writing, were also essential to success.[24]

Although he had run out of time to prepare, Wilberforce had armed himself with a few clear notes, set out in two columns, giving a structure to the speech which he broadly followed. But by now he also had the advantage of being completely steeped in the subject, and knowing the arguments on each side as well as any man alive. Such knowledge would now be deployed in the most important speech of his career thus far.

To a twenty-first-century audience a speech of three and a half hours would undoubtedly seem to be of inordinate, if not intolerable, dimensions. Yet in the eighteenth-century House of Commons a speech of this length, particularly when introducing a debate on a subject of great importance, was neither unusual nor considered inappropriate. Two hundred years later, the advent of television and the circulation of a mass of information both electronically and in print about every controversial subject would reduce parliamentary speeches to the role of summarising an argument or delivering a spoken press release, primarily intended to be read elsewhere. But at the time at which Wilberforce was speaking, Members of Parliament relied on key speeches from their leaders to supply the bulk of the information and the arguments with which it was necessary that they become acquainted. If a case was not fully explained to them on the floor of the House of Commons, they would probably never hear it at all. Wilberforce therefore had to present the whole of his argument in a single speech, even though the arguments were set out in a growing number of pamphlets: then, as now, Members of the House of Commons were the people least likely to read publications designed to influence them.

Furthermore, the readiness of Members of Parliament to switch their votes according to the arguments presented, particularly on an issue such as this where party loyalties did not apply, placed a premium on oratorical ability and persuasiveness which the subsequent rise of disciplined political parties would ultimately render almost worthless. The prospect that a speech could make all the difference to the result generally brought out the best in those speaking, just as the disconnection between the quality of the speech and the result obtained would by the late twentieth century produce speeches of stultifying morbidity. In the House of Commons of 1789, eloquence mattered.

Faced with such requirements, Wilberforce would cast off his physical fragility that afternoon to deliver a speech which, even set against the centuries of debates in the House of Commons, stands out as one of the true masterpieces of parliamentary oratory. He knew what sort of speech he had to give: one which would call others to share in the detestation of the slave trade he had developed, but would do so on the basis of clear facts and marshalled arguments, and would also reassure his listeners that the consequences of what he proposed could be both controlled and beneficial. The Members of the House of Commons would not be won over by appeals for Christian morality or human compassion: they 'no more dreamt of a seat in the House in order to benefit humanity than a child dreams of a birthday cake that others may eat it'.[25] They had to be persuaded that the abolition of the slave trade was not merely desirable, but was consistent with the interests of an enterprising and seafaring nation, and of an Empire that was never free from the encroachments and competition of its rivals.

Wilberforce's speech, recorded more accurately than most of the time because it was printed and circulated afterwards, is worth studying not only for his use of language, but also for his employment of eight separate devices of parliamentary persuasion, each one of them skilfully and sometimes cunningly employed. The first such technique was that of disarming what was undoubtedly a sceptical audience:

> When I consider the magnitude of the subject which I am to bring before the House – a subject, in which the interests, not of this country, nor of Europe alone, but of the whole world, and of posterity, are involved . . . it is impossible for me not to feel both terrified and concerned at my own inadequacies for such a task.[26]

Furthermore, he explained, he wished to guard against entering into the subject with too much passion: 'It is not their passions I shall appeal to – I ask only for their cool and impartial reason';[27] and, most important of all in his initial disarming manoeuvre, he said he would avoid accusations of guilt:

I mean not to accuse any one, but to take the shame upon myself, in common, indeed, with the whole parliament of Great Britain, for having suffered this horrid trade to be carried on under their authority. We are all guilty – we ought all to plead guilty, and not to exculpate ourselves by throwing the blame on others.[28]

After explaining the consequences of the trade for Africa – 'Does not every one see that a slave trade, carried on around her coasts, must carry violence and desolation to her very centre?'[29] – he deployed his second device: flattery. Those who had given evidence to the Privy Council inquiry, he reminded the House, had often come to conclusions of their own, but 'I mean to lay it down as my principle, that evidences, and especially interested evidences, are not to be judges of the argument.'[30] Only they, the Members of Parliament, were able to judge the truth: 'I trust gentlemen will judge for themselves, whether parliament is to rest satisfied that there are no abuses in Africa, in spite of all the positive proofs of so many witnesses on the spot to the contrary.'[31] Having assured his colleagues, most of whom had never left the shores of Britain, that they alone were equipped to assess these matters, he moved on to his third technique: the inclusion of his opponents in his feelings of outrage. Speaking of the transporting of slaves across the Atlantic, he declared:

This I confess, in my own opinion, is the most wretched part of the whole subject. So much misery condensed in so little room, is more than the human imagination had ever before conceived. I will not accuse the Liverpool merchants: I will allow them, nay, I will believe them, to be men of humanity ... I verily believe therefore, if the wretchedness of any one of the many hundred negroes stowed in each ship could be brought before their view, and remain within the sight of the African merchant, that there is no one among them whose heart would bear it. Let anyone imagine to himself 6 or 700 of these wretches chained two and two, surrounded with every object that is nauseous and disgusting, diseased, and struggling under every kind of wretchedness! How can we bear to think of such a scene as this?[32]

Fourth, he moved on to the most cherished practice of parliamentary orators throughout the ages: picking the weakest part of an opponent's case and ridiculing it. He singled out the evidence to the Privy Council of Captain Robert Norris, who had argued that the slaves were happy to leave Africa, that they were well fed and given plenty of water on the way, that their quarters were perfumed with frankincense and lime juice, and that they happily danced and made ornaments. Wilberforce chose Norris's evidence for a lacerating response:

> What will the House think when ... the true history is laid open? The slaves who are sometimes described as rejoicing at their captivity, are so wrung with misery at leaving their country, that it is the constant practice to set sail in the night, lest they should be sensible of their departure ... the scantiness, both of water and provision, was suggested by the very legislature of Jamaica in the report of their committee to be a subject that called for the interference of parliament. Mr Norris talks of frankincense and lime juice; when the surgeons tell you the slaves are stowed so close, that there is not room to tread among them: and when you have it in evidence from Sir George Yonge, that even in a ship which wanted 200 of her complement, the stench was intolerable. The song and the dance, says Mr Norris, are promoted. It had been more fair, perhaps, if he had explained that word promoted. The truth is, that for the sake of exercise, these miserable wretches, loaded with chains, oppressed with disease and wretchedness, are forced to dance by the terror of the lash, and sometimes by the actual use of it ... Such, then is the meaning of the word promoted ... As to their singing, what shall we say when we are told that their songs are songs of lamentation upon their departure which, while they sing, are always in tears insomuch, that one Captain ... threatened one of the women with a flogging, because the mournfulness of her song was too painful for his feelings.[33]

He proceeded to explain the terrible death rate among the slaves, and used the evidence to pass on to his fifth technique: that of arguing that the consequences of current policies were so terrible that it was necessary at least to think of alternatives to them:

Such enormities as these having once come within my knowledge I should not have been faithful to the sight of my eyes, to the use of my senses and my reason, if I had shrunk from attempting the abolition: it is true, indeed, my mind was harassed beyond measure; for when West-Indian planters and merchants retorted it upon me that it was the British parliament had authorized this trade ... It became difficult, indeed, what to answer; if the ruin of the West-Indies threatened us on the one hand, while this load of wickedness pressed upon us on the other, the alternative, indeed, was awful. It naturally suggested itself to me, how strange it was that providence, however mysterious in its ways should so have constituted the world, as to make one part of it depend for its existence on the depopulation and devastation of another. I could not therefore, help distrusting the arguments of those, who insisted that the plundering of Africa was necessary for the cultivation of the West-Indies. I could not believe that the same Being who forbids rapine and bloodshed, had made rapine and bloodshed necessary to the well-being of any part of his universe.[34]

He thus arrived naturally at his sixth purpose, to reassure: 'I hope now to prove, by authentic evidence, that, in truth, the West-Indies have nothing to fear from the total and immediate abolition of the slave trade';[35] and it was here that the many days he had spent in painstaking analysis of population numbers bore fruit. Improvements in the treatment of slaves in recent decades, he maintained, had made it possible for the slave population to grow naturally: 'In Jamaica there is at this time an actual increase of population among the slaves begun.'[36] This development could be hastened by slave-trade abolition: 'When the manager shall know that a fresh importation is not to be had from Africa, and that he cannot retrieve the deaths he occasions by any new purchases, humanity must be introduced; an improvement in the system of treating them will thus infallibly be effected, an assiduous care of their health and of their morals, marriage institutions, and many other things as yet little thought of, will take place; because they will be absolutely necessary.'[37]

In widening his message of reassurance, Wilberforce now employed

one of the time-honoured tricks of parliamentary debate, that of inviting his opponents to agree with a proposition before immediately
showing that it is groundless, thus discouraging others from showing
agreement with them for the remainder of the debate. Carefully, he
invited his opponents into the trap:

> I have in my hand the extract from a pamphlet which states, in
> very dreadful colours, what thousands and tens of thousands will
> be ruined; how our wealth will be impaired; one third of our
> commerce cut off for ever; how our manufactures will droop in
> consequence, our land-tax will be raised, our marine destroyed,
> while France, our natural enemy and rival, will strengthen herself
> by our weakness.[38]

His critics obligingly fell into the trap: with 'a cry of assent being
heard from several parts of the House',[39] Wilberforce revealed that the
pamphlet had been written fifteen years before, about the independence of the American colonies.

> I would therefore ask gentlemen, whether it is indeed fulfilled? Is
> our wealth decayed? Our commerce cut-off? Are our manufac-
> tures and our marines destroyed? Is France raised upon our ruins?
> On the contrary, do we not see, by the instance of this pamphlet,
> how men in a desponding moment will picture to themselves
> the most gloomy consequences, from causes by no means to be
> apprehended?[40]

Seventh, he appealed to British self-interest: 'The next subject which I
shall touch upon, is, the influence of the slave trade upon our marine;
and instead of being a benefit to our sailors as some have ignorantly
argued, I do assert it is their grave.'[41] Running through the all-too-
revealing statistics which Thomas Clarkson had assembled in Liverpool
and Bristol, he concluded that 'many of these valuable subjects are,
from sickness and the dire necessity from entering into foreign employ
for maintenance, lost to the British nation'.[42]

    Finally, he gave his audience a choice between inspirational reform
or guilty inaction. If Britain led the way, France would follow, for its
new leader, Monsieur Necker, 'has actually recorded his abhorrence of

the slave trade'.[43] It was Britain that could escape from the 'mortification' the country should feel at 'having so long neglected to think of
our guilt, or to attempt any reparation!'[44] Instead, the nation could
'withdraw from these wretched Africans those temptations to fraud,
violence, cruelty and injustice, which the slave trade furnishes';[45] and
now he presented the inescapable choice to those around him:

> There is a principle above every thing which is political; and when
> I reflect on the command which says, 'Thou shalt do no murder'
> believing the authority to be divine, how can I dare to set up any
> reasonings of my own against it? ... The nature and all the
> circumstances of this trade are now laid open to us; we can no
> longer plead ignorance, we cannot evade it, it is now an object
> placed before us, we cannot pass it; we may spurn it, we may kick
> it out of our way, but we cannot turn aside so as to avoid seeing
> it; for it is brought now so directly before our eyes, that this House
> must decide, and must justify to all the world, and to their own
> consciences, the rectitude of the ground and principles of their
> decision ... Let not parliament be the only body that is insensible
> to the principles of national justice. Let us make reparation to
> Africa, so far as we can, by establishing a trade upon true commer-
> cial principles, and we shall soon find the rectitude of our conduct
> rewarded, by the benefits of a regular and growing commerce.[46]

Wilberforce then moved twelve resolutions setting out the facts of the
slave trade as he knew them, and inviting the Commons to agree with
a series of statements concerning the potential for a more civilised
trade with Africa and for the slave population of the West Indies to
increase naturally. As it was now well into the evening, he said he did
not expect a full debate on these resolutions that night.

His speech had been finely calculated: while disdaining passion at
the outset, its factual contents and call for action could not fail to
arouse the passions of those who agreed with him, and by speaking of
the 'avowed end'[47] of his proposals as 'the total abolition of the slave
trade' while making no reference to slavery itself, and dwelling at great
length on the potential for reproduction among the slave population,
he had rigidly adhered to the strategy of the abolitionist campaign. He

was not being dishonest: he believed very strongly that the abolition of the trade would lead quickly to a better life for those who remained enslaved, but he was advancing towards his long-term goal of the end of slavery with extreme stealth, to say the least. Such an approach was politically essential – it was vital that a sceptical Parliament was asked to adopt a measure of just and practical policy rather than the idealistic overthrow of the social fabric and economic system of its colonies.

Delivered masterfully within these constraints, Wilberforce's speech represented a compelling case for the immediate abolition of the slave trade. As a comprehensive statement of the arguments, it has stood the test of time. As an example of a reasoned appeal to legislators to find a happy combination of enlightened self-interest and humanitarian principle, it has few equals down the ages. Many saw it in such terms at the time, Burke immediately hailing it as 'most masterly, impressive and eloquent. Principles so admirable, laid down with so much order and force, were equal to anything he had ever heard of in modern oratory; and perhaps were not excelled by anything to be met with in Demosthenes'.[48] William Grenville came down from the Speaker's chair* to hail 'one of the most masterly and eloquent speeches he had ever heard; a speech which could not fail to reflect the greatest lustre upon his hon. friend'.[49] Pitt himself spoke up in support, and another MP said that the speech had made him 'more proud of being an Englishman, than he had ever been before'.[50]

The opponents of abolition, however, were ready too. As Wilberforce noted, 'All my assertions were flatly contradicted.'[51] Lord Penrhyn was on his feet within seconds of Wilberforce sitting down, to claim 'that no reliance whatever could be placed on the picture he had chosen to exhibit'.[52] Mr Gascoyne was up next, telling the House that there was scarcely an assertion Wilberforce had made 'that was not contradicted by respectable authority'.[53] Sir William Young rose to argue that abolition would result in a clandestine trade being created, in which 'the sufferings of the Africans would be ten times greater than any they

---

* In those days the Speaker was allowed to leave the chair to give his own opinions, a practice forbidden in more recent times.

now felt'.[54] And Alderman Newnham of London declared that 'he could not give his consent to a proposition which . . . would fill the city with men suffering as much as the poor Africans'.[55] These speeches were the first sign of vigorous opposition in the Commons. There seems little doubt, as Clarkson later claimed, that the opponents of abolition had been thrown onto the defensive by the mass of evidence presented to the Privy Council which favoured the abolitionist cause, and by the detailed information with which Wilberforce could support his arguments. But in the nine days between 12 May and the resumption of the debate on the twenty-first, they regrouped and coordinated their tactics to good effect. Apparently judging that they were too weak in numbers simply to vote down the resolutions Wilberforce had moved, they abandoned the previous assumption that they could knock the whole project on the head, and played instead for the maximum possible delay. To the frustration of Pitt and Fox, a string of MPs argued that the Privy Council evidence was insufficient, and that the House of Commons must hear its own evidence: failure to do so would 'abandon their privileges, and furnish an example fundamentally injurious to their own rights'.[56] With some reluctance, Wilberforce agreed that evidence for and against the trade would be examined by the House of Commons as a whole, with witnesses called before it.

This apparent failure by Wilberforce to press home his advantage and bring his resolutions to a vote, with the parliamentary session of 1789 less than two months from its end, has generally been judged harshly by historians. In later life, Wilberforce felt it necessary to take issue with one historian who argued that he 'ought to have availed myself of the favourable feelings towards our cause which were then generally prevalent, whereas by my dilatory course I suffered them to die away'.[57] More recent writers have accused Wilberforce of being too 'gentlemanly'[58] and acting 'as if his opponents had only the best of intentions',[59] while being 'a poor strategist'.[60] Others have thought that his moving of twelve weighty resolutions rather than a simple motion in favour of abolition allowed the Commons to 'wander down into a maze where his opponents could regain the initiative'.[61]

It is certainly true, with the benefit of hindsight, that the summer of 1789 represented a most propitious time for assembling a majority in favour of abolition, and that events beyond the shores of Britain in the succeeding years would only make Wilberforce's task harder. However, he can hardly be faulted for not foreseeing events which no one in the world expected. Even had he enjoyed such powers of foresight, it is hard to see that his cause could have benefited from him acting otherwise than as he did, given the parliamentary procedures and the balance of opinion at the time. As he put it himself in his own defence: 'Tho' a resolution condemning the Slave Trade in general might have been obtained, it was only thro' the medium of an Act of Parliament that such a Resolution could be carried into effect,'[62] and this would no doubt have required the taking of a good deal of evidence, and would thus have made no difference to what now transpired. Later experience would additionally show that the idea that the passing of a motion condemning the slave trade would necessarily be followed in the next year by Parliament outlawing it was a fallacy. In any case, it seems likely that the result of bringing the matter to an immediate vote could not have been predicted with certainty: while the opponents of abolition lacked the numbers to quash the idea entirely, Wilberforce almost certainly also lacked the numbers to bring matters to a head without first giving his opponents every opportunity to present their case. Furthermore, a rushed decision by the House of Commons would have been flatly rejected in the House of Lords, with the outcome that matters would have moved no further forward at all.

Only a united cabinet with a reliable majority on this issue in both Houses of Parliament could have secured the quick abolition of the slave trade in 1789, but none of these factors was applicable. Wilberforce may have been gentlemanly, but he was already an experienced parliamentarian who was alert to all the opportunities of Commons procedures. He was also advised and counselled throughout this period by William Pitt, whose recent triumph in the Regency crisis had revealed him to be one of the foremost procedural tacticians of the age. The idea that these two men had a weaker grasp of the procedural possibilities open to them than the commentators of two hundred years later should be discounted.

Politically necessary though the hearing of more evidence was, Wilberforce evidently had no idea of the sheer grinding length of the parliamentary stalemate which would now ensue. His opponents took up time so effectively that after four full days of hearing evidence on the floor of the Commons, only two witnesses had been examined. Subsequent days were thinly attended, and the end of the session approached: on 23 June the whole matter was deferred until the following year. Dolben's regulations of the previous year were renewed, but only after Liverpool MPs had succeeded in blocking any move to increase the amount of deck space available to each slave. The opening manoeuvres of the battle to abolish the slave trade were over. The long war of attrition had begun. Muncaster's view, written to Wilberforce in May from the vantage point of the House of Lords, had proved correct: 'It appears to me that you will not make any effectual progress this year . . . Immediate abolition will not go down in our House and gradual will be stifled in the other.'[63]

It was a sad summer for the abolitionists. On 21 July James Ramsay died at Teston, his declining health apparently broken by the vituperative attacks on him launched by Crisp Molineaux MP in the debate of 21 May. Molineaux, a hard-line opponent of abolition, had few regrets. 'Ramsay is dead,' he told his son. 'I have killed him.'[64]

It had been an exhausting session of Parliament for Wilberforce, but by the beginning of the summer recess in June he was planning to go to Paris. The Commons debates had shown that the prospect of the French continuing with the slave trade while Britain abolished it represented a huge difficulty in the minds of many MPs; now, as the French Third Estate formed itself into a National Assembly and the demands for liberty and equality echoed through the streets of Paris, there was a revived prospect that the French would abolish the trade themselves. As Thomas Clarkson recalled, 'Mr Wilberforce, always solicitous for the good of this great cause, was of the opinion that, as commotions have taken place in France, which then aimed at political reforms, it was possible that the leading persons concerned in them might, if an application were made to them judiciously, be induced to take the slave trade into their consideration, and incorporated among the abuses to be done away.'[65] With the leading French Minister, Jacques Necker, publicly in favour of abolition, Wilberforce's hopes were high.

By mid-July the disorder in Paris was reaching such a pitch that senior MPs were advising Wilberforce that it was neither safe nor wise to travel there. On the night of 13 July he 'determined not to go abroad'.[66] It was on the very next day that Louis XVI lost control of his capital, the revolutionary crowds taking the hated Bastille by storm. Instead it was Clarkson who went to Paris at the behest of Wilberforce and the Committee in early August, finding many sympathisers with abolition but a Revolution that was spinning out of anyone's control. In the fevered atmosphere prevailing in Paris, Clarkson was welcomed by leading figures such as the comte de Mirabeau, but accused by others of being a British government spy. Spying was indeed taking place, since Clarkson discovered that two of the six-man committee ostensibly supporting him were actually in the pay of French slave merchants and reporting back to them. It was October before he could arrange a meeting he desired with sympathetic members of the National Assembly, but as bad luck would have it this coincided with the next crucial moment in the Revolution: the forcible removal of the King and Queen from Versailles and their return to Paris as prisoners of the crowd – 'After this, things were in such an unsettled state for a few days, and the members of the National Assembly were so occupied . . . that my little meeting of which it had cost me so much time and trouble to procure the appointment, was entirely prevented.'[67]

Clarkson was to find many converts to his cause in France. The Archbishop of Aix, on seeing the diagram of the *Brookes*, 'was so struck with horror, that he could scarcely speak'.[68] Yet even at a time of egalitarian idealism, the French baulked at approving abolition. Many mistrusted Britain for having discussed it at length and taken no decision. The French plantation-owners of Saint-Domingue (present-day Haiti) knew they were sitting on a powderkeg of discontent among the black slave majority on their island, and were fearful of anything which tended towards emancipation. French slave traders, less democratic in their instincts than their filibustering counterparts at Westminster, issued death threats to Clarkson and his collaborators, claiming that three hundred people had sworn to kill them if necessary. After six months, the valiant Clarkson left Paris in deep disappointment. The beginnings of the French Revolution had looked like a wonderful opportunity for the abolitionists; soon its violent and all-encompassing nature would become the biggest obstacle to their efforts.

It was as well that Wilberforce did not go to Paris himself, for his health was still uncertain. Instead, he set off to Bath in late July, taking the waters with his sister and his cousin Henry Thornton, whom he thought an 'excellent, upright, pure, and generous young man'.[69] Once restored to some extent at Bath, his summer progress around the country was vintage Wilberforce. Staying with Hannah More and her sisters at Cheddar Gorge, he was distracted from the scenery by the sad state of the local population, and started thinking of schemes to provide for the education of their children. Recording his progress in life the day before his thirtieth birthday, he concluded: 'What shame ought to cover me when I review my past life in all its circumstances! With full knowledge of my Master's will, how little have I practised it!';[70] and after he had reported his weak state of health to William Hey, September found him in Buxton, where he fell in with the Archbishop of Canterbury and simultaneously resolved 'to endeavour a new plan of thought . . . to keep the account plus and minus'.[71] Visiting his constituents in Sheffield in late October, and thereafter calling on his relatives in Nottinghamshire, reading and visiting all the time, he did not arrive back in London until November. By New Year's Day 1790 he was bemoaning his condition, conscious of the political struggle to come: 'My health is very bad, a little thing disorders me, at thirty and a half I am in constitution sixty. "The night cometh when no man can work" . . . Oh may divine grace protect and support me throughout the ensuing campaign.'[72]

When Parliament resumed that January, Wilberforce returned to the political equivalent of trench warfare in the Commons. Seeing that the continued hearings of evidence on the floor of the House would become so protracted and tedious that they would peter out altogether, Wilberforce moved at the end of January that a small committee should be appointed to do the job, albeit one that any Member could choose to attend. This essential manoeuvre raised many protests from the other side, but it certainly speeded up the hearing of evidence, and led to a small band of MPs devoting many hours a day to the slave trade for the next four months. At first there were four or five MPs on each side, then eventually only two or three, with Wilberforce enjoying the constant support and companionship of William Smith, a Unitarian wholesale grocer who was Member for Sudbury. His days were as busy as they had ever been, with the committee sitting from 10 a.m. to 3 p.m. and the evenings taken up with other business on the floor of the Commons, and any spare time used for preparing witnesses and cross-examinations for the next sitting of the committee. The team who assisted with this daily labour of research, including Clarkson and his brother, became known as Wilberforce's 'White Negroes', slaving in their own way at a task which never seemed to end.

Despite the crushing weight of such work, Wilberforce was careful not to neglect other issues. He continued to be in and out of Downing Street for discussions with Pitt every few days, and found time in March to give speeches on Parliamentary Reform and the proposed repeal of the Test and Corporation Acts. He agonised at length over how to vote on the latter question, on which the carrying of repeal would have opened up the holding of public office to people outside the Church of England. It may seem surprising in a later age that an ardent Evangelical, who shared much common ground with the Methodists who were about to break away from the Church of England, should in the end decide to vote against the extension of the rights of religious dissenters. Wilberforce, however, always saw himself as working within the established Church rather than in opposition to it, and was by nature institutionally conservative. At length he came to the view that an increase in the influence of dissenters would further weaken the standing and principles of the Church. On 3 March 1790 he was part of the overwhelming parliamentary majority which kept the bar on dissenters in place for another generation.

Notwithstanding the distraction of other issues, Wilberforce had to remain ever vigilant as his committee's examination of witnesses ground on. In mid-April the defenders of the trade sprang a fresh procedural surprise: having finished the calling of their own witnesses, they moved for the House to make an immediate decision without hearing any abolitionist witnesses at all. Suddenly it was Wilberforce who was accused of delaying matters, with Bamber Gascoyne asking the House 'to consider the destructive consequences of delaying this business', even though he and his colleagues had now been obstructing it for a year.[73] Wilberforce was outraged, fearing that the abolitionist side of the argument would never be put in detail, and hurried over to Downing Street, where he 'Saw Pitt in bed, and talked with him on the enemy's impudent attempt to resist our calling evidence: at his suggestion went to Fox and saw him; also called on Burke.'[74]

This lobbying of all the parliamentary leaders secured the continuation of his committee and the hearing of his own witnesses. The assembling of volunteers to appear in this capacity was no easy matter: Clarkson combed the country for them, and Wilberforce even had to resort to enticing, as his sons wrote, 'a reluctant witness through the resistless influence of the Duchess of Gordon';[75] some sixty abolitionist witnesses presented their case over the subsequent few weeks. It would be easy, once again, to judge that Wilberforce made a tactical error in producing abolitionist witnesses rather than bringing the matter to the floor of the House for a vote. But it appears to have been the unanimous view of the abolitionist side that they would have been unlikely to win in a division held after such one-sided proceedings in the committee. As Clarkson put it:

> It was certain therefore, if the decision were to be made upon this basis, that it must be entirely in their favour. Will it then be believed that in an English House of Commons there could be found persons, who could move to prevent the hearing of any other witnesses on this subject; and, what is more remarkable, that they should charge Mr Wilberforce, because he proposed the hearing of them, with the intention solely of delay? Yes.[76]

Those witnesses who came forward were given a hard time by the anti-abolitionists. In Clarkson's words again:

> It is perhaps difficult to conceive the illiberal manner, in which our witnesses were treated by those on the other side of the question. Men, who had left the trade upon principle, and who had come forward, against their apparent interest, to serve the cause of humanity and justice, were looked upon as mercenaries and culprits, or as men of doubtful and suspicious character. They were browbeaten ... It was however highly to their honour, that they were found in no one instance to prevaricate, nor to waver as to the certainty of their facts.[77]

The evidence provided by these witnesses in what remained of the 1790 session and the opening months of 1791 was fearful and compelling, sufficiently so that Wilberforce supervised the circulation of extracts of it to all Members of Parliament. The accounts of sickening mistreatment of slaves demolished the notion that Africans were being transported into a happier world.

The committee heard an account from Grenada of a slave thrown into boiling cane juice, and dying four days later.[78] They heard that 'it is *no uncommon thing* for persons to neglect and turn off their slaves, when past labour, to *plunder, beg or starve*. General Tottenham has often met them and once in particular, an old woman past labour, who told him that her master had *set her adrift to shift for herself*. He saw her about three days afterwards, *lying dead* in the same place.'[79] The same General gave an account of seeing 'a youth, about nineteen, walking the streets, in a most deplorable situation; *entirely naked, and with an iron collar about his neck, with five long projecting spikes. His body, before and behind, his breech, belly, and thighs, were almost cut to pieces; and with running sores all over them; and you might put your finger in some of the wheals. He could not sit down ... and it was impossible for him to lie down, from the projection of the prongs.*'[80] As he could not work, his master would give him nothing to eat. Other accounts were of slaves murdered and thrown into the road, or gibbeted alive in chains.

Such evidence might be thought to have been overwhelming, but it was being heard by a small and partisan committee, while the political world had its mind on other things. And in June 1790 its proceedings were interrupted when, six years into a Parliament elected for a maximum of seven, Pitt called a general election. Wilberforce had to drop everything and hasten to Yorkshire.

The calling of a general election meant anxious moments for an eighteenth-century county Member, for if the early canvassing showed him in any way vulnerable, it would be followed by an all-out and very expensive contest. Wilberforce had won his seat in 1784 in exceptional circumstances, and it had been judged by his opponents that 'He came in in consequence of a fine speech of his own and through the momentary delirium of the County of which he could not avail himself again.'[81] They also recognised, however, that 'His visits among his Constituents in the populous parts . . . have been very frequent and thought very flattering. His attention to their correspondence has also been much spoke of and his assiduity every way in cultivating their good opinion has been unwearied.'[82] Backed by these advantages of incumbency, Wilberforce was soon rushing around Yorkshire to deter potential opponents. As it turned out, the Whigs whom he had so unexpectedly ousted six years before concluded that the general respect and affection he had now built up made him once again unbeatable, and they concentrated their efforts, successfully, on recovering one of the seats for Hull instead. Re-elected by acclamation, with Duncombe once again as his colleague, Wilberforce came closer to physical than political disaster, when he narrowly escaped from his carriage overturning and being 'dashed to pieces' on a road near Bridlington.[83] He took it as a reminder of his purpose in life: 'How many have been killed by such accidents, and I unhurt! O let me endeavour to turn to Thee.'[84]

With the new Parliament not meeting for months, Wilberforce was once again free to embark on his summer travels, soon taking in Buxton and Teston, then heading northwards again for the marriage of his sister at Buxton, and on to north Wales with Thomas Babington. It was with Babington, the Squire of Rothley Temple in Leicestershire, who had known him at Cambridge and would himself become an MP in 1800, that Wilberforce renewed his determination that October to master every detail of the evidence so far presented on the slave trade. Staying at Yoxall Lodge in Staffordshire, the home of Thomas Gisborne, who had lived in neighbouring rooms as an undergraduate, Wilberforce turned his friend's house into an abolitionist library: according to Marianne Thornton, Wilberforce and Babington 'have never appeared downstairs ... except to take a hasty dinner, and for half an hour after we have supped: the Slave Trade now occupies them nine hours daily. Mr Babington told me last night, that he had 1400 folio pages to read, to detect the contradictions, and to collect the answers which corroborate Mr W's assertions in his speeches: these, with more than 2000 papers to be abridged, must be done within a fortnight. They talk of sitting up one night in each week to accomplish it. The two friends begin to look very ill, but they are in excellent spirits, and at this moment I hear them laughing at some absurd questions in the examination, proposed by a friend of Mr Wilberforce's.'[85]

Wilberforce knew that he must bring matters to a head in the first session of the new Parliament. He returned to London in late November, armed with a total command of the facts, but only to find every other leading figure completely distracted by other issues. For one thing, Pitt was about to present a crucial budget; but it was foreign affairs which had now come to dominate the political scene.

The autumn had brought a confrontation with Spain over the right of settlement on the west coast of America, culminating in a diplomatic triumph for Pitt. Wilberforce was soon on his feet in the Commons supporting his friend. Loyally, he would do so again over war in India two months later, and then again over the far less propitious circumstances of Pitt's abortive threat of war against Russia and his humiliating climbdown before the intransigence of Catherine the Great. Most ominously of all, the French Revolution was going far beyond the establishment of a constitutional monarchy on British lines:

titles were being abolished, the Church attacked, and moderate leaders such as Necker had been driven from office. While Charles James Fox continued to commend the revolutionaries and celebrate their achievements, his long-standing ally Edmund Burke published his *Reflections on the Revolution in France*, condemning the Revolution's attack on property and abandonment of justice. Even Wilberforce found that within days of returning to Westminster, 'My mind is distracted, I get little business done and variety of affairs embarrasses me';[86] but it was of far greater consequence for him and his cause that many MPs were becoming alarmed about the future, and suspicious of radical change.

At first, Wilberforce had to fight for parliamentary time even to resurrect his committee. 'Dec 16th. Debate on taxes and my slave business put off till after Christmas ... I very angry, but I fear it was rather my wounded pride.'[87] By early February 1791 he had his committee back in action, although not without encountering opposition, and by early March, 'Never was I more busy; besides the daily examinations of the Slave Trade witnesses, there are public and private letters, county matters &c. Pray for me that I may preserve a sober mind and a single eye amidst all my distractions.'[88] The giving of evidence completed, he sought the long-awaited full-scale debate in April; the date for it was first set for the second, then the twelfth, and finally the eighteenth. It was to be the debate he had worked towards for years, with the House asked to vote on a simple motion 'to bring in a bill to prevent the farther importation of Slaves into the British colonies in the West Indies'.[89] It was obvious that the abolitionist campaign was approaching a crucial moment. Wilberforce resolved 'on as much diligent application to slave business as my health will allow'.[90] In one of the last acts of his life, John Wesley had written to him on 24 February: 'Unless God has raised you up for this very thing, you will be worn out by the opposition of men and devils; but if God be for you who can be against you. Are all of them together stronger than God? Oh, be not weary of well-doing.'[91]

Yet the terrible truth was that events had turned against the abolitionists. Despite their busy circulation of the overwhelming testimonies of the outrages of the slave trade, the abolitionist Committee had failed to maintain the activity and petitioning which had climaxed ahead of the debate of May 1789. Now it was April 1791, and as Clarkson put it, 'We had the mortification to find, that our cause was going down in estimation, where it was then most important that it should have increased in favour.'[92] The unabated violence of the French Revolution, the sweeping assertions of Thomas Paine's widely circulated *Rights of Man*, and, worse still, the emerging accounts of slave revolts in the West Indies, gave the attitudes of Members of Parliament a sharp jolt in a very conservative direction. Reports of fighting in Saint-Domingue, accompanied by atrocities committed against the white population, had reached England. In the weeks before the debate it was also known that the slaves of Martinique had risen in revolt. There were rumours of a slave uprising in Dominica; in Clarkson's words, 'Nothing less than an insurrection in Dominica – Yes! – An insurrection in a British island. This was the very event for our opponents.'[93] Wilberforce's adversaries were not slow to try to lay the blame for this at his door. When he rose on 8 April to urge Members to read the actual evidence presented to the House, other Members rose and said that the slaves of Dominica 'had conceived an idea . . . that the Governor had the authority of the British Parliament, and of "Massa King Wilberforce" for a regulation, by which they should not be obliged to work more than three days a week, and be paid two shillings a day . . . Their design had been to cut the throats of all the white inhabitants at a given hour at supper, and to possess themselves of the island.'[94]

On the afternoon of 18 April 1791 Wilberforce duly rose to deliver his denunciation of the slave trade. Armed with more evidence than ever after the sittings of his committee, he added to his assertions of two years earlier by showing that British ports were in no way dependent on the slave trade, and that slaving voyages were often in any case unprofitable: 'Long might she [Liverpool] be rich and flourishing, provided it was by fair and honest gains! but it was not by this detestable traffic that she had risen to her present opulence; and that not only because it composed but a thirtieth part of her export trade, but also because it was a mere lottery – profitable, indeed, to some individuals, but a losing trade on the whole.'[95] He spoke for four hours, and even then thought, 'By God's blessing got through pretty well to others' satisfaction but very little to my own – I knowing how much omitted.'[96]

Once again he presented his case in masterly fashion, and once again he received the strong support of the two leading politicians of the land: Pitt backed his calculations in detail, while the honours of eloquence went this time to Fox: 'Here, in England, such was our indignation at every act of injustice, that a highwayman, a pickpocket, or even a pilferer, was, by law condemned to death; so jealous were we in cases where our own property was concerned! But we permitted to go unpunished crimes committed in consequence of the slave trade, in comparison with which the criminal practices of England were innocence itself.'[97] Yet the mood of the House was not with its leaders. The first speaker after Wilberforce was Colonel Tarleton, now elected for Liverpool, who said that abolition 'would instantly annihilate a trade which annually employed upwards of 5,500 sailors, upwards of 160 ships', and a huge amount of exports.[98] The next speaker summed up the mood of the Commons all too well: 'He must acknowledge that the slave trade was an unamiable trade; but he would not gratify his humanity at the expense of the interests of his country, and he thought we should not too curiously inquire into the unpleasant circumstances with which it was perhaps attended.'[99]

Wilberforce was beaten, and he knew it. In the peroration of his opening speech he revealingly declared that 'he was comparatively indifferent as to the present decision of the House. Whatever they might do, the people of Great Britain, he was confident, would abolish the slave trade, when, as would now soon happen, its injustice and cruelty should be fairly laid before them. It was a nest of serpents, which would never have endured so long, but for the darkness in which they lay hid.'[100] As for himself, 'He was engaged in a work he would never abandon . . . it is a blessed cause, and success ere long, will crown our exertion.'[101]

Looking at the sullen ranks of the House of Commons, he closed his speech with this:

Never, never, will we desist till we have wiped away this scandal from the Christian name, released ourselves from the load of guilt, under which we at present labour, and extinguished every trace of this bloody traffic, of which our posterity, looking back to the history of these enlightened times, will scarce believe that it has been suffered to exist so long a disgrace and dishonour to this country.[102]

When the House divided at 3.30 a.m. on 20 April 1791, eighty-eight MPs voted for Wilberforce's motion. One hundred and sixty-three voted against. Four years on from its confident beginning, the abolitionist cause had met outright defeat.

9

'An Overflowing Mind'

------◆◆◆------

I resolve to endeavour henceforth to live more for the glory of God,
and the good of my fellow creatures – to live more by rule, as in the
presence of him by whom I shall finally be judged.

WILLIAM WILBERFORCE, January 1789[1]

He addressed himself to the promotion of every scheme which ingenuity, his own or others, could devise for the religious, and intellectual,
and social improvement, either of the rich or of the poor.

SIR JAMES STEPHEN, *Essays in Ecclesiastical Biography* (1849)[2]

THE YEARS BETWEEN the launch of the abolition campaign in
1787 and the heavy Commons defeat of 1791 had seen the slave
trade become the central preoccupation of Wilberforce's life. It would
remain so for decades to come. Yet despite the sometimes exhausting
demands this made on him, those same years saw him quite deliberately
expand his interests, knowledge and contacts, leading him to take up
a multiplicity of other causes in the years that followed. It was in these
years that he developed the habits, friendships and methods which
would define his days for the rest of his life. Fighting to live up to his
ideals, he waged an incessant internal struggle against what he saw as
his own weakness and frailty, while simultaneously turning in other
people's eyes into an extraordinary combination of gregariousness,
generosity and strength. While still in his early thirties, he would
become the inspiration and mainstay of one of the most influential

and altruistic groups of men ever to set out to use the British political system to advance their ideals.

There is no doubt that Wilberforce was a changed character in the eyes of his friends. Marianne Sykes recorded: 'He is now never riotous nor noisy but always very cheerful, and sometimes lively but he talks a great deal more upon serious subjects than he used to do. Eating beyond what is absolutely necessary for his existence seems quite given up. He has a very slight breakfast, beef or mutton and nothing else for dinner, no more that day except some bread about ten o'clock.'[3] The combination of his tiny physical frame, devoid of spare flesh or striking features, with an uplifting and endlessly enquiring personality, would always strike observers and friends of Wilberforce. Somewhat later in life, another friend, John Harford, would comment:

> His frame was at all times extremely spare, and seemed to indicate that the ethereal inhabitant within was burdened with as little as possible of corporeal adjuncts; but from this form so slight proceeded a voice of uncommon compass and richness, whose varying and impressive tones, even in common conversation, bespoke the powers of the orator. His eyes, though small, beamed with the expression of acute intelligence, and of comprehension quick as lightning, blended with cordial kindness and warmth of heart. A peculiar sweetness and playfulness characterised his mouth, his forehead was ample, and his head well formed; and though there was not a single handsome feature, yet the mingled emanations of imagination and intellect, of benevolence and vivacity, diffused over his countenance a sunny radiance, which irresistibly attracted the hearts of all who approached him.[4]

While Wilberforce's appearance was utterly traditional – he wore powder in his hair long after Pitt's taxes would drive it from fashion, and maintained a standard of dress and appearance which 'were those of a thorough gentleman of the old school'[5] – there was nothing stiff about his manner: 'No one could be in his company without hearing his noble sentiments, or allusions to schemes of benevolence, or expressions of sympathy and kindness propounded in the silvery tones of his voice, in the most natural and easy manner.'[6] Even as a child he had been highly sociable: now his natural love of company had found a purpose, that of 'bringing together all Men who are like-minded, and who may probably at some time or other combine and concert for the public good'.[7] 'Never omit any opportunity,' he would later tell his son Samuel, 'of getting acquainted with any good or useful man.'[8] Sir James Stephen, son of the James Stephen who had become an important ally in Wilberforce's abolitionist work, recalled that Wilberforce was endowed with such 'genial warmth and graciousness of temper' that his kindness to all who met him 'expanded with such a happy promptitude, that ... he might have passed for the brother of every man, and for the lover of every woman with whom he conversed'.[9] Society was 'the necessity of his existence', and whoever he was with, he was among 'the most eminent in wit, in genius and learning'.[10]

It was at mealtimes that Wilberforce's irrepressible sociability was most regularly on display, Harford enjoying observing him 'carrying on a discussion while in the act of carving a large joint – often addressed by others interlacing his subject with exclamations at the bluntness of the knife, or paying little attentions to his guests, and then taking up the broken thread of his subject and pursuing it amidst the same sort of interruptions'.[11] Wilberforce considered that 'It was one of the distinctions between us and animals, that the latter sat munching their food by themselves, but that men have the faculty of exercising their mental powers while they satisfy the requirements of nature.'[12] He considered breakfast, then usually held mid-morning, as an important social occasion. Late at night he would still be ranging over every subject and considering his future plans – 'the midnight hour was his zenith'.[13]

Such a ready acceptance of human company, when coupled with his attentiveness to causes and constituents, and the proximity of his house to the main doors of the Palace of Westminster, was a recipe for near pandemonium when Parliament was sitting. Yorkshire manufacturers and landowners, foreign ambassadors, slave-trade experts, eager Evangelicals and hungry Members of Parliament regularly thronged his residence. Hannah More considered it like 'Noah's Ark, full of beasts clean and unclean'.[14] According to his sons, 'his ante-room was thronged from an early hour: its first occupants being generally invited to his breakfast table; and its later tenants only quitting it when he himself went out on business. Like every other room in his house it was well stored with books; and the experience of its necessity had led to the exchange of the smaller volumes with which it was originally furnished, for cumbrous folios "which could not be carried off by accident in the pocket of a coat".'[15] By three o'clock in the afternoon, MPs preparing for that day's sitting – serious business on the floor of the House usually began around 4.30 or 5 p.m. – would turn up in anticipation of lunch, sometimes numbering twenty at a time. Yet Wilberforce, and his cousin Henry Thornton, who had taken to lodging with him at 4 Old Palace Yard, never seemed to tire of such invasions: 'It delighted us to see our friends in this way, especially as it gave us the opportunity of talking upon any important points of public business without any great sacrifice of time. Those who came in late put up with a mutton-chop or beef-steak.'[16]

This happily chaotic scene of readily accepted intrusions was hardly conducive to the methodical conduct of routine business, and as a result Wilberforce's failure to keep up with the mass of correspondence, which came through his door even more rapidly than his visitors, was chronic. Even Pitt, also a hopeless correspondent on less important matters, was sometimes reduced to writing 'Pray write one line' to try to get an urgent response from him.[17] Bags of letters would accompany Wilberforce on his journeys, many of them still not attended to even when he returned. 'Again and again I have resolved to write to you,'[18] he would often have to explain, while coming up with charming excuses for his closest friends. To Muncaster he wrote: 'Another and another and another post you will say, and no letter . . . Indeed, my dear fellow, I am not to blame. In intention I have written to you again and again. But again and again has the progress of this *Intention* into *Act* been interrupted.'[19] On another occasion he wrote: 'I am over head and ears, plunged in letters to which I owe answers, and my eyes are bedusted and weak, but I could not defer writing to you.'[20] Never ceasing to bemoan the weight of mail which awaited his attention, he would write to his constituent Samuel Roberts in later life: 'My dear Sir, Did you but see the list of my unanswered correspondents, you would own that my sending back even three hasty lines in return for your kind letter was a friendly attention.'[21] It did not help matters that he was so often surrounded by frenetic activity, and letters flying in all directions, that he often could not remember whether he had replied to a letter or not. Letters would emerge several weeks after they had been received, from the inside of newspapers or, in the case of a letter from the future President of the United States John Quincy Adams, stuck to the top of a desk drawer. When he did put pen to paper, however, the results were as lively and as charming as his conversation. He would write hurriedly and directly, as if speaking, with similar diversions and allusions written 'with all the unguarded haste of intimacy'.[22] He would often complain that he was 'Much employed in answering an immense arrear of letters, and continual fresh masses coming in.'[23]

Charm was one reason why Wilberforce could get away with being such a dilatory correspondent, but he was also forgiven by his friends and clients because they knew that a letter to him was far more likely to produce the appropriate action or concern than it would have been if sent to most other Members of Parliament. But the result of being so busy was, in his own words, that 'Both my body and mind suffer from over-occupation.'[24] That his mind was too busy and his eyes failing him were his most familiar complaints; he wrote to one friend in January 1792: 'My eyes are but indifferent today, and I have much work for them ... Such a crowd of ideas rush into my mind, that I scarce know how to discriminate or select them.'[25] His diary entries in the autumn of 1790 had a regular refrain: 'October 8th. Unwell. Hard work – slave evidence. 9th. Eyes bad. Hard at work. 18th. Hard at work again – slave business. November 1st. Slept ill. Not being well partly through working too much.'[26] He found it difficult to still his mind, writing to William Hey: 'I am wakeful in bed, even when free from pain or disorder, if I have been reading or thinking in the evening; and I never sustain the loss of the nourishment and refreshment of sleep without feeling like a hunted hare all the next day, and being very unfit for any strenuous occupation.'[27]

It was not only slave-trade business that filled his mind with activity: his closeness to Pitt meant that he was rapidly caught up in any major political event, such as the Regency crisis, while Wyvill would regularly impress on him the need to pursue various measures of electoral reform. When Duncombe and Wilberforce took their time over bringing in a fresh Yorkshire Register Bill before the 1790 general election, Wyvill sharply reminded them that 'If you wish your Re-election to be carried with as much éclat as your first Election, you must jointly exert yourself to promote the measures in question: with-out which the zeal of many friends will abate.'[28] The effect was some-times to leave Wilberforce exhausted, Farington recalling on one occasion: 'He told me that yesterday he did not feel well, he wanted more rest; – without nine hours rest he cannot go on comfortably, on which account when he has been kept up in the House of Commons till four or five o'clock in the morning he always lays in bed till twelve or one o'clock that day.'[29]

Yet, in common with most other public figures who are drained by the almost irreconcilable demands made of them, Wilberforce drew great strength from his private moments and passions. Mentally, he seemed to be sustained and fortified by his voracious reading. Books of huge variety, according to James Stephen, 'were all in turn either lightly skimmed, or diligently studied . . . He searched them to detect the various springs of human action, and their influence on the welfare of the great brotherhood he loved so well.'[30] He read sermons, speeches, theology, the Greek New Testament, missionary accounts, legal com-mentaries, biographies and collections of letters, carrying a large number of books with him wherever he went so that he could skip from one to the other and enjoy favourite passages once more. As Harford observed:

> His mental energy never flagged. We were often amused at the capacities of his pockets, which carried a greater number of books than would seem . . . credible: and his local memory was such that, drawing out any author, he seemed instantaneously to light on the passage which he wanted. In addition to the stores of his pockets, a large green bag full of books filled a corner of his carriage, and when we stopped at our inn in the evening it was

his delight to have this bag into the parlour, and to spread part
of its stores over the table. He kindled at the very sight of books.[31]

His love of reading is confirmation that, alongside his enjoyment of
company, Wilberforce was rarely unhappy with solitude. His favourite
moments in the Lake District had been 'when in the early morning I
used to row out alone, and find an oratory under one of the woody
islands in the middle of the Lake'.[32] For Wilberforce, reading, travelling
and gazing out on the countryside joined together as a splendid opportunity both to learn and to contemplate his actions. He had always
adored rural England: like so many of his earliest characteristics, this
passion seemed to have been enhanced and fortified by his later faith
– 'Whoever was his companion was sure to see him full of delight
at the various beauties or wonders of nature.'[33] Marianne Thornton
reported that 'He used to go into ecstasies especially about flowers.'[34]
Harford said that 'Of flowers he was peculiarly fond. He delighted to
gaze upon their colours and to investigate their structure; and most of
his favourite pocket authors were thickly set with them in a dried state.
It was often hard to persuade him to quit the garden for the breakfast
table, and when he made his appearance it was generally with a flower
in his hand. Once there, he was sure to be the life of the party.'[35]

It was through nature that Wilberforce put politics into perspective.
Writing to Muncaster of 'enjoying the first greetings of summer – the
nightingales are abundant', he could say, 'my heart is warmed and
thankful for the unequalled blessings I enjoy. I look down with unaffected superiority on the contentious sparrings of our political parties.'[36]
He saw flowers as 'the smiles of the deity. How delightful an ordinance
of Providence is the smile. What cheerfulness does it diffuse around!'[37]
On another occasion he exclaimed, 'what should we think of a friend
who had furnished us with a magnificent house and all we needed,
and then coming in to see that all had been provided according to his
wishes, should be hurt to find that no scents had been placed in rooms?
Yet so has God dealt with us. Surely flowers are the smiles of his
goodness.'[38]

Flowers, books, and occasional solitude in the parliamentary recess in the second half of each year fought a running battle in Wilberforce's mind with the endless distractions and temptations which buffeted him in the parliamentary sittings of each winter and spring. While nature allowed him to feel close to God, political machinations often had the opposite effect, as extracts from his diary in December 1790 seem to show:

> December 1st. Dined R. Smith's – Pitt . . . Dundas, Bankes – staid too long – came home heart-sick. My heart cold in religious exercises. 2nd. My mind is distracted – I am embarrassed by too great a variety of objects. 13th . . . I have lately been tempted to vanity and pride. Many symptoms occur to my recollection. Pleased with flattery. To Pitt's, where a great circle of House of Commons chiefly on taxes &c. Oh how foolish do they seem so to neglect heavenly things![39]

He found he had to fight against the inevitable desire, shared by most men involved in British politics from the Norman Conquest to the present day, to be awarded a peerage. After spending time with Pitt and Dundas,

> I used to find myself gradually led away into their way of talking about things and of estimating them, at about places, and titles &c. I often detected myself in thinking, 'why should not I get a title and soon?' How difficult it is to keep our obligation to God continually in company now. How often have I carried a paper in my pocket to look at, to put me in mind of such things. I remember once putting a stone in my shoe when I was in high spirits, and was going to spend the evening in company.[40]

The result was a long-running internal tug-of-war, with regular affirmations of his good intentions followed by almost equally regular confessions to himself that he was not living up to them. While the struggle against the slave trade was the greatest challenge he faced in the world outside his own mind, inside it he waged a contest which he often found even more difficult, trying again and again to stick to his adopted principles while surrounded by the plots, manoeuvres and heavy drinking sessions of his long-standing friends. Time and again he adopted rules by which he intended to live, as when he arrived at Rayrigg in the summer of 1788: '1. To be for the ensuing week moderate at table. 2. Hours as early as can contrive. Redeeming the time.'[41] At the end of that year he began to keep tabular records of how he had used his time each day. A typical day when Parliament was sitting would include seven and a half hours of House of Commons business, eight and a quarter hours in bed, five and a half hours of 'requisite company &c visits &c', three-quarters of an hour of serious reading and meditation, a quarter of an hour unaccounted for or dressing, and one hour 'squandered'.[42] Yet often in the years that followed he would be writing, 'exceeding my rules. I re-resolve humbly imploring pardon for Christ's sake,'[43] or noting on the last day of the parliamentary session in 1789, 'Henceforth a reform to be attempted. Earlier hours. Attention to health – bodily, mental, intellectual.'[44] Only a few months later he was bemoaning: 'Oh how difficult it is to keep alive in the soul any spark of the true spirit of religion! . . . For the ensuing week let it be my main care to exterminate a sensual spirit rather by substituting better regards in its place.'[45] After the defeat of his motion in 1791 he noted, 'I thank God that this town season is nearly over, I hope the next will be better. I now resolve on – more temperance, mens regl,* more devotion, more solitude (Milner's hint), no company after House at night, less bustle by day.'[46]

Wilberforce's self-criticism was relentless. Most of the time, his own assessment of how he performed against a daily list of desired objectives was 'baddish', 'very bad' or 'forgot', and only occasionally did he record 'middling' or 'rather better'. No observer could have considered his assessment of himself in August 1791, while staying at Temple Rothley, to be fair to one who had spearheaded the abolitionist campaign for four demanding years while simultaneously attending to a multitude of other matters:

> My eyes being indifferent I cannot note down at large the particu-
> lars of my state . . . Alas! Could I now write at large I should have

---

* 'Mensa' meaning 'table' in Latin. This phrase meant 'table regulations': his rules on moderation at meals.

only to record my own disgrace. (What advantages have I possessed how shamefully have I abused them: I scarce dare to believe
myself a child of God, for though I don't give in to many pastimes
of worldly men, though I abstain from gross vice; how little can
I say I have the renewed mind) ... My besetting sin seems to be
a volatility of mind ... (Again – I suffer much from a carnal
sensual disposition ...) – my peace of conscience disturbed ... I
have been sadly inattentive when engaged in study: let me henceforth be not slothful in business.[47]

Three weeks later he considered himself little better, writing out an
alphabetical list of his faults which included:

A = Forgetfulness of God and Christ and losing sight of them
B = Too sensual a mind, and too earthly
C = Mensa: Regl. Freq.
D = Inattentive in study
E = Peevish towards inferiors
F = Not friend enough to Mother and Sally
G = Not thoughtful for friends spiritual good. I in general too
    selfish
H = Vain and conceited and captious in company
J = Evil speaking
K = Wandering in Prayer – particularly at family devotions: and
    little seriousness in reading scripture
L = Little or no gratitude to God for my many comforts (at
    meals), friends &c &c.[48]

A week later he considered himself as barely improved at all:

My eyes being bad, I cannot write by candlelight yet let me take
up a pen for one moment to record my own sad failures. Alas!
Alas! How weak am I! ... Today also I have gone to the patience
of the bounds of temperance too far for Sunday, too far to allow
me to relish spiritual things – and then must I reproach myself
with having failed last week in No.s A,B,E,F,G,H,J,K, L ... this
week I will endeavour by his Grace to attend particularly to the
faults.[49]

This was a struggle in which 'religion is still too much a toil to me, and not enough of a delight'.[50] Yet, for all the agonising struggle going on inside him, the reality in the eyes of other people was that an ever stronger and more principled man was steadily succeeding in applying his ideals. For one thing, the same frankness and humility with which he scribbled in his diary became reflected in his outward character. He once told a beggar that 'I am only a poor sinner like yourself,'[51] and was known to ask friends, 'In all your conversation and correspondence with me, be candid and open, and point out all my faults.'[52] He was revolted by flattery. Gisborne apparently 'never saw in him so much display of temper as when he received a servile letter from someone wishing to become ingratiated with Pitt, exclaiming "How much rather would I have the man spit in my face!"'[53] His readiness to confront others over their behaviour in a straightforward way sometimes brought unexpected dividends:

> A gentleman came to my house who was a good deal in the habit of swearing, & he did so whilst in my house. I thought it right to let him know that I had observed it & thought it very wrong & therefore I wrote to him & told him of it, saying at the same time that no one else but ourselves knew it. Well he wrote back to me in a very angry manner, & begged me to return him a book which he had given me as a pledge of kindness. I wrote to him again sending back the book but of course assuring him again that no one but ourselves knew any thing of the matter. He wrote back to me as soon as he was cool & thanked me for the whole affair and sent me back another book![54]

The keeping of the Sabbath, and its proper use for reflection and study, became of high importance to Wilberforce. His son Samuel wrote that 'He spoke much of the delight of the Sunday as a day specially appointed for the consideration of high and heavenly things. Especially to those who like himself were harassed during the week by perpetual business.'[55] Sometimes he would note that he was 'much affected all day with a sense of heavenly things' on Sunday,[56] but on other Sundays he would record: 'for want of a plan lost the value of this day sadly'.[57] Just as he managed to turn away from most offensive activities on the

Sabbath, so he increasingly succeeded in distancing himself from various pleasures and festivals of which he disapproved. Most Members
for Yorkshire would have considered it political suicide to resign the
stewardship of York races and divert the subscription to a hospital,
while also refusing to attend other summer festivities, but Wilberforce
did all of this without seeming to pay any political penalty: 'I could
not consistently with my principles frequent the theatre and ballroom
and I knew that I should give offence by staying away were I actually
at York; but no discontent was ever expressed at my not presenting
myself to the county on these occasions. My friends appeared tacitly
to admit to my claim to the command of my own time during the
recess.'[58] His diligence in attending to Yorkshire's affairs thus gave
him the freedom to regulate his own conduct and maintain personal
standards which most of his constituents would have found strange.

It was trickier, however, for him to resist another common practice
of the late eighteenth century: a challenge to a duel. In a Commons
debate of April 1792, Wilberforce would bring up the cruelty to slaves
meted out by a Captain John Kimber, who had allegedly flogged to
death a pregnant slave girl aged fifteen. Kimber was subsequently tried
for murder but acquitted, following which he pursued Wilberforce
with menace and the threat of violence. Demanding 'a public apology,
£5,000 in money, and such a place in the government as would make
me comfortable',[59] he began to call regularly at Wilberforce's house
and to lie in wait for him in the street. Kimber was eventually persuaded
to back off by Lord Sheffield, a senior defender of the slave trade but
one who deprecated such threats to Wilberforce, although what means
of persuasion were employed is not known. Even so, at one stage that
summer Wilberforce took an armed bodyguard with him on his travels
in addition to his usual contingent of a private secretary and a valet,
while maintaining a philosophical air in correspondence with his
friends: 'I can't say I apprehend much, and I really believe, that if he
were to commit any act of violence it would be beneficial rather than
injurious to *the cause*.'[60]

That summer he received a direct challenge to a duel from another
naval captain. Never in his life had he wanted for courage, but duelling

was rising high up his list of unacceptable behaviour, and he opted for 'a proper and easy explanation of my determination and views in respect to duelling' rather than taking up the challenge.[61] Honour would normally have demanded meeting such a challenge, but no one seems to have accused Wilberforce of cowardice or thought it appropriate that this increasingly distinguished Member of Parliament should have to bother about duelling with discontented naval officers. By now Wilberforce was used to threats, either of violence or libel. In the summer of 1787, as he embarked on the abolitionist campaign, he received abusive letters from a Wimbledon man, Anthony Fearon, who threatened to publish a serious libel. Its contents have never become known. Public figures, then as now, were used to putting up with unsubstantiated rumours circulating about them: Pitt was the subject of frequent innuendo about his sexuality or mental stability and, with more certain justification, his heavy drinking. In the case of Wilberforce, the rumours varied from him having owned slaves in the West Indies and sold them just before taking up the abolitionist cause, to him having secretly married his sister's maid. Whatever Fearon's allegations, they caused Wilberforce some anxiety – '*at all events* he must not be permitted to publish'[62] – but the threatened publication never took place.

Wilberforce's reaction to such a threat was a charitable one – 'It is very painful to me to think that his family may want the necessities of life'[63] – and although he would not send money openly in the face of attempted blackmail, he arranged for his friend Henry Addington, shortly to be Speaker of the House of Commons, to find some employment for Fearon's wife. This can be interpreted as generosity of spirit, or alternatively as indirectly buying off a blackmailer. Wilberforce was at pains, however, to ensure that Fearon, who would die in 1790, did not know the origin of the help he would receive, writing to Addington, 'Tho' even here great caution is necessary lest with the circumstances . . . it might seem as if you had regarded him as an injured man, and I had therefore taken him under your patronage.'[64]

For this to have been a simple act of generosity would in no way be surprising, for Wilberforce was hugely and routinely generous to many individuals and causes when he became aware of their needs. Never having been interested in his wealth when he first came into it, his conversion had brought out in him a disdain for the possession of large amounts of money for its own sake: 'It was not for instance asked in the House of Commons when a man had made an able speech "How much is he worth?"'[65] By the early 1790s he was giving away £2,000 a year (the equivalent of around £200,000 today), which approximated to about a quarter of his income. His son Samuel later wrote: 'He spoke of a sum of money which had been unexpectedly paid him. He said he thought it was an absolute duty always to spend a considerable portion of such money in charity. That it was giving to God according to your increase, and that he believed that there was an especial present blessing on such conduct.'[66] When he agreed to a request for money, he always tried to ensure that the applicant used it to improve his or her condition for the future; but he was reluctant to leave anyone destitute, writing in one case: 'I do it only because it would be ruin to him to withhold it . . . I have solemnly assured him it should be the last time of my assisting him and have given him parting advice . . . He dislikes me and feels no gratitude to me, I know, for what I have done.'[67]

The beneficiaries of Wilberforce's philanthropy varied from a debt-ridden naval officer who needed a uniform, to clergymen wishing to distribute money among the poor and, later in his life, to people imprisoned for their debts. Above all, they included young people who needed support for their education, particularly if they could go on to a place in the Church. He gave generously and consistently to the Elland Society, run by his friend William Hey, which supported bright but poor students from Yorkshire. With his need to educate himself belatedly after the wasted years of his youth always pressing on his mind, the education of others became a passion for him, and one which found a powerful outlet from the summer of 1789 when he stayed with Hannah More and her sisters in Somerset. His acquaintance with Hannah More was to become one of the greatest friendships of his life. With many mutual friends and interests, they hit it off at once. She regarded Wilberforce as 'one of the most extraordinary men I ever knew for talent, virtue and piety. It is difficult not to grow wiser and better every time one converses with him.'[68] Fairly extraordinary herself, More wrote tragedies and poetry, was a close friend of David Garrick and lived in fashionable circles, whilst slowly joining Wilberforce in Evangelical beliefs.

It was More who introduced Wilberforce to Charles Wesley, who blessed Wilberforce, with the result that 'I don't think I ever was so much affected, he had such a fine appearance, and it was the first time I had ever seen him; I quite burst into tears, I could not at all contain myself.'[69] It was More too who helped to mobilise the growing spirit of philanthropy with which he regarded his wealth. When they visited the Cheddar Gorge and were appalled by the absence of any education for the children there, Wilberforce said to her, 'If you will be at the trouble, I will be at the expense,' opening up several years in which More battled to establish schools with Wilberforce's money. This was often in the teeth of local opposition: one civic leader begged her not to think 'of bringing any religion into the country, it was the worst thing in the world for the poor, for it made them lazy and useless'. The More sisters persisted, and within two years Wilberforce was able, on another visit to Cheddar, to visit a large congregation of children being educated at his expense, and hear them sing 'Praise God, from whom all blessings flow'.[70]

Alongside his bountiful public charity, Wilberforce increasingly succeeded in getting himself to think carefully about what he could do for each of the people he knew. Eventually he made long lists of how he could help his friends, enjoining himself to study the list every Sunday:

> S— and Mrs. What books reading? To give them good ones.
> Walker's Sermons. Call on Mrs S and talk a little . . . Education
> of their children, to inquire about . . .
> The J—'s. Call and sound them on religion. Give them money
> to give away, &c. Little presents.
> Lord and Lady J. See them. Get them through G. Discover what
> books reading.

S— and Mrs. Call – Civility, &c . . . Countenance them with
their relations . . .

J— and G—S—. More civil to.

Dr and Mrs W. Civility. Him to dinner, &c. Call on her, and
find what books proper, and give them. Query, family prayer?

W.B—. Present to, and try and talk with her.

H.M and R.B—. More civil to, and inquire . . .

Lady E—. Speak pretty openly, yet tenderly.

Lady A— and Sir R. Has he read Doddridge? . . .

Mr and Mrs M—. Encourage to family prayer, &c.

Mrs R.S— and R. Kindness and attention. Hints to her, and
showing that more within, if I durst let it out. Tell her my own
story.

J.E—. Talk with, to give him favourable impressions of his
brother's religion.

W—. Find occasions of conciliating . . .[71]

Incredibly, at least by the standards of most politicians, Wilberforce's
concern for individuals even extended to trying to heal divisions
between political opponents. In May 1791 the long-standing alliance
between Edmund Burke and Charles James Fox was rent asunder by
their violently opposed views on the French Revolution; Wilberforce
noted in his diary 'the quarrel between Burke and Fox, which I had
endeavoured to prevent'.[72] Even though these two principal opposition
figures were strong supporters of abolition, they had both hitherto
been hardline opponents of Wilberforce's great friend Pitt, who, in
greater conformity with traditional parliamentary behaviour, did nothing but aggravate the quarrel between them.

Towards Pitt himself, Wilberforce remained an affectionate friend
and a dependable political ally, constantly in and out of Downing
Street and up and down the road to Holwood. Yet the boisterous
and frivolous nature of their early friendship had gone for good, and
Wilberforce's unending admiration for Pitt was tinged with sorrow.
Harford recalled that Wilberforce 'seldom mentioned Mr Pitt's name
without an affectionate epithet, and he once said to me: "I certainly
never knew, on the whole, so extraordinary a man." Occasionally, thus

speaking of him I had heard him express his deep regret, that owing to Mr Pitt being so entirely absorbed in politics, he had never allowed himself time fairly to turn his attention to religion, or to examine scripture as the rule of life.'[73] To Wilberforce, this was a distressing and serious failing. While on the one hand he could say of Pitt that he 'knew all his most private plans, and I am sure that if they had been dictated by an angel from Heaven there could not have been greater purity or a more sincere desire to do everything for the good of the country',[74] on the other hand, 'The moral improvement of the people is the great end which a Minister ought to have in view, which he, in the modern way left to itself.'[75] As a result, Wilberforce, while considering Pitt always to have acted from good motives, regarded him as not doing so in a sufficiently comprehensive way, for Pitt had not set out to create a country 'where everyone acted upon Xtian principles'.[76] Such views meant his loyalty to Pitt was no longer blind, nor was it permanently guaranteed. If Wilberforce considered that his intimate and powerful partnership with Pitt was outweighed by higher considerations, he would no longer avoid differing openly from his friend, as events were soon to show.

Wilberforce's social circle had now moved on from the Goostree set of young parliamentarians who had once frolicked in his garden at Wimbledon. Central to his new set of acquaintances was his cousin Henry Thornton, only a year younger than himself and leading an astonishingly parallel life. The son of John Thornton, Henry, like Wilberforce, inherited a sizeable fortune which had been made in the Baltic trade, but in his case he went on to expand it further with a successful banking career. Adopting the same Evangelical beliefs as his cousin, Henry gave away up to six-sevenths of his even larger income in the early 1790s, and was a banker of such integrity that he personally paid £20,000 to investors who had lost their money in a venture he had recommended to them. Having considered standing for Hull in succession to Wilberforce in 1784, he desisted when he realised he would have to buy votes in the time-honoured way, and instead became MP for Southwark, where bribery was not the fashion. He joined Wilberforce as a welcoming host in 4 Old Palace Yard and was, naturally, a stern supporter of most of the causes Wilberforce adopted.

As Wilberforce travelled the country each summer, he stayed with friends and built deep friendships with them, turning to advantage the fact that he no longer had any base of his own outside Westminster. Turning westward each year, he could visit the More sisters in Somerset while making his way to and from the Bath waters which were still deemed essential for his often faltering health. Once there, he could draw Edward Eliot to join him – 'Spa water in company will do better for me than Bath water in solitude'[77] – before doing the rounds of several country houses and taking up residence in each of them, with servants and huge quantities of books, enjoying the countryside while forever seeking a still deeper understanding of the slave trade. In the summer of 1791, in the aftermath of his defeat in the Commons, he spent much time at Rothley Temple, the house of Thomas Babington, which was 'a singularly unaltered specimen of an old English home', with an air of 'having been put to rights at the date of the Armada and left alone ever since'.[78] For Wilberforce's hosts his visits could mean some serious work, involving extended religious conversation and reading history to each other while Wilberforce applied himself to the development of further skills. While staying with Babington, he noted, 'I mean to apply to public speaking preparation'[79] – a further instance of the hunger for self-improvement in a man who was already one of the most accomplished orators of his time. From Babington's house Wilberforce liked to progress to that of Thomas Gisborne, writing to Babington with a twinkle in his eye: 'I understand he is rather more uncertain than you whether he can take me in, having taken the precaution of unroofing his house. He has not even the merit of originality, for it is an old expedient for turning out an unwelcome occupier.'[80]

Deliberately or not, Wilberforce was quietly establishing a network of friends who not only rejoiced in his company but were happy to get to know each other. When Henry Thornton employed his great wealth to buy and extend a large house at Battersea Rise in Clapham, a few miles south of Westminster, this expanding network of wealthy

Evangelicals and high-minded politicians increasingly bumped into each other there. It was the start of one of the most extraordinary and influential coalitions British society had ever seen, known to history as the Clapham Sect.

Clapham had been an isolated and swampy place until the mid-eighteenth century, when its common was drained. By 1791 it was a 'pleasant village of nightingales', with a population of 2,700 and decent roads giving easy access to the heart of London. Wilberforce had been a regular visitor in the late 1780s, once he had sold up in nearby Wimbledon, staying with his wealthy uncle John Thornton, Henry Thornton's father, when he needed respite from Westminster. When Thornton died in 1790, Henry's brothers Robert and Samuel took on the family estate at Clapham, while Henry bought Battersea Rise, a large Queen Anne house on the west side of the common.

It is difficult to escape the conclusion that Henry Thornton deliberately set out to create a colony of like-minded people in and around Battersea Rise. For one thing, he had two wings added almost immediately, creating a house which had thirty-four bedrooms in total, along with a library the plan of which was sketched out by Pitt. For another, he built two further houses in the garden. One of these, to be known as Grant Glenelg, was soon occupied by his friend Charles Grant, an Evangelical who had made a fortune in India and had returned to Britain with an utter determination that the gospel should be preached to the Indian people. Into the other house, Broomfield, came Edward Eliot, who after his wife's death had become the religious soulmate of Wilberforce, in addition to being the most intimate friend and brother-in-law of Pitt. Most important of all, Wilberforce himself took up residence in Battersea Rise when Henry Thornton settled there in 1792, both of them moving freely between this spacious new home and their cramped alternative quarters in Old Palace Yard. Wilberforce was undoubtedly the central figure in the growth of the group which now began to take shape. In later life, Henry Thornton would write:

Few men have been blessed with worthier and better friends than it has been my lot to be. Mr Wilberforce stands at the head of these, for he was the friend of my youth. I owed much to him in every sense soon after I came out in life, for my education had been narrow, and his enlarged mind, his affectionate and understanding manners and his very superior piety were exactly calculated to supply what was wanting to my improvement and my establishment in a right course. It is chiefly through him that I have been introduced to a variety of other most valuable associates, to my friends Babington and Gisborne and their worthy families, to Lord Teignmouth and his family, to Mrs Hannah More and her sisters; to Mr Stephen and to not a few respectable Members of Parliament. Second to only Mr Wilberforce in my esteem is now the family of Mr Grant.[81]

This was the nucleus of the Clapham Sect, although it was not a sect as such, and this term was never used during Wilberforce's lifetime. The Clapham group, as it might more accurately be called, thus consisted at the outset of Wilberforce, Henry Thornton, Edward Eliot and Charles Grant. Their regular visitors and lodgers included Babington, Gisborne, Hannah More and Isaac Milner, all drawn to the place by Wilberforce, while his parliamentary ally William Smith and the grandfather of the abolitionist campaign, Granville Sharp, soon moved in there. In later years they would be joined by James Stephen, when he left the Caribbean for good, Lord Teignmouth (formerly John Shore), when he came back from five impressive years as Governor General of India, and Zachary Macaulay, once he had struggled to implement in Africa one of the Clapham group's most ambitious projects. Leading Evangelicals such as Charles Simeon, resident in Cambridge, were drawn on regular visits to Clapham to commune with this powerful grouping, as was the poet William Cowper. Giving unity and spiritual guidance to them all was John Venn, the rector of Clapham parish church from 1792, son of Henry Venn, who had been a prime mover in eighteenth-century Evangelism. John was brought in by the Thorntons to preach a more openly Evangelical gospel than the one to which the Clapham congregation had been accustomed. Wilberforce found his first sermon impressive: 'Venn preached an excellent introductory sermon – I received the sacrament and had much serious reflection. Oh may it be for good! I renewed all my solemn resolves, and purpose to lay afresh my foundations.'[82] Before long, Venn was attracting large congregations, and Wilberforce was thinking that Pitt should make him a bishop.

The community created by these impressive individuals was probably also unique in its atmosphere. Wholly relaxed in each other's company, they observed no restrictions in wandering into each other's homes and gardens, discussing any great cause or biblical text that came to mind. Henry Thornton would note in his diary: 'Talked with Wilber a few hours on politics gaining much information from him ... Hurried off to dine with Dr Milner and Wilber – talked two or three hours . . .'[83] The intimacy they developed was remarkable, it being their custom 'to consider every member of that coterie as forming part of a large united family, who should behave to each other with the same simplicity and absence of formality, which, in the usual way, characterises intercourse only among the nearest relatives'. Some of the members of the group were, of course, already related to each other. In addition, Thomas Gisborne had married Babington's sister. Eventually, to confuse matters utterly, Babington married Macaulay's sister and introduced him to the group, Macaulay married one of Hannah More's pupils, James Stephen married Wilberforce's sister, and John Venn's sister married another member of the group, Charles Eliot. The Clapham group were soon bound together not only by their shared activity and philosophy, but by multiple ties of family.

Wilberforce himself seemed unlikely to submit to these matrimonial temptations. He had persistently warned himself against being taken over by sensual feelings, although when he returned to Yoxall Lodge at the end of 1791 and saw Babington being greeted by his family, he noted, 'Glad to see my friends again, and felt sadly the want of a wife and children to hail my return; yet looked up to Heaven as the true object of desire.'[84] Two years earlier he appears to have fallen briefly in love with a Miss Hammond, sister-in-law of his friend Henry Addington, who had to break it to Wilberforce that Miss Hammond had accepted another man's proposal. Wilberforce consoled himself with the reflection that such was the difference in their views and 'Plans of Life' that 'two people of as much sensibility as she and I could not have been happy together'.[85] He did not rush to find an alternative partner, concluding: 'It is very likely I shall never change my condition; nor do I feel solicitous whether I do or not.'[86] Dorothy Wordsworth considered him 'as unlikely as any man ever to marry at all as any I know'.[87]

Yet Wilberforce, while being 'the Agamemnon of the host . . . the very sun of the Claphamic system',[88] was a playful presence at Clapham, popular with children and adults alike. Some years later, when Henry Thornton had married, his young daughter Marianne felt that:

> Mr Wilberforce seemed so entirely one of our family that I cannot describe my first impression of him any more than of my own father . . . He was as restless and as volatile as a child himself, and during the long and grave discussions that went between him and my father and others, he was most thankful to refresh himself by throwing a ball or a bunch of flowers at me, or opening the glass door and going off with me for a race on the lawn 'to warm his feet' . . . I know one of my first lessons was I must never disturb Papa when he was talking or reading, but no such prohibition existed with Mr Wilberforce. His love for, and enjoyment in, all children was remarkable.[89]

The 'long and grave discussions' observed by Marianne Thornton would ultimately lead to one of the greatest varieties and volumes of charitable activity ever launched by any group of people in any age. In the twelve years that followed 1792 the Claphamites would promote charity schools in Ireland, found an asylum for the deaf and dumb children of the poor, offer relief to the poor of the City of London, launch education initiatives in Africa, and create a refuge for orphan girls. They founded the Society for Religious Instructions to the Negroes in the West Indies, the London Missionary Society, the Society for Bettering the Condition and Increasing the Comforts of the Poor, the Church Missionary Society, the Religious Tract Society, the Society for Promoting the Religious Instruction of Youth, the Society for the

Relief of the Industrious Poor, the British National Endeavour for the Orphans of Soldiers and Sailors, the Naval Society for the Support of the Orphans and Children of British Sailors and Marines, the Institution for the Protection of Young Girls, the Society for the Suppression of Vice, the Sunday School Union, the Society for Superseding the Necessity for Climbing-Boys in Cleansing Chimneys, the British and Foreign Bible Society, and the wonderfully named Friendly Female Society, for the Relief of Poor, Infirm, Aged Widows, and Single Women of Good Character, Who Have Seen Better Days. In their concern for the health of the population, Claphamites would also lead the establishment in London alone of a cancer hospital, a fever hospital, two eye clinics and a large number of other medical societies and dispensaries. Nor were these even their principal endeavours. The abolition of the slave trade remained the central cause of Claphamite thinking, and coming up behind it came two other great causes, both of them concerned with people thousands of miles from Britain.

The first was that of sending Christian missionaries to India. It demonstrated the power of the Clapham system that Charles Grant was able to infuse other members of the group, particularly Wilberforce and Charles Simeon, with this rising passion of his life, and that Wilberforce was able to take the matter to Pitt, and was soon moving an amendment in Parliament to the Charter of the East India Company, requiring it to admit Christian missionaries. As with the slave trade, this 'emphatically Claphamic' cause had a simply-stated objective, but would require many years of diligent application to bring it about. The East India Company resented such interference, and feared religious trouble in India. It managed to muster sufficient parliamentary support to have Wilberforce's amendments rejected, leaving him sadly lamenting in 1793, 'All my clauses were last night struck out on the third reading of the Bill and . . . millions of people . . . are left . . . to the Providential protection of – Brama.'[90]

The second such cause stood out still more for its unbridled idealism, and would involve the taking of huge risks with both Clapham capital and human life: the founding of a free colony on the west coast of Africa which would demonstrate to the world that a vigorous trade could be carried on without resort to slavery, and that black and white people could live together harmoniously as equals. The roots of this idea lay in Granville Sharp's famous victory of 1772, when he had forced from Lord Mansfield the judgement which showed that slavery was incompatible with British law. While any slaves held at that time in the British Isles had consequently been set free, there had been little provision or demand to enable them to find alternative employment. By the 1780s, 'the streets of London swarming with a number of Blacks in the most distressed situation, who had no prospect of subsisting in this country but by depredations on the public or by common charity, the humanity of some respectable Gentlemen was excited towards these unhappy objects'.[91] Granville Sharp was once again foremost in promoting this endeavour: 'They were accordingly collected to the number of above 400, and together with 60 whites, chiefly women of the lowest sort, in ill health, and of bad character, they were sent out at the charge of government to Sierra Leone. It was hoped that the necessity of their situation might bring them into some tolerable habits of industry and good order; and a grant of land to his Majesty from King Thom, the then neighbouring chief, was obtained for their use.'[92] Sharp set out to equip this land of liberty, on the west coast of Africa, with a constitution and fundamental laws of his own design. Settlers had to sign a contract binding themselves to the other settlers 'for the Protection and Preservation of their common Freedom'.[93] Headmen were chosen to conduct the affairs of government, householders had a voice and a Common Council, and every ten householders would form a tithing, with every ten tithings forming a hundred. Thus was the old English system of frankpledge combined with late-eighteenth-century notions of freedom. The use of money was to be resisted, with individual labour providing the medium of exchange, and a special tax levied on those unwilling to work. Indeed, the certificates given to the settlers to protect them from slave traders announced that they were free citizens of 'the colony of Sierra Leone or the land of freedom'.

Such noble ideals were to prove extremely difficult to put into practice in a land two thousand miles away, of which the scheme's designers knew little in terms of terrain and climate. A report of 1791, commenting on the initial wave of settlers of 1787, listed the difficulties as 'excessive drinking and other debaucheries; they were landed in the wet season; there was no order of regularity established amongst them; and from these causes a very great proportion of them being exposed to the weather, died very soon'.[94] Sharp was disappointed, writing: 'The greatest blame of all is to be charged on the intemperance of the people themselves; for the most of them ... became so besotted during the voyage that they were totally unfit for business when they landed, and could hardly be prevailed on to assist in erecting their huts.'[95]

These opening calamities were a mere hint of what was to come. Over the following three years, some of the surviving settlers deserted – one even becoming a slave trader himself – others struggled to survive, and at the end of 1789 a local chieftain wreaked revenge for the misbehaviour of a British warship by burning the little settlement to the ground. Sharp looked for help in salvaging his project, and it was only natural that he would go straight to Henry Thornton, William Wilberforce and others who would soon be his fellow Claphamites. With Pitt and the Treasury deaf to Sharp's requests for further financial assistance, Wilberforce was to be found, in January 1790, lobbying the Treasury for the gift of a ship, the *Lapwing*, that was about to be sold. The St George's Bay Company, soon to be renamed the Sierra Leone Company, was formed that year, with Sharp as president, Henry Thornton as chairman, and directors who included Babington, Charles Grant, Thomas Clarkson and Wilberforce. Thornton set about the administration while Wilberforce raised money, the directors resolving to raise capital of £100,000 (the equivalent of around £10 million today) to ensure that the next attempt to reinforce the colony would be well-equipped. Wilberforce and Thornton themselves subscribed liberally – another example of their generosity, given the dubious prospects of receiving any return on the money. Soon the efforts to found a durable colony became an inseparable adjunct of the abolitionist campaign, with Alexander Falconbridge sent out to reorganise the colony, and Thomas Clarkson's younger brother John in charge of the expedition which would bring a new wave of settlers to Sierra Leone. Wilberforce himself devoted huge amounts of time to the project from the beginning of 1790 onwards, his diary being littered with such comments as, 'Meeting on Sierra Leone business, morning and evening till 11 o'clock at night.'[96] Such priority did he give to these matters that he could even be wrenched from one of his favourite watering holes, Yoxall Lodge, in mid-December 1792 – 'On Thursday night last I was suddenly summoned to Town on the Sierra Leone business, and, though very reluctantly, I of course obeyed.'[97]

Given the immense practical difficulties inherent in the project, some of which were obvious even then, it may seem that the Sierra Leone Company was an ill-advised distraction for the leading abolitionists, whose time was already so heavily committed to contending for abolition itself. Yet, while perhaps less didactic than Sharp in their view of how the free settlers should live, Wilberforce and his fellow directors shared powerful idealistic motives for their enthusiasm for this project. If it were successful, they believed it would demonstrate that people formerly held as slaves were entirely capable of free and productive labour. Furthermore, it would be shown that British goods could be exported to Africa in return for local products which did not include slaves. And, in the longer term, a successful free colony could become a model for the conduct of affairs in Africa and a bridgehead from which Christianity could spread across the entire continent. Wilberforce would always be excited at the prospect of a golden future for Africa, writing to John Clarkson in 1791 that he should find 'some proper person on whom you can depend for sending up into the interior country, accounts of our settlement, specimens of our manufactures, offers to educate any promising young men, well recommended &c &c. We know there are some considerable talents in Africa, and if we could once establish connection with them it might be productive of the most intensive benefit . . . I think this idea of providing the means of *probing* the interior is never to be lost sight of. It may be attended by the most *splendid* and the most blessed consequence.'[98]

The defeat of 1791 thus gave a new impetus to the idea of making the most of Sierra Leone and attacking the very root of the slave trade. Before long, Falconbridge had found the sixty-four survivors of the original settlement, while John Clarkson was scouring the bleak villages of Nova Scotia for recruits among the four thousand former slaves who had ended up there, rather pointlessly, at the end of the American War of Independence. Promised freedom from the British, they had been taken to Nova Scotia when British forces decamped from the United States, but had been given no land there, and had found it was scarcely the place of their dreams. Now, more than a thousand joined Clarkson's voyage across the Atlantic under the auspices of the Sierra Leone Company, every settler being promised twenty acres of land for himself, ten for his wife and five for each child. The charter of the company also provided for schools to be established, for black and white settlers to be 'equally governed', and made clear that 'They will always have a large store of European goods for sale, and a force sufficient to defend it.'[99]

Wilberforce was much impressed by John Clarkson, whom he referred to as 'the Admiral', and was constantly solicitous of his welfare: 'I conceive it probable from your having left England so suddenly, that you may not have carried with you many of those little conveniences in which *you Naval gentlemen* generally *abound*, and I send you by one of the ships that are now going out a writing desk which is fitted out for dressing of which I beg your acceptance, as a token of my affectionate remembrance. The Cabinet Maker says you must keep it as much as possible both from damp and heat, but if it is injured by the climate it can be restored when you return.'[100]

Clarkson oversaw the establishment of the new colony before passing on his duties to the young Zachary Macaulay, another future Claphamite, who turned out to be an extraordinarily able administrator. Appalled by his experiences of slavery in the West Indies, he had become an Evangelical convert under Babington's guidance. He would spend most of the 1790s in Sierra Leone, guiding the fragile little colony through the worst that could be flung at it: malaria, fire, mutiny and war. The worst setback would be the virtual destruction of the entire settlement by French warships in 1794. By the time Macaulay left Sierra Leone in 1799, it was a neat and largely self-supporting settlement of 1,200 people, with wharves, fishing boats and farms. There would be fresh civil disorder there the following year, but further settlers continued to arrive, with the impressive total of eighteen thousand former slaves arriving by 1825. It was transferred to the Crown as a full-scale British colony in 1808. The site of the original settlement, Freetown, is still the capital of the twenty-first-century country of Sierra Leone. As a transformational influence on Africa and on European attitudes to Africans, it cannot be said that Sierra Leone lived up to Wilberforce's expectations. But it showed more than anything else that he and his friends, talking and playing in their gardens at Clapham, were no mere debating society. They were prepared to put their money, time and reputation behind ideas which had the potential to change the whole way in which their compatriots thought about their world.

Defeated as he had been, and distracted by a multitude of other causes as he certainly was, Wilberforce at the beginning of 1792 had no doubt about his central objective. 'I mean,' he wrote to Muncaster, 'to bring on the slave business within a month after Parliament meets, that we may then, being defeated, sound the alarm throughout the land.'[101] For the reaction of the abolitionists to their crushing defeat the previous year was one of stubbornness and determination. The greatest assault yet made on the slave trade was about to begin.

IO

The Independent

I do foresee a gathering storm, and I cannot help fearing that a
country which . . . has so long been blessed beyond all example with
every spiritual and temporal good, will incur those judgements of an
incensed God, which in the prophets are so often denounced against
those who forget the Author of all their mercies.

WILBERFORCE TO WILLIAM HEY, 1792[1]

Mr Wilberforce is a very respectable gentleman, but he is not the
people of England.

EDMUND BURKE TO WILLIAM PITT, 1795[2]

THE DEFENDERS of the slave trade had been quick to celebrate
their defeat of Wilberforce in 1791. In Bristol, church bells were
rung, a bonfire was lit, and a half-day's holiday was awarded to sailors
and workers. In the words of Thomas Clarkson, the Commons debate
of that April was viewed 'as the last spiteful effort of a vanquished and
dying animal, and they supposed that they had consigned the question
to eternal sleep'.[3] Yet although the first four years of the abolitionists'
efforts had brought a clear numerical defeat on the floor of the Commons, they had nevertheless given them something of inestimable value
for the future: an overwhelming moral advantage. Defeat did not, as
it turned out, end the debates about the slave trade. Furthermore, the
weight of evidence which the abolitionists had presented to successive
inquiries, and which could now be disseminated throughout the land,
had changed the terms of those debates forever. Ironically, from the

moment of their victory onwards, the trade's defenders rarely attempted any further substantive defence of it on its merits. The endless accounts of deaths, kidnappings, floggings and unspeakable conditions on the Middle Passage meant that efforts to portray the slave trade in a happier light could no longer credibly be attempted. In future, the defence could only be that it was not timely, politic or convenient to abolish the trade at any particular moment. Such an argument would prove immensely strong in the dark and turbulent years which lay immediately ahead, but supremely fragile when time and circumstances changed.

The convincing nature of the evidence accumulated against the slave trade is the conclusive answer to those who might have thought Wilberforce to have been dilatory in pushing forward proceedings in Parliament between 1787 and 1791. An attempt to bring matters to a head more speedily would have foundered in any case. As it was, the abolitionists emerged from the ashes of defeat bearing the crucial pillars of their evidence, published as a thirty-two-page summary, printed in many thousands of copies and sold at four pence a time. Clarkson toured the country seeking popular support, while Wilberforce wrote to friends and contacts across the country asking for supportive petitions to Parliament in advance of a fresh debate planned for early 1792: 'It is on the general impression and feeling of the nation we must rely, rather than on the political conscience of the House of Commons.'[4] At the same time, large numbers of people began refusing to use West Indian sugar (the word 'boycott' did not then exist). In Clarkson's words: 'These were of all ranks and parties. Rich and poor, churchmen and dissenters, had adopted the measure. Even grocers had left off trading in the article, in some places . . . By the best computation I was able to make from notes taken down in my journey, no fewer than three hundred thousand persons had abandoned the use of sugar.'[5]

Wilberforce was unsure about such a tactic, conscious as ever of the need to work within the system and win over the political class, and seeking a legitimate demonstration of opinion rather than that the population at large should take matters into its own hands. The result exceeded all expectations. Petitions came in from every part of the kingdom, eventually comprising 519 in total bearing some half a million signatures – the greatest such demonstration of popular opinion British politics had ever known. Even Manchester petitioned for abolition, while only four petitions were received in defence of the trade. On no other issue had the people of Britain given voice to such a collective and overwhelming conscience.

Such massive support brought renewed optimism for the abolitionists, and opened up the prospect of real progress in 1792. In many other respects too, the current of opinion was flowing in their direction. William Grenville, a convinced abolitionist, had become Pitt's Foreign Secretary in 1791. Abroad, the US Congress had decided in 1790 to outlaw the supplying of slaves to foreign ports, although this law was little enforced and the new nation's vigorous slave trade continued. In March 1792, Denmark became the first country to abolish the import of slaves from Africa to its own colonies, albeit with effect only from 1803. The cause of abolition was once again on the advance. In an otherwise static world, the prospects of securing it might have been greater than ever before.

Tragically, however, for Wilberforce and for hundreds of thousands of people who would be enslaved in the years to come, events elsewhere were soon to overshadow and eventually to engulf these signs of progress. While the current of opinion may have been in their favour, the entire tide of the political world was about to move against them. The French Revolution had initially been seen by many as a passing convulsion which would result in France becoming a constitutional monarchy, and a more peaceful neighbour for Britain. But now it was taking a course so violent, anarchic and threatening that it was becoming the defining political event of the age.

It would be difficult to overstate the impact of the French Revolution on the politics of Britain in the 1790s and the decades that followed. Clearly, the overthrow not merely of a government but of an entire system of government in Britain's nearest neighbour was an important event in itself. France was the most powerful country in Europe, and thereby in the world, at that time. Her population was around two and a half times that of the entire British Isles. For European leaders, French kings had been indispensable allies or unconquerable menaces for centuries. Yet by the summer of 1791 the French monarchy was on its knees: Louis XVI's attempt to flee the country had ended in him being hauled back to Paris, suspended from his duties and imprisoned in the Tuileries, at the apparent mercy of the mob. An ever more radicalised revolution, steadily overturning all accepted notions of monarchy, aristocracy, property, religion and justice, was not yet an immediate physical threat to its neighbours – but the ideas on which it was based increasingly were. Those ideas, of violent revolution and an end to all hereditary government, could be communicated to huge numbers of people by means of the improved printing techniques and developing transport networks which had never before been available. In the open society of Britain, radical groupings such as the Society for Constitutional Information and the London Corresponding Society expanded rapidly in size and activity, while Thomas Paine's *Rights of Man* had sold 200,000 copies within weeks of going on sale in 1791. Meanwhile, across Continental Europe, kings and emperors shifted uneasily in their palaces and readied themselves to take up arms against revolutionary doctrines. And thousands of miles away in the West Indies, news of the Revolution inspired slave communities to speak of liberty and to plan revolt.

Saint-Domingue was by far the largest French colony in the West Indies: its population of forty thousand whites and fifty thousand mixed-raced mulattos was far outnumbered by 450,000 black slaves. While the revolutionary National Assembly in Paris equivocated about whether liberty and equality were notions which should automatically be extended to slaves, the slaves of Saint-Domingue took matters into their own hands. On 22 August 1791 they rose and butchered their masters in perhaps the bloodiest and most massive slave revolt the world has ever seen. A thousand plantations were set ablaze at the beginning of what would become years of brutal violence and warfare. Whites in the plantations were murdered, raped and tortured to death amidst terrible atrocities, children bayoneted along with the rest.

Months later, when blood-curdling news of the uprising arrived in London, it added hugely to the hostility towards liberalising measures which the French Revolution had already begun to create. If the tales of the atrocities were true, one writer told the *Gentleman's Magazine*, 'It is to be hoped, for Heaven's sake we shall hear no more of abolishing the slave trade . . . the Negro race are but a set of wild beasts let loose.'[6]

In such circumstances, Wilberforce was pressed to delay any further motion on the slave trade: 'People here are all panic-struck with the transactions in St. Domingo, and the apprehension or pretend apprehension of the like in Jamaica and other of our islands. I am pressed on all hands, except by W. Smith and the committee who hear little of the matter, to defer my motion till next year.'[7] Even Pitt thought it was impossible to proceed, Wilberforce recording, 'Pitt threw out against slave motion on St. Domingo account. I must repose myself on God.'[8] But to Wilberforce's eternal credit he decided to press on – 'This is a matter wherein all personal, much more all ministerial attachments must be as dust in the balance.'[9] Looked at purely rationally, the events in Saint-Domingue were as much an argument in favour of abolition as against it: if slave populations were prone to rebellion, what sense was there in making them even larger, rather than concentrating on improving their conditions? Wilberforce was not expecting to win the debate on such arguments, but there was no tactical sense in further postponing it. The petitions were pouring in, the evidence was complete, and time and events might only make things harder. And so, on 2 April 1792, he once again prepared himself to call on the House of Commons to vote for the abolition of the slave trade, opening a debate which Edmund Burke would later describe as exhibiting 'the greatest eloquence ever displayed in the House'.[10]

Wilberforce once again emphasised at the outset of his speech that he was not calling for emancipation of the slaves. This was 'an intention he could never have entertained for a moment. He was exceedingly sensible that they were in a state far from being prepared for the reception of such an enjoyment.'[11] But he enjoyed pouring scorn on the shattered arguments of his opponents: 'When they were asked questions upon this subject, they gave first one answer and then another, going from one corner to another, and shifting their ground to conceal the real infamy of the traffic, until closely pressed and unable to defend themselves any longer, they retired from it altogether, and, like the rat, when the house was in flames, changed their station, and hid themselves in the corner of another building.'[12] Dangers such as those evidenced in Saint-Domingue, he said, 'were multiplied tenfold by the importation of Negroes; for those just arrived, being less inured to, must be more displeased with the system carried on in the West Indies'.[13]

It was a speech which demonstrated Wilberforce's confidence in his faith – 'True liberty was a plant of celestial growth, and none could perceive its beauties, but those who had employed the nobler faculties of the human soul in contemplating the goodness of the divine essence from whence it sprung'[14] – and in the evidence he had now established:

> Africa, Africa, your sufferings have been the theme that has arrested and engages my heart – your sufferings no tongue can express; no language impart! . . . It was the restoration of these poor distressed people to their rights that he had nearest at heart . . . a point which he would never abandon, until he had obtained his object; and to be entitled to it, he had made out a case so clear, so plain, so forcible, so just, so irrefragable, that he was confident there was not one person, even among those who wished well to the trade, who would deny the truth of his assertion.[15]

The conclusion of his speech, perhaps a less effective one than on other occasions, was about his own feelings: 'In his exertions for the present cause, he had found happiness, though hitherto not success; . . . it enlivened his waking, and soothed his evening hours; . . . he carried the topic with him to his repose, and often had the bliss of remembering, that he demanded justice for millions, who could not ask it for themselves.'[16]

The speech was predictably assailed by Tarleton and others, who once again argued that 'If we were disposed to sacrifice our African trade, other nations would not enter into so ruinous a plan,'[17] and attacked the authenticity of many signatures on the petitions. Predictably too, Charles James Fox and, in the early hours of the next morning, William Pitt, weighed in with their support. In what would be remembered by all those who heard it as one of his greatest speeches, Pitt set out a vision of a free and prosperous Africa, a subject with which Wilberforce had enthused him:

> We were once as obscure among the nations of the earth, as savage in our manners, as debased in our morals, as degraded in our understandings, as these unhappy Africans are at present. But in the lapse of a long series of years ... we have become rich in a variety of acquirements, favoured above measure in the gifts of Providence, unrivalled in commerce, pre-eminent in arts, foremost in the pursuits of philosophy and science, and established in all the blessings of civil society: we are in the possession of peace, or happiness, and of liberty; we are under the guidance of a mild and beneficent religion; and we are protected by impartial laws, and the purest administration of justice ... From all these blessings, we must forever have been shut out, had there been any truth in those principles which some gentlemen have not hesitated to lay down as applicable to the case of Africa ... Had other nations applied to Great Britain the reasoning which some of the Senators of this very island apply to Africa, ages might have passed without our emerging from barbarism; and we, who are enjoying the blessings of a British civilisation, of British laws, and British liberty, might, at this hour, have been little superior, either in morals, in knowledge, or refinement, to the rude inhabitants of the Coast of Guinea ... God forbid that we should any longer subject Africa to the same dreadful scourge, and preclude the light of knowledge, which has reached every other quarter of the globe from having access to her coasts![18]

As the morning sun broke through the east windows of the House of Commons, Pitt, in a brilliant shaft of spontaneous oratory, called on Parliament to extricate Africa from darkness in a peroration which left even the opposition commenting on 'one of the most extraordinary displays of eloquence they had ever heard'.[19] Wilberforce recorded that 'Never did Mr Pitt feel more warmly or enforce his arguments with

more convincing reasoning or more impressive eloquence.'[20] Yet while
it was Pitt who won the battle of the orators that night, it was his
cabinet colleague Henry Dundas who won the war of the tacticians.

In the 1790s Dundas, now the Secretary of State for Home and
Colonial Affairs, was second in political power only to Pitt himself.
Under a Prime Minister who was uninterested in patronage, Dundas,
who had been an indispensable ally to Pitt in the turbulent events of
1783, had moved in as the arch-fixer, the man who commanded votes
and dispensed power. Controlling as he did almost the entire parliamentary representation of Scotland, a good deal of patronage in India
and appointments across the rest of the Empire, while also having the
ear of Pitt to a greater extent than anyone else – including Wilberforce
– his opinion on any subject mattered enormously. His relationship
with Wilberforce had always been cordial, not close, and he had never
joined his senior colleagues Pitt and Grenville in passionate advocacy
of abolition. As he was always concerned with the maintenance and
expansion of Britain's colonial empire, his intervention was unlikely to
be helpful to the abolitionists. And in this debate, for the first time, he
intervened.

This author has argued elsewhere that Dundas would not have
acted as he did without prior consultation with Pitt.* Pitt and Dundas
were simply too close, in the hourly conduct of government business
and the nightly consumption of serious quantities of port, to take part
in the same debate without discussing it in advance. This is not to
imply that Pitt was in agreement with what Dundas now proposed,
but it is probably fair to assume that he regarded it as a second-best
solution which would achieve the ultimate objective of abolition while
ending the divisive debates about it in the meantime. For what Dundas
proposed was simple in language and beguiling for the majority of
MPs, who were torn between the undeniable case against the slave
trade on the one hand, and their fears of the immediate consequences
of its abolition on the other. He moved that the word 'gradually'
be inserted into Wilberforce's motion for abolition, his object being

---

* See *William Pitt the Younger*, pp.301–2.

'gradually and experimentally to prove the practicability of the abolition of the trade, and to provide the means of cultivation, to increase
the population, and to evince that all the alarms which were now
entertained of danger from the measure were ill-founded'.[21]

There was no doubt that the gradualist proposition represented an
acceptable outcome for most MPs: it did not so much catch their mood
as provide them with a window of escape from the need either to
defend the slave trade or to align themselves with anything remotely
radical in the troubled circumstances of the time. In a series of divisions, the shelving of all further debate was defeated by 234 to eighty-
seven; the insertion of the word 'gradually' was carried by 193 to 125;
and the amended motion 'that the slave trade ought to be gradually
abolished' was carried by 230 votes to eighty-five.

The voting was concluded at 6.30 on the morning of 3 April.
Wilberforce walked across to Old Palace Yard and scribbled a letter to
William Hey:

> I take up my pen for a single moment to inform you that, after a
> very long debate ... my motion for immediate Abolition was put
> by; though supported strenuously by Mr Fox, and by Mr Pitt with
> more energy and ability than were almost ever exerted in the
> House of Commons ... We carried a motion however afterwards
> for gradual Abolition ... I am congratulated on all hands, yet I
> cannot but feel hurt and humiliated. We must endeavour to force
> the gradual Abolitionists in their Bill (for I will never myself bring
> forward a parliamentary licence to rob and murder) to allow as
> short a term as possible, and under as many limitations.[22]

It was an anti-climax: the Commons had voted for the first time for
abolition, but it was not clear what their vote would mean. Wilberforce
was right to be suspicious. Decades later he would state his conviction
that gradualism was a cloak under which 'many who could not avow-
edly oppose us became our most dangerous enemies'.[23] For in practice,
the word 'gradually' would turn out to mean very little at all.

*   *   *

The battle over the meaning of the word 'gradually' was soon joined in earnest. On 23 April 1792 Dundas proposed that the trade be abolished from 1 January 1800, a proposition strenuously opposed by Wilberforce and his colleagues, in the knowledge that hundreds of thousands of slaves would be captured and transported in the eight years to come. Their own counter-proposition that the date be set as 1 January 1795 was defeated by forty votes, but they managed to carry 1 January 1796 – less than four years distant – by nineteen votes, after further debates on 25 and 27 April. Wilberforce concluded that 'On the whole this is more than I expected two months ago, and I have much cause for thankfulness.' He wrote to John Clarkson, 'I cannot help regretting we have been able to do no more; yet on the whole we have reason to be thankful for what we have obtained.'[24]

Such thankfulness proved mistaken for several reasons. The first was that the date of 1796 left the House of Commons almost evenly divided on its practicability. While Pitt thought that 'the sentence of death was passed and that in 4 years the sentence would assuredly be executed',[25] Bishop Porteus, a long-standing Wilberforce supporter, commented on the substitution of 1796 for 1800: 'This alteration I most sincerely regret, as I fear it will occasion the entire loss of the Question. The term of eight years is a reasonable term and would probably have prevented further opposition. Mr Dundas himself told me that the West India Planters and Merchants would have acquiesced in the annihilation of the trade in the year 1800.'[26] It is not at all clear, of course, that there would have been such acquiescence, and in any case there remained a second formidable obstacle, in the shape of the House of Lords.

When the Lords debated the motion from the Commons, the Duke of Clarence took the opportunity to make his maiden speech. Firmly entrenched among the small number who continued to contest the truth of the evidence presented, he argued that 'The negroes were not treated in the manner which had so much agitated the public mind. He had been an attentive observer of the state of the negroes, and had no doubt . . . that, when the various ranks of society were considered, they were comparatively in a state of humble happiness.' He went on to argue, in good obstructionist style, that the Lords should veto the plans of the Commons simply to make a point: 'an implicit obedience to the House of Commons, much as he respected that House, would render the House of Peers useless, and thus the natural and constituent balance in the constitution would be endangered. This he never would endure.'[27] The following year this future King would, in a speech described by his elder brother the Prince of Wales as 'incomparable', argue that Wilberforce was either a fanatic or a hypocrite, although he apologised after being upbraided by Grenville. Still opposed to abolition, the Lords insisted on hearing their own evidence at the bar of the House, a process which previous experience in the Commons suggested could be interminable. The giving of evidence had not even started when Parliament rose for the summer.

It was to be the last summer of peace, and by the time a new parliamentary session began the prospect of even gradual abolition would have receded sharply. For it was during that summer that the French Revolution broke through all remaining restraints and crashed in its fullest fury against the interests of the other nations of Europe. On 10 August the Tuileries was stormed and the Swiss guards defending Louis XVI slaughtered by the mob. In a series of despicable massacres at the beginning of September, prisoners, priests and princesses were savagely murdered. Most important of all, the hitherto invincible Prussian army, sent into France in the expectation that it would easily crush the Revolution on behalf of the monarchs of Europe, was to be found by late September pathetically retreating after enduring a robust cannonade from the Revolutionary French forces at the Battle of Valmy. After Valmy the confidence of the revolutionaries knew no bounds. By the end of November, French troops had invaded the Austrian Netherlands, thereby threatening the security of Holland, long since regarded as a vital British interest. At the same time, Savoy had been annexed to France, assistance offered to revolutionaries in all other nations and Louis XVI put on trial for his life. Intoxicated and inflamed, the Revolution now knew no frontiers, and nor did its leaders in Paris consider themselves bound by any previous international agreements. Europe's descent into one of its greatest cataclysms was underway.

At home, with the radical societies mushrooming in strength, a poor harvest adding to serious discontent, and the *Rights of Man* in full circulation, domestic instability joined international danger in setting the scene for a powerful conservative reaction. Such was the effect on British politics that Pitt himself now turned emphatically against parliamentary reform – it would be defeated by 282 votes to forty-one in a debate of 1793 – despite having been its passionate champion throughout his early career. The unity of the opposition was simultaneously collapsing under the strain: in January 1793 a leading Whig, Lord Loughborough, would join Pitt's government as Lord Chancellor and thus begin a major realignment of political parties. Any progressive measure was off the agenda. As Samuel Romilly ruefully commented, 'If any person be desirous of having an adequate idea of the mischievous effects produced in this country by the French Revolution ... he should attempt some reform on humane and liberal principles.'[28] While the normal alliances of British politics fell apart, Wilberforce found his own traditional supporters on opposing sides: Wyvill was a sympathiser with the Revolution and favoured radical change within Britain, while most other Yorkshire freeholders would have no truck at all with revolutionary ideas.

Wilberforce himself was never likely to be in sympathy with ideas which, as practised in France, represented the overthrow of all law, authority and religion. To one of Thomas Paine's supporters he wrote: 'Surely the disposition to fall in with such doctrines as are contained in the writings of these miscalled champions out for *freedom* is, at bottom, pride and fullness bred of irreligion.'[29] Yet he suffered the embarrassment of being voted a citizen of France by the revolutionaries of 1792, an honour which he never fully disowned, and he found himself bracketed in the reactionary mind with Paine and other radicals. A pamphlet of late 1792 attacked 'the Jacobins of England, the Wilberforces, the Coopers, the Paines and the Clarksons', and asked, 'By what motives the promoters of the Abolition have been actuated? The answer is plain, Fanaticism and False Philosophy had exalted their imagination, and obscured their reason ... They saw the means of establishing such a Government as best suited to their wild ephemeral theory.'[30]

The support for abolition of the radical societies further damaged it as a cause in the view of those who feared instability. A Hull correspondent wrote to Wilberforce: 'People connect democratic principles with the Abolition of the Slave Trade and will not hear it mentioned. This is, I hear, precisely the case in Norfolk.'[31] After reaching an unprecedented peak of public support in early 1792 as a force for good and reason the abolitionist cause was, within a matter of months, regarded by many as one that was contaminated by revolutionary fellow-travellers.

Wilberforce reacted with inner calm to these deeply depressing misfortunes for his cause. He went as usual that August to Bath and Somerset, and found his way in the autumn to Teston (where Lady Middleton had died), Yoxall Lodge and Rothley Temple. In addition, he took in a visit to Walmer Castle on the Kent coast where Pitt, having become Lord Warden of the Cinque Ports at George III's insistence, was now in occasional residence. Pitt was evidently adept at keeping Wilberforce off the subject of religion: 'October 4th. At night alone with Pitt, but talked politics only – did not find myself equal to better talk. I came here hoping that I might really find an opportunity of talking seriously with Pitt, what a wretch am I to do so with any one. O Christ, help me.'[32]

Wilberforce's diary for late 1792 continues to show considerable inner torment. There is still the conviction that he is unworthy, that he has put his talents 'to so little purpose! I am now entering my thirty-fourth year; above the half of my life is spent. Oh spare me yet, Thou God of mercy, and render me yet an ornament to my Christian profession.'[33] He continued to struggle with his various resolutions, noting variously while at Yoxall Lodge that November, 'This day I have gone on but very poorly in spite of all repentance of yesterday,'[34] and, 'Alas! This week I have been going on too much as usual, violating all my resolutions.'[35] Yet on the whole he was steadily gaining greater strength from his religion: 'By God's grace still I will preserve, with more earnestness than ever, labouring to work out my own salvation in an entire and habitual dependence upon him.'[36] These feelings coincided with the start of the Clapham group and his habitual residence there. The political world was about to bring him his greatest trials, but physically and spiritually Wilberforce felt increasingly at home.

By the end of 1792, all other questions in British politics had been overtaken by a very simple one: war or peace. Pitt and Grenville had been determined to stay out of the European war. By mid-November, however, Dutch territory was being violated by the French, the British government stated its readiness to fight for Dutch independence, and naval mobilisation was begun. Last-ditch negotiations took place in December and in January 1793, hampered by the fact that Britain no longer recognised the French government. Wilberforce recorded on 3 December, 'Heard of the militia being called out, and Parliament summoned – talked politics, and of the state of the country, which seems very critical.'[37] On the basis of having been a regular visitor to 10 Downing Street in the weeks that followed, Wilberforce always defended Pitt against the charge that he had all along been seeking war with France. But he found himself in clear disagreement with the conclusion that Pitt and Grenville had reached by the end of January, that war was inevitable and necessary. Deeply concerned about the consequences of war, he explained his attitude in a letter to Wyvill: 'I own to you I cannot quite acquit Administration of *all* blame, or I should rather say, I don't believe I should have acted quite as they have done; yet from my heart I declare I cannot condemn them . . . what a dreadful, what a monstrous idea is that of two great Kingdoms using all the talents which God gave for the promotion of general happiness, for their material misery and destruction.'[38]

Wilberforce knew that Pitt had put forward to the French and other European powers a proposal under which the French Republic would be recognised and left in peace provided France ended its aggression towards other countries, but he was intensely frustrated that Pitt would not reveal this plan in public – 'I never was so earnest with Mr Pitt on any other occasion, as I was in my entreaties before the war broke out, that he would declare openly in the House of Commons, that he had been, and then was, negotiating this Treaty.'[39] Wilberforce was probably naïve in his expectation that this 'might possibly produce an immediate effect in France',[40] but he thought it would provide the basis for Britain to refrain from hostilities for the moment and, ultimately, to have added justification for war if the proposal were rejected. In Pitt's judgement, however, the opportunity for negotiation had passed, and the credibility of commitments entered into by the Parisian revolutionaries could not be relied upon. The execution of Louis XVI on 21 January 1793 had shocked the British establishment. In the Commons debate of 1 February, as Pitt prepared the country for war, he showed once again his ability, for the moment, to control Wilberforce. Having resolved to get to his feet and declare that war was not yet necessary, Wilberforce found that 'I was actually upon my legs to open my mind fully upon the subject, when Pitt sent Bankes to me earnestly desiring me not to do so that day assuring me that my speaking then might do irreparable mischief, and pledging himself that I should have another opportunity before war should be declared.'[41] He sat down. But there was no further opportunity. On the very same day in Paris, France declared war on Britain and Holland.

Given that France had now picked a fight with much of the rest of Europe – entering into war simultaneously with Britain, Holland, Prussia, Austria, Spain, Sardinia and many German and Italian states – there was a widespread assumption that it would be defeated within one or two years. Those involved could not have known that they were embarking on a quarter of a century of nearly continuous warfare, in the greatest conflict Europe had ever witnessed. Wilberforce's immediate priority was to maintain the momentum for abolition, introducing a motion on 26 February for further consideration of the abolition of the slave trade. Yet even this simple step, which was a procedural prerequisite for renewing the motion for gradual abolition passed the previous year, was voted down, by sixty-one votes to fifty-three.

It was the beginning of the darkest and most dispiriting time of all for the abolitionist campaign. The House of Lords continued with its examination of witnesses, but not without some debate as to whether to bother doing even that, and managed to get through the grand total of seven witnesses in the whole of 1793. In May, Wilberforce adopted a new tactic. This was to bring in a Bill, not to abolish the slave trade outright, but to forbid the supply of slaves to foreign colonies by British ships. Granville Sharp considered that the measure would facilitate 'the future general abolition of *the trade*, by cutting off a considerable part of the interested opposition against us',[42] and in proposing this idea the abolitionists were indeed on to a most important manoeuvre, albeit one that could not succeed in the circumstances then prevailing. MPs associated with the West Indian plantations were inclined towards the Bill because, as one of them put it, 'It would be for the benefit of himself and the rest of the Planters as they should have their slaves at a cheaper rate.'[43] It was thus possible that greed for a lower market price for fresh slaves could seriously divide the opponents of abolition.

When Wilberforce proposed the same measure again the following year, Stephen Fuller worried that it could 'be fatal to the cause, as the African Merchants have many friends in the House who will certainly leave us if we leave them'.[44] Even so, it proved impossible to pilot such a measure through Parliament: Wilberforce won a small majority in 1793, but lost the Bill at its third reading. In 1794 he laboured for weeks to carry it through the Commons, only to find that discussion of it was postponed in the House of Lords, with the semi-acquiescence of Grenville. In the midst of a war, his supporters in the government had their minds on other things. He wrote to Muncaster: 'I have, I confess, no hopes of its getting through the Lords, yet I do not relish its being suffered to lie upon the shelf, and therefore am half vexed at Grenville. However in all the disappointments of life of every kind, we must learn to say "Thy will be done." '[45] On the issue of general abolition, the Lords contented themselves with hearing a mere two witnesses in the course of 1794.

It was a time of near despair for Wilberforce's allies. While Parliament dawdled and the war intensified, Jamaica boomed, increasing its population of slaves by fifty thousand between 1791 and 1797. The outrages which the abolitionists had fought for so long to prevent went on not only unchecked but even exacerbated. When Wilberforce's next motion for general abolition was defeated outright – by seventy-eight votes to sixty-one – in February 1795, Samuel Hoare of the London Abolition Committee wrote to his Philadelphia colleagues: 'We have never addressed you under circumstances of greater discouragement ... The acts and sophistry of interested men have been proved sufficient to induce the House of Commons to desert a duty the incumbency of which after a long investigation it had solemnly acknowledged. Although fully disposed to renew ... exertions whenever opportunities may encourage them; the Meetings of this Committee are now held only occasionally.'[46] Thomas Clarkson had reached the end of his tether: 'The Committee were therefore reduced to this; – either they must exert themselves without hope, or they must wait till some change should take place in their favour. As far as I myself was concerned, all exertion was then over. The nervous system was almost shattered to pieces. Both my memory and my hearing failed me.'[47]

Thus Clarkson, one of the great driving forces behind the abolition campaign, retired from it sick and broken. Wilberforce organised financial support for him, writing to Muncaster: 'The truth is that he has expended a considerable part of his little fortune, and though not perhaps very prudently or even necessarily, yet I think, judging liberally, that he who has sacrificed so much time, and strength, and talents, should not be suffered to be out of pocket too.'[48] This was in spite of Clarkson's sharp words to Wilberforce over the failure to secure a promotion for his brother in the navy. Wilberforce was never keen on using his position to secure promotion and patronage for others: he told Pitt that same year that he was writing about 'the last case of patronage about which I will ever worry you'.[49] Clarkson thought his brother had been treated 'in a very scandalous manner', writing to Wilberforce that 'your own timidity has been the occasion of his miscarrying his promotion'.[50] Wilberforce wrote a brilliant and uncompromising reply, in which he reminded Clarkson that 'We have long acted together in the greatest cause which ever engaged the efforts of public men, and so I trust we shall still continue to act with one heart and one hand,'[51] and said of his complaint: 'The fact is, I am used to such remonstrances. It is the mode wherein I am accustomed to be addressed by people who, having for themselves or their friends expected the favours of government in consequence of my solicitations, have had their too sanguine hopes disappointed or deferred: they always, like you, seem rather to approve of one's delicacy in the general, but claim a dispensation from it in their own particular instance.'[52]

Through it all, Wilberforce maintained his own resolution and determination to keep the cause alive. In response to rumours that he was preparing to give up the fight he wrote in a letter to James Currie of Liverpool:

> ... though I shall not enter on the topicks contained in your letter I notice one of them – that I mean of my being supposed to be as you delicately express it 'fainting in my course'. Nothing, I assure you is farther from the truth; it is one of those calumnies (for such I account it) to which every public man is exposed and of which though I have had a tolerable proportion, I cannot complain of having had more than my fair share. In the case of every question of political expediency, there appears to me room for the consideration of times and the seasons – at one period under one set of circumstances it may be proper to push, at another and in other circumstances to withhold our efforts. But in the present instance where the actual commission of guilt is in question, a man who *fears God* is not at liberty ... If I thought the immediate Abolition of the Slave Trade would cause an insurrection in our islands, I should not for an instant remit my most strenuous endeavours.[53]

Such remarks demonstrate the gulf which had now opened up between Wilberforce and leading ministers. To Dundas, whom Wilberforce now considered 'most false and double; but poor fellow! Much to be pitied',[54] an insurrection in the West Indian islands would have been one of the greatest imaginable calamities. When Wilberforce asked him to support the Foreign Slave Bill he responded: 'Your Bill will be considered by the Colonies as an encroachment upon their legislative rights and they will not submit to it unless compelled. Upon that ground I have used all the influence to prevent any question on the subject being agitated during the war at least.'[55]

In spite of all these vicissitudes, Wilberforce seemed able to draw on an inner strength even as the whole political and military scene darkened. In the summer of 1793 he was to be found at Bath as usual, and once again with Hannah More and her sister at their home at Cowslip Green in Somerset, accompanied throughout by John Venn. At the end of the summer he spent two months in Battersea Rise, enjoying the solidarity and purposefulness of Clapham, having 'laid the first timbers of my tract'[56] – the beginning of work on a book in which he intended to explain his Evangelical philosophy to the nation. Autumn saw him once again at Yoxall Lodge and Rothley Temple, much engaged in the early stages of this work and characteristically berating himself for attaching any pride to it – 'With what shame do I discover my worldly heart desirous of gaining credit by my tract! I have been more diligent and self-denying lately: I have found this morning the advantages of a little religious solitude.'[57] Engaged in a similar progress in the summer and autumn of 1794, he spent time at Teston reading Tom Paine's *Age of Reason* – 'God defend us from such poison'[58] – and finished up at Yoxall Lodge in November, where 'I left off my tract till next year, and began to apply to politics.'[59]

Throughout these two years, Wilberforce remained a close friend and confidant of Pitt, now a Prime Minister at war. His diary is littered with notes such as 'To Town 14th September to see Pitt – a great map spread out before him,' or 'Off for Holwood. Pitt and I tête-à-tête – he very open, and we discussed much.'[60] Few backbenchers in history have ever enjoyed such intimacy with a Prime Minister weighed down by wartime responsibilities. His opinion of Pitt was as high as ever: 'If the flame of pure disinterested patriotism burns in any human bosom, it does in his.'[61] But Wilberforce watched at close quarters as the high hopes for a quick war were replaced by the mounting shock of accumulating defeats: the disaster of the attempted siege of Dunkirk and the French recapture of Toulon in 1793; the French advance into Germany, Italy, Belgium and Spain, and the heavy British losses in the West Indies in 1794.

On the positive side, the government consolidated an overwhelmingly strong domestic political position by bringing leading Whigs into the cabinet in the summer of 1794, leaving Fox in opposition in an isolated and tiny minority. And occasionally there was good news from the high seas, particularly after 'the Glorious First of June' of 1794, in which Admiral Howe mauled the French navy in the Atlantic, bringing ecstatic crowds to welcome the fleet home at Portsmouth. 'Would it not have surprised you,' Wilberforce wrote to Muncaster at the end of June, 'when the wind had a little cleared away the smoke in which the royal salute had enveloped the skies, to have seen Harry Thornton and C. Grant and your humble servant perched on the poop of the *Queen* at Spithead. Yet so it was. We thought Portsmouth might be a highly useful as well as an interesting spectacle, and accordingly went thither a couple of days and should have stayed longer (I at least) if the Royal family being there had not made the place so very bustling and kept away some persons we principally wished to see. We found matter of lasting reflection.'[62]

He was indeed reflecting not merely on seeing the wounded men come ashore, but on the wisdom of continuing a war in which Britain seemed to be obtaining no advantage other than the acquisition of colonies into which it would then wish to import slaves. The French had turned out to be fighting on an entirely different basis from the other nations of Europe, fired by revolution and able to mobilise one and a half million men in the opening two years of the war, the greatest such number the modern world had ever witnessed. He was struck by meeting the Abbé de Lageard, whom he and Pitt had met eleven years before on their visit to France, who had escaped France after being hunted for a year and a half, and argued that 'Only the French can conquer the French.'[63] In response to the claim, often advanced by Pitt, that France would soon be beaten because its financial resources were limited, the Abbé was said to have commented, 'I should like to know who was Chancellor of the Exchequer to Attila.'[64]

Increasingly, Wilberforce found that he did not believe in the strategy his great friend was pursuing. Hating the bellicose language of the conflict, he noted in his diary after one of Pitt's stirring Commons speeches in July 1794, 'Pitt much too strong for war.'[65] It was a war which was not only preventing the fulfilment of his abolitionist objectives, but one he felt he had to challenge even on its own merits. He had already laid claim to the luxury of political independence. Now he was to discovery its agony.

Wilberforce had reached the view, one that would be confirmed by subsequent events, that the French Revolution had reached the stage at which it could not be reversed by external force of arms. Royalist revolts within France had been comprehensively crushed, invaders invariably repelled, and the most extreme and violent phase of the Revolution appeared to have run its course when the arch-proponent of the guillotine, Robespierre, was himself executed beneath it in July 1794. Britain's allies were faltering, and the French had averted starvation by managing to bring a huge grain convoy across the Atlantic despite the tactical British success of the Glorious First of June. In these circumstances, Wilberforce thought that Britain should at least be open to a negotiated peace, but that the insistence on the restoration of the French monarchy into which British policy had slid in the course of 1793 would make any negotiation impossible. As he explained in a letter to Henry Bankes:

> Remember, all the French know of the intentions of Great Britain is from our declarations, and from Pitt's speeches, and these have been uniformly point-blank against any accommodation with the existing system of government in France, or in other words, against a republic. Therefore unless we make some new declaration, they can have no idea but that we mean to fight against the republic ... I would gladly get an end put to this war without Pitt's being turned out of office, which will hardly be possible I fear if it continue much longer. Much however as this weighs with me, and that not merely on private grounds, the other obvious considerations are far more important. I am quite sick I own of such a scene of havoc and misery, and unless I am quite clear I shall not dare vote for its continuance.[66]

The letter to Bankes was one of several efforts by Wilberforce to obtain the views of those who were friends to both him and to Pitt, seeking their opinions but also preparing them for the grave controversy he

would cause by openly opposing Pitt's central policy. A few days before
Parliament was due to meet at the end of the year he wrote to Edward
Eliot, one of the dearest friends of both of them:

> I am sure your affectionate heart will be not a little hurt, to hear
> that I fear I must differ from Pitt on the important point of
> continuing the war . . . I need hardly say that the prospect of a
> public difference with Pitt is extremely painful to me, and though
> I trust his friendship for me has sunk too deep in his heart to be
> soon worn out, I confess it hangs on me like a weight I cannot
> remove . . . My spirits are hardly equal to the encounter. However,
> I hope it will please God to enable me to act the part of an honest
> man in this trying occasion.[67]

Pitt had always been relaxed about his personal friends taking up
independent political positions, and had indulged those who had differed from him on such matters as parliamentary reform in the 1780s.
But this was an entirely different matter. The country was at war, and
in an increasingly dangerous situation. Wilberforce had been a close
friend for the entire duration of their political lives to that date, was
privy to all his personal and political plans, and was an almost daily
visitor who would walk into 10 Downing Street and discuss any subject
with Pitt, whether he was in the cabinet room or his bedroom. For
such a friend to launch a political attack at a testing moment of national
crisis could not help but be a wounding personal blow. Furthermore,
Wilberforce was now a respected and senior Member of Parliament;
his views carried weight and his opposition to the war would inevitably
feed the growing discontent with it.

Such considerations weighed heavily on Wilberforce. He considered
it his duty to speak his mind, but 'No one,' he would write a quarter
of a century later, 'who has not seen a good deal of public life, and felt
how difficult and painful it is to differ widely from those with whom
you wish to agree, can judge at what an expense of feeling such duties
are performed.'[68] The pain of it disturbed his nights, but as the opening
of Parliament approached on 30 December 1794, he was clear that he
must go ahead. He had already decided that his differing from Pitt,

while 'lessening my popularity; shewing me my insignificance, may not be bad for my spirituality and becomes me on entering a sense of increased temptations',[69] and that he would have to be ready 'in particular to bear with kindness the slights and sarcasm I must expect from all political causes'.[70] While the cabinet held their traditional eve of Parliament dinner in Downing Street, Wilberforce dined in Old Palace Yard with his own 'cabinet' – Duncombe, Muncaster, Henry Thornton and Bankes – confirming his intentions and drawing strength for the coming ordeal.

The next day, under Pitt's hurt and reproachful gaze, he rose in the Commons 'To perform,' as he put it, 'a painful act of duty . . . expressing . . . a difference with those with whom it had been the happiness of his political life so generally to agree.'[71] Arguing that the House had to 'change its conduct when the state of affairs had so materially changed', he moved an amendment to the Address to the King stating that: 'Upon full consideration of all the events and circumstances of the present war . . . we think it advisable and expedient to endeavour to restore the blessings of peace to his Majesty's subjects, and to his allies, upon just and reasonable terms.'[72] He did not, of course, carry the House: seventy-three MPs voted for his amendment and 246 against, but this was a larger show of opposition to the war than the Commons was used to. Pitt refrained from any public attack on his old friend, but was said to have himself lost sleep over the breach between them, while the Duke of Portland, one of the Whig grandees who had now joined Pitt's coalition government, considered that 'Pitt seemed pretty seriously hurt by it.'[73] Inevitably, new friends of Pitt such as Portland quietly enjoyed any event which showed his old friends to be of less value. Portland thought that Wilberforce and Bankes were 'pretended friends' of Pitt, and enjoyed hearing George III say, 'I always told Mr Pitt they were hypocrites and not to be trusted.'[74]

Wilberforce's speech produced a strong reaction. While Fox came to see him to say that 'You will soon see that you must join us altogether'[75] – in the opposition – many Yorkshire constituents were appalled, and George III cut him at a royal *levée*. Windham, another Whig who had recently joined the cabinet, called him a 'wicked little fanatical imp'.[76] Milner wrote to say that 'I never conceived that you intended to take so decided a part in this business as to lead the Opposition against Pitt . . . I wish I may be mistaken, yet as I understand your Amendment and the consequent division, it will certainly tend to weaken the government and divide the sentiments of the country to strengthen a factious opposition, and to encourage the French convention.'[77]

It did not even help matters that Wilberforce went out of his way to support the government on other matters a few days later. With the opposition calling for the repeal of the Habeas Corpus Suspension Act, by which Pitt had introduced internment without trial as a means of quelling public disorder, Wilberforce argued that 'In the present state of the country, the true policy to be observed was by all safe means to conciliate the minds of the well intentioned part of the community on the one hand, and on the other to strengthen the hands of government for the repression and punishment of factions.'[78] Such a position was in no way inconsistent with his support for negotiations with France, but because most politicians who opposed the war also opposed the suspension of Habeas Corpus, while those who supported the war supported the suspension, Wilberforce's straddling of the two positions laid him open to further attack. Portland called it 'a pretended recantation . . . It is a ruse which cannot be mistaken.'[79] Wilberforce was suspected of wanting to set up his own political party, Milner warning him that 'both opposition and your disgusted friends of administration are inclined to admit a notion that you are endeavouring to raise a consequential party of your own',[80] while a supporter from Yorkshire wrote that 'faction begins to claim you . . . It is of infinite importance that you should not appear to the country as a leader of opposition.'[81]

Beset as he was by troubled friends and indignant opponents, Wilberforce maintained his course, strengthened in his view that the war was futile by the crushing defeats the French inflicted on the Dutch in January 1795. On the twenty-sixth of that month he renewed his call for negotiation, arguing that he thought 'a counter revolution more likely to take place if Peace should be made than during the continuance of War'.[82] He would do so again at the end of May, raising the anti-war vote in the Commons to a total of eighty-six MPs, while giving a vigorous defence of his right to differ from a Prime Minister who was his friend: 'My high opinion of the Minister's integrity, (and of no man's political integrity do I think more highly,) ... ought certainly to make me give due weight to what I know are his opinions.' But, he added, 'I am sent here by my constituents not to gratify my private feelings, but to discharge a great political trust; and for the faithful administration of the power vested in me, I must answer to my country and my God.'[83]

For good measure, Wilberforce also opposed that month, May 1795, the settlement of the Prince of Wales's debts painstakingly negotiated by Pitt. Prince George had managed to run up personal debts of around £600,000 (an amount nearing £50 million in today's money) even while taxes were being raised and the rest of the country was tightening its belt to support the war. This was in spite of the large sums given to him over the previous twelve years, and it further fed the utter disgust felt for him by his father, George III. It was only in return for a settlement of his debt that the errant Prince agreed to marry Caroline of Brunswick, in what would become one of the most disastrous marriages in the entire history of the royal family, and it was Pitt's task to agree a financial settlement which King, Prince and Parliament could all agree to. Pitt was not amused when the delicately constructed compromise of a grant of £125,000 a year for the Prince, on condition that some of it went for debt repayment, ran into robust opposition in Parliament, with Wilberforce once again at the forefront, reminding the House of 'the distresses which at this moment the lower orders were experiencing from the unequalled price of every necessity of life'.[84]

Many personal and political relationships would have been ruptured forever by such persistent and varied opposition. Wilberforce was indeed excluded from Pitt's inner circle in the weeks that followed his initial opposition to the war. It was noted that when there was a 'party of *the old firm* at the Speaker's'[85] at the beginning of February – in other words the former members of Goostree's, such as Pitt, Dudley Ryder and Thomas Steele, along with later additions such as William Grenville and Henry Addington – he was no longer invited. For a time, 'all the hot Pittites would scarcely speak to me'.[86] Yet it would soon turn out that the long friendship between Pitt and Wilberforce was too deep, and the strength of each of their good natures too strong, for this major political difference to lead to personal animosity or even separation. Pitt had led the way with his magnanimous response, speaking solidly for Wilberforce's latest ill-fated motion to abolish the slave trade that February. By 21 March, Robert Smith had brought them together at dinner: 'For the first time since our political difference – I think both meaning to be kind to each other – both a little embarrassed.'[87]

By 25 April, Wilberforce was noting, 'To Battersea Rise – called Eliot's, knowing that Pitt was there, and that Eliot knew I knew it, and thinking therefore it would seem unkind not to do it.'[88] The following day: 'I had meant to be quiet to-day, and had hoped to be able to employ myself in devotional exercises, when after church Pitt came with Eliot; and considering he did it out of kindness, I could not but walk back with him.'[89] In May, just before the row over the Prince's allowance, 'Eliot called and asked me to dine at Battersea Rise to meet Pitt and Ryder – called and staid two hours with them all; walking, foining, and laughing, and reading verses, as before.'[90] Most of Pitt's ministerial colleagues did not share this taste for reconciliation: when Wilberforce called at Downing Street in late May he 'found Grenville, Dundas, Pepper Arden, Ryder, and Pitt – last very kind, first shy, second sour, and my pride wounded, alas!'[91] Wilberforce's hostility to the war had exacerbated the mistrust between him and Dundas, who wrote to him: 'I have a very decided opinion that some of your late political conduct and the lead you have taken in Parliamentary discussions have done irreparable mischief,'[92] while he in turn suspected Dundas of persuading Pitt to continue the war for the sake of colonial conquest.

Dundas had good reason to be angry with Wilberforce, for the reconciliation between him and Pitt was becoming a matter of substance as well as sentiment. By the summer of 1795 the strategic position of Britain was worsening rapidly: the humiliated Dutch had signed a treaty with France, Spain was in the process of changing sides, the French were gaining ground in the West Indies, and a British-inspired expeditionary force of French émigrés who were landed on the coast of Brittany was annihilated. Food shortages at home were causing mounting unrest and public disorder. At the end of June London saw a gathering of a hundred thousand people demanding peace, reform and lower food prices. Pitt was coming round to Wilberforce's view: a negotiated peace might avert disaster, and if it was rejected by the French the nation would be more united in pursuing the war.

The King and much of the cabinet were deeply suspicious of any attempt to make peace with France. It would be early 1796 before the first feelers were extended towards the French, and these would be rejected. Nevertheless, the shift in Pitt's views behind the scenes helped bring Wilberforce back to supporting the administration in the autumn of 1795. Pitt wrote to him on 24 October:

> It is hardly possible to form any precise opinion of what is to be done till we see the immediate issue of the crisis just now depending, but I cannot help thinking that it will shortly lead to a state of things in which I hope our opinions cannot materially differ. I need not say how much personal comfort it will give me if my expectation in this respect is realised. Yours sincerely and affectionately, W Pitt.[93]

In the days that followed Wilberforce was once again to be found advising Pitt, this time on the tactics for the opening of the next session of Parliament, at which the tone of the King's Speech – referring to 'the Restoration of Peace' – was markedly different from that to which Wilberforce had objected so strongly only ten months before.

Wilberforce felt vindicated, as well as believing that Pitt was 'more deeply devoted to his country's welfare than any other political man'.[94] He had shown no sign of wavering under the opprobrium heaped upon him that year, although he had taken what was for him the unusual step of touring Yorkshire that summer to mitigate the anger of his constituents. Since the Parliament was five years old and a general election was likely in the following year, he could not afford to ignore them. He encountered some serious hostility: 'In one family of my most zealous partisans, when I visited Yorkshire even as late as the

middle of the summer, the ladies would scarcely speak to me.'[95] Others
were 'violently incensed by my political conduct',[96] but on the whole
he had a reasonable reception, and many Yorkshire freeholders were
in any case becoming dissatisfied with Pitt's government.

Wilberforce had provided a striking example of political courage
and independence. What is more, his attention to good personal
relations had meant he had done so without doing irreparable harm
to the relationships he valued the most. While his revolt against Pitt
was fairly short-lived, arousing the suspicions of the opposition that
the two of them had actually been in collusion for a good part of it, it
would fortify his reputation for integrity and reason. Furthermore, it
seems likely to have been one of the factors which did influence Pitt
to make an attempt for peace, predisposing him to do so on further
occasions in the future, and thus had a major effect on the conduct of
government at the height of a war. Windham, despite being Secretary
at War, was complaining by the end of 1795 that Britain was 'not
governed by Mr Pitt and others, that we naturally should be, but by
Mr Wilberforce and Mr This-and t'other that I could name, and who
have not only low and narrow notions of things, but their own little
private interest to serve'.[97] In general, however, there was relief in
government ranks that the debates of 1795 saw Wilberforce and his
fellow 'Saints' come back on board. Pitt's young protégé George
Canning commented that 'Wilberforce and his conscientious followers,
the *effusion-of-human-blood party*, all came back to us.'[98]

Not only was Wilberforce back, but he was about to provide crucial
support for Pitt in the deepening domestic crisis which the combined
circumstances of war and a poor harvest had now produced. Vast
crowds surrounded Parliament when the King opened it that October,
demanding peace and bread. A window of the King's coach was shattered; it was thought by a bullet. Amidst fears of uncontrollable disorder Pitt introduced two highly controversial measures; the Seditious
Meetings Bill and the Treasonable Practices Bill, rapidly known as
Pitt's 'Gagging Bills'. They imposed draconian penalties on those who
attacked the constitution, banned meetings of more than fifty people
at a time, and allowed anyone addressing such a meeting to be arrested.

Fox led the outraged opposition to these drastic moves: 'Say at once, that a free Constitution is no longer suitable to us; say at once, in a manly manner, that upon an ample review of the state of the world, a free Constitution is not fit for you . . . But do not mock the understandings and feelings of mankind by telling the world that you are free.'[99] But the vast majority of the Commons thought the time had come for such measures, even if they amounted to repression. Wilberforce, back in favour at Downing Street, worked with Pitt to draw up the Bills and make them acceptable. On 9 November he rose in the House to give full backing to the government: 'He had always considered it as the grand preservative of the British constitution that there was a popular assembly, the House of Commons, in which all popular grievances might be freely and safely discussed to which the people might be encouraged to bring their complaints, wherein they might be sure there would never be wanting those who would stand forth to assert the cause of the injured or oppressed; here in short, all the national humour might be suffered to ferment without danger.'[100] It was not acceptable that outside Parliament 'lectures were given, and harangues delivered, of the most inflammatory nature; hand bills and prints of the most atrocious description were circulated'.[101]

Such views were pure Wilberforce: for although he spearheaded the abolitionist campaign and led so many other endeavours on the basis of justice, fairness, and concern for the poor or destitute, he was no political radical. He was utterly conservative when it came to the defence of the constitution or the existing political order, seeing revolution or anything approaching it as hostile both to religion and to wise and considered leadership. Once again, he saw no contradiction between his firm support for public order and his earlier opposition to the war, but to those in regular opposition he yet again appeared as a hypocrite. 'I am now an object of popular odium,' he noted. 'O how fleeting is popular favour. I greatly fear some civil war or embroilment and my cowardly heart shrinks from the dangers and difficulties . . . But find thy heart in God O my Soul! Riot is expected from the Westminster meeting. The people I hear are much exasperated against me. The printers are all angry at the Sedition Bills. O how vain now appears all successful ambition. Poor Pitt! Alas! Alas! O if he knew the way of life.'[102]

Yorkshire appeared bitterly divided over the Gagging Bills. Wyvill, who had now lost all patience with Pitt, decided to call a county meeting at York to raise a petition against the Bills, deliberately doing so on a Friday, 27 November 1795, when it was too late for weekly newspapers to carry the news that the meeting had been called for only four days later, on Tuesday, 1 December. It was the Sunday morning before Wilberforce, on his way to church in Westminster, heard that Wyvill's supporters were secretly bringing together a huge meeting of freeholders to condemn the government. The result was one of the most dramatic journeys of eighteenth-century politics. Wilberforce first walked around to Downing Street to consult with Pitt. They agreed that he must try to get to the meeting in York to prevent Yorkshire, one of the most powerful political counties in the land, being plunged into outright opposition to Pitt's government. There would be less than forty-eight hours to make a journey of some two hundred miles, which would be a close call even with the fittest horses and toughest of passengers.

When Wilberforce found that his carriage could not be readied in time, Pitt said, 'Mine is ready, set off in that.'[103] One observer commented: 'If they find out whose carriage you have got you will run the risk of being murdered.'[104] But by half-past two that Sunday afternoon, Wilberforce was hurtling north in Pitt's carriage. Monday morning saw him at Alconbury, with still over 130 miles to go, while vast numbers of freeholders were already arriving in York: 'There went through Hatton Turnpike,' one observer wrote that day, 'above three thousand horsemen.'[105] Wilberforce covered over 110 miles that day on the Great North Road,* to reach Ferrybridge in Yorkshire. At eleven o'clock on the Tuesday morning, Wyvill and his supporters were attempting to conduct a divided meeting in the York Guildhall, with huge crowds gathered outside, when Wilberforce's carriage, completely unexpected

---

* The Great North Road, roughly corresponding to the modern A1, was by 1787 in good condition the whole way from London to Edinburgh. Its compulsory milestones had the incidental consequence of making universal the measurement of the standard mile.

by all concerned, turned the corner and came into view. 'What a row did I make,' he observed to his sons more than thirty years later at the same spot, 'when I turned this corner in 1795; it seemed as if the whole place must come down together.'[106] Amidst tumultuous cheering and hats filling the air, Wilberforce stepped into the Guildhall and demanded that Wyvill debate with him out in the Castle Yard so that the entire crowd could listen. When Wyvill refused, Wilberforce went to the Castle Yard anyway, and addressed 'perhaps the largest assemblage of gentlemen and freeholders which ever met in Yorkshire'.[107] Those who heard his defence of Pitt and his Bills considered it the greatest speech he had ever delivered. Characteristically, Wilberforce himself was dissatisfied with his effort, complaining to William Hey the following week, 'I should have said much more,'[108] but others thought it was 'a most incomparable speech indeed'.[109] Fifteen years later a Colonel Cockell wrote to him to say: 'I never felt the power of eloquence until that day. You made my blood tingle with delight . . . you breathed energy and vigour into the desponding souls of timid loyalists, and sent us home with joy and delight.' A Leeds merchant wrote at the time: 'The burst of applause spontaneously flowing from constituents brought there by no influence whatever, save that of disinterested independence and purest civic principle . . . applause from such hearts, and so uprightly earned . . . will ever sound in your ears.'[110] The threatened petitions against the government were reversed, and by the Friday Wilberforce was back in the House of Commons presenting petitions in full support of the Gagging Bills. Where Yorkshire had led, many other counties rapidly followed. Pitt must have reflected that rarely had forgiveness been so rapidly rewarded.

Within two weeks of returning from Yorkshire, Wilberforce was giving notice that he would once again raise the question of the slave trade in the Commons, for it was now, he said, 'when we are checking the progress of licentiousness, now is the very time to show our true principles, by stopping a practice which violates all the real rights of human nature'.[111] 1 January 1796 was about to arrive, the date by which the House of Commons had voted in 1792 the slave trade should be abolished. Yet the truth was that it was no nearer at all to abolition.

II

Consuming Passions

———— ⋅ɪOɪ⋅ ————

Accustom yourself to look first to the dreadful consequences of failure;
then fix your eye on the glorious prize which is before you; and when
your strength begins to fail, and your spirits are well nigh exhausted,
let the animating view rekindle your resolution, and call forth in
renewed vigour the fainting energies of your soul.

WILLIAM WILBERFORCE, *A Practical View* (1797)[1]

Oh, how wonderful are his ways! An eventful year for me – my book,
my marriage, health restored in sickness.

WILLIAM WILBERFORCE, 31 December 1797[2]

'IT WAS HARDLY NECESSARY for him to state to the House,' said
Wilberforce when he rose in the Commons on 18 February 1796,
'that there was something very peculiar in the present time, as connected with this unfortunate subject. Gentlemen could not but recollect,
that the 1st January 1796, was the time when the House had declared
that the slave trade should end. The first January, 1796 was past, but
alas! the detestable traffic proceeded with undiminished spirit.' Taking
the resolution of that House 'that the slave trade should be abolished
in January 1796' for his ground, he 'stood upon a foundation that
could not be shaken. This was the sentence of the House, formally and
deliberately pronounced, after a more elaborate discussion than any
question had ever undergone. It became his duty, therefore, to call
upon the House for the execution of its sentence.'[3] If it was disorder
and revolution that were now the primary fears of his colleagues,

Wilberforce argued, then it was ludicrous to import still larger numbers of discontented slaves to the islands of the West Indies, since 'it was manifest that every fresh importation of African negroes was a fresh accumulation of inflammable matter into the islands ... How much less would the danger have been, if the 150,000 wretched Africans, who have been imported within the last four years, had not been added to the most dangerous of all the negroes.'[4]

This was a compelling argument – sound policy combined with human justice: 'If gentlemen felt no impulse from the principles of justice and common humanity they should at least hearken to the dictates of policy and common sense, and give to self interest what they might be disposed to refuse to the calls of compassion, justice, and virtue.'[5] Narrowly, and with the emphatic support of Pitt and Fox, Wilberforce overcame the views of those like Robert Jenkinson, the future Lord Liverpool, who argued that the effect of abolishing the trade at such a moment 'would be to destroy all subordination, and to endanger the present state of the West India islands'.[6] Wilberforce was given leave to bring in his Bill by a vote of ninety-three to sixty-seven. At last, feeling 'surprise and joy',[7] he thought he might be on the brink of success. He spent the following few days flitting between Downing Street, Old Palace Yard and the chamber of the Commons, working on his Bill with Pitt himself and finding great utility in living in a house so close to the doors of the Commons: on 22 February he 'Crossed from dinner, and finding the House in a good state brought in Slave Bill without opposition, and recrossed.'[8] The following week he was dining at home when a hostile MP moved the second reading of his Bill, hoping to have it defeated in a thin House while Wilberforce was not there, but he 'Hurried from dinner at home over to House to the second reading of the Slave Bill. Spoke against time till many came. Carried it 63 to 31.'[9]

By 7 March he had got the Bill through its committee stage, despite the continual unhelpfulness of Dundas – 'Admitting the African slave trade to be founded upon injustice and inhumanity ... this was not the proper time for the abolition'[10] – an obstacle so persistent that Wilberforce would be unlikely ever to forget it. As the Bill approached its final hurdle in the Commons, its third reading on 15 March, Wilberforce's hopes were high. He had consistently won a majority in the previous week, and the House seemed well attended that night, his main concern being that five or six of his supporters had gone to the opera to hear a new work from Italy. As it turned out, their absence was to be crucial: he mustered seventy votes for the third reading of the Abolition Bill. There were seventy-four against.

To Wilberforce, now nine years into his campaign for abolition, the defeat of 1796 was the cruellest he had yet suffered. He walked across Old Palace Yard utterly dejected, noting in his diary: 'Enough at the Opera to have carried it. Very much vexed and incensed at our opponents.'[11] Stephen Fuller's rather honest assessment made in 1788 still seemed to run true: 'The stream of popularity runs against us; but I trust nevertheless that common sense is with us, and that wicked as we are when compared with the abolishers, the wisdom and policy of this country will protect us.'[12] It seemed impossible to overcome the 'wisdom and policy' of the British establishment. In May, a Bill further to improve the conditions in which slaves were carried was 'counted out', the device of calling a vote in order to demonstrate that a quorum was not present being used successfully by its opponents. Wilberforce's regular attempts to persuade Pitt to desist from the conquest of further West Indian islands, into which fresh slaves were then imported, were dashed by Pitt's need for military successes and by the immense influence of Dundas.

The strain of his efforts and of these shattering disappointments told on Wilberforce. In early April he was on his feet in the Commons arguing in favour of a Dog Tax – 'Everything should be done that had a tendency to abridge the excessive number of those animals'[13] – but after that he fell seriously ill. Milner hurried down from Cambridge with his remedies and his fortifying presence; Wilberforce would write later that year: 'He was the means, if not of saving my life, at least of sparing me a long and dangerous fit of sickness . . . When he is at an *uncomeatable* distance I never have the same sense of security.'[14] Even so, it took him some time to recover from the physical and mental strain. He regularly felt faint and weak, on one occasion to the extent of not being able to see Pitt and Dundas when they called at his house. And after ten days of confinement he noted that 'I have lately felt and now feel a sort of terror on re-entering the world.'[15] Yet in the coming weeks he would be required to re-enter the world with a vengeance. When he travelled with Pitt to Cambridge on 20 May he learned that a general election was imminent. After the crushing defeats and low spirits of the spring of 1796, the months to come would demonstrate once again his extraordinary resilience and reveal much about the source of such strength. He set off immediately for Hull.

In common with most politicians through the centuries, Wilberforce found that intensive contact with the electorate revived his spirits rather than drained them. After feeling 'permanently hurt' following that year's defeat of abolition,[16] he showed no sign of it as he bustled about Hull attempting to secure the election of Samuel Thornton, brother of Henry and another member of the Clapham group. It was only after Thornton had been brought in 'with difficulty' that Wilberforce set out for York,[17] dining in the carriage to save time, while being assured by all he met that his election was guaranteed. Indeed it was: with Duncombe standing down, all of his possible replacements promised to give their second vote to Wilberforce, and there seemed to be scarcely any opposition to his re-election. It was only one year since he had offended many in Yorkshire by opposing Pitt over the war, and for many years he had disdained most of the ritual festivities and county events which a Member for Yorkshire would normally attend. Yet set against all of that, Wilberforce had now reached the point in his political career where his reputation for integrity, independence and meticulous attention to Yorkshire matters in the Commons outweighed all other considerations in the minds of his constituents.

The one danger to him in Yorkshire, as ever in a two-Member constituency, was that a contest for the other seat would require him to face the vast expense and canvassing of a contested election. The result was that it was very much in his interests to try to settle the election of his colleague without a contest – and, given his popularity, it was very much in the interests of the other candidates to receive his endorsement. It was difficult, however, for Wilberforce openly to support either of the other two candidates: Walter Fawkes, the candidate of the opposition Whigs, and Henry Lascelles, a Pittite but the heir to the Harewood family fortune, derived from sugar and slaves. With some of Wilberforce's supporters threatening to leave him if he did not team up with Lascelles, he nevertheless held firm and was spared a contest by Fawkes retiring from the field. Fawkes only discovered after he had quit that he had been sent a letter of support by the Dukes of Norfolk and Devonshire and Earl Fitzwilliam – support so useful that he would have forced a contest – which had lain unopened as he made his decision. As it was, Wilberforce, the leading abolitionist, and Lascelles, the plantation-owner, were declared elected for Yorkshire. Following the ceremony on 7 June, at which he was carried through the streets of York amidst tumultuous scenes, Wilberforce noted, 'Home about seven and prayed. Much affected, and shed many tears.'[18]

After calling in at Hull to see his mother, whose health was beginning to fail, and making a progress through the West Riding in which he found 'all this dining publicly and incessant company . . . sad work',[19] Wilberforce arrived by the end of June in Buxton, where he was to spend some weeks resting, reading and taking the waters on the advice of William Hey. At Buxton he fell into one of his contemplative periods, characteristically appearing 'vain and gay'[20] to his friends, while making a sad assessment of the political scene and his own role in private. Writing to Muncaster of public affairs, he said: 'Seldom have they offered a more gloomy spectacle. To me, I own, they wear a still darker aspect; because I see nothing of that proper temper of mind in our great men which I should hail as the dawning of the day after a night of darkness and horror.'[21] He was irritated that he could not enjoy a short walk in Buxton without people joining him, and that he had made no progress on his 'tract'. This combination of outward sociability with inner seriousness had always been a Wilberforce characteristic. In old age he would write: 'I sometimes think I have the art . . . of concealing from my most intimate associates my real character . . . I am at times much more disposed to melancholy than you would imagine'.[22] To some extent he believed that this was how a Christian should behave, writing in 1795 of 'the peculiar character of a Christian; gravity in the House, cheerfulness, kindness, and placability, with a secret guard and hidden seriousness'.[23]

Both sides of his character were, of course, indispensable to him, and in any case, innate. But his refusal to reveal any inner torment to most companions meant that only a few knew when he was distressed or in doubt about the future. John Newton, who had always encouraged Wilberforce to maintain his political career, was one of those few. Now, as Wilberforce briefly contemplated retirement from public life, Newton sent him a powerful and persuasive letter. God had not dismissed him from the House of Commons; it was impossible to measure the amount of good that he might be doing there:

> The example, and even the presence of a consistent character, may have a powerful, though unobserved effect upon others. You are not only a representative for Yorkshire, you have the far greater honour of being a representative for the Lord, in a place where many know him not ... It is true that you live in the midst of difficulties and snares, and you need a double guard of watchfulness and prayer. But since you know both of your need of help, and where to look for it, I may say to you as Darius to Daniel 'Thy God whom thou servest continually is able to preserve and deliver you' ... Indeed the great point for our comfort in life is to have a well grounded persuasion that we are, where, all things considered, we ought to be.[24]

By early September 1796, fortified by such persuasion, Wilberforce was drawing up a list of the many things he could be thankful for: his recovery from illness, protection from danger, and 'my being providentially engaged in the slave trade business'.[25] He then returned to London, unusually early in the year for him, 'prompted by the possible hope of doing good in pressing Pitt to peace – not to stipulate for islands – perhaps include Slave Trade in treaty',[26] his mind already moving on to how the concomitant horrors of the continuing war and the booming slave trade could be brought simultaneously to an end in a comprehensive peace treaty with France. That autumn there was a bout of optimism about the prospects for peace. Although Spain was about to enter the war again on the French side, the Austrians were advancing against the French in Germany, British troops had taken St Vincent, St Lucia and Grenada in the West Indies, and Catherine the Great of Russia seemed to be preparing to enter the war. With the French additionally beset by internal troubles, Pitt sent the Earl of Malmesbury to Paris in September in the hope that he could negotiate an honourable peace, an expedition undertaken with the warm approval of Wilberforce.

Wilberforce in the autumn of 1796 seemed fully recovered from the depression of earlier in the year. He bustled about Westminster on a wide variety of business. He pursued with Pitt and Dundas his idea that all the slave-trading powers would be brought together at the time of peace in a general abolition convention, considering that peace was made more likely by the internal state of France, which was itself the judgement of Providence – 'A neighbouring country has been severely punished for its infidelity and wickedness.'[27] He stoutly defended Pitt in a series of Commons speeches, bringing him into sharp exchanges with Fox and Sheridan: on 2 November he said 'He had felt himself impelled by an invincible impression'[28] to accuse Fox of making an invasion of the country more likely, bringing forth the wrath of Sheridan for 'the most extraordinary and unprovoked libel I ever heard in this House',[29] and being 'invincibly called' to utter words that were either 'political or fanatical'.[30] He protested against plans to drill the militia on Sundays, but otherwise gave full support to the war effort, and attended so many ministerial dinners and consultations that he might almost as well have been in the cabinet. He lobbied hard for the building of more churches and for help for destitute French émigrés. He argued strongly, early the following year, for relieving Quakers of the necessity of paying tithes, in protest at which some of them had gone to prison. He immersed himself in the affairs of St Bartholomew's hospital, having discovered that serious abuses of patients were taking place there, and spent much time reordering the hospital's affairs. And as if all this did not provide sufficient distraction at the time at which he was meant to be writing a book, he kept a close eye on the affairs of Sierra Leone, while also expending a huge amount of effort in support of the philosopher Jeremy Bentham, whose efforts to design a model prison or 'panopticon' had first been encouraged by the government and then frustrated (because it was to be built near to the estate of a member of the cabinet, Earl Spencer), resulting in serious financial losses. Wilberforce considered Bentham to have been 'cruelly used',[31] and intervened with ministers, while Bentham was happy to become an abolitionist in return: 'If to be an anti-slavist is to be a Saint, Saintship for me.'[32]

In December 1796 the hopes for peace came to nothing, but Wilberforce nonetheless ended the year with another trenchant defence of Pitt, and a sharp difference with Fox over Pitt's advancing of subsidies to the Austrian Emperor without the full knowledge of Parliament. It was little wonder that the opposition was sometimes exasperated by Wilberforce's profession of political independence, for after the revolt of the previous year he had rarely failed to support his friend in Downing Street. When the Commons discussed the failure of the peace negotiations on 30 December, Wilberforce noted, 'Pitt very earnest with me not to speak,' and he obeyed.[33]

The two friends had stuck together through 1796; 1797 would turn out to be a decisive year for both of them, but in very different ways. Pitt was about to face the most difficult year of the war so far. He would finish it with his health declining and no end in sight to the continuing national crisis. With rumours of marriage early that year discounted, his life would narrow down to that of a beleaguered war leader with increasingly failing health. For Wilberforce, by contrast, 1797 would be the year in which his life broadened out. He would finish it not just as an assiduous parliamentarian and a foremost abolitionist, but as a serious influence on the religion and philosophy of his countrymen, and he would do so whilst simultaneously bringing a deep and lasting happiness to his domestic life.

In the opening days of 1797 Wilberforce was suddenly taken so ill that he feared his life would be imperilled as much as in 1788. He noted on

2 January: 'I had a severe seizure of complaint in bowels, I used the usual remedies. I thank God they succeeded . . . I took in twenty-four hours six grains of opium.'[34] He even considered that he 'Had death, as probable, in view, and felt resigned but no ardour or warmth';[35] but within a week he was able to travel to Bath, fortified by the thought that he could have died into finally putting several weeks of concentrated work towards finishing what he had always referred to as his 'tract'. Despite having 'sixty or seventy' visitors in the month or so that he spent there,[36] he nevertheless managed to finish the book by working hard in the mornings, and returned to London in mid-February to take it to his printer, while also playing his part in the first of the many great crises of that year. Although the landing of a rather pathetic French force on the coast of Wales was easily crushed,* following the aborted French invasion of Ireland only weeks earlier, concern about the possibility of a successful invasion of Britain exacerbated a run on the Bank of England, whose reserves were almost exhausted by the end of February.

After Pitt had taken emergency action to restore confidence and to permit the issuing of a far larger quantity of paper currency, Wilberforce once again defended him in the House, and was appointed to a parliamentary committee to examine the solvency of the Bank. The need for the committee to sit for several days continually into the first weekend of March affords an interesting glimpse into both Wilberforce's trenchant insistence on his religious principles and his ambivalent political position. So great was the atmosphere of crisis that the previous weekend Pitt had called a meeting of the Privy Council on the Sunday, involving King George III himself, at Buckingham House. Yet the following weekend, with the committee still partway through its work, Wilberforce successfully insisted that a committee of which he was a member could not possibly sit on a Sunday. On the Saturday, Pitt appeared before the committee to defend his handling of the Bank's affairs. Wilberforce was part of the committee which had to hold him to account. Despite this formal role, over the next few days

---

* To the present day this was the last landing of foreign troops on the British mainland.

he spent a good deal of time at Downing Street, dining with Pitt and discussing the entire political scene, arguing all the time for a further attempt at peace. Such was Wilberforce's standing in Parliament that it was thought entirely in order for him to be on a committee scrutinising a minister while simultaneously behaving as one of his best friends.

As the crisis at the Bank passed, Wilberforce once again had to shift his parliamentary focus to the issue of the slave trade. Not only did he intend yet again to bring in his now-annual motion for abolition that spring, but 1797 was a year in which both sides could begin to see what they thought was the endgame. It was clear by now that when peace eventually came, Wilberforce would use every ounce of his influence with Pitt to attempt to obtain an international prohibition of the slave trade in the treaty. It was also clear that it was the continuation of the war and the fear of revolution, rather than any remaining belief that the slave trade could be justified on its merits, which induced Parliament to desist from abolishing it. West Indian planters began to see very clearly that they had to come up with some sort of solution of their own if the trade were to be saved once the war was over. Sir William Young, an MP who had been foremost in the dogged opposition, told the Leeward Islands Assembly that 'Many persons who have hitherto opposed the measures of Mr Wilberforce will feel themselves under the necessity of submitting to them, unless some plan of regulation shall be brought forward,' and that 'for the joint purposes of opposing the plan of Mr Wilberforce and establishing the Character of the West India body, it is essential that they should manifest their willingness to promote actively the cause of Humanity by such steps as shall be consistent with safety to the prospects of Individuals and the general interests of the Colonies'.[37]

In line with this stratagem, on 6 April 1797 another of the West India planters, Charles Ellis MP, introduced into the Commons a proposal for 'the Amelioration of the Condition of the Negroes in the West Indies'. This involved calling for improvements to living conditions, and the beginnings of education for the slaves, with a view to eventual abolition. It remitted the responsibility for carrying this out entirely to the colonial legislatures. Wilberforce was quick to see the plan for what it really was, and to oppose it, telling the House that 'from the present plan, it was impossible the slave trade should ever be put an end to',[38] since the Jamaican legislature had never yet looked upon the trade as an evil. To his great frustration, the resolution was carried by a majority of thirty votes. Its passage had no binding effect, but it demonstrated all too clearly that any assumption that abolition would follow on automatically from the end of the war could prove to be a false one. In these circumstances, the responsibility resting on Wilberforce's shoulders to sustain the parliamentary battle, develop new lines of attack against wily opponents, and keep the hopes of the abolitionists alive at a time when so many had lost heart or abandoned the fight, was immense. Looked at from the standpoint of the twenty-first century, Wilberforce's ultimate victory was inevitable. But looked at from his own standpoint in April 1797, after such a string of deeply discouraging defeats, the workings of inevitability would have seemed very hard to discern.

Parliamentary battles often exposed Wilberforce's psychological strains and physical fragility, but those of early 1797 appeared to have no effect on his sense of well-being. On the contrary, the month of April 1797, which as it happened would be one of deep crisis in the affairs of the British state, would prove to be a watershed in Wilberforce's life, and one that would leave him with a deeper sense of contentment and achievement than he had ever yet known. One of the two components of this swelling sense of happiness was literary, for on 12 April the book on which he had laboured for so long, *A Practical View of the Prevailing Religious System of Professed Christians, in the Higher and Middle Classes in this Country, Contrasted with Real Christianity*, was published. How exactly this book of some 110,000 words had emerged from the extended parliamentary sittings, continual travelling and chaotic heaps of correspondence which represented Wilberforce's daily burdens was a mystery to some of his friends. In the words of Sir James Stephen, the son of Wilberforce's abolitionist collaborator: 'To build up a literary edifice, in which chapter was to rise upon chapter, in architectural proportion, was a task which suited him as ill as the labours of the collier would agree with the taste of an aeronaut.'[39]

Wilberforce admitted in his foreword that he had long been 'looking forward to some vacant season, in which he might devote his whole time and attention to this interesting service, free from the interruption of all other concerns', but that 'meanwhile life is wearing away, and he daily becomes more and more convinced, that he might wait in vain for this season of complete vacancy'.[40] He would therefore 'throw himself on the Reader's indulgence for the pardon of such imperfections as the opportunity of undiverted and more mature reflection might have enabled him to discover and correct'.[41]

Milner warned Wilberforce about the difficulties of writing a book on religion, and the danger it might pose for his reputation. Eight years earlier, Wilberforce had written a list of reasons 'For' and 'Contra' publishing a religious book. The reasons 'For' included: 'Even to the careless whom I know, I can hardly open myself at least with sufficient plainness in private'; 'the really well disposed taught the difference between almost and altogether Christians'; and 'My way cleared of many difficulties by this explicit avowal of my sentiments; unjust conclusions will no longer be drawn from my cheerfulness or my not making religion the matter of frequent conversations.' The 'Contra' arguments included: 'the dread of an over righteous man would deter people from cooperating with me for national reform . . . I should be looked upon as morose and uncharitable. Bishops would fear me . . . I may effect this without such a publication by private conversation with friends, and by public declarations.'

At that time he had resolved 'on the whole not to publish', but the atmosphere of the 1790s was very different from that of the late 1780s. In a national crisis which he associated with the workings of Providence, he became determined to communicate his beliefs to the country. Despite all the distractions he persisted in the attempt, driven on by a feeling that the truth and logic of his beliefs were so overwhelming, if presented to anyone who professed to be a Christian, that they had to be set down in some form that people could study and consider. It is said that his efforts to bring together the various passages which emerged from days snatched during the parliamentary recesses of the preceding years were much assisted when he stayed with the Gisbornes,

Mrs Gisborne apparently gathering up 'the scattered leaves with which her guest had enriched her drawing room, or her conservatory', and putting them in a more orderly state when he wasn't looking. When she finally saw the finished volume, she is said to have remarked that its existence persuaded her 'that a fortuitous concourse of atoms might, by some felicitous chance, combine themselves into the most perfect of forms, – a moss-rose or a bird of paradise'.[42]

When Wilberforce took the finished manuscript to a well-known publisher in the Strand, Thomas Cadell, he found himself treated as 'an amiable enthusiast',[43] and was told that there was so little demand for religious publications that even a book with his name on it, followed by his title 'Member of Parliament for the County of York', would only call for the printing of five hundred copies. Even this did not deflate him, and he happily made amendments to the proofs in March before sending out copies to his friends at the time of publication. There were, indeed, some critical reactions and reviews. One reader was quick to write, reflecting Pitt's doubtful popularity at the time, that 'It was my primary intention to examine your publication in detail; but this object I soon abandoned, as tedious, from the prolixity of your effusions; as unprofitable, from their wildness; as impracticable, from their indistinction ... you stand impeached at the bar of Religion, Reason, and Humanity, of that high crime and misdemeanour, – a long, and uniform, and ardent support, in your political capacity, of WILLIAM PITT.'[44] Other reviewers, less politicised and more intellectual, took advantage of Wilberforce's effusive writing to argue that his book was too vague, or did not fit in with any of the established schools of scriptural analysis: 'He has neglected to give a definition or a clear explanation of the doctrines which he so strongly inculcates, and ... has left his readers to collect them as they are able, from hints incidentally thrown out in different parts of his work.'[45] Yet the overall reaction was hugely positive. From Wilberforce's friends came predictable but genuine praise: with the country seeming to be on its knees, Bishop Porteus wrote that he was 'truly thankful to Providence that a work of this nature has made its appearance at this tremendous moment'.[46] John Newton wrote: 'What a phenomenon has Mr. Wilberforce sent abroad! *Such* a book, by *such* a man, and at *such* a time!'[47] Muncaster wrote: 'As a friend I thank you for it; as a man I doubly thank you; but as a member of the Christian world, I render you all gratitude and acknowledgement. I thought I knew you well, but I know you better now, my dearest excellent Wilber.'[48]

The praise for *A Practical View* was by no means confined to Wilberforce's closest friends. The dying Edmund Burke read it and drew comfort from it in his final days, remarking that 'if he lived he should thank Wilberforce for having sent such a book into the world'.[49] Arthur Young, an innovative writer on agricultural matters whom Wilberforce had never met but who became an important ally in the future, wrote that the book 'made so much impression upon me that I scarcely knew how to lay it aside',[50] and the clergyman and writer Legh Richmond said that Wilberforce's book 'humbled my heart, and brought me to seek the love and blessing of that Saviour who alone can afford a peace which the world cannot give'.[51]

One of the reasons for the enthusiastic reception the book received seemed to be the trying nature of the times, when people were looking for an explanation of what was happening to them, and a better way to live. Criticisms of the book made by people steeped in academic interpretations of the Bible bore the appearance of intellectual snobbery, and quite possibly created a reaction in its favour. In addition, Wilberforce's standing in Britain meant that writings which in another author might have gone unnoticed commanded a large audience. As one historian explained it a century later, 'Written by a layman who was well known as an accomplished debater in Parliament – a man who was on terms of intimacy with the most eminent statesmen of the day, and an eminent statesman himself, a man of wit and talent who had been a brilliant ornament to society, a man of extraordinary philanthropy and benevolence, the parliamentary representative of the largest county in England – it came with a force which no work of any clergyman or of any unknown layman could possibly possess.'[52]

The combined result of all of this was that the pessimistic publisher was confounded: the five hundred copies were sold out within a few days, and a reprint urgently begun. Within six months, 7,500 copies had been sold – a best-seller by late-eighteenth-century standards – in five editions. During Wilberforce's lifetime it would go through at least fifteen editions in Britain and twenty-five in America, while also being translated into French, Italian, Spanish, Dutch and German. Within a century there were fifty editions. Wilberforce would presumably be surprised and gratified if he knew that a modern edition is still readily available in the first decade of the twenty-first century.

As a book, *A Practical View* certainly has deficiencies. It is often repetitive, its contents are arranged in a somewhat haphazard way, and its chapter structure seems unbalanced – with Chapter IV being ten times as long as Chapter V, for instance. Yet its strengths: the sincerity, eloquence, and enthusiasm of its language; the relevance of its analysis for the parlous condition of Britain at the time; and the hope it extended to individuals and to the entire country if they could find it within themselves to accept the full meaning of a religion they already professed to support, far overcome these weaknesses. In later years Wilberforce told one of his sons 'that he was sensible that his book on Christianity might be very much censured by many persons for the diffusiveness of its style, but that was in part intended by himself, because a book, which, like his was intended for popular effect is more likely to obtain its object, when its style is diffusive'.[53]

The book begins with Wilberforce's own motivation for writing it – 'It is the duty of every man to promote the happiness of his fellow-creatures to the utmost of his power'[54] – and concludes with a summary of his analysis that 'To the decline of Religion and Morality our national difficulties must both directly and indirectly be chiefly ascribed; and that my only solid hopes for the well-being of my country depend, not so much on her fleets and armies, not so much on the wisdom of her rulers, or the spirit of her people, as on the persuasion, that she still contains many, who love and obey the Gospel of Christ; that their intercessions may yet prevail; that for the sake of these, Heaven may still look upon us with an eye of favour.'[55] Everything in between is a comprehensive statement of the views Wilberforce had developed over the previous eleven years: 'the result of observation, serious inquiry, much reading and long and repeated consideration'.[56] The influence of

Doddridge's writings on his mind is evident throughout, and there are many signs too of his close study of the treatises of the seventeenth-century Puritan non-conformist John Owen. Wilberforce's book, however, would command a circulation vastly greater than these earlier works, and was expressed in more direct and uplifting language:

> Beat the world at its own best weapons. Let your love be more affectionate, your mildness less open to irritation, your diligence more laborious, your activity more wakeful and persevering. Consider sweetness of temper and activity of mind, if they naturally belong to you, as talents of special worth and utility, for which you will have to give account. Carefully watch against whatever might impair them, cherish them with constant assiduity, keep them in continual exercise, and direct them to their noblest ends.[57]

Wilberforce had said, 'I believe, were I not a real Christian . . . I should probably be an atheist,'[58] and at the heart of *A Practical View* is his driving belief that the teachings of Christianity, if they are true, must be taken to a logical conclusion in terms of human behaviour. There was no point in being a Christian without taking it seriously. His analysis of the behaviour of the bulk of professed Christians in the country was acute as well as scathing:

> If we listen to their conversation, virtue is praised, and vice is censured; piety perhaps applauded, and profaneness condemned. So far all is well: but let any one, who would not be deceived by these 'barren generalities' examine a little more closely, and he will find, that not to Christianity in particular, but at best to Religion in general, perhaps to mere Morality, their homage is intended to be paid . . . The Bible lies on the shelf unopened: and they would be wholly ignorant of its contents, except for what they hear occasionally at church, or from the faint traces which their memories may still retain of the lessons of their earliest infancy.[59]

By contrast, Wilberforce calls on Christians '*specially* to believe the doctrines, imbibe the principles, and practise the precepts of Christ'.[60]

The book is peppered with quotations from the Bible, emphasising

the importance Wilberforce attached to its continual study. He repeatedly emphasises the need to fear God: 'As all nature bears witness to
his irresistible power, so we read in scripture that nothing can escape
his observation, or elude his discovery; not our actions only, but our
most secret cogitations are open to his view. "He is about our path
and about our bed, and spieth thou all our ways [Psalm 139:3]."'[61]
Wilberforce advocates for the true Christian the virtues which he himself had struggled to develop over the previous eleven years. One is to
serve God and promote His glory, to be active also, and useful: 'Let
not your precious time be wasted "in shapeless idleness"; an admonition which, in our days, is rendered but too necessary by the relaxed
habits of persons even of real piety.'[62] It is not surprising that such a
sentiment came from the pen of a man who noted in his diary a few
months earlier, 'May I be enlightened, and purified, and quickened;
and having sadly wasted my precious faculties even since my thinking
more seriously, may I now more constantly act as an accountable
creature, who may be called away suddenly to his reckoning.'[63]

Another virtue he presses upon his readers is the importance of
self-examination and watchfulness, particularly when excelling and
receiving praise. If a man, he explains in Chapter IV, 'finds himself
pursuing wealth, or dignity, or reputation, with earnestness and solicitude; if these things engage many of his thoughts; if his mind naturally
and inadvertently runs out into contemplations of them; if success in
these respects greatly gladdens, and disappointments dispirit and distress his mind; he has but too plain grounds for self-condemnation.
"No man can serve two masters."'[64] In addition, Christians should
have a burning passion for God, from which great joy is obtained:

> If we look to the most eminent of the Scripture characters, we
> shall find them warm, zealous and affectionate. When engaged in
> their favourite work of celebrating the goodness of their Supreme
> Benefactor, their souls appear to burn within them, their hearts
> kindle into rapture; the powers of language are inadequate to the
> expression of their transports; and they call on all nature to swell
> the chorus, and to unite with them in hallelujahs of gratitude,
> and joy, and praise.[65]

These and other virtues come together to give a clear prescription for action:

> Let true Christians then ... strive in all things to recommend their profession, and to put to silence the vain scoffs of ignorant objectors. Let them boldly assert the cause of Christ in an age when so many who bear the name of Christians are ashamed of Him ... Let them be active, useful, and generous toward others; manifestly moderate and self-denying in themselves. Let them be ashamed of idleness ... Let them evince ... a manifest moderation in all temporal things; as becomes those whose affections are set on higher objectives than any which this world affords, and who possess, within their own bosoms, a fund of satisfaction and comfort, which the world seeks in vanity and dissipation ... Let them countenance men of real piety wherever they are found; and encourage in others every attempt to repress the progress of vice, and to revive and diffuse the influence of Religion and Virtue ... Let them pray continually for their country in this season of national difficulty.[66]

It is such passages that give Wilberforce's book its power. He had poured into it the strengths of his beliefs, expressed through his natural eloquence, with the result that critics seemed churlish or nitpicking. Furthermore, he embraced within this comprehensive statement of his philosophy his purpose as a politician: 'Nor is it only by their personal conduct (though this mode will always be the most efficacious) that men of authority and influence may promote the cause of good morals ... Let them enforce the laws by which the wisdom of our forefathers has guarded against the grosser infractions of morals ... Let them favour and take part in any plans which may be formed for the advancement of morality.'[67] While, he explains, 'Religion is the business of everyone,' he considers that 'its advancement or decline in any country is so intimately connected with the temporal interests of society, as to render it the peculiar concern of a political man'.[68] And in a section of the book to which he, rather optimistically, drew Pitt's attention, he argues that 'If a principle of true religion should ... gain ground, there is no estimating the effects on public morals, and the consequent influence on our political welfare.'[69] While Wilberforce may have flirted with the idea of political retirement less than a year earlier, *A Practical View* revealed that he had totally united in his mind his role as a politician with the advancement of Evangelical thinking. His book showed that his walk would always remain a public one. In it he reaffirmed that he would never desist from the causes, such as the abolition of the slave trade, which he had adopted in previous years. Someone who showed zeal in God's service would be 'supported by a courage which no danger can intimidate, and a quiet constancy which no hardships can exhaust',[70] and in a passage which could have served to address his own thoughts after each parliamentary defeat for abolition, he wrote: 'Accustom yourself to look first to the dreadful consequences of failure; then fix your eye on the glorious prize which is before you; and when your strength begins to fail, and your spirits are well nigh exhausted, let the animating view rekindle your resolution, and call forth in renewed vigour the fainting energies of your soul.'[71]

Wilberforce had underscored his purpose as a politician. Yet he had also shown once again, as he had done when creating the Proclamation Society, that his ambitions for what he could achieve went far beyond the parliamentary and the political. He believed it was imperative to attempt to change the morals of an entire nation, and ultimately of the entire world. Speeches in Parliament were therefore not enough: it was necessary to communicate what he felt in a more durable and transmissible form. Driven by the need to do so, he had produced something his contemporaries found arresting and astonishing, while, in keeping with his own advice, he showed no undue satisfaction about the flattery and excitement his book caused. And before many hours had passed he did something which was, at least in the view of his friends, more astonishing still.

Now thirty-seven years old, Wilberforce had himself expressed scepticism about ever marrying. 'I doubt,' he wrote the previous year, 'if I shall ever change my situation; the state of public affairs concurs with other causes in making me believe "I must finish my journey alone"

... Then consider how extremely I am occupied. What should I have done had I been a family man for the last three weeks, worried from morning till night?[72] Yet there was something about the way Wilberforce considered his 'solitary state' to have 'some advantages', such as impressing on him 'the duty of looking for and hastening to a better country', that was not wholly convincing.[73] Furthermore, letters in earlier years contained several hints that he would like to marry if the opportunity arose. In June 1791, after spending a month with old friends such as Henry Thornton and Edward Eliot, he wrote, 'I must beware of this sort of old bachelor's life,'[74] and it was on that visit that he noted how he missed having a family to welcome him home. In *A Practical View* he idealised marriage as a means of mutually strengthening religious devotion:

> The wedded state seems to afford to the married man the means of rendering an active share in the business of life more compatible, than it would otherwise be with the liveliest devotional feelings; that when the husband should return to his family, worn and harassed by worldly cares or professional labours, the wife, habitually preserving a warmer and more unimpaired spirit of devotion than is perhaps constituent with being immersed in the bustle of life, might revive his languid piety; and that the religious impressions of both might derive new force and tenderness from the animating sympathies of conjugal affection.[75]

In 1796, any instinct that led Wilberforce to think he should still be looking for a wife received a very sharp prod. In that year his cousin and housemate Henry Thornton married, breaking up the companionship of Old Palace Yard and temporarily reducing Wilberforce's status at Clapham to that of a guest of a married couple. There can be little doubt that this turn of events made him feel the loneliness of bachelorhood to a far greater extent than ever before, and in later years Henry Thornton's daughter Marianne would report that 'I once heard him say that the union between her [Marianne's mother] and my father gave him such a delightful idea of domestic life that it made him determined to marry also.'[76] Further underlining the supposition that he was predisposed to marry at the beginning of 1797 is the sheer rapidity of what now transpired.

In the same week as the publication of *A Practical View*, Wilberforce travelled to Bath, and noted there, on 13 April, the Thursday before Easter: 'Babington has strongly recommended Miss Spooner for wife for me. We talked about it.'[77] The 'Miss Spooner' in question was Barbara Ann Spooner, the third of ten children of a wealthy Birmingham businessman. She was twenty years old, regarded as 'extremely handsome',[78] with an attractive face and large, soulful eyes, and was an Evangelical who, possibly at Babington's prompting, had written to Wilberforce for spiritual advice. As she was resident in Bath that Easter, Babington took the opportunity to bring the two of them together on the Saturday. Wilberforce appears to have fallen in love instantly, writing and underlining *'Pleased with Miss Spooner'* in his diary that night.[79] By the following day, he was fearing that he was suffering from 'too much animal *heat* and emotion, partly from ideal forms of conjugal happiness to which Miss Spooner has led me. What a blessed Sunday have I been permitted to spend, how happy at dinner and in love.'[80]

On the Monday, Wilberforce received the news of one of the most alarming events it was possible to imagine in wartime eighteenth-century England: that the Channel fleet, based at Spithead in Hampshire, had refused orders to put to sea, and mutinied. With the country already in danger of invasion, Pitt was in Downing Street facing the gravest crisis he had ever encountered. It is a measure of Wilberforce's sudden obsession with Miss Spooner that even in these circumstances he remained firmly rooted in Bath for the following week. By that evening, rumours of a connection between them were rife around the city, but even so, Babington managed to engineer a simultaneous visit to the Pump Room for them on the Wednesday. The same thing happened on the Thursday, Wilberforce's notes reporting that he was even 'More pleased with her,'[81] and on the Friday, 'Slept well tonight, every other kept awake thinking of her.'[82] By that weekend he was in an agony of love and indecision, and being counselled by Henry Thornton and Hannah More not to be too hasty. Yet on the Sunday, 23 April, having known Barbara for precisely eight days, he wrote to her proposing marriage, was talked out of such precipitate action by Babington, discovered the letter had already been sent, and by the evening had received her acceptance. His diary captures the agony of the day:

> Sunday 23rd April. After sad night haunted with Miss Spooner rose to prayer. Miss Spooner to Pump Room, Randolphs. Much affected and at length I fear too hastily wrote. I fear rather too hastily declaring to Miss Spooner state of my mind and she dined with us. Afternoon. Babington rather advised me to put off to 2 or 3 days. I vexed, having got over the Struggle. But at length gave way. When going to Miss Babington found that my letter had actually gone. That night I had a formal favourable answer – kept awake all night.[83]

Wilberforce then spent a few more contented days in Bath with Barbara, and was awaiting the arrival of several friends, including Milner, to join him for the rest of his stay. But with the marriage agreed, the turn of international events and the anxious nature of a letter he received from Pitt persuaded him that he could linger no longer. On top of the naval mutiny came the fear that the Austrian Empire was about to pull out of the war against France, leaving Britain to fight on alone. As Pitt needed urgent parliamentary approval for a fresh loan to Vienna, Wilberforce reluctantly departed for London – Milner arriving in Bath to find his carriage at the door ready to leave – where he spent several weeks in the thick of the mounting crisis, and amid some personal controversy.

The controversy arose from the rumour that Wilberforce, following the demands of sailors for better pay and conditions, was helping to foment trouble in the army on similar grounds. On 13 May 'Pitt sends to me about soldiers' and asked for the truth.[84] Thankfully for Wilberforce, the truth was soon uncovered: a degenerate clergyman named Williams, to whom Wilberforce had given money but then refused further help in the light of him wasting it, had been visiting army barracks armed with Wilberforce's genuine letter and signature, but reading out from it a fictional message of support for the grievances of the soldiers. Wilberforce helped the government to track down 'wicked Williams' and put an end to the matter, but in the same week he was pitched into the debate on his annual motion to abolish the slave trade. This was the first test of opinion on the issue in the extremely conservative House of Commons produced by the general election of the preceding year, and it was not an encouraging one: his motion was defeated by eighty-two votes to seventy-four. Wilberforce, still elated by the prospect of marriage, was more sanguine than usual about the result: 'I did not want Christian love to keep me from falling out of temper, and I have been too long used to it to feel much disappointment from losing my motion.'[85] The slave trade had shrunk to a minor item on the nation's political agenda: by the end of the month the naval mutiny had spread, the army was rioting in its London barracks, and Austria had made peace with France. Wilberforce observed: 'Pitt and the others now convinced that things *in extremis* yet no apparent sense of God. I now feel exceedingly hunted and shattered.'[86]

The next day, Monday, 29 May, he left for Bath, and on Tuesday the thirtieth was married to Barbara. It was six weeks and three days since he had first set eyes on her. In spite of their short acquaintance and the age gap of nearly eighteen years between them, he was utterly certain that he was marrying the right person. He had written to Matthew Montagu: 'Above all the women I ever knew she is qualified *in all respects* to make me a good wife.'[87] Elsewhere he noted: 'I believe indeed she is admirably suited to me and . . . I believe her to be a real Christian, affectionate, sensible, rational in habits, moderate in desires and pursuits, capable of bearing prosperity without intoxication, and adversity without repining.'[88]

After four days' honeymoon alone, the couple spent their first married weekend with the More sisters at Cowslip Green, Barbara later remembering: 'We arrived on Saturday to dinner and were most hospitably welcomed with a frankness and cordiality and almost over-whelming expressions of delight that seldom met with in the more polished circles and which owed their charm to being believed to be truly sincere.'[89] She was bemused by the sisters and charmed by the scenery. 'Early on Sunday morning, all was alive in the little mansion and after breakfast our chariot and a chaise were at the door,'[90] ready for a church service where a wedding psalm was sung and the school-children being educated through Wilberforce's and Hannah More's philanthropy were duly assembled to meet the bride. Unconventional as this may have been for part of a honeymoon, Barbara showed no sign of minding it.

For his part, Wilberforce was overjoyed to have his 'dearest B' by his side. Neither then nor on any day of the remaining thirty-six years of his life did he show anything other than delight and satisfaction in the choice he had made. His friends, though in some cases worried about the speed of it all, were generally approving. Hannah More thought Barbara 'a pretty, pleasing, pious young woman',[91] and Henry Thornton commented that 'She is a very pleasing young woman about twenty-five, rather handsome than otherwise, with much feeling, great openness and simplicity of character, and unquestionably of a pious disposition ... Her fortune is small (£5,000) and the family is not by any means grand, her father being merely a thriving merchant and a country banker with a large family ... The match is not what the world would account to be a good match – that is to say he has not insisted on some things which the world most esteems, because he has thought it indispensable that the lady should have certain other qualities.'[92]

Thornton's comments underline the fact that Barbara was no society lady. She would prefer a quiet, domestic life, and as a result would not always be popular with her husband's friends. Wilberforce saw this tendency as one of her attractions, remarking many years later: 'How thankful should I be for having a wife who is not of the fashionable sort,'[93] and even noting in 1803: 'I find reason to thank God for my marriage which, by shutting me out more from the world, has tended to keep me from its infection.'[94] But to others it often seemed that Barbara was too timid, and too prone to worrying, for a man who liked to travel so much, and too cautious with money for one who was so generous. Dorothy Wordsworth would write many years later: 'Mrs W looked very interesting, for she was full of delight ... but I must say that she has never since appeared to me to such advantage. Yet I like her very well – admire her goodness and patience and meekness – but that slowness and whininess of manner – tending to be self-righteousness, I do not like.'[95] Marianne Thornton, who had believed that her mother and father's marriage helped to prompt that of Wilberforce, thought that he 'was not equally fortunate in his choice'. Barbara, she thought, 'was extremely handsome and in some ways very clever but very deficient in common sense, a woman with narrow views and selfish aims, that is if selfishness can be so called when it took the shape of idolatry of her husband, and thinking everything in the world ought to give way to what she thought expedient for him. Instead of helping him forward in the great work which Providence had given him to do, she always considered she was hardly used when he left her side and instead of making his home attractive to the crowds of superior people that he invited, her love of economy made her anything but a hospitable hostess.'[96] The huge Isaac Milner, whose appetite matched his frame, would complain 'there was nothing on earth to eat' in the Wilberforce household, and after commanding the servants to bring food without limit would be thanked by Wilberforce 'for seeing to these things, Mrs Wilberforce is not strong eno' to meddle much in domestic matters'.[97]

Whatever his wife's failings might later turn out to be, Wilberforce would never admit them, and he was hugely fortified in spirit by what had happened to him. Worrying within days of the wedding that he was not being sufficiently diligent in his parliamentary work, he was back in London with his bride early in June, renting Broomfield at Clapham from Eliot for the rest of the parliamentary term. 'Let me go forth,' he noted, 'remembering ... that my political station is most important, my means of doing good, numerous and great; my cup full of blessings, above all spiritual. The times how critical! Death perhaps at hand. May God be with me for Christ's sake.'[98]

This new era was a fraught one on the political front, with Pitt struggling on against a France increasingly dominated by Bonaparte. On the personal front, it brought little but tragedy for Wilberforce. Travelling northwards in early August to take his new wife to York, he received news of the sudden death of his sister's husband, Dr Clarke, aged only forty-five. With his sister in mourning and his mother in 'great decrepitude', he spent the next three weeks in Hull comforting them, while securing for Joseph Milner the position of vicar of Hull, in succession to his deceased brother-in-law.

By mid-September Wilberforce and Barbara were in Bath, hoping that Edward Eliot would join them for a while, but instead the post brought fresh tragic news. Eliot, one of Wilberforce's closest friends, was not coming to stay: at the age of thirty-seven he too was dead. Wilberforce had lost a great companion, in evangelicalism and in politics, and was 'deeply hurt by Eliot's death – kept awake at night by it'.[99] He also worried about Pitt, beleaguered in Downing Street as the latest peace talks with France failed. George Rose, Pitt's Secretary to the Treasury, had written to him to say: 'The effect produced on Mr Pitt [by the news of Eliot's death] was, as you may imagine, beyond description; it has not happened to me to be a witness of such a one, as I saw him immediately after his getting Lord Eliot's letter by the common post, and reading it among others, not knowing the writing; it is difficult even to conceive the impression made by the misfortune and the manner of hearing it.'[100] Wilberforce had wanted Pitt to appoint Eliot as Governor General of India, to combine good government with Christian activity there, yet deeply saddened as he was, his reaction to Eliot's death demonstrated the strength he now drew from his faith. Eliot's last letters to him had shown his own humility and religious character. Wilberforce asked Hannah More why newspapers should refer to '*poor* Eliot',[101] and wrote to Muncaster, 'I have the solid satisfaction of knowing that his mind was just in the state I should have wished, had I been aware of the awful change which awaited him. May my last end be like his!'[102]

Eliot's death led to Wilberforce buying Broomfield from his executors, giving him a permanent residence in Clapham. It is not surprising that Barbara preferred the house there to Old Palace Yard, with its endless procession of political visitors, and Wilberforce was, as a result, travelling more than ever the four miles between his two homes. But, fortified by his personal happiness, he threw himself back into parliamentary affairs when the new session began in November 1797. The refusal of France to contemplate any reasonable peace terms had hardened his attitude to the war: Pitt had tried everything he could to attain an honourable peace; now, as he tried to rally the country for an indefinite war, he enjoyed the support of Wilberforce. 'Englishmen should feel the necessity,' he told the Commons, 'of coming forward in preservation of the Constitution; and to secure those objects should draw hand and heart together and proclaim to the world that if divided before, they could unite whenever union became necessary.'[103] He was soon feeling 'Hurried beyond all comfortable bearing, and having more to do than I can execute,'[104] all the more so because he was closely consulted by Pitt, a Prime Minister struggling to cope with permanent warfare and massive holes in his cherished public finances. When Pitt announced a massive tax rise in his budget that November, amounting to a tripling of most taxes, Wilberforce thought, erroneously, that he would have to back down. Yet Pitt persisted, albeit with some amendments, and in the end Wilberforce spoke in his favour, much to the irritation of the opposition. He had by now earned a reputation for integrity, sincerity and independence of thought, and his suggestion of an alternative to the huge tax increases in the form of voluntary contributions by wealthy people – he himself contributed an eighth of his income that year – was subsequently taken up as an additional source of revenue. But his high standing did not make him immune from the sharp cutting edges of political debate. The year 1798 and early 1799 saw Wilberforce involved in a series of controversies which led to acrimonious disagreement with members of the Foxite Whig opposition, and to his being accused of excessive conservatism or harshness.

One such controversy arose from the prosecution in 1797 of a poor printer, Thomas Williams, for distributing cheap editions of Paine's *The Age of Reason*. It was at the behest of the Proclamation Society that Williams was prosecuted for circulating this pro-revolution and anti-religious work, and largely as a result of the Society's unexpected employment of the leading liberal advocate Thomas Erskine that he was convicted. Erskine, however, wanted the Proclamation Society to drop the case before judgement was passed, apparently after having come across Williams's sick and poverty-stricken wife and family. He asked them to show Christian charity, but the committee of the Society, including Wilberforce, decided that they could not ask for leniency or drop the case without suggesting that the blasphemy contained in *The Age of Reason* was not significant. Williams received a sentence of a year's hard labour in Cold Bath Fields prison. The dispute over the true circumstances of his family has continued ever since, with fresh evidence coming to light in 1972 suggesting that they were far better off than Erskine had suggested. Nevertheless, Wilberforce and his colleagues could henceforth be accused of unmerciful behaviour.

Cold Bath Fields, at Clerkenwell in London, was the prison in which many state prisoners, interned without trial or convicted of sedition, were held. On 21 December 1798 the Commons debated the continued suspension of Habeas Corpus, which Wilberforce supported as an undesirable but necessary barrier to revolution. When he entered the chamber that night he found himself under attack from John Courtenay, the MP for Tamworth, who suggested that Wilberforce, well known for his concern for prisoners and 'celebrated for his humanity', had not visited Cold Bath Fields, otherwise his 'principles of "vital Christianity" would have induced him to exert himself to ameliorate the condition of these unhappy people', who were treated worse than the famous prisoners of the Bastille.[105] 'I am certain,' he finished, 'the honourable gentleman will no longer suffer it to be said by the unfortunate, "I was in prison and you visited me not."'[106]

Wilberforce gave a vigorous response. He had indeed visited the prison in the past, and had just received a report from a visiting magistrate from which he quoted, 'showing that the food intended for the prisoners consisted of as good legs of mutton and pieces of beef as he had ever seen at his own table, that the utmost cleanliness prevailed throughout the place and that nothing could be more satisfactory than this account of the state of the prison and the health and treatment of the prisoners'.[107]

The following week Courtenay raised the matter again, accusing Wilberforce of 'Christian rancour and religious facetiousness' towards him. Wilberforce responded that 'a religious man might sometimes be facetious', while 'the irreligious did not of necessity escape being dull'.[108] He soon regretted this, noting in his journal: 'How jealous of character and greedy of applause! Alas! Alas!'[109] But in years to come he would have greater cause to regret his defence of Cold Bath Fields. The prisoners held there became a *cause célèbre* for radical MPs, notably Sir Francis Burdett, whose persistent enquiries eventually led to the admission that those interned there without trial were treated in the same way as those who had been convicted, and that prisoners who were unable to buy immunity from prosecution were given short rations, solitary confinement, beatings and forced labour. Given the earlier lack of any official knowledge of these practices, Wilberforce's mistake was understandable, but nevertheless it did not add to his reputation.

Wilberforce's political positions in the late 1790s underlined the fact that, while he called for the transformation of British society through an improvement in the moral behaviour of individuals, he was adamantly opposed to anything that smacked of political revolution. For one thing, his championing of the abolitionist cause would have stood no chance at all if his name had been associated with radical measures in general; but Wilberforce saw no contradiction between his concern for the poor and unfortunate and his defence of what was seen as repressive measures. Revolution as witnessed in France was thoroughly anti-Christian in character, and the moral improvements he sought could not take place without an ordered society. Furthermore, he subscribed, along with Pitt and other disciples of Adam Smith, to a view of economics which favoured free markets rather than government intervention: the same views which led him to support freer trade with Ireland and France in the 1780s caused him to oppose earlier attempts to form trade unions in the 1790s. In 1799 he spoke in favour of new laws to prevent the combination of workers into unions, to be known as the Combination Act, saying that these unions would be 'a general disease in our society; and for which he thought the remedy should be general; so as not only to cure the complaint for the present, but to preclude its return'.[110] All such views must be judged against the background of the times: a bloody revolution in France, a destructive war then in its eighth year, and economic troubles which seemed to bring even closer the danger of insurrection at home. But they also demonstrate how strongly Wilberforce believed that the many reforms for which he campaigned could only be secured within the political and parliamentary system to which he so much belonged.

It was this combination of being such an active Member of Parliament on day-to-day issues, as well as being the foremost moral crusader of the nation, which made his life so hurried. In the course of 1798 he could be found speaking in the Commons on the regulation of newspapers, in favour of the fateful introduction of income tax, reluctantly supporting sending the militia overseas, or vociferously complaining about the misrepresentation of Members' speeches in the press. At the same time, he was redoubling his efforts to introduce Christianity to India, leading to the formation two years later of the Church Missionary Society for Africa and the East. His support for the government kept him close to Pitt, whom he continued to think 'has more disinterested patriotism and a purer mind than almost (I scarce need say almost) any man, not under the influence of Christian principles I ever knew'.[111]

On Sunday, 27 May 1798, however, Pitt did something which led Wilberforce to be 'more shocked than almost ever'.[112] Having accused the leading opposition MP George Tierney, in an angry debate the previous Friday, of obstructing the defence of the country, he had refused to retract the allegation, and accepted a challenge to a duel. On the Sunday afternoon the British Prime Minister and another Member of Parliament had accordingly met on Putney Heath, each taken twelve paces and then fired their pistols at each other. As it happened, neither party was injured, and in conformity with the standards of the time, honour was deemed to have been satisfied all round.

Wilberforce was outraged three times over. For one thing, his close friend the Prime Minister had risked his life at a time of deep national crisis and possibly imminent invasion. As an angry George III wrote to Pitt: 'I trust what has happened will never be repeated ... Public characters have no right to weigh alone what they owe to themselves; they must consider also what is due to their country.'[113] Secondly, Wilberforce had come to consider duelling as one of the least Christian activities engaged in by the British upper classes. In *A Practical View* he had argued that the practice was 'the disgrace of a Christian society',[114] and 'its essential guilt' was that 'It is a deliberate preference of the favour of man, before the favour and approbation of God ... wherein we run the risk of rushing into the presence of our Maker in the very act of offending him.'[115] These considerations placed 'the crime of Duelling' on a different footing from almost any other: 'Indeed perhaps there is No Other, which mankind habitually and deliberately resolve to practise whenever the temptation shall occur.'[116] Third and for good measure, Pitt had chosen to commit what Wilberforce saw as this nefarious crime on a Sunday, making his action as unacceptable as it could possibly be.

This was not the sort of thing that Wilberforce was going to let pass. When he heard about it on the Monday he 'resolved to do something if possible', and by the Wednesday had put down a Commons motion condemning duelling and calling for it to be outlawed in future. In his haste and outrage, however, he had not thought things through, for Pitt's reaction to his motion left him in the position he always found most agonising – caught between his conscience on the one hand and a personal appeal from his great friend on the other. Pitt wrote from Downing Street that night explaining that he regarded a motion on duelling at that particular moment as a motion of censure against him: 'I feel it a real duty to say to you frankly that your motion is one for my removal. If any step on the subject is proposed in parliament and agreed to, I shall feel from that moment that I can be of more use out of office than in it: for in it, according to the feelings I entertain, I could be of none.'[117]

Wilberforce thought this was 'a strange length to which he carries the point of honour',[118] but he was now in a quandary. Either his motion would be defeated, or the carrying of it would remove a Prime Minister of fifteen years' standing to no other purpose. He agonised for three days before deciding that, wholly capable of independence as he had previously shown himself to be, he could not push the point in these circumstances. He wrote to Pitt: 'I am sure, my dear P. that I need not tell you that the idea of my being compelled by duty to do any thing painful or embarrassing to you has hurt me not a little . . . I will only hint at the pain you have been the occasion of my suffering on the subject itself . . . It is my sincere prayer, my dear Pitt, that you may here be the honoured instrument of Providence for your country's good,'[119] and thus he would withdraw his motion. Pitt's reply thanked him for his 'cordial friendship and kindness on all occasions, as well where we differ as where we agree'.[120]

Pitt's duel opened up what was to be a difficult summer, on every political and personal front. Ministers were labouring to create a new international coalition against France in a deadlocked war. Bonaparte, now emerging as a dominant figure in French politics, was known to be at large in the Mediterranean with a French army and fleet which even Nelson could not find. Pitt disappeared for several weeks from public view, the accumulating strains of war leadership and excessive drinking producing his most severe bout yet of physical collapse. It was even rumoured that he had gone insane, a report Wilberforce dismissed as 'altogether without foundation'.[121] Wilberforce too was unwell that June, suddenly 'taken ill . . . four or five days very threatening'.[122] As he attempted to settle down for a peaceful rest at Broomfield in the recess, he found that Barbara, now pregnant, was also unwell, and received the news that his mother had died at Hull. He travelled north for the funeral, and wrote to Barbara: 'My dear Mother did not suffer in death, and I trust she is happy . . . It was a solemn and an affecting scene to me, yesterday evening, to be in my mother's room, and see the bed where I was born, and where my father and my mother died, and where she then lay in her coffin. I was alone, and I need not say to you, or seek to conceal from you, I put up my prayers that the scene might work its due effect.'[123]

Wilberforce's feelings at such a time are little to be wondered at. Relieved to find his wife well when he returned to London, he noted: 'What a humbling impression have I of my own inability; that all my happiness, and all that belongs to me, is at the disposal of the Supreme

Being! . . . Whatever may be God's will now, may I submit with humble, acquiescing confidence . . . May I be enabled to do better in the time to come; and if God should give me an offspring, may I bring it up in His faith, and fear, and love, as a Christian should be educated to go through such a world as this.'[124] It was a turning point in his fortunes that year. On 21 July his first son, William, was born, and by September Wilberforce was able to take a fully recovered wife and a healthy son to some of his favourite haunts, at Yoxall Lodge and Bath. There, in late October, they heard the news that caused Britain to rejoice: in early August Nelson had annihilated an entire French fleet at the Battle of the Nile. Back in London by November, Wilberforce found Pitt once again in high spirits and apparently recovered, amidst growing optimism about the war.

It seemed the nation had forgotten about the slave trade, yet through all of these multiple distractions Wilberforce fought doggedly on for the cause he could never abandon. Each year he presented his annual motion for abolition. It was defeated by eighty-seven votes to eighty-three in April 1798 and by eighty-four to fifty-four in March 1799. These debates had become something of a ritual, enlivened only a little by some of the more talented Members elected in 1796, such as Bryan Edwards on the side of the West Indian plantation-owners and the young George Canning, Pitt's protégé, arguing eloquently for abolition.

Finding their main line of attack so firmly blocked, Wilberforce and the 'Saints' in Parliament increasingly focused on other measures to undermine the trade. Wilberforce worked strenuously behind the scenes to persuade Pitt that the export of slaves to newly conquered colonies in the West Indies should not be permitted. The abolitionists had been horrified when a Proclamation of 1797 permitted planters and traders in Jamaica and Barbados to export rum and Negroes to Trinidad, captured from the Spanish, and to other conquered islands. Slaves sold from the British colonies were of course replaced by fresh imports from across the Atlantic. James Stephen was beside himself that Pitt could permit such a thing, demonstrating the beginnings of serious doubts among some abolitionists as to whether Pitt could be relied on as an ally. While it would be 'wrong in his capacity to suppose him such a miserable dupe', he wrote to Wilberforce, why had he not interfered in the matter, or at least consulted them? What would now happen was that 'the poor creole negroes bought or removed for this purpose, instead of an amelioration of their lot, as your exertions and the aspect of events promised them, will be torn from all the little comforts they possess, and from almost all their connexions for ever; even from their immediate families in general, for few, if any, women or children are sent to clear and settle new lands; and all this for no end, but that new imported wretches may be broken in to their miserable destiny upon their old estates instead of new ones'.[125] Rejecting Stephen's complaint that he had been 'improperly silent',[126] Wilberforce exerted all his private influence with Pitt, and in April 1798 'at last got the Proclamation about slaves rescinded'.[127]

Such disputes showed that the abolitionists were having to fight hard even to stand still. But early in 1799 they did succeed in narrowly carrying through both Houses of Parliament a Bill, piloted by William Smith, to increase further the amount of space on a ship allocated to each slave. Building on this success, Henry Thornton took charge of a further measure, the Slave Trade Limitation Bill, which aimed to prohibit the export of slaves from a substantial northerly area of the West African coast. After heated debate in the Commons it was passed (by fifty-nine votes to twenty-three), but in the Lords 'the question was canvassed in its progress with greater interest and zeal than any that has occurred since the Regency'.[128] Arch-conservatives such as Lord Thurlow combined with the Duke of Clarence to try to knock this measure on the head. George III himself was clearly not sympathetic, Wilberforce noting in his diary, 'Slave Limitation Bill not popular at Court.'[129] Proxy votes were issued from all corners of the kingdom. On 5 July the Bill was defeated at its second reading by thirty-two votes to twenty-seven, with thirty-six proxies on each side.

To Wilberforce, whose health was once again failing that summer, this narrow defeat was one of the bitterest blows he had ever suffered, all the more so since a mistake had been made over the proxies, and it appeared afterwards, but too late, that the Bill should have been carried. 'Never so disappointed by any defeat and grieved,'[130] he wrote the following day. Twelve arduous years after he had started his campaign, the slave trade was flourishing as never before.

12

Darkness Before Dawn

———————=·◦·=———————

It was truly humiliating to see, in the House of Lords, four of the
Royal Family come down to vote against the poor, helpless, friendless
Slaves.

WILLIAM WILBERFORCE, 1804[1]

Your heart would ache could I . . . make you a partaker of my political
grievances.

WILBERFORCE TO BABINGTON, 22 March 1803[2]

THIRTEEN YEARS AFTER the abolitionist committee had first
convened in London, and eight years after half a million people
had petitioned Parliament to abolish the slave trade, the eighteenth
century closed with the committee inactive and the slave trade
operating on its greatest ever scale. In the years from 1791 to 1800,
British slave traders surpassed all previous records, purchasing or kidnapping no fewer than 400,000 Africans and transporting them to the
Americas. 1798 alone saw 150 ships leave the port of Liverpool bound
for Africa, the highest number ever recorded. The booming price of
sugar in the 1790s, caused partly by the interruption of supply from
French colonies which had been seized by Britain or, like Saint-
Domingue, collapsed into civil war, gave the plantation-owners of
Jamaica and Barbados the incentive to invest in new slaves. Added to
this traditional demand now came an insatiable appetite for slave
imports from the rapidly expanding economy of Brazil – largely supplied in Portuguese ships – and a parallel growth of slave imports into

Cuba. At one stage around the turn of the century, Cuba was importing nearly fourteen thousand slaves a year, mainly carried in British and American ships. US laws against supplying foreigners with slaves were rarely enforced, and early in the new century the state of South Carolina would once again open up its own market for slaves, bringing in forty thousand in only four years – and half of those from British traders. Not only did European nations rely for their precious supplies of sugar on the labour of the slaves of their colonies, but they had become similarly dependent for their supplies of cotton on the slave-based economy. As James Stephen put it in 1804, 'The monster, instead of being cut off, as the first burst of honest indignation promised, has been more fondly nourished than before; and fattened with fuller meals of misery and murder.'[3]

For several years since the mid-1790s, Wilberforce and his small band of parliamentary 'Saints' had borne the brunt of keeping alive what often seemed to be a futile campaign. They had fought on tenaciously even as popular enthusiasm flagged and the organisational machinery of the abolitionist campaign had atrophied. Wilberforce had shown himself to be a living example of the duty to be active and to continue in a chosen course regardless of the obstacles that he had so powerfully expressed in *A Practical View*, but it was a duty which often came up against his always frail physique. In February 1799 he complained of 'a serious return of illness, availing itself of the very severe and cheerless north-eastern blasts', which had 'stuck to me more obstinately than usual'.[4] He responded to this by dining out less and trying to find some quiet working hours in the evenings, but by August of that year he was nevertheless exhausted. Finding that his physician was 'earnest with me to lie by, and relax – and sure (just as Milner) that I shall break down otherwise',[5] he refused to take the full sabbatical year strongly recommended to him, but decided to spend the whole of that autumn in Bath, resting with his family. It was a rapidly growing family, baby Barbara having been born on 21 July 1799 – coincidentally one year to the day since the birth of William Junior – and Wilberforce was soon to discover a whole new level of happiness at being at home with his children. Eventually there would be six of them, with Elizabeth born in 1801, Robert in 1802, Samuel in 1805, and Henry in 1807. Unusually for the times, the Wilberforces managed to produce a large number of children without any infant deaths, and his family gave Wilberforce what he described in 1802 as 'Domestic happiness beyond what could have been conceived possible.'[6]

Wilberforce loved being at home with his children, and always considered 'that retired, domestic life is by far the most happy for me'.[7] He broke off a letter to Hannah More with the words: 'Here I am irresistibly summoned to a contest at marbles, and in these days of the rights of man, as I would not furnish any valid ground for rebellion . . . I obeyed the call.'[8] Not only did he adore all of his children, but he idealised Barbara's care for them as a mother, writing to his son Samuel more than twenty years later, 'You will never know your mother's feelings because there is a tenderness in a mother's heart which exists in no other place.'[9] He would always defend her – 'Sat up too long, but poor B had a load of grievances and indeed she is to be pitied being very nervous and bearing the load of domestic cares chiefly or solely rather'[10] – and the results of her poor management and his tenderness of heart resulted in a chaotic household, with long-serving but incompetent servants kept on the family payroll whatever their shortcomings. The Wilberforces had some thirteen or fourteen servants, a perfectly normal number for a large household of the time, including a coach driver who even when he was 'driving like a madman' was kept in his job.[11]

The children would run about in the Broomfield gardens, and even had a number of young black boys as their playmates: Zachary Macaulay had returned from his stint in Sierra Leone in 1799 with forty African children to be educated in England. A high proportion of them died from a climate and diseases they were unused to, but those who survived found an atmosphere of racial equality among the Claphamites which would have been unknown anywhere else in the British Isles at the time. This was even taken to the point that when the boys played at soldiers, the Africans played the role of Negro bandsmen and, just as in the real army, carried out the role of 'flogging' the other soldiers, particularly William Junior. Charles Shore noted the irony of 'the son receiving such treatment at the hand of a negro just when and where his father was exerting his strenuous efforts to rescue the negro from the similar usage of the white'.[12]

This chaotic domestic scene was completed by the regular arrival of as many letters and visitors as it was ever possible to cope with. At the end of the summer recess in 1802, Wilberforce noted: 'the last fortnight has run insensibly away. My letters are an incessant toil and trouble to me.' Nevertheless, he had managed to read 'part of Boswell's Johnson; Ferguson's Roman History; a little of D'Arnay's Private Life of Romans; Epistle to the Romans . . . Bettering [of the Poor] Reports; Goldberry's French Account of Africa'.[13] In 1801 he explained to Muncaster when writing from Broomfield, 'I have been reproaching myself for not writing to you; but at this place I am even more pressed for time than in London. The explanation is that I have brought with me a mass of unanswered letters, and that I find here a good library; the latter tempts me from the former, and the rest follows of course.'[14]

Letters would be kept waiting, but visitors would not. During the attempt to rest in Bath in the autumn of 1799, Henry Thornton commented, 'He is a man, who, were he in Norway or Siberia, would find himself infested by company; since he would even produce a population for the sake of his society in the regions of the earth where it is the least. His heart also is so large that he never will be able to refrain from inviting people to his house.'[15] This was true enough: two years later Wilberforce would be writing to Gisborne from Bath, 'As I cannot think it right to say, through my servant, "not at home", and am not allowed to tell people so myself, I may be interrupted before I have done writing the letter I have promised you.'[16] It was the flow of visitors that resulted from his combination of a welcoming nature with a central role in so many of the issues of the day that generally overpowered his regular initiatives to find more time to think and work.

In 1800 James Stephen, his increasingly close collaborator on slave-trade matters, married Wilberforce's widowed sister Sally, not without some misgivings on Wilberforce's part, but with the result that the Clapham group was bound together even more tightly by marriage. It was their son, later Sir James Stephen, who wrote in 1849 his own eyewitness account of Wilberforce in company, and it helps to explain why there were always so many callers at the door:

> Mr Wilberforce was, by the gift of nature, amongst the most consummate actors of his times. Imagine David Garrick – talking not as a mime, but from the resources of his own mind, and the impulses of his own nature – to have personated in some other society the friends with whom he had been dining at the Literary Club, – now uttering maxims of wisdom with Johnsonian dignity – then haranguing with a rapture like that of Burke – telling a good story with the unction of James Boswell – chuckling over a ludicrous jest with the child-like glee of Oliver Goldsmith . . . and there will emerge an image of the social William Wilberforce, ever the same, and ever multiform, constraining his companions to laugh, to weep, to admire, to exult, and to mediate at his bidding.
>
> This rare felicity in running over the whole scale of feeling, and the refinement which rescued him, at each successive passage, from every taint of affectation or of coarseness, gave to his discourse a far deeper interest than would have belonged to the mere words he uttered, if falling from any lips but his own. A certain air of originality embellished the most trite and familiar of his observations. There was still an impress of novelty when he repeated for the twentieth time some favourite maxim, or told over again some well-known story, or resumed the discussion of yesterday from the very beginning . . .
>
> He did not dispose of a laughable incident by one terse and pregnant jest; he rather used it as a toy to be tossed about and played with for a while, and then thrown aside. Even his wisdom demanded a certain breadth of space for its development; for it incorporated every illustration, pleasant or pathetic which fell in his way and left behind it an impression more delightful than definite. Being himself amused and interested by everything, whatever he said became amusing or interesting.[17]

It was this love of society and of discussion and argument, along with his powerful sense of duty, which meant that Wilberforce could not lead a 'retired, common domestic life', even if he could occasionally persuade himself that that was what would make him happiest. However much he regretted being 'often absent from my family from Monday morning to Saturday night or Sunday morning', and however much he lamented at the end of each recess – 'Now it is gone like a dream, and I am about to plunge into the bustle of life again'[18] – he never wished to be parted permanently from such bustle. He could afford to live anywhere he wished in England, with a happy family and a chance to read and be tranquil for the rest of his life. Yet in spite of this temptation and his frequent ailments, he simply could not tear himself away from the centre of political action, and from his deepest conviction that he would one day be held accountable for how he had spent his time.

Thus Wilberforce disregarded his doctors and returned to London in January 1800, only to find a political landscape as bleak as any he had known in his lifetime. The disastrous harvest of 1799 had inaugurated a period of spiralling food prices and grain shortages, which exacerbated popular discontent with the government and with the war. His attempts to abolish the slave trade had run into the sand. And on the Continent, France was being delivered by the military brilliance of Napoleon from the near-certain defeat which had faced it the previous year to repelling yet again the powerful coalition assembled against her. Wilberforce's return to Westminster would have seemed a mixed blessing to Pitt and his ministers: on Christmas Day 1799 Napoleon had written a personal letter to George III proposing peace, and a fierce parliamentary debate was anticipated on the government's rejection of any such negotiations. Wilberforce fully expected to oppose his old friends again, on the same issue as in 1795, and was prepared to do so, noting 'I am grieved to the heart' when Napoleon's offer was spurned, and 'fearful that I must differ but leave off consideration until indispensable, and I can hear what Pitt says'.[19]

Pitt had learned his lesson: he could not afford another Wilberforce revolt, and spent considerable time slowly persuading him that Napoleon was not a reliable partner with whom to make peace. In the debate of 7 February 1800, Wilberforce was therefore to be found defending the continuation of the war, reminding MPs that 'The danger to which this country has been exposed, was one of the greatest extent; not merely threatening, as in the case of former wars, the diminution of territory and population, but the loss of everything which served to render society, and life itself comfortable ... if peace were now made with France, he could not consider that there was a prospect of its being attended with security to this country.'[20]

Wilberforce immersed himself more than ever that year in the full range of political debate, notwithstanding his near collapse the previous summer. He supported the continued suspension of Habeas Corpus, and spoke regularly on Pitt's proposed Union of the Westminster and Dublin parliaments – something of which he was 'tremulously uncertain',[21] given that it would add to the Commons one hundred Irish Members who might be less independent than he desired in their voting habits. He spoke, not surprisingly, with great force on the Adultery Prevention Bill, which he considered a subject 'of much more importance than any question about Peace or War, or any Constitutional question', because it 'went to the inmost recesses of domestic happiness; to the very foundations of civil society ... unchecked, nothing could have a greater tendency to destroy the whole fabric of society'.[22] At the same time he became involved in efforts to ban bull-baiting, a cruel sport which in later debates he would say 'degraded human nature to a level with the brutes', when 'the common people of England had surely a sufficient number of innocent amusements in their festivals, their gambles, their athletic exercises'.[23] Out of public view, he worked strenuously to persuade Pitt that a proposed Limiting of Toleration Bill, pushed forward by Pitt's close friend George Prety-man, now Bishop of Lincoln, and allowing magistrates to refuse licences to preachers who they thought might be seditious, would be an unwarranted interference in religious freedom. Wilberforce knew that the House of Commons was so little interested in religion that if the government proposed such a measure it would be easily carried. He went to the root of the problem by taking his case to Pitt. On this occasion his influence was decisive, and the Bill was withdrawn. Most of all, however, in that session he occupied himself with the central question of the day, and one of huge importance to his Yorkshire constituents: the shortage of food.

After a poor harvest in 1798, that of 1799 had been ruined by torrential rains in August. By the winter of 1799–1800, parts of Britain were approaching famine. No such situation had been known in Wilberforce's lifetime. For all his acceptance of the prevailing faith in market forces – he reread Adam Smith that year to try to improve his understanding of how economics should work – he also thought it was inexcusable to make no attempt to help the poorer people who were the worst-affected. While Wilberforce always accepted the social structures of his time, and was living in an age far removed from the idealistic notions of eliminating poverty which would animate later generations of politicians, he had always had a powerful sense of the duty owed by higher to lower classes. The whole basis of the Proclamation Society and of *A Practical View* had been that the higher reaches of British society had a responsibility to set an example which others would then follow; similarly, he believed that those with wealth, such as himself, had a duty to give a significant part of their income to those in need. For many years now he had set a rare example in this regard, giving away thousands of pounds of his own money each year, much of it to clergymen to distribute in their parishes. His records of personal donations made in the late 1790s say much about his character:

> For St Anne's school annually £31 10s
>
> Mr Charles's schools in Wales, annually £21
>
> Lent Robert Wells £13, which never expect again – he has a wife and six children to maintain, and ekes out a scanty income by trade in old clothes.
>
> Sent Dr Chapman 5 guineas for a book which not read, and impertinently sent me; but Irving says he is a worthy man, and he must be distressed to act in this manner.
>
> Lent M. £100, not very willingly, because though I sincerely wish to serve him, I think this plan of paying off all his debts will not make him economise. It is Mr Pitt's plan.
>
> Rev. Mr Scott, half a year of his son's College allowance, £15.
>
> Given W.C £63 to enable him to refund what he has taken of the

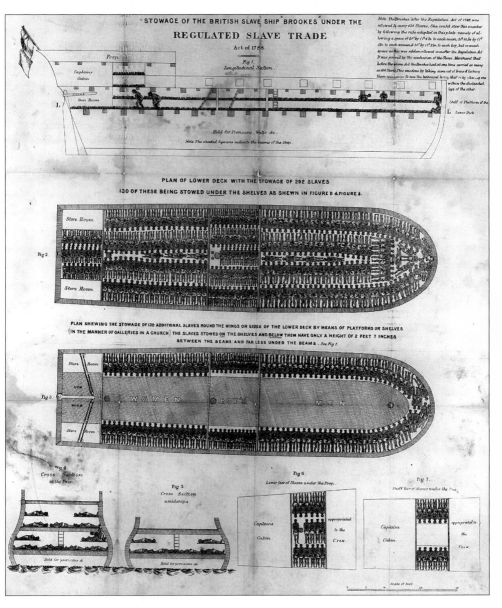

The diagram of the *Brookes*, showing how 482 slaves could be crammed into a small ship, was widely circulated by the abolitionists.

Thomas Clarkson, whose research and travels provided compelling evidence against the slave trade. After writing his celebrated essay on slavery in 1785 he resolved that 'some person should see these calamities to their end'.

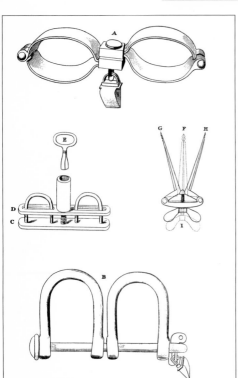

Josiah Wedgwood's classic medallion showing a kneeling slave in chains became the emblem of the abolitionists, widely worn in fashionable society.

Clarkson toured the country with thumbscrews and shackles from the slave trade to illustrate its horrors to the people of Britain.

Left: Granville Sharp, the first in a series of exceptional individuals who devoted much of their lives to opposing slavery.

Middle: James Stephen. An ingenious lawyer and intellectual mainstay of the abolitionist campaign, he would become one of Wilberforce's closest friends, and indeed his brother-in-law.

Right: Zachary Macaulay. A lifelong ally of Wilberforce's, he was appointed the first Governor of Sierra Leone and founded the Anti-Slavery Society.

The Clapham group, one of the most extraordinary and influential coalitions British society has ever known, gathered in the library at Battersea Rise. Wilberforce, hunched, stands in the centre, with members of the Thornton family around him.

Wilberforce's allegations in 1792 that Captain John Kimber had brutally whipped an African girl onboard his ship were depicted in this print. Kimber would later challenge Wilberforce to a duel.

Barbarities in the West Indias, by Gillray. In support of Wilberforce's anti-slave-trade speech of 1791, a slave is shown held down in a vat of boiling sugar; black body parts are nailed to the wall.

Charles James Fox, by
Sir Thomas Lawrence.
Fox's short tenure as
Foreign Secretary before his
death in 1806 would help
open the way to abolition.

William Pitt the Younger,
Prime Minister for nineteen
years. He considered that of
all politicians, Wilberforce had
'the greatest natural eloquence'.
He did not live to see the
slave trade abolished.

The storming of the Bastille in Paris on 14 July 1789. The French Revolution would become the greatest obstacle to abolition of the slave trade, creating a powerful reaction in Britain against radical ideas.

The town of Cap-Français in flames, 22 August 1791, as hundreds of thousands of slaves in the colony of Saint-Domingue rose in violent rebellion against their French masters.

Slave revolts had always been crushed with pitiless harshness, as depicted in this image of a living slave suspended by the ribs in Surinam in 1796...

...but after years of bloody warfare French troops were never able to regain control of Saint-Domingue, leading to the creation of independent Hayti.

Barbara Wilberforce: 'Above all the women I ever knew she is qualified in all respects to make me a good wife.'

Gore House, Kensington, situated where the Royal Albert Hall now stands. Wilberforce would go into the garden at a late hour to listen to the nightingales and to 'read aloud fine passages from his favourite poet, Cowper'.

Board's money. I do it only because it would be ruin to him to
withhold it ... As I have told him plainly, I fear he cannot be
saved from ruin. I have had much anxiety and vexation from him,
my only comfort is that I treat him like a Christian, he me as a
man of the world.[24]

The same feeling of the responsibility to give help when it was needed
now led Wilberforce to be foremost among the MPs seeking to alleviate
the effects of high grain prices and food shortages. He thought that
Adam Smith's principles should not be 'pushed to a vicious extreme',[25]
and became a member of the parliamentary committee set up to
examine the situation. In spite of all his other burdens he vowed not
to leave the meetings of the committee 'for any other business whatever',[26] even though, as he told Muncaster, 'I have not for one morning
omitted to take my place at the committee, and that cut such a solid
lump out of the day as to leave the rest composed but of fragments.'[27]
Much in correspondence with Arthur Young, who had also come to
the conclusion that action had to be taken to help the agricultural
poor, Wilberforce wrote, 'I own *I am shocked at the languor which
prevails on this important subject in sensible and feeling men. God forgive
them ... My poor rough friends in the West of Yorkshire* are suffering
with admirable patience, living on bad barley and oat meal mixed with
bean meal and damaged wheat meal when they can get it.'[28] Young
persuaded Wilberforce that a scheme for the mass planting of potatoes
was part of the answer; when Wilberforce advocated this in the Commons he was so upset that the press reports jested that he had attributed
his own tiny physique to not being given potatoes as a child that he
called them 'a farrago of unintelligible nonsense'.[29]

Action was taken to try to improve matters, including the importing
of more grain and limited versions of a potato scheme, but Wilberforce
thought the measures were too weak, and that he had been unable to
give ministers a sufficient 'sense of the necessity of taking effectual
steps for the relief of the lower orders'.[30] He would have liked to have
seen a maximum price set for grain, and was furious with the Duke of
Portland for denouncing the idea, wanted to see landowners give back
grazing rights to poorer people from land that had been enclosed, and

generally wanted to see the better-off 'gain the hearts of our people by declaring our determination to abridge our luxuries, and comforts, and superfluities'.[31] Always setting an example, he gave away so much money in 1800 that he spent £3,000 (over £160,000 in today's money) more than his income. It pained him deeply that others among the better-off did not share his sense of responsibility, and he found their opposition to some of the policies he favoured 'really *shocking*, and though used to the *conduct* of country gentlemen on such occasions, I find it hard to bear it with due temper and charity'.[32]

It was a harrowing year for Wilberforce. Although 'panting' to see the Lake District again, he thought it was easier to take his family in the recess to the coast at Bognor. There his wife became dangerously ill, to the point that Wilberforce thought she would die. As ever, he drew the lesson from this that the adoption of true Christian behaviour could never be postponed for another day. The postscript he wrote on a letter to one friend said, 'My dear wife has been delirious ever since we knew she was seized. How little could we have attended to her spiritual state if it had been before neglected, and we had wished to prepare for death! What a practical lesson to us all!'[33] Henry Thornton thought that Wilberforce 'seems more softened and melted than terrified or agonised, and shows the truly Christian character under this very severe and trying dispensation'.[34]

It was some three weeks before Barbara's condition improved, in mid-October. Wilberforce would not, after all, have to bring up three children without his wife, but he had been through a sore personal trial. 'God has in His chastisement remembered mercy; my beloved wife is spared to me,' he noted,[35] and he was soon back in London attending to the continuing scarcity of grain. Yet even in this deeply trying year, his lonely battle against the slave trade had gone on. He continued to work on Pitt with a view to the eventual peace treaty, whenever the war should end, bringing an end to the slave trade by international agreement. He received sufficient encouragement from Pitt about the prospects for this that he was always able to assure Stephen that the prospects for success, and the commitment of the Prime Minister, were more solid than he might think. In addition, there were further indications that the West Indian lobby thought they would be on weak ground once the war ended. Early in 1800 they went so far as to propose a compromise, by which the slave trade would be suspended for five years. Pitt clutched at this opportunity: for a Prime Minister inundated with problems, such an arrangement would take the issue off the table for some years to come. But in the end agreement did not materialise, lacking sufficient support among the slave-trade lobby as well as the consent of Dundas.

With such negotiations in train, Wilberforce had not proposed his annual motion for abolition in 1800. Nor would he do so in 1801. By then the negotiation of a peace treaty with France was imminent, and the rejection of abolition in the House of Commons would have weakened Wilberforce's hand in trying to secure its inclusion in the treaty. The moment Wilberforce had been waiting for was imminent, but against all his expectations he would soon face fresh obstacles. For the France with which Britain would be negotiating would no longer be a country fighting for liberty and equality, but a country turning back towards absolutist monarchy. And having been in and out of Downing Street for over seventeen years, working in harness with William Pitt, Wilberforce was about to have to face a situation in which William Pitt was no longer Prime Minister.

On 5 February 1801 George III accepted the resignation of William Pitt as First Lord of the Treasury, and thereby Prime Minister. On 14 March Pitt surrendered the seals of office, after seventeen years and eighty-five days in power. The background to his resignation was complex – a deadlocked war, deteriorating relations with the King, and increasingly severe recurrences of debilitating illness – but the immediate cause was a single issue: Catholic emancipation. That the Prime Minister had resigned over this matter was surprising to parliamentarians and their observers alike, since discussion of it had been going on within the government in private, but there was no doubting the power of the issue to break governments and burst upon the political scene.

It was little more than a hundred years since William III's overthrow of James II, and the subsequent Battle of the Boyne that had secured the Protestant succession to the British Crown. It was little more than fifty years, within the memory of many people still alive in 1801, that Bonnie Prince Charlie had mounted the Jacobite attempt to recapture the Crown. In late-eighteenth-century England, suspicion of Catholics, because of their potential cooperation with foreign powers, remained strong. The admission of Catholics into the army, necessitated by the American War of Independence, had been a key factor behind the devastating popular uprising of the Gordon Riots in 1780. But over the years that followed a new generation of ministers, with Pitt and Grenville at the centre, became convinced that these suspicions were obsolete, and that Catholics should be allowed to stand for election, sit in Parliament and hold public office. Furthermore, they considered that the union of the British and Irish parliaments in 1800 made such a measure imperative, since without it the majority Catholic population in Ireland would not become reconciled to the rule of a London parliament.

In many ways, Catholic emancipation became a parallel issue to that of the slave trade, favoured by opposition figures such as Fox and liberal-minded ministers led by Pitt, but opposed by the real conservatives in the administration such as Lord Hawkesbury (the future Earl of Liverpool), the Duke of Portland and Lord Lough-borough, the Lord Chancellor. Most difficult of all, the King was adamantly opposed to emancipation, and whereas members of the royal family opposed abolition of the slave trade on the floor of the House of Lords, George III considered emancipation as something which could not even be discussed at all. For him, the matter was above politics, 'beyond any Cabinet of Ministers',[36] as he once put it, since the admission of Catholics into office would, at least in his view, have represented the direct violation of his coronation oath to defend the Protestant faith. When he heard that ministers were none-theless about to propose the measure, he exploded in public, 'I will tell you, that I shall look on every Man as my personal Enemy who proposes that Question to me.'[37] Pitt, unwilling to live with the King's public expression of views in opposition to his own ministers, tendered his resignation. George III, unwilling to retract his opinions, accepted it.

Pitt's fall from power over Catholic emancipation underlines how difficult it would have been for him to make abolition of the slave trade a government measure in the preceding years. His government had been a coalition of men with widely differing views on such matters, and was still far more susceptible to royal influence than would be the case with governments of later decades. When his ministers were united he could generally persuade the King of the merits of a policy – although on the Catholic issue even this would not have sufficed – but on questions where ministers were divided and the King was opposed to him he was unable to put the weight of the government behind a particular policy without breaking his administration apart. Catholic emancipation and slave-trade abolition were two of the issues which Pitt had to sit astride. The intersection of these two faultlines would give Wilberforce some of his most difficult moments in the years ahead.

The successor to Pitt as Prime Minister was Henry Addington, the respected Speaker of the House of Commons who had been re-elected with Wilberforce's warm approval only a few weeks before. He was only two years older than Pitt and Wilberforce, being forty-four in the year he became Prime Minister. He was well-known to both of them socially, and indeed liked. Pitt went so far as to designate Addington as his successor, to the dismay of seasoned senior ministers such as Dundas and Grenville – who thereupon left office with Pitt – and of Pittite zealots like Canning, who would forever disparage Addington as 'the Doctor', and would eventually come up with insulting judgements such as 'Pitt is to Addington as London is to Paddington'. It was true that Addington's political abilities fell far short of those of Pitt, and that after twelve years in the Speaker's chair he was not remotely used to governmental decisions. Between the announcement of Pitt's resignation and its taking effect, a period which was extended by the King suffering a fresh bout of mental instability, a serious move was made by Pitt's friends to persuade him to stay in office and to attack Addington for unfairly taking advantage of his honourable intention to resign. With customary frankness, Wilberforce went to Addington to tell him what was being said:

> I set off for Addington and told him honestly what was said of him – well I acted the part of an honest man. I told him that it was universally said that Pitt had employed him to prevent misunderstanding with the King and that he had used his situation to gain the King's confidence for himself and had been too ready to receive his favour. I told him that I did not believe it was so. He was very angry at first; but we parted good friends.[38]

Addington did indeed take office, with a weakened government composed of his own friends and the most conservative elements of the old one. The new government was pledged from the outset to resist Catholic emancipation, and its general disposition did not present an encouraging prospect for abolition. Momentarily, Wilberforce seems to have wondered about joining the new cabinet himself, perhaps an indication that it had been Pitt's decision as much as his, so many years before, that he should not enter ministerial office. On one Sunday during the change of administration, he noted, 'I was for a little intoxicated, and had risings of ambition. Blessed be God for this day of rest and religious occupation, wherein earthly things assume their true size and comparative insignificance; ambition is stunted, and I hope my affections in some degree rise to things above.'[39] Any toying with the idea of entering office cannot have been very serious: Wilberforce would have had to abandon the pursuit of many of his cherished causes, and could hardly have joined any government that was not committed outright to abolition. In addition, he considered Addington as 'a man of talents and integrity, and of generous feelings', but one who was 'not qualified for such rough and rude work as he may have to encounter'.[40]

Wilberforce therefore had serious doubts about the new government, but like Pitt, whom he regarded as acting 'most magnanimously and patriotically',[41] he was prepared to give it a chance, and even to regard it as an opportunity. Under Pitt's long government he had come to define his political independence as meaning giving general support

to ministers but opposing any particular actions of which he dis-
approved, rather than ever entering into systematic opposition. He
initially approached Addington's government in the same manner, and
very much approved of its evident intention to make peace as soon as
possible. Britain's allies had once again deserted her, although military
successes that spring in Egypt and at Copenhagen allowed negotiations
with France to begin in the summer on a satisfactory footing. Wilberforce was as active as ever on the floor of the House, calling for the
regulation of cast iron and cutleryware in order to prevent unfair
competition with Yorkshire manufacturers, and supporting the establishment of a military training college, something of a British after-
thought at the end of eight full years of warfare. In the summer recess
he took his family to visit the Gisbornes, and then on to Bath.

By the time Parliament met in the autumn, Addington and
Hawkesbury, his Foreign Secretary, had agreed the Preliminaries of
Peace with France. Wilberforce was fully approving of the terms, on
which Pitt had been consulted throughout, but hardliners such as
Dundas, Grenville and Windham were outraged: Britain was to give
back all her colonial conquests except for Trinidad and Ceylon. Malta,
a key strategic bastion, was to be returned to the control of the Knights
of the Order of St John. Wilberforce's defence of these terms, in a
debate of 4 November, was a classic expression of his generally pacific
views on foreign affairs:

> As to the restitution of our conquests, he commended it. We had
> as many settlements as we could want or manage. It had become
> a matter of jealousy against us, that we had engrossed the com-
> merce of the world. He had no idea of growing rich by the
> exclusion of others: let all grow rich together. It was an erroneous
> opinion, that in order to derive commercial advantages from any
> country, it was necessary that that country should be under our
> dominion. America was a proof of the contrary.[42]

He did not say so in Parliament, but he would probably have preferred
Trinidad to have been given away as well, for its retention by Britain
would reopen the issue of whether it could be settled with slaves. He

was soon exerting himself to prevent this, although largely having to rely on lobbying Pitt to lobby Addington in turn, since the instant access to Downing Street that he had enjoyed for seventeen years had now come to an end. The issue troubled him greatly: 'Oh what an eternal blot would it be on the character of parliament, if, after having resolved by an immense majority that the Slave Trade should be gradually abolished, we should enter on the cultivation of a new settlement, the complete peopling of which with negro slaves, reckoning the number always lost in opening uncleared lands, would take near a million of human beings!'[43] Having few opportunities for easy conversation with Addington, and having been informed by the French Foreign Minister, perhaps rather misleadingly, that France would be quite likely to agree to general abolition of the slave trade if it was proposed by Britain, Wilberforce took great trouble over a deeply persuasive and very generous letter to Addington in advance of the final treaty negotiations at Amiens. In a letter dated 2 January 1802, written from Old Palace Yard, he said:

> After much very serious ... and anxious reflection, lest this momentous business, which Providence seems in some sort to have committed to my care, should suffer from my mismanagement, I have determined to lay before you in writing a few thoughts, for which I claim your grave and deliberate consideration. By being committed to paper, they will not be of the fugitive and transitory nature of opinions communicated, however earnestly, and heard however attentively, in conversation, but will be a solemn and lasting record of my sentiments, and of the proposal I have found on them.

He reminded Addington of the early debates on the slave trade, and said he wished 'that it were possible to revive in their full force the emotions which were then excited', and went on to explain his current tactics:

> I have stated to the friends of the cause in private, that if defeated in the main question, I would try the subordinate ones; such as, abolishing the trade for supplying foreigners with slaves;

exempting from the Slave Trade a certain district round Sierra
Leone; and, above all, prohibiting the Trade in slaves for clearing
and opening new lands, a motion which the acquisition of Trinidad renders peculiarly necessary; and, finally, the instituting of a
negotiation for effecting a general Abolition of the Slave Trade.

I own to you however that I shall go to the performance of this
duty with a heavy heart; for I am not sanguine in my hopes of
effecting much through the medium of parliament, whatever part
you may take in the House; though I am more sanguine in my
hopes of gradually opening the eyes of the people of England to
the ruinous impolicy of our West Indian system. But I must do
my duty and acquit my conscience. Yet what neither I, nor possibly
even you, can effect through parliament, you may accomplish far
more extensively in another manner.

The key objection of colleagues such as Hawkesbury had been that
other nations would carry on the trade if Britain abolished it, but now:

I scarce need suggest that all the European powers by whom the
Slave Trade has ever been carried on, will be engaged in the
negotiation at Amiens; and that the ascendancy possessed by Great
Britain and France over their respective allies, affords means and
facilities for effecting the desired object, which may never again
occur . . . I have good reason to believe that America would gladly
unite in the engagement.

He explained why the proposal would have to come from Britain,
and finally, with a selflessness uncommon among politicians, offered
Addington the leadership of the abolitionist cause:

I will only add a few words from myself. It is not (to a friend I
may make the avowal) without emotion that I relinquish the idea
of being myself the active and chief agent in terminating this
greatest of all human evils; but you will readily believe me when
I say that any unpleasant sensations on this head vanish at once
before the prospect of effecting the desired object far more rad-
ically and completely than by any springs I could set in motion.
I hope I can truly assure you also, that it helps reconcile me to
my loss on this occasion, that it would be your gain; and I should

look on with joy, if the Disposer of all human events, who has already rendered you the instrument of good to mankind in the termination of one of the most bloody wars that has raged in modern times, should further honour you, by making you His agent in dispensing to the world this greatest and most extended of all earthly benefits. To your serious consideration I submit these reflections.[44]

In all but the physical sense, Wilberforce was a big man: Addington was not. Not only did he and Hawkesbury not succeed in negotiating a general abolition, but they did not even try. To be fair to them, it is highly unlikely that they would have been successful, and their over-riding concern was to end the war; they were probably aware that French assurances on the issue of the slave trade were a pretence. The French Revolution was over, leaving Napoleon in charge, and later in 1802 he went out of his way to revive the slave trade, as well as to send a force of twenty-five thousand troops to reconquer the still turbulent island of Saint-Domingue. But Wilberforce was convinced that, had Pitt still been in office, at least an attempt would have been made to outlaw the trade, and Britain would have stood on higher moral ground. Now, the hopes that he had nurtured through the many years of parliamentary defeats, that Pitt would be able to sort matters out at the time of the peace and that a revolutionary France would be willing to agree appropriate terms, were dashed to pieces.

Wilberforce could have been forgiven if he had wept. Worse still, his disappointments with Addington were only beginning. He had once again postponed his annual motion on abolition until a debate could be held on a motion by Canning aimed at stopping the settlement of Trinidad with slaves. Although Canning was an ardent abolitionist, his real purpose was to divide Pitt from Addington and to foment more opposition to the new government; not surprisingly, Addington managed to delay for some months the holding of the debate. When it was finally held, on 27 May 1802, Addington got out of the situation by promising an inquiry the following year, once the island had been surveyed. There was no groundswell in the Commons for anything else; Wilberforce thought it was a 'sad and most unprincipled speech', and he 'grieved to the heart'.[45] He was never able to move his motion for abolition that year, for in June Addington called a general election.

Wilberforce followed what had now become a six-yearly ritual after his re-election in 1790 and 1796. First of all he would 'quite abhor the prospect of a general election' and 'pant for quiet and retirement',[46] seriously considering retiring rather than standing. Then he would set off nonetheless up the Great North Road to the familiar scenes in the Castle Yard at York. Having got there, he would be swept up in the excitement, enjoying himself enormously, and would be buoyed by the 'august and interesting scene; not one hand was lifted up against him, and surrounding countenances were expressive of the greatest delight and esteem towards him'.[47]

Safely re-elected, he spent much of the rest of the summer in Yorkshire, sometimes musing as he approached his forty-third birthday about the purpose of his life. He considered the further development of his knowledge and oratory to be important – in a man who was already one of the most knowledgeable commentators and captivating public speakers of his time – but his main object would be 'the promotion of his moral and religious usefulness'. Politically, his aim was clear in his mind: 'Whatever dreams of ambition I may have indulged, it now seems clear, that my part is to give the example of an independent member of parliament, and a man of religion, discharging with activity and fidelity the duties of his trust, and not seeking to render his parliamentary station a ladder by which to rise to a higher eminence.'[48]

William Wilberforce, who aspired to change the morals, habits and policies of a nation, had conclusively reconciled himself to pursuing these goals without ever holding ministerial office. But as he returned to Westminster in November 1802, the realisation of his principal objective seemed as distant as ever. Fox considered at this time that the slave trade would never be abolished while George III was alive. Addington, who had voted for abolition in 1792, was clearly unmoved to do anything as Prime Minister ten years later. Wilberforce moved steadily into a position of hostility towards the Addington government. At the same time, Pitt, for separate and sometimes more personal reasons, was doing the same.

Wilberforce was livid when he heard that British ships were being used to carry French supplies and soldiers to Saint-Domingue to wage war against the former slaves, and he used his speech at the opening of Parliament to attack the idea of fresh alliances with Continental powers which could not be relied upon, and would entangle Britain in further wars. Once again, he would be unable to move his motion for abolition in the parliamentary session in 1803: first he was struck down by 'flu, and was more seriously ill than he had been for some years, and second came the worst news he could conceive – that after only one year of formal peace, Britain and France were again sliding towards war. France had invaded Switzerland and annexed parts of northern Italy, while Britain had thought better of giving up possession of Malta. When France refused to heed an ultimatum, Britain declared war on 18 May 1803. Five days later, a packed House of Commons heard Pitt far outshine Addington in his stirring call for the successful prosecution of the war. But Wilberforce, no longer constrained by ties of friendship to the Prime Minister of the day, denounced outright the resumption of conflict. He questioned the decision to hold on to Malta – 'Why this Malta in perpetuity for ourselves?'[49] – and argued that 'The real security, the true interest of this country strongly enforced the expediency of avoiding war, if possible, in the present situation of our affairs and, what is more, I cannot but believe that his Majesty's ministers have plunged into it rashly and unnecessarily.'[50] He was one of sixty-seven MPs who voted against the resumption of war. Three hundred and ninety-eight voted in favour.

Wilberforce's attitude to the war was straightforward, as it had been when he opposed Pitt in 1795. He was against the conflict, but he was utterly loyal to his country, and wanted it fought effectively and successfully if it had to be fought at all. He was never drawn, as Fox had been during the time of the American War of Independence and the French Revolutionary wars, into any suggestion that he sympathised with the enemy's cause. Accordingly, he grew increasingly disgusted, along with Pitt, at the failure of Addington and his ministers to provide energy, leadership and preparation for the war they had entered into. As volunteer companies were formed that summer for defence against French invasion, he revealed in a letter to Muncaster his feelings about the government, as well as his fears about his own physical state:

> My dear Muncaster, you and I disagree about the ground and policy of the war, but I am sure you would have said, if you had foreseen how languid the government would have been in such trying circumstances, that we had better not have ventured so bold a line of conduct ... I sometimes think I should go to Yorkshire this summer as my proper post. But then again when I call to mind my weakly body, that I often cannot walk half a mile, never can ride one, that I must have my meals and sleep with perfect regularity, that I cannot bear a drop of rain, &c. I am afraid of getting into circumstances in which people, seeing me in good spirits and able to talk, but not knowing my bodily infirmities, might attribute my inactivity to cowardice and luke-warmness; and I might disgrace myself, and damp the exertions of others.[51]

He continued to oppose Sunday drilling, but gave £500 to the Yorkshire volunteers, and denounced the government when it proved unable to cope with the vast throngs of volunteers who came forward, and had to limit the numbers. At the end of July he steeled himself to make a short visit to Yorkshire, delivering a stirring speech at the scene of his greatest triumphs, the Castle Yard at York, and he was back in the Commons in August, 'expressing a confidence that the country was equal to the situation it was placed in, and would finally triumph over its difficulties'.[52] Despite his mounting dissatisfaction with the Addington government he scolded himself in his diaries for not being nicer to Addington himself, and did his best to help the increasingly urgent but ultimately unsuccessful efforts to stop Pitt and Addington moving into direct political confrontation. After a short stay in Hertfordshire, he repaired as usual to a rented villa in the vicinity of Bath with his family, looking forward to 'a prospect of my living in more quiet than I have long enjoyed'.[53] There he caught up with reading and letters, enjoyed his children, and made long lists of his blessings and failings. He managed to spend nearly three months thus secluded, although receiving visitors as usual and finding the Pump Room at Bath full of people dissatisfied with the conduct of the government at a time when a French invasion was thought to be imminent.

The prospect of the French army arriving at any time often created in him a fatalistic mood. 'Who knows,' he noted that Christmas, 'but that it may be my last preparation for eternity.'[54] With the country yearning for stronger leadership, the new year brought escalating attacks on the government from all quarters: Grenville, leading the 'new opposition', Fox, leading the 'old opposition', and Pitt, launching an all-out parliamentary assault on the ministers he had nominated to succeed him. In mid-March 1804 Wilberforce joined Pitt in attacking the inadequate state of the navy, having been briefed by Charles Middleton that the government had been 'strangely negligent'.[55] Such were the parliamentary demands at this time that he was unable to attend the first general meeting of yet another Evangelical project in which he was closely involved: the formation of the British and Foreign Bible Society. He did manage to attend the next meeting, on 2 May, when he made 'a speech of equal animation and judgement',[56] helping to launch on its way another initiative dear to his heart. Over the next twenty years the Bible Society would distribute more than four million Bibles, translated into 140 languages and dialects, in more than fifty of which it had never appeared before.

By then the Addington government was collapsing. George III, somewhat reluctantly at first, once again sent for Pitt. On 18 May 1804 he returned to office as Prime Minister, but the King's continuing veto over the inclusion of Fox in any government meant that Pitt could include neither Fox nor his old mainstay Grenville, now loosely allied to Fox, in the government. It would be a government with a narrow parliamentary majority, led by a Prime Minister who was well past the peak of his physical strength and political support, but it was one that Wilberforce could instinctively support in his independent way. Although Grenville had always been an ally on the slave trade, Wilberforce thought that he and his friends, such as Windham, were too hawkish in war. He wrote to Muncaster, 'I am not sure that this arrangement is not the very best possible; the Grenvilles are so wrong-headed and warlike.'[57] From Wilberforce's point of view, however, the new government was hardly ideal. Pitt included very conservative figures such as Hawkesbury, and brought back Dundas (now Lord Melville), this time as First Lord of the Admiralty. It would not be a government dedicated to abolition of the slave trade any more than was its predecessor. With the war resumed, invasion thought to be imminent, George III still on the throne and unhelpful cabinet ministers in power, it might have seemed an unpropitious time to mount a fresh assault on the slave trade. But Wilberforce, having failed for good but frustrating reasons to move his annual abolition motion in each of the previous four years, was determined to renew, yet again, his interminable struggle against the trade he was dedicated to destroy.

If 1792 had been the year in which the cause of abolition faltered, then 1804 was the year in which it was revived. Given past experiences of insurmountable parliamentary obstacles and the expectation that the renewed war would last for some years, Wilberforce's first thought was to make a fresh attempt at a negotiated suspension of the trade. No doubt he imagined that any such suspension would demonstrate that the world could live without it, that Liverpool would still prosper and the existing slaves of the West Indies could be better cared for. From the point of view of the plantation-owners there was a clear self-interest for many in halting the supply of new slaves. The price of sugar had fallen from its peak, and the market was no longer expanding as rapidly as it had been. Newly conquered lands such as Demerara in Dutch Guiana possessed extremely fertile soils and large uncultivated areas, so the existing planters had a vested interest in preventing their full exploitation. This realisation opened up a serious division in the West Indian ranks.

The negotiations seemed more likely to succeed than the earlier effort in 1800, with Wilberforce being assured in the spring of 1804 that the great West Indian merchants and planters would approve the idea of a five-year suspension. To avoid the planters having to accept anything which came with his name attached to it, Wilberforce tried to persuade Addington, still Prime Minister at this stage, to propose the suspension himself. He still clung to the idea that Addington was a good man at heart, partly because he was such a serious Christian, but found that the offer was once again spurned, 'from a natural aversion to come forward just at this moment'.[58] By mid-May, not only was Addington leaving office, but a general meeting of planters and merchants at a London tavern totally rejected the idea of a suspension and voted 'that every legal and proper step should be taken to oppose the progress of any Bill which may be brought into Parliament either to suspend or abolish the Slave Trade'.[59] They had probably realised, along with Wilberforce, that once the trade was suspended it was unlikely ever to be resumed. As a result, Pitt, as the incoming Prime Minister, and 'having had no time to settle any thing with any part of the Cabinet',[60] as he explained to Wilberforce, could see no merit in moving for a suspension which had not been agreed.

With all hope of compromise gone, Wilberforce once again set out on his lonely task of proposing yet another Bill to outlaw the slave trade, to be trenchantly opposed in both the Commons and the Lords. Yet he was to find that he was in stronger company that year than at any time in the previous decade. For one thing, the London Abolition Committee resumed its meetings for the first time since 1795, and did so fortified by the inclusion of James Stephen and Zachary Macaulay, who had helped Wilberforce keep the flame of their cause alive through the darkest years. Thomas Clarkson himself came back on the scene, and correspondence with the Pennsylvania Abolition Committee was resumed. Strengthening the transatlantic ties, Wilberforce wrote to the future US President James Monroe, who was in London negotiating a commercial treaty, for assurances that certain states had not revived the slave trade. Monroe's assurances to him in response were inaccurate, but at least fortified the abolitionists' belief in American solidarity. In addition, they were strengthened by the arrival on the scene of new and younger adherents, particularly the brilliant young liberal lawyer Henry Brougham, a future Lord Chancellor, who joined the Committee in 1804 and offered to tour Europe, in the guise of an American, in the abolitionist cause.

At least two factors seemed to have sparked the discernible uplift in abolitionist activity in the spring of 1804. One was the evident divisions and uncertainties among the West Indian planters: their signs of weakness, even if now retracted, inevitably emboldened their opponents. But more important was the wider change in the British political atmosphere. The abolitionists had fallen short of their expectations in the early 1790s because the entire political landscape had changed to their disadvantage. The French Revolution had brought an extremely cautious and reactionary atmosphere to Westminster and public debate. By 1804, France was very much still the enemy, indeed an enemy more feared than in 1792, but the nature of France had changed. No longer was Britain fighting a set of revolutionary ideas which threatened to overturn all established institutions of state, Church and society. It was now fighting something much easier to understand: the despotic power of a dictator, Napoleon, who proclaimed himself hereditary Emperor of the French on the very day Pitt returned as Prime Minister. Moreover, this was a dictator who defended slavery and gave succour to the slave trade, and whose troops were even now waging war against the rebellious slaves of Saint-Domingue. Thus while abolition in the 1790s may have seemed to have something dangerously in common with Britain's enemies, abolition in 1804 was very happily combined with opposition to everything French.

These factors may have contributed to the pleasant surprise Wilberforce enjoyed when he asked the Commons for a first reading of his Abolition Bill on 30 May, and found at the end of the debate that there were only forty-nine votes against. The greater surprise, however, was the size of the vote in favour, which revealed another fresh source of strength. Since the last full-scale debates on the slave trade in 1799, a hundred Irish Members had been added to the House of Commons. Many of them, it turned out, were well-disposed to abolition. On the day of the debate, it happened that a large number of them were dining together and decided that they would walk *en bloc* into the division lobby for Wilberforce's Bill. The result was that he mustered a surprising 124 votes in favour, a majority of seventy-five.

This was the most unambiguous victory Wilberforce had ever gained in this cause. He went home that night to find great excitement in his house – Stephen, Macaulay, Grant, Henry Thornton and William Smith all gathered to discuss the details of the Bill and the tactics they should adopt. It was much easier now to believe in eventual success. Wilberforce wrote the next day, to an archdeacon, 'Well – the Supreme Disposer of all things can turn the hearts of men, and before him difficulties vanish.'[61] Suddenly he was awash with support and letters of congratulation, but there were many more hurdles to jump. The second reading debate of 7 June produced anti-abolition speeches from a leading member of Pitt's government, Viscount Castlereagh, and a leading member of the opposition, William Windham. Even so, it went through by one hundred votes to forty-two, the Irish Members still doing their bit. Throughout the debate, Wilberforce was once again at pains to stress that the slave trade could be abolished without dispensing with slavery itself. Indeed, he used fresh data gathered over the twelve years since the key debate of 1792 to strengthen his argument that, if cared for, the Negro population of the West Indian islands would increase of its own accord. He suggested that evidence from the United States showed that 'in the ten years from 1791 to 1801, the American Negroes had increased in such proportion as to hold out a fair prospect of doubling their number in twenty-five years'.[62] On 27 June he carried the Bill at third reading by ninety-nine votes to thirty-three, with Pitt in warm support and Addington 'much vexatious'.[63] The abolitionists had shown their strength, but it must have been clear for most of these proceedings that the year was already too far advanced to get the Bill through the much more difficult House of Lords before the summer recess intervened and the parliamentary session came to an end. The Commons debates had therefore been more of a demonstration than an actual making of law. Even so, Wilberforce was disappointed when Pitt advised that a passage through the Lords was impracticable. He wrote to Muncaster:

> It was truly humiliating to see, in the House of Lords, four of
> the Royal Family come down to vote against the poor, helpless,

friendless Slaves. I sometimes think the Almighty can scarcely
suffer us to be rid of such a load of wickedness, to which we cling
so fondly, without making us suffer for our bigoted attachment.
It is often the way of Heaven to let the error bring its own
punishment along with it. Well, my friend, it will one day be
consoling, that you and I exerted ourselves to clear the ship of
this stinking cargo.[64]

Nevertheless, he also thought that 'we are somewhat advanced on our
way; though I am far from being so sanguine as many were, even in
1792'.[65] Furthermore, he had discovered in his preparation for debates
in the House of Lords that Grenville, still in opposition, would be a
powerful supporter when the time really came. He had never had a
high opinion of Grenville, once thinking him 'a shabby man bent on
amassing money', but he was now coming to regard him in a more
positive light. The readiness to cooperate of these two men would be
of great significance in the future.

At the beginning of September an exhausted Wilberforce took his
family off to Lyme in Dorset, where he at last found tranquillity: 'I
never was at any place where I had so much the command of my own
time, and the power of living as I please.'[66] He nevertheless busied
himself for much of the time with writing articles – under the pseudo-
nym 'Scrutator' – for the *Christian Observer*, another Evangelical project recently launched, reading widely, and answering the usual arrears
of letters. He corresponded with Stephen about a new abolitionist tract,
and worried about Pitt and the war. Pitt was labouring to construct a
Third Coalition against France by bringing Austria, Russia and Prussia
into the war on Britain's side. Wilberforce was privately sceptical: 'Pitt
is the most upright political character I ever knew or heard of; but
with all public men it is extremely dangerous for a country that they
should be under a temptation to fight it out, to try their fortune again
after having been unsuccessful in a formal war. Their own character
and glory, and the national interest, are so apt to become identified in
their judgment, that they are too forward to consider as conducive to
the latter whatever measures they are prompted to undertake from
their solicitude for the former.'[67]

High though his opinion of Pitt remained, 1805 would bring Wilberforce great vexation and disappointment with his old friend. Pitt was now struggling, bearing a huge weight of the work of government himself despite his failing energy, often at odds with George III, enjoying only a narrow control over the House of Commons – and all while the country was at greater danger of imminent invasion than at any time in living memory. The pressures on him were intense, making him more prone than ever to what Wilberforce referred to as 'dilatoriness and procrastination, his great vices'.[68] Not only did Pitt not have the time for anything he considered unnecessary, but there was no way he could deliver the support of his government in general for Wilberforce's next attempt at abolition. Leading ministers such as Hawkesbury, Castlereagh and Melville would have had none of it. Addington, who returned to the government in January 1805 ennobled as Lord Sidmouth, had already shown his total lack of enthusiasm, and the King and his court remained opposed. Pitt had neither the physical nor the political strength to deliver support for Wilberforce.

For Wilberforce, Pitt's distractions would make 1805 one of his most frustrating years ever, all the more so after the false dawn of 1804. When he again brought this Abolition Bill to the floor of the Commons, in March this time so there would be more hope of getting it through the Lords, the Irish let him down and his enemies mobilised, so that he was actually defeated by seventy-seven votes to seventy. He was distraught: 'I never felt so much on any parliamentary occasion. I could not sleep after first waking at night. The poor blacks rushed into my mind, and the guilt of our wicked land.'[69] The following day he told Muncaster he hardly had the spirit to write. It was the first abolition debate in which Pitt had not risen to support him. And at the same time, Wilberforce was in an agony of frustration attempting to secure from Pitt a ban on the British sale of slaves to Guiana.

Wilberforce thought that stopping the Guiana trade would prevent the sale of some twelve to fifteen thousand slaves annually. Many of the West Indian planters themselves were not opposed to it, on account of their own self-interest. Stopping it would be in line with previous action on Trinidad in the earlier wars. When he had tackled Pitt about this in the summer of 1804, Pitt 'positively said he had no doubt of stopping the Trade by Royal Proclamation. Very strong on this, and against any vote of Parliament.'[70] All that was necessary was for Pitt or his ministers to prepare an Order in Council for submission to the King and the Privy Council, but the delay in carrying out this apparently simple task now went on for many months. After eight months of waiting, Wilberforce went to see Pitt on 9 March 1805, six days after the defeat of his Bill, and told him that if he did not prepare the Order in Council then a group of Members from all sides would try to force the issue in Parliament. It seemed the only way to get Pitt's attention. Pitt duly promised to act, and work on the Order in Council began, but by now he had pushed Wilberforce into cooperation with the opposition. At the end of that month, Wilberforce and one of his 'Saints', Henry Bankes, went to a meeting at Lansdowne House with Charles James Fox, his lieutenant Charles Grey, and a new young hope of the Whigs, Lord Henry Petty. Petty was another significant recruit to the abolitionist campaign. Wilberforce's increasing readiness to coordinate his tactics with leading opposition figures ranging from Fox to Grenville, and their readiness to work with him, was another telling event. The Order in Council finally went through on 13 September 1805. For Wilberforce, it was a signal achievement: 'This is preventing the importation of a vast number of poor creatures, who would otherwise, as in the last war, have been the victims of our great capitalists.'[71] But it had been another exhausting effort.

Wilberforce was only able to operate in this way because all shades of opinion had eventually come to accept that he was a genuine independent. And as it happened, one of the greatest tests of that independence was about to arise. On 18 March Wilberforce was with Pitt in Downing Street discussing the Guiana trade when an envelope arrived which Pitt had been awaiting. 'I shall never forget,' recorded Wilberforce, 'the way in which he seized it, and how eagerly he looked into the leaves without waiting even to cut them open.'[72] The document was the Tenth Report of the Commission of Naval Enquiry, and its importance was that it contained direct criticism of the conduct of Dundas, now Lord Melville, when he had been Treasurer of the Navy in Pitt's earlier government. Melville stood accused of turning a blind eye to the misuse of Admiralty funds by one of his assistants, who had used public money for private transactions. The taxpayer had suffered no loss, but what had happened was more in keeping with the practices of the 1740s than the 1790s, and Melville was further accused of having sometimes been in possession, perhaps unwittingly, of some of the money himself. Since Melville was now again in government as First Lord of the Admiralty, the opposition were bound to make a huge issue out of this report. The rivalry between Pittites, Foxites, Grenvillites and Addingtonians had brought Westminster to one of the most acrimonious phases of its history, notwithstanding the fact that the country was engaged in a war for national survival. It was not many hours before the radical MP Samuel Whitbread had tabled a motion attacking Melville for acting 'in a manner inconsistent with his duty, and incompatible with those securities which the legislature has provided for the proper application of the public money'.[73]

For the opposition, then, the ensuing debate scheduled for 8 April was an opportunity to punch a big hole in Pitt's administration. For Pitt, it was a tiresome distraction from the business of fighting the war. Defeat in the debate would be a serious blow, but so would dismissing Melville, when he thought he needed him at the Admiralty and no taxpayers' money had been lost. In any case, Pitt would have reckoned he would have been able to win the debate if the government's normal supporters stayed firm.

The debate of 8 April was therefore of great importance. Pitt loyally defended Melville, but it was not one of his best speeches, perhaps understandably so, after an entire career strongly opposed to financial irregularities. Wilberforce knew from private conversations that Pitt was not really happy with Melville's conduct: 'People thought that they were most closely united together, tho' I knew, that in fact they were not on such good terms as they had been.'[74] Wilberforce, it was said, had not decided which way to vote until he heard the arguments advanced earlier in the debate. Whatever he said could be crucial in determining the outcome. Would he stay by his great friend when he really needed him? Or would he confirm his reputation for independence and his long-standing dedication to probity in public office, by joining in censuring a public minister who was at fault? It is impossible to know for sure whether any personal considerations entered into what Wilberforce did next. While he would have felt sympathy for Pitt, he had also become more exasperated with him than ever before in the immediately preceding weeks. To Melville, he owed no favours at all, for he more than anyone else had succeeded in obstructing the progress of abolition during the endless debates of the 1790s, and had refused to assist Wilberforce's lobbying of the House of Lords the previous year. He had always been, in Wilberforce's eyes, a bad influence on Pitt, and a minister too dedicated to colonial acquisition.

To any normal politician these factors would have been easily sufficient to produce a vote for censuring the unfortunate minister. Yet such was Wilberforce's determination always to judge 'measures not men', and his conviction that he would have to account for his actions to God, that the decision he came to was almost certainly based on his considered and dispassionate judgement. As Wilberforce rose to speak late that night, Pitt turned around from the front bench and looked straight at him. 'It required no little effort,' Wilberforce later reflected, 'to resist the fascination of that penetrating eye'[75] – but resist it he did. To him, the defence that no money had been lost to the taxpayer was beside the point: 'As to the argument that there has been no actual loss to the public by these transactions: when we reflect upon the consequences that might arise from the detention of money intended for the payment of so great a department as the navy of this country, when we might reflect upon the lengths to which men may be induced to go if the mind is once accustomed to such abuses, and when we consider the expense such conduct must inevitably have upon all the inferior departments, I do contend that the loss, in a pecuniary view, may have been to an extent almost incalculable.'[76] 'Here is my Lord Melville,' he said, 'publicly declaring on his oath that he has tolerated his dependant in a gross breach of an Act of Parliament for the purposes of private emolument. I really cannot find language sufficiently strong to express my utter detestation of such conduct.'[77] In a powerful speech of condemnation, he concluded, 'We it is who are now truly on our trial before the moral sense of England; and if we shrink from it, deeply shall we hereafter repent our conduct.'[78]

It was a decisive speech. Forty votes were said to be influenced by it, and when the vote was taken in the early hours the result was a tie, 216 for the Ayes and 216 for the Noes. The Speaker, Charles Abbott, went white, adjourned the House for ten minutes and then returned to give his casting vote against Melville. The House adjourned at half past five in the morning. Wilberforce went home and 'Could not get cool in body or mind. Bed, and slept till twelve.'[79] No one would ever doubt again that he was an independent.

Melville was ruined. He resigned from the government, suffered his name being erased from the Privy Council, and spent the next year defending himself against impeachment – ultimately with success. As for Pitt, he had suffered a grievous political blow, and some observers recorded him that night as jamming his hat deeply over his forehead and 'the tears trickling down his cheeks'.[80] Others subsequently saw in his humiliation that night the beginning of his end. Wilberforce always rejected the idea that what had happened injured Pitt's health. It was indeed the end of November 1805 before Pitt's health collapsed. By then Britain had lived through a tense and arduous summer, expecting a French invasion that never came and eventually, in early November, hearing the news of Nelson's overwhelming defeat of the French fleet at Trafalgar. Indirectly, Wilberforce's condemnation of Melville had helped to bring about this great victory, for the new First Lord of the Admiralty was none other than his old friend the naval expert Sir Charles Middleton, now ennobled as Lord Barham, whose management of the navy was producing a sharp improvement in its organisation. As the nation rejoiced, Wilberforce was 'so overcome that he could not go on reading for tears'.[81] Late December, however, brought news of grim familiarity: at the Battle of Austerlitz, Napoleon had vanquished the Emperors of Austria and Russia, destroying their armies and leaving Britain alone, once again, in an interminable war.

In the days that followed the news of Austerlitz, Pitt fell into a sickness from which he would never recover. Wilberforce was spending Christmas at Yoxall Lodge, and it was not until he returned to London on 21 January 1806 that he realised the seriousness of Pitt's condition. By the twenty-second he was 'quite unsettled and uneasy about Pitt', but he had no chance to visit him in his house at Putney Heath, because no visitors were being admitted by Pretyman and the Stanhopes, who were nursing him till the end. On the twenty-third Pitt was dead, at the age of forty-six.

Wilberforce always considered that the stress of war had killed Pitt, 'and the accounts from the armies struck a death blow within'.[82] He wrote in his diary: 'Deeply rather than pathetically affected by it. Pitt killed by the enemy as much as Nelson. Babington went to dine at Lord Teignmouth's but I had no mind to go out.'[83] He was appalled that Pretyman had waited until within twenty-four hours of the end before asking Pitt to pray with him, although he was perhaps unaware that Pitt had replied that he had 'neglected prayer too much to allow him to hope it could be very efficacious now'.[84] He wrote to Muncaster, 'There is something peculiarly affecting in the time and circumstances of poor Pitt's death. I own I have a thousand times (aye, times without number) wished and hoped that a quiet interval would be afforded him, perhaps in the evening of life, in which he and I might confer freely on the most important of all subjects. But the scene is closed – for ever.'[85] To William Hey, he wrote of Pitt on 12 February, 'for personal purity, disinterestedness, integrity, and love of country, I have never known his equal'.[86] He turned himself to trying to find private subscribers to pay off Pitt's vast personal debts, having contributed to a similar fund when Pitt left office as Prime Minister in 1801, but on this occasion the debts of £46,000 (the equivalent of some £2.7 million today) were too great for such an operation, and he reluctantly had to agree that they should be paid off at public expense.

On 22 February 1806, as Pitt's funeral cortège processed from Westminster Hall to his resting place in the north transept of Westminster Abbey, Wilberforce helped to carry the banner in front of the coffin. It would soon be twenty years since Pitt had helped to prompt him to take up the cause of the slave trade. Now he would have to complete the task of securing the abolition of the trade without his friend in Downing Street. Yet as Wilberforce watched Pitt's coffin join that of his great father in his tomb, he would have had no idea how close he was to success. It would be one of the ironies of history that the departure from the scene of his great friend would be one of several crucial events which meant that victory was now at hand.

13

Abolition

———————◆◆◆◆◆———————

Here then after a glorious struggle of eighteen years a final period is
at length put in this country to the most execrable and inhuman
traffic that ever disgraced the Christian world.

BISHOP PORTEUS, Memoranda Book[1]

How God can turn the hearts of men!

WILLIAM WILBERFORCE, diary, April 1806[2]

FOR NEARLY TWO DECADES, as Wilberforce had struggled on
with the campaign against the slave trade, he had done so on the
basis of certain assumptions: that the abolitionist cause was assisted by
the presence in Downing Street of a sympathetic William Pitt; that
abolition could best be sold to reluctant British MPs on the basis of
an international agreement with France and other European powers;
that it was easier to pass such a measure in peacetime than during a
war; and that the House of Lords could only ever be induced to pass
the necessary legislation if it had already gone through the House of
Commons with emphatic support. Yet when success arrived, as it was
about to do with the speed and force of a political avalanche, it came
only when all of these assumptions could be stood on their head.
Within weeks of the death of Pitt, the success of abolition would seem
beyond doubt, and a year and a day after he had been laid to rest in
Westminster Abbey it would have passed every parliamentary hurdle.
It would have done so with the arguments advanced in its favour
strengthened by the need to wage war, and in the absence of any

327

agreement with Continental nations. Those who voted in the final divisions in the House of Commons would be emboldened by success in the House of Lords, rather than the other way round. And as a final irony, a campaign which had fought for years to elevate public concern and focus attention on its demands would take the decisive steps to success by means of an extraordinary manoeuvre of legislative stealth. After so many years in which events had conspired with wily opponents to frustrate every assault on the slave trade, 1806 saw every circumstance swing in the abolitionists' favour, aided by their own persistence and ingenuity.

The first crucial ingredient of the success to come was a change of government. Pitt's death made that inevitable. The ministers he left behind – Hawkesbury, Castlereagh, Canning, Spencer Perceval: 'Pitt's friends', as they would soon become known, for want of any other collective description – were highly capable, but not immediately able to fill his shoes. The ministry had already been lacking a sufficient parliamentary majority to feel secure; without Pitt their position was untenable. George III had no alternative but to turn to a leading opposition figure to form a government, and since his relations with Charles James Fox had always been characterised by unlimited enmity, his choice fell naturally on Lord Grenville. Thus Grenville, who had sat with Pitt and Wilberforce in the grounds of Holwood as they discussed the slave trade in 1787, became the man who would ultimately preside over its abolition.

Grenville had been insistent for several years that the desperate circumstances of the country required a broadly-based government supported by all the main political factions. It was on these grounds that he had refused to take office with Pitt in 1804, since George III's adamant exclusion of Fox from the cabinet made such a union impossible. Now, however, the King bowed to the inevitable, knowing that Grenville would once again insist on the inclusion of Fox, and that the country could not be left with no government at all. In February 1806 Grenville became First Lord of the Treasury, with Fox as Foreign Secretary and Sidmouth as Lord Privy Seal, making a coalition of three parliamentary factions. It was a government that would become known to history as 'the Ministry of all the Talents', although the failure to attract some of 'Pitt's friends' and the exclusion of the rest of them meant that this was not an accurate description. Nevertheless, in the midst of a military struggle with Napoleon, Britain now had a government with a large parliamentary majority, and one that stretched further across the political spectrum than any of recent times: Grenville, the hard-line Foreign Secretary of the 1790s, had come to office in harness with Fox, the long-standing opponent of war with France.

It was a government assembled for the purpose of making peace with Napoleon if possible, but leading a united nation in war if not. For the moment, its military strategy would be to contain further French aggression on the Continent while using Britain's newly won mastery of the seas to put the maximum pressure on Napoleon. It happened also to be a government which was, with the exception of a small minority including Sidmouth, much more sympathetic to Catholic emancipation than its predecessor, a factor which would ultimately lead it to follow Pitt's path of five years earlier into fatal confrontation with the King. But also as it happened, it was, at last, a government in which a majority of members were ardently in favour of the abolition of the slave trade. Sidmouth, as Wilberforce knew to his cost, was no enthusiast for abolition. But most of the other leading ministers opposed to abolition, such as Castlereagh and Hawkesbury, had now left office. In the new administration, the two dominant figures of Grenville and Fox had been stout abolitionists for the whole of their political lives. Rising stars who came in with them, and whom Wilberforce had grown to know through his conferring with the opposition the previous year, were of a similar mind. In particular, Lord Henry Petty now became Chancellor of the Exchequer, and Charles Grey was installed as First Lord of the Admiralty. The ministerial ranks were suddenly dominated by politicians who regarded abolition as a fundamental part of their beliefs.

Although the absence of complete unanimity in the cabinet meant Grenville could not make abolition a government measure, he was clearly in a position to put the weight of his administration behind it in a way that Pitt had never felt able to do. Furthermore, since Catholic emancipation seemed impossible while George III was alive, abolition of the slave trade would have appeared to Grenville and Fox as one of the few important measures on which they were united and which could actually be carried through. One uncertain flank was the position of the Prince of Wales, whose influence was growing as the abilities of George III decayed, and with whom the new ministers had close political links. They had already taken the precaution of appointing the Prince's adviser, Lord Moira, to the cabinet, but the Prince had in earlier years endorsed the trenchant opposition of his younger brother, the Duke of Clarence, to abolition. Now, however, Fox persuaded the Prince 'not to stir adversely',[3] and the way was open for Grenville and Fox to use their power in the interests of abolition.

Wilberforce reacted to the new situation with a series of astute tactical judgements, combined with several displays of his now unquestionable independence. He rejected the idea put forward by James Stephen of making a formal pact with the new government to give it general support in Parliament if it would proceed with abolition – 'The idea is inadmissible for many reasons. The two parties would infallibly have different ideas of the practical extent of the obligation, and mutual misunderstanding, crimination, and recrimination would infallibly ensue'[4] – but he also thought they 'ought to contrive that the effect intended by it may be produced'[5] without any formal arrangement. It would have been utterly against his nature to bind himself to supporting any government's wider measures. Indeed, he immediately attacked the new government when it took the unprecedented (and unrepeated) step of including a senior judge, the Lord Chief Justice, Lord Ellenborough, in the cabinet. Wilberforce's attacks on the wisdom and propriety of such an appointment illustrate his remarkable ability to remain on good terms with those he opposed politically. He wrote to Ellenborough to explain his objections, which he described in a letter to Henry Bankes as 'the mischievous consequences of subjecting the decisions of our courts of justice to the influence of party attachments ... the most injurious blow our constitution has sustained'.[6] The two men nevertheless remained friends, and when Ellenborough left office the following year he is meant to have said, 'Well, Wilberforce, I hope I have not done much mischief after all.'[7]

Next, Wilberforce exercised his unrestrained independence to give unexpected support to the government, to the chagrin of some of his long-standing friends. Pitt's death had created a by-election in his constituency of Cambridge University at the same time as Lord Henry Petty was required to stand for re-election to the Commons because of his appointment as Chancellor of the Exchequer. Petty took the opportunity to elevate his political importance by standing for Pitt's prestigious old seat, and Wilberforce, who liked him and his opinions, declared his open support. That Wilberforce should support an opponent of Pitt to represent Pitt's old constituency was astonishing to some of his friends, with Pittite Claphamites like Milner and Simeon writing angry letters. Milner said he was 'vexed from the heart', and ended rather scornfully, 'Did I tell you, they say Lord H. Petty must have gained you by praying extempore?'[8] Wilberforce conceded to his diary, but evidently to no one else, that he had probably pledged his support to Petty too hastily, but in the event Petty was elected and Wilberforce's strong personal connections with senior members of the new government were reinforced.* However hasty his judgement in this case, it was certainly not unwise.

With such new ministers in place, all seemed set for Wilberforce to have a fairer than usual crack at his annual ritual, a fresh frontal assault on the slave trade. In March he conferred with Grenville, Fox and Petty, who all agreed to support a renewed motion for abolition. The assumption was that, as in so many preceding years, the motion would be carried by the House of Commons but would face major obstacles in the Lords. It was, therefore, entirely possible that the long stalemate of the previous two decades would have continued. But Wilberforce did not put down his usual motion, and nor would he ever do so again. Later in March, as he was on the point of crossing Old Palace Yard to table it, James Stephen came to him with an

---

* Petty's defeated opponent was Lord Palmerston, then an unknown youth but later one of the great Prime Ministers of the nineteenth century.

alternative plan. It was an ingenious one, and it would seal the fate of the British slave trade.

By 1806, Wilberforce well knew that any measure he proposed which rested 'on general Abolition principles or is grounded on justice and humanity', thereby suffered from 'an imputation which I am aware would prove fatal to it'.[9] His mind was therefore fully open to a more indirect way of achieving his objectives. The events of the previous year, and James Stephen's careful thinking, now provided one.

At the end of 1805, Stephen had published a book, *The War in Disguise*, which was already having a major impact on the thinking of Britain's political and military leaders. His thesis was that, in spite of Britain's great maritime power, the colonies of her enemies were prospering in wartime circumstances because of their freedom to use the ships of neutral countries. Cargoes destined for France were being shipped across the Atlantic under neutral flags, and then diverted to their true destination once they reached coastal waters. Other cargoes were being sent to the United States and then re-designated as American before crossing the Atlantic. Not only was this allowing the colonies of France and Spain to prosper, but it was giving them an actual advantage over British colonies, whose produce, being carried in British ships which were subject to enemy attack, was delayed in transit by convoy arrangements and was subject to higher insurance rates. To add insult to injury, British seamen were being induced to fly neutral flags in order to carry on trade with enemy colonies. It was no wonder, Stephen argued, that

> Bonaparte has recently boasted, that Martinique and Guadaloupe are flourishing, in despite of our hostilities ... The neutral flag gives them not only protection, but advantages before unknown. The gigantic infancy of agriculture in Cuba, far from being checked is greatly aided in its portentous growth during the war, by the boundless liberty of trade, and the perfect security of carriage ... In short, all the hostile colonies, whether Spanish, French, or Batavian, derive from the enmity of Great Britain, their

ancient scourge and terror, not inconvenience but advantage: far from being impoverished or distressed by our hostilities as formerly, they find in war the best sources of supply, and new means of agricultural, as well as commercial prosperity.[10]

Stephen's conclusion, one which informed opinion in London found impossible to contest, was that the interests of Britain's colonies and their plantations, as well as the wider British interest of actually winning the war, meant that existing policy towards neutral shipping needed to be overturned. The Royal Navy should be set free to interdict trade between enemy colonies and their home country. This would, of course, involve searching or seizing neutral shipping when necessary. What is more, in the aftermath of Trafalgar, this was a policy that it had the power to carry out.

The War in Disguise was hugely persuasive, and from the beginning of 1807 measures against neutral shipping along the lines of its recommendations would indeed be taken. Stephen had used his intimate legal knowledge of shipping and trade materially to assist the British war effort, and there is no doubt that he fully intended to do so. But the true brilliance of *The War in Disguise* was that it contained within itself the disguise of a second purpose. It was a policy proposal with another one hidden within it. For while the slave trade was mentioned only once in passing in the entire book, Stephen knew full well that the consequences for it of the implementation of his proposals would be devastating.

The prevention wherever possible of neutral vessels going to and from the ports of enemy colonies would deliver a triple blow to the slave trade. France and Spain, already unable to ship slaves to their colonies under their own flags for fear of British attack, would in future be unable to do so in neutral shipping either. Second, and more importantly, the inability of their Caribbean colonies to receive supplies and manufactures from Europe, or to export tropical produce, would lead to the complete collapse of their economies, and an end to their demand for more slaves. And thirdly, to the extent that such colonies were indirectly supplied by British slave ships – which they sometimes were, by the device of landing slave cargoes on Danish islands for onward shipment to the French and Spanish – the British slave trade would itself be reduced. These measures would not eliminate the supply of slaves to British colonies in British ships, nor the supply to the United States in British and American ships, nor the vast trade to Brazil in Portuguese ships, but they would eliminate, for the moment, the rest of the foreign slave trade. Added to the major impact of the Guiana Order finally enacted in 1805, the total effect on the British slave trade would be to reduce it by more than half. Yet it was hard to oppose such an idea without opposing the successful prosecution of the war.

The next part of Stephen's plan completed its ingenuity. The new leading ministers, however firmly opposed to the slave trade, were unable to make general abolition a government measure which all members of the government would have to support. However, they could bring in a Bill to turn the previous year's Order in Council relating to Guiana into a more permanent Act of Parliament, and since this would be confirmation of an existing government policy, it would indeed be a government measure. Furthermore, the supply of slaves to foreign colonies with which Britain was at war was so manifestly against the national interest that the prohibition of it could be made general. It would be illegal to be in any way involved in the supply of slaves to colonies captured from the enemy, or to those which they still held. On 24 March Wilberforce wrote to Grenville to propose this strategy:

> Since I had the pleasure of seeing your Lordship the other day, an idea has been suggested by Mr. Stephen . . . which has prevented my giving notice according to the intention I then stated. This is, that an Act of Parliament has often, or generally, been found necessary for rendering an Order of His Majesty in Council really effectual; and that in the instance of the order for stopping the supply of slaves to Dutch Guiana, issued about last August, an act of Parliament is peculiarly requisite. The next step to which we were led, was, that on the very same principles as those on which the Guiana Order and the proposed act for rendering it effectual would rest, the British slave trade for supplying all foreign colonies ought also to be prohibited. And as the order was supported

by those members of administration who were most adverse to
abolition principles, we thought that a further measure grounded
on the same principle might probably without difficulty obtain
the support of all the members of the present administration . . .
It is obvious, however, that as the stopping of the foreign slave
trade may be justified even to the satisfaction of the opponents of
General Abolition, it would be imprudent to embark them both
in the same bottom, and therefore it would be highly desirable
that Government should give notice of the measure I have suggested, before my motion is made which would include the foreign
slave trade as part of the whole.[11]

In other words, this considerable blow to the slave trade would be
delivered while Wilberforce stayed quiet about the subject of abolition
in general. Grenville saw the opportunity, and acted immediately.
Wilberforce had already lobbied Fox and Petty, and only three days
after Wilberforce's letter to Grenville, the Attorney General, Sir Arthur
Piggott, was on his feet in the House of Commons giving notice of the
introduction of the Slave Importation Bill. Piggott unfortunately got
the details wrong, omitting all mention of Dutch Guiana for instance,
and Wilberforce had to write an urgent note to be taken in to Fox at
dinner to get this rectified, but matters were indeed put right and a
Bill in exact conformity with Stephen's plans was introduced to the
House of Commons.

With the approval of the entire cabinet, including those opposed to
abolition, the Bill went largely unnoticed at each stage of the legislative
process that April. The hard-line opponents of abolition were by no
means so stupid as not to notice that something serious was afoot, but
they were devoid of any support within the government, confounded
by the fact that much of what was in the Bill had previously been
agreed to, and could not stir their friends to take the trouble to come
to Westminster in order to oppose a measure which would manifestly
make it easier to win the war. In vain did Tarleton suggest, in a debate
of 25 April, that 'ever since he had had a seat in parliament we have
had an annual debate on this subject, and as the measure could not be
carried in its general form, they were now coming by a side wind on

the planters',[12] for his normal allies were simply not there. To the extent that any argument at all was made against the Bill, it was that its effect would be to turn the trade over to the Americans, 'by whom the slaves would be treated with much more cruelty; for it appeared that they had lost 152 men on the passage in one instance, and yet made a profitable voyage'.[13] That Wilberforce had outmanoeuvred his opponents was evident from their repeatedly asking what had happened to his usual motion for abolition, and why it was not being discussed at the same time. But in a masterly display of self-restraint, he simply said nothing at all during the passage through Parliament of the Slave Importation Bill. He offered no clarification to his opponents, and gave every appearance that the Bill was nothing to do with him. His silence during the debates was all the more stark for the fact that he was almost continually on his feet in the months of April and May discussing nearly every other subject that came before Parliament. He pleased his Yorkshire constituents by speaking several times against the introduction of a tax on pig iron; made a plea, well before his time, for the introduction of child tax allowances in relation to property duties; spoke warmly of granting an annuity and an estate to the heirs of Nelson; and intervened on a wide range of other subjects, ranging from the affairs of India to compensation for losses sustained in the importation of Swedish herrings.

On the slave trade, however, Wilberforce was silent, as were all the other 'Saints'. 'The Foreign Slave Trade Bill is going quietly on,' he noted in early April.[14] Ministers happily joined in on the conspiracy of stealth. When one or two more anti-abolitionists woke up to what was happening, such as Sir Robert Peel (father of the Prime Minister of thirty years later), who complained that 'He had not attended earlier stages of the Bill because "he had not been aware that it was a Bill so mischievous in its nature as he now found it to be".'[15] Fox was all innocence in reply. 'He only wished', he said, that the Bill would have the effect on the slave trade that its small number of opponents asserted: 'As to this Bill having an operation gradually to abolish the slave trade, as some gentlemen seemed to apprehend, he owned he could not flatter himself in the hope that it would produce such a consequence; and if he thought it would have such a tendency, instead of that being with him an argument against the Bill, it was one which would render him ten times more enamoured of it.'[16]

Taken together, the silence of Wilberforce and the denials of Fox amounted to one of the most masterly exercises in laying smoke in the long annals of parliamentary manoeuvres. That it was made possible by Wilberforce's intimate cooperation with new ministers to whom he had largely been opposed for much of their political lives was a tribute to his skill in maintaining good relations on all sides and to their respect for his independence. It was twenty years since the Testonites had selected Wilberforce as having the right combination of talents to fight for abolition in Parliament, and as the weeks passed in 1806 they were proved to have chosen well. The Slave Importation Bill passed its final stage in the House of Commons, the third reading, by thirty-five votes to thirteen, in a thin House on the night of 1 May.

The same trick now had to be performed in the House of Lords, which long experience had shown was more likely to be a difficult matter. Wilberforce was worried that the Duke of Clarence and Lord Sheffield would try to dilute the Bill by amending it. In keeping with the tiptoeing tactics which had so far worked so well, he did not even sit in the gallery of the House of Lords to listen to the debates, but once again pretended that it was just a piece of government business. Although he waited anxiously to hear what had happened, he need not have worried, for even in the House of Lords the abolitionists now possessed three fresh advantages. One was that in Grenville the Lords now had the Prime Minister himself as one of their own number, for the first time in nearly a quarter of a century after the long dominance of Pitt. This undoubtedly added weight to the government's strength in that House. Secondly, the arguments used by Grenville when he introduced the Bill himself on 7 May, utterly in line with Stephen's thinking and based on notes prepared by him, were as difficult to refute in the Lords as they had been in the Commons:

> The islands in the West Indies were now nearly all of them in the possession of this country, or of our enemies; and, if it was a clear

and obvious policy that we should not give advantages to our enemies, it was surely equally clear that we should not supply their colonies with slaves, thereby affording them additional means of cultivation, contributing to increase the produce of their islands, and thus enabling them to meet us in the market upon equal terms of competition, or perhaps to undersell us. This appeared to him so obvious, that he thought it unnecessary to argue it. The first object of the bill, therefore, was to prevent British subjects from supplying foreign colonies with slaves. The same principle was also applicable to the supply of colonies captured from the enemy, and only held until peace. In the islands captured in the last war, and which were given up at the peace, British capital was employed to so great an extent, that the exports from those islands equalled the exports from Jamaica. All this went to benefit and enrich the enemy, and to increase their means of rivalry. Another object of the bill, therefore, was to enforce the order of council, issued to restrain this species of trade, enacting, at the same time, additional regulation, in order to prevent the importation of slaves into the islands thus conquered from the enemy, and the consequent investiture in them of a large portion of British capital.[17]

Not only were opponents thus out-argued, but there was a third factor working in the Bill's favour, which was that abolitionist opinion had at last gained some ground even in the upper House. The Bishops had become more active in their support for it,* and while the Duke of Clarence was opposed, another younger royal duke, the Duke of Gloucester, declared his support for the Bill, and indeed for total abolition. Gloucester had been befriended by Wilberforce over the previous years, and one of the products of their conversations was now revealed: the Duke had become an abolitionist.

As the debates went on, Grenville had no difficulty swatting away the objections raised that other countries, and in particular America, would take up the trade instead: 'Did we not ride everywhere unrivalled on the ocean? Could any power pretend to engross this trade, while

---

* Then, as now, leading Bishops were given seats in the House of Lords.

we commanded from the shores of Africa to the western extremities of the Atlantic? America had been represented as likely to succeed us in the trade; but were not noble Lords aware, that there was a majority of the United States decidedly hostile to this traffic?'[18] In addition, with the Bill only minutes from its final approval on 16 May, Grenville, as he later wrote to Wilberforce, 'saw our strength and thought the occasion was favourable for launching out a little beyond what the measure itself actually required'.[19] While he continued to reject the idea that the Bill was 'abolition in disguise', he went on to say, highly significantly, that:

> Were this true, he should be glad indeed, not of the disguise, but of the abolition. It would be an event most grateful to his feelings to witness the abolition of a traffic that was an outrage to human-ity, and that trampled on the rights of mankind. But he could see no reason for disguise, on such a subject. He had heard of fraud in disguise, or injustice and oppression in disguise; but justice and humanity required no disguise. Those who felt those virtues would also be proud to acknowledge them.[20]

The Lords passed the Bill by forty-three votes to eighteen. In letting the mask slip a little at the last moment, Grenville had probably taken a calculated risk. By then he knew the Bill would be carried anyway, but by stating so clearly at the same time the moral case for total abolition he had prepared the ground perfectly for what might be the next stage of the rapid but step-by-step approach. It was a classic incremental strategy. Just as the Guiana Order of Council the previous year had made it easier to argue for the Bill about to be carried, on the grounds that much of it had already been agreed to, so it would now become easier to argue for general abolition once a large proportion of the slave trade had been outlawed anyway. Wilberforce was understand-ably delighted to have arrived at this position, writing in his diary: 'Sunday 18th. We have carried the Foreign Slave Bill, and we are now deliberating whether we should push the main question. Oh Lord, do Thou guide us right, and enable me to maintain a spiritual mind amid all my hurry of worldly business, having my conversation in heaven.'[21]

The abolitionists had made a huge advance, and could see that their chances of carrying general abolition were now better than they had ever been. Nevertheless, the parliamentary session, which would normally end in July or early August, was well advanced, and Grenville was doubtful that such an important and controversial Bill could be carried through both Houses before its end. Wilberforce, though, was ready to do anything to make it possible. Yet again, in a repeat of his offer to Addington in 1802, he offered to give up the leading role in bringing forward an abolition Bill if that would help it to be carried. He wrote to Grenville on 20 May that 'If the measure is to be brought forward at all, it had better be, not by me, but by Mr Fox. The circumstance of your patronising the measure in the House of Lords and Mr Fox in the House of Commons will have, I trust, great weight in neutralising some who might be active enemies and converting into decided friends some who otherwise might be neutral.'[22] Grenville, however, was worried that it was rushing things too much to expect a Bill for total abolition to go through the House of Lords in a matter of days or weeks, 'and if we fail now we do irretrievable mischief to the cause'.[23] Various alternatives were considered, including Grenville's own idea that high duties should be imposed on the slave trade in order to strangle it over a period, but Wilberforce understandably rejected this. The conclusion was that Fox in the Commons and Grenville in the Lords would move motions condemning the slave trade in the course of June, in effect binding Parliament to act on total abolition in the near future. The actual wording of the motion duly moved by Fox on 10 June 1806, 'This House ... will, with all practicable expedition, proceed to take effectual measures for abolishing the said trade, in such a manner, and in such a period as may be deemed advisable,'[24] was calculated to win the support of those who still favoured 'gradual' abolition, including cabinet members such as Sidmouth.

In fact, the wording of the resolution represented a further instalment of the softly-softly strategy of that year. Wilberforce, Fox and Grenville had every intention of using the passage of such a motion to justify immediate abolition at the beginning of the next session of

Parliament, early in 1807. When it came to the debate, Fox poured forth the persuasive eloquence for which he was famed. Not knowing that he was making one of the last speeches of his life, he declared:

> So fully am I impressed with the vast importance and necessity of attaining what will be the object of my motion this day, that if, during the almost forty years that I have now had the honour of a seat in parliament, I had been so fortunate as to accomplish that, and that only, I should think I had done enough, and could retire from public life with comfort, and conscious satisfaction that I had done my duty.[25]

Tarleton and Gascoyne fought a rearguard action, the latter concluding with the quote from Leviticus that had been used to give biblical authority to the slave trade. Wilberforce, no longer holding back, was immediately on his feet: 'If the honourable gentleman could believe that slavery was sanctioned by our holy religion, he should only feel disposed to pity his weakness and error, and should endeavour to rectify his mistake in the spirit of mildness and conciliation. It was the glory of our religion, that it not only forbade all those odious means by which slaves were procured but expressly prohibited the practice of man stealing, and called us to act on a principle of universal philanthropy, and kind goodwill to all men.'[26] Stirred by his opponents, and throwing off the tactics of disguise, he called for a Bill early in the next session to abolish a trade which 'would ultimately be found rotten to the core'.[27] In a clear demonstration of how much the atmosphere had changed, the motions condemning the trade were carried by 114 to fifteen in the Commons and by forty-one to twenty-one in the Lords, where success could not have been guaranteed without the 'gradualists' on board. Wilberforce additionally proposed an Address to the King calling for 'negotiations with Foreign Powers with a view to the General Abolition of the Slave Trade',[28] which was carried without a division.

While much of the momentum for the sudden breakthrough by the abolitionists had come from a determination to defeat the French, Wilberforce had an eye on the peace negotiations then opening in

Paris. If peace was made without international agreement on abolition, as in 1802, much of what had just been gained would be reversed, and the final passage of an Abolition Bill would become harder to secure. So as the barriers to abolition came crashing down in the summer of 1806, Wilberforce continually assessed the issue from every angle, and tried to guard against every eventuality. After the many years of disappointments, he was utterly determined not to be beaten now. Although congratulations poured in, and he allowed himself to recognise that things 'looked more promising than for many years', he also noted, 'I am sick of the bustle, and long for quiet but I will not leave the poor slaves in the lurch.'[29] Later estimates would suggest that the Bill of 1806 would destroy as much as three-quarters of the British slave trade; but general and permanent abolition had still not been enacted. And before it could be secured, two wholly unexpected events were about to occur.

Charles James Fox had waited twenty-three years to return to power after his ejection from it by George III in 1783, until Pitt's death and his alliance with Grenville at last made it possible. But within months he was himself dying, as a distressed William Smith reported to Wilberforce on 27 June. For Wilberforce, Fox's condition, diagnosed as dropsy, created a double concern. Fox had been a tower of strength for the abolitionists in the preceding months, and his presence in government weighted it heavily in their direction. Wilberforce had known that Fox was unwell after the Commons vote of 10 June, when he noted, 'If it pleased God to spare the health of Fox and to keep him and Grenville together, I hope we shall see next year the termination of all our labours.'[30] A government without Fox leading it in the Commons would be a less certain quantity. In addition, Wilberforce had always maintained a personal fondness and respect for Fox, even though they had been on the opposing side of most political questions in the previous quarter of a century, and Fox had led a private life devoted to gambling and womanising to an almost unimaginable degree. His reflections on Fox's imminent demise, as set out in a letter to William

Hey on 1 August, are pure Wilberforce, typifying his approach to death, religion, and politics:

> How affecting an instance of the precarious nature of all human enjoyments is exhibited in Mr Fox's present situation! No sooner is he able to grasp the prize, after which he has been so many years stretching in vain, and which, now that his great rival is no more, he might hope to possess without a competitor, than, behold, the bubble bursts in his hand, and he discovers the hollowness of all sublunary good. But I cannot help thinking that Mr Fox had, even before his illness begun to taste that the gratifications of ambition are less sweet in the enjoyment than in the expectation. And many of his partisans who had anticipated a sort of golden age from his administration, begin to find that matters go on very much after the old sort. I have myself long ceased to expect much from any men who are destitute of true religion. But then as I do not look for so much good from the men of the world, whose talents and even political and moral principles I approve in the main; so neither do I apprehend as much evil from the government of which I disapprove. – I have long thought the remark in Mr Hume's Essays very wise; wherein he counsels moderation in our political expectancies, either of good or evil – especially in a country where the constitution contains so many safeguards against evil as ours does.[31]

Fox died on 13 September: after an entire political life intertwined with that of Pitt, he had taken only eight months to follow him to the grave. Wilberforce need not have worried, however, about the effect this would have on the political outlook of the government. After an aborted attempt to split the Pittites by recruiting Canning (who was in any case an out-and-out abolitionist) to the cabinet, Grenville replaced Fox as Foreign Secretary with Charles Grey, now Lord Howick, who had also been in close cooperation with Wilberforce the previous year.* Howick would not be able to offer anything like the eloquence

---

* Although Grey had become Lord Howick, this was a courtesy title and enabled him to continue to sit in the House of Commons. It was only when he succeeded his father as Earl Grey that he would have no choice but to move to the House of Lords.

and force of Fox in the House of Commons, but there was no doubt that he would be just as keen to press forward with abolition in the new session.

By this time Wilberforce had taken himself and his family off for their usual late-summer retreat. Once again they made for Dorset, and 'slipped into the snug and retired harbour of Lyme, for the purpose of careening and refitting'.[32] As usual, even though Wilberforce was taking a physical rest from the late nights of Westminster, he had no intention of taking an intellectual one. His first book had been a great success: now he felt the need to write another one, and indeed to complete the entire work from beginning to end in only a few months. It would be a comprehensive restatement of the case for abolition, which he felt was necessary given that the taking of evidence and the early debates of principle were now a decade and a half in the past. He intended to publish it just before the Abolition Bill arrived in the House of Lords, so that it might be 'like a shot which hits between wind and water; it might prove of decisive efficiency'.[33] He was well engaged in this work when, on 15 October, it was brought to a total stop. He was, he confessed to his diary, 'Shocked by a letter from Lord Grenville announcing a dissolution of parliament.'[34] Only just over four years into the seven-year parliamentary term, Grenville had decided on a general election.

Grenville had good reasons for calling an election in the autumn of 1806, and his decision to do so would be vindicated by the overall outcome. Prime Ministers of the eighteenth and early nineteenth centuries could use an election to 'make' a Parliament, with more of their allies included in it, taking full advantage of the powers of patronage and Treasury money. The current Parliament had been elected under Sidmouth in 1802, and Grenville felt, quite correctly, that he could increase his majority with fresh elections. Furthermore, the death of Fox and the turn of international events meant that he needed to strengthen his position in the Commons sooner rather than later. The Paris peace talks had collapsed in early October – taking with them what little hope there was of uniting with France in abolishing the slave trade – and the intensification of war and the fresh alliance with

Prussia that this would entail persuaded Grenville that he should bolster his position while he could.

For three reasons, the calling of the 1806 election was immensely inconvenient for Wilberforce. For one thing, it meant that the work on his new book was violently interrupted, putting it irretrievably behind the schedule he had in mind. More ominously, there was immediate talk of a contest in Yorkshire: the return to government of the Whigs had greatly enhanced their electoral confidence, and they would be highly likely to make an attempt on one of the Yorkshire seats, currently held by Wilberforce and Lascelles. Finally, the election came before an intense controversy over the future of the West Riding woollen industry had had time to die down, putting the Yorkshire MPs at the mercy of some very disgruntled constituents.

The debate about manufacturing methods in the woollen industry had preoccupied Wilberforce for much of May and June, even while the manoeuvrings on the slave trade were at their height, and was a powerful example of the political and social tensions caused by the continuing advance of the Industrial Revolution. The burgeoning clothing industry of the Yorkshire West Riding had hitherto been dominated by cottage weavers, who made their goods at home and sold them in the cloth halls through cooperative arrangements. By the beginning of the nineteenth century these clothiers, whose numbers made them a constituency which could not be ignored, were threatened by the arrival of copious amounts of fresh capital and mechanised mills. As a result, they wanted Parliament to restrict competition by legislating against the production of cloth in large factories. Wilberforce was assiduous in attending the parliamentary committee which inquired into the woollen trade, and 'never but one day was prevented from attending it'.[35] Their report, largely written by Wilberforce despite the distractions of slave-trade motions, opposition to pig-iron duty, and renewed protests against the Sunday drilling of the militia, was a compromise which sensibly allowed the expansion of mills but also called for safeguards for the weavers. Although the compromise was highly regarded in the House of Commons, it did not impress the Yorkshire clothiers, who were left unenthusiastic about Wilberforce and militantly opposed to Lascelles, who had been less than sympathetic to their concerns.

It was not surprising in these circumstances that the Whigs saw their chance to elect Walter Fawkes, who had narrowly backed off from a contest in 1796. This time there was no doubting that the great Whig grandees of the county, such as Earl Fitzwilliam, were behind him, with unlimited spending power. Lascelles in turn had huge support from the landed gentry and nobility. Wilberforce was in a tricky position, since siding with either of them would enrage the followers of the other, and he would need the second vote of each side's supporters. On the other hand, maintaining neutrality would also cost him a great deal of support. The Whigs could not work directly against Wilberforce, because Grenville had been absolutely clear with them that he wanted him re-elected – 'Mr Wilberforce *must* be supported by the Government interest but not one farthing of money from the Treasury.'[36] Wilberforce was also no mean campaigner. At election times he had always shown himself to be a serious political operator. Fitzwilliam calculated that Wilberforce would do better to align himself with Fawkes, and, in a remark which shows that Wilberforce was not always regarded as a man of pure principle, said that he would not 'be surprised to see the little man's cunning guiding him towards that course'.[37] Nevertheless, Wilberforce, whether on principle or by calculation, resisted taking sides, and tore into the campaign with his customary energy. Initially he had to overcome rumours that he was not standing by sending a letter affirming his candidacy from Nottingham as he travelled northwards. By then he was receiving reports from his agents that 'the clothiers . . . are violent beyond all conception' against Lascelles;[38] and by the time he was in Leeds on 28 October he could see the mood for himself:

> Tuesday. Went with merchants to Hall. Most kindly received. Then Whitehall, after speechifying. Drawn to the inn and home by the people. Friends met in the evening. Cloth Hall trustees called, and agreed to canvass for me. A most violent cry against Lascelles among the clothiers, but not for matter but manner of committee business. I heard that if he had come with me to the Hall, they

would have let me pass, and then shoved down cloth in his way to stop him.[39]

Having secured his flank with the clothiers, he found an ecstatic reception among the heavier industries of Sheffield. Wilberforce's diary entries give some idea of the magnificent chaos of the elections of the time:

> Meant to go to Cutlers' Hall, and thence to Town Hall; but populace would drag us to Town Hall, where joined and thanked by cutlers for Iron-tax opposition – speechified them, and afterwards people, from Hall steps. Immense concourse. Sea of faces. I endeavoured to walk, but soon forced to take to carriage and dragged all round for half an hour (several run over, but not much hurt); and to Angel again, where dined.[40]

That had been the Wednesday; by the Friday he was in Wakefield, where he was 'met a mile off, and drawn by people into town to inn, where addressed the people in the marketplace – vast crowd . . . off for Dewsbury, where dragged and addressed again. Carriage broke and stopped . . . Speechified again – dreadful roads . . .'[41]

It is worth remembering that these were the scenes even before it was clear that there would be a contest for the Yorkshire seats at all. This was merely the trial of strength, during which the candidates assessed whether they should take the extraordinary step of forcing the matter to an actual poll of the voters. Wilberforce was soon clear as to what the outcome would be under that eventuality, writing to Grenville on 1 November that he hoped there would not be a poll, 'for certainly I *whisper* to you IN PERFECT CONFIDENCE (what I cannot be as glad of as you, from my personal goodwill to Mr. Lascelles, though I am most scrupulously and *conscientiously* neutral between him and his opponent) that Mr. Fawkes also will be victorious'.[42] It was a remarkable feature of Wilberforce's approach to politics that he retained such goodwill towards a colleague who had always been opposed to the abolition of the slave trade, and whose family had greatly profited from it themselves. In the event, Lascelles could also see that the game was up, and that the expense of an all-out election could not be justified. He quit the contest on 1 November, leaving Wilberforce and Fawkes elected. Yorkshire had thus provided one of the more than forty gains which added to the Commons majority of Grenville and his allies and secured them in office. Or so any reasonable observer might have thought.

Elected for the fifth time to represent Yorkshire, and obviously with huge popular support, Wilberforce wrote to a friend of his great thankfulness. He thought that he 'can only ascribe it to that gracious Providence which can control at will the affections of men . . . I never attend races or even assizes, which members for Yorkshire before me used to do . . . It really shows that there is still some public spirit among us; and that if a member of parliament will act an honest and independent part, his constituents (such at least of them as are themselves independent) will not desert him.'[43] But he did not linger long in Yorkshire. Grenville now told him that when the new Parliament met in January he intended to introduce a Bill to abolish the slave trade almost immediately, and what was more, to introduce it in the House of Lords. Emboldened by the evident shift of opinion in the Lords the previous summer, he would take the Bill through its toughest test at the very beginning: if it passed the Lords it would then be unstoppable in the Commons. The whole matter of the slave trade in British law would finally be decided. And in Wilberforce's eyes, the need to finish his book was now desperately urgent. He made haste for London.

The Members who gathered for the opening of the new Parliament on 15 December 1806, and to listen to Wilberforce, as a senior MP of twenty-six years' standing, second the re-election of Charles Abbott as Speaker of the Commons, would have had every expectation that the Grenville administration was now set fair for some years. In fact, it would be turned out within a matter of months, with Pitt's friends returned to power for a generation, and its imminent fall would make the now-anticipated passage of the Abolition Bill a very fine race against time. The fortunes of the abolitionists as they neared victory would therefore to some extent become bound up with the fate of the government, as, in spite of Pitt's earlier example, it embarked on a collision course with the King on the familiar and divisive issue of the status of Roman Catholics.

The root cause of the political upheavals of 1807 that would accompany the final push for abolition was military. In November 1806 Napoleon had descended on the Prussians, crushed them at the Battle of Jena, occupied Berlin and declared a Continental economic blockade of Britain. One of the measures that had been contemplated within the government for some months to enlarge the pool of British military manpower was to raise Catholic regiments in Ireland. In order to do this, ministers wanted to relax the rules on Catholic army officers, who under the Irish Act of 1793 were able to serve in the army below the rank of General, but were only allowed to serve and worship in Ireland, not in Britain. The need to put this right and to head off mounting pressure in Ireland for general Catholic emancipation made Grenville and his colleagues determined to act, but in the course of February 1807 they wedded themselves to a position of allowing Catholics to serve right up to the rank of General, and George III had become equally committed to preventing them doing so. After forty-seven years on the throne refusing to budge on most aspects of the Catholic question, the King was not going to suffer a major defeat now. Such was the impasse, even though some flexibility on the part of ministers could have given them most of what they wanted while still leaving the situation acceptable to the King, that by early March Sidmouth would have resigned from the cabinet in protest and by mid-March the King would be looking for an alternative government. There would not be many weeks in which to pilot an Abolition Bill through both Houses of Parliament before the ministers who were so crucial to it were no longer in place. Wilberforce himself would be of no help to the government on the Catholic issue. In early March he would oppose part of its proposals, a special grant to the Irish Roman Catholic college at Maynooth, on the grounds that special favours for Catholics would inhibit the growth of Protestantism in Ireland. While 'he allowed it was not only criminal but cruel in the highest degree to oppress or restrain the Catholic religion', he felt that 'as a sincere friend to the Protestant religion, he was unwilling to extend an establishment which would prevent the propagation of that religion'.[44] Although no friend to Catholicism, Wilberforce was therefore more balanced on this subject than most of his countrymen: England would soon be echoing once again to the cry of 'No Popery!'

In such circumstances it was immensely fortunate that several powerful forces now came together to make the passage of an Abolition Act both rapid and overwhelming. The first of these was the utter determination of Grenville to deal with abolition at the very beginning of the new Parliament. Obstinacy and rigidity had always been among his political failings, and would be material to his forthcoming débâcle with George III, but in the case of the slave trade at the beginning of 1807 such characteristics in a Prime Minister created unstoppable momentum. Even while the election results had still been coming in during early November 1806, Grenville had written to Wilberforce saying that he proposed to introduce in the Lords 'a Bill simply abolishing the trade and declaring the being engaged in it to be a misdemeanour punishable as such at law'.[45] Throughout December, the draft of the Bill was circulated between Grenville, his officials, Wilberforce, Stephen and the Duke of Gloucester. It was published in January 1807, and the key debate and vote at second reading would take place in the first week of February.

In the meantime, powerful support was on its way from another and more distant quarter, for in December 1806 President Thomas Jefferson of the United States attacked the 'violations of human rights which have been so long continued on the unoffending inhabitants of Africa',[46] and called on Congress to use the forthcoming expiry of the constitutional limitation of twenty years totally to abolish the slave trade in the course of 1807. A Bill to outlaw the slave trade passed through the Senate in January and the House of Representatives in February, and was signed by the President on 2 March, making it illegal from 1 January 1808 to bring to the United States any 'negro, mulatto, or person of colour as a slave'. The Act would prove to be weakly enforced, and much of the continuing American slave trade would prove to be internal. The United States was in a wholly different position from the Caribbean because its slave population was expanding so rapidly by natural means that the maintenance of slavery in no way depended on the slave trade – that is why the Southern states were prepared to agree to abolition – but even so, America's declarations shattered the argument of British opponents that the slave trade would be taken up by American ships.

The successful passage of the American Act was not known in Britain at the time of the climactic debate in Westminster, but its likelihood was. And a yet further force which hit the House of Lords just days before the crucial deliberations was Wilberforce's book. What he had always described as a 'tract' or a 'pamphlet' had become a work of some eighty thousand words in nearly four hundred pages. Theoretically addressed to his constituents, it was entitled *A Letter on the Abolition of the Slave Trade addressed to the Freeholders and Other Inhabitants of Yorkshire*. He managed to finish it on the evening of 27 January, and it was published in hard covers four days later (a feat totally unheard of in the twenty-first century). In it, Wilberforce summed up the arguments he had presented over the previous twenty years. His introductory words to his constituents argued that 'If the Slave Trade be indeed the foulest blot that ever stained our National character, you will not deem your Representative to have been unworthily employed, in having been among the foremost in wiping it away.'[47] He wrote much, as ever, of the need to fear God's judgement:

> That the Almighty Creator of the universe governs the world which he has made; that the sufferings of nations are to be regarded as the punishment of national crimes ... If these truths be admitted, and if it be also true, that fraud, oppression, and cruelty are crimes of the blackest dye, and that guilt is aggravated in proportion as the criminal acts in defiance of clearer light, and of stronger motives to virtue (and these are positions to which we cannot refuse our assent, without rejecting the authority not only of revealed, but even of natural religion); have we not abundant cause for serious apprehension?[48]

It was therefore vital 'to lighten the vessel of the state of such a load of guilt and infamy'.[49] He tore into those who had argued that Negroes were a different species 'with disgust',[50] and, moving for once into the evils of slavery itself, gave 'decisive proof' that the argument that slaves were happy was utterly unfounded. For in those instances where slaves managed to save any money for themselves, what did they do with it? 'When the savings of many years have, at length, accumulated to a considerable amount, how do they dispose of it? With this sum, for which they have been struggling during the whole course of their lives, they go to their masters, and buy their freedom. By the sacrifice of their last shilling, they purchase their release from that situation which the West Indians would persuade us is a condition of superior comfort.'[51] It was in his writing, rather than in parliamentary speeches, that Wilberforce best displayed the unity of his political and religious beliefs. He summed up:

> Providence governs the world. But if we are not blind to the course of human events, as well as utterly deaf to the plain instructions of Revelation, we must believe that a continued course of wickedness, oppression, and cruelty, obstinately maintained in spite of the fullest knowledge and the loudest warnings, must infallibly bring down upon us the heaviest judgements of the Almighty. We may ascribe our fall to weak counsels or unskilful generals; to a factious and overburthened people; to storms which waste our fleets, to diseases which thin our armies; to mutiny among our soldiers and sailors, which may even turn against us our own force; to the diminution of our revenues and the excessive increase of our debt: men may complain on one side of a venal ministry, on the other of a factious opposition; while amid mutual recriminations, the nation is gradually verging to its fate. Providence will easily provide means for the accomplishment of its own purposes ... we have, as I firmly believe, the means within ourselves of arresting the progress of this decline. We have been eminently blessed; we have been long spared; Let us not presume too far on the forbearance of the Almighty.[52]

Wilberforce's book still serves as yet another monument to his determination to use every legitimate means of shifting opinion. Whether it made a serious difference at such a late stage cannot be known, although copies of it were rushed to the House of Lords and circulated widely as soon as it came off the presses. What it certainly demonstrated was that the abolitionist campaign in its final stages threw off the cloak of national self-interest, under which it had advanced so much the previous year, and resumed its frontal assault on the inhumanity of the slave trade. Stephen's brilliant arguments had got them a good deal of the way to their target, but such arguments could get them no further. Abolition of the remaining British slave trade could not be justified on grounds of national self-interest. As William Smith put it to Wilberforce the previous August, the final step could only be taken if Parliament 'will do this heroic deed in some fit of heroism'.[53] That the abolitionist strategy had to be changed in this way at the beginning of 1807 is the conclusive answer to those, such as Eric Williams in his 1944 work *Capitalism and Slavery*, who argued that global overproduction of sugar 'demanded abolition' in 1807.[54] Britain's naval power gave her at that time the power to stop almost all other production and maintain her own for the future, something which was generally accepted at the time to require slavery, and still widely thought to require a slave trade. As Roger Anstey showed in *The Atlantic Slave Trade and British Abolition* (1975), 'The crushingly obvious definition of Britain's national interest lay in maintaining the slave trade to her own possessions whilst denying it to her enemies and competitors.'[55]

The moral framework in which Wilberforce had always placed his practical arguments therefore mattered as the issue came to a head in 1807, as did his own indefatigable efforts to move parliamentary opinion over the previous twenty years. He was no mere agent of something that had always been inevitable. Abolition was not bound to happen in 1807: it required a conjunction of forces of which Wilberforce and his band of 'Saints' were a truly indispensable component. That Wilberforce's role had been crucial was never doubted by those serving in Parliament at the time, from the Prime Minister downwards. As Grenville introduced the Bill to the Lords in one of his finest speeches, relying heavily on the moral arguments which had been largely unspoken the year before, he concluded with an effusive tribute to Wilberforce:

> I cannot conceive any consciousness more truly gratifying than must be enjoyed by that person, on finding a measure to which he has devoted the colour of his life, carried into effect – a measure so truly benevolent, so admirably conducive to the virtuous prosperity of his country, and the welfare of mankind – a measure which will diffuse happiness amongst millions, now in existence and for which his memory will be blessed by millions as yet unborn.[56]

The remaining opponents of abolition had no doubt either who was to blame for their predicament. Lord Westmorland attacked the influence of Wilberforce, although Wilberforce, listening in the gallery, thought 'it was a double pleasure to be praised by Lord Grenville and abused by Lord Westmorland'.[57] Grenville had thought he could count on fifty-six votes a few days before the Lords debate, then perhaps seventy, but when it came to it the tide of opinion had overwhelmed even the last bastion of reaction: the House of Lords carried the Abolition Bill by one hundred votes to thirty-four. It was the death knell of the British slave trade.

By the night of 23 February, the triumph of the House of Lords had been repeated in the House of Commons, the tears streaming down Wilberforce's cheeks and the eulogies of his colleagues ringing in his ears as even the recalcitrant recognised the inevitable and the Bill was carried by 283 votes to sixteen. Even though it was nearly five o'clock in the morning, Old Palace Yard teemed with well-wishers. It was the culmination of one of the greatest campaigns of British history. As William Smith tried to work out which sixteen MPs had voted the other way, Wilberforce commented, 'Never mind the miserable sixteen, let us think of our glorious 283.' 'Well, Henry,' he said to Thornton, 'what shall we abolish next?' 'The lottery, I think,'[58] came the reply.

To Bishop Porteus the victory was the end of 'a glorious struggle' which would put a stop to 'the most execrable and inhuman traffic that ever disgraced the Christian world', and which would 'reflect immortal honour on the British Parliament, the British nation and all the illustrious men who were the principal promoters of it. I am truly thankful to Providence for permitting me to see this great work brought to a conclusion.'[59] To all opponents of the slave trade it was a time of almost unrestrained excitement, with Wilberforce able to use the commanding parliamentary majority to insert fresh clauses into the Bill, naming the fines and penalties which were to be incurred for breaking the new law. But when some overexcited supporters started to propose the abolition of slavery itself, and one opponent within the cabinet, William Windham, suggested that those who opposed the slave trade should have the logical consistency to do so, Wilberforce was clear that further change would take time: 'They had for the present no object immediately before them, but that of putting stop directly to the carrying of men in British ships to be sold as slaves in the British Islands, in the West Indies . . . Still, he must confess, that he should have another object after that in view and that he looked forward to a still more happy change in the state of the negroes in the West India islands.'[60] For now, 'we were not to say that because a man had two wounds we should refrain from curing one, because it was not in our power to heal both the wounds immediately'.[61]

Wilberforce spoke these words on 16 March. On 18 March, the Bill returned to the House of Lords for the amendments to it to be considered. On the nineteenth the King in effect dismissed Grenville and the entire government over the Catholic question, and started his search for a new Prime Minister. With the last hours of Grenville's administration ticking away, Wilberforce had to rush around Westminster on 23 March seeking agreement to the correction of clerical errors in some of the amendments to the Bill. It was, in any event, too late for a new administration to stand in the way of the Bill, and politically impossible to do so, since it had been carried by such large majorities. Grenville and Wilberforce had won the race against time. On 24 March, Grenville's last day as Prime Minister, he obtained the formal consent of George III for the Abolition Bill. At noon on Wednesday, 25 March 1807, the Speaker of the House of Commons announced the enactment of the Slave Trade Abolition Act. From 1 May that year its provisions would take effect. The trade which had taken millions of Africans to the colonies of the British Empire was now outside the law.

14

High Respect; Low Politics

While the slave masters are pouring out their maledictions on Wilberforce, the slaves are at the same time roaring out and wishing the best
of blessings to light upon the head of the *Godlike Emancipator!*

JOHN HILL, a missionary, to the British and Foreign Bible Society, 1808[1]

I am always very slow to decide on points of great importance, when
I know I have but very inadequate grounds on which to rest my
opinion. But I have to suspect that those who have more and better
grounds, have not always sufficient.

WILBERFORCE TO BANKES, 26 July 1809[2]

T HE PASSAGE of the Abolition Act was an immense achievement
for Wilberforce, and was seen to be so at the time. Although his
own view was that he was 'only one among many fellow labourers',[3]
he was now accorded by much of the rest of the world the status of a
statesman and veteran campaigner. While slaves were hailing him as a
'*Godlike Emancipator*', Sir James Mackintosh was writing from India,
'Hundreds and thousands will be animated by Mr. Wilberforce's
example, by his success and . . . by a renown that can only perish with
the world, to attack all the forms of corruption and cruelty that scourge
mankind. Oh what twenty years in the life of one man those were,
which abolished the Slave Trade!'[4] Even the previous year, once the
struggle looked certain to be won, the *Edinburgh Review* had said, 'Let
our gratitude be testified to that man who has begun and led through
this glorious struggle – who has devoted to its success all his days and

all his talents – who has retired from all recompence for his labours, save the satisfaction of doing good to his fellow creatures – who, giving up to mankind what others have sacrificed to party, has preferred the glory of living in the recollection of a grateful world to the shining rewards of a limited ambition.'[5]

It was widely judged that for persistence, selflessness, integrity and fair-mindedness, Wilberforce had set a standard that was rarely attained in politics. Given such a reputation, and the fact that he was only forty-seven years old and was one of the most assiduous of all Members of Parliament, he was much courted by rival factions as their fortunes were once again dramatically reversed. By the time Parliament was informed of the Royal Assent to the Slave Trade Abolition Act, Grenville was already sitting on the opposition benches, to which he had gone with good grace, and evidently no small measure of relief that he would no longer have to bear the burdens of government. Instead, George III reverted to Pitt's old friends, with the ageing Duke of Portland nominally leading a government in which the real power would lie with several of the younger former adherents of Pitt.

The result was that, although Wilberforce had worked happily with Grenville and his colleagues, with astonishingly productive results, he found the new government by no means uncongenial either. Inevitably, it included very conservative figures such as Castlereagh and Hawkesbury, who had been no friends of abolition, but abolition had now been enacted, and no one proposed to reverse it. In any case, the central figures in the new government had been strong supporters of abolition: George Canning became Foreign Secretary, and the young Spencer Perceval rose rapidly to lead for the new government in the House of Commons and take the office of Chancellor of the Exchequer. In Wilberforce's eyes, Perceval had many advantages. He was not only an abolitionist but also an Evangelical Christian, and had not only been an ardent disciple of Pitt, but was a highly able speaker in the House of Commons. Within two years he would succeed Portland as the recognised as well as the *de facto* Prime Minister. Wilberforce would come to regard Perceval as 'one of the most conscientious men I ever knew; the most instinctively obedient to the dictates of conscience, the least disposed to give pain to others, the most charitable and truly kind and generous creature I ever knew'.[6] Furthermore, the new administration was united in the view which had now brought them to power, opposition to Catholic emancipation, and it was one which at that time Wilberforce shared. They were more adamant for continued war than their predecessors, but the failure of the Grenville–Fox peace negotiations and the ever more aggressive behaviour of Napoleon hardened the view of Wilberforce and other doubters that the war must go on. Wilberforce was therefore prepared to approach the incoming government in the same spirit as the outgoing one, by giving qualified support to its existence, working closely with its leading members, and voting on its measures according to how he saw their merits. In practice, this often meant giving help to ministers when they needed it: Wilberforce told a colleague who commented on the difficulties of being an independent that he 'would find that I do not so entirely forswear all Party connection as you may suppose from my general and unqualified language'.[7]

How could Wilberforce so easily transfer his working relationships from one faction to another at a time of intense partisanship between the two sides? In later decades, any leading Member of Parliament who slipped so easily from working in the inner circle of one set of ministers in March to that of their foremost rivals in April would be regarded with suspicion, if not incredulity. There was, indeed, a little bit of cynicism at the time, for when the Whigs put down a Commons motion to condemn the new government a week after it took office, Wilberforce suffered a serious outbreak of his old bowel complaint at the remarkably convenient time of the debate and the actual vote, thus uncharacteristically missing the occasion altogether. It would not have been in his character to lie about an illness, and there is no suggestion that he did, but he had told Pretyman that day, 'I should enter the House with a most painful and embarrassing set of conflicting opinions and feelings.'[8] Yet the fact that Perceval was able to fight off the attack that day in a House of Commons which had been elected only a few months earlier to support an alternative government demonstrates that Wilberforce was not alone in his view that the King's government should be given a chance. Many MPs, exhibiting forms of political independence rather different from that embodied by Wilberforce, were still happy to take their cue from the King or to have their support purchased – through titles, pensions, or promises for their friends – by the government of the day. Some of them were only loosely associated with one of several competing factions, and could easily switch their support between them.

Nevertheless, the change of government in 1807 would come to be seen in later decades as an important milestone in British politics. It would mark the end of a period of multiple factions and the reassertion of the existence of two great parties. The group of 'Pitt's friends' who came to power in 1807 would, against all expectations of the time, in some combination lead the country without interruption for the whole of the next twenty-three years. Opposed to Catholic emancipation and parliamentary reform, and beholden to market forces and the defeat of France, their partnership would take on a permanent form which would become the nineteenth-century Tory Party. At the same time, on the opposition benches Grenville and his faction would become indistinguishable from the former colleagues of Fox, merging together in a new Whig coalition. The foundations of the modern Conservative and Liberal parties were therefore being laid. Eventually such parties would squeeze out independent representation, but in 1807 the beginnings of a wider franchise and stronger party organisations in constituencies were still a quarter of a century away. It was still possible for independents, whatever their motives, to hold serious sway: Wilberforce was now in such a position. And theoretically it was still possible for an independent, even in a vast constituency like Yorkshire with a large number of electors, to defeat both of the emerging parties in a fully contested electoral battle. Wilberforce had no inkling, however, that his ability to do so was about to be put to the test.

For most of April 1807, the business of Parliament seemed to go on much as before, albeit with a new set of ministers in charge. On 17 April Wilberforce was back on his feet, supporting Samuel Whitbread's Bill to revise the Poor Laws. Wilberforce considered that the new government's ability to win its first key vote, 'which I was prevented from joining by a real, and for a time serious, indisposition, has removed my fears of a dissolution of parliament'.[9] But, unbeknown to him, the new ministers were understandably enticed by the possibility of obtaining a Parliament in which they would have a more comfortable margin. The fact that their opponents had in effect been ejected from office by the King, and that they could ask for support on the popular basis of opposition to Catholic emancipation, led them to think this was the best opportunity they would have to increase their majority. On 29 April Parliament was dissolved, and a fresh general election announced, Wilberforce noting in his diary that he was 'astonished by a letter from Perceval announcing a dissolution'.[10] The Parliament had lasted only a little over four months, making it the shortest-lived of modern times.*

Although Wilberforce had been re-elected with acclaim in 1806, it was clear that a three-way contest for the two seats had been only narrowly averted when Lascelles stood down. With a new election following so immediately, it soon became apparent that the chances of an all-out and highly expensive contest for Yorkshire were much increased. Wilberforce's new colleague, Walter Fawkes, quit in disgust, stating 'that after what had lately passed, a Seat in the House of Commons, which was the first wish of his heart had ceased to be the object of his ambition; and that he could not consistently, with the duty he owed to a numerous and increasing family, consent to expose himself to the danger of these sudden and unexpected dissolutions'.[11] Fawkes' departure from the scene removed any doubts Lascelles might have had about mounting a strong campaign to recover his old seat, with all the great wealth of the Harewood estates behind him. On the other side, there was no way that the Whigs, having triumphed over Lascelles only the previous November, were going to sit back and let his seat be returned to him. With or without Fawkes, they would fight tooth and nail, nominating the twenty-one-year-old Viscount Milton, son of Earl Fitzwilliam, and thereby guaranteeing access to perhaps the

---

* It is still the shortest-lived, being some six weeks shorter in its duration than the Parliament of March–September 1974.

greatest landed wealth in the whole of the north of England. Hailed as a legislative hero as he might have been that March, Wilberforce could see at the end of April that unless he stood down from representing Yorkshire he was about to be caught up in a no-holds-barred electoral battle the like of which had not been seen in living memory. Even though he was 'sickened at a contest',[12] he turned aside the advice of those friends who said he should now seek a different seat. He would not be driven out of Yorkshire by money, or abandon a constituency in which he had received so much support. The stage was set for one of the most hard-fought and expensive elections for a single constituency in the whole course of British history.

Wilberforce had already been elected on five occasions to represent the county of Yorkshire. In three of those elections, those of 1784, 1796 and 1806, a struggle for the two seats had been averted when the third-placed candidate resigned the contest, and in the other two, 1790 and 1802, only Wilberforce and the one other candidate had ever taken the field. In 1807, Wilberforce's two rivals were too determined and too evenly matched for a similarly satisfactory outcome to be achieved, and the consequence was an event unique not only in Wilberforce's career, but in his entire lifetime: a county election in Yorkshire in which the voters actually had to go to the polls. Since such a thing had not happened since 1742, and then only for a by-election for one of the seats, 'the under-sheriff for that year could find no precedent for the arrangements to be made'.[13] All that was clear at the outset was that in this election the Earl of Harewood was 'ready to spend in it his whole Barbadoes property'[14] to elect Henry Lascelles, and Earl Fitzwilliam was assembling a vast organisation to elect Lord Milton. Horses, carriages and paid agents were rapidly hired by the two rival aristocratic families, both in order to move their voters to the polling booths at York and to deny such assistance to the other candidates.

At the outset, Wilberforce suffered the double disadvantage of having no comparable organisation in place, and, as the only incumbent standing for re-election, being far away in London when the other candidates began their scramble for votes. He headed north hurriedly, apparently having a narrow escape from breaking his leg when he set out, and reached Yorkshire to find the election in full swing. When he arrived at the southern boundaries of the county on the Great North Road he 'Halted afternoon at Doncaster. Heard for certain Lord Milton standing. But I doing well at Doncaster.'[15] But it was not until 4 May that he was able to bring his principal supporters together in York to coordinate an organisation, having established that 'Mr. Lascelles and Lord Milton had already engaged canvassing agents, houses of entertainment and every species of conveyance in every considerable town'.[16] Even so, Wilberforce and his supporters were quietly confident. He was, after all, highly popular with his constituents, as the canvass of the previous year had shown, his achievement in leading abolition was widely admired, and he was well placed to receive the second vote of both Lascelles' and Milton's supporters. This was, of course, his trump card: he was the first choice of many voters, but he was also the second choice of almost all the others, in an election in which each elector had two votes. The government, in the person of Spencer Perceval, had no wish to oust him, although it had not helped by giving Lascelles advance notice of the calling of the election; and the opposition, taking the form of Earl Fitzwilliam, the Duke of Norfolk and the representatives of the clothiers, had no wish to oust him either, provided he did not team up with Lascelles.

Maintaining neutrality in such a bitterly disputed election, however, was not as easy as it looked. First of all, the two rival camps were soon putting it about that Wilberforce was so safe that he did not need any second votes – the supporters of Milton or Lascelles could therefore give their man his best chance by using only a single vote, known as a 'plumper'. Then it was said that Wilberforce would not be able to join in paying the travelling and accommodation expenses of all those who gave him one of their two votes, unlike the other candidates, who could pay in full. More damagingly, the suspicion began to grow in the Milton camp that Wilberforce, who they regarded as 'a very artful man',[17] was saying he was neutral, but was actually cooperating with Lascelles. Unfortunately for Wilberforce, there was some evidence for this, albeit created inadvertently on his part. Lascelles, even though he was an anti-abolitionist, was a firm Pittite, and was running on a 'No Popery' ticket, and his supporters were more likely to overlap with those of Wilberforce than were Milton's Whiggish organisers. It was not surprising, therefore, that many of Lascelles' supporters also canvassed for Wilberforce, and vice versa, in an area spread over many thousands of square miles and in which Wilberforce, still assembling an organisation, could not easily control what was done on his behalf. In addition, whether by chance or through the coordinated work of their election committees, Wilberforce and Lascelles visited the same towns on the same days in early May – Wakefield, Bradford, Halifax, Huddersfield and Leeds.

Lascelles' arrival at the Leeds Cloth Hall on 5 May, with the clothiers almost as strongly opposed to him as they had been the previous year, gives some hint of the strong emotions involved: 'Popular feeling ran so strongly against him that he could not obtain a hearing, and was obliged to retire amidst a tremendous and long continued thunder of groans and hisses.' Milton, on the other hand, admittedly according to an admirer, 'astonished everyone who heard him; and from this moment the cry of "No infant legislator" descended to the tomb, with its relative "No popery" which was the same morning exploded by the discovery that Mr Lascelles had a gentleman of the Roman Catholic persuasion upon his great committee in Leeds'. Each such event was immediately followed by a leaflet war about what had really happened. The next day Lascelles' committee published this:

> THE Friends of Mr. LASCELLES do avow that the attendance on that Gentleman to the two Cloth Halls was highly respectable, and his reception highly flattering: that the Hooting and Hissing, so universally tremendous, proceeded only from a description of people on a level of the writer of the bill entitled 'Mr Lascelles's Speech,' viz. A parcel of 'DISAFFECTED RAGAMUFFINS,' hired for the purpose and not the respectable Clothiers and Freeholders; and that his short Speech was not, like Lord Milton's, written on a card . . .[18]

Milton's committee thereupon replied with this:

... We have no doubt, that these 'Disaffected Ragamuffins,' will, on the Day of Election, convince the Country, that they have more weight in the County of York, than the Son of a Barbadoes Planter. But Mr Lascelles having told the Clothiers of Yorkshire that he did not care a D..n for them all, it is perfectly in character for his friends to call the Clothiers of the Cloth-hall, 'A parcel of Disaffected Ragamuffins.'[19]

They went on to recall that

Mr Lascelles had his speech written for him at the last County Meeting, he could not read the writing of the friend to whom he was indebted for its composition, but after having taken it from his pocket, and made halve [sic] a dozen fruitless attempts to read it, he sat down in a pet, amidst the burning blushes of his disgusted friends ... So much for written speeches. The friends of Mr Lascelles, like a man in a quagmire, at every step they take, sink deeper in the mud![20]

Soon the leaflets of both sides became blunter. Those for Lascelles read: 'No Imbecile Infant of a factious Aristocracy. No trampling on Kings. No Popery. No Irish Papists. No Milton.'[21] Those for Milton read: 'NO Tyranny. No enemy to the Clothiers. No Juggling Union of Candidates. No Defenders of Melville ... No Plunder. No Slave-dealing Lord. No Yorkshire Votes purchased with African Blood. No Lascelles, no never! Milton for Ever! God save the King!'[22]

It did not take long for the Yorkshire air to become thick with accusations – slave dealing, popery, hypocrisy and electoral skulduggery. Lascelles declared that he would oppose any attempt to repeal the abolition of the slave trade, and his leaflets asked: 'Who voted against the abolition of the Slave Trade? Earl Fitzwilliam, the Father of Lord MILTON, and Lord Dundas, the Father-in-law of LORD MILTON, deny it who can?'[23] Milton's leaflets said they rejoiced that 'the Son of a Slave dealer has to seek ... popularity', and considered 'this sudden conversion to the cause of humanity, either as altogether miraculous, or as a trap to catch the support of the humane and unwary'.[24] Those electors seeking a higher level of political intercourse were entertained by the campaigning poetry that was never far from the elections of that era. Here one of the best efforts came from the Wilberforce campaign:

WILBERFORCE FOR EVER!
NO SLAVERY

Fame let thy trumpet thro' Yorkshire resound
And gather the Friends of fair Freedom around;
Unawed by the Great and unbribed by the Court
The pride of our Country shall have our support.

Chorus – Wilberforce is the Man, our Rights to maintain,
The longer we prove him,
The better we love him;
We'll support him for Yorkshire again and again.

Shall he, who has serv'd us the best of our days,
Unstain'd by a Bribe without Pension or Place;
Whose conduct to come we may judge by the past,
Be rejected, dishonour'd, deserted at last?

Chorus – Ah! No, we'll maintain Wilberforce to a Man;
Him we can confide in,
We've proved and we've tried him,
We'll support him for Yorkshire again and again.

Let the foes of our Friend and his noble Designs,
Repeat their worst charge that he cants and he whines;
O we've heard of his Cants in Humanity's Cause
While the Senate was hush'd, and the land wept applause.

Chorus – Then shew us the Man, that talk like him can,
Our Interest we find in
Such canting and whining,
He shall cant for the County again and again.[25]

At 11 a.m. on Wednesday, 13 May, the nomination meeting was held on the hustings erected in the Castle Yard at York, with all three candidates' names duly placed in nomination. Now began much haggling between the rival camps as to the construction of the polling booths, their openness to public view, and the arrangements for the freeholders to queue while waiting to vote. The votes were not secret, and Milton's supporters argued that the actual casting of the vote should be open to public view so that the crowds could give their verdict on each vote cast, but the sensible conclusion of the authorities was that 'a wooden partition seems necessary to prevent those taking the poll from being stunned from the noise usually prevalent at elections, as well as to guard them from interruption and disturbances, which the assistance of constables would be inadequate to prevent. Those who have witnessed the taking of the poll for Middlesex, where no such precaution is used, describe it as a scene of confusion and uproar.'[26]

The arguments over whether the barriers to hold back the queuing voters should be in a straight line or at an angle give a further flavour of the atmosphere of a contested election: 'The making the passage in a straight line (which Lord Milton's friends recommended, by way of shortening the confinement in the passage,) would have enabled a mob to pour through the passage in spite of constables, to break down the bars and sweep away the voter from his post; . . . the sheriff and his assistants would have been at the mercy of a mob.'[27] The so-called constables were thus widely expected to be overrun at the first opportunity, and their credibility was further damaged by the fact that each of the candidates was allowed to recommend thirty of the hundred constables concerned, 'a circumstance which produced inconvenience, both from the men considering themselves too much as the retainers of the candidates, and from their being nominated without much attention to personal activity or fitness for the undertaking'.[28]

When a show of hands was taken in support of each nomination, Wilberforce seemed to have almost unanimous support. Confident in how matters were proceeding, he set off for Hull, where he spoke to a huge crowd of his approach to politics and his long friendship with Pitt: 'I . . . had the satisfaction of finding the dictates of public duty coincide with the impulse of private friendship. But I never addicted myself to him so closely as not to consider every question and every measure with impartiality and freedom; and I supported or opposed him as my judgement and conscience prescribed.'[29] He had not lost his powers of speech-making: 'Gentlemen, so long as you thus understand the constitution under which you live, and know its nature, so long you will be safe and happy; and notwithstanding the varieties of political opinion which will ever exist in the free country, you will present a firm and united front against every foreign enemy. Great countries are perhaps never conquered solely from without, and while this spirit of patriotism and its effects continue to flourish, you may, with the favour of Providence, bid defiance to the power of the greatest of our adversaries.'[30]

Wilberforce should have been set for a reasonably comfortable victory. But when the great throng assembled at York for the beginning of polling on 20 May, this time with the Lascelles and Milton organisations working in full swing, the show of hands placed him last. It was, therefore, Wilberforce who had to demand that the poll take place, or accept the loss of his seat. Worse still, the first two days of voting – out of what was expected to be a poll of fifteen days – also showed him in bottom place, with 1,674 votes, compared to 1,688 for Lascelles and 1,951 for Milton. Suddenly his re-election seemed to be in danger. He was being out-organised. When Henry Thornton, James Stephen and his sons, and other friends tried to travel up the Great North Road to assist, they found that Lord Milton had hired all the post-horses between London and York (since some Yorkshire freeholders would have to travel all the way from London to vote), and ended up travelling on the mail coach. Yet Wilberforce kept his nerve, and his speech in the Castle Yard of 20 May, demanding a poll and asking for financial support, was soon circulated throughout the county. He said he had been assured of majority support, and 'I cannot bring myself to believe that the Freeholders of Yorkshire are capable of breaking their word with me. Therefore, notwithstanding the Sheriff's having decided that the show of hands was in favour of the two other Candidates, I have thought it right to demand a poll.'[31] He went on to explain that the immense extent of the county and the huge number of freeholders meant the expense of fighting the election 'would far exceed the powers of a private gentleman's fortune',[32] and went on to make his appeal:

This, Gentlemen, is an expence which I cannot undertake to defray; for ... I should not with comfort enter the House of Commons in a situation, which might subject me to the imputation of wishing to render my seat in Parliament subservient to the reparation of my broken fortunes. The kindness of many of my more particular friends has prompted them to subscribe ... But ... a far more general effort must be made, or else I must retire from the contest with a considerable majority in my favour. A comparatively small minority will then send representatives to Parliament; and if, when the sense of the county is so clear, you give up the hope of carrying that sense into effect, on account of the expence is it too much to say that the independence of Yorkshire is lost for ever? ... If the Freeholders of all ranks would contribute, each according to his means, towards asserting the independence of his County, some perhaps by coming to poll at their own charge entirely; others doing it in part; some, suppose, forming a local fund or helping to execute some plan for conveying the voters at a cheap rate ... no more would be required ... to suffer a comparatively small minority of Freeholders to choose a member, in opposition to the general sense, would be to suffer the County to sink, perhaps for ever, into dependence and insignificance.[33]

This appeal had its effect. He had already received a donation from none other than Spencer Perceval himself, but he now received much more local support. While a visiting London barrister who was meant to be advising him was reduced to saying, 'Mr. Wilberforce has obviously no chance, and the sooner he resigns the better,'[34] many stubbornly independent Yorkshire freeholders had other ideas. £18,000 was raised at once, with his old friend Charles Duncombe, now Lord Feversham, organising the money and debarring him from making any contribution himself. As one freeholder put it, 'It is impossible that we can desert Mr. Wilberforce and therefore put down my name for £500.'[35] Eventually his fund would reach £64,544, although he would only spend £28,600 and the rest was returned to the subscribers. Lascelles and Milton each spent around £100,000 (the rough equivalent of £6.2 million today), and now, on all the roads to York there arose an extraordinary spectacle: thousands of men setting out to queue at the polling booths. The *York Herald* reported:

> Nothing since the days of the revolution has ever presented to the world such a scene as this great county for fifteen days and nights. Repose or rest have been unknown in it, except it was seen in a messenger asleep upon his post-horse, or in his carriage. Every day the roads in every direction to and from every remote corner of the county have been covered with vehicles loaded with voters; and barouches, curricles, gigs, flying waggons, and military cars with eight horses, crowded sometimes with forty voters, have been scouring the country, leaving not the slightest chance for the quiet traveller to urge his humble journey, or find a chair at an inn to sit down upon.[36]

Many Wilberforce supporters responded to the appeal to come at their own expense. A letter from Hull reported, 'No carriages are to be procured, but boats are proceeding up the river heavily laden with voters: farmers lend their waggons; even donkeys have the honour of carrying voters for Wilberforce and hundreds are proceeding on foot. This is just as it should be. No money can convey all the voters; but if their feelings are roused, his election is secure.'[37] One freeholder published a letter on 22 May which read:

> WHAT are you doing? Is Wilberforce last upon the Poll? That friend of humanity – that enemy of the Slave Trade – that tried, that faithful, that upright Senator, is he last upon the Poll? Shame where is thy blush! Are you willing to desert him? Forbid it every principle of gratitude. Exert yourselves without delay! Rouse from your apathy! Come forwards like men!
> VOTE FOR WILBERFORCE,
> And convince the world that he is dear to every honest Yorkshireman.
> A FREEHOLDER.[38]

And come forward they did. When a large body of Wensleydale voters were met on the road and asked their intentions they responded, 'Wilberforce, to a man.'[39] A voter from Rotherham refused any expenses for his journey because he had managed to travel for free: 'Sure enow I cam all'd-way ahint Lord Milton's carriage!'[40] Wilberforce wrote to his wife: 'My having been left behind on the poll seemed to rouse the zeal of my friends, (I should rather say, of my fervent adherents,) they exerted themselves, and have mended my condition.'[41] After five days' voting, Wilberforce was leading the poll with 5,910 votes, ahead of Lascelles on 5,297 and Milton on 5,195. It was time for Milton's last throw.

The tactics employed against Wilberforce by the Milton campaign for the remainder of the election stand as a reminder to all politicians that great achievements and wide respect offer no immunity against the lowest means of electoral attack. Milton only needed to overhaul Lascelles' narrow advantage in order to become one of the two Members elected, and it is unclear why he decided to focus so much fire on Wilberforce instead. The answer probably lies in a mixture of two factors: the election was sufficiently finely balanced between all three candidates for one of them to gain substantially by winning 'plumpers' who voted for him alone; and the Milton campaigners probably felt that they were being hoodwinked by secret cooperation between Wilberforce and Lascelles, and could damage both their opponents by revealing this. With whatever motivation, they set about a vicious campaign against Wilberforce, starting with the hiring of 'twenty bruisers' to disrupt his meetings and to prevent his speeches on the hustings from being heard. These characters included 'Firby the young ruffian'[42] and John Gully, a champion boxer who would himself become a Member of Parliament twenty-five years later. So Wilberforce, whose speeches in the House of Commons commanded such attention, found himself being heckled every moment he attempted to speak in the heart of his own constituency. In wit, he was more than a match for his assailants, Thornton recalling of one occasion:

> While Wilberforce was speaking the other day, the mob of Milton interrupted him: he was attempting to explain a point which had been misrepresented; he endeavoured to be heard again and again but the cry against him always revived. 'Print, print,' cried a friend of Wilberforce from the crowd, 'print what you have to say in a handbill, and let them read it, since they will not hear you.' 'They

read indeed,' cried Wilberforce; 'what, do you suppose that men who make such a noise as those fellows can read?' holding up both his hands; 'no men that make such noises as those can read, I'll promise you. They must hear me now, or they'll know nothing about the matter.' Immediately there was a fine Yorkshire grin over some thousand friendly faces.[43]

Often, however, he could not be heard at all. The cry of 'No coalition!' was raised against him whenever he opened his mouth, and the charge was that he had broken his promise of neutrality to make a hypocritical alliance with a slave-owner in order to save his seat. 'SUGAR-CANE TO BE SOLD BY AUCTION *by Messrs Slavery and Juggle*', mocked the Milton leaflets:

> A large Quantity of Damaged SUGAR-CANE, of a blue colour, tinctured with a few red spots resembling drops of African blood, recently imported from Barbadoes, and brought to the hammer to pay the expenses of a monstrous Coalition, formed betwixt a saint and a sinner, and which expences it was originally intended to pay out of the 'Harewood Poor Box'.
>
> Samples may be seen at Messrs. W—, and L—'s Committee-rooms, which have been united for the convenience of sale.
>
> No Clothier, Methodist, Quaker, or any other honest elector need apply, as the Cane being hollow within, will not bear their scrutinizing examination.[44]

For those who preferred their election literature in verse, the Milton campaign soon had this rolling off the presses:

THE MONSTROUS COALITION!!

> We've heard of Coalitions strange
> Between a Whig & Tory;
> But, Nature sure herself must change
> Ere you believe This Story!!
>
> What! Shall the friend of human kind,
> The advocate of Freedom,
> Join with the MAN, whose fetters bind,
> Whose guilty lashes bleed'em!!

Shall HE who purged us from this ill
Join with a Negro Dealer;
Who of his ever honour'd BILL
Would fain be the REPEALER!!

What! Shall the Patriot condescend
(Lord MELVILLE'S firm Detector)
To join with TROTTER'S bosom friend,
And MELVILLE'S warm PROTECTOR!!

Such junction can have no excuse;
And future times will wonder
How e'er the Foe to all abuse
Should join the FRIEND OF PLUNDER![45]

Wilberforce considered these attacks to have no basis. As he told the story: 'And at last the cry of my having joined Lascelles was raised. This conduct of Lord Milton's friends is shameful; since, by seeing the poll-books, they must have known that I was not connected with him. Then, "No coalition, and Milton a plumper" was mounted; and he would bring up none else.'[46] But in reality he had laid himself open to the attack through lacking the preparation and tight organisation which would have been necessary for him to enforce his intended neutrality. The Milton campaign could come up with plenty of evidence to support their assertions:

> The committees of Mr Wilberforce and Mr Lascelles have always acted in concert with each other: . . . A caution was published by each Committee couched in precisely the same words, printed on the same paper, and which was undoubtedly the production of the same pen.

> Mr Wilberforce's agent at Scarbro', Mr Woodall, requested the friends of Mr Wilberforce to divide their votes with Mr Lascelles.[47]

Milton thus asked his voters to come to a clear conclusion:

FREEHOLDERS OF YORKSHIRE,
    You have a fair statement of the case between Lord Milton's friends and Mr Wilberforce; it is for you to draw the conclusion.

You have on one side a number of decisive FACTS. On the other – what? A number of unfulfilled PROMISES. If Mr Wilberforce had been as anxious to act an upright part as to secure his election, he would, when he discovered the unfair proceedings of his committee, have instantly interfered to stop them, or if he had found his authority insufficient to effect this honourable purpose, he should have declared in the face of the County, that though he disclaimed all coalition himself, his friends had acted as though it existed, this would have been worthy of Mr Wilberforce's character: But Mr Wilberforce has not acted thus. His conduct to say the least of it, has been suspicious and disingenuous, and has had the effect of deceiving many of Lord Milton's friends. But the hour of delusion is past, those independent Freeholders, who detest trick and collusion, will no longer divide their votes with Mr Wilberforce but give Lord MILTON a PLUMPER.[48]

So it was that, twenty-seven years into a political career based on frankness and truth, Wilberforce found himself accused in his own backyard of being deceitful and disingenuous. He had always enjoyed elections once they got going, but his diary suggests that this one was drudgery: 'Breakfasted daily at the tavern – cold meat at two – addressed the people at half-past five or six – at half-past six dined, forty or fifty, and sat with them. Latterly the people would not hear me, and shameful treatment. On Sundays allowed to be very quiet, to dine alone, and go twice to church.'[49] In York, church meant the Minster, 'the largest and finest Gothic building probably in the world', where, he wrote to Barbara, 'the sublimity of the whole scene nearly overcame me'.[50] To add to his woes, the teeming city of York acquired bugs and germs along with its thousands of voters, and he was confined to bed for the final days of polling, suffering the further damaging rumour that he was dead. It says much for his calm nature and constant faith that he bore a situation in which 'everyone was now so firmly convinced of the coalition between Mr Wilberforce and Lascelles that even the Quakers gave plumpers to Lord Milton, so disgusted were all honest people by his deceitful behaviour',[51] with a complete absence of either vengefulness or despair. He defended himself, but avoided attacks on his opponents, and he paid for the votes and expenses of those supporters who requested it, but went without the expensive parades and networks of paid agents employed by the other candidates. And each evening one of his agents heard him repeating the same stanza from Cowper:

> The calm retreat, the silent shade,
> With prayer and praise agree,
> And seem by Thy sweet bounty made
> For those that follow Thee.[52]

There is no doubt that Wilberforce was damaged by weak organisation and the vituperative attacks of Milton. Milton told his father that Wilberforce was 'quite out of temper and did not know what to say . . . he is now accused of hypocrisy and duplicity in his conduct during the election; it is delightful to see that people begin to find him out'.[53] Among the clothiers of the West Riding Wilberforce received only 331 votes, compared to 273 for Lascelles and 1,081 for Milton. In the east and north of Yorkshire, however, his support remained strong. Clothiers notwithstanding, the county's electorate also consisted of blacksmiths, butchers, clerks, farmers, grocers, gentlemen, merchants, school-masters, shoemakers and yeomen, who generally stood by a man they had come to respect over the years. After ten days of voting, Wilberforce was still in the lead, with 10,026 votes to 9,047 for Lascelles and 8,717 for Milton. In the final days, Milton's spirited campaign and the com-placency of the Lascelles organisers, who neglected to bring up all their voters from London, pushed Milton into second place. On 3 June 1807, at 'about half past five o'clock on Friday afternoon, Richard Fountayne Wilson, Esq, the High Sheriff, announced the final result of one of the most arduous electioneering contests that this or any other county ever witnessed'.[54] The result was:

Wilberforce 11,808
Milton 11,177
Lascelles 10,990

Nine thousand of the votes for Milton were plumpers, but Wilberforce had prevailed, coming top of the poll in a bitter contest despite spending little more than a quarter of the money dispensed by each of his opponents. No other independent parliamentarian of the time could have come out victorious against the most powerful of his local landed aristocrats. Yet it had been an uncomfortably close shave: a thousand votes fewer, and the man for whom the House of Commons had stood and cheered at the end of February would have been ejected from it by the beginning of June. Wilberforce knew that his victory should have been greater, writing to Hannah More a few days after the result, 'Had I not been defrauded of promised votes, I should have had 20,000. However it is unspeakable cause for thankfulness to come out of the battle ruined neither in health, character or fortune.'[55] In an open letter to his constituents he confessed that he had 'too much neglected pride, and pomp, and circumstance; the procession, and the music, and the streamers, and all the other purchased decorations which catch the vulgar eye', but since it was 'not my money but that of my kind and public-spirited supporters, which was expended, no liberal mind will wonder at my having earnestly wished to be parsimonious'.

His success, he argued, should be known for its quality rather than its quantity: 'We may perhaps have too much indulged our love of simplicity; but to our eyes and feelings, the entrance of a set of common freeholders on their own, and those often not the best, horses, or riding in their carts and waggons, often equipped in a style of rustic plainness, was far more gratifying, than the best arranged and pompous cavalcade.'[56] He had, nevertheless, compromised his principles to some extent, as for the first time since his conversion it had been necessary for him to pay for votes; if he had refused to do so, his defeat would have been certain. No one expected or argued, however, that he should withhold such expenditure in these circumstances. And in the end he had topped the poll in a famous contest, and was able to return to Westminster elected for the sixth time as a Member for the county of Yorkshire, noting as he did so, 'O Lord, direct me to some new line of usefulness, for Thy Glory, and the good of my fellow-creatures.'[57]

*   *   *

According to Henry Thornton, the William Wilberforce of 1807 was 'thin and old beyond his years, but still he is a horse well capable of work'.[58] As Wilberforce approached his forty-eighth birthday that year he must have been conscious that Pitt, almost his exact contemporary, had died at the age of forty-six, Charles James Fox at fifty-seven, and his dear friend Edward Eliot had died suddenly when thirty-seven years old. Thin from his self-imposed moderation at table, fragile by nature, and often worn down by the boisterous electioneering and ceaseless campaigns he had taken part in, he did not cut a robust figure. Yet even now, abolition at last enacted and his seat secure, he did not countenance idleness. Indeed, he considered lying in bed late in the morning to be positively dangerous: 'there was scarcely anything equally injurious: that God frequently made self-indulgence its own punishment, and that a decline in religion generally began in this way as it led to a hurrying over of the morning devotions. That he had seen many instances of it, when from lying in bed late private prayers had been neglected and the soul had always suffered in consequence.'[59] In any case, business crowded in on him: his fame after abolition brought ever more correspondence in its wake; the accelerating industrialisation of Yorkshire added continually to the burdens of its Members of Parliament in securing legislation for the building of roads; and with the country still at war and Napoleon nearing the height of his power, Parliament was rarely free from controversy and crisis.

In no sense, therefore, did Wilberforce see the enactment of abolition as an opportunity either to relax or to lengthen his stride. But he did want to see more of his children, and to be able to combine more easily the late-night sittings of Parliament with a genuine family life. It was to that end in 1808 that he moved his family out of Clapham, some four miles from the Palace of Westminster, and bought a sizeable mansion, Gore House, in Kensington Gore, less than half that distance away. He said he dreaded 'the separation which my leaving Broomfield would make for my chief friends, the Thorntons, Teignmouths, Stephens, Venn, Macaulay, with whom I now live like a brother',[60] but buying the twenty-five-year lease in Kensington had the additional advantages of saving money by requiring him to maintain one home instead of two, and would, he supposed, 'withdraw me from company and give me more time'.[61] He would be less vulnerable to callers than in Old Palace Yard, which had become all too convenient as a place for the whole of Parliament and its observers to find him.

The new Wilberforce residence was located on the precise spot where the Albert Hall was to be built a few decades later, but at that time its environs were still charmingly rural. It was, he wrote to William Huskinsson in 1810, 'but a mimicry of the *real* country',[62] but from there he could hear the nightingales, walk across Hyde Park and Green Park to the House of Commons in half an hour, and his children could play in a three-acre garden. It was an area of country lanes, with deer running about in the nearby Kensington Gardens. Once a dining room had been added and vast numbers of books shipped in, Kensington Gore became the ideal Wilberforce location, combining rural air, proximity to Parliament, space for the whole family, and a good place to read and reflect.

Wilberforce's fears that he would be separated from his friends were to prove as groundless as his hopes that he would be more elusive for other callers. James Stephen, himself an MP from 1808, was eventually to be found living in neighbouring Hyde Park Gate. Other Claphamites were happy to come to Kensington for dinner, although John Venn arrived one evening to find that Wilberforce had completely forgotten he was coming, and had gone out somewhere else. Other visitors were not at all confounded by the change of address, since Kensington was not far away, and Wilberforce was now more reliably to be found at one location. Thornton complained that Wilberforce invited far too many people to join him for mid-morning breakfast, and 'obstructed his usefulness by not sorting his guests'.[63] As a result he was besieged by good causes and charitable requests, and 'continues to overflow with tenderness and to complain much of want of time to do more than half the benevolent things which he meditated'.[64] After breakfast, the hall of the house would fill up with people requiring favours, money, advice or constituency attention, and Wilberforce would complain within a few years that 'the inconvenience which I suffer from it is extreme. For my servants assure me, that in spite of all they can say, of my being engaged, of my not seeing persons unless they come by appointment, (Yorkshire men however are excepted from this rule,) people will force their way in, and then you may conceive the consequence.'[65]

Overall, however, the move to Kensington was a success. While he was irritated by the 'frequent invitations, difficult and painful to resist', he found that he could get some peace by stealing off into an adjoining house, '*the Nuisance*', which he had also purchased, although 'Even there I should be no more safe, if it were known that I had such a lurking-hole, than a fox would be near Mr Meynell's kennel.'[66] Yet he clearly delighted in his new home, writing to the American Ambassador John Jay in 1810, 'We are just one mile from the turnpike-gate at Hyde Park Corner . . . yet, having about three acres of pleasure-ground around my house, or rather behind it, and several old trees, walnut and mulberry, of thick foliage. I can sit and read under their shade, which I delight in doing, with as much admiration of the beauties of nature (remembering at the same time the words of my favourite poet [William Cowper], "Nature is but a name for an effect, whose cause is God") as if I were 200 miles from the great city.'[67]

Furthermore, he really did see more of his children, not only taking them to Brighton or Eastbourne each summer, but also showing them the British Museum and generally adopting an indulgent attitude to the household din they generated. 'How can I be worried with such trifles,' he asked a visitor when his conversation was interrupted by children crashing about on the floor above, 'when I have such constant remembrances of God's goodness to me?'[68] His children were to be educated at a small private school rather than any of the prestigious public schools, which the Evangelicals considered to give a poor preparation for the resisting of temptation and vice. He ate with them and played cricket with them despite his appalling eyesight, and when he badly injured his foot while doing so in 1810 he was disappointed that this meant he missed several days of the House of Commons, but took it as 'the indication of Providence that I am to be quiet'.[69] His only strictness with his children was requiring them to attend prayers each day, usually at 9.45 in the morning, along with Barbara and all their

servants. When they were all together in the dining room he 'knelt at
a table in the middle of the room, and after a little pause began to
read a prayer, which he did very slowly in a low, solemnly awful voice.
This was followed by two other prayers and the grace.'[70] The whole
family would, of course, observe the special nature of Sunday. John
Harford, who first met Wilberforce in this period, was struck first by
his sociability, remembering him 'coming in with a smiling animated
countenance, and a lively vivacity of movement and manner, exchanging kind salutations with his friends, whose faces lighted up with
pleasure at his entry'.[71] On Sundays at Kensington, Harford recalled:

> During the long days at the close of spring he sometimes went
> into the garden at a late hour to listen to the nightingales which
> then abounded at Kensington. None but a few select friends who
> liked to spend their time as he did were invited to his house on
> Sundays. In the evenings he sometimes read aloud fine passages
> from his favourite poet, Cowper, imparting to them the fullest
> effect by the tones of his musical voice, and he was always ready
> for conversation at once elevating and instructive.[72]

Despite such moments, Wilberforce could never find enough respite
for his own liking, particularly from the huge volume of letters which
continued to pour in on him: when he took his family to Eastbourne
in July 1809, after leaving London by 'cutting the cables, rather than
regularly unmooring',[73] he took with him so many unanswered letters
that he had to spend three and a half hours simply sorting them out
and putting them in some order of priority. After several weeks working
his way through the pile, he wrote to one friend who had complained
of never receiving a reply:

> I really was not aware that I was your epistolary debtor, but in
> truth I have for eight weeks past doing little else than paying off
> a heavy arrears of letters. By the way, this great correspondence
> has been for some time, I had almost said, the sole business of
> my life. Its size does not arise so much for my having been for
> many years Member for Yorkshire – though that circumstance
> must doubtless have some effect – but it proceeds from my having

been for near thirty years in public life, with the character of not
turning a deaf ear to those who state their several sufferings.[74]

His friends, he said, 'according to their different tempers', suggested
varying solutions, from Stephen's 'never answer them' to Henry Thornton's advice to assign a certain amount of time each day to answering
letters and preventing a backlog from developing: 'But this, without
reference to the quantity I have to write, and to my being sometimes
so entirely engrossed otherwise for days together, is to apply a standing
measure to a line varying in all degrees from a point to a line almost
illimitable.' The whole business had become 'a standing grievance to
me',[75] and the previous year, after a whole month at Eastbourne, he
had written to Babington, 'I am vexed beyond measure, to tell you that
I really have done little since I came here but write letters.'[76]

Yet the truth was that the role Wilberforce had taken on in life
made it inevitable that letters would pile up 'until they form a mass
that is absolutely terrific',[77] and that his methods of answering them
only exacerbated the problem. He had associated himself with so many
charities and causes, and had proved so generous to those who came
to him in need, that he was bound to be subject to innumerable further
requests for advice and assistance. People from all over Britain wrote
to consult him about the erection of a new chapel or church, the
propriety of singing, the usefulness of new inventions, and the need to
use his influence to help various youths who had been led astray, or
criminals who had been condemned. One letter from a clergyman in
Ireland thanked him for saving from the gallows 'a thoughtless youth'
who was only 'a knavish boy': 'You discovered the mistake and procured
him a pardon a few hours before he was to have suffered.' In addition,
'My next application was for a poor distressed widow once in affluence
and though what was procured was very small yet your goodwill was
equally the same,'[78] and now he went on to ask for another young
criminal to be saved from hanging, and banished instead. In such cases
Wilberforce would always do his best, writing to the Home Secretary,
or the Duke of Gloucester, or whoever might be able to intervene,
although presumably some unfortunates found themselves jailed or

hanged before he managed to sort through his correspondence in the summer. At the same time he was in communication with influential Americans, administrators in Sierra Leone, naval captains and a great number of his accumulated friends. His mode of answering them made matters still worse, since he generally wrote as he spoke, expansively and discursively, flitting from one subject to another and going on at unnecessary length.

He wrote to one Yorkshire friend, 'You will, I know, suggest to yourself an excuse for me if I return you a short and hurried reply, and you see that, having my own proneness to garrulity when engaged in a friendly tête à tête, I have taken against it the precaution of a small sheet of paper being resolved not to encroach on a second' – but he ended up using seven more sheets nevertheless.[79] He would send off other letters while omitting the most important point he wanted to mention, realising that he had done so a few hours later and sending off an addendum. Sometimes bemused ministers would receive the second of these missives without the first one ever having been posted, causing still greater confusion. And sometimes, when he received a letter from someone previously unknown to him, he would reply with such warmth and enthusiasm that he added a further regular correspondent to his burdens. A notable example of this was his long correspondence with Samuel Roberts, a Sheffield constituent, who had an appointment in June 1811 to call on Wilberforce at Kensington and discuss a local issue. Arriving there to find that Wilberforce had forgotten the appointment and gone out, Roberts bumped into another Yorkshireman who informed him that such treatment was only too typical.

What was far more typical, however, was that Wilberforce used Roberts' resulting letter of complaint to turn him into a great friend: 'Wrote to Mr Roberts, from whom I received a most frank and honest letter; too strongly charging me with deceiving people, though ascribing it to my attempting more business than I can execute. I love his frankness, and thanked him for it.'[80] He told Roberts that he considered him 'as entitled to my warmest gratitude for what I must deem a signal act of friendship. Two of the best friends I have had in the world, have endeared themselves to me in no small degree by the same friendly frankness. Amongst other advantages which follow thus openly, is this, that if a man be not in fault, or not in fault greatly, he has an opportunity of vindicating himself in whole or in part; or if he be in fault, he has the opportunity of acknowledging, and as far as possible of repairing it.'[81] Fortified by this disarming attitude, Wilberforce more than made up for his erratic working methods with his characteristic mixture of frankness, humility and sheer effectiveness at dealing with a matter when it finally grabbed his attention.

Just as Wilberforce's willingness to help involved him in so many personal cases that his correspondence became disordered, so his determination to be a regular attender of the House of Commons and to consider all sides of the questions debated there sometimes gave an erratic appearance to his politics. There had never, of course, been any question as to where he stood on his adopted issues such as the slave trade and observance of the Sabbath – he even wrote to Spencer Perceval in 1808 to complain that the summoning of Parliament back from its Christmas recess on a Monday would require Members to travel on a Sunday, and Perceval had taken this sufficiently seriously to extend the recess by several days. But on some other issues, particularly as the wearing on of a deadlocked war presented agonisingly difficult choices, his determination to be fair and to be influenced by the actual arguments presented gave him something of a reputation for wavering and indecisiveness. He was a daily fixture in the House of Commons, sitting on the front bench so that he could hear more easily, looking even smaller than he was from hunching over notes so copious and detailed that it was sometimes difficult for him to extract the main points from among them, peering through his eyeglass as he scribbled so furiously that other Members would edge away from him to avoid being splashed with his ink. He could sometimes empathise with both sides of an issue to such an extent that he appeared to speak in support of each, and Samuel Whitbread once brought the House down by accusing him of doing so. He was known to apologise to bemused ministers for voting a certain way then regretting it: Lord Liverpool, as Hawkesbury had now become, once commented that he did not know how Wilberforce had voted the previous night, but he was sure that 'in whatever way he voted he repents of his vote this morning!'[82] In 1809 he spoke strongly in favour of parliamentary reform, in line with his long-held views, but ended up opposing the actual Bill presented, in the hope that there would be a better one in the future.

The most difficult decisions of all for British parliamentarians after 1807 concerned the conduct of the war, now fifteen years in length save for the brief interruption of the Treaty of Amiens. In July 1807, Napoleon, having vanquished the Prussians, held his celebrated meeting with Tsar Alexander of Russia on a raft on the river Niemen, culminating in the Treaty of Tilsit. Franco–Russian cooperation allowed Napoleon to attempt all-out economic warfare against Britain by closing the ports of the entire European Continent to British shipping. The intention of the French and Russians to force Denmark and Sweden into their alliance presented British ministers with a terrible choice: to risk the Danish fleet falling into the hands of the French, or to attack Denmark themselves to render her fleet useless, even though she was a neutral nation who meant Britain no harm. They had little alternative but to proceed against the Danes, and after they had refused to surrender their fleet peacefully, it was taken from them by force amidst the devastating bombardment of Copenhagen that September.

Wilberforce would not have made a good war leader. He agonised about this action at the time: 'Alas, alas! I cannot but greatly doubt the policy of changing so great a number of men from cold into most willing and energetic allies of France. They must think us the most unjust and cruel of bullying despots.'[83] The importance attached to Wilberforce's opinion is shown by the fact that both Perceval and the commander of the British naval force at Copenhagen, Admiral John Gambier, who had the advantage of being a devout Christian and a personal friend, made great efforts to persuade him of the necessity of what they had done. Two months later he was still reflecting to Babington 'that I doubt if I should have dared to advise the expedition, if I had been in the Cabinet'.[84] Yet by March of the following year he joined in the Commons' approval for the sending of the British expedition, saying 'a superior duty had outweighed a lesser',[85] while launching a subscription for assisting the poorest Danes to rebuild their homes.

Other British efforts to take the war to the enemy in these years came in for his criticism or uncertain support. He thought the ill-fated attempt to capture Buenos Aires from the Spanish in 1807 was 'the most absurd in conception, and the worst planned as to execution',[86] and was much troubled by the still more disastrous Walcheren expedition of 1809, in which British forces seized an island in the Scheldt estuary to open a second front against Napoleon while he was engaged in fresh war against the Austrians. The expedition was a military and strategic fiasco, not least because the Austrians were rapidly crushed by Napoleon. By the time it was abandoned in December 1809, with heavy losses, Wilberforce had become a regular critic of ministers. He sat on the parliamentary committee which inquired into what had gone wrong, but in the resulting censure debate refused to support either the government or the opposition – 'I voted against opposition's strong resolutions of censure, but could not say the plan was justifiable, or acquit of all blame.'[87] This meant that he had voted with the government on the overall conduct of Walcheren, but with the opposition on many of the details.

What was ambivalence and indecisiveness to his critics was to him, however, the rigorous and fair pursuit of independence. The criticisms he made of British strategy towards South America and over Walcheren were fully justified by events, and he wisely refrained from criticism of another sequence of expeditions which seemed rather hopeless at the time, but which would ultimately provide a fundamental turning point in the Napoleonic wars. To ensure the closing of Europe to the British, Napoleon needed not only the acquiescence of Denmark but that of Portugal, which was consequently invaded by the French in late 1807, followed by the proclamation of Napoleon's brother, Joseph Bonaparte, as King of Spain. By the summer of 1808 a small British force under Sir Arthur Wellesley had landed in Portugal and performed the then remarkable feat of defeating the French army in a land battle at Vimiero. For several years the Peninsular War, as it would become known, was severely criticised by the opposition in Westminster, and the routing of another British force in northern Spain in early 1809 gave them plenty of ammunition. But Wilberforce believed that Napoleon had overreached himself in Spain, considering that the imposition of his brother's rule over the Spanish was 'so heaping insult on injury, that he might have foreseen that human nature would scarcely bear it'.[88] In this he was right, for the Spanish revolt against French rule would become one of the bloodiest guerrilla wars in the history of Europe, draining the lifeblood of France while British forces under Wellesley, soon to become Duke of Wellington, repelled every French attempt to conquer Portugal. Ultimately, around a quarter of a million French soldiers would die in the Peninsula, and Napoleon would one day find that the British commander and his tiny army who had landed in Portugal would be the authors of his doom at Waterloo.

It would be some years before the scale of the French catastrophe in Spain became clear, and it was not until 1812 that Napoleon compounded the error with his march on Moscow, leaving the balance of war tipped decisively against him. In the meantime British politics, devoid of the massive coalition which had sustained Pitt in the 1790s, or of the party truces which would characterise the global conflicts of the twentieth century, was the scene of bitter controversies and closely contested votes. Wilberforce was foremost amongst the swing voters in the Commons whose opinions thus mattered greatly, whether ministers liked it or not. Spencer Perceval went to great lengths to please him and to keep him informed as the Tory government survived a series of seemingly insurmountable crises.

When the Duke of Portland retired as First Lord of the Treasury in 1809, Perceval succeeded him, but only after the Foreign Secretary, Canning, and the War Secretary, Castlereagh, had both resigned from the government after fighting a duel with each other. Canning had been plotting for months to get Castlereagh removed from the government; when Castlereagh discovered this he issued the challenge to the duel, and wounded Canning in the leg. Wilberforce's views on this resumption by politicians of his least favourite activity were not surprising: 'The reflection which forces itself on my mind throughout the whole transaction is, that the public interest seems to have been forgotten by almost all parties';[89] and the duel had the added effect of removing from a struggling government two of its principal talents. An attempt to bring the opposition, led by Grey and Grenville, into coalition proved abortive, partly because George III would not stoop to asking them himself, and eventually Perceval was able to form a cabinet and soldier on. Wilberforce, as usual, was happy to give this government his broad support while freely criticising its measures, considering Perceval and his ministers 'men superior in ministerial talents to the other set'.[90] He thought it would be seriously short of effective parliamentary speakers, but that ministers should not always be judged on their speaking ability: 'It is sad work that we should take measure by the false standard of oratory, as to the fitness of men for ministerial situations: it was excusable in the commonalty of Athens, but is scarcely so in the British House of Commons.'[91] Even so, he was missing the oratory of Pitt, Fox and Burke, which had dominated the Commons for so long, and thought the debates were 'poor compared with former times; yet Perceval improved, and Canning extremely clever'.[92]

It is not surprising that in such circumstances ministers tried hard to secure the approbation of Wilberforce, and to hear his 'silvery tones'[93] – as a young Gladstone described his voice in later years – coming to their aid. Wilberforce did indeed have disadvantages as a Commons speaker, Sir James Stephen considering that 'The habit of digression, the parenthetical structure of his periods and the minute qualifications suggested by his reverence for truth impeded the flow of his discourse, and frequently obscured its object,' but despite all that, 'he was still a great Parliamentary speaker'.[94] Whatever his defects, Wilberforce always retained a naturally captivating style that had led even Pitt to consider him to have 'the greatest natural eloquence' he had ever known.[95] Another accomplished speaker, the American Edward Everett, would say of Wilberforce's speaking style a few years later that although he was 'quite diminutive and unprepossessing, and his air much hurt by his extreme near sightedness', nevertheless, 'His fluency – happy use of metaphor – affectionate and cordial manner of allusion to the persons or topicks in question – make him one of the happiest speakers I ever heard.'[96] With such easy command of language allied to nearly three decades of parliamentary experience, Wilberforce remained a formidable asset to any cause he chose, and away from the finely balanced judgements of military tactics his eloquence was fortified by moral certainty. As another of Stephen's sons, George, would put it:

> Men might doubt about his vote on minor issues, but where the interests of morality, or humanity, or religion were involved, there Wilberforce's perception of what was right appeared intuitive, and his vote was certain: neither rank, nor power, nor eloquence bewildered him for a moment then. All the honours, all the wealth, all the seductions that the world could furnish, would not have tempted him to offend his conscience by even a momentary hesitation; he at once rose above all infirmities of habit, firm as a rock upon the spiritual foundation on which he rested.[97]

An example of the weight he carried came early in 1809 when the Duke of York, George III's second son, became embroiled in a classic royal scandal. Commander-in-Chief of the Army, he had fallen out with a former mistress, Mrs Clarke, who, it was now alleged by a radical MP called Colonel Wardle, had taken bribes from army officers seeking promotion, with the full knowledge of the Duke. Soon Mrs Clarke was being cross-examined at the bar of the House of Commons, which was predictably packed with MPs. Wilberforce was mortified that the matter was being investigated in public rather than in a private committee: 'This melancholy business will do irreparable mischief to public morals, by accustoming the public to hear without emotion of shameless violations of decency.'[98] As the proceedings advanced he wrote to William Hey:

> What a scene are we exhibiting to the world! It is no more than was to be foreseen by any one who was ever so little acquainted with the House of Commons. We are alive to the political offence, but to the moral crime we seem utterly insensible; and the reception which every *doûble entendre* meets in the House, must injure our character greatly with all religious minds.[99]

With Perceval determined to defend the Duke and the opposition Members out to get him, Wilberforce and the 'Saints' took a middle line, not believing the Duke guilty of corruption, but thinking he must have had a good idea of what was going on, and being appalled at the example his behaviour was setting. They were determined that he should resign, notwithstanding the government's defence of him, and Wilberforce wrote to Muncaster on 18 March that

> Unless the Duke of York should resign before Monday, I am sanguine in my expectation, that we should either carry the question for his removal, or for some measure which must lead to it ... If we believe the Bible, we must believe that the vices of the great, both directly and consequentially, call down the judgments of the Almighty; and I may say to you that I am strongly influenced by the persuasion, that by marking such shameful debauchery, thus publicly disclosed, with the stigma of the House of Commons, we should be acting in a manner that would be pleasing to God, and directly beneficial to the morals of the community.[100]

The government could do the arithmetic. The Duke resigned before the Commons could vote him out, Henry Thornton being told that the King and all the royal family were extremely angry with Wilberforce. But Wilberforce was happy with his own conduct – 'What could I do as an honest man short of what I have done?'[101] He was similarly clear about other matters which aroused his ire, attacking the national lottery in May 1809 as 'peculiarly objectionable, because it diffused a spirit of gambling among the people, while it produced no benefit to the public Treasury in any degree commensurate to the injury it inflicted in the interest of the community'. He could 'never reconcile his mind to the existence of a law for the toleration of that which was obviously wrong'.[102] He continued to oppose the petitions presented to Parliament in favour of Roman Catholic emancipation, spoke strongly in favour of a reduction in the number of capital offences, and enthusiastically supported Sir Samuel Romilly's amendments of the Criminal Law and proposals for prison reform. He involved himself in so many issues and debates that Stephen sometimes had to remind him that their work on the slave trade was far from complete. Sending him a paper on the trade in 1810, Stephen bemoaned the fact that 'it will sink under the weight of your daily epistles'. Wilberforce would be much better as a reformer if he 'disdained, in his grand projects of universal good, all petty objects of individual charity or duty. Why, if you were my Lord Wellington and I, Massena [Wellington's French opponent], I would undertake to draw off your whole attention to my grand movements, and ruin your army unperceived, by teasing your piquets and burning a few cottages on your flanks.'[103]

Such teasing criticism of Wilberforce was no doubt necessary from time to time in order to get his attention, but he had been anything but slow in following up the passage of the Abolition Act. Within three days of its enactment he was writing, on 28 March 1807, to the Duke of Gloucester to present his plans for an African Institution 'for promoting the Civilisation and Improvement of Africa'.[104] This was one of his grandest visions: that with the curse of the slave trade removed, Africans could begin to become prosperous, educated, peaceful and, of course, Christian. Installed as Chairman of the African Institution, with the Duke of Portland as President and Zachary Macaulay as Honorary Secretary and a cross-party alliance of MPs in dutiful support, Wilberforce had developed plans by the summer of 1807 for a protectorate around Sierra Leone which would allow the steady expansion of investment, European trading and missionary work into the rest of West Africa. Such high hopes for the future of Africa were soon to be dashed, for Sierra Leone was itself still a struggling entity, African traders were highly resistant to Europeans intruding on their networks, and trade in new products inevitably took time to develop. A further obstacle was, of course, that a very large slave trade was still going on.

The vast majority of the British slave trade was indeed annihilated by the Abolition Act of 1807. Some of the Liverpool slave-trading merchants even made a successful transition to the importation of palm oil, demand for which was soaring as the Industrial Revolution intensified. There was also a growing trade in gum, hides and beeswax. To deter those British traders who might try to continue the slave trade nonetheless, the British West Africa Squadron was created, starting with two small warships stationed off the African coast from 1808, with instructions to intercept illegal British traders and the incentive of a bounty to be paid (£60 for a male, £30 for a female and £10 for a child) for each slave liberated. Even so, a small minority of British traders attempted to continue slaving, generally under the guise of a foreign flag. Thus on one occasion when the Royal Navy stopped and searched a ship which contained over a hundred slaves, calling itself the *Marques Romaino* and flying a Spanish flag, further investigation revealed that it was the *Prince William* from Liverpool.

It was not until 1811 that the British slave trade was truly eradicated. In that year the British West Africa Squadron was greatly strengthened, and Henry Brougham piloted through Parliament, with the strong support of Wilberforce, the Slave Trade Felony Act, which made slave trading by British subjects punishable by transportation to Australia for fourteen years. Yet although the British slave trade had been undeniably crushed, this in no way meant that the enslavement of Africans was at an end. British abolition had been greeted by African rulers and traders with a certain amount of perplexity. Since they continued to acquire large numbers of slaves themselves, they saw no reason why they should not be able to sell them to others, and were sometimes offended by being unable to do so. As the British Company of Merchants trading to Africa explained to Parliament:

> Can the wildest theorist expect that a mere act of the British legislature should, in a moment, inspire ... natives of the vast continent of Africa, and persuade them, nay more, make them practically believe and feel that it is for their interests to contribute to, or even to acquiesce in, the destruction of a trade not inconsistent with their prejudices, their laws, or their notions of morality and religion, and by which alone they have been hitherto accustomed to acquire wealth and purchase all the foreign luxuries and conveniences of life?[105]

Internal wars in Africa continued to yield vast numbers of slaves. Although the trans-Saharan trade supplying the countries of north Africa was much smaller than the slave traffic across the Atlantic, it was entirely unaffected by British abolition. But most important of all, the transatlantic trade was itself still very busy. Although the French slave trade was suspended by virtue of the fact that no French ship could operate safely on the high seas while France was at war with Britain, no such constraint applied to Britain's Portuguese allies, soon to be joined by the Spanish once France and Spain were at war. Indeed, the prospect of British naval power being used to exterminate the remainder of the transatlantic slave trade produced a mini-boom in slave traffic after 1807, as the slave traders of Brazil and Cuba stocked up on slaves while they could. The forty-two slave ships that arrived in Rio in 1810 represented the largest number ever recorded.

Under British duress, the Anglo–Portuguese Treaty of Alliance was made to include an article committing Portugal to the 'gradual abolition of the slave trade', and the Portuguese additionally undertook not to increase the area of the West African coast from which they took slaves. It nevertheless remained the fact that the Portuguese trade was still carried on, and indeed flourished at a higher level, and that when the strengthened West African Squadron overzealously interpreted the Anglo–Portuguese Treaty to capture twenty-four Portuguese slave ships between 1810 and 1813, it had to be reined in by the British Foreign Office. As Foreign Secretary between 1807 and 1809, George Canning also sought to persuade the Spanish to agree to gradual abolition throughout their empire, but efforts by liberal Deputies in the Spanish Cortes to bring Spain into line with Britain met such adamant and united opposition from Cuba that Spanish leaders feared the loss of their most productive colony if they proceeded.

Such was the scale of the continuing trade and the difficulty of securing abolition by Spain and Portugal, not to mention the problems that would arise if peace were made with France without a French commitment to abolition, that it was soon apparent to Wilberforce and Stephen that their work was far from done. Wilberforce was always active in lobbying to put pressure on other countries and in monitoring the progress of efforts to prevent illegal trading. When Zachary Macaulay was involved in the seizure of a slave ship in 1809, Wilberforce wrote one of the most excited letters he ever penned:

Near Newport Pagnell, October 19th 1809

My Dear Macaulay,

I am in the state of a full charged bottle of electrical fluid, which wants some conductor to empty itself by. Mrs W indeed takes her part in my joy, but I want you, or Stephen, or Babington, or H Thornton. You really deserve a statue. But more serious and sober matter for rejoicing remains, after the first riotous effervescence has, or rather shall have, fumed away, for this is far from being yet the case with me; and with as much sobriety as I can, I compose myself into a grateful acknowledgement of the goodness of Providence, in blessing your endeavours with success. It may be useful to put down exactly the whole story, from the first faint and distant view you had of the thief with scarcely lights sufficient to ascertain his substance and features, till this moment, when he is dragged into open day in all his deformity . . . I should like to see Stephen's face when he first hears of the seizure. Farewell. With full kind regards to Mrs M, I am, ever affectionately yours,

W Wilberforce.[106]

Most of all, Wilberforce concentrated his persuasive power in these years on the United States. Although the USA had abolished the slave trade almost simultaneously with Britain, enforcement of the American ban was a far more difficult proposition than that of the British. There was no diminution in the demand for slaves in the American Deep South, and since internal and coastal trading of slaves had not been abolished, it was extremely difficult to identify and prevent the international trade once it reached American waters. There was even a two-way traffic, with Virginia planters actually breeding slaves in order to sell them in Charleston or New Orleans, sometimes for onward and illegal transportation to Cuba. President Madison told Congress in December 1811 that American citizens were still 'instrumental in carrying on a traffic in enslaved Africans, equally in violation or the laws of humanity and those of their own country'.[107] The Americans also had no naval squadron off Africa to enforce their own prohibition: illegal slavers were therefore able to fly the American flag and claim that the British navy had no right to interfere in their business.

The nightmare of a large illegal trade prospering in the absence of adequate American enforcement deeply worried Wilberforce. In September 1808 he wrote to James Monroe in Virginia explaining that 'all our hopes of success in our endeavours for the eternal benefit of Africa must be grounded on our preventing these infractions of the law'.[108] He enclosed another letter for the then President Thomas Jefferson, calling for Anglo–American agreement on rights of mutual intervention 'allowing each country to take the others' slaves ships'.[109] He went on: 'A compact formed between our two countries for the benevolent purpose of stopping, perhaps, the most destructive scourge that ever afflicted the human race, may lead to similar agreements with other countries, until at length all the other civilised nations of the earth shall have come into this *concert of benevolence*.'[110]

Wilberforce followed this up by lobbying his American Evangelical friend in Britain, John Jay, who also interceded with the American government. And when the British Appeal Court ruled in 1809 that the Royal Navy could interdict American ships engaged in slavery because their activity was illegal under American law, Wilberforce was delighted. It was from 1808, however, that Anglo–American relations began a sharp deterioration. The United States was caught in the middle of the all-out economic warfare between Britain and France. As Napoleon attempted to tighten the closure of all Continental ports to British shipping, the British government responded with its famous 'Orders in Council' which barred all neutral shipping from French and allied ports unless it had first entered a British port, reconsigned the cargo as British and paid duty on it. Efforts to enforce these rules inevitably brought Royal Navy ships into regular confrontation with American trading vessels. Friction also arose over the growing trend for press-ganged British sailors to desert to American ships and acquire American citizenship within a matter of weeks. British warships would then stop and search American merchant ships looking for these deserters and take back into the navy sailors who were now officially American, as well as others who had been American for much longer.

The Orders in Council were a natural extension of Britain's use of her sea power to wage economic war, an approach which had done so much damage to the slave trade in the run-up to abolition. Stephen, as the author of *The War in Disguise*, was strongly in favour of them, and from 1808 to 1812 the policy they enshrined was adamantly defended by Perceval's government amidst increasingly bitter political acrimony about its effects. Since the policy caused great offence to neutral nations, including the United States, and intensified the economic effects of the war, arguably exacerbating the recession which hit the British economy in 1811, the opposition took up the cause of rescinding the Orders in Council, and the issue became the subject of a clear Tory–Whig divide. Brougham was foremost among the opponents, and made celebrated parliamentary attacks on the Orders in 1810 and 1811. This was the sort of issue on which Wilberforce found it very difficult to decide the best course of action: his abolitionist friends were divided, the extent to which British economic troubles were caused by the Orders was highly debatable, and while the war with France had to be won he dreaded the prospect of a consequent war with the United States, which would destroy any immediate prospect of Anglo–American agreement on action to extinguish the slave trade. As the Commons rose for its summer recess in July 1811, he gave a speech full of foreboding: 'Deeply, sir, do I deplore the gloom which I see spreading over the western horizon; and I most earnestly trust that we are not to be involved in the misfortune of a new war, aggravated by possessing almost the character of civil strife – a war between two nations, who are children of the same family, and brothers in the same inheritance of common liberty.'[111]

He was right to be gloomy. The year 1812 would bring him a great deal of anguish.

15

The Struggle Renewed

—————— ◆◦◆ ——————

If to profess humanity to our fellow creatures, and to endeavour with zeal to carry into execution whatever measures lay in my power for promoting their welfare, were the hon. Gentleman's definition of fanaticism, I am afraid that I am a most incorrigible fanatic.

WILLIAM WILBERFORCE, 1816[1]

Your indefatigable exertions to effect the abolition of an execrable traffic . . . have enrolled your name among the illustrious benefactors of mankind.

Address to William Wilberforce from the freemen of Hull, 1812[2]

HAD HE LIVED, Spencer Perceval would probably have become one of the longest-serving Prime Ministers in British history. As he walked over from 10 Downing Street to the House of Commons on Monday, 11 May 1812, he was a man who had repeatedly defied all expectation of political defeat: suddenly taking office with the other Tories in 1807, managing against the odds to form his own government without Castlereagh and Canning in 1809, and, most astonishingly of all in the eyes of contemporaries, remaining in office in 1811 even when the Prince of Wales finally took over the powers of the throne as Regent. It had been the universal expectation for a quarter of a century that the moment Prince George had the power to install a Whig administration he would do so. In fact, on 1 February 1811 the Duke of York was 'sent to acquaint Lords Grey and Grenville, who were employed upon arrangements for a new administration, that it was

not his Royal Highness's intention to make any change at present'.[3] Fox would have turned in his grave, while Pitt would have cheered from his, as Perceval's growing reputation allowed him to remain in office through the economic crisis of that year. 'All acknowledge,' as Wilberforce put it, 'the talent, spirit, integrity, good humour and various excellences of Perceval.'[4]

Fifty years old and at the height of his powers, Perceval hastened that day down Parliament Street and into the crowded lobby of the House of Commons, knowing that he was late for a debate in which Brougham was holding forth against the Orders in Council. Standing by the door of the lobby was a tall man in tradesman's dress named John Bellingham, who blamed his financial ruin and early confinement in a Russian debtors' prison on the British authorities. As Perceval entered the lobby, Bellingham pulled out a pistol and shot him in the heart. Perceval took one or two more steps, managed to say, 'Oh, I am murdered,' and fell down dead, the only British Prime Minister ever to have been assassinated.

Bellingham was seized by onlookers; within a week he would be hanged.* In the immediate aftermath of the shooting, confusion reigned in the House of Commons itself, where the shot had been clearly heard. While word went round 'that someone has been shot', William Smith actually thought it was Wilberforce who was slumped on the floor of the lobby. Ironically, Wilberforce was dining at Thomas Babington's house in Downing Street, and discussing Perceval's virtues, when Babington tore in 'agitated greatly'.[5] Wilberforce rushed first to Perceval's house to see his wife and children, and then to the prison rooms of the Commons, 'where the poor wretch Bellingham was, they were examining him. I carefully perused his face for some time, close to him – a striking face: at times he shed tears, or had shed them; but strikingly composed and mild, though haggard ... Poor Lord Arden quite wild with grief – "No, I know he is not here, he is gone to a better world." '[6]

* One of Bellingham's present-day kinsmen, Henry Bellingham, is Conservative Member of Parliament for North-West Norfolk, but is of a milder disposition.

The political world was, of course, horrified, although beyond Westminster popular discontent with the government was demonstrated by the fact that exultant mobs lit bonfires in London, Nottingham and Leicester. Wilberforce was one of the senior Members summoned by the Speaker the next day to agree that the Commons vote £50,000 for Perceval's family and £2,000 a year for his widow for the rest of her life. When a larger amount was proposed by Perceval's friends Wilberforce loyally supported them, but noted down his thorough disapproval: 'How very low and mercenary people are! I see plainly that many of P's friends think getting ever so little more money, to be got, if at all, with a struggle, and as a triumph of a party, worth all the handsome and the honourable in the world; forgetting all the invidious constructions which will be put upon it in the present state of the country.'[7]

Most of all, Wilberforce reflected, as he would often do in subsequent years after the death of friends, on the great power of faith in the midst of such events. He thought Christianity had never been seen 'in a more lovely form than in the conduct and emotions it has produced in several on the occasion of poor dear Perceval's death. Stephen, who had been so much overcome by the stroke, had been this morning, I found, praying for the wretched murderer, and thinking that his being known to be a friend of Perceval's might affect him, he went and devoted himself to trying to bring him to repentance ... Poor Mrs Perceval after the first grew very moderate and resigned, and with all her children knelt down by the body, and prayed for them and for the murderer's forgiveness. Oh wonderful power of Christianity! Is this the same person who could not bear to have him opposed by anyone?'[8]

Perceval's assassination was followed by several weeks during which Britain went without an effective government at the height of a war. The Regent decided to stick with the Tories, asking Robert Jenkinson, 2nd Lord Liverpool (formerly Lord Hawkesbury), to form a government. Liverpool was faced with an immediate motion of no confidence in the Commons, which Wilberforce took an active part in opposing, while privately conceding that 'I own I do not see how the ministry can stand the battering of the House of Commons.'[9] Duly defeated by

a majority of four, the new government was immediately ousted, but after all efforts by other potential Prime Ministers, such as Marquess Wellesley and Lord Moira, had come to nought, the political merry-go-round came back to Lord Liverpool. Despite having been defeated in May, he won a large majority in the Commons in June, with Castlereagh as the new Foreign Secretary, Sidmouth as Home Secretary, and Canning, much to Wilberforce's disappointment, still unwilling to join the cabinet unless he could be clearly senior to Castlereagh. From this chaotic beginning, Liverpool would go on to govern for fifteen years until 1827, becoming the third-longest-serving Prime Minister in British history, after Walpole and Pitt.

On 16 June 1812, within days of taking office, the new ministers decided to cave in to popular pressure and abandon the controversial Orders in Council. Wilberforce had noted months earlier that he was 'sick at heart from the sad prospect of war with America',[10] and the abandonment of the Orders in Council would remove the biggest single source of Anglo–American tension. It was a further tragedy of the year 1812, however, that the news of this major British concession travelled westwards across the Atlantic at the same time as America's declaration of war travelled eastwards. On 4 June, President Madison had asked Congress to declare war on Britain; the Senate had agreed on 18 June, albeit only by a majority of six.

The so-called 'War of 1812' was thus an unnecessary war, although quite apart from trade issues, the Americans had high hopes of sweeping the British from Canada and claiming it as their own. Wilberforce was utterly distressed by the prospect of it all: 'Alas! Alas! This sad war with America! I never felt any public incident so deeply. Yet on the whole I thank God I can lay my head on my pillow in peace, for our government is not chargeable with the blood-guiltiness; but Maddison [sic], Jefferson, &c.'[11] The war would be an inconclusive one, dragging on for more than two years as all American efforts to invade Canada were repulsed. In August 1814, British forces would land near Washington, capture the American capital and burn down the White House itself, before themselves being defeated. In the meantime, all Wilberforce's efforts to secure cooperation between Britain and America in policing their abolition of the slave trade were inevitably suspended. Ultimately, the war would be ended by the Treaty of Ghent of December 1814, which committed both countries 'to use their best endeavours' to put an end to the slave trade,[12] but the implacable resistance of the United States to American-flagged ships being searched by other nations had been fully demonstrated by the outbreak of war, and would always be maintained in the years to come.

For all these disappointments, 1812 would nevertheless be the year in which the scales of war tipped decisively against Napoleon. In July of that year in Spain, Wellington inflicted a severe defeat on the French at the Battle of Salamanca. By the autumn, Napoleon was retreating from Moscow with the bodies of hundreds of thousands of his soldiers and horses strewn behind him. It is a measure of Wilberforce's lack of warlike instincts that he saw these calamities for France as an opportunity to negotiate for peace, while the governments of Britain, Spain and Russia began to glimpse at last the possibility of crushing Napoleon once and for all. The diary entry he made after speaking in the Commons on 1 December 1812 was typical Wilberforce, both for its complaint about poor press reporting and for the rather convoluted nature of his reasoning on matters of war:

> I meant to speak rather for peace, but expressed my meaning imperfectly, and the newspapers which I have seen putting in only what is calculated, as they conceive, to make me unpopular, and leaving out all the rest, I am made to be far more warlike than I am, or should have been supposed to be, if I had been silent. They omitted all I said about my thinking it a favourable time for treating, and that I hoped they would take every fair opening; but that giving them credit for this intention . . . I would not hamper them, and probably injure the country's cause by instructing them to treat by a parliamentary direction; when they would feel bound to obey, and the enemy of course conclude that he might treat on terms proportionably more favourable.[13]

Tormented as he was by the exigencies of war, Wilberforce had spent much of the preceding year and a half agonising over a more personal decision. Although the Parliament to which he had been narrowly elected in 1807 could theoretically sit until 1814, the serious possibility of the death of George III before that time meant that an early general election had to be anticipated, since a new Parliament was always elected on the accession of a new monarch. By the summer of 1811, Wilberforce was worried that he would not be able to maintain the rigorous workload of a Member for Yorkshire, but his assiduous nature made him unwilling to remain a county Member unless he was equal to constant attendance in Parliament. He took this view even though other county Members often had far less consistent records of attendance. As he described his own methods himself:

> I make all other business bend and give way to that of parliament. I refuse all invitations for days on which the House sits. I commonly attend all the debate, instead of going away after the private business is over for two or three hours, and coming down again after a comfortable dinner; on the contrary I snatch a hasty meal, as I may, before the public business begins, in the short interval sometimes between the end of the private and the beginning of the public. I see little or nothing of my family during the session of parliament (though, blessed be God, of a more tender, excellent wife no man ever received 'The gift from the Lord' ...) and I have staid till the very end of the session every year of the last twenty-three or twenty-four.[14]

In August 1811 he set aside a day 'specially to devote to the important purpose of seeking God's direction on the important question whether or not to resign Yorkshire and if so, whether to come in for a small borough'.[15] He had already received the offer from Barbara's first cousin, Lord Calthorpe, of becoming one of the two Members for the borough of Bramber in Sussex – Calthorpe, as the owner of twenty of the thirty-six local burgages, therefore being able to elect whomever he liked. As so often when he had a difficult decision to make, Wilberforce set down the arguments on paper, stating the main reasons for retiring from Yorkshire as:

> 1. The state of my family – my eldest son just turned thirteen, and three other boys, and two girls. Now though I should commit

the learning of my boys to others, yet the moral part of education should be greatly carried on by myself. They claim a father's heart, eye, and voice, and friendly intercourse. Now as long as I am MP for Yorkshire, it will, I fear, be impossible for me to give my heart and time to the work as I ought, unless I become a negligent MP such as does not become our great county. I even doubt whether I ought not to quit public life altogether, on the ground that if I remain in the House even for Bramber, which Lord Calthorpe kindly offers, I shall still be so much of a political man, that the work of education will not be set too heartily. This consideration of education is, in great measure, the turning point with me; but,

2. The state of my body and mind, especially the latter, intimate to me the solve senescentem, – particularly my memory, of the failure of which I find decisive proofs continually . . .[16]

It did not help that his close friends were divided about the best course of action: Charles Grant and Henry Thornton were against him leaving Yorkshire, while Thomas Babington was in favour of his complete retirement. Although John Harford noted that 'He was serene, cheerful and happy, and at the age of fifty-two had the gaiety and the spirits of a young man of twenty,'[17] there was no doubt that Wilberforce was deteriorating physically. Chest trouble came on top of his long-standing bowel complaints, and he would soon develop a curvature of the spine which within a few years would require him to wear 'a steel girdle cased in leather and an additional part to support the arms'.[18] In July 1811, James Stephen sent him a frank assessment of his faults, health and habits in an effort to guide his decision. Coming from one so close to him, it must stand as one of the finest insights into Wilberforce's condition and character.

Stephen began by rejecting the idea that Wilberforce was declining mentally:

As to the intellectual decay, I am disposed to say that it is not real; I never heard you speak better than the last time, pitch of voice excepted; and I think you are better and better heard there, in the parliamentary sense of the word. Your great defect always has been want of preparation in cases that demand, and, – with those who do not know your habits, – raise the expectation of it. No man does so little justice to his own powers. That you stand so high as you do, is because you could stand much higher if you would ie. if you could and would take time to arrange your matter. At the same time I do think your faculties, in one respect, are the worse for wear; I mean your memory. I perceive it to decline even as fast as my own, and that is a bold word. Yet were I continually as hurried as you are, I could remember nothing and do nothing.

He went on to say that Wilberforce was clearly deteriorating physically:

> I lament, my dear Wilberforce, to say, that of late I have at times seen or conceived I saw symptoms of deterioration in your bodily appearance, as if you were getting old faster than I could wish, or rather losing the promise of long abiding strength . . . Your spirits too, I have thought not uniformly so high and so long on the wing as they used to be . . . If you could be content with a very limited attendance, coming down only on special or important occasions, and leaving the ordinary business of the House to younger and stronger men, you might do much good there without hurting yourself, or neglecting your private duties.

He went on to develop the argument that a Member of Parliament did not have to turn up every hour of the day:

> Is a representative unfaithful, or does he serve his country ill because he does not give all his time to political labours during the enormous portion of the year now occupied by a session? Then let celibacy become a qualification for parliament as well as for the popish priesthood. A man has no right to be a husband and a father unless he will give to those relations an adequate portion of his time . . . For my part, I even fancy you coming down like the great Chatham, or some other veteran on great occasions, exciting an interest even by the rarity of your presence, much more by your opinion delivered with all the aid of preparation, and perhaps doing more good in that way than you have ever yet done. Three-fourths of our debates are on questions hardly fit for you, and not worthy of your time. They are such as

embarrass you on the middle ground you occupy and make it
difficult for you to act without a real or apparent inconsistency.

Finally, Stephen gave a wonderful piece of advice, which went against
Wilberforce's entire *modus operandi* as a Member of Parliament:

> You seem to think that a man can never hear too much, or read
> or talk too much on any subject, before he votes on it but for my
> part I hold that a man goes as often wrong from too much as
> from too little discussion. Besides, the newspapers, bad as they
> are, give general ideas enough to enable a man who will take time
> in his library to make up a sound opinion on most questions
> before their ultimate decision. I am clear you would be oftener
> right if you consulted only your own judgement and your books,
> and not what is said by others, either in or out of the House.

He ended with: 'My opinion strongly inclines that you should not sit
again for Yorkshire.'[19]

Yet the decision remained a difficult one for Wilberforce, who
did not want it to be thought that he feared defeat, and who was
understandably attached to a constituency he had already represented
for twenty-seven years. While the testimony of his sons about this time
confirms that 'Delicacy of health had indeed set on him already some
of the external marks of age, and a stoop which he contracted early,
and which lessened his apparent stature, added much to this effect,'
they insisted too that 'The agility of his step, the quickness of all his
senses, (though he only heard with one ear), his sparkling eye, and the
compass and beauty of his voice, contradicted all these first appearances.'[20] As no election materialised in 1811, Wilberforce continued his
internal debate on the matter throughout much of 1812. He dismissed
out of hand any idea of going to the House of Lords, reminding Samuel
Roberts that 'My intimacy with Mr Pitt for so many years may be
supposed to have rendered it not difficult for me to obtain such an
elevation,'[21] partly because he steadfastly refused to use a public position to benefit his relatives.

Eventually, when the Parliament was dissolved in 1812 – not by the
death of the King, who would remain stubbornly alive for another

eight years, but by the calculation of ministers that they could fortify their majority – Wilberforce was forced to a reluctant decision. He considered that leaving the House would be 'like closing my account, and I seem to have done so little, and there seem some things which it would be so desirable to try to do before I quit parliament, that I shrink from retiring as from extinction',[22] and so he decided to give up Yorkshire, acknowledging that he would be more likely to stand for it again if he was being seriously opposed, and take the offer of Bramber instead. He would never have to take part in a contested election again, and as battle was joined across the constituencies he wrote that he felt 'somewhat like an old retired hunter, who grazing in a park, and hearing the cry of the hounds pricks up his ears and can scarce keep quiet or refrain from breaking out to join them'.[23]

Wilberforce rejected several offers of seats elsewhere, along with the entreaties of some of his Yorkshire constituents who thought he was merely angling for a renewed invitation to represent them. Thoroughly disappointed by his confirmed decision, the freeholders gathered in York to vote him thanks for twenty-eight years' service as their representative in Parliament, 'for his unremitting and impartial attention to the private business of the county; and for his independent and honest performance of his trust upon every public occasion'. Eight days later the freemen of Hull voted their own address, thanking him in terms which can rarely have been equalled by the tributes paid to any other Member of Parliament in history:

> In common with a large portion of Yorkshire freeholders, we deeply regret the necessity of your retirement to a station of comparative leisure; still some consolation is derived from the assurance that the benefit of your talents will not be withdrawn from the country at a period of unprecedented danger and difficulty ... We cannot however pass unnoticed your indefatigable exertions to effect the abolition of an execrable traffic, alike inconsistent with British feeling and Christian principle – exertions which have enrolled your name among the illustrious benefactors of mankind ... Among other subjects of praise, it is not the least that on retiring from the representation of this county after a

faithful service of twenty-eight years, and possessed of the influence which your station must necessarily command, you have not
during that period accepted a place, pension or rank, and have
acquired no other than the distinguished title of the 'Friend of
Man'.[24]

Thus Wilberforce attended the opening of the new Parliament in
November 1812 as the Member for a rotten borough, albeit one given
to him with no conditions attached. From now on he could lighten
his load and attend the House of Commons a good deal less than in
previous years. But James Stephen had been right. Far from marking
the decline of his parliamentary role, his new situation would help to
give him the time and the freedom to spearhead a series of major and
unrelenting campaigns.

Wilberforce does not seem to have anticipated how much of his time
would continue to be taken up by politics in the years to come. At the
end of 1812 he wrote out a plan for his life which had his children as
its first object, then Parliament, and 'Thirdly; When I can spare time,
my pen to be employed in religious writing.'[25] He also intended to
spend more time on daily religious devotions, considering that anything less than an hour spent in private prayer each morning was
inadequate. But he still considered it his duty to speak out on major
issues, even those on which he found it difficult to come to a decision;
and one such issue was once again at the forefront of parliamentary
debate early in 1813: Catholic emancipation.

Wilberforce had slowly and laboriously been changing his mind on
the issue of whether Catholics could be admitted to Parliament. He
had always taken a dim view of the Catholic Church, considering
Ireland to suffer from 'irreligion and immorality' which 'popery has
increased and fomented'.[26] Friends such as Milner and William Hey
regularly counselled him against supporting Catholic emancipation.
As Irish Members pressed the issue hard in early 1813 he had, however,
come to his own independent view, even without the weeks of study
he had intended to give to the issue, and with relevant 'pamphlets and

other documents' lying 'unopened on my table'.[27] He decided that the existing situation, whereby Catholics were able to vote in elections but not to be elected themselves, created the worst of both worlds: MPs who were nominally Protestants in effect represented the views of their Catholic constituents, while the Catholics continued to nurse the grievance of being unrepresented. Such a situation was dangerous to British security, and, as Wilberforce put it to William Hey, 'Where can be the wisdom of retaining the prison dress, when you have set the men at liberty?'[28] He thus rose to speak on 9 March 1813 to give his fresh and considered view: whatever else could be said of him, he could not be accused of being too proud to change his mind. He wrote afterwards that he 'did not feel at home, and rather lost the thread of my argument',[29] but one observer, Thomas Barnes, wrote that 'He has at length broke the chain of his scruples, and . . . with a warmth of language and manner quite his own, unequivocally recommended the abolition of penal statutes in matters of religion.'[30] Wilberforce told the House that 'they were leaning on a broken reed – they were relying on a false security. Political power had already been granted to the Catholics, and by leaving them in their present state, the legislature would not be acting with policy for the security of the country.'[31] It was an enlightened view: 'Light and knowledge were spreading in Ireland, and the more they extended, the more would the Catholics of Ireland desire to enjoy all the privileges of free men.'[32] He had shifted his ground, and it was a precursor of his more tolerant attitude to Catholicism in later years. In the Commons, a narrow majority agreed with him, but liberality towards Catholics had still not arrived in the House of Lords. It would be 1829 before Roman Catholics won the right to sit in the British Parliament.

While he was still pronouncing on the weighty matters of the day, Wilberforce's release from the burdens of representing Yorkshire allowed him to home in on the principal causes he wished to advance, just as Stephen had argued it would. He had always taken the view that an MP should try to concentrate on selected issues, writing to his son William a few years later: 'If you come into parliament . . . choose out for yourself some specific object, some line of usefulness. Make yourself thoroughly acquainted with your subject, and you will not only be listened to with attention, but you will, please God, do great good. This is the mode in which I have often advised young men to proceed, but they seldom would be wise enough to follow my counsel, and hence you hear of many of them making one or two good speeches, and then all is over.'[33] His relentless campaigning on the slave trade had been one of the ultimate examples of the discipline he recommended, in spite of all the other distractions of those years.

Now, after trying to do too much in recent years, he recovered this strategic sense, being prepared to turn down great causes as well as to take them up. To the repeated entreaties of Samuel Roberts that he adopt the cause of abolishing the lottery he responded, 'I dare not make any engagement to take up this subject, because I am pre-engaged to another grievance, if I may use a word implying unity, to denote a whole long series of physical and moral evils . . . And when there is no prospect of success, and when our opinion has been declared again and again with the utmost solemnity, it scarcely seems advisable to employ on any evil that time and trouble which, otherwise directed, might be productive of practical benefit.'[34] Although the lottery was therefore safe from anything other than his occasional criticisms, the arrival of the year 1813 opened up the prospect of fighting for a cause on which Wilberforce had passionate views and a clear prospect of success.

In 1793 he had tried and failed to open up India to Christian missionaries when the Charter of the East India Company had been renewed. The Charter had been granted for twenty years, and all that time Wilberforce, a patient predator, had lain in wait. His detestation of certain Hindu practices, particularly that of *suttee* (wives having to throw themselves alive onto the funeral pyres of their deceased husbands), and his horror that India remained closed to Christianity, almost surpassed description. To him, it was 'next to the slave trade, the foulest blot on the moral character of our country' that the Indian population was left to exist 'under the grossest, the darkest, and most depraving system of idolatrous superstition that almost ever existed upon earth'. The opportunity to rectify this, he wrote early in 1812, was something he had 'long been looking forward to', even if he had to 'call into action the whole force of the religious world'.[35] From February to June 1813, Wilberforce applied himself remorselessly to this cause, using all the lessons of campaigning that he had learnt in the endless struggle against the slave trade. It was, after all, almost certainly the last opportunity he would have in his lifetime to defeat the Anglo-Indian presumption that the introduction of a new religion would stir up trouble in India and make mutinies more likely. He therefore threw into it the whole force of his personality and power.

Methodically, Wilberforce lobbied the senior members of the government for fully twelve months beforehand, losing some ground when the sympathetic Perceval was assassinated. By early 1813 he was heavily devoted to calling for petitions from all round the country, while the *Christian Observer*, the Church Missionary Society and all of his 'Saints' busied themselves in support. By now they were expert at such work, and the 837 petitions which poured in on Parliament surpassed all previous experience, their half a million signatures rivalling the scale of the petitions against the slave trade in 1792. As the table of the House of Commons groaned beneath the mass of paper, Wilberforce followed up this evidence of popular support with visits to all of the leading figures in Parliament, government and opposition alike: 'You know enough of life,' he wrote to Hannah More, 'to be aware that in parliamentary measures of importance, more is to be done out of the House than in it.'[36] He had learnt, too, always to prepare the ground in the Lords as well as the Commons, writing to the former Lord Chancellor, Lord Erskine: 'We have too many in both Houses who seem to think our dominions safer under Brahma and Vishnu, than under that of the Almighty . . . we sadly want in the Committee of the H. of Lords, friends to the diffusion in India of Christianity . . . Surely your Lordship will not fail us in such an emergency.'[37]

It was a model campaign, and by the end of May 1813 the government had capitulated, Castlereagh telling Wilberforce on 27 May that the government would support everything he wanted. Even so, Parliament still had to be persuaded. By the time Wilberforce rose to speak on 22 June to support the 'East India Christianizing Resolution' moved by Castlereagh, MPs were thoroughly fed up with the many weeks they had already spent considering the East India Company's affairs. Wilberforce had only readied himself for the speech that morning, despite Stephen imploring him to prepare more thoroughly, but he rose and delivered a passionate speech, three hours in length, which gripped the attention of the Commons and which was afterwards printed and sold by Hatchard's in Piccadilly.

Wilberforce launched into a searing attack on attributes of Hinduism, starting with the caste system, 'a detestable expedient for keeping the lower orders of the community bowed down in an abject state of hopeless and irremediable vassalage . . . Even where slavery has existed, it has commonly been possible . . . for individuals to burst their bonds . . . But the more cruel shackles of Caste are never to be shaken.'[38] He attacked the various practices of polygamy, infanticide and *suttee*, and the worshipping of gods who 'are absolute monsters of lust, injustice, wickedness and cruelty. In short, their religious system is one grand abomination . . . Our religion is sublime, pure and beneficent. Theirs is mean, licentious and cruel';[39] and he stressed that he blamed the British, not the Indians, for this situation:

> I indignantly repel the charge which has been unjustly brought against me, that I am bringing an indictment against the whole native population of India; and 'what have they done to provoke my enmity?' Sir, I have lived long enough to learn the important lesson, that flatterers are not friends: nay, Sir, they are the deadliest enemies. Let not our opponents, therefore, lay to their souls this flattering unction, that they are acting a friendly part towards the Hindoos. No, Sir: they, not I, are the real enemies of the natives of India, who, with the language of hollow adulation . . . on their tongues, are in reality recommending the course which is to keep those miserable beings bowed down under the heavy yoke which now oppresses them . . . For true friendship, Sir, is apprehensive and solicitous: it is often jealous and suspicious of evil; often it even dreads the worst concerning the objects of its affection, from the solicitude it feels for their wellbeing, and its earnestness to promote their happiness.[40]

Barnes, who disagreed with Wilberforce, nevertheless recorded, 'He spoke three hours, but nobody seemed fatigued: all indeed were pleased, some with the ingenious artifices of his manner, but most with the glowing language of his heart ... He never speaks without exciting a wish that he would say more.'[41] In the debates of subsequent days Wilberforce took pains to point out that he was not advocating compulsory conversion to Christianity, but simply the opening up of India to missionaries – 'Compulsion and Christianity! Why, the very terms are at variance with each other: the ideas are incompatible.'[42]

The resolution was carried by eighty-nine votes to thirty-six, dispelling Wilberforce's fears and much exceeding his expectations. After a further month of debates and manoeuvres his triumph was confirmed, an event which he placed on a par with the achievement of abolition. Bishops and missionaries were soon on their way to India, although over time both Wilberforce's great hopes and his opponents' fears would turn out to be exaggerated. Christianity would indeed spread in India, but Wilberforce's unshakeable faith and lack of any direct experience of other continents made it difficult for him to see that mass Christian conversions in India or Africa were a naïve hope. Two hundred years later, in an age in which tolerance of other religions is regarded as a virtue, his attacks on the basic precepts of Hinduism may seem strange. But the Evangelicalism of Wilberforce's time did not allow for inhuman practices to be defended on the grounds of adherence to a different religion, and for him conversion to true Christianity was as essential for the moral framework and salvation of other nations as he had already argued it was for Britain. At the very least, he had once again demonstrated the sheer breadth of his ambitions for Christian ideals, and the formidable power he was now able to bring to a well-chosen political cause.

This notable success did not mean that the summer of 1813 was without its disappointments. Both John Venn and Granville Sharp died that July, and Wilberforce was engaged in writing lengthy letters to Castlereagh opposing a treaty with Portugal which would still not prevent her from carrying on a large slave trade. By mid-August he was happy to be with his entire family at Sandgate on the south-east coast of Kent, adopting the ritual which, for him, counted as a holiday: 'I get up about seven; then serious time and devotions for an hour; then dressing and hearing one of the children read to me for three-quarters of an hour – after breakfast, letters, and writing; dictating &c. We dine together early, and some of the children read till we walk out, from about six till eight; then coming in I have an hour serious. Then family prayers, supper, and bed about eleven. I must try to see more of the children, and to obtain more time for study; hitherto I have done little but write letters.'[43] Notwithstanding his giving up of Yorkshire, the growth of his great heaps of correspondence barely slackened, and he would complain for years to come that he could not even read during a whole day the letters that arrived each morning.

That autumn Wilberforce lost another dear friend – his lifelong correspondent, Lord Muncaster – but managed to visit Hannah More in Somerset, which he had not done for seven years. He missed the opening of Parliament in November, for the first time in nearly thirty years, and was true to his promise to spend more time with his children, while news poured in of fresh allied victories over the French. In June, Wellington had shattered the French armies in Spain at the Battle of Vitoria. On 25 November Wilberforce could hear the booming of the guns at the Tower of London, celebrating the breach of the French lines in the Pyrenees, opening France itself to the advance of the Anglo-Spanish armies. In central Europe, the French were capitulating in Dresden. Russian and Austrian armies were advancing relentlessly on France. While Parliament eagerly anticipated final victory, Wilberforce was so moved by accounts of the wartime suffering of the civilian German population that he added the creation of a relief fund for them to the list of his great causes. Lords, MPs and clergy found themselves bombarded by letters from Wilberforce asking them to add a subscription or attend a meeting. He managed to assemble a great meeting at the Freemasons' Hall in March 1814, badgering the Archbishop of Canterbury to attend it, the Duke of York to chair it and the Home Secretary to ask the Prince Regent for a grant. He was disappointed by the Duke of York's chaotic chairing of the event, but was eventually called on to speak, which he did 'in the silver tones of a seraph',[44] and was greeted with such thunderous cheers that 'Poor B[arbara]burst into tears and wept at seeing me so applauded.'[45]

In the audience that day in the Freemasons' Hall was Madame de Staël, who since Pitt had refused her hand in marriage thirty-one years before had turned into an indomitable force – a combination of writer, thinker, conversationalist, lover and hostess which made her one of the acclaimed figures of early-nineteenth-century Europe. Her Swiss château had become 'the headquarters of European thought'. Her liberal ideas had brought her banishment from France by Napoleon, while she did her utmost in return to encourage the Fourth Coalition which was now bent on his destruction. It is evidence of Wilberforce's international renown by this time that Madame de Staël was utterly determined to see as much of him as possible during her stay in London. Despite his distaste for grand dinners, late-night parties and eating too much, he eventually agreed that she could hold a dinner in his honour after she had told Romilly that 'she wished more to be acquainted with me than with any other person'.[46] Once there, he was engaged by her in discussion about everything from Rousseau to Paley, from the causes of creation to the nature of beauty, and he tore himself away at half past eleven reflecting on an experience that 'was intoxicating even to me'.[47] He avoided further such dinners, which disturbed both his concentration and his digestion, but he had already made a strong impression. Madame de Staël told Sir James Mackintosh that 'Mr Wilberforce is the best converser I have met with in this country. I have always heard that he was the most religious, but I now find that he is the wittiest man in England.'[48] She would be a vociferous opponent of the slave trade when she returned to Paris.

Wilberforce was indeed now something of a revered figure, and one of international fame. An Italian visitor would comment a few years later that 'When Mr Wilberforce passes through the crowd on the day of the Opening of Parliament, everyone contemplates this little old man, worn with age, and his head sunk upon his shoulders, as a sacred relic; as the Washington of humanity.'[49] Independent Haiti would soon name a naval vessel after him, which would distinguish itself in

1819 by seizing a Spanish slave ship. In the summer of 1814, with Napoleon banished to exile in Elba and London filling up with celebrating and victorious allies, Wilberforce was sought after by the Prince of Poland and the King of Prussia, and praised by the great Prussian General Marshal Blücher in a speech at the City of London tavern for his efforts to help the suffering Germans.

France had been defeated, and Wilberforce only wished that Pitt had been alive to see it. He took his children to see the Cossacks, the famed destroyers of French armies, at a London barracks, and watched as London led the tumult of rejoicing. But for Wilberforce the hour of victory became a deeply worrying time, and one that would lead him back, yet again, to fight as hard as ever for the cause he had championed for most of his life. For the unfortunate truth was that the abolition of the British slave trade had not led to the wider consequences which its supporters had predicted for it. Other nations were still heavily engaged in it, most notably Britain's Spanish and Portuguese allies, and they could soon be joined by a renewed French trade, unless the forthcoming peace treaty enshrined its abolition. Ships of other nations were engaged in an illegal trade which continued to feed British colonies, among others, with fresh supplies of slaves. The gradual improvement in the conditions in which slaves were kept, forecast by Wilberforce on the grounds that the supply of them would be constrained, was not in evidence. On 3 June 1814 he heard that the proposed peace treaty with France being negotiated in Paris by Castlereagh would only provide for French abolition of the slave trade five years later. 'Alas! Alas!' he noted in his diary, 'how can we hope that in five years' time, with so many additional motives to cling to the Trade, she will give it up? . . . Let all who would not be partakers of the guilt, protest against it.'[50]

Castlereagh returned from Paris the following week. When MPs saw him enter the chamber with the peace treaty under his arm they rose to greet him with a great burst of cheering. But as the whole House erupted around him, Wilberforce remained firmly in his seat. Shortly afterwards he rose to tell Castlereagh and the House that 'I cannot but conceive that I behold in his hand the death-warrant of a multitude of innocent victims men, women, and children, whom I had fondly indulged the hope of having myself rescued from destruction ... For my own part indeed I frankly declare no considerations could have induced me to consent to it ... My noble friend must allow for my extreme regret, if when at length, after a laborious contention of so many years, I had seemed to myself in some degree in possession of the great object of my life – if then, when the cup is at my lips, it is rudely dashed from them, for a term of years at least, if not forever.'[51] Nearly fifty-five years old, and well past the peak of his energy, Wilberforce now mobilised himself once again in the greatest cause of his life.

As it became evident in the years after British abolition that a huge foreign slave trade continued unabated, Wilberforce and his fellow abolitionists had adopted a two-pronged strategy aimed at destroying it. The first prong was something which once again could be accomplished within the British Empire: a complete register of all existing slaves. Anecdotal evidence suggested that British West Indian plantation-owners were illegally purchasing slaves from foreign colonies in the West Indies, which were in turn receiving fresh supplies of slaves via Portuguese, Spanish and American traders. The result was that the continuing slave trade was still partly sponsored by British money even though it was no longer conducted in British ships, and as long as this situation continued the long-predicted need of the planters to improve the condition of their existing slaves would not arise.

Yet again, it was Stephen's fertile mind from which the solution emerged: if planters were forced to keep a register of all the slaves in their ownership, showing their age, sex, name, height, colour, distinguishing marks and country of origin, their circumvention of the Abolition Act could be detected and suppressed. The first target for this measure was Trinidad, since its recent conquest meant that it had no colonial assembly, and the laws governing the island could therefore easily and unquestionably be made in London. In 1810 Wilberforce had introduced a Trinidad Registry Bill in order to put pressure on the government to act, and by the beginning of 1812 he, Brougham, Stephen and Romilly had persuaded Perceval to institute a Trinidad registration scheme by means of an Order in Council. While this was important progress, few other islands were to follow this example voluntarily. It was clear that a fresh Act of Parliament would be required in order to force registration on the rest of the British colonies, something to which they were implacably opposed on grounds of excessive interference in their affairs and the absence of undisputed evidence that smuggling was continuing on a large scale. With Liverpool more sceptical of the need for action than Perceval had been, and Parliament preoccupied with war and economic crisis, Wilberforce held off from an all-out attempt to pass a Register Bill until the second prong of the abolitionist strategy had been tested – the international agreement on abolition which he had always craved.

The independence movement taking shape in Spain's South American colonies generally incorporated hostility to the slave trade. In 1811 newly independent Venezuela outlawed the trade; the following year the revolutionaries in Buenos Aires did the same; while in Bolivia the hero of independence, Simón Bolívar, declared the abolition of slavery itself. But the story in Brazil and Cuba was very different, the Cubans threatening the Spanish with a declaration of independence if Spain acted against the slave trade. Despite debates in the Cortes, Spain baulked at abolition, and did little to prevent British and American slave ships from sailing under Spanish colours, notwithstanding strong pressure from Marquess Wellesley, elder brother of the Duke of Wellington and British Ambassador to Spain, asking her 'to take all necessary action'.[52] There began to surface among Spanish politicians the sentiment which would provide a huge obstruction to British statesmen in the succeeding years: Britain had taken twenty years to abolish the slave trade, yet now expected other countries to do so without notice, and after a period of warfare in which their supplies had often been interrupted; this was merely Britain seeking economic advantage from the powerful naval position with which she was emerging from the war.

Portugal similarly, while introducing tighter regulations on the transport of slaves in 1813, and nominally committing herself to gradual abolition and ending slave trading from parts of Africa outside her zone of influence, nevertheless hotly resented any British attempts to interfere with the prospering slave trade originating from areas such as Angola and Mozambique. Wilberforce was furious that Spain and Portugal, having preserved or recovered their independence with the assistance of British arms, should now be able to carry on their slave trading as a result, writing to Castlereagh:

> When I consider how closely we have been intertwining the inter-
> ests of the Portuguese with our own, and how freely our blood
> and treasure have been lavished to preserve them in existence, I
> grow warmer, if not more indignant than I ought to be at such
> treatment, and indeed at such conduct considered in itself – that
> with declarations in their mouths that they consider the Slave
> Trade unjust and inhuman ... they should be striving for the
> right of availing themselves of the protection of our flag, for the
> purpose of bringing on the natives of Africa miseries five times
> greater than any from which we have delivered them![53]

Although international efforts to build a consensus against the slave trade made some progress, they had little overall impact. Sweden agreed to condemn and outlaw the trade upon becoming a British ally in 1813, but any Swedish slave trading had been negligible. It was when Napoleon surrendered in 1814 that the long-awaited opportunity to secure international abolition was at hand. Wilberforce, who thought that 'never surely was the hand of the Almighty more strikingly manifested' than in the fall of Napoleon, considered that a convention of the great powers for the abolition of the trade 'would be indeed a glorious termination of the hurricane'.[54] His hopes for such an achievement were inevitably mingled with apprehension about what would other-wise happen. Writing to Gisborne, he said:

> It would be too shocking to restore to Europe the blessings of
> peace with professions of our reverence with the principles of
> justice and humanity, and at the same moment to be creating, for
> so it would really be doing wherever the Slave Trade is extinct,
> this traffic in the persons of our fellow creatures. We are much

occupied with the grand object of prevailing on all the great European powers to agree to a convention for the general Abolition of the Slave Trade. O may God turn the hearts of these men! What a great and blessed close it would be of the twenty-two years drama![55]

Wilberforce and Stephen soon agreed that in these circumstances their plans for a Register Bill should be set aside, so that the anticipated West Indian reaction to it would not alarm European leaders who might otherwise join in compelling Spain and Portugal to join in abolition. Wilberforce now flung everything at this objective. Chastising himself that 'I wish I had been prepared as I ought with works in all modern languages about the Slave Trade,'[56] he set about writing a long letter to Tsar Alexander in the hope that the pressure for general abolition would come from Russia as well as from Britain. Russia had no vested interest in the slave trade, and the Tsar was not only the most powerful man on the Continent of Europe after his humbling of Napoleon, but was also known to sympathise with modern and humane causes. The writing of the letter to Alexander turned into another marathon of toil, after much of which Wilberforce told Harford that he was 'only going on because I had begun and that the time already spent on the work would be wasted if I should not finish it, yet it is now a very wretched business'.[57] The finished work set out for the Tsar the history of what had happened in Britain and the risks of the revival of the trade in France, and appealed to him: 'But though the guilt and infamy of this wicked traffic no longer attaches to Great Britain, yet the Trade itself still exists; and it is in the hope, sire, of leading you to employ your powerful influence in suppressing it, that in the name of religion, justice and humanity, I implore your notice.'[58]

Wilberforce wrote additionally to the French Foreign Minister, Talleyrand, joined in the African Institution's decision to send Macaulay to Paris to argue the case for abolition, after having regretted once again that he was not available to go himself, and proposed an Address to the Regent in the Commons on 3 May, unanimously carried, instructing ministers to negotiate for general abolition. His letter to Talleyrand, like that to the Tsar, turned into a sizeable pamphlet, combining the logic of the current French situation – 'France had not now the poor excuse to plead, that the abolition would demand sacrifices, which she cannot afford to make. Not one solitary vessel, not a single seaman, not a livre of capital is now employed in the Slave Trade . . .'[59] – with a plea to avoid ineffective and hypocritical regulations: 'Your enmity they can understand, your cruelty they can endure, sometimes even despise; but insult them not by your humanity, and allow not yourself, in the practice of these detestable and wicked barbarities, to indulge in complacencies of humanity and virtue.'[60]

After mounting these efforts, it is not surprising that Wilberforce was devastated when Castlereagh returned from Paris in early June with nothing more than a French commitment to abolition in five years' time. In the two weeks that followed, he mustered a triple response. First, he attacked the peace terms in the House of Commons. Secondly, he went straight to the highest authorities in Europe, beginning with the Tsar, who had now arrived in Britain. The arrival of Alexander caused immense excitement in London, although within a few days he had so offended the Regent and the aristocrats with whom he mixed that Lord Grey thought him 'a vain, silly fellow'.[61] Wilberforce was nevertheless delighted to be summoned to his presence. Before going to meet him at Pulteney's Hotel on Sunday, 12 June, he prayed at the Locke Chapel at Hyde Park Corner 'for a blessing on my interview',[62] and then arrived to find the Tsar himself was still at church. When the great monarch arrived he shook Wilberforce's hand with great warmth, assured him 'that he was much interested for my object', and asked him to keep him informed by letter. Despite the assurances of sympathy, it was not clear that the Tsar was interested in expending Russian power on this issue rather than on his final objectives in the forthcoming negotiations. After initially saying, 'We must make them,' in reference to French abolition, he shifted his commitment to 'We must keep them to it,'[63] and blamed the failure to agree on immediate abolition on Castlereagh – 'What could be done, when your own Ambassador gave way?'[64]

An increasingly agitated Wilberforce was soon round at Castlereagh's office the next morning, and then took his arguments to the

Prime Minister, Lord Liverpool. Liverpool told him that it had been impossible to secure French agreement to immediate abolition because French ministers were totally opposed to it. They considered British arguments of justice and humanity to be mere hypocrisy, and notwithstanding their defeat in the war, had been utterly intransigent on this point, although acquiescing in many others. Finding no satisfaction among heads of state and government, Wilberforce resorted to his third tactic, the mobilisation of enormous popular support. On 17 June a packed abolitionist meeting was held at the Freemasons' Hall, where the arrival of Wilberforce was greeted with a storm of cheering. The meeting agreed to petition Parliament and to call for petitions from throughout the kingdom, once again entrusting the parliamentary leadership of their efforts to 'William Wilberforce, the father of our great cause'.[65]

Ten days later as hundreds of petitions circulated in the towns and cities of Britain, and after coordinating his tactics with Grenville in the Lords, Wilberforce rose in the Commons to propose an Address to the Regent on the international congress shortly to be held in Vienna. His motion, expressing 'profound regret that more has not been accomplished in this great work',[66] called on ministers to negotiate 'a general and solemn engagement'[67] for the universal abolition of the slave trade, and for tougher terms to be imposed on France so that the French slave trade would be outlawed in less than five years, and excluded immediately from all regions of Africa where British abolition had had effect. He implored ministers to see the importance of what was now at hand:

> When the heads of all those now living were laid low, and the facts that now excited such powerful feelings, were related by the pen of the cold, impartial historian; when it was seen that an opportunity like the present had been lost, that the first act of the restored King of France was the restoration of a trade in slavery and blood, what would be the estimate formed of the exertions this country had employed, or of the effect they had produced upon a nation under such weighty obligations? Surely, no very

high opinion could be indulged either of British influence or of French gratitude.[68]

Castlereagh, regretting the French position, had no option but to align himself with the motion as it was unanimously approved, although Wellington, also in London at the time, wrote to his brother Marquess Wellesley that he was astonished at the pressure exerted by Wilberforce and his allies, and that they seemed to want 'to go to war to put an end to that abominable traffic; and many wish that we should take the field in this new crusade ... I was not aware till I had been here some time of the degree of frenzy existing ... about the slave trade.'[69] Unaware as he might have been, the nation left him in no doubt of it: after only a few weeks over a quarter of a million signatures had been gathered on 806 petitions, standing as a sharp public rebuke to the government for not having tried harder. As Castlereagh set off for the Congress of Vienna, due to open on 1 October 1814 to settle the details of the European peace, he was all too aware that he could not afford to return without additional progress on the slave trade. Wilberforce busied himself with Stephen, preparing information on the trade for Castlereagh, and briefings for Wellington who had now become Ambassador in Paris. He made sure that if they failed to improve on the terms of the peace, it would not be for want of arguments.

The Congress of Vienna, beset with arguments over the fate of Saxony and Poland, would drag on into the new year. Wilberforce spent much of the autumn of 1814 with his family at Sandgate. He received regular personal reports from the British negotiators overseas, sometimes encouragingly, as when Castlereagh assured him that he had given copies of Wilberforce's book on abolition to all of the sovereigns meeting in Vienna, and sometimes discouragingly, as when Wellington told him that he could find no one in Paris other than Louis XVIII who agreed with the idea of French abolition. He continued his correspondence with Talleyrand, trying 'to chase away that base and detestable suspicion which I hear is so common in France, that we are acting from mercenary or malicious motives, notwithstanding all we talk about Justice and Humanity'.[70]

The Wilberforces spent Christmas 1814 at Barham Court at Teston, having borrowed the house from Lady Barham (Lord Barham, formerly Charles Middleton, had died the previous year) while lending Kensington Gore to Henry Thornton, who was seriously ill with tuberculosis. After visiting him on 13 January, Wilberforce wrote to Macaulay: 'Our dear friend is continually before my mind's eye, and his emaciated figure and face are very affecting. Above all, seeing poor Mrs Thornton with her nine children makes my heart bleed. May it please God to raise him up again, in answer to the prayers of his many friends.'[71] The prayers went unanswered: Thornton was dead a few days later. Wilberforce hastened back to London, where 'I stood for some time looking upon his poor emaciated frame; I cannot say countenance for that was no more. I should not have known him so ghastly was the face, so discoloured, so meagre . . . the faithful nurse who had led him into the death room began to weep. I observed to her, *This* is not our friend. This is but the earthly garment which he has thrown off. The man himself, the vital spirit has already begun to be clothed with immortality.'[72] Their partnership of thirty years was over, and within a few months Henry's wife Marianne would die of the same illness. Yet Wilberforce always showed great resilience in the face of personal loss, and although Hannah More worried that 'he has lost a great part of himself – his right hand in all great and useful measures',[73] he was as immersed as ever in late January 1815 in his efforts to secure general abolition.

The setbacks for general abolition in 1814 fortified the determination of Wilberforce and his colleagues to push forward with a Register Bill in the 1815 session of Parliament, but they found ministers averse to their efforts. Stephen was so disgusted that the Liverpool ministry, which he had generally supported, was unwilling to give the crucial support needed for the passage of such a Bill that he threatened to resign from Parliament altogether. Wilberforce tried to stave this off, persuading him with some difficulty to await the return of Castlereagh from Vienna in early March, when the prospects for international abolition and the government's final attitude to a Register Bill would become clearer. Castlereagh would arrive in London on 4 March with

European peace, so it seemed, successfully concluded. Within ten days, ministers had made clear that they would not support the Register Bill, and Stephen duly resigned his seat, Wilberforce considering that 'His integrity is great. I believe after what he has stated, he can act no other wise.'[74] On 17 March Wilberforce wrote to Liverpool, warning him that this decision would weaken his own support for the government, and that he would not rest content if the abolition of the slave trade did not produce the steady improvement in the condition of the slaves which had always been a key Wilberforce objective:

> It really would, on all accounts, grieve me to find myself opposed to your Lordship's government on these great questions of the deepest interest to every man of religion as well as humanity. Hitherto I have abstained from bringing into notice the miseries of the Black population, and I would still abstain, if without divulging them they might gradually be removed; but life is wearing away, and I should indeed be sorry if mine were to terminate before at least a foundation had been laid of a system of reformation, which I verily believe would scarcely be more for the comfort of the slaves and free coloured population than it would be for the ultimate security of the West India colonies themselves. I remain, with real respect and regard, my dear Lord Liverpool, your Lordship's very sincerely, W Wilberforce.[75]

This was a clear reaffirmation that the ending of the slave trade was not an end in itself: if it did not produce the desired effect, then other measures would have to be taken. But Wilberforce could at least be pleased by the international declaration Castlereagh had brought back from Vienna once British public opinion had stiffened his spine. At Castlereagh's behest, the governments of Britain, France, Spain, Sweden, Austria, Prussia, Russia and Portugal jointly declared that 'the commerce known by the name of the African slave trade is repugnant to the principles of humanity and universal mortality', and that it was their 'duty and necessity' to abolish it as soon as they could.[76] Wilberforce accepted that 'all done that could be done'.[77] Furthermore, Castlereagh had negotiated a new treaty with Portugal, ending the Portuguese slave trade north of the equator, which admittedly left most of it intact, and agreeing on complete abolition eventually. It was further agreed that the ships of each country could be inspected by those of the other, which in practice meant British warships policing both, and in the first instance of Britain paying other countries to abolish the slave trade a British loan to Portugal was written off and compensation was paid for some thirty Portuguese slaving ships seized by the Royal Navy in earlier years.

Later that same year Castlereagh would also conclude a fresh treaty with Spain, by which the Spanish abolished their slave trade north of a line ten degrees north of the equator and committed themselves to complete abolition by 1823. For ardent abolitionists these treaties were a long way from complete success, but Castlereagh could at least point to some serious progress, and ministers no doubt felt that they were doing quite enough to satisfy Wilberforce's opinions, Castlereagh at one stage referring to him as 'the most damned intractable fellow with whom I ever had to deal'. The British government was in any case beset in March 1815 by two monumental crises which would have made arguments over the slave trade a relatively minor consideration in the minds of Liverpool and Castlereagh. The first of these was the agricultural recession, which led the government to propose a tightening of the Corn Laws, protecting domestic agriculture by raising the price at which foreign corn could be admitted into the country to eighty shillings a quarter. Thirty years later the Corn Laws would produce a devastating split in Robert Peel's Conservative Party, but in 1815 the Tories united to avoid the ruin of British agriculture even at the price of violent disorder as people rebelled against the escalating price of food. One MP was pulled out of his carriage by the mob as he approached the House of Commons, riots took place in which the houses of some government supporters were set on fire, and Wilberforce found himself taking in friends who dared not venture to their own homes – 'Charles Grant, and Mr Arthur Young, the agriculturalist, slept with us for security on Tuesday.'[78]

As ministers pressed Wilberforce to speak up in their support on the Corn Laws he toyed with the idea of only doing so if they would support his Register Bill, but in the end decided to speak anyway, telling his son William, 'I thought that if I remained silent, many might say Mr Wilberforce professes to trust in the protection of God, but you see when there is a danger to be apprehended from speaking out, he takes care to protect himself by being silent.'[79] The result was that Kensington Gore had to be heavily protected: 'Were you to enter the dining-room at family prayer time without having received some explanation of our appearance, you would probably begin to think that we were expecting a visit from the ex-Emperor and his followers at Kensington Gore, and had prepared a military force to repel his assault. For you would see four soldiers and a sergeant . . . we had some reason to apprehend mischief for our house, in consequence of the part which I judged it my duty to take on the Corn Bill; and as your mother . . . was advised to evacuate the place, I preferred the expedient . . . of having four or five soldiers in my house – the very knowledge of their being there, rendering an attack improbable.'[80] There is no doubt that Wilberforce was genuinely in favour of the Corn Laws, although he noted that he would have preferred a price of seventy-six shillings rather than eighty. Although his generation had been influenced by Adam Smith and others to believe in freer trade, they did not feel this should be extended to the point of ruining the country's landed interest and food production, without which both the social order and national security would be threatened. And the second great crisis of 1815 reminded them that even after winning a war twenty-three years in length, the country was far from secure. On 1 March Napoleon had returned to France from exile in Elba. By mid-March, with the French army rallying to their former Emperor, Louis XVIII was in flight and the recognised government in Paris had collapsed.

The return of Napoleon once again exposed Wilberforce's lack of appetite for war: 'If Bonaparte could be unhorsed, it would, humanly speaking, be a blessing to the European world; indeed to all nations. And government ought to know both his force and their own. Yet I greatly dread their being deceived, remembering how Pitt was.'[81] Napoleon also gained some credit in abolitionist circles by announcing the immediate and total abolition of the French slave trade. But as Wilberforce welcomed William Wordsworth to Kensington Gore –

'29th [of May]. Wordsworth the poet breakfasted with us, and walked garden – and it being the first time, staid long – much pleased with him'[82] – Wellington and Marshal Blücher were manoeuvring in Belgium for their climactic battle with Napoleon. He worked hard that June to prepare for the forthcoming debate on the Register Bill, spending Sunday, 18 June at Taplow in Buckinghamshire, where his family had been enjoying a week's holiday. He walked through the village and to the church, enjoying 'a quiet day',[83] unaware that just across the English Channel the greatest battle of the entire nineteenth century was being fought at Waterloo. It was not until four days after the battle, on the following Thursday, that the definitive news reached London that Napoleon had been vanquished once and for all. Wilberforce joined in the rejoicing, his note of how Wellington should be rewarded illustrating how differently MPs thought in the early nineteenth century from their counterparts in a later age: 'I preferring infinitely a palace to be built, to buying one ready made.'[84]

Wilberforce renewed his efforts to send relief to suffering Germans, prompted partly by the victorious Blücher, who not only sent his aide-de-camp to brief Wilberforce on everything that had happened, but wrote to the committee raising funds for Germany: 'I have fought two pitched battles, five engagements, masked three fortresses, taken two, but I have lost twenty-two thousand men. Will the people of England be satisfied with me now? Desire Mr Wilberforce to bestir himself.'[85] Wilberforce also introduced his Register Bill into the Commons, knowing he could take it no further that session without support from the government. But as the allied powers gave a harsher edge to the peace terms they imposed on newly defeated France, not only providing for a strong Netherlands but fining France seven hundred million francs, imposing an army of occupation, restricting her frontiers to those of 1790 and exiling Napoleon to distant St Helena, Wilberforce would have had every right to be pleased with the news concerning the slave trade. The Bourbon government, restored for the second time in fifteen months, would not attempt to reverse Napoleon's abolition of the trade. Castlereagh wrote to Wilberforce from Paris on 31 July: 'I have the pleasure of acquainting you that the long desired object is accomplished ... the unqualified and total abolition of the Slave Trade throughout the dominions of France.'[86]

Yet even now the slave trade was far from being at an end. The governments of Spain, Portugal and France would prove far less willing or able to enforce their commitments than the government of Britain. It was, ironically, just as France made her unequivocal announcement on abolition that the first French slaving ships to sail for many years put to sea from Bordeaux.

16

Under Attack

No Wilberforces. Think of *that*! No Wilberforces!

William Cobbett on arrival in the United States, 1818[1]

May we be enabled to maintain a Christian frame of spirit amidst all these irritating hostilities, and remember that they will by and by appear only like the barking of the cottage curs on our passing through a village, when on our progress in the journey of life.

WILLIAM WILBERFORCE, 1816[2]

T HE WILLIAM WILBERFORCE who approached his fifty-sixth birthday in the summer of 1815 was still incurably addicted to the persistent habits which gave his life its character of unfailing generosity amidst unavailing chaos. The state of his correspondence made him feel that he was 'sinking into an abyss of unanswered letters and unfinished business'. He wrote to Hannah More on 19 July, 'I cannot tell how it has hurt me to hear that you had been throwing out a plaint of never hearing from me . . . If I had written to you as often as I had thought of you, I can truly say you would have had no more frequent correspondent.'[3] He then went on to recount how the previous day 'a young female of twenty came into my library, whose first words when we were alone were "I have run away Mr Wilberforce,"'[4] causing him to spend many hours assisting a young fugitive whom he had never met before. He then set off, despite his attachment to his family, on a five-week tour of southern England, taking him first to Oxfordshire to see Blenheim Palace, then to Cirencester, on to Bristol and into Somer-

Philanthropic Consolations after the loss of the Slave Bill. After yet another defeat in 1796, Wilberforce is imagined by Gillray to have consoled himself by cavorting with black women.

The Weather Cock of St Stephen's. Wilberforce's plea for peace with France in 1795, in opposition to Pitt, upset many of his friends and led to him being accused of being blown too easily by the political wind.

A procession at Wootton Bassett in Wiltshire celebrates the end of the British slave trade. Popular pressure and mass petitions had been a major component of the campaign for abolition.

William Wyndham Grenville, Pitt's hard-line Foreign Secretary. Trenchantly opposed to the slave trade, he presided as Prime Minister over its abolition in 1807.

Fast brigantines able to outrun patrol vessels were used for the illegal trade. The slaver *Antonio* is shown here taking on slaves in the Bonny River, West Africa.

Gillray's *Sketch of the Interior of St Stephen's* depicts the House of Commons with Addington (standing) as Prime Minister. Addington, later Lord Sidmouth, did little to help the campaign of Wilberforce, who is unflatteringly portrayed sitting behind him, holding a staff.

The 'trial' of Queen Caroline in the House of Lords. Vast crowds gathered outside and the entire peerage assembled inside, in the midst of a crisis that threatened to engulf the monarchy.

Henry Brougham, an ardent abolitionist who led Wilberforce into an ill-fated attempt to settle the acrimonious dispute between George IV and Queen Caroline.

William Wilberforce Junior, Wilberforce's first son, born in 1798 and photographed in 1875. His disastrous venture into farming destroyed the family fortune.

Inset: Wilberforce in 1820.

Wilberforce in the last year of his life, painted by George Richmond. His son Henry wrote, 'He speaks very little as if looking forward to future happiness; but he seems more like a person in the actual enjoyment of heaven within.'

set and Devon. Despite his curving spine, troublesome bowels, dependence on opium, poor eyesight, difficulty in hearing, and the need to
transport large quantities of books and letters wherever he went along
the jolting roads, he insisted that 'travelling suits me admirably'.[5] Insati-
ably curious, he could not bear to sit still during the parliamentary
recess, and such was his reputation that he always found a welcome,
whether in country homes or in village inns, sometimes with church
bells ringing in his honour when local inhabitants discovered he was
in the vicinity.

Arriving in Brighton in late August, he was finally reunited with
his family, and spent most of the autumn there, albeit interrupted by
the funeral of Henry Thornton's widow in London that October. By
mid-November, the Prince Regent himself was holding court in Brighton, making full use of the magnificent Pavilion which he had ordered
to be built. It was a measure of the acceptance by British society of the
abolition of the slave trade that Wilberforce now found himself a
very welcome guest at the Regent's table. It did not remotely suit his
constitution and habits to be invited each day to the long and sumptuous parties the Prince insisted on holding, and he told Hannah More,
'It is sad work. Dinner comes on table at six; at nine the dinner party
goes into the other rooms, in one of which is music, in another cards
. . . and a long gallery 160 feet long, walking about, till about a quarter
or half-past twelve, and then, on the Prince's retiring, all of us depart.
But really it is a large part of existence, from six to half-past twelve
daily, or rather nightly.'[6] Yet he was also flattered to be invited, all the
more so after the long years of the royal family's hostility to his campaign against the slave trade. He told Stephen that it had reinforced
his view that he had no need of any titles or a seat in the House of
Lords: 'I am not afraid of declaring that I shall go out of the world
plain William Wilberforce . . . For really had I been covered with titles
and ribands, I should not have been treated with more real, unaffected,
unapparently condescending, and therefore more unostentatious
civility.'[7]

Wilberforce had never been so closely incorporated into the court.
Even so, the experience left him 'feeling peculiar pity for the great and

high of the earth',[8] and he was delighted when the Prince excused him from attending nightly and simply asked him to turn up for dinner whenever it suited his convenience. Wilberforce had become something of a revered figure, whose dogged persistence in pursuing his beliefs for thirty years had brought respect for his habits of life, while his company was universally sought in polite society. Although the deaths of the Thorntons caused a great change 'in the circle of my acquaintance',[9] his openness to good company meant that he was never short of new and admiring friends. One of these was the leading Quaker, Joseph John Gurney, who met Wilberforce for the first time in the summer of 1816. Wilberforce had taken his family to Lowestoft on the Suffolk coast, possibly to avoid the intrusions of the Prince Regent into a second annual family holiday, and Gurney went to visit him 'partly for the purpose of seeing so great a man, and partly for that of persuading him to join our party at the time of the approaching anniversaries of the Norfolk Bible and Church Missionary Societies'.[10]

Gurney's experience was a familiar one: 'I was then young; but he bore my intrusion with the utmost kindness and good humour, and I was much delighted with the affability of his manners, as well as with the fluency and brightness of his conversation.'[11] Gurney then discovered one of the hazards of inviting Wilberforce to stay with him, that he ended up accommodating 'not only himself, but his whole family group – consisting of his amiable lady and several of their children, two clergymen who acted in the capacity of tutors, his private secretary, servants, &c.'.[12] When Wilberforce moved with his family he did not travel light: William and Dorothy Wordsworth found them a house in the Lake District for the late summer of 1818, and discovered that space was needed for nineteen people, with the addition of a small cavalcade of horses. No one ever seemed to mind the inconvenience this could sometimes create, Dorothy Wordsworth concluding that 'he is made up of benevolence and lovingkindness, and though shattered in constitution and feeble in body he is as lively and animated as in the days of his youth'.[13]

Similarly, Gurney later wrote: 'I venture that no-one who has been accustomed to observe Wilberforce will ever find the slightest difficulty in picturing him on the tablet of the mind. Who that knew him, can fail to recall the rapid movements of his somewhat diminutive form, the eliminations of his expressive countenance, and the nimble finger with which he used to seize on every little object that happened to adorn or diversify his path? Much less can we forget his vivacious wit – so playful, yet so harmless – the glow of his affections – the urbanity of his manners – and the wondrous celerity with which he was ever wont to turn from one bright thought to another.'[14] Southey, another poet who received a visit from the Wilberforces during their Lake District holiday, recalled with amusement 'such a *straggling* visitor – he was longer *going, going, going* than a bad bale of goods at an auction; and even when he began to go, he brought to at the bookcase on the staircase, and again in the parlour, to the utter despair of his wife, who resigns herself with comical composure to all his comicalities'.[15]

As Wilberforce moved into old age, these happy social qualities remained an enduring attribute, saving him from ever being considered morose or tedious amidst the pursuit of so many serious causes. When Benjamin Rush was appointed American Ambassador to London in 1817 he expected to find Wilberforce 'grave', but in fact 'he was full of animation. He led, without engrossing the conversation. His manner gave point to all that he said, and in his voice there were peculiarly eloquent intonations.'[16] He was playful, charming, and always curious about people, and his good humour seemed able to survive any setbacks, fortified as he was by a faith which had long since become absolute. When his sister Sally died in the autumn of 1816, sending Stephen into terrible grief, Wilberforce was at first shaken to see his sister's fixed features in death, but reflected, 'O it is the spirit, the inhabitant of the earthly tenement, not the tenement itself, which was the real object of our affection. How unspeakably valuable are the Christian doctrines and hopes in such circumstances as ours!'[17] His resilience made Wilberforce a huge comfort to Stephen and to other friends in distress.

Beyond his friends, Wilberforce's public reputation was such that, according to Southey, 'the weight with which his opinion came to the public' was 'far greater than [that] of any other individual'.[18] He was less active on a daily basis in the House of Commons by 1816, but he was still a powerful voice on the side of any argument, and remained a captivating public speaker, whose rising to his feet generally caused him to shed the often flitting nature of his conversation. When Edward Everett heard him speak at a meeting of the Church Missionary Society in 1818, he remembered that Wilberforce

> spoke to great effect. His manner, as far as respects movement and gesture are bad – his figure quite diminutive and unprepossessing, and his air much hurt by his extreme near-sightedness. But his fluency – happy use of metaphor – affectionate and cordial manner of allusion to the persons or topicks in question – make him one of the happiest speakers I ever heard: nothing can be imagined more hearty than the welcome given him: and to one, who has only seen him in private, nothing can be more unexpected than his power as an orator. In private, he is distracted – flies from topick to topick – seems whirled around in a vortex of affairs: nervous and restless. When he gets up, all this subsides – he rises above himself, and his immediate personality ... It is a curious reverse of what happens in most men, who, though they be calm and tranquil in private, are thrown into trepidation whenever they address the publick.[19]

To others, such as Sir James Stephen, Wilberforce's speeches in the Commons maintained the strongest attributes of his conversation, being characterised by 'natural and varied cadences ... animation and ease ... and ... affectionate, lively, and graceful talk'. He thought that 'no member, except the leaders of the great contending parties, addressed the House with an authority equal to that of Mr Wilberforce'.[20]

Ironically, it was as Wilberforce reached this peak of reputation and authority in his late fifties that he was to come under the most severe personal attacks he had ever experienced. Lauded by Evangelicals, abolitionists, American observers and the upper echelons of British society, he would nevertheless find his character assaulted and his politics abused amidst the fresh crises which were to hit Britain in the years after the defeat of Napoleon. Edward Everett would note that 'the miserable infection of party spirit goes so far here that it is getting to be quite fashionable to abuse him in the papers, and . . . speak contemptuously of him'.[21] For not only was the battle to suppress the foreign slave trade far from won, but the intensity of domestic politics would bring Wilberforce up against a rising tide of bitterness.

The first wave of attacks, in 1816, came from the unsurprising quarter of the West Indies. Wilberforce was about to make a fresh attempt to legislate for the compulsory registration of all slaves in British colonies, a proposition that was anathema to the owners of the plantations. The petition they presented to Parliament insisted that there was no evidence of the mistreatment of the slaves, and 'that it is contrary to the principles of British jurisprudence, the birthright of Englishmen, and the natural privileges of freeborn subjects, to suffer penalty, either in person, character, or estate but for offences legally charged and strictly proved; that the proposed Bill is evidently viewed by the colonists not only as oppressive in itself, and in direct violation of the unalterable principles before laid down, but as introductory to a more extended system of interference with their municipal regulations and domestic concerns'.[22] In pamphlets their language became far more extreme, particularly after the slaves of Barbados had mounted a violent insurrection in the spring of 1816. The slaves were said to have revolted because of what they had heard of Wilberforce's Register Bill and the hopes it had given them; he was accused of fomenting revolution and murder.

Wilberforce considered such attacks to be 'scandalous', but was 'rather animated than discouraged' by them.[23] On 19 June 1816 he delivered a combative speech in the House of Commons which was revealing about his attitude to slavery at this time, as well as demonstrating that he was in no way retiring into a timid old age. He ridiculed the planters for attributing the insurrection to him, saying that it was not his proposal for a register that had created violence, but the extreme language of the planters in opposing it – 'There would have been no insurrection if the business had been less spoken of'[24] – and he was now prepared to make a public denunciation of slavery itself: 'It is in no case safe that man should be entrusted with arbitrary power; but, in the present instance above all others, every circumstance conspires to provoke an abuse of arbitrary power.'[25] The distance of the plantation managers from authority made it impossible to ensure that they would behave in a humane way, and 'by an immutable moral law, the effects of slavery extended not only to the sufferer, but operated a corresponding degradation of the mind of the inflictor of the suffering'.[26] Nevertheless, he reaffirmed that he was not seeking instant emancipation: 'They had always thought the slaves incapable of liberty at present, but hoped that by degrees a change might take place as the natural result of the abolition.'[27] He claimed that even Lord Melville had once argued that after a certain date all newborn slaves should be born free, with the clear implication that he would favour such an approach now. For in the absence of any visible improvement in the condition of the slaves, and in view of the evident continuation of an illicit trade, Wilberforce was adamant that additional measures now needed to be taken.

By the time he made this speech, Wilberforce already knew that he would not be able to secure the passage of a Register Bill that year; but he continued to raise the subject in order to put pressure on the government and on the colonial legislatures. Castlereagh, joined by the Colonial Secretary, Lord Bathurst, urged him not to press the matter, so as not to create a huge British row over slavery at a time when they were making progress in negotiations over the Spanish slave trade. Their arguments were strong, and opposition abolitionists such as Romilly and Brougham urged the same course; after consultations with these latter two as well as with William Smith, Zachary Macaulay and Stephen, Wilberforce determined not to bring the Register Bill to a vote that year.

In return, he expected real progress from Castlereagh towards securing Spanish abolition. He regularly harangued him on the matter both in private and on the floor of the Commons, knowing that a huge slave trade was still being carried on, legally by Spanish and Portuguese ships south of the line designated for them, and illegally by French and American ships, many of the latter flying Spanish flags.

Over-zealous British seizures of foreign-owned ships created an outcry in the countries concerned, where the alleged abuse of British naval power was much resented. In the course of 1816, thirty-six ships left French ports on slaving voyages even though this was now technically illegal, while a pusillanimous and divided French government did nothing about it. The African Institution calculated at the end of the year that sixty thousand slaves were being shipped across the Atlantic each year, a quarter of them in American ships under Spanish colours. To make matters worse, illegal traders often used ships which had not been designed for holding slaves at all, cramming them into the holds of converted warships and other vessels which gave the victims even less space than in the days when the British trade was legal and regulated. Wilberforce's denunciations of such practices, delivered in a speech in the Commons in June 1817 as he moved an Address to the Prince Regent to press for renewed international pressure for abolition, were as evocative of the horrors of the trade as any he had delivered in the previous thirty years. He described to the House the conditions of slaves forced into ships built 'for fast sailing, not for stowage'. In such vessels,

> The slaves were all stowed together, perfectly naked, and nothing but rough unplaned planks to crouch down upon, in a hold situated over their water and provisions, the place being little more than two feet in height, and the space allowed to each slave being so small, that it was impossible for them to avoid touching and pressing upon those immediately surrounding; the greatest part of them were fastened, some three together, by one leg each, in heavy iron shackles, a very large proportion of them having the flux; that they were compelled to perform their natural evacuations under these dreadful circumstances, without being able to move, and to remain amidst their own excrement, which could not be cleared away until the said slaves were all disembarked.[28]

He described the terrible mortality on such voyages, and brought evidence that a vessel of only 120 tons had conveyed six hundred slaves. He denounced a captain of a slave ship who had said his slaves 'enjoyed tolerable comfort; but being asked whether they had room to lie on their backs, he said they had not. What idea of comfort this person had it was difficult to conceive.'[29]

Castlereagh, once an opponent of abolition, had over the years become sufficiently impressed by the unfairness of other countries continuing with the trade, and sufficiently prodded by Wilberforce and public opinion, that he had become a persuasive advocate for international abolition. By 1816 he was exasperated with the conduct of Britain's allies, considering the Portuguese as 'odious' and saying that the Spanish and Portuguese governments were 'well matched in dishonesty and shabbiness'.[30] He invoked the agreement on gradual abolition signed at Vienna to convene a series of international conferences between 1816 and 1819 aimed at international abolition, the first time the great powers had been led to attend a programme of multilateral conferences to settle their differences, other than at a time of determining peace or war. International pressure did produce some dividends: the Dutch abolished the slave trade by treaty with Britain in 1818, agreeing as they did so to the British right to search their ships. The French government produced fresh directives against the trade in 1817, although with no discernible effect on the activities of their traders. The unequivocal abolition of the French slave trade in 1818 was followed only by a continuing increase in the illegal trade.

In bilateral negotiations with other nations, however, Castlereagh was making serious progress by 1817, particularly when he was able to pay British money in exchange for foreign abolition. One small example from that year was an agreement with the King of eastern Madagascar to end the slave traffic from his country in return for payments from Britain for the following three years. But the real prize for Castlereagh was a bilateral agreement with Spain on rapid abolition, and it was not long before Wilberforce considered that the Foreign Secretary had 'done famously'.[31] On 9 October 1817, Wilberforce was able to write to Zachary Macaulay from Stansted in Essex, where he was taking his autumn sojourn:

However pressed for time, I must tell you without delay, or renounce forever all claims to being capable of the relations of peace and amity, that a very friendly and handsome letter from Castlereagh informs me, that he has actually received the Treaty with Spain (signed) for abolishing the Slave Trade, generally and finally in May, 1820, and immediately to the north of the Line. Also, which is scarcely less valuable, that a system of mutual search is agreed to be established for enforcing the Abolition law. Well may we praise God.[32]

The treaty with Spain was a significant achievement for Castlereagh, but it came at the price of £400,000 from the British taxpayer as inflated compensation for the Spanish ships damaged or confiscated by the Royal Navy over the previous ten years. It was undoubtedly the most serious blow to the slave trade since British abolition in 1807, but it would take far longer to have that effect. Wilberforce, Castlereagh and the British political establishment in general continued to place unwarranted faith in the sincerity with which other nations would implement their obligations: the 1817 Spanish treaty was followed by a huge surge in slave imports to Cuba, accompanied by urgent requests for women slaves so that more slaves could be born there in future. This was followed by various attempts to extend and circumvent the 1820 deadline when it finally arrived, and by weak attempts at enforcement thereafter. Similarly, a fresh treaty signed with Portugal in July 1817 was followed by a considerable increase in slave imports to Brazil. The Spanish and Portuguese authorities faced a particular problem, as their largest colonies, Cuba and Brazil respectively, were militantly opposed to the abolition of the slave trade, to the extent of being prepared to contemplate independence in order to avert it. Cuba drew back from this after a phase of massive slave imports and with the prospect of continuing smaller-scale illegal trading, but for Brazil the prospect of Portuguese acquiescence to British demands gave further fuel to the growing movement for independence.

Thirty years on from his first resolve to eradicate the slave trade, Wilberforce and his parliamentary collaborators were still finding that international abolition was a treacherous affair. Nevertheless, the treaty with Spain was an important landmark, for all the comments of the Whig Member of Parliament Sir Oswald Mosley* that 'It was not for us to teach Spain humanity.' Furthermore, British colonies were beginning to contemplate bringing in their own schemes of registration in order to avoid the encroachment, and no doubt the detailed provisions of legislation, on the matter from Westminster. Wilberforce would have been justified in believing that his efforts were not in vain. But by January 1817 he was feeling the pressure of other issues, and, perhaps for the first time in his life, was being deflected in some of his efforts against the slave trade by the seriousness of the domestic political crises. That month he wrote to Macaulay:

> I have for some time been unwillingly yielding to a secret suggestion that it would be better perhaps to lie upon our oars in the Registry Bill, and West Indian cause. When parliament meets, the whole nation, depend upon it, will be looking up for relief from its own burthens, and it would betray an ignorance of all tact to talk to them in such circumstances of the sufferings of the slaves in the West Indies. We should specially guard against appearing to have a world of our own, and to have little sympathy with the sufferings of our countrymen.[33]

Wilberforce had been stung by criticism that he cared relatively little for what was happening in his own backyard. He had been accused in 1816 of provoking revolt in the West Indies. But by the beginning of the following year it seemed to many of his colleagues at Westminster that it was Britain itself that was on the brink of revolution.

The end of the Napoleonic wars in 1815 was followed by a deep recession in Britain. Politicians of the time saw it as their job to manage the finances of the government, but not to try to control the economic situation of the entire country, and their priorities after Napoleon was vanquished were to stop the rapid growth of the national debt, reduce

---

* This Sir Oswald Mosley was the great-great-grandfather of the twentieth-century politician of the same name.

government expenditure and demobilise a large part of the armed forces. In retrospect it may seem obvious that the sudden application of such measures would bring economic hardship, but the rapid growth of manufacturing in the previous decades meant that the ministers of the time were in uncharted territory, and there were no modern theories of Keynesian demand management or statistics for money-supply growth to guide them. Pitt had left them a belief in opening up trade where possible, though not so much as to desist from the protection of British agriculture, and in balancing the Treasury's books the market would take care of the rest. But as the harvest of 1816 turned into a disaster, adding food shortages and high prices to the pain of an industrial contraction, huge numbers of British people were reduced to a state of anger or despair.

The voice of such intense discontent was provided by a variety of radical writers and politicians: Sir Francis Burdett, who had regularly clashed with Wilberforce in the past, and who now demanded annual parliamentary elections and a vote for every household; William Cobbett, prolific writer and scourge of the establishment, whose *Political Register* was sold at two pence a copy to the masses to avoid stamp duty and poured scorn on complacent ministers; and Henry Hunt, known as 'Orator' Hunt for the rabble-rousing speeches with which he brought vast meetings to a state of rebellious anger against the authorities. In November 1816 Hunt spoke to a crowd of tens of thousands at Spa Fields in London, asking them to show that 'the whole people of England were petitioning for their rights'.[34] While the vast majority of those who attended were well-behaved and simply wanted a petition to be sent to the Prince Regent, who twice refused to receive it, the presence at the rally of a cap on the end of a pike, as well as the flying of a British version of the tricolour, followed by a small riot in the City of London, rang every possible alarm bell at Westminster.

With similar meetings being held throughout the major cities and the ugly atmosphere continuing into the new year, the last straw for the government was the hissing at the Prince Regent as he travelled from the opening of Parliament in January 1817 and the shattering of two windowpanes of his coach either by a stone or a bullet. Ministers reacted in similar fashion to that adopted in a parallel situation in 1795, although then the country had been at war. A secret committee of MPs was set up to inquire into the disturbances and the ringleaders, with Wilberforce as one of its members. For a time this kept him, he said, as busy as he had ever been in Parliament, although he found time to write to Barbara, whom he had left with the family at Hastings, that she should 'pray in earnest against sedition, privy conspiracy and rebellion', and that although 'Hunt seems a foolish, mischief-making fellow' he was 'no conspirator',[35] and it was other ringleaders who had to be seized.

The report of the secret committee pointed to a plot to seize the Bank of England and the Tower of London while causing a mutiny in the army: those thought to be responsible were arrested that January. The rest of the government response closely followed the precedent of 1795, with legislation rapidly passing through Parliament to impose severe restrictions on the right to hold public meetings and, through the suspension of Habeas Corpus, the reintroduction of internment without trial. Such measures were passed through Parliament by huge majorities, although predictably scorned by the likes of Cobbett: 'They sigh for a Plot ... They are working and slaving and fretting and stewing; they are sweating all over; they are absolutely pining and dying for a Plot!'[36]

The radicals would gain additional ammunition later that year when it turned out that an alleged conspiracy to march on London had not only been revealed to the authorities by a government spy named Oliver, but also largely fomented by him so that he could get the credit for reporting on it. But the revolutionary tinge to radical agitation meant that even the opposition Whigs in Parliament could show little sympathy for it, and the back of the protests was broken by the clampdown of the authorities, a better harvest and a general economic recovery throughout 1817. Fearing arrest, Cobbett fled to America. He had always defended slavery while calling for better conditions for British workers, and in the years to come would intensify his attacks on what he saw as the hypocrisy of Wilberforce in campaigning for better conditions for Negro slaves abroad while British people lived in desperate conditions at home in the new manufacturing towns. In 1818 he wrote his famous description of the paradise he had found in America:

> ... A hundred brace of woodcocks a day – think of that! ... And never to see the hangdog face of a tax gatherer. Think of that! No alien acts here. No long-sworded and whiskered Captains. No Judges escorted from town to town and sitting under the guard of dragoons. No packed juries of tenants ... No hangings and rippings up ... No Cannings, Liverpools, Castlereaghs ... or Sidmouths ... No Wilberforces. Think of that! No Wilberforces![37]

This line of attack on Wilberforce, that his espousal of various Evangelical causes was hypocritical when he appeared to be happily complicit in political repression and economic stagnation in domestic politics, would gain ground in subsequent years. There was something of a lull in such controversies during 1818, a year which saw Habeas Corpus restored and a brief return to domestic peace, leaving the harsh measures of the previous year seeming vindicated in the eyes of the authorities, and exposed as unnecessary in the eyes of their critics. But it was a false dawn: a bad harvest that year and renewed industrial downturn plunged the country into an even more intense social and economic crisis in the course of 1819. The people of Birmingham and Manchester attempted to elect their own representatives to demand reform. On 16 August 1819, when Hunt began to address a crowd of sixty thousand at St Peter's Fields near Manchester, the magistrates hesitated to act but then sent in cavalry to arrest him, causing panic and violence which resulted in eleven deaths.

The 'Peterloo massacre', as it became known, was a watershed in British politics, providing Whig and radical reformers in subsequent years with the perfect illustration of the dangers of repressive and unrepresentative government. The action of the magistrates was sternly defended by Sidmouth, the Home Secretary, and indeed by the Prince Regent, causing yet more uproar in response. Even the more liberal supporters of the Tory government considered that no other policy was possible, George Canning writing: 'To let down the magistrates would be to invite their resignations and to lose all gratuitous service in the counties liable to disturbance forever. It is, to be sure, very provoking that the magistrates, right as they were in principle, and nearly right in practice, should have spoilt the completeness of their case by half an hour's precipitation.'[38] But the country was divided, and much respectable opinion appalled. The Corporation of London and the freeholders of Yorkshire called for an inquiry, Earl Fitzwilliam being forced to resign as Lord Lieutenant for the West Riding because of his agreement with them. Wilberforce was worried that the country was in a state of 'something nearer to civil war, than this land has exhibited since 1646',[39] but he had no doubt as to where he stood. He was flatly against an inquiry into Peterloo, which 'would be the means of producing more discord and bloodshed than any other measure that could be devised',[40] and he supported the government's Six Acts which once again clamped down on seditious meetings and writings.

Wilberforce's stance on Peterloo, added to his previous support of the government in facing down any symptom of discontent in the previous years, brought much vituperative comment. The radical commentator Francis Place described him as 'an ugly epitome of the devil'. The essayist William Hazlitt described him as 'as fine a specimen of moral equivocation as can well be concerted', who 'preaches vital Christianity to untutored savages, and tolerates its worst abuses in civilised states'.[41] Hazlitt considered that Wilberforce meant well, but would never risk becoming unpopular with the ruling establishment: 'He ... reaps the credit of independence without the obloquy ... He has all the air of the most perfect independence, and gains a character for impartiality and candour, when he is only striking a balance between the *éclat* of differing from a Minister on some vantage ground, and the risk or odium that may attend it.'[42]

In some of the debates of this period Wilberforce was indeed on shaky ground – for example, criticising the use of government spies but refusing to vote for an inquiry into their activities, which occasionally left him sounding critical of the government but unwilling to become unpopular with its members. In one debate the Whig spokesman George Tierney said that Wilberforce's 'phraseology was happily adapted to suit either party; and if now and then he lost the balance of his argument, and tended a little to one side he quickly recovered himself, and deviated as much in an opposite direction as would make a fair division of his speech on both sides of the question'.[43] Other opposition figures who were normally close to Wilberforce, such as Brougham, thought he was naïve to accept the word of the government whenever matters came to a crunch: his refusal to believe that a man such as Lord Sidmouth would abuse his powers was 'the simplicity of innocence'.[44]

As a rule, Wilberforce had always been careful not to make personal attacks on political opponents. His refraining from doing so was in line with his Christianity, his independence and his need to muster a majority from all quarters on the issues he most cared about. Now, however, the insults flung at him on the floor of the House of Commons itself sometimes brought him to make a sharp retort. He told Tierney that he had known him long enough 'to know that he always appears most confident when his cause is desperate'.[45] And in the debates on the suspension of Habeas Corpus in 1817 he had a celebrated exchange with his chief parliamentary tormentor, Sir Francis Burdett, who broke House of Commons conventions to describe Wilberforce as an 'honourable and religious member': 'The honourable and religious member was shocked the other day at the description of the Africans chained and carried into slavery. How happened it that the honourable and religious member (Order! Order!) was not shocked at Englishmen being taken up under this act and treated like African slaves?'[46] Wilberforce noted in his diary that 'He forced me up in self-defence,' and retaliated with a sharp personal attack on Burdett: 'If I could be base enough to seek the destruction of those institutions which we both profess to revere, I would tell him what instrument I would choose. I would take a man of great wealth, of patrician family, of personal popularity, aye and of respectable talents, and I am satisfied that such a one, while he scattered abroad the firebrands of sedition under pretence that he went all lengths for the people, would in reality be the best agent in the malevolent purpose of destroying their liberties and happiness.'[47] Burdett was much taller than Wilberforce, but as the counterblast continued, one MP, Sir Thomas Acland, thought the spectacle was 'like a giant dangling a dwarf'. Romilly thought that Wilberforce's response was evidence more of his 'virtue than of his genius, for who but he was ever possessed of such a formidable weapon, and never used it!'[48]

It is largely because of Wilberforce's attitude towards domestic discontent after the war that he has sometimes been seen as having a narrow and unbending view of British society, confirming the impression made to history by his support for the Combination Act in the 1790s that he was the enemy of many progressive political causes. Yet it is all too easy to look back from later centuries with accusations of inconsistency or excessive conservatism while forgetting both the pressures and the prevailing thinking of the time. The politicians of 1819 had lived through one of the most turbulent periods in history, and had emerged from nearly a quarter of a century of warfare only to find themselves riding economic crises and social changes which were difficult either to foresee or to understand. They had witnessed a bloody revolution in their nearest neighbour within their lifetimes, and when vast crowds gathered to demand change they had no opinion polls or mass-membership political parties to guide them as to what people would settle for. Furthermore, previous crises had taught them that restrictive laws were generally effective at suppressing discontent in Britain until better economic times arrived. It should not be surprising that they readily turned to the same remedy and always erred on the side of caution and authority.

It might be thought that Wilberforce had no need to place himself in such prominent defence of the Liverpool government's actions, but a failure to do so on his part would not have helped the causes for which he was fighting, nor would it have been in line with his most deeply held beliefs. Although he was a man of principle he was also a practical politician, and he wrote to Macaulay in 1817 that he had 'again and again been silent when I should have spoken' in defence of the government, 'but for the consciousness that I had to look to the opposition rather than to government as our supporters in the Registry Bill and West Indian matters'.[49] To have actually lined up with the

Whigs and radicals when the crisis became intense, however, would have caused catastrophic damage to his fight against the slave trade and his emerging work against slavery, since he would have been thought by the government and much of the country to have been dangerously revolutionary in his inclinations. In addition, he considered it his duty to back the government 'if the ship were in danger of going down',[50] and at times in 1817 and 1819 that did indeed appear to be the case. He had always believed in moderate reform and evolutionary change in social and political institutions. Thus he believed that a modest reform of parliamentary representation was the right way to make progress, and the gradual alleviation of the burdens of slavery was the right way to bring about its destruction. He saved his campaigns for dramatic change for the removal of barriers to such evolutionary reform, of which the continuation of the slave trade and the bar on Christianity in India had been outstanding examples. The clamour for instant and radical reform made by people like Burdett and Hunt went totally against Wilberforce's instincts.

On a personal level, it is not surprising that Wilberforce sided with politicians such as Liverpool, Sidmouth and Castlereagh, with whom he had worked in varying degrees of cooperation for several decades, rather than with figures such as Cobbett, who had attacked him over the years for everything from opposing bear-baiting, to encouraging the growing of potatoes, to being concerned about the welfare of slaves. But to think that Wilberforce simply stuck with the perceptions of the circle within which he was comfortable would be to forget the number of occasions on which he had challenged their thinking in the past. His objection to the views of the radicals went much deeper than any resentment he might have felt at being attacked by them. For Wilberforce, the worst aspect of revolution as practised in France, and radical reform as advocated in Britain, was that it was utterly divorced from Christianity. Radicals, he wrote in 1819, 'would exclude religion from life, and substitute knowledge in its stead', but 'it is only by educating our people in Christian principles that we can advance in strength, greatness and happiness'.[51] Cobbett's writings were not only subversive of politics but of religion, and 'the blasphemous songs and papers of the seditious will disgust all who have any religion or any decency'.[52] This was his great fear: that religion and morality would go out of the window with political and social stability, as indeed had happened in France. On the suspension of Habeas Corpus he had argued that he 'could readily conceive how the lower orders, that valuable portion of the community whose labour was so essential to the social system under which we live, might be tempted by the delusive and wicked principles instilled into their minds to direct their strength to the destruction of the government, and to the overthrow of every civil and religious establishment'.[53]

Wilberforce would never, therefore, support reform that was anti-thetical to religion, as his dealings with the early idealistic socialist Robert Owen well showed. Owen had found Wilberforce a sympathetic listener when he first visited him in 1812, and he was soon invited back to dinner at Kensington to read a paper on his ideas for education. The paper had proved sufficiently turgid for Wilberforce to sleep through much of it, but Owen had observed to him earlier that 'one of my great principles is that persons ought to place themselves in the situation of others, and act as they would wish themselves to be treated'. A deadpan Wilberforce then enquired, 'Is that quite a new principle, Mr Owen? I think I had read something very like it in a book called the New Testament.' Owen's answer was 'Very possibly it may be so,'[54] but the socialist model of manufacturing he set up at his New Lanark mill in Scotland made no allowance for Christianity, and when Owen's plans were discussed in the Commons in 1819, Wilberforce was 'forced to speak against it on the Christian ground'.[55]

Wilberforce continued to believe that the real revolution that was required was in morals and education, so that people could become fit for the greater power they sought: education and religion would make them 'less likely to become the dupes of designing and factious men'.[56] He showed great interest throughout this time in ideas for the improvement and expansion of education. His efforts in the immediate post-war years, alongside his persistent harassment of the international slave trade, were also applied to a wide range of other reforming causes. It is these efforts, above all, that dispel the one-dimensional idea of

Wilberforce as a repressive arch-conservative after 1815. He spoke up in support of legislation to improve the conditions in which chimney-sweeps had to work, and assisted attempts to limit the working day of children in the textile industry – a limit initially set at thirteen and a half hours. He attacked the Game Laws, which imposed severe punishment including transportation for even minor acts of poaching, and he became energetically involved in prison reform, under the influence of Fowell Buxton and Elizabeth Fry. Fry was yet another practical reformer invited to dinner at Kensington to discuss her ideas; the very next morning Wilberforce was to be found with her in Newgate Prison, where she had improved the behaviour of women prisoners by educating them. He joined in the campaign to restrict capital punishment to the most serious crimes and presented Gurney's Quaker petitions on the matter to Parliament in 1818 after Romilly, parliamentary leader of this campaign, had committed suicide.

There can be no doubt, amidst the controversy and invective of the politics of the time, that Wilberforce's hopes and ideals were still alive. And while the recriminations and fear of revolution had taken hold in Britain, he had been quietly getting on with putting his ideals into practice in another country altogether, where a revolution had already taken place.

The great slave rebellion that had erupted in the French colony of Saint-Domingue in 1791 had precipitated two decades of warfare, but by the time of the defeat of Napoleon, with all French expeditions to recover the island defeated or aborted, a semblance of stable government had emerged there. Renamed Hayti, the forerunner of the modern Haiti, the island was now entirely populated and ruled by the former slaves. In the northern part of the island, power had been seized by Henri Christophe, a former slave born on St Kitt's who had become President and then declared himself King Henry I. With remarkable energy he set about improving the education, agriculture and commerce of the first black-ruled country of the West Indies.

In 1815 Wilberforce entered into correspondence with Christophe, taking care to inform Lord Liverpool of what he was doing but to conceal it from as many other people as possible. Early the following year a black teacher from Massachusetts, who had travelled to Hayti on Wilberforce's recommendation with a supply of vaccines, returned to England with a request from Christophe for aid in the form of professors who could educate his people. The idea of helping Christophe create a free and flourishing black state soon gripped Wilberforce's imagination, since it opened the prospect of demonstrating that the West Indies could enjoy a peaceful and prosperous future without any need for slavery at all. Even more in Christophe's favour, in Wilberforce's mind, was that the long war with the French had inclined him towards everything English: he wanted help in the teaching of the English language and the conversion of his people from Catholicism to a reformed Church.

Wilberforce became so excited at the possibilities that he called in much of the old Clapham Sect, while deeply regretting that he was too old to go out to Hayti himself. Asking Macaulay to scour the country for suitable academics, he explained to Stephen that 'the King has requested me to get for him seven schoolmasters, a tutor for his son, and seven different professors for a Royal College he desires to found. Amongst these are a classical professor, a medical, a surgical, a mathematical, and a pharmaceutical chemist.'[57] He wrote to Charles Simeon of the prospect of 'sowing the seeds of civilisation, and still more of Christian faith, in this hitherto blighted quarter of the world, where, when they have once taken root, they will gradually diffuse themselves throughout all the coloured inhabitants of the western hemisphere'.[58]

It did not prove easy to find any academics of talent who were prepared to go to Hayti, other than those who had fallen on hard times, but Wilberforce beavered away at a continual stream of letters of advice to Christophe, which was eventually accompanied by two small detachments of teachers and a large quantity of Bibles. He told Grenville that these efforts had to be kept confidential for the moment, since 'I have seen such proofs of the terror of Black Improvement even among the better kinds of West Indians ... that every degree of opposition may be anticipated.'[59] While defending the reputation of Christophe against various libels – such as that he had shot his right-hand man in public, which indeed turned out to be untrue – he went to enormous trouble to help a King whom he concluded was 'a very extraordinary man',[60] corresponding with his collaborators throughout the country, putting his own money into the project in advance of any payments from Christophe, and spending days at a time with each of the people who were going out to Hayti at his behest. All of this was coordinated with Thomas Clarkson, who was in Paris trying to stir the French into enforcing abolition, and who now set to work on a peace treaty between Hayti and France.

In 1818, the combination of excitement at the prospects for Hayti, frustration at the inability to impose a general register of slaves or fully to eradicate the slave trade, and shock at some of the punishments still meted out to slaves in the West Indies, persuaded Wilberforce to begin to focus his attention on the institution of slavery itself. At a dinner at the end of January 1818 with the leading abolitionists Stephen, Romilly, Brougham, Macaulay, William Smith and Sir James Mackintosh, Wilberforce spoke of bringing about 'a full inquiry into the state of the slaves, and for a radical improvement'.[61] He was unsure at this stage of how to proceed, Castlereagh telling him the following day of the 'danger of pressing for too entire a change, in short for slaves' emancipation, till abolition by other powers secured – the French, Dutch, and American right of search. Much struck with his remarks and information.'[62] It had begun to be clear to him, however, that the gradual improvement in the conditions of the slaves which he had always held in mind might never take place without a campaign for further measures. In the spring of 1818, faced with a general election, he decided once again to be elected for Bramber – no actual voting being necessary – and to sit in Parliament for at least another two years: 'Thus Providence seems to fashion my ways and if I should go entirely out of public life in two years, I hope to have previously sown the seeds and laid the foundation of the West Indian reform.'[63] He still did not think of outright and instant emancipation as practically poss-ible or politically saleable, but was turning over in his head schemes for improving the education, religion and rights of the slaves so that one day they could be free.

Sadly, Hayti did not for long provide the example of enlightened government which Wilberforce had longed for and done so much to assist. Christophe had been hugely grateful for Wilberforce's help, sending him his portrait and naming a ship after him, but he became steadily more tyrannical and unpopular. 1820 would see a sick and desperate Christophe abandon Christianity, revert to voodoo, suffer a mutiny among his army and aristocrats, and finally shoot himself. He had never done much in the event about his intention of converting his subjects from Catholicism, but Wilberforce was much saddened by the news of his death, and always defended his memory, arguing that the excessive discipline and hoarding of money for which Christophe had been criticised had been essential in case France had attacked him. 'He was a great man,' Wilberforce concluded, 'intent on the improvement of his people, but he furnishes a striking instance of the truth, that by too earnestly pursuing a good object you directly defeat it.'[64] It was a thought that summed up Wilberforce's ever-present awareness that tactical cunning had to be combined with good principles in order to attain a political objective. He almost certainly had in mind that his efforts to combat the injustices of slavery would require such an approach. But while he was feeling for the best way forward against slavery, he became controversially embroiled in the affairs of another branch of royalty; this time not through the ambitions of the King of a remote West Indian island, but of the Queen of England herself.

17

Trials of Faith

─────────·○·─────────

To be told before all the world, that on me and my conduct depends
the fate of the Empire, is enough to make a man anxious.
WILLIAM WILBERFORCE, August 1820[1]

To her damnation, may she never return.
THE PRINCE REGENT, August 1814[2]

O F ALL THE TROUBLED MARRIAGES of the modern royal family,
that between George, Prince of Wales – the future George IV – and
Caroline of Brunswick must rank as by far the most catastrophic.
Wilberforce would later reflect that 'We marry our Kings and Queens
contrary to the laws of God and nature,'[3] and the preparation for the
wedding of the Prince and Princess in 1795 had provided a perfect
illustration of this truth. For one thing, the Prince had already secretly
married Mrs Maria Fitzherbert, perpetrating the double offence firstly
of breaking the Royal Marriages Act, which required the King's permission for one of his children to marry, and secondly of marrying a
Catholic, in defiance of the Act of Settlement, which guaranteed the
Protestant line to the throne. For another, he had a further favourite,
Lady Jersey, at the time the marriage was proposed, with whom he
remained infatuated and whom he had the indelicacy to send on his
behalf to greet his bride when she arrived at Greenwich. And for good
measure, he had only agreed to get married at all in order to help
persuade his father to give him a senior commission in the army and

to secure a deal with the government which would provide him with an increased income, given his accumulation of no less than £630,000 of debt (the rough equivalent of £50 million today).

By the time the wedding day arrived, George III had informed his son that he would on no account give him a military command, and the increased allowances for which he was desperate were facing a difficult reception in Parliament, leaving him with very little motive to be married at all. The only way to devise a less successful prospect for a marriage was to present the Prince with a bride who did not conform to his social and physical tastes, and this was duly accomplished: the dandified Prince, who loved to dress with extreme extravagance and who could take his pick from the ladies of London society, was presented with a wife who knew little of the ways of the English court, was not strikingly beautiful, and had nothing like the dress sense to which he was accustomed. According to the Earl of Malmesbury, who had been sent out to collect the Princess and instruct her in her future life, 'She has quick parts, without a sound or distinguishing understanding ... a ready conception, but no judgement ... some natural, but no required morality, and no strong innate notions of its value and necessity; warm feelings and nothing to counterbalance them ... She has no governing powers, although her mind is *physically* strong.'[4] He was not impressed with her dental condition or her habits of personal hygiene, about which he felt bound to speak to her.

When Lady Jersey went to greet the Princess she set off deliberately late, but took the trouble to make her change into an ill-fitting dress and, so it is alleged, placed a foul-smelling substance in her hair, in order to aggravate further her natural disadvantages. The first meeting of bride and groom was scarcely auspicious, with the Prince saying barely a word, embracing her once, calling for a glass of brandy and leaving forthwith. The Princess was left asking whether he was always like that, and commenting that he seemed very fat and nothing like as handsome as his portrait. The wedding ceremony, conducted on 8 April 1795 at the Chapel Royal, St James's, was scarcely more encouraging. While the Archbishop of Canterbury paused significantly at the passage concerning the disclosure of 'any lawful impediment', and twice went over the part requiring the Prince 'to live from that time in nuptial fidelity with his consort', the Prince was already drunk, 'looked like death . . . as if he wanted to hide himself from the looks of the whole world',[5] and had to be prompted in his responses by his father. He spent most of that night collapsed in the fireplace of his bedroom, the Princess later recalling that he 'passed the greatest part of his bridal night in the grate where he fell, and where I left him'.[6]

It was a minor miracle that the Princess became pregnant almost immediately, for within three weeks they were effectively separated. While the Princess lived for several years in Carlton House, the Prince's residence, it was Lady Jersey who accompanied the Prince on his nights of social frivolity, with Caroline being left behind with her baby, Princess Charlotte. When she reacted to this by trying to make her own social and travel plans, the Prince responded with horror, and refused to allow her to live anywhere else with their child. As a result, she spent 'many solitary hours' at Carlton House, generally shunned by both the Prince and the Queen, until she finally revolted with these words:

> I have been two and a half years in this house. You have treated me neither as your wife, nor as the mother of your child, nor as the Princess of Wales. I advise you that from this moment I have nothing more to say to you, that I regard myself as being no longer subject to your orders, or your rules.[7]

From that day on she did indeed abandon the rules and habits of the royal family, becoming hugely popular as she did so, since she was seen by the public as the victim of an ungrateful Prince and an unwelcoming Queen. She set up house in Blackheath, to the south-east of London, where she entertained a wide variety of visitors – including senior politicians such as Canning – and flirted freely with them if they were male. Gossip turned to accusations, particularly that a child she had taken in and adopted was in fact her own, and a committee of cabinet ministers was established in 1806 to inquire into her conduct, finding that the child was not hers at all, but that 'other particulars concerning the conduct of Her Royal Highness . . . necessarily give occasion to very unfavourable interpretations'.[8] There is no doubt that she had adulterous relationships, but equally no doubt that the Prince did the same. They continued to lead separate lives, with relations so bad that in 1814 Caroline was not included in the great celebrations of the allied victory over Napoleon and was never invited to meet the great conquerors, the Tsar of Russia and the King of Prussia, when they arrived in London. Disgusted, she left Britain for a new life in Italy, travelling through Naples, Genoa, Rome and Milan and acquiring a handsome Italian courier, Bartolomeo Pergami, who soon became her lover.

The Princess's lifestyle in Italy and her continued enjoyment of a level of popularity in Britain which far exceeded that of the Prince, caused him huge embarrassment and anguish. By 1818 he was turning his

> whole thoughts to the endeavouring to extricate myself from the cruellest as well as the most unjust predicament that ever even the lowest individual, much more a Prince ever was placed in, by unshackling myself from the woman who has for the last three and twenty years not alone been the bane and curse of my existence, but who now stands prominent in the eyes of the whole world, characterised by a flagrancy of abandonment unparalleled in the history of women, and stamped with disgrace and dishonour.[9]

When she had left Britain he had drunk 'to her damnation, may she never return',[10] and his greatest dread was that she would come back to England and claim her rights not only as a Princess but eventually as Queen. To avoid this calamity, efforts were made in 1819 to mediate an agreed separation. The interlocutor between Prince and Princess was Henry Brougham, close collaborator of Wilberforce in the campaign against the slave trade, and one of the opposition politicians who had gravitated to the Princess as the Prince and the Tory government had become entrenched together. The Prince wanted a complete divorce, believing that the so-called 'Milan Commissioners' sent out to gather evidence against the Princess would return with overwhelming evidence of her adultery. The cabinet, however, believed that the pursuit of divorce proceedings by an unpopular Prince Regent and government against a popular Princess, added to the atmosphere of crisis already prevailing, would present 'a serious hazard to the interests and peace of the Kingdom',[11] and would have been happy to settle for a separation. Brougham had indeed proposed a separation on behalf of the Princess, involving her remaining abroad and renouncing her right to be crowned Queen in return for a much-increased annuity, but never seems to have told the Princess that the cabinet were ready to settle for this. Brougham appears to have played a double game, negotiating on behalf of the Princess but posing to the Prince as the one man who could secure the divorce that he wanted; and since divorce rather than separation was never acceptable to the Princess, agreement was never reached. Thus it was that when George III finally died in January 1820, the Prince Regent became King George IV and the Princess he loathed, sitting in her self-imposed Mediterranean exile, became Queen of England. The stage was set for one of the most bizarre and celebrated confrontations of British history.

The royal crisis into which William Wilberforce would be plunged in 1820 turned on what might seem in retrospect to have been a very small point: whether the name of Queen Caroline should be included in the Anglican Liturgy. According to Castlereagh, it was on the day after the death of his father that George IV attended church and realised that every congregation of the Church of England would now be asked to pray not only for him but for his wife, and 'the horror of having the Queen made an object of the prayers of his people haunted his imagination and distracted his rest'.[12] The cabinet reluctantly agreed to the omission of the Queen's name from the Liturgy, but continued to be very cautious about a divorce, with the King consequently threatening to dismiss them. The ministers nevertheless stood their ground, and promised divorce proceedings only if the Queen were to commit the provocative act of returning to England for the coronation. This was thought very unlikely, and in any case the political world in March 1820 was thoroughly distracted by other developments: the discovery of the Cato Street Conspiracy, involving a radical plot to murder the entire cabinet at dinner, heightened the atmosphere of national crisis, while a general election was held – in which Wilberforce was once again returned automatically for Bramber – and the King failed to find any set of ministers able and willing to replace the Liverpool government on his terms. But by April one of the cabinet's worst nightmares was coming true. Notwithstanding the risk of public divorce proceedings and the exposure of her affairs, the Queen was so incensed at her treatment and the exclusion of her name from the Liturgy, which she saw as an admission of guilt if she agreed to it, that her carriages in Italy were being loaded with all her clothes, jewels and china, and she was heading for England. On 5 June she arrived at Dover, to a royal salute from the castle, and to be greeted everywhere by cheering crowds shouting 'Long live Queen Caroline!'

The government was now in a serious situation. Committed to going ahead with the divorce proceedings they had tried to avoid, ministers were forced to lay on the tables of the Commons and Lords what became the famous 'green bag' of accumulated evidence against the Queen, with a proposal that the contents be examined in a secret committee. Opposition MPs leapt to the defence of the Queen, while thousands of people gathered outside the home of one of her supporters, Alderman Wood, where she had taken up residence. The crowds saw the Queen as a martyr, a victim like them of royal indifference and governmental incompetence. It was this conjunction of general public rebelliousness with the Queen's daring act of return which made the crisis of 1820 a very dangerous one for the authorities. Charges and counter-charges of adultery flying between King and Queen could prove the final ruin of the reputation of the royal family. Public sympathy and support for the Queen could become uncontrollable, with rumours abounding that the army could not be relied on in such circumstances. The government took the precaution of moving some army units out of London because of their apparent loyalty to the Queen. In such circumstances, many MPs looked for one of their number who could speak independently of party and help bring about a sensible solution. Inevitably, they turned to Wilberforce.

On 7 June, Castlereagh moved in the Commons for the inquiry into the Queen's conduct to begin. He was preceded by Brougham telling MPs on behalf of the Queen that 'She solemnly protests against the formation of a secret tribunal to examine documents privately prepared by her adversaries, as a proceeding unknown to the law of the land, and a flagrant violation of all the principles of justice.'[13] The debate went back and forth, with ministers determined to carry the motion in order to fulfil their commitment to the King. It was only after lengthy speeches by Castlereagh, Tierney and Brougham that Wilberforce rose to his feet. He told the House that 'He was acquainted with no circumstance in history which was followed by evils in his opinion exceeded by those to be apprehended from the present case ... there was no true lover of his country, who would not be glad and wish to see by all means the fatal extremity averted.'[14] He then 'proposed an adjournment of the question till Friday upon pure motives of charity to spare the public the *horrid and disgusting* details of the King's green bag and of the green bag which the Queen might bring against the King'.[15]

This would only be a two-day delay, but it was one Wilberforce argued might still allow 'an accommodation' to be made. Other MPs rushed to support his motion, and Castlereagh, in effect defeated, agreed in the early hours of the morning to adjourn the House without the motion being carried. Not for the first time, Wilberforce had upset the parliamentary calculations of ministers: the King was left fuming, ministers embarrassed and Parliament seething with rumour. Yet the more positive result was that negotiations between King and Queen were intensified, with Castlereagh adjourning the House again when the Friday came so that these could be continued. In the light of later events, Wilberforce's efforts can easily be seen as futile or pointless interfering, but in June 1820 he played a part which actually came very close to resolving the national crisis.

The morning after carrying his motion, Wilberforce sent a letter to the King, conveyed to Carlton House by his son William, imploring him to restore the Queen's name to the Liturgy and warning him that otherwise 'the country should be in a fury, and soldiers might some of them change'.[16] The King did indeed make major concessions some days later, agreeing to his wife's recognition as Queen provided she lived abroad, and consenting to give her the money that she wanted and even a royal yacht. Wilberforce, now placed at the heart of efforts to achieve a settlement by virtue of his powerful role in the Commons, was in constant touch with Brougham and Canning as they worked for a solution, and allowed himself a day or two of optimism. 'I hope,' he noted, 'I am averting a great evil.'[17] But the King could not bring himself to restore the Queen's name to the Liturgy, and in the light of his having made so many other concessions, Wilberforce and other MPs who had supported his call for compromise decided that the only solution was to persuade the Queen to yield on this point. He further came up with the idea that the Queen would agree to do this at the specific request of the House of Commons rather than as a concession to the King, permitting her to concede the point with dignity.

A solution seemed entirely possible. The King, having toyed with the idea of bringing in the Whigs even at the price of granting Catholic emancipation, recovered from his rage with his ministers and negotiated in good faith. The Queen was advised by Brougham to accept the terms she was now offered, while he assured Wilberforce that the sort of compromise he had in mind would do the trick. It was after discussing matters with Brougham on 17 June that Wilberforce came to the conclusion that he could play a final and decisive part in resolving matters by moving an address to the Queen in the House of Commons recognising her position – so that she would always be treated as a Queen when abroad – in return for her dropping of her insistence to be included in the Liturgy. He wrote to Macaulay that the papers Brougham had brought him showed that the Queen's legal advisers 'had suggested that they pressed the restoration of her name to the Liturgy for the recognition of her rights and vindication of her character and they added that if it could not be granted in substance, an equivalent might be found for it, for instance the recommendation of the Queen to any Court on the Continent. Well then said I, surely the Address of the House of Commons . . . would be at least as good an equivalent as presenting at a foreign state. In truth, it would have been a much better, and Mr Brougham felt so . . .'[18]

The error into which Wilberforce was thus led was a wholly under-standable one. He had worked with Brougham for some sixteen years on slave-trade matters and, despite their differences on other issues, Brougham had always acted in good faith. He was now the Queen's official Attorney General, and was known to have been one of her closest counsellors for several years. Wilberforce could not have known that Brougham was in no position to give the assurance that the Queen would agree to this compromise. The truth was that she was now livid with Brougham on two counts: for trying to dissuade her from coming back to England at the last minute, and for concealing from her the earlier readiness of the cabinet to settle matters broadly on her terms, a fact which her direct contact with Liverpool had now revealed to her. Furthermore, she was buoyed by the ecstatic reception she had received from the crowds, and believed her position to be strengthening. Wilber-force was therefore about to place his parliamentary weight and repu-tation on the line for a delicately constructed compromise proposal with which the Queen did not actually agree.

By Monday, 19 June, Wilberforce believed that his compromise might work, and that in the unrelenting atmosphere of crisis it was his duty to propose it. Rumours continued to circulate of serious discon-tent in the army, notwithstanding the removal of the mutinous Third Foot Guards from London, and troops stationed at Hampton Court were reported to be drinking to the Queen's health. It was not con-sidered over-fanciful around the coffee houses of Westminster that the Queen could actually seize power by force, in the style of Catherine the Great in 1762. On 20 June Wilberforce gave notice that he would move an address to the Queen the following day, but without giving details of what would be in it. The House buzzed with anticipation, and he went home to bed. Unfortunately, 'Just as I was going upstairs to bed last night I heard a knocking about kitchen stairs door and Charles' [the footman] voice "Sir, a letter from the Queen."'[19] This letter, apparently written at the instigation of Alderman Wood, who remained a hard-line advocate of the Queen's cause but without full knowledge of all her past misdemeanours, told Wilberforce that:

The Queen has heard with the greatest surprise and regret that such a religious and worthy character as Mr Wilberforce should have given notice in the House of Commons this evening of his intention to move an Address to Her Majesty; the substance of which she is informed, is to renounce that most important right, of being restored to the Liturgy.

A right which is so justly due to Her Majesty's conscience and her honour, against the foul accusations and slanderous attacks on her character.

Her Majesty assures Mr Wilberforce that she never will abandon this point – as her honour is dearer to her than her life; therefore trusts Mr Wilberforce will take this into his serious consideration and not propose such a motion in the House . . .[20]

Wilberforce managed to sleep well despite the terrible quandary into which he was now placed. The need to postpone moving his much-anticipated motion caused him great embarrassment in the Commons. As the official parliamentary record puts it, 'Mr Wilberforce having been called on by the Speaker, an interval of several minutes elapsed before he made his appearance. When he at length entered the House, he rose and observed, that he should certainly have persevered in bringing the subject of his promised motion before the House that day, but for some cause which it was not in his power to avoid.'[21] One observer noted that the House had been 'as full as it could hold in expectation of Wilberforce's motion . . . Wilberforce called by Speaker – did not appear – at last he came and said he begged to put off his motion until next day . . . There was a cry of No No – but the House finally consented . . . All business at a stand.'[22]

Eventually, following renewed reassurances from Brougham, Wilberforce and his supporting 'Peace Party', led by Stuart Wortley, Henry Bankes and Sir Thomas Dyke Acland, decided to go ahead with a slightly amended motion. Brougham brought Wilberforce a second 'more moderate' letter from the Queen, and on 22 June wrote to him: 'she will accede to your address, I pledge myself'.[23] Emboldened by such powerful reassurance, Wilberforce duly moved his motion that

day in a packed House of Commons. He apologised to the House for the previous day's delay, expressed his awareness 'of the great task which he had undertaken',[24] and declared that 'he was not actuated by feelings of partiality either on one side or the other on this delicate and vastly important question. He only desired most ardently to avoid the opening of that fatal Green Bag.'[25] The commencement of an inquiry was something 'the evils of which could never be overestimated, and which must be productive of the most injurious consequences to all parties concerned in them, as well as to the welfare and morals of the empire at large'.[26]

Opposed by the Queen's ardent adherents, including Brougham, who maintained his public firmness on her behalf while privately negotiating, Wilberforce's motion imploring the Queen to yield on the remaining points at issue was carried by 391 votes to 124 – 'I seldom have known so full a House.'[27] While Wilberforce had acted entirely honourably, and had used his great prestige in the House of Commons to make an attempt at a peaceful accommodation which few others could have mounted, outside the House his motion looked like a further attempt by the political establishment to remove from the Queen what was rightly hers. When Wilberforce, Wortley, Acland and Bankes, attired in full court dress, arrived in a carriage at the Queen's residence on Saturday, 24 June, they were greeted by much hooting and hissing from the crowd. For his efforts, Wilberforce was now popularly known as 'Dr Cantwell', a nickname which was resounding in his ears as he entered the presence of the Queen.

In an upstairs drawing room, Wilberforce and party were presented to Queen Caroline, who was flanked by Brougham, her Attorney General, and Thomas Denman, her Solicitor General. Brougham had drafted her acceptance of the address from the House of Commons, Denman her rejection. It was Denman who prevailed, as Wilberforce recounted to Barbara in a letter later that day: 'I grieve from the bottom of my heart to say that with my brother messengers I am lately returned from our visit to the Queen, bringing back her answer, civil in terms to the House of Commons, but positively rejecting our proposal. Her manner was extremely dignified, but very stern and haughty. There

was a great mob about the door, which if it had been night would have been very dangerous, but no stones were thrown . . .'[28]

The arrival of the MPs back into the street equipped only with the Queen's blunt rejection of their mediation brought much derision and exultation from the crowd outside. Jeered and spat at, Wilberforce retreated from the scene, his careful work of the previous three weeks in ruins. He was disturbed by the obloquy now heaped on him – 'What a lesson it is to a man not to set his heart on low popularity, when after 40 years disinterested public service, I'm believed by the Bulk to be a Hypocritical Rascal!',[29] but on the whole his reaction to the attacks being made on him reflected the healthy philosophical air with which he regarded political misfortune. He wrote to Barbara, who was at Bath with the family:

> I got the nineteen Sunday newspapers once for all the other day, that I might the better judge their contents; and assuredly such a selection of ribaldry and profaneness never before disgraced my library, and I trust never will again. Of course many of the writers honour me with a peculiar share of attention but this will soon blow over, and by and by all the well-disposed part of the community will do me justice, and above all, the Lord will protect. This is as fine a summer's day as I ever knew, and I have been quite delighting in the garden . . .[30]

Adding to the public misunderstanding of his role, Wilberforce never revealed the secret pledge given to him by Brougham, leaving the impression that the motion he had put to the Commons was the product of his own meddling, and that he had had no firm reason for believing it would be accepted. But he seems to have believed that Brougham did his best to persuade the Queen to accept the deal, and it was simply not in his character to make damaging revelations about a colleague in order to save himself from embarrassment. Strikingly for a politician, Wilberforce was not a vengeful or bitter man. History must judge his intervention in the affairs of the Queen far more kindly than did observers at the time. And in the end the big loser from the Queen's rejection of Wilberforce's good offices was the Queen her-

self, for the opportunity to come to a dignified settlement would not recur.

Notwithstanding the virulent hostility of the London mob, the King would now brook no further compromise. On 4 July Lord Liverpool gave notice in the House of Lords of the introduction of a Bill of Pains and Penalties, a proposal to strip the Queen of her title and dissolve her marriage by Act of Parliament. The preamble to the Bill referred to her 'licentious disgraceful and adulterous intercourse' with 'a foreigner of low station'.[31] The procedure for passing such a Bill involved parliamentary hearings to ascertain the truth of the preamble, with witnesses called and counsel heard in the manner of a trial. With the House of Lords due to begin consideration of the Bill in mid-August, waiting for the Italian witnesses to arrive, Members of Parliament began their summer holidays amidst a continued atmosphere of alarm. George Canning, who had regularly flirted with the Queen in her days at Blackheath, but who now remained in the cabinet whilst absenting himself from its decisions – despite the fulminations of the King – wrote that he had left for Italy in early August 'to bring my wife and family safe out of the reach of revolutions'.[32]

Wilberforce chafed at the lack of true religion in the royal family but before setting out for Weymouth to join his wife and children he called on another royal, the Duchess of Kent. She 'received me with her fine animated child on the floor by her with its playthings, of which I soon became one'.[33] This one-year-old child was destined to be Queen Victoria. In late July Wilberforce set off for Weymouth, calling on his way at the home of Henry Bankes and reflecting on the times nearly forty years before when he had stayed there with Pitt and 'the old set'.[34] Within a few days he was on his way back to the capital, noting in his diary that 'the accounts from London are most alarming', and being prodded by a variety of public and private appeals to make a further attempt to reconcile the King and Queen. One of these was an open letter to him from the opposition peer Lord John Russell, published in The Times on 5 August, which said that Wilberforce was the only man in the country who could succeed. Much might Cobbett, one of the Queen's unequivocal supporters, mock the spectacle of 'the proud Whig crawling to the obsolete Saint',[35], but many others thought the same as Russell, with William Lamb – one day to be Prime Minister as Lord Melbourne – writing, 'if anything is to be done, your presence and influence will do it'.[36]

Advised that the fate of the country was in his hands, a worried Wilberforce thought it best to return to London: 'to be told before all the world, that on me and my conduct depend the fate of the Empire, is enough to make a man anxious'.[37] As things turned out, there was nothing to be done there. The King would deal with no one on the matter but his ministers, who were utterly committed to the passage of the Bill of Pains and Penalties. The Queen still enjoyed huge popular support, and was moving into the splendid Brandenburgh House on the Thames near Hammersmith, with Brougham ready to lead her defence in the House of Lords. No compromise was available, and Wilberforce repaired once again to Weymouth, writing to Bankes, 'Alas! Surely we never were in such a scrape',[38] while on 17 August, 258 peers took their seats in the House of Lords for the trial of their Queen.

The 'trial' of Queen Caroline was one of the great set-piece confrontations of British history. The massed ranks of the Lords attended in force at a time of year when they would normally have been reclining in their country estates, observers from all over the world hung on each morsel of news, newspapers printed the proceedings in minute detail, artists were commissioned to paint the scene, and vast crowds gathered outside to plague the arrival of government peers and applaud the almost daily coming and going of the Queen herself. Her first arrival for the proceedings brought 'a universal cheering from a countless multitude',[39] while the Duke of Wellington was heckled: either he or Lord Anglesey is meant to have shouted at the jostling crowd, 'God Save the Queen – and may all your wives be like her.' From the beginning, the poor performance of witnesses meant matters did not go well for the government cause: the one crucial witness who had actually seen the Queen and Pergami in the act of adultery did not come forward until after the trial. The first day's witness, who had produced all the circumstantial evidence of connecting doors, sharing of tents on board ships, and apparent sharing of bathwater, was demolished by Brougham on the second day by being shown to have an unreliable memory for almost any other material facts. Weeks of doubtful evidence produced a conflict in the minds of the Lords between their loyalty to the King and their general assumption that the Queen was guilty of adultery on the one hand, and the obviously doubtful nature of the procedure now being used against 'this defenceless woman', as Brougham put it, on the other. By the time the evidence had been heard and the debate on it begun, the Lord Chancellor was having to admit that some of the endeavours to procure evidence might have been corrupt, while the Whig peer Lord Erskine, despite fainting in the middle of his speech, was able to argue that the whole case had begun in corruption, been carried on by perjury, and if successful would be the triumph of 'foul injustice and cruelty'. The second reading of the Bill was carried by only twenty-eight votes, the third reading by only nine.

Victory for the King by such a narrow majority in the House of Lords was a moral triumph for the Queen, particularly since there was now little prospect that the Bill could make headway in the House of Commons. Cities across Britain exploded in rejoicing, with London experiencing 'all the unmitigated extravagances of a popular triumph; popular meetings, addresses, illuminations, squibs, bonfires, and breaking of windows'.[40] In the minds of the populace, the Queen had been acquitted, and Wilberforce, now at Bath, heard the news as coaches arrived from London covered in white ribbons to celebrate her victory. For several weeks the political crisis seemed to intensify. The Queen had become identified with radical politics, and appealed directly to the people of the country. Canning had resigned from the government, unable any longer to sit on both sides of the fence. The King fumed and threatened to abdicate, while once again being unable to dismiss his ministers because Grenville would not accept the poisoned chalice of bringing the opposition to power at such a time. At the end of November a huge celebration was held at St Paul's Cathedral in honour of the Queen, a crowd of fifty thousand cheering her on. Wilberforce returned to London with foreboding, wishing that he 'had anything to call me away' from the House of Commons.[41]

Although Queen Caroline had won a political and moral triumph, her earlier unwillingness to compromise meant that in reality she was no further forward than before. The King had failed to destroy her, but her name was still not restored to the Liturgy, and she was running short of funds since the financial settlement the government had proposed would only come into force when she left the country. The celebrations at St Paul's would prove to be the high-water mark of her political appeal, since events were soon to prove, just as earlier moments of popular disturbance and discontent the previous year and in the 1790s had suggested, that the British population was more stable and the British state more solid than many observers and even its leaders had a tendency to think. As the controversy over the Bill of Pains and Penalties receded and the general state of the country improved, so the agitation in support of the Queen began to diminish. In a final attempt to help a negotiated end to the matter, Wilberforce spoke and voted on 13 February 1821 in favour of the restoration of her name to the Liturgy, but found the majority of the House of Commons firmly against him. At the beginning of March, the Queen accepted an increase in her annuity from the cabinet to £50,000, notwithstanding her previous insistence that she would only take more money if her name was included in the Liturgy. Her popularity collapsed. Additionally, the beginning of an economic recovery that year reduced the general discontent for which she had provided a rallying-point. She ceased to be a royal champion in the eyes of the people, and was seen as yet another money-grabbing public figure.

Wilberforce, ever the conciliator, suggested to ministers that the King now generously give the Queen liturgical recognition as a matter of grace and favour, but George IV had not come this far through the crisis to give any ground now. The Queen's attempt further to improve her financial settlement by threatening to attend the coronation, much postponed but finally set for 19 July 1821, did not faze the King or cabinet.

Wilberforce was more worried than most about what might happen, writing to his son Robert about whether he should see the splendid event, 'probably if I were your age I should like to witness it. I have but one objection which I do not like to state to your mother. I shall not be at all surprised if there is some visit on the Queen's account then the troops will be called to quell it and I suppose they should refuse to act against the populace. There is no saying what the consequences might be. Do not even, I beg of you, mention this apprehension to anyone, still less mention its having been suggested by me.'[42]

In reality the Queen's power had gone. Arriving at Westminster Hall on the morning of the coronation and uttering to the sentry her tragic cry, 'Let me pass; I am your Queen,'[43] she found only that the pages slammed the door in her face. Her attempt to enter Westminster Abbey itself was also repelled, the fickle crowd hissing her as she disappeared and cheering the newly-crowned King George IV as he emerged resplendent from the ceremony. Utterly broken, she soon fell ill, and on 7 August she was dead. The King heard the news as he prepared to embark on a ship for Dublin. Arriving there the next morning he told his first, rather embarrassed, audience that it was 'one of the happiest moments of my life'.[44]

Just as the nation and the royal family were buffeted by crises at the beginning of the 1820s, so Wilberforce himself would experience in these years more loss, sorrow and misfortune than he had ever previously known. One growing preoccupation for him was the indolence and ill-discipline of his eldest son, William – 'I fear he has no energy of character or solid principle of action,' Wilberforce confided to his diary.[45] Like the other children, William had been educated at home, but even the best efforts of the young Oxford clergyman who was his tutor produced in him no particular religious inclination and no aptitude for the one career Wilberforce had in mind for his sons, that of the cloth.

By 1816, when William was eighteen years old, Wilberforce wrote, 'O my heart is quite sick about William, and that while there are some good traits, there should be such sad qualities. O how much I see the effects of our own indulgence, selfishness in one form or another, his grand vice.'[46] Despite his own closeness to Cambridge, or perhaps because of his own youthful experiences there, Wilberforce formed a view that the appropriate place for the instilling of religion and discipline into his sons was Oriel College, Oxford. The second and third sons, Robert and Samuel, would eventually gain admission and do well there, but no place at Oriel could be found for William as he turned nineteen in the summer of 1817. He was sent instead to Trinity College, Cambridge, where his habits did not improve. He did not read much, dissipated the generous allowance he received from his father, and was easily taken advantage of by other undergraduates who enjoyed making use of his money and tarnishing the Wilberforce reputation. In January 1819 Wilberforce was bemoaning the fact that William 'was buying another horse for sixty guineas and not behaving well about it thou' I most honourably to him'.[47] Advised by Henry Venn, son of John Venn, that he should withdraw William from college rather than let him become licentious and corrupted, he decided to cancel his allowance to teach him a lesson. William seemed to accept this with good grace; he was always 'very kind and attentive' to his father, and for a moment seemed to have learnt his lesson.[48] But events at the end of March that year were to be the last straw: William had become utterly drunk on a Sunday evening, forced his presence on friends who were 'piously disposed',[49] ignored the fact that the body of one of his good friends was lying in the neighbouring set of rooms awaiting the funeral the next day, and then told lies about the whole incident afterwards. It would have been difficult to come up with a set of misdemeanours more offensive to his father, and William found himself removed from Cambridge, with Wilberforce noting with some anguish in his diary, 'O my poor Willm. How strange he can make so miserable those who love him best and whom really he loves.'[50]

William was sent to study under the stricter and lonelier regime of John Owen, the secretary of the Bible Society. The affection between father and son was undiminished, and possibly even strengthened by what had happened. At the beginning of 1820 William married Owen's daughter Mary. Wilberforce could console himself with the thought that his eldest son could still have a happy future, albeit not the one he originally had in mind. Not suspecting the disasters that William could still inflict on his father and family, Wilberforce was temporarily able to consider his son well settled.

By the time of William's marriage, Wilberforce was facing much sorrow in other ways. His great friend Isaac Milner, whose companionship and intellect had turned him to religion, came to stay at Kensington Gore that February, but fell ill and was soon dying. Wilberforce spent many hours with his friend in the last few weeks of his life and, as ever, was equable and thankful when confronted by the death of those close to him: 'Never was there an easier dismission, which is the more observable because he had fears of the pain of dying; when he was told he was in danger he grew more composed and calm than he had been before. It is very odd, but I felt rather stunned than melted. Spent the morning, after a short prayer, chiefly in writing to different friends.'[51]

At the same time, Wilberforce's own advancing years began to tell. His brother-in-law, William Spooner, wrote to Lord Calthorpe in May 1821, 'I do not hear without pain the reports from various quarters of the very ill looks of Mr Wilberforce. He is very generally thought to be greatly aged of late; and much less adequate to Parliamentary fatigues. My sister has kept him at Bath as long as she could; ... she returns to London with many uneasy apprehensions and her fears are extremely in accordance with the remarks of various friends who have seen him lately.'[52] At nearly sixty-two years of age and with a constitution that had never been strong, Wilberforce was in all probability suffering from the effects of decades of opium consumption as well as the chronic complaints of bowels, lungs and spine. His eyes were now so bad that it was difficult for him to read or work without help; when his secretary was late one day that February he complained that 'it is a sad business to have my eyes in another person's keeping'.[53] Illness kept him away from the Commons a good deal in the spring, and although he was full of thankfulness as usual for his eventual recovery, remembering that his imminent demise had been foretold by his doctor thirty-three years before, he noted that he should always be ready for death from now on: 'How wonderful is it that I continue unto this day! But I shall probably have little warning: let me remember therefore Christ's admonition, "Be ye also ready".'[54]

Yet to add to his trials that year it would not be his own death he had to face, but that of one of his children. His eldest daughter Barbara had fallen ill with consumption in the summer of 1820. After a brief recovery, she was very ill again by September 1821. Wilberforce had spent much time with her, often long into the night. When she died on 30 December, at the age of twenty-two, he was once again fortified by his faith, writing to his friend John Harford, 'Blessed be God, the pain of the stroke was alleviated by many gracious mitigations – above all, by the assured persuasion Mrs W and I have been able to indulge that our dear child has gone to a better world.' He thought his daughter's patience and confidence in the face of great suffering had been 'delightful evidence of her being prepared for the great change',[55] and 'the assured persuasion of Barbara's happiness has taken away the sting of death'.[56]

Barbara was at Stephen's house in London when she died, so she could be close to good medical attention, for by that time Wilberforce had been through the further sorrow of selling Kensington Gore, instead taking a lease on a house at Marden Park in Surrey, fifteen miles south of Westminster. Although no note seems to have survived of his feelings at the time, he cannot have been happy to leave a house that suited him so well, and where the garden and nightingales were such a joy to him. But the sad truth was that the financial burden of such a large house had become too great to him: the man who had always had more than enough money was now having to retrench. His combination of generosity to his sons, philanthropy to all and sundry, maintenance of servants who were no longer useful, lowering of rents on properties he owned, and inattention to investments which were often mismanaged by his friends and family, meant that the considerable fortune he had inherited was much reduced.

Surrounded, then, in 1821 by the death of loved ones, his own frailty and diminishing finances, Wilberforce could have been forgiven some sadness or disillusionment. He did indeed remark to one of his sons at about this time, 'My dear boy, do not be a politician; it is the most unprofitable of all subjects; it has been my business and my life, but I hope that you are meant for something better.'[57] Yet such was his natural optimism and his burning faith that on the day of his daughter's funeral, once he had said goodbye to her coffin and to his friends, he retreated to a small room at the top of his stairs and made a list of the many blessings of his life. These, he said, 'have been of every kind, and of long continuance', including 'a kindly natural temper, a plentiful fortune' and his being a Member of Parliament for so many years, 'my being made the instrument of bringing forward the Abolition; my helping powerfully the cause of Christianity in India; my never having been discredited, but being always supported on public occasions'. He was thankful for marrying as late as his thirties, 'yet finding one of the most affectionate of wives', for having children, 'all of them attached to me beyond measure', for having 'so many kind friends', and for the fact that 'the great and noble now all treat me with respect, because they see I am independent of them'. Above all, he noted down his thankfulness for 'having been rendered the instrument of much spiritual good by my work on Christianity', and alongside his thanks to God finished with his desire 'more than I ever yet have done to dedicate my faculties to Thy glory and service'.[58] His work was not yet done.

Efforts to suppress the illegal slave trade had ground on into the 1820s. In 1818, faced with the continued smuggling of thousands of slaves each year into the United States from Spanish-held Florida and islands off the coast of Honduras, the US Congress had passed an Anti-Slaving Act, increasing the penalties for the smuggling of slaves and improving the rewards for informers. In 1820, President Monroe went further, for the first time dispatching American forces to another continent by sending a small flotilla of warships to the coast of West Africa to intercept American vessels illegally purchasing slaves. Most of the ships concerned still flew Spanish flags, but some of them were indeed captured, amidst hearty cooperation between the American and British navies. But suspicion of British intentions and entrenched American hostility to any British right to search American ships continued to prevent any agreement between the two countries involving a mutual right of search, the one thing that would have allowed the Royal Navy to deliver a death blow to the illegal American trade. Even though a committee of the House of Representatives recommended such an agreement in 1820 and again in 1821, these proposals became lost without much trace in the Senate. Most estimates suggest that between American abolition of the slave trade in 1807 and the beginning of the Civil War in 1861, some fifty thousand slaves were imported into the United States in defiance of the law.

The limited American initiatives to act against the trade earned some praise from Wilberforce when he rose in the House of Commons on 26 June 1821 – fully thirty-two years after his first parliamentary onslaught on the slave trade – to propose an Address to the King condemning the European nations for their continuing toleration of the trade and calling for more effective international action against it. While praising Castlereagh's efforts as Foreign Secretary, he told the House that 'notwithstanding all the steps which had been taken, however, he was sorry to say that the slave trade was still carried on to an immense extent, and in many instances with a degree of barbarity sufficient to exhaust human suffering on the one hand, and human cruelty on the other'.[59] A mutual right of search among all nations was what was needed, for the commitment of Spain and Portugal to their treaties was doubtful, and as for the French, 'it was impossible, indeed, for any man acquainted with the character of the French, not to feel extremely disappointed at the disposition of that people to persevere in this odious traffic, after it was abandoned by England, and its nefarious practices were universally proclaimed'.[60] French slaving ships had recently been discovered from which slaves, in a haunting reminder of the *Zong*, had been stowed in casks and thrown overboard in order to avoid search parties. So although Britain had destroyed its slave trade, Wilberforce appealed to the Commons that 'the work of humanity and justice must still be incomplete while the other nations were engaged in it'.[61]

Wilberforce was no longer in daily attendance in the House of Commons, and his illness in the spring of 1821 had kept him away from it for some weeks, but he continued to speak on a wide range of subjects, and to show a level of activity which would have put many younger Members to shame. Having only recently emerged from the trauma of the debates on Queen Caroline, he was to be heard in the Commons in 1821 calling for the punishments for the crime of forgery to be made less harsh, for the size of the army to be reduced, and, remounting an old hobbyhorse, for fresh efforts to be made to prevent the burning of Hindu widows in India. The following year he was speaking up for the beleaguered Christians of Greece and, becoming unusually bellicose, calling on the powers of Europe to drive back the Turks, 'a nation of barbarians, the ancient and inveterate enemies of Christianity and freedom, into Asia'.[62] He intervened frequently on a Bill regulating colonial trade to ensure that none of its provisions would make easier the illicit trading of slaves, and he mounted a major effort in July 1822 to persuade the government to investigate and extinguish the emerging signs of slavery in new settlements being founded at the Cape of Good Hope, the future South Africa. In words all too prophetic of the late twentieth century he warned that any distinctions between Europeans and other races there would create 'dangerous animosities', and 'the growth of mutual goodwill and civilisation must be materially obstructed' by them.[63]

Whilst still performing this vigilant parliamentary patrolling of all issues and laws connected to the slave trade, Wilberforce knew that his days at the head of the anti-trade campaign were almost over. He still worked hard at it: dictating letters to leading Frenchmen about their numerous illegal traders – 'the common pests of mankind';[64] preparing a fresh pamphlet to Tsar Alexander to be distributed to all the members of parliament in France, Spain, Portugal and Belgium; endlessly lobbying Castlereagh and Liverpool; writing to members of the US Congress; yet nevertheless always wishing he could do more – 'it is vexatious beyond measure to have my time frittered away, but my eyes are the chief hindrance'.[65] He rejoiced when the Spanish Cortes legislated for severe penalties against slave traders: 'I really have not for years received such welcome intelligence. Thank God for disposing the hearts of the Spaniards for this act of mercy.'[66] But he knew that the state of his eyes and his health meant that such activity could not long be continued, and he knew too something he had not known at the time of Abolition in 1807: that the difficulties of enforcing a ban on slave trading were so great, and the mistreatment of slaves in the plantations was so prevalent, that these horrors could only be finally extinguished through the abolition of slavery itself.

To destroy slavery altogether would require a fresh campaign and a great deal of time – Wilberforce himself continued to believe that freedom for the slaves could only come about in stages, with education, religion and morality instituted among them in advance of complete liberation. Reflecting at Bath in 1820, he had considered 'five or six years' to be the maximum remaining time for which he could be useful in the House of Commons, 'yet I should greatly like to lay a foundation for some future measures for the emancipation of the poor slaves'.[67] By the end of 1822, his language concerning this hope was becoming more that of action: 'my conscience reproaches me with having too long suffered this horrible evil to go on. We must now call upon all good men throughout the kingdom to join us in abolishing this wicked system, and striving to render the degraded race by degrees a free peasantry. O may God bless our attempt.'[68] Seeing that this was a campaign he himself would be unlikely to complete, he carefully and deliberately devolved the future leadership of it onto one of his colleagues. Those who had worked loyally with him over the decades – Stephen, Bankes, William Smith – were also too old, so Wilberforce's choice fell on Fowell Buxton, still in his mid-thirties.

Buxton was still inexperienced in Parliament, and was no man of means, but he had the great merits of being an Evangelical who was eloquent and fearless. He had impressed Wilberforce with his denunciations of the penal code and the excessive use of capital punishment, and impressed him still more when he attended a meeting of the African Institution in January 1821 and attacked its ineffectiveness. Wilberforce, he recalled, 'thanked me for the boldness and openness of my remarks and said they had penetrated deeply into his heart'.[69] Rather than taking offence at the criticism, Wilberforce wrote to Buxton that May to ask for his assurance that in the war for the emancipation of the slaves,

If I should be unable to commence the War (certainly not to be declared in this Session) and still more, if commenced, I should (as certainly would, I fear be the case) be unable to finish it you would kindly continue to prosecute it. Your assurance to this effect would give me the greatest pleasure, pleasure is a bad term, let me rather say peace and consolation; for alas my friend I feel but too deeply how little I have been duly assiduous and faithful in employing the talents committed to my stewardship ... Both my head and heart are quite full to overflowing, but besides that my eyes are tired, the time which by snatches I have seized amidst continuing interruptions for penning this hasty scrawl all gone and I must conclude. Let me then intreat you to form an alliance with me, that may truly be termed *Holy*.[70]

Buxton took his time about deciding whether to accede to this request, but by the end of 1822 he was ready to do so. By then some progress against the slave trade had been made, this time by France, where the government had begun to make denunciations of the trade, and even to take modest action against it. Attempting to follow up this advantage, Wilberforce engaged in feverish lobbying of the British government to make measures against the slave trade a key point at the forthcoming international congress which was to be held at Verona, and to put pressure on the French government to allow 'the fair use of the press for enlightening the public mind'.[71] He continued to fire off letters in the summer of 1822, while reliving his old summer tours of stately houses on a progress which led him once more to Rothley Temple and Yoxall Lodge.

As he travelled that summer, the talk of his hosts and the political world would have been dominated by one event: Castlereagh, Foreign Secretary for the last ten years, had committed suicide. Overworked and seemingly mentally unbalanced in the final weeks of his life, he was also being blackmailed over a homosexual episode. Wilberforce wrote that he 'never was so shocked by any incident'.[72] Castlereagh had been a reluctant convert to the cause of abolition, but in recent years had won the praise of Wilberforce and Brougham for his steady determination to destroy the slave trade in his negotiations with the other powers. His suicide, coming on top of the similar fate of other MPs Wilberforce admired – Whitbread and Romilly – had, Wilberforce told Bankes, 'strongly enforced on my mind the unspeakable benefit of the institution of the Lord's Day . . . I am persuaded that to withdraw the mind one day in seven from its ordinary trains of thought and passion, and to occupy it in contemplating subjects of a higher order, which by their magnitude make worldly interests shrink into littleness, has the happiest effect on the intellectual and moral system. It gives us back on the Monday to the contemplation of our week-day business cooled and quieted, and it is to be hoped with resentments abated and prejudices softened.'[73]

Castlereagh was replaced as Foreign Secretary by his arch-rival George Canning, Wilberforce's friend for nearly thirty years on the basis of their mutual closeness to Pitt and united hostility to the slave trade. Canning found within weeks that among the penalties of being Foreign Secretary was to be bombarded with letters from Wilberforce. One of the first matters with which he had to deal was the prospect of Brazilian independence, first broached with him unofficially in November 1822. Asked by Wilberforce whether he would acknowledge Brazilian independence, Canning replied, 'Shall we be justified in making the Abolition of the Slave Trade by Brazil a *sine qua non* condition of any such acknowledgement? I incline to think so.'[74] In the event, Brazilian reluctance to embrace immediate abolition meant that it was delayed long after independence in 1823, with a consequent delay in British recognition and a vast Cuban-style upsurge in slave imports through the late 1820s in anticipation of the legal trade coming to an end.

There was little more that Canning could have done to bring about instant abolition by Brazil. His heart was in the right place, and he allowed Wilberforce to know the details of many international negotiations, as well as dealing with his plethora of requests for other efforts and interventions, particularly to secure toleration for Protestants in South America and northern Italy. Progress was certainly being made in destroying the slave trade, but with the Congress of Verona failing to adopt any further practical measures, the abolitionists were disappointed in the achievements of the government, and further fortified in their view that emancipation must now be the goal.

For some years ministers had remonstrated with Wilberforce to hold back on pressing for emancipation so as not to prejudice their efforts to win greater international agreement on the trade. Now the abolitionists all believed that the time for waiting was over, and Wilberforce's sense of guilt that he had not previously mounted an all-out assault on slavery grew stronger. He set to work on an anti-slavery manifesto, although, failing to complete it when he had hoped at the end of January 1823, he wrote to Thomas Babington, 'I am become heavy and lumbering, and not able at once to start into a canter, as I could twenty years ago. Happily, it is a good road and in a right direction.'[75]

When it was finished, Wilberforce's *Appeal to the Religion, Justice, and Humanity of the Inhabitants of the British Empire, in behalf of the Negro Slaves in the West Indies* was distributed throughout Britain, and was the call summoning the abolitionists to their last great campaign. By the time it was published, Thomas Clarkson had distributed his own anti-slavery tract, and the Anti-Slavery Society had been founded on 31 January with the Duke of Gloucester as President. As Wilberforce, in his sixty-fourth year, hoped that 'he might yet live to see the fruit of his present labours',[76] the campaign to abolish slavery throughout the whole of the British Empire had begun.

18

'An Increase of Enjoyments'

——————=:Oɪ=——————

We have indeed the prospect of brave and able recruits to fill our
ranks, but the guiding spirit will long be missed.

William Smith on the retirement of Wilberforce, 1825[1]

I am a bee which has lost its sting.

WILLIAM WILBERFORCE, 1827[2]

T HE ANTI-SLAVERY MANIFESTO published by Wilberforce in
1823 called on his fellow Britons 'to commence, without delay, the
preparatory measures for putting an end to a national crime of the
deepest moral malignity'.[3] Before coming to its stirring conclusion –
'justice, humanity, and sound policy prescribe our course . . . our
exertions will be ardent, and our perseverance invincible'[4] – he admitted that the abolitionists had been too sanguine about the effects of
the abolition of the slave trade on the behaviour of the West Indian
colonies: 'We judged too favourably of human nature; we thought too
well of the colonial assemblies; we did not allow weight enough to the
effects of rooted prejudice and inveterate habits.'[5]

For the abolitionists, it was now established fact that the colonial
legislatures could never be relied upon to take measures to improve
the welfare of slaves, or to do anything that would begin to elevate
them from their degrading status. Wilberforce evinced no doubt in his
manifesto that a deliberate programme leading to the end of all slavery
on British territory must be instigated by the Westminster Parliament.

Yet again, however, he had come to this conclusion well before senior ministers and many other MPs were prepared to support it. As a result, the earlier appeals to bring an end to slavery received a mixed reception in the House of Commons and a sympathetic but ineffective response from the government of the day, in exact parallel to the early appeals against the slave trade thirty-four years earlier. Parliamentary apathy and delaying tactics would once again be the chief obstacles in the way of the abolitionist cause.

On 18 March 1823 it was Wilberforce, rising in the Commons to present a petition from the Quakers, who delivered the first considered parliamentary assault on the very existence of slavery. Although he noted afterwards that 'fatigue rather stupefied me, and I forgot the most important points',[6] his speech was nonetheless clear and powerful. He said that he regretted 'that he had not before now attempted to put an end, not merely to the evils of the slave trade, but to the evils of slavery itself';[7] explained that their hopes for more care to be taken with the health and religious instruction of the slaves had been dashed; countenanced if necessary the payment of compensation to slave-owners when the slaves were emancipated; and told the Commons with his customary eloquence that it was 'an extraordinary anomaly, that the freest nation that ever existed on the face of the earth ... in which the blessings of equal law were extended to the whole community – that such a country should be chargeable with the guilt and inconsistency of allowing slavery in any place under its control'.[8]

What happened next left Wilberforce fuming: 'Never almost in my life was I so vexed by a parliamentary proceeding.'[9] Canning simply refused to engage in the debate. He enquired as to whether Wilberforce was putting down a specific motion for abolition, and then sat down, catching the abolitionists unprepared and allowing the next parliamentary business to commence. For decades Canning had been a zealous supporter of the abolition of the trade, but as Foreign Secretary he was in a difficult position once the arguments moved on to slavery itself: lack of agreement within the cabinet, shortage of funds to pay the compensation that might be required, and an unwillingness to provoke a total upheaval in the West Indian colonies, with unknowable economic consequences, all played their part.

By the time the abolitionists secured a full-scale debate on slavery, on 15 May 1823, with Fowell Buxton taking the lead, Canning was ready with an alternative proposal. Even though Wilberforce, who made a lengthy attack on slavery in the debate, argued that all experience showed that the colonial legislatures would not embark on reform of their own accord, Canning was able to persuade the House to adopt a set of resolutions calling on the colonies to take measures to ameliorate the condition of their slave populations, and ultimately looking forward to 'a progressive improvement in the character of the slave population, such as may prepare them for participation in their civil rights and privileges which are enjoyed in other classes of His Majesty's subjects'.[10] In one sense this was an important advance, for the government and Parliament had now admitted that action needed to be taken, and 'looked forward' to the eventual destruction of slavery. On the other hand, that was left as a very distant prospect, and the measures to be taken in the meantime were still entrusted to colonial legislatures, among which the slave-owners were still predominant.

Wilberforce's reaction was to continue to express great scepticism that the colonies would do anything, but to think that the debate had performed a 'good service'.[11] In any case, as he admitted to his diary, the abolitionists did not at that stage command sufficient votes to achieve any more.

With the chances of passing a parliamentary motion explicitly calling for abolition as soon as possible thus blocked, May 1823 saw the abolitionists outmanoeuvred by Canning. They would be attacked, and repeatedly so, by later commentators for being insufficiently radical or effective. Buxton's motion had called for slavery to be gradually abolished, albeit as quickly as slaves could be made ready for freedom and plantation-owners could be compensated or otherwise adjust to the change. That the abolitionists themselves were at this stage only in favour of a gradual emancipation can seem surprising to later generations. Wilberforce's own detestation of slavery cannot be doubted: 'a system of the grossest injustice, of the most heathenish irreligion and immorality, of the most unprecedented degradation, and unrelenting cruelty'[12] is how he had described it in his manifesto. Yet he had been clear at every point that he thought its destruction would have to take place in stages.

Why did Wilberforce advocate gradual rather than immediate abolition of slavery? Part of the answer lies in the importance he attached to the slaves having been left destitute of religion: 'though many of the physical evils of our colonial slavery are cruel and odious, and pernicious, the almost universal destitution of religious and moral instruction among the slaves is the most serious of all the vices of the West Indian system'.[13] For Wilberforce, this was the ultimate condemnation of the system, as it left the slaves 'practically strangers to the multiplied blessings of the Christian Revelation'.[14] Having maintained for forty years that the people of Britain needed stronger religious and moral guidance, Wilberforce clearly believed that this applied all the more to people who had enjoyed little exposure to Christian teaching, and his view that this was so may have been reinforced by the somewhat chequered histories of Haiti and Sierra Leone.

In addition, there were other factors which caused the entire abolitionist leadership, including Fowell Buxton and Thomas Clarkson, to adopt a gradualist agenda. The assumption they had adopted from the very beginning of their efforts in 1787 (Buxton obviously excepted) was that the abolition of slavery was a vastly more difficult undertaking even than the abolition of the slave trade. Their twenty-year struggle to secure legislation against the trade would inevitably have led them to think that the immediate abolition of slavery would be too frightening, too expensive and too dramatic to succeed. The initial reaction of Parliament and government would have confirmed that impression. They were used to inching their way forward in a conservative political world and, being predominately old men with nearly forty years of unchanging methods and procedures behind them, could not appreciate how much that world was about to change.

A final factor would have been that the vituperative attacks made on them for proposing the abolition of slavery could not have left them feeling anything other than timid. In August 1823, William Cobbett penned the most excoriating of his onslaughts on Wilberforce. Cobbett was particularly enraged that Wilberforce persisted in calling for the slaves to be given the freedoms and privileges of British labourers, and his attack on Wilberforce's manifesto did not mince words: 'There is a great deal of canting trash; a great deal of lying; a great deal of that cool impudent falsehood for which the Quakers are famed; a monstrous quantity of hypocrisy is there evident in these seventy-seven pages of yours.'[15] He attacked Wilberforce as 'a most consummate hypocrite . . . have you, Wilberforce, have you ever done anything to mitigate the laws which exist in this country with regard to those free British labourers with which you so cantingly talk? Never have you done one single act, in favour of the labourers of this country.'[16] Wilberforce had argued that the killing of slaves went unpunished. Cobbett's response was Peterloo:

> this [the killing of slaves] is perfectly damnable, to be sure: this is tyranny: here is horrible slavery: the tyrants ought to be stricken down by thunderbolts, or to be otherwise destroyed. But, Wilberforce, listen to me a bit; did you ever hear of a parcel of people, who were assembled at Manchester on 16 August 1819. These were persons whom you call free British labourers. Well, then, these labourers had not run away from any masters. They had committed no crimes or misdemeanours towards their masters. About five hundred of them were, nevertheless, killed or wounded . . . and pray, Wilberforce, was anybody punished for killing and wounding them? Did anybody pay any fines for killing and wounding these free British labourers? Were not those who committed the killing and wounding thanked for their good conduct on that occasion? Did you ever object to those thanks? Did you not object to any parliamentary enquiry into the conduct of those who caused that killing and wounding? . . . You make your appeal in Piccadilly, London, amongst those who are wallowing in luxuries, proceeding from the labour of the people. You should have gone to the gravel-pits, and made your appeal to the wretched creatures with bits of sacks round their shoulders and with haybands round their legs; you should have gone to the roadside, and made your appeal to the emaciated, half-dead things who are

there cracking stones as level as a die for the tax-eaters to ride on. What an insult it is, and what an unfeeling, what a cold-blooded hypocrite must he be that can send it forth . . .[17]

In summary:

> you seem to have a great affection for the fat and lazy and laughing and singing and dancing Negroes; . . . I feel for the care-worn, the ragged, the hard-pinched, the ill-treated, and beaten down and trampled upon labouring classes of England, Scotland and Ireland to whom . . . you do all the mischief that it is in your power to do; because you describe their situation as being good, and because you do, at any rate, draw the attention from their sufferings.[18]

Furthermore, Wilberforce and Buxton soon found that a slave insurrection in Demerara that year was blamed on them. Following up Canning's resolutions in the House of Commons the Colonial Secretary, Lord Bathurst, had told the Governor of this particular colony that the planters could no longer use whips to drive the slaves in their fields. This order created great consternation: first among the planters, who held anxious meetings about how they would maintain their authority; and then among the slaves, who got wind of the fact that the planters were trying to deny them a measure of freedom granted in Westminster. The result was a full-scale revolt that August by thirteen thousand slaves, which was eventually suppressed with much brutality, including many hangings.

To opponents of abolition, the Demerara revolt was further evidence that the abolitionists were putting lives at risk by raising the slaves' hopes for emancipation. Wilberforce received one three-word letter which simply read 'thou vile hypocrite'.[19] Zachary Macaulay told him that even Canning's private secretary had stated that 'the insurrection in Demerara had been instigated by Wilberforce, Buxton, and co.'.[20] To the abolitionists, by contrast, the revolt demonstrated that the government and the colonies were proceeding in an incompetent way. As Macaulay explained, 'the whip is the grand badge of slavery and the apprehension of the slaves, who feel it as the prominent mark of their servile state; its removal would naturally be but another name for emancipation. Our plan was certainly of a very different kind. They should have begun by all those reforms which would have had a wonderful influence, without seeming directly and suddenly to weaken the Masters' authority.'[21]

Wilberforce very much agreed with Macaulay's assessment, recommending that the abolitionists counterattack and blame the government directly for the insurrection. He argued that measures taken to improve the conditions of the slaves should be properly explained to them, and that the removal of the whip from the fields need not have meant the destruction of all authority if the slaves still knew that they could be flogged afterwards, at night. This recommendation has been used to mock Wilberforce, and further to imply that he was not really interested in freedom for the slaves. It must, however, be understood in its context: Wilberforce was arguing that the Demerara revolt could have been prevented, at a time when the practical reality was that slavery was still very much in existence. He had spoken of his abhorrence of the use of the whip on countless occasions, and in his manifesto had set out to destroy the argument 'that without the driving whip' the slaves 'never would willingly engage in agricultural labour'.[22] He was no advocate of the whip, or defender of any of the degrading practices of slavery.

While the gradual abolitionists and their opponents indulged in a war of words over the Demerara revolt, its eventual irony was that it undermined the arguments of both sides, and helped to pave the way for rapid emancipation. For one thing, it showed that the slaves were increasingly ready to take matters into their own hands, a fact which Wilberforce used to full effect in a further Commons debate on 16 March 1824, albeit still in the context of arguing for gradual abolition. He told the House that 'they were now standing on the brink of a precipice, and if they did not take great care, they would find that the more they paused, the less energetic they were, the greater was the danger likely to become'.[23] The slaves, 'despairing of relief from the British Parliament . . . would take the cause into their own hands, and endeavour to affect their own liberation'.[24] It would now be very foolish to proceed only with 'hesitating steps'.[25]

In addition, Demerara created a martyr for the abolitionist cause, in the form of John Smith, a non-conformist missionary based on one of the plantations where the revolt had started. Accused of having had full knowledge of the uprising but of having done nothing to alert the authorities, he was arrested, tried by court martial, convicted and sentenced to death. Although he was likely to have been reprieved by the London government, he died in prison, and his case helped to galvanise abolitionist opinion and to expose the arbitrary nature of law enforcement in the colonies. Wilberforce noted in his diary, 'Poor Smith the missionary died in prison at Demerara! The day of reckoning will come.'[26]

In June 1824 the Smith case brought Wilberforce to the Commons for one of his last parliamentary speeches. In late March and April he had been seriously ill with pneumonia. Confined to his bed for some weeks, he wrote to his son Henry that 'Your dear mother so strenuously resisted my taking up my pen that I began to be afraid I should lose the faculty of writing. Indeed my life has been to a great degree of the animalised kind – eating drinking airing napping being its *daily business*.'[27] Nevertheless, on 11 June he was back on his feet in the Commons, attacking the trial of Smith by court martial and the prejudices of the planters, and telling MPs that they themselves were now on trial, for 'by our decision on the present question men will judge'.[28] It was, however, far from one of his finest speeches, and he knew it, noting that, 'I quite forgot my topics for a speech, and made sad work of it . . . I greatly doubt if I had not better give up taking part in the House of Commons.'[29]

The end of Wilberforce's parliamentary career was approaching. Four days after disappointing himself with his speech on Smith, he returned to the House to present a petition for the abolition of slavery from the town of Carlow in Ireland. His remarks on this petition would turn out to be the last of his many hundreds of parliamentary interventions over forty-five years as an MP, but neither he nor his hearers knew that at the time. He attacked the way in which Demerara, Barbados and Jamaica were being administered, and told Canning that his plan of relying on the colonies to improve matters, 'which depends for its success on the members on the West Indian legislatures gradually laying aside their prejudices ... is fundamentally hopeless; the expectation appears to me utterly vain'.[30] Parliament had to act: 'let but the Imperial legislature assume its proper tone, and maintain its just authority ... and you will soon witness with delight the accomplishment of your benevolent purposes'.[31] The next day he attended the founding meeting of the Society for the Prevention of Cruelty to Animals. The following week he was present at the first-anniversary meeting of the Anti-Slavery Society at the Freemasons' Hall. It was an occasion which symbolised more than any other that the leadership of the anti-slavery campaign was beginning to pass to a new generation.

The packed meeting was electrified by the speech of Zachary Macaulay's son Thomas Babington Macaulay, a recent Cambridge graduate who would become one of the great historians of the nineteenth century, whose denunciation of the colonies, according to Marianne Thornton, caused such an ovation that 'the very walls seemed to be coming down with the thunders of applause'.[32] The contrast between 'the young Alexander',[33] as Wilberforce described him, and Wilberforce's own hunched and ageing figure must have been stark. He summoned up the mood in his own speech: 'We have been engaged in many a long and arduous contest, and we also have had to contend with calumny and falsehood. But we are more than repaid, by the success that has already attended our efforts, and by the anticipations which we may derive from what we have witnessed this very day, when, if our sun be setting, we see that other luminaries are arising to shine with far greater lustre and more efficient strength.'[34]

At the same time, far beyond the gatherings of distinguished figures in London halls, the nature of the anti-slavery campaign was beginning to change. Clarkson reported from his tours that 'everywhere People are asking me about *immediate abolition*, and whether that would not be the best'.[35] There was a growing demand for West Indian sugar to be avoided, and an emerging groundswell of opposition to slavery among people otherwise uninvolved in political affairs. One of them was Elizabeth Heyrick, a former schoolteacher who published a well-argued and crisply written pamphlet on *Immediate, not Gradual Aboli-*

tion, in which she stated that 'the abolitionists have shown a great deal too much politeness and accommodation' towards the West Indian planters. While paying due credit to Wilberforce, Clarkson and their colleagues for what they had achieved, she attacked their caution. That 'they should "fear where no fear is", should swallow the bait, so manifestly laid to draw them aside from their great object; that they should be so credulous, so easily imposed upon, is marvellous'.[36] Maintaining that the abstinence of one-tenth of the inhabitants of Britain from West Indian sugar would lead to the collapse of slavery, she called on people to take matters into their own hands, and for Parliament forthwith to 'break the iron yoke from off the neck of our own slaves ... Then, and not till then, we shall speak to the surrounding nations with the awe-commanding eloquence of sincerity and truth and our persuasions will be backed by the irresistible argument of consistent example.'[37]

Heyrick was one of a number of women who waged active campaigns against slavery in the 1820s, with women's societies in Worcester and Sheffield adding to her own work in Leicester to organise sugar boycotts and demand immediate emancipation. Occurring as this did nearly a century before women would be given the vote in Britain, it was difficult for the male leaders of the Anti-Slavery Society to adjust to it. Yet it was a strong indication that popular pressure within the country would soon become sufficiently powerful that, when allied to the growing restiveness of the slaves themselves, it would ensure that both gradualism and hostility to freedom for the slaves could soon be swept away.

Whatever the fate of the anti-slavery campaign, it was clear to all concerned by the summer of 1824 that Wilberforce was no longer physically able to be at the forefront of it. The day after speaking at the Freemasons' Hall he was once again taken seriously ill, this time while travelling with Barbara to stay with his old friend Lord Gambier in Buckinghamshire. Immediately put to bed when they arrived, 'it was not until I woke at about four o'clock next morning that I found I had my clothes on and that a part of them could be put off',[38] and he was confined to bed for most of the following month. Living in relative seclusion for some weeks, he then spent much of the autumn taking the waters at Bath, musing about writing an autobiography, or a Life of Pitt, or a further religious book. Any parliamentary exertions were, in the opinion of Barbara and his doctor, beyond him.

Wilberforce thought that Lord Liverpool might call a general election early in 1825, which would provide a convenient moment for leaving the Commons. Many admirers believed he should be given a peerage, allowing him to take up a seat in the House of Lords. He himself rejected this idea, partly because he thought a hereditary peerage had a damaging effect on the morals and piety of the next generation, and his eldest son William was already problem enough. When one admirer, Sir John Sinclair, came up with the idea of a peerage to be passed on only to those born after its granting, a kind of life peerage, he still rejected it. He admitted that 'there have been periods in my life, when on worldly principles, the attainment of a permanent, easy and quiet seat in the legislature, would have been a pretty strong temptation to me. But, I thank God, I was strengthened against yielding to it.'[39] For Wilberforce was a natural House of Commons man: he had spent his early years there watching Pitt ruthlessly exploit the cravings of so many for a peerage that the Lords had grown inflated in size. Such a spectacle had almost certainly strengthened his contempt for any seeking of a place there. In addition, he probably felt that constraint peculiar to parliamentarians who have spent many decades in the House of Commons – Winston Churchill and Edward Heath being twentieth-century examples – and that the Commons had been such a special place for him, and so central to his life, that no other chamber could ever be a substitute for it. Thus disdaining a peerage, and finding no general election forthcoming as the new session began in 1825, he sat down on 1 February to the familiar task of writing down the reasoning behind a decision, in this case his retirement from public life:

REASONS FOR RETIRING NOW FROM PARLIAMENT

I have long meant to retire when this parliament should terminate; consequently, the only doubt is whether to retire now or at the end of the approaching session.

The question then is, whether my qualified attendance during this session affords such a prospect of doing good as to warrant my continuance in parliament for its term?

Dr Chambers does not deem it necessary to forbid my attendance altogether, but intermits fears that if an illness should occur, I might not have strength to stand it.

Had I no other promising course of usefulness, it might or rather would be right to run the risk of a seizure, in my present line. But,

　1. I hope I may employ my pen to advantage if I retire into private life; and, 2. My life is just now peculiarly valuable to my family – all at periods of life and in circumstances which render it extremely desirable, according to appearances, that I should be continued to them.

I am not now much wanted in parliament; our cause has powerful advocates who have now taken their stations.

The example of a man's retiring when he feels his bodily and mental powers beginning to fail him, might probably be useful. The public have been so used to see persons turning a long-continued seat in parliament to a count of obtaining rank, &c. that the contrary example the more needed ought to be exhibited by one who professes to act on Christian principles.[40]

Wilberforce's sense of still not having done enough remained: he wrote to Babington at about this time that 'when I consider that my public life has nearly expired . . . I am filled with the deepest compunction and the consciousness of my having made so poor a use of the talents committed to my stewardship.'[41] But when, on 17 February, he wrote to Buxton to ask him to apply to the Chiltern Hundreds on his behalf, the mechanism by which Members of Parliament can resign their position, this was not, of course, the view of his colleagues. Buxton reminded Wilberforce that 'the Carthaginians put upon Hannibal's tomb, "We vehemently desired him in the day of battle,"'[42] and said that that exactly described his feelings. Southey wrote: 'I hope you have retired in time, and will therefore live longer as well as more for yourself; but that House will not look upon your like again.'[43]

Wilberforce left the House of Commons without fanfare and without visiting it. There was no valedictory speech or ceremony of departure. His letter to Buxton brought an end to a parliamentary career spanning forty-five consecutive years. 'Thank God,' wrote Barbara, 'the Die is cast.'[44]

'I am a bee which has lost its sting,'[45] is how Wilberforce described his life after leaving Parliament, although he also noted that 'a man need not be idle because he ceases to be loquacious'.[46] Idle he was certainly not, always fearing that he might waste precious time and continuing to deal with a steady flow of letters, visitors and travels. He paid a nostalgic visit to Lord Grenville, continued on to see Thomas Gisborne, visited Walmer on the Kent coast, 'to see the Castle where I had been above thirty years ago, in poor Pitt's time',[47] and by autumn of 1825 was once again enjoying the waters and society of Bath. He was plagued by the weakness of his eyes, often adding to the end of a letter a comment such as 'I must no longer trespass on my slender stock of eyesight,'[48] but by having books read to him he managed to get through a huge quantity of literature, including being able to indulge a new passion for the works of Sir Walter Scott. While renting a small house at Uxbridge to the west of London, he also enjoyed himself looking for the ideal residence for his retirement, and eventually found it at Highwood Hill, just to the north of London and only two miles from the Great North Road, on which he had travelled so often to Yorkshire. He told Gisborne that 'I shall be a little zemindar, one hundred and forty acres of land, cottages of my own &c,'[49] and the Wilberforces were finally able to move there in June 1826, complete with the usual chaos – 'Had a too hasty prayer for first settlement in a new house – all in confusion.'[50]

No sooner had Wilberforce arrived in his new home than young William, his wife, son and nurse all took up residence there too, William's attempt to become a barrister having been written off as hopeless. The next prospective career was to be farming: he took to looking after the fields of the new property, and was persuaded by a Major Close to invest in a dairy farm at St John's Wood, a little to the south and on the edge of London. Wilberforce, hoping that his eldest son would at last find satisfaction and success, supported this investment, even borrowing money to do so, and allowed William to invest all the capital he had settled on him.

In the meantime the other sons were forging ahead in a manner much more pleasing to their father. Robert and Samuel both graduated from Oxford with first-class degrees, and Henry followed in their footsteps to Oriel College. Robert went on to become a Fellow and Tutor there, and thus remained in Oxford while Samuel was still a student, the latter becoming President of the newly founded Oxford Union, and determining to enter a career in the Church. All three of the sons who went to Oxford would become deeply committed Christians, although of a more establishment and less Evangelical variety than their father: indeed, Robert and Henry would eventually become Roman Catholics. They were, of course, caught up in the intellectual changes of their times, which saw the start of the Oxford Movement and the Tractarians, who agreed that Anglicanism, Orthodoxy and Roman Catholicism were three branches of the one 'Catholic Church'. Wilberforce, whose letters constantly scolded, nagged and encouraged his sons, did not seem to mind their drifting from Evangelical thinking – 'My three Oxonians are strong friends to High Church and King doctrines' – and was delighted with their progress.

To his new home, Wilberforce brought the same group of shuffling servants he could not bear to sack. Marianne Thornton described the scene: 'Things go on in the old way, the house thronged with servants who are all lame or impotent or blind, or kept from charity, an ex-secretary kept because he is grateful, and his wife because she nursed poor Barbara, and an old butler who they wish would not stay but then he is so attached, and his wife who was a cook but now she is so infirm. All this is rather as it should be, however, for one rather likes to see him so completely in character and would willingly despair of getting one's place changed at dinner and hear a chorus of Bells all day which nobody answers for the sake of seeing Mr Wilberforce in his element.'[51] For the combination of books, family, visits and a new residence in the countryside made Wilberforce a happy man. 'Here am I,' he told Marianne Thornton, 'a wreck left over for the next tide but yet a-bounding in enjoyment and blessings.'[52]

There was no sense of melancholy in Wilberforce's retirement. One American visitor, William Sprague, found him 'small in stature, extremely rapid in his movements, very near-sighted and crocked almost to deformity', but also 'perfectly radiant with intelligence and benignity'.[53] Visitors revelled in his conversation, the Bishop of Calcutta recalling that his 'natural eloquence was poured out, strokes of gentle playfulness and satire fell on all sides, and the company was soon absorbed in admiration'.[54] He rarely ventured into London, and when he did it was to preside at an anti-slavery gathering, but he enjoyed planning a huge tour of Yorkshire for the summer of 1827. It was to be the last visit of his life to the county he had represented for so long. Everywhere he went he was welcomed enthusiastically; he wrote to Stephen, 'I can truly say that the magnitude, wealth and industrious population of our vast county have made me feel even more than when I represented it in parliament the importance of the trust then committed to my care.'[55] His final visit on the tour was to Wentworth Woodhouse, the seat of Earl Fitzwilliam, from which efforts to prevent his election had been managed and financed in 1784 and 1807. Fitzwilliam, he thought, 'might well have been forgiven if he had conceived an inconquerable antipathy to me',[56] yet Wilberforce was received with a friendliness and generosity which brought tears to his eyes. He departed happy and grateful from the county he loved, and would never see again.

By October 1827 he was back at Highwood Hill, praying, having books read to him and dictating letters in the morning, walking in his garden in the afternoon, dining by five o'clock, taking a nap for an hour or two, after which he would 'rise for a new term of existence, and sparkle through a long evening to the astonishment of those who expected, at his time of life, to see his mind and spirits flag'.[57] Wilberforce showed no sign of missing politics, although he kept up a busy correspondence with Stephen, Macaulay and Buxton, bemoaning to Buxton 'the utter hopelessness of any honest co-operation from the Colonial Assemblies',[58] and reminding him that the destruction of the remaining slave trade should be the 'prime and grand object' of his parliamentary activities.[59]

Liverpool had left office as Prime Minister early in 1827, to be succeeded by Canning, who was dead within a matter of months. Very much an independent in his old age, Wilberforce hoped that the long period of Tory rule would now be over, and that the Whigs would come to power on a programme of reform. Such a dramatic change would not occur until 1830, after the Duke of Wellington's two-year premiership, but the dam which had held back so many reforming causes was now beginning to crack. Catholic emancipation, the issue on which Pitt and Grenville had broken their governments a quarter of a century before, was finally granted in 1829. Popular agitation against slavery continued, and the Whigs, under Grey and Brougham, were determined that when they came to office they would at last enact the reform of parliamentary representation which Wilberforce had advocated nearly fifty years before. One by-product of such reform, bringing as it would the direct representation of manufacturing towns and cities, would be a Parliament much readier to condemn the institution of slavery.

In the spring of 1828, Wilberforce paid a two-month visit to London, calling on the Bishop of London and the Duke of Wellington, sitting for Sir Thomas Lawrence for a portrait, and attending meetings of the African Institution, the Anti-Slavery Society, and the Naval and Military Bible Society. But he also had another, more local purpose, which was to obtain permission from the Church Commissioners to erect a new chapel on Highwood Hill. When he had purchased Highwood in 1825 he had found its only disadvantage to be that the parish church of Hendon was some three miles distant. His plans to rectify this by building a chapel had at first been welcomed by the vicar of Hendon, Theodore Williams. Once the necessary permission had been granted and the building begun, however, Williams underwent a violent change of attitude, circulating a pamphlet which claimed that

Wilberforce was 'prosecuting by the grossest falsehood' the scheme for the chapel for the sake of his own pecuniary gain.

The reasons for Williams's sudden opposition to Wilberforce's cherished project are unclear, but he was known to dislike Evangelicals, and may have reacted against the chapel being built under an Act which allowed the founder of it to appoint the vicar. The building work had to be delayed while the Church Commissioners checked their legal powers, and Wilberforce was reduced to the task of writing around his friends to urge them not to believe what was being said about him. He considered Williams to be 'somewhat deranged', and noted that he was in debt for £30,000 'in books, horses, pictures &c'.[60] At the age of seventy it was a controversy he could have done without, and his letters betray some anxiety and loss of spirits. He wrote to warn one friend, Lady Olivia Sparrow, that she should be prepared for 'any rumours you might hear of my being discovered at seventy and upwards to be a liar, a covetous rogue and a hypocrite'.[61] The controversy dragged on well into 1830: Wilberforce would not live to see his chapel consecrated for public worship. But a far greater disaster was about to test his patience and equanimity, and one that would mean that he would soon have to sell Highwood Hill and live as a much poorer man.

William's departure from Cambridge and failure to become a barrister had been disappointments for his father, but the misfortune he brought upon his whole family in 1830 was of an entirely different order. The Major Close with whom he had invested turned out to be untrustworthy, and as the dairy business ran into huge losses William concealed from his father the true extent of his financial plight, borrowing more money and making his eventual liabilities bigger still. When his debts were ultimately revealed as creditors closed in, they amounted to more than £50,000 (the equivalent of £3.8 million today). Wilberforce's income from his land in Yorkshire was at this time unusually low, with the combination of an agricultural depression and his own persistent generosity meaning that little rent was coming in. William's losses consumed most of his remaining wealth. By the end of 1830, he and Barbara had decided that they must move out of Highwood and let it, in order to live more modestly and have something left to leave to their children. All offers of financial help were refused, including one from Earl Fitzwilliam to pay off William's entire debts.

Wilberforce's reaction to these events was perhaps stronger testimony to his character than any other occurrence in his life. He had been accustomed to considerable wealth since his earliest youth; now as an old, frail man he had to do without it and part with the home he had carefully selected for the evening of his days. Yet he never showed any bitterness towards William, who left for Italy for a time, Wilberforce writing to Babington in 1831, 'I must allow William £600 per annum more when I am able,'[62] a larger amount than he was giving to his other children. He wrote to friends that 'it is *some* trial to me to be compelled to quit my garden and still more my books and more than this have no residence to which I can ask an old friend to take a dinner or a bed with me'.[63] But in one of his last letters from Highwood he also wrote, 'I am bound to recognise . . . the gracious mitigation of the severity of the stroke. It was not suffered to take place till all my children were educated, and nearly all of them placed out in one way or another; and by the delay, Mrs Wilberforce and I are supplied with a delightful asylum under the roofs of two of our own children. And what better could we desire?'[64] For forty-five years he had believed in Providence; he was not going to stop now.

To Wilberforce, this was something that was meant to happen, and he would make the best of it. By the summer of 1831 he and Barbara were living temporarily in Samuel's rectory at Brighstone on the Isle of Wight. Samuel had married Emily Sargent in 1828. All of Wilberforce's living offspring, except William, were soon dependent on Church livings because his surviving daughter, Lizzy, had married a curate early in 1830. Robert would have to move out of Oriel College when he married Agnes Wrangham,* and it was at this point that

---

* Wilberforce's great-great-grandson, C.E. Wrangham, edited Wilberforce's 1779 diary of his 'Journey to the Lake District from Cambridge', which was published in 1983. He also collected the papers descended through the families of his ancestor Robert Wilberforce and his brother Henry. The entire collection was bought and placed in the Bodleian Library, Oxford, in 1998.

Wilberforce's freedom from personal animosities in politics reboun-
ded in his favour. Eleven years earlier he had never revealed how
Brougham's secret but worthless assurances had led him into such
unpopularity in his approach to the affairs of Queen Caroline. Now
Brougham was Lord Chancellor in the new Whig government, and
when he heard of Wilberforce's financial losses he offered to Robert
the living of East Farleigh in Kent, as well as securing the parish of
Rawmarsh near Rotherham for Lizzy's husband. Admittedly, Brougham
could not resist following this up by asking Wilberforce to write round
his Cambridge friends soliciting votes for Palmerston, their Whig candidate. Wilberforce replied, 'In truth I have entirely done with politics,'
and that he had to acknowledge 'what I daily feel, the infirmities of
advanced and continually advancing years',[65] but nevertheless considered Brougham to have behaved handsomely towards him.

Once Robert and Agnes had taken up residence at East Farleigh in
the summer of 1832, their readiness to welcome Wilberforce and
Barbara to stay with them on an almost permanent basis did much to
bring comfort and happiness to Wilberforce as old age overcame him.
It was a year that would bring two further great personal sorrows. In
February Wilberforce had rushed to Samuel's house on the Isle of
Wight, where his thirty-year-old daughter Lizzy was suffering from a
severe chest infection. She died soon after he arrived. As ever, his faith
made him resilient in the face of such a blow, writing, 'my poor
son-in-law and his little infant are indeed much to be pitied . . . but I
am cheered by the strong persuasion that my dear Elizabeth has gone
to a better world'.[66] In October, James Stephen, his great friend,
brother-in-law and intellectual mainstay for some forty years died at
Bath. Wilberforce, whose own demise had been predicted so often, was
living to see many of his lifelong associates go to their graves. Early
the next year, Hannah More fell seriously ill. 'I cannot understand,'
wrote Wilberforce, 'why my life is spared so long, except that it does
show that a man can be as happy without a fortune as with one.'[67]

Such was Wilberforce's love of society and aptitude for making
new friends at every stage of life that even now he was not without
companions. He enjoyed the company of Harford, and of Sir James

Mackintosh, an MP who had been one of his most regular supporters. Seventy-three years old in 1832, he still managed to visit Bath and Battersea Rise. Above all, he overflowed with gratitude for his sons and his daughters-in-law. He had always been fond of nautical allusions to describe his whereabouts and movements, referring to 'riding at single anchor' if he was on alert for a return to Westminster, or 'cutting the cables rather than regularly unmooring' when making a swift exit from London to seek rural air. Now, he described himself and Barbara as having 'great cause for thankfulness in being moored in our latter days in our peaceful haven which we enjoy (after all my tossings during my long and stormy voyage in the sea of politics) under the roofs of our sons in Kent and in the Isle of Wight, relieved from all the worry of family cares and witnessing the respectability, usefulness and domestic happiness of those most dear to us'.[68] At each location he was able to listen to his sons preach in their churches. At East Farleigh Robert and Agnes had a special walk levelled for him in their garden: 'Robts. garden sheltered (from North and East) gravel walk made expressly for me by dear Robt. is extremely valuable. I was not out of the garden all the week. It is so clean and smooth and sheltered.'[69] A steady flow of visitors added to the contented scene. East Farleigh in the winter of 1832–33 witnessed the arrival of Lord Barham (grandson of the late Sir Charles Middleton, who had done so much to persuade Wilberforce to take up the issue of the slave trade), the young James Stephen, Wilberforce's fourth son Henry and even Prince Czartoryski of Poland, the former Foreign Minister of Tsar Alexander. Wilberforce loved to spend hours chatting to each of them, and when dressing or resting continued to have books read to him – Jane Austen's *Mansfield Park*, Walter Scott's *Woodstock*, Maria Edgeworth's *Ennui* and Sharon Turner's *History of England*. He regarded himself as extremely fortunate, writing, 'had not the state of my finances rendered it absolutely necessary, I fear I should hardly have thought myself warranted in giving up my only residence, but it is really true, speaking unaffectedly, that our heavy loss has led to the solid and great increase of our enjoyments'.[70]

Wilberforce was now far detached from day-to-day politics, but he continued to do everything he could to encourage the opponents of slavery. On 15 May 1830 he had presided for the last time at a meeting of the Anti-Slavery Society, feeling physically unequal to the task in subsequent years. It had been a meeting at which the impatience of the young abolitionists had finally exploded: two thousand people packed the Freemasons' Hall, many of them to demand slavery's entire and immediate abolition. It was Clarkson who moved that Wilberforce, 'the great leader in our cause',[71] should take the chair, and it was therefore Wilberforce who had to try to control a meeting in which the caution of the old politicians was criticised and the motion that 'From and after 1st January 1830 every slave born within the King's dominions shall be free' was proposed, amidst thunderous cheers. As George Stephen described it, when Wilberforce rose to put this motion to the vote it 'was carried with a burst of exalting triumph which would have made the Falls of Niagara inaudible at equal distance'.[72] The result was a split in the anti-slavery movement, with a new Agency Committee coordinating the work of radical abolitionists and increasingly superseding the more traditional approach of Buxton, Brougham, Clarkson, Macaulay and Wilberforce. But over the next two years, the old guard of the abolitionists, Wilberforce included, endorsed the Agency Committee and moved into line with its more urgent ambitions, as the prospects for immediate success steadily grew.

Although Wilberforce was pleased that the Whigs had come to power in 1830, he was worried that their Reform Bill, extending the franchise, abolishing rotten boroughs and redistributing parliamentary seats to the main centres of population, went too far in one go. Once it was carried, however, and became the Reform Act of 1832, the general election held on the new basis produced intense popular pressure in many areas for the abolition of slavery, and an increasing number of candidates felt bound to commit themselves to it. Adding to the urgency, in January 1832 the slaves of Jamaica had risen in a revolt which took British troops several weeks to put down. The opinion of ministers in London was that freeing the slaves had become essential if uncontainable rebellions were to be averted. Wilberforce wrote to Buxton from East Farleigh in November 1832, 'I feel, and shall feel this affair the more, because I myself am not guiltless. I myself ought to have stirred in it more than I did before I left the House of Commons, and now that I am there no longer, I consider you as my heir at law.'[73]

Any need for gradualism was over. On New Year's Day 1833 Wilberforce wrote to Macaulay to congratulate him on 'having entered on the year which I trust will be distinguished by your seeing at last the mortal stroke given to the accursed Slave Trade, and the emancipation of the West Indian slaves at length accomplished'.[74] That spring, petitions against slavery poured in on Parliament. Wilberforce was prevailed on to make the short journey from East Farleigh to the town of Maidstone, to propose the local petition for total abolition. It was to be the last speech of his life, as he lifted his frail voice for the final time to denounce the horror and immorality of slavery and to finish with the words, 'I trust that we now approach the very end of our career.'[75] He had recovered from influenza that winter, but his chest was weak and his body very frail. One month later, on 14 May, the Colonial Secretary, Lord Stanley, stood at the dispatch box in the Commons to propose a government motion for the abolition of slavery. He did so with a glowing salute to Wilberforce: 'Wilberforce still remains to see, I trust, the final consummation of the great and glorious work which he was one of the first to commence; and to exclaim, like the last of the prophets ... "Lord, now let thy servant depart in peace." '[76] As his bodily strength drained away, the liberation for which William Wilberforce had hoped and worked almost all of his adult life came at last into view.

19

His Feet on the Rock

———

What more could any man wish at the close of life, than to be attended
by his own children, and his own wife, and all treating him with such
uniform kindness and affection?

WILLIAM WILBERFORCE, 1833[1]

I N THE SUMMER OF 1833, William Wilberforce knew that he was
dying. He wrote to Lord Calthorpe that he was being 'favoured with a
gradual exit',[2] and would say to visitors, 'I am like a clock which is almost
run down.'[3] He spoke repeatedly of his gratitude for his life and for his
relative freedom from pain at the end of it, and gave little outward sign
of being anxious about his approaching end or its imminence.

It was less obvious to Wilberforce's family and friends that he
would die that summer, although he was clearly in serious physical
decline. He left East Farleigh on 20 April for a brief visit to the Isle of
Wight, and then continued on to his familiar haven at Bath. Joseph
John Gurney visited him there and found him 'reclining on a sofa,
with his feet wrapped in flannel; and his countenance bespeaking
increased age since I had last seen him, as well as much delicacy'.
Nevertheless, 'he received me with the warmest marks of affection, and
seemed to be delighted by the unexpected arrival of an old friend . . .
the illuminated expression of his furrowed countenance, with his
clasped and uplifted hands, were indicative of profound devotion and
holy joy'.[4] To his sons he gave the instruction that 'you must always
join with me in praying that the short remainder of my life may be

spent in gaining that spirituality of mind which will fit me for heaven. And there I hope to meet all of you.'[5]

More hunched and frail than ever, and never fully recovering from the influenza that had struck him early that year, Wilberforce might easily have died at Bath. In mid-July, however, the consensus among his family and doctors was that he could benefit from seeing his London physician, Dr Chambers, who had looked after him for most of the previous decade. On 17 July the little figure who had travelled so incessantly across England for more than half a century was seated in the back of his coach for the final journey of his life. He arrived two days later in London and took up residence in the home of his cousin Lucy Smith, at 44 Cadogan Place, near Sloane Street. His return to London was – at least on the part of others – in no way in anticipation of his approaching death, but as it happened it reunited him for the final ten days of his life with the people and events of the political world among whom he had felt at home for so long. He was full of reflections and little pieces of wisdom, telling the Reverend William Jay before he left Bath that 'the best way to reduce an undue attachment to the subordinate things in religion . . . is to keep up a supreme regard to the more important ones . . . then we shall have little time and less inclination to engage in the strivings and strives of bigots'.[6] He was optimistic about the moral state of the world: 'I think real religion is spreading; and I am persuaded, will increasingly spread, till the earth is filled with the knowledge of the Lord, as the waters cover the sea.'[7] To another visitor he advised that 'Popularity is certainly a dangerous thing – the antidote is chiefly in the feeling one has; how very differently they would regard me, if they knew me really!'[8]

Any doubting of his faith within his own mind had been vanquished decades before. 'I should be always cheerful too, if I could make myself as sure as he does that I was going to Heaven,'[9] one friend had commented several years before. Wilberforce often noted that he was ashamed of his luxuries, that he was suffering very little compared to others and compared to Christ, and that he was deeply thankful to be surrounded by his wife, sons and friends who cared for him so well. Above all, he hoped that 'No man on earth has a stronger sense of sinfulness and unworthiness before God than I.'[10] Only one political issue remained fixed in his mind as his health deteriorated that year. As the debates about the abolition of slavery gathered pace in the House of Commons, he wrote to William Smith on 25 June, 'future ages will justly regard the work as a grand national victory over wickedness and cruelty'.[11] He had followed the debates closely, on one occasion rising from the table at dinner when told that a debate on the emancipation of the slaves would just be starting, to cry, 'Hear! Hear! Hear!' On 25 July he received, with his son Henry, a young and keen Evangelical Member of Parliament for breakfast. The MP in question was to be another of the greatest campaigners and indefatigable note-takers of British political history: William Ewart Gladstone. It was the only time that Gladstone, then twenty-three years old and no friend to abolition, would meet Wilberforce. He wrote in his diary: 'Went to breakfast with old Mr. Wilberforce – heard him pray with his family. Blessing and honour are upon his head.'[12]

On Friday, 26 July, Wilberforce seemed to be well enough to take some air outside, and he was carried in his chair to the steps in front of the house, where 'he presented a most striking appearance, looking forth with calm delight upon trees and grass, the freshness and vigour of which contrasted with his own decay'.[13] That evening he seemed to improve, and it was thought that within a few days he could be on the road again, presumably to return to East Farleigh. But his son Henry noted that night, 'he is strongly impressed with a feeling that he is near his end; much nearer than from what his physician says I trust is the case. He speaks very little as if looking forward to future happiness; but he seems more like a person in the actual enjoyment of heaven within.'[14]

It seems that it was on this day, Friday, 26 July 1833, that Wilberforce received the news that the Abolition of Slavery Bill, requiring the end of slavery throughout the whole of the British Empire and the payment of £20 million to the slave-owners in compensation, was secure in its passage through the House of Commons.* The young Tom Macaulay,

---

* Most previous books on Wilberforce repeat the error made by his sons in their biography in stating that the crucial second reading, or alternatively the third reading, of the Abolition of Slavery Bill took place on Friday, 26 July. In fact, the parliamentary records show that

present at the time, wrote that Wilberforce 'excelled in the success which we obtained ... as much as the youngest and most partisan could have done'.[15] 'Thank God,' said Wilberforce, 'that I should have lived to witness a day in which England is willing to give twenty millions sterling for the Abolition of Slavery.'[16] The Bill's passage meant that from August 1834 the 800,000 slaves in the colonies of the British Empire would technically be free. And so, with extraordinary poignancy and symmetry, the man who had laboured for nearly fifty years to promote measures that would one day lead to the emancipation of the slaves knew, at the very end of the seventy-three years and eleven months of his life, that this goal had been accomplished.

Within twenty-four hours of this event, on the Saturday night, Wilberforce's condition deteriorated sharply. By the Sunday he was having fainting fits and sometimes losing his memory. If he had been more distant from London he might never have known for sure that abolition had been secured. On the Sunday evening, conscious for a while, he said to Henry and Barbara, 'I am in a very distressed state.' 'Yes,' replied Henry, 'but you have your feet on the Rock.'[17] With his last recorded words, Wilberforce responded, 'I do not venture to speak so positively; but I hope I have.'[18] At 3 a.m. on Monday, 29 July 1833, his body exhausted but his mind hopeful and fulfilled, his earthly life was over.

✳ ✳ ✳

---

this particular day was one of the few in that week and the succeeding one on which slavery was not discussed at all in the House of Commons. The Bill actually received its second reading on Monday, 22 July, and was carried without a vote. Of greater importance was the detailed consideration of its provisions on the Wednesday and Thursday, 24 and 25 July, during which the abolitionists, led by Buxton, came within seven votes of defeating the government on its plans for the slaves to serve a twelve-year apprenticeship to their former masters; these would in effect tie them to working at the same places, albeit in return for wages and with restricted hours. By the Thursday the government had made a major concession on this point, reducing the apprenticeship period to seven years (as matters turned out, the whole apprenticeship idea was abandoned by 1838). The news that Wilberforce received on Friday, 26 July would not therefore have been that the Bill had passed its second reading, but that the apprenticeship system had been watered down, that the £20 million grant to the planters was not in doubt, and that the abolitionists had shown sufficient strength during the proceedings on the Bill to be sure that it would be carried in a satisfactory form. The Bill completed its passage through the House of Commons the following week, and was passed by the House of Lords on 20 August.

Wilberforce had left instructions that he was to be buried at Stoke Newington, to the north of the City of London, in the same vault as his sister and his daughter Barbara. The British body politic, however, had other ideas, with leading members immediately writing to Henry:

> We, the undersigned Members of both Houses of Parliament, being anxious upon public grounds to show our respect for the memory of the late William Wilberforce, and being also satisfied that public honours can never be more fitly bestowed than upon such benefactors of mankind, earnestly request that he may be buried in Westminster Abbey; and that we, and others who may agree with us in these sentiments may have permission to attend his funeral.[19]

Such was the honour this represented that there seems to have been little hesitation in the Wilberforce family before acceding to the request. On Saturday, 3 August, as the Abbey bell 'tolled slowly and solemnly',[20] Wilberforce's coffin, draped in black velvet with a border of white satin, was borne to its resting place by pallbearers who included some of the highest-ranking figures in the land: the Duke of Gloucester, the Marquis of Westminster, the Speaker of the House of Commons, and the Lord Chancellor, Henry Brougham. In burying him as they did, and where they did, close to the graves of Pitt, Fox and Canning, the parliamentarians of the time made clear their view that William Wilberforce was to be ranked on a par with the greatest statesmen of their age.

Two centuries later, what should be our estimation of Wilberforce? In his own lifetime he called forth extremes of opinion about his own career, from being 'one of the illustrious benefactors of mankind', in the words of the voters of Hull, to the 'canting hypocrite' denounced by Cobbett. He had not long been dead when two of his sons differed sharply with Thomas Clarkson, as described in Chapter 7, about the extent of his pre-eminence in the campaign to abolish the slave trade. He has been hailed as the ultimate principled campaigner, but sometimes criticised as a temporising compromiser. Lauded by Evangelicals to the present day as a heroic figure who demonstrated that Christian virtues could be given practical effect, he has nevertheless been regarded with suspicion by political radicals, who have considered his lack of sympathy for the workers of the Industrial Revolution to reveal his reactionary instincts. The seeming contradictions of Wilberforce's life have always made him difficult to unravel and understand: a man of conservative disposition who devoted much of his life to one of the great progressive causes of his time; a politician who loved being close to those in power but never seemed to need the possession of it himself; a wit with a love of society who was appalled by dances or the theatre – Wilberforce's views and habits were not made for easy categorisation.

Wilberforce's endearing attributes of character, however, are easy to agree on, for they were not only remarkable, but were applauded by his contemporaries with total unanimity. Sir James Stephen (the son) wrote that 'nature herself endowed him with that genial warmth and graciousness of temper which, by a constant succession of spontaneous impulses, pours itself into all the channels of social intercourse . . . When Pitt, and Burke and Sheridan were not to be had, he would take the most cordial pleasure in the talk of the most woollen of his constituents at Leeds. When Madame de Staël and Mrs Crewe were away, some dowager from the Cathedral Whist Club became his inspiring muse . . . Dullness fled at his approach.'[21] Henry Brougham wrote that Wilberforce 'was naturally a person of great quickness and even subtlety of mind, with a lively imagination . . . he had wit in an unmeasured abundance, and in all its varieties; for he was endowed with an exquisite sense of the ludicrous in character, the foundation of humour, as well as with the perception of remote resemblances, the essence of wit'. At the same time, 'his nature was mild and amiable beyond that of most men; fearful of giving the least pain in any quarter, even while heated with the zeal of controversy on questions that roused all his passions; and more anxious, if it were possible, to gain over rather than to overpower an adversary – to disarm him by kindness, or the force of reason, or awakening appeals to his feelings, rather than defeat him by hostile attack'.[22]

It was this rolling together of playfulness with persuasiveness, geniality with solemn purposes, that made Wilberforce an ever-popular companion or guest. His instruction to his sons to 'never omit any opportunity to become acquainted with any good or useful man' was one he unfailingly followed himself; since his position made it possible for him to meet all the leading figures of the nation, many of those of Europe, and thousands of his constituents and correspondents, this gregarious attitude made his list of acquaintances very long indeed. The happy chaos of his daily existence, with more callers than could be seen, more letters than could be responded to, and more issues to consider than could fit into his head, only made his friends enjoy his company the more, while marvelling that he never seemed to lose his calm temper and generous disposition. Personally loyal to his friends and thoughtful enough to write down lists of how he could help them, there is no doubt that Wilberforce would have been a good person to have known.

That Wilberforce was a great parliamentary performer is also beyond question. Brougham thought that 'his eloquence was of a very high order. It was persuasive and pathetic in an eminent degree; but it was occasionally bold and impassioned, animated with the inspiration which deep feeling alone can breathe into spoken thought.'[23] Not all his speeches were great ones, but he spoke so often, and frequently with so little preparation, in the Commons that to expect a permanent gold standard is unrealistic. William Lecky, the great historian, thought that Wilberforce 'could not be compared in intellectual power with Pitt, Fox, Burke, or Sheridan but he stood high in the second line of parliamentary debaters';[24] yet the opinion of Wilberforce's speeches held by these great orators themselves was much higher. His opening speech against the slave trade in 1789 was compared by Burke to the work of Demosthenes; Pitt is often quoted as having said, 'of all the men I ever knew, Wilberforce has the greatest natural eloquence'.[25] An obituary of September 1833 said that 'Mr Wilberforce possessed in perfection the two most essential attributes of popular declamation – the choicest flow of pure and glowing English, and the finest modulation of the sweet and powerful voice.'[26] It was said that however long or rambling some of his speeches became, the presence within them of five to ten minutes of real brilliance could always be relied on.

As a Member of Parliament, Wilberforce added application to eloquence, never failing in his heyday to attend Parliament whenever it
was sitting. In an age when many MPs barely opened their mouths in
the chamber, he spoke on the vast majority of the most important
subjects, and an extraordinary variety of minor ones. In addition, he
worked on the problems of his constituents with an assiduousness that
was exceptional for that time, although he was partly required to do
so by taking on the representation of Yorkshire, not only the largest
county in England but one not generally known for tolerating neglect.

These three qualities – sociability, speaking ability and capacity for
work – would have made Wilberforce an effective politician at any
time and in most circumstances. Together, they are enough to create a
popular, fairly senior figure in the political world. But the decisive
factor in making his achievements possible was, as usual in human
life, not his qualities but the use to which he decided to put them:
indeed, his belief that he was wasting his considerable talents seems to
have been one of the forces which produced his Evangelical conversion,
leading in turn to his adoption of clear objectives and a deep sense of
being held to account. That he never held a government post is highly
likely to have been the result of Prime Ministers – even including his
best friend of the time – deciding that he was not suited to ministerial
office. In that judgement they were almost certainly correct. Wilberforce had the persistence and persuasiveness of a campaigner, but not
the rapid decisiveness sometimes required of those who hold high
executive office. His readiness to consider all points of view, assume
the best of human nature in his opponents, and change his opinions
if necessary, were all features that should be rated highly in a politician,
but he possessed them to such a degree that the overall effect at a
cabinet table or in charge of a department of state would probably
have been disastrous. As another of Stephen's sons, George Stephen,
put it, 'his essential fault was that of busy indolence; he worked out
nothing for himself; he was destitute of system, and desultory in his
habits; he depended on others for information, and laid himself open
to misguidance ... From this habit sprung another failing, of no
trifling importance in a public man – he was indecisive; he wanted the

confidence which he might have justly placed in his own judgement. It was a common saying of him ... that you might safely predicate his vote, for it was certain to be opposed to his speech.'[27] For fully half of the forty-five years Wilberforce sat in Parliament, Britain was at war; he would not have made a war minister.

The two great friends who entered the Parliament of 1780, Pitt and Wilberforce, would therefore become extreme examples of two contrasting approaches to political life. Pitt became perhaps the ultimate career minister, in office for almost all his adult life and the second-longest-serving Prime Minister in British history. Wilberforce became the ultimate non-career politician, following up the absence of any appointment to ministerial office in his early years by deliberately eschewing it for the rest of his life. Instead, it was his Evangelical convictions which gave unity and coherence to his work. The arrival of those convictions did not change his character, but it did reinforce some of his best attributes, intensifying his intellectual curiosity and readiness to apply himself to Parliament, while giving him a stubborn persistence in trying to reveal the truth and a pronounced ability to accept setbacks and overcome them.

It was, of course, a fortunate chance of history that Wilberforce was donning the armour of religious faith and political determination at the very moment when the battle over the existence of the slave trade was ready to be fought. As demonstrated in Chapter 6, the spread of Enlightenment values in the eighteenth century produced a mounting hostility to the slave trade, at least among some Britons and Americans. If Wilberforce had lived and undergone his conversion half a century earlier, no amount of effort on his part could have destroyed the trade; half a century later and he would have found it accomplished already. The opportunity for individuals to change history is shaped by the great social and intellectual forces of their times. Yet it is also true that such forces can only act through the agency of enterprising individuals. Abolition of the slave trade would have occurred eventually, but without the efforts of Wilberforce, Clarkson, Sharp, Stephen, Macaulay and their colleagues, it would not have happened when it did.

To argue over who should take the lion's share of the credit for the abolition campaign is futile and unnecessary. Wilberforce and Clarkson, the two most celebrated abolitionist figures, clearly each regarded the work of the other man as indispensable to his own. Without Wilberforce, Clarkson and the extra-parliamentary campaigners would have lacked a general on the battlefield that mattered most; without Clarkson, Wilberforce would have lacked both ammunition and an army. Equally, Wilberforce could not have waged the campaign he did in Parliament without his band of 'Saints', and he could not have brought it to a successful conclusion without the exceptional knowledge and ingenuity of James Stephen. But given the politically charged and highly controversial nature of the subject, complete with upheavals in world affairs and domestic politics along the way, the parliamentary campaign against the slave trade required a most unusual combination of qualities in its leader: a thirst for the truth, an ability to win allies across the political spectrum, a refusal to accept defeat so strong as to be an inability to do so, a command of parliamentary oratory, and an understanding of how to anchor detailed and practical arguments in the context of great moral force. In the pursuit of abolition, this was precisely the combination of abilities that William Wilberforce brought to bear.

The abolitionists always intended that the ending of the slave trade would make the institution of slavery impossible to maintain. In retrospect, however, they were mistaken in thinking that, in Clarkson's words, destroying the trade would be 'laying the axe at the very root' of slavery. The reality turned out to be precisely the other way round: the slave trade, in all its illegal and multinational forms, could only finally be eradicated once slavery too had been abolished. Human ingenuity is such that illegal trading will always take place if a sufficient profit is to be had from the end-user, as the twenty-first-century traffic in drugs, arms and people continues to demonstrate. Where slavery remained legal after Wilberforce's death, a slave trade of some kind continued, legal or not. In the United States, only the Civil War and the defeat of the Southern states, leading to the end of slavery, finally extinguished the illicit slave trade. In the case of Brazil, whose slave trade remained legal into the 1850s, the quarter of a century after Wilberforce's death saw a further half a million slaves imported from Africa. Hundreds of thousands were sold in the same decades to the planters of Cuba, who remained the most zealous of all defenders of slavery. The last recorded landing of slaves in Cuba was in 1870, not long before slavery there came to an end. The final abolition of slavery in the Portuguese Empire did not take place until 1875, and in Brazil in 1888.

Elements of the international slave trade therefore survived the efforts of the abolitionists for almost a century. It turned out that, far from taking an axe to the very root of slavery, they had spent decades hacking off its branches while much of it continued to flourish. Mistaken though they were, and disappointed though they would become in thinking that the 1807 Abolition Act would itself spell doom for slavery, they nevertheless had little alternative in the late eighteenth century to tilting at the trade before anything else, for the outright destruction of slavery would have been beyond them. Nor should the central importance of their achievement in securing the abolition of the trade of Britain, the world's foremost maritime power, ever be underestimated. Within the space of twenty years, and in the face of political misfortunes on a scale that only a revolution in Paris could bring, they converted the people and the entire political establishment of Britain to the cause of abolition, turning their country after 1807 into one that bullied, harassed and bribed other nations into giving up their own similarly detestable traffic.

As described in Chapter 13, national self-interest played a significant role in the events of 1807, and afterwards it strengthened the motivation of successive British governments to annihilate internationally the trade that Britain had forsaken. But Britain's total abolition of the trade in 1807 went beyond national economic or political interest, and it did so because Wilberforce and his colleagues had demonstrated beyond argument that the slave trade was incompatible with values British people regarded themselves as proud to uphold. The moral authority they attached to their case did much to embolden those who later built on British abolition, whether it was restless slaves seeking their freedom in Jamaica, Royal Navy captains patrolling the coast of West Africa or, half a century later, Palmerston declaring that one of his greatest achievements as British Prime Minister had been to help ensure the extinction of the Brazilian slave trade. In the avalanche of condemnation that descended on slavery in the nineteenth century, the abolition of the British slave trade in 1807 represented the early fall of the mightiest possible boulder.

Wilberforce, then, deserved the many tributes that have been paid to his almost lifelong campaign against the slave trade. The achievements were not remotely his alone, but it must never be forgotten that at times in the late 1790s he kept the cause alive when many others had forgotten it. That he was regarded as pre-eminent among the abolitionists in his own time is clear from his ability to designate a chosen successor, Fowell Buxton, as the leading parliamentary spokesman on slavery issues. Clarkson could not have moved at the 1830 meeting of the Anti-Slavery Society that Wilberforce take the chair as 'the father of our great cause' unless that had been how he was perceived. Wilberforce had succeeded in providing not only parliamentary leadership but genuine inspiration, and the latter spread not only across Britain but to many other parts of the world. 'Everyone should know Wilberforce,' reflected Abraham Lincoln, one of the greatest emancipators of them all.

As the leader of a cause, Wilberforce certainly had his faults. He was sometimes too credulous and too trusting towards those in power, at home or abroad, and particularly if they were his personal friends. As George Stephen put it, he 'felt perhaps unconsciously, too much deferential regard for rank and power, irrespective, not of the morality, but of the sterling worth of their possessors'.[28] He found it hard to believe that a real gentleman like Sidmouth was beyond persuasion, however many times he was disappointed by him, and even harder to think that a man as rational as Pitt would not summon the power and courage always to do the right thing. To work with, rather than confront, those in high authority was his natural inclination and style. Sometimes this held him back, but mostly it served as a natural complement to the agitation out of doors that colleagues like Clarkson were able to create. The threat of popular pressure could not alone have brought an early end to the slave trade, as the successful resistance of eighteenth-century governments to widespread national opinion regularly showed. The success of abolition required reassurance at the highest levels of the state, and Wilberforce was ideally suited to provide it.

Wilberforce might have been quicker in the 1820s to see that the rapid emancipation of the slaves was an attainable goal, but his gradualist instincts were in line with those of all of his senior colleagues, and he was happy to support a more ambitious programme when the whole British political environment changed after 1830. The more wounding criticism levelled at him over the years has been the echo of Cobbett: that he was insensitive to the conditions of workers closer to home, and actually damaged their cause by supporting repressive legislation and unsympathetic ministers. It is possible to answer this, as one commentator did, by saying that it is like criticising Columbus for not discovering Australia as well; but if Wilberforce were here to defend himself he would be likely to make three more substantial points. The first is that he gave strong personal and political support to a variety of reforming causes such as prison reform, and was involved in a mass of charitable activity, often aimed at improving the conditions of the poor. Where practical measures could be taken, he was generally in their support.

Secondly, independent as he was, he could not support one cause without considering its effect on another: if he had been a spokesman for radicalism in general he could not have been the effective persuader and campaigner on slavery in particular. His cautious and conservative disposition on the maintenance of the domestic political and economic order ensured that his views on the slave trade were listened to, and the withholding or giving of support to ministers on issues of great importance to them affected their willingness to do his bidding on matters of importance to him. He demonstrated a level of political independence which many people found surprising even then, and which would be rendered almost impossible for MPs of later generations as the age of universal suffrage, mass communication and party machines arrived. But in politics, true independence is impotence, and Wilberforce knew, and at times confessed, that he had to support ministers on certain issues in order to press them harder on others.

Perhaps most important of all, a third defence of Wilberforce is that all his views, some of which are seen as progressive and some as reactionary from the standpoint of a later age, were rooted in a consistent view of the importance of religion, morality and education. Just as the state of slavery was destructive of true religion, morality and any sense of responsibility, so was a state of revolution. The French Revolution had cast aside all Christian heritage and teaching: anything which threatened Britain with the same must therefore be forcefully resisted. Wilberforce did not believe in unlicensed freedom, but rather that liberty could only responsibly be exercised within a strong moral and institutional framework. To him, the existence of slavery and proposals for great domestic upheaval were both obstacles to such a framework, and there was no inconsistency in being an enemy to them simultaneously.

Abolition of the slave trade was William Wilberforce's central tangible achievement, but his belief that the moral strength of society is the foundation of all else made his contribution to history far greater than one Act of Parliament. While disdaining political ambition of the conventional kind, he set out after his conversion on the most ambitious programme of them all, namely to change the entire moral climate of his country and a good deal of the world. His opposition to the slave trade was a mere manifestation of an insistence on the value of Christian principles which, when he gave voice to it, caused any hesitation or indecision to fall away. His son Samuel wrote that Wilberforce 'said of all his public life he looked back with the greatest pleasure on his religious publication'.[29] His great vision of moral and spiritual enrichment was what he lived for, whether in defending the institution of marriage, attacking the practices of the slave trade or emphatically defending the Sabbath day. And just as he fought shy of political factionalism, so he steered clear of religious factionalism too: his Christianity was of a unifying, effusive and ecumenical kind. His vociferous attacks on other religions, particularly Hinduism, sound harsh and intolerant to a twenty-first-century ear, but they reinforce the boldness of his concept of an entire Christian world. It is surprising, not that someone who lived so long ago had views which now seem old-fashioned, but that he left behind him so many prophetic truths, such as his stark warning about the dangers of making racial distinctions in southern Africa, and his notable reflection that 'wars are popular in their commencement and pernicious in their course'.[30]

Wilberforce was a legislator for almost the whole of his adult life, but central to his beliefs was the view that laws must be underpinned by a common understanding of ethics and conduct. His ambitious and energetic promotion of his views may well have contributed to the changed social conventions which dominated the Victorian age after his death, creating a British society very different from the licentious London against which he had revolted in the 1780s. As one of the 'Fathers of the Victorians' his views once again seem dated when seen from the vantage point of the more relaxed morality of later times, but in relation to his basic view that the long-term happiness of a society depends on how individuals behave towards each other, how families hold together, and how leaders keep the trust of people, who can say with confidence that he was wrong?

Wilberforce's pursuit of a broad and uplifting vision of society elevates him far above the general ranks of politicians. But the fact that he managed to live according to his own principles, and constantly reflect his beliefs in his own character, is his crowning glory. It may be easier to disdain money and to give much of it away if you inherit a large amount of it, but few people born in that position actually do so. It is easy to think that a Member of Parliament can resist all temptations of seeking high office if he has a great cause as an alternative, but it is still a rare event. Wilberforce exercised a genuine and remarkable self-discipline, and managed to do so while maintaining an optimistic and vivacious disposition. His conduct as a husband, father or elected representative is hard to fault. His generosity to those who came to him in need of help became an outstanding example of the virtues he called for in others. He showed how a political career could be conducted differently, pursuing long-term objectives deeply rooted in certain principles, strengthened in his indifference to holding power by his understanding of its transitory nature. As a result, he defied the axiom that political careers necessarily end in failure, going to his grave fulfilled by the knowledge of what he had helped to do, while those politicians to whom power alone is important decline in their old age into bitterness and despair.

It is the combination of Wilberforce's achievements and his qualities that mark him out as a figure rare indeed. Judged all round, his achievements were greater than those of most of the occupants of the highest offices in the land. But the reason he is a lasting inspiration rather than a mere notable parliamentarian is that in a long and arduous public life, he showed unyielding reverence for truth, loyalty, integrity and principle as he understood it, setting an example that has stirred the hearts and elevated the minds of generations who followed. In the dark historical landscape of violence, treachery and hate, the life of William Wilberforce stands out as a beacon of light, which the passing of two centuries has scarcely dimmed.

NOTES
BIBLIOGRAPHY
INDEX

NOTES

ABBREVIATIONS

Correspondence: R. and S. Wilberforce, *Correspondence of William Wilberforce*, Vols I–II, Perkins, Philadelphia, 1841

Life: R. and S. Wilberforce, *Life of Wilberforce*, Vols I–V, John Murray, London, 1838

PD: Parliamentary Debates from the Year 1803 to the Present Time. London: Hansard, 1812 and later years

PH: Parliamentary History of England, from the Earliest Period to the Year 1803. London: Hansard, 1814

PR: Parliamentary Register: or History of the proceedings and debates of the House of Commons (and House of Lords) containing the most interesting speeches, etc., London, 1775–1813

Private Papers: A.M. Wilberforce, *Private Papers of William Wilberforce*, Fisher Unwin, London, 1897

PROLOGUE

1 23 Feb 1807, PD VIII col. 947
2 ibid col. 968
3 ibid col. 972
4 ibid col. 987
5 Clarkson, History Vol I p. 1
6 ibid Vol II p. 579
7 12 May 1789, PH XXVII col. 48
8 ibid col. 68
9 23 Feb 1807, PD VIII col. 967
10 ibid col. 978–9
11 Life III p. 297, Wilberforce to Hey, 2 Mar 1807, Life III p. 297

ONE: **One Boy, Two Paths**

1 Wilberforce Mss c.43 f.1
2 Life I p. 8
3 Fiennes p. 69
4 Robert Wilberforce's will, East Riding of Yorkshire Archives, Wilberforce Papers, DDHB 35/61
5 Jackson p. 313
6 Life I p. 3
7 Porter p. 185
8 Horace Walpole to Sir Horace Mann, 13 Dec 1759, Walpole
9 Wilberforce Mss c.43 f.1

10 Milner, Rev. I. p.vi
11 ibid p.iv
12 Scott pp. 56–7
13 Pryme p. 25
14 Corlass p. 11
15 Milner, Rev. I. p.xiii
16 Life I p. 4
17 Wilberforce Mss c.43 f.1
18 Wilberforce Mss e.11 f.122
19 Wilberforce Mss d.56 f.187
20 Milward p. 32
21 Harford p. 198
22 Wilberforce Mss d.56 f.187–8
23 Townsend Vol I p. 139
24 Whiteley p. 339–40
25 ibid
26 Brown p. 34
27 Venn, Rev. H. p. 76
28 Milner, Rev. I., Works Vol VIII p. 190
29 Watkins and Shoberl p. 355
30 Brown p. 33
31 Gunning Vol II p. 63
32 Wearmouth p. 135
33 Wade p. 22
34 Cole p. 52
35 Carpenter p. 75n
36 Boswell Vol III p. 200
37 Wearmouth p. 243
38 ibid p. 244
39 ibid pp. 243–4
40 Rupp pp. 389, 259
41 Horace Walpole to Sir Horace Mann, Letter 3 May 1749, Walpole
42 Carpenter p. 198
43 Namier p. 421
44 Life I p. 5
45 Harford p. 218
46 Life I p. 6
47 Wilberforce Mss d.56 f.187
48 Wilberforce Mss d.56 f.186
49 Wilberforce Mss e.11 f.123
50 Wilberforce Mss e.11 f.124
51 Life I p. 7
52 Wilberforce Mss d.56 f.186
53 Life I p. 7
54 Milner, Rev. I. p.xxiv
55 Lyles p. 40
56 Smith pp. 96–7, 'Methodism', Article in the *Edinburgh Review*, 1808
57 Goldsmith p. 7

58 Porter p. 49
59 Wilberforce Mss c.43 f.3
60 ibid
61 ibid
62 15 Nov 1771, Wilberforce Mss c.51 f.99
63 29 Nov 1771, Wilberforce Mss c.51 f.100
64 9 Aug 1772, Wilberforce Mss c.51 f.104
65 Sep 1772, Wilberforce Mss c.51 f.106
66 Wilberforce Mss c.4 f.2
67 Wilberforce Mss c.4 f.3
68 Wilberforce Mss c.4 f.11
69 14 Apr 1797, Wilberforce Mss c.40 f.106
70 Wilkinson, Patentee Vol I p. 111
71 Wilkinson, Memoirs Vol IV p. 52
72 11 Nov 1788, *Hull Packet*, Tickell p. 644
73 Jackson p. 267
74 Life I p. 8
75 Wilberforce Mss e.11 f.125
76 Wilberforce Mss c.43 f.3
77 Wilberforce Mss e.11 f.124
78 Wilberforce Mss e.11 f.126

TWO: **Ambition and Election**

1 Wilberforce Mss e.11 f.134
2 Wilberforce Mss d.56 f.186
3 Wilberforce Mss c.43 f.3
4 Life I p. 10
5 Winstanley p. 210
6 Hardwicke Papers Add Mss 35626 f.25
7 Mullinger p. 226
8 Baker p. 1086
9 Wilberforce Mss d.56 f.186
10 Porter p. 162
11 ibid
12 Life I p. 11
13 Wilberforce Mss e.11 f.126
14 College examinations book 1776–78, St John's College Cambridge c15.6
15 Life I p. 11
16 Wilberforce Mss c.43 f.3
17 Wilberforce to S. Roberts, 2 Apr 1817, Life I p. 12
18 Gisborne to William Smith, 15 Apr 1834, Wilberforce Mss c.65 f.112–14
19 ibid
20 Life III p. 58
21 Wilberforce Mss e.11 f.134

22 Wilberforce Mss e.11 f.127
23 Russell, Memoirs Vol I p. 127
24 ibid p. 139
25 Hague p. 34
26 Wilberforce Mss e.11 f.117
27 Pitt to Edward Eliot, 14 Mar 1780
   Pretyman Mss HA 119.T108.39.250
28 Pitt to Lady Chatham, 21 Jan 1775,
   Taylor and Pringle pp. 376–7
29 Stanhope, Life of the Rt. Hon.
   William Pitt Vol I p. 27
30 Pitt to Lady Chatham, 27 Mar 1780,
   Chatham Papers, PRO 30/8/12 fol.155
31 Wraxall Vol III p. 124
32 Life I p. 14
33 Pollock p. 10
34 Hadley p. 491
35 O'Gorman p. 154n
36 ibid p. 152
37 Namier and Brooke Vol III p. 617
38 O'Gorman p. 92
39 Pollock p. 11
40 ibid
41 Life I p. 14
42 ibid
43 Wilberforce Mss c.43 f.5
44 Wilberforce Mss d.56 f.181
45 Wilberforce Mss c.43 f.5
46 Pitt to Westmorland, 26 Jul 1779,
   Hague p. 56
47 17 May 1781, PR Vol III p. 350
48 5 Dec 1781, PH Vol XXII col. 800
49 ibid
50 Boulton Vol I p. 147
51 Timbs Vol I p. 110
52 ibid p. 111
53 Boulton p. 148
54 Timbs p. 116
55 Wilberforce Mss e.11 f.129
56 ibid
57 Life I p. 19
58 Porter pp. 264–5
59 Lord Macaulay's Journal, 16 May 1850,
   Trinity Mss O.152 f.318
60 Life I p. 30
61 Wilberforce Mss e.11 f.41
62 G. Edwards to Wilberforce, 5 Dec
   1782, Wilberforce Mss d.13.183
63 Wilberforce to Thompson, 9 Jun 1781,
   Wilberforce Mss c.51 f.12–13

THREE: **The Devoted Acolyte**

1 Philip Francis to Wyvill, 26 Dec 1794,
   Wyvill Mss ZFW 7.2.91.13
2 Life I p. 55
3 Black p. 234
4 ibid
5 Wraxall Vol II p. 139
6 22 Feb 1782, PR VI p. 274
7 Wilberforce Mss c.43 f.9
8 Stanhope, Life of the Rt. Hon.
   William Pitt Vol I p. 70
9 Wilberforce Mss c.43 f.5
10 Russell, Life Vol I p. 285
11 Wilberforce Mss c.43 f.5
12 Furneaux p. 21
13 Wilberforce Mss c.43 f.11
14 Pitt to Wilberforce, 6 Aug 1782, Duke
   Mss, Wilberforce Papers, Box I, Folder
   II
15 Diary, Wilberforce Ms Don e.164 f.12
16 Furneaux p. 22
17 Wilberforce Mss e.11 f.31
18 Wilberforce Mss e.11 f.32–3
19 Life I p. 32
20 ibid p. 33
21 ibid p. 23
22 Pollock p. 20
23 Wilberforce to Eliot, 15 Oct 1782,
   Stanhope Mss 731 (11)
24 Diary, Wilberforce Ms Don e.164 f.3
25 17 Feb 1783, PD Vol XXIII col. 441
26 Diary, 17 Feb 1783, Wilberforce Ms
   Don e.164 f.3
27 Wilberforce Mss c.43 f.7
28 Fitzmaurice Vol III p. 375
29 George III to Lord Temple, 1 Apr 1783,
   Fortescue Vol VI, no. 4272 p. 330
30 Diary, 24 Mar 1783, Wilberforce Ms
   Don e.164 f.4
31 Diary, 31 Mar and 3 Apr 1783,
   Wilberforce Ms Don e.164 f.7
32 Pitt to Wilberforce, 6 Aug 1783,
   Private Papers pp. 4–5
33 ibid p. 4
34 Diary, 20 Mar 1783, Wilberforce Ms
   Don e.164 f.6
35 Diary, 23 May 1783, Wilberforce Ms
   Don e.164 f.4
36 Pollock p. 18

37 Pitt to Wilberforce, 6 Aug 1783, Private Papers p. 5
38 Pitt to Wilberforce, 22 Aug 1783, Correspondence I p. 25
39 Life I p. 34
40 Wilberforce to Bankes, Life I p. 35
41 ibid
42 ibid p. 36
43 ibid
44 ibid
45 ibid
46 Wilberforce to Bankes, 28 Oct 1783, Life I p. 44
47 ibid
48 Diary, 17 Oct 1783, Wilberforce Ms Don e.164 f.16
49 Pollock p. 23
50 Wilberforce to Henry Bankes, 28 Oct 1783, Life I p. 43
51 Wilberforce Mss c.43 f.9
52 Hathaway Vol I p. 93
53 20 Nov 1783, PH XXXIII col. 1247
54 Buckingham Vol I pp. 288–9
55 Wraxall Vol III p. 191
56 ibid p. 195
57 Diary, 22 Dec 1783, Wilberforce Ms Don e.164 f.18
58 Diary, 23 Dec 1783, Wilberforce Ms Don e.164 f.19
59 Life I p. 48
60 1 Mar 1784, PH Vol XXIV col. 704
61 Diary, 1 Mar 1784, Wilberforce Ms Don e.164 f.21
62 Wilberforce Mss e.11 f.130
63 Life I p. 52
64 Diary, 25 Mar 1784, Wilberforce Ms Don e.164 f.22
65 Wilberforce Mss c.43 f.9
66 Life I p. 53
67 ibid p. 54
68 ibid
69 Account of the Debate at the Meeting at York, on the 25th day of March, 1784, Wyvill Political Papers Vol II p. 349
70 ibid pp. 349–50
71 Pitt to Wilberforce, 24 Mar 1784, Duke Mss, Wilberforce Papers, Box I, Folder II
72 Life I p. 57
73 ibid
74 Wilberforce Mss d.56 f.185
75 Wilberforce Mss c.43 f.9
76 Wilberforce Mss d.56 f.186
77 'Yorkshire Election Poll Book', Wilberforce Ms Don e.165 f.10
78 ibid f.14–15
79 ibid f.2
80 Diary, 27 Mar 1784, Wilberforce Ms Don e.164 f.23
81 Diary, 30 Mar 1784, Wilberforce Ms Don e.164 f.23
82 Diary, 3 and 5 Apr 1784, Wilberforce Ms Don e.164 f.23
83 Pollock p. 30
84 Diary, 7 and 8 Apr 1784, Wilberforce Ms Don e.164 f.23
85 Pitt to Wilberforce, 10 Apr 1784, Duke Mss, Wilberforce Papers, Box I, Folder II
86 Richard Sykes to Fitzwilliam, 16 Apr 1784, Fitzwilliam Mss (Northants)
87 ibid
88 Wilberforce to Hey, 3 Nov 1790, Correspondence I p. 75
89 ibid

FOUR: **Agony and Purpose**

1 Diary, 27 Nov 1785, Life I p. 91
2 Furneaux p. 48
3 Diary, 19 Sep 1784, Wilberforce Mss e.164 f.32
4 Wilberforce to Muncaster, 12 Nov 1784, Life I p. 67
5 ibid p. 68
6 ibid p. 67
7 ibid p. 68
8 Forster p. 43
9 Gunning Vol I p. 257
10 Pollock p. 32
11 Diary, 10–30 Nov 1784, Wilberforce Ms Don e.164 f.35–6, Wilberforce Mss c.43 f.11
12 Wilberforce Mss e.11 f.131
13 Life I p. 76
14 Wilberforce Mss c.43 f.11
15 Life I p. 75
16 Wilberforce Mss c.43 f.13
17 Pitt to Wilberforce, 19 Dec 1784, Private Papers p. 9

18 Furneaux p34
19 Wilberforce to Elizabeth Wilberforce, 30 Nov 1816, Private Papers p. 169
20 Doddridge, Rise p. 34
21 ibid p. 109
22 ibid p. 237
23 Life I p. 77
24 Wilberforce Mss c.43 f.13
25 Milner, M. p. 19
26 Wilberforce Mss c.43 f.13
27 ibid
28 Diary, May 1785, Wilberforce Ms Don e.164 f.42
29 18 Apr 1785, PD XXV col. 462
30 Diary, 23 May 1785, Life I p. 78
31 Diary, 19 Apr 1785, Wilberforce Ms Don e.164 f.41
32 Diary, 19 Apr 1785, Wilberforce Ms Don e.164 f.43
33 Pollock p. 36
34 Wilberforce to Mr Clapham, 14 May 1785, Pollock p. 36
35 Pitt to Wilberforce, 30 Sep 1785, Duke Mss, Wilberforce Papers, Box I, Folder II
36 Diary, 14 Apr 1785, Furneaux p. 34
37 Harford pp. 207–8
38 Life I pp. 83–4
39 ibid p. 88
40 Wilberforce to Eliot, 28 Sep 1785, Stanhope Mss 731 (11)
41 Wilberforce Mss e.11 f.132
42 Life I p. 88
43 Wesley, C., Journal pp. 146–7
44 Doddridge, Life p. 24
45 ibid p. 25
46 ibid p. 28
47 Wesley J., Journal Vol I p. 51
48 Cecil p. 60
49 ibid p. 77
50 Huntington pp. 111–12
51 Newton, Memoirs p. 8
52 Wilberforce to Samuel Wilberforce, 13 Sep 1814, Wilberforce Mss d.16 f.88
53 Wilberforce Mss e.11 f.131
54 Bullock p. 197
55 ibid p. 198
56 ibid p. 192
57 Life I p. 90

58 ibid p. 89
59 Starbuck p. 58
60 Diary, 28–30 Nov 1785, Life I pp. 90–2
61 Wilberforce Mss e.11 f.132
62 Life IV p. 338
63 Life I p. 90
64 ibid p. 98
65 Furneaux p. 48
66 Pitt to Wilberforce, 2 Dec 1785, Private Papers p. 12
67 ibid
68 ibid p. 13
69 ibid pp. 13–15
70 Life I p. 95
71 ibid p. 93
72 ibid p. 96
73 ibid p. 97
74 Newton to Cowper, 30 Jan 1786, Hannay Collection, CO134
75 Newton to Wilberforce, 12 Sep 1788, Correspondence I p. 64
76 Wilberforce Mss c.49 f.71
77 Thornton to Wilberforce, 24 Dec 1785, Life I pp. 103–4
78 Life I pp. 101–2
79 Wilberforce Mss c.43 f.14
80 Life I p. 106
81 Saunders p. 79
82 Wilberforce to Sally Wilberforce, 16 Apr 1786, Life I p. 111
83 Wilberforce to Mr O'Hara, 27 Jun 1795, Wilberforce Mss d.15 f.207
84 ibid
85 ibid
86 Belmonte p. 96
87 Overton p. 47
88 ibid p. 50
89 Life III p. 357
90 Life IV p. 242
91 ibid p. 248
92 Life I p. 99
93 Russell, Household of Faith p. 232
94 Wilberforce Mss c.43 f.14
95 Newton to Wilberforce, 21 Mar 1786, Wilberforce Mss c.49 f.4

FIVE: **Diligence and New Causes**

1 Life I p. 119
2 Catherine King to George King, 1 Nov

1786, Church Missionary Society Mss, Venn Papers ACC81 c23 f.16

3 Wilberforce to Samuel Wilberforce, 5 Dec 1822, Private Papers p. 206

4 Wilberforce to Wyvill, 16 Oct 1788, Wilberforce Mss d.56 f.19

5 1 Jun 1786, PH XXVI col. 60

6 Life V p. 341

7 Hathaway Vol I p. 331

8 Hague p. 234

9 Furneaux p. 49

10 15 Feb 1787, PH XXVI col. 441–2

11 Duncombe to Wyvill, 29 Jun 1786, Wyvill Mss 7.2.54

12 *Gentleman's Magazine*, Apr 1787 p. 179

13 Stirling, Annals II pp. 250–1

14 *Kentish Gazette*, Saturday 22– Wednesday 26 Jul 1769, in Morsley, News from the English Countryside p. 67

15 Pollock p. 41

16 5 Jul 1786, PH XIX col. 198

17 Journal, 8 Oct 1786, Life I p. 123

18 Life I pp. 118–19

19 ibid

20 Pollock p. 46

21 Hennell, 'Evangelical Spirituality', p. 138

22 Doddridge, Rise p. 150

23 Journal, 21 Jun 1786, Life I p. 116

24 Journal, 22 Jun 1786, Life I p. 117

25 Journal, 2 Jul 1786, Life I p. 118

26 30 Nov and 16 Dec 1786, Wilberforce Mss c.4 f.15–16

27 Life I p. 119

28 Wilberforce Mss c.43 f.14

29 Catherine King to George King, 1 Nov 1786, Church Missionary Society Mss, Venn Papers ACC81 c23 f.16

30 Wilberforce to Muncaster, 20 Oct 1786, Life I p. 124

31 ibid p. 125

32 Pollock p. 66

33 ibid p. 68

34 Hague p. 238

35 Life I p. 198

36 Pollock p. 59

37 Wilberforce Mss d.56 f.180–1

38 Life I p. 131

39 Pollock p. 60

40 Life I p. 130

41 Wilberforce to Hey, 12 Jun 1787, Life I p. 131

42 Egan I pp. 18–19

43 Sydney Smith to John Murray, 24 Oct 1830, Holland Vol II p. 310

44 Anonymous, A Dissertation upon Drunkenness, 1727, title page

45 22 Feb 1743, PH XII col. 1238

46 George Rose to Wilberforce, 4 Nov 1790, Duke Mss, Wilberforce Papers, Box I, Folder III

47 Egan I p. 19

48 Colquhoun pp.vii–xi

49 Porteus Mss 2103 f.8

50 ibid

51 Wilberforce to Hey, 29 May 1787, Correspondence I p. 52

52 Proclamation for the Encouragement of Piety and Virtue, and for Preventing and Punishing of Vice, Profaneness and Immorality, George III, June 1787

53 Manchester to Wilberforce, 18 Sep 1787, Duke Mss, Wilberforce Papers, Box 1, Folder II

54 Fitzwilliam to Revd Zouch, 2 Sep 1787, Fitzwilliam Wentworth Woodhouse Mss e.234.14

55 More, Thoughts pp. 119–20

56 Smith, *Edinburgh Review*, Jan 1809 p. 134

57 Wilberforce to D. Ryder, 27 Sep 1787, Pollock p. 64

58 ibid

59 Hazlitt p. 219

60 Furneaux p. 299

61 Radzinowicz III p. 496

62 Webb pp. 53, 84

63 Robert Smith to Wilberforce, 1786, Correspondence I p. 44

64 Wilberforce to Sally Wilberforce, 1787, Correspondence II pp. 60–1

65 Pollock p. 50

six: **The Trade in Flesh and Blood**

1 Aristotle Book I

2 Davis p. 61

3 Thomas p. 69
4 ibid p. 89
5 ibid p. 155
6 ibid p. 156
7 ibid
8 Donnan Vol IV p. 49
9 Thomas p. 196
10 ibid
11 ibid p. 247
12 An African Merchant p. 7
13 Equiano pp. 48–50
14 Thomas p. 370
15 Newton, Journal p. 109
16 Wadstrom pp. 1–2
17 Donnan Vol II p. 570
18 ibid p. 445
19 Falconbridge pp. 12–13
20 Newton, Journal pp. 29, 31, 32
21 Falconbridge pp. 14–15
22 Equiano Vol I p. 71
23 Newton, Journal p. 105
24 ibid p. 75
25 Thomas pp. 404–5
26 Equiano pp. 78–9
27 Falconbridge p. 28
28 ibid p. 25
29 Thomas p. 422
30 ibid p. 410
31 Isaac Parker, Evidence to the Select Committee Appointed to take Examination of Witnesses on the Slave Trade, Vol LXXIII p. 123
32 ibid
33 Newton, Journal p. 104
34 Frezier p. 301
35 Falconbridge p. 34
36 Equiano pp. 86–7
37 28 May 1777, PH XIX col. 305
38 Montesquieu Bk XV, Ch I, trans Cohler, Miller and Stone p. 246
39 Rousseau Bk I, Ch IV, trans Cele p. 10
40 Ferguson pp. 201–2
41 Thomas p. 468
42 Smith, A., Book III Chapter II pp. 488–9
43 Paley Ch III p. 49
44 Klingberg p. 31
45 Wesley, J., Thoughts pp. 24–7
46 Clarkson, History Vol I p. 138

47 Bruns p.xxii
48 ibid pp.xxiii–iv
49 Kolchin pp. 76–7
50 Bruns p.xxix
51 ibid
52 Benezet p. 33
53 Anstey, The Atlantic Slave Trade p. 244
54 Sharp pp. 6–7
55 Pollock p. 11
56 Wilberforce Mss c.43 f.20
57 Hoare Vol I p. 239
58 ibid p. 241
59 Pollock p. 51
60 Clarkson, Essay p. 75
61 Clarkson, History Vol I p. 210
62 La Trobe p. 22
63 Porteus Diary, 16 March 1807, Porteus Mss 2104, f.95
64 Wilberforce to James Stephen, 15 Jan 1817, Life I p. 149
65 Clarkson, History I p. 241
66 ibid p. 254
67 Journal, 28 Oct 1787, Life I p. 149
68 12 May 1789, PH XXVIII col. 48

SEVEN: **Early Optimism**

1 Wilberforce to Wyvill, 25 Jan 1788, Wyvill Mss ZWF 7.2.59.13
2 Letter, 5 Mar 1788, *Gentleman's Magazine*, April 1788 p. 311
3 Life I p. 131
4 Wilberforce to Eden, Jan 1788, Auckland Papers BM Add Mss 34427.402
5 Howse p. 32
6 Harford p. 139
7 Pollock p. 58
8 Life I p. 151
9 Wilberforce Mss c.43 f.31–2
10 Fairminute book, 22 May 1787, Add Mss 21.254 f.2
11 ibid
12 ibid fol.5
13 Clarkson, History Vol I p. 286
14 ibid p. 284
15 Pollock p. 71
16 Anstey, Liverpool p. 186
17 Drescher p. 207n

18 Fairminute book, 16 Oct 1787, Add Mss 21.254 f.16
19 Clarkson, History Vol II pp. 191–2
20 ibid p. 111
21 Wilberforce to Lord Stanhope, 25 Jan 1788, Stanhope, G. and G. p. 72
22 Wilberforce to Wyvill, 25 Jan 1788, Wyvill Mss ZWF 7.2.59.13
23 Wyvill to Wilberforce, 17 Mar 1788, Wyvill Mss ZWF 7.2.59.16
24 Walvin in Hayward p. 36
25 Clarkson, History Vol I p. 412n
26 ibid p. 323
27 ibid p. 324
28 ibid pp. 324–5
29 ibid p. 325
30 ibid p. 359
31 ibid p. 293
32 ibid p. 365
33 ibid p. 386
34 ibid p. 409
35 ibid p. 410
36 Robert Wilberforce to Clarkson, 18 Jul 1834, Clarkson, Strictures p. 7
37 Wilberforce to Macaulay, 6 Aug 1811, Duke Mss, Wilberforce Papers
38 Life I p. 152
39 Taylor p. 25
40 Clarkson, Strictures p. 52
41 Life I p. 153
42 Diary, Dec 1787–Jan 1788, Wilberforce Mss b.2 f.3
43 Wilberforce to Eden, 23 Nov 1787, Auckland Papers BM Add 34427.123
44 Wilberforce to Eden, 7 Dec 1787, Auckland Papers BM Add 34427.183–4
45 Life I p. 158
46 Diary, 24 Jan 1788, Life I p. 161
47 Report of the Lords of the Committee of the Council appointed for the Consideration of all Matters relating to Trade and Foreign Plantations; submitting to His Majesty's consideration the Evidence and Information they have collected in consequence of his Majesty's Order in Council, cover page
48 Diary, Jan 1788, Wilberforce Mss b.2 f.3
49 Clarkson, History Vol I p. 292
50 Diary, 19 Feb 1788, Wilberforce Mss b.2 f.3
51 Pollock p. 78
52 Wilberforce to Wyvill, 8 Mar 1788, Wilberforce Mss d.56 f.16
53 Harford p. 90
54 Life I p. 169
55 Rob Harris to Wyvill 27 Mar 1788, Wyvill Mss ZWF 7.2.59.19
56 Wilberforce to Wyvill, 25 Apr 1788, Wilberforce Mss d.56 f.16
57 9 May 1788, PD col. 502
58 ibid col. 504
59 Wilberforce Mss c.43 f.27
60 17 Jun 1788, PH XXVII col. 598
61 Hague p. 298
62 Pitt to Grenville, 29 Jun 1788, Fortescue Vol I p. 342
63 Wilberforce Mss b.2 f.4
64 ibid
65 Pollock p. 82
66 ibid pp. 81–2
67 Pereira Vol II p. 1758
68 Milner to Wilberforce, 16 Nov 1793, Wilberforce Mss d.15 f.32
69 Life I p. 174
70 Jones pp. 23–5, 32,
71 Diary, 3 Apr, 1 Mar 1818, Wilberforce Mss c.37, f.120, 112
72 Pollock p. 79
73 Life I p. 175
74 Journal, 7 Jun 1788, Life I p. 176
75 ibid
76 Life I p. 181
77 ibid p. 179
78 ibid p. 183
79 ibid p. 181
80 ibid p. 182
81 Wilberforce Mss b.2 f.9
82 ibid
83 Wilberforce to Wyvill, 25 Apr 1788, Wilberforce Mss d.56 f.17
84 Wilberforce to Freeholders of the County of York, Wyvill Mss ZWF 7.2.59.34
85 Wyvill to Wilberforce, 4 Oct 1788, Wyvill Mss ZWF 7.2.59.24
86 Wilberforce Mss d.56 f.20
87 Diary, 11 Nov 1788, Wilberforce Mss b.2 f.7

88 Thomas Steele to Wilberforce, Wilberforce Mss c.50 f.49
89 Wilberforce to Wyvill, 6 Dec 1788, Wilberforce Mss d.56 f.23
90 Diary, 17 Jan 1789, Wilberforce Mss b.2 f.9
91 19 Jan 1789, PR XXV p. 283
92 Wilberforce Mss b.2 f.8
93 ibid
94 Wilberforce to Wyvill, 17 Nov 1788, Wilberforce Mss d.56 f.22
95 Journal, 20 Mar 1789, Life I p. 210

EIGHT: **Eloquence Without Victory**

1 12 May 1789, PD XXVIII col. 63
2 Life I pp. 296–7
3 Fuller to Jamaica Committee of Correspondence, 30 Jan 1788, Duke Mss, Fuller Letter Book
4 Fuller to Lord Sydney, 29 Jan 1788, Duke Mss, Fuller Letter Book
5 Fuller to Jamaica Committee of Correspondence, 6 Feb 1788, Duke Mss, Fuller Letter Book
6 ibid
7 Report of the Lords of the Committee of the Council appointed for the Consideration of all Matters relating to Trade and Foreign Plantations; submitting to His Majesty's consideration the Evidence and Information they have collected in consequence of his Majesty's Order in Council p. 224
8 ibid p. 44
9 ibid pp. 122–3
10 ibid p. 123
11 ibid p. 119
12 ibid p. 40
13 ibid p. 117
14 Harris, R. p. 287
15 Beckford pp. 270–1
16 McNeill, 'Review of New Publications', *Gentleman's Magazine*, Dec 1788 p. 1094
17 Letter, 23 Apr 1789, *Gentleman's Magazine*, Apr 1789 p. 334
18 'Review of New Publications', *Gentleman's Magazine*, Jul 1789 p. 633

19 Picton p. 260
20 Diary, 8 Apr 1789, Wilberforce Mss b.2 f.12
21 Petition to the House of Commons, 12 May 1789, Donnan Vol II pp. 605–6
22 ibid p. 611
23 Diary, 8 Apr 1789, Wilberforce Mss b.2 f.13
24 Harford pp. 44–5
25 Namier p. 2
26 12 May 1789, PH XXVIII col. 41–2
27 ibid col. 42
28 ibid
29 ibid col. 43
30 ibid col. 44
31 ibid
32 ibid col. 45–6
33 ibid col. 46–7
34 ibid col. 48
35 ibid col. 49
36 ibid col. 53
37 ibid col. 52
38 ibid col. 54
39 ibid
40 ibid col. 54–5
41 ibid col. 55
42 ibid col. 57
43 ibid col. 59
44 ibid col. 60
45 ibid col. 61
46 ibid col. 63
47 ibid col. 42
48 ibid col. 68
49 ibid col. 76
50 ibid
51 Wilberforce Mss c.43 f.25
52 12 May 1789, PH XXVIII col. 67
53 ibid col. 68
54 ibid col. 73
55 ibid col. 76
56 ibid col. 92
57 Wilberforce Mss c.43 f.22
58 Hochschild p. 161
59 ibid pp. 161–2
60 ibid p. 161
61 Pollock p. 90
62 Wilberforce Mss c.43 f.22
63 Life I pp. 294–5
64 Furneaux p. 93
65 Clarkson, History Vol II p. 122

66 Diary, 13 Jul 1789, Wilberforce Mss b.2
    f.16
67 Clarkson, History Vol II pp. 137–8
68 ibid p. 153
69 Life I p. 236
70 Diary, 23 Aug 1789, Wilberforce Mss
    b.2 f.18
71 Diary, 6 Sep 1789, Wilberforce Mss b.2
    f.18
72 Diary, 1 Jan 1790, Wilberforce Mss b.2
    f.19
73 23 Apr 1790, PH XVIII col. 712
74 Diary, 20 Apr 1790, Wilberforce Mss
    b.2 f.20
75 Life I p. 222
76 Clarkson, History Vol II p. 179
77 ibid p. 200
78 Extracts from the Evidence delivered
    before a Select Committee of the
    House of Commons, in the Years 1790
    and 1791; on the part of the
    Petitioners for the Abolition of the
    Slave Trade p. 18
79 ibid p. 19
80 ibid
81 J. Beckett to Fitzwilliam, 24 Mar 1788,
    Fitzwilliam Wentworth Woodhouse
    Mss F.34, 160
82 ibid
83 Life I p. 272
84 ibid
85 ibid p. 282
86 Diary, 2 Dec 1790, Wilberforce Mss
    b.2 f.23
87 Diary, 16 Dec 1790, Wilberforce Mss
    b.2 f.23
88 Life I p. 288
89 18 Apr 1791, PH XXIX col. 278
90 Diary, 18 Mar 1791, Wilberforce Mss
    b.2 f.25
91 Life I p. 297
92 Clarkson, History Vol II p. 208
93 ibid pp. 210–11
94 8 Apr 1791, PH XXIX col. 363
95 18 Apr 1791, PH XXIX col. 271
96 Diary, 18 Apr 1791. Wilberforce Mss
    b2. f.25
97 18 Apr 1791, PH XXIX col. 352
98 ibid col. 281
99 ibid col. 282
100 ibid. col. 278
101 ibid
102 ibid

NINE: 'An Overflowing Mind'

1 Life I p. 193
2 Stephen, Sir J. Vol II p. 213
3 Pollock p. 103
4 Harford p. 3
5 ibid
6 ibid p. 255
7 Wilberforce to Samuel Wilberforce, 14
   Jun 1823, Wilberforce Mss c.1 f.52
8 ibid
9 Stephen, Sir J. Vol II p. 142
10 ibid
11 Harford p. 259
12 ibid p. 258
13 Gurney p. 15
14 Life I p. 257
15 ibid p. 256
16 Harford pp. 97–8
17 Life I p. 163
18 Wilberforce to Mornington, 20 Apr
    1799, Wellesley Papers, Add Mss 37308
    f.228
19 Wilberforce to Muncaster, 24 Aug
    1798, Pollock p. 98
20 Wilberforce to Muncaster, 16 Jun 1791,
    Correspondence I p. 79
21 Wilberforce to Samuel Roberts, 31 Dec
    1813, Correspondence II p. 127
22 Wilberforce to Wyvill, 23 Feb 1796,
    Wyvill Mss ZFW 7.2.106.19
23 Wilberforce to Hannah More, 28 Sep
    1804, Life III p. 194
24 Life I p. 328
25 Wilberforce to William Manning, 20
    Jan 1792, Life I p. 330
26 Diary, 8, 9 and 11 Oct 1790,
    Wilberforce Mss b.2 f.22–3
27 Life I p. 282
28 Wyvill to Wilberforce, 11 Nov 1789,
    Duke Mss, Wilberforce Papers, Box I,
    Folder II
29 Farington p. 2828
30 Stephen, Sir J. Vol II p. 145
31 Harford p. 70
32 Furneaux p. 80

33 Harford p. 258
34 Forster p. 19
35 Harford p. 258
36 Wilberforce to Muncaster, 10 May 1804, Life III pp. 157–8
37 Wilberforce Mss e.11 f.80
38 Life V pp. 286–7
39 Diary, 1, 2 and 13 Dec 1790, Wilberforce Mss b.2 f.23
40 Wilberforce Mss d.56 f.169
41 Life I p. 182
42 Diary, Jan–Feb 1789, Wilberforce Mss b.2 f.10
43 Life I p. 198
44 Diary, 15 Jul 1789, Wilberforce Mss b.2 f.16
45 Life I pp. 250–1
46 Diary, 22 May 1791, Wilberforce Mss b.2 f.25
47 Journal, 28 Aug 1791, Wilberforce Mss c.40 f.3–4
48 Journal, 18 Sep 1791, Wilberforce Mss c.40 f.5
49 Journal, 25 Sep 1791, Wilberforce Mss c.40 f.6
50 Journal, 29 Aug 1791, Life I p. 313
51 Price p. 89
52 ibid p. 88
53 Life V p. 345
54 Wilberforce Mss e.11 f.84–5
55 Wilberforce Mss e.11 f.25
56 Diary, 15 Feb 1789, Wilberforce Mss b.2 f.10
57 Diary, 27 Nov 1790, Wilberforce Mss b.2 f.23
58 Life I p. 309
59 ibid p. 358
60 ibid p. 359
61 ibid p. 356
62 Wilberforce to Addington, 30 Jul 1787, Pollock p. 71
63 Wilberforce to Addington, 23 Jul 1787, Sidmouth Mss 152M.C1787.OZ2
64 ibid
65 Wilberforce Mss e.11 f.16–17
66 Wilberforce Mss e.11 f.16
67 Life II pp. 304–5
68 Life I p. 138
69 Wilberforce Mss d.56 f.160
70 Diary, 2 Jul 1791, Life I p. 305

71 Friends' paper, 12 Jan 1794, Life II p. 405
72 Diary, 4 May 1791, Life I p. 300
73 Harford p. 157
74 Wilberforce Mss d.56 f.155
75 Wilberforce Mss d.56 f.182
76 Wilberforce Mss d.56 f.180
77 Wilberforce to Eliot, 20 Jul 1792, Stanhope Mss 731 (11)
78 Trevelyan Vol I pp. 166–7
79 Journal, 24 Aug 1791, Life I p. 312
80 Wilberforce to Babington, 22 Jul 1791, Life I p. 310
81 Howse p. 16
82 Furneaux p. 117
83 Diary, 14 Jan, and nd 1795, Thornton Mss 7674 I.R
84 Diary, 13 Dec 1791, Life p. 322
85 Pollock p. 94
86 ibid p. 95
87 Dorothy Wordsworth to Jane Pollard, 30 Apr 1790, Selincourt p. 27
88 Stephen, Sir J. Vol II p. 194
89 Forster p. 42
90 Furneaux p. 120
91 Sierra Leone Company, 19 Oct 1791 p. 3
92 ibid
93 Fyfe p. 16
94 Sierra Leone Company, 19 Oct 1791 pp. 4–5
95 Sharp to Mrs. —, 12 Jan 1788, Hoare, Granville Sharp p. 313
96 Diary, 2 Aug 1791, Life I p. 307
97 Wilberforce to Wyvill, 17 Dec 1792, Life I p. 325
98 Wilberforce to John Clarkson, 28 Dec 1791, BL Add Mss 41626 A f.28
99 Sierra Leone Company, 19 Oct 1791 p. 51
100 Wilberforce to John Clarkson, 28 Dec 1791, BL Add Mss 41626 A f.28
101 Life I p. 333

TEN: **The Independent**

1 Life II p. 4
2 ibid p. 72
3 Clarkson, History Vol II p. 346
4 Wilberforce to Hey, 21 Feb 1792, Life I p. 334

5 Clarkson, History Vol II pp. 349–50

6 Anonymous Letter, 31 Dec 1794, *Gentleman's Magazine*, December 1794

7 Life I p. 340

8 ibid p. 341

9 ibid

10 Pollock p. 115

11 2 Apr 1792, PH XXIX col. 1057

12 ibid col. 1058

13 ibid col. 1061

14 ibid

15 ibid col. 1065

16 ibid col. 1073

17 ibid col. 1091

18 ibid col. 1156–7

19 Pitt to Dundas, 25 Nov 1792, Pitt Mss

20 Wilberforce Mss c.43 f.33

21 2 Apr 1792, PH XXIX col. 1107

22 Wilberforce to Hey, 3 Apr 1792, Life I pp. 345–6

23 Life I p. 351

24 Wilberforce to John Clarkson, 27 Apr 1792, BL Add Mss 41626 A f.83

25 Wilberforce Mss c.43 f.23

26 Porteus Diary, 25 Apr 1792, Porteus Mss 2100 f.57–8

27 3 May 1792, PH XXIX col. 1439–50

28 Thomas p. 523

29 Wilberforce to Anon, 6 Nov 1792, Wilberforce Mss d.15.174

30 Anonymous, A Very New Pamphlet Indeed! pp. 3–4

31 Life II p. 18

32 Journal, 4 Oct 1792, Wilberforce Mss c.40 f.48

33 Journal, 24 Aug 1792, Wilberforce Mss c.40 f.42–3

34 Journal, 4 Nov 1792, Wilberforce Mss c.40 f.50

35 Journal, 11 Nov 1792, Wilberforce Mss c.40 f.50

36 Journal, Wilberforce Mss c.40 f.51

37 Diary, 3 Dec 1792, Life II p. 1

38 Wilberforce to Wyvill, 14 Feb 1793, Wyvill Mss 7.2.82.2

39 Wilberforce to Hey, 14 Feb 1801, Life II p. 13

40 ibid

41 Life II p. 11

42 Sharp to Archbishop —, 7 Jun 1793, Hoare, II p. 247

43 Fuller to Jamaica Committee of Correspondence, 5 June 1793, Duke Mss, Fuller Letterbook

44 ibid 4 March 1794

45 Wilberforce to Lord Muncaster, 5 Apr 1794, Life II p. 50

46 Hoare to Philadelphia Abolition Society, 14 Aug 1795, Philadelphia Abolition Society Am S. 081, Anstey, Atlantic Slave Trade p. 280

47 Clarkson, History Vol II p. 469

48 Wilberforce to Muncaster, 19 May 1794, Life II pp. 52–3

49 Pollock p. 130

50 Life II p. 39

51 ibid p. 44

52 ibid p. 40

53 Wilberforce to James Currie, 13 Apr 1793, Currie Mss 920 Cur 50

54 Life II p. 27

55 Dundas to Wilberforce, 7 Mar 1794, Wilberforce Mss d.17 f.74

56 Diary, 3 Aug 1793, Life II p. 33

57 Journal, 8 Dec 1793, Wilberforce Mss c.41 f.5

58 Diary, 9 Aug 1794, Wilberforce Mss c.34 f.33

59 Diary, 8 Nov 1794, Wilberforce Mss c.34 f.36

60 Diary, 14 Oct 1793, Life II p. 45

61 Wilberforce to Currie, 13 Aug 1793, Currie Mss 920 Cur 50

62 Wilberforce to Muncaster, 30 Jun 1794, Wilberforce Mss d.15 f.192

63 Wilberforce to Muncaster, 3 Nov 1794, Wilberforce Mss d.15 f.201

64 Life II p. 92

65 Diary, 10 Jul 1794, Wilberforce Mss c.34 f.30

66 Life II p. 67

67 Wilberforce to Eliot, 22 Dec 1794, Stanhope Mss U1590 S5 O4/11

68 Wilberforce to Archdeacon Wrangham, 20 Dec 1820, Life II p. 71

69 Wilberforce Mss c.41 f.28

70 ibid

71 31 Dec 1794, col. 1016
72 ibid col. 1026
73 Portland to Fitzwilliam, 7 Jan 1795, Fitzwilliam Mss f.31.36
74 ibid
75 Life II p. 72
76 Feiling p. 203
77 Milner to Wilberforce, 4 Jan 1795, Life II pp. 75–6
78 5 Jan 1795, PH XXXI col. 1129
79 Fitzwilliam Mss F.31.36, Portland to Fitzwilliam, 7 Jan 1795
80 Life II p. 74
81 ibid p. 78
82 26 Jan 1795, PH XXXI col. 1234
83 Life II p. 90
84 14 May 1795, PH XXXI col. 1492
85 Diary, 12 Feb 1795, Wilberforce Mss c.34 f.47
86 Wilberforce to S. Roberts, 2 April 1817, Pollock p.130
87 Diary, 21 Mar 1795, Wilberforce Mss c.34 f.52
88 Diary, 25 Apr 1795, Wilberforce Mss c.34 f.58
89 Diary, 26 Apr 1795, Wilberforce Mss c.34 f.58
90 Diary, 12 May 1795, Wilberforce Mss c.34 f.61
91 Diary, 21 May 1795, Wilberforce Mss c.34 f.63
92 Pollock p. 131
93 Life II p. 110
94 Wilberforce to Camden, 18 June 1795, Camden Mss
95 Life II p. 80
96 Furneaux p. 134
97 Baring p. 336
98 Aspinall, Later Correspondence of George III Vol II p. 416n
99 9 Nov 1795, PH Vol XXXII col. 279
100 ibid col. 294
101 ibid col. 293
102 Journal, 22 Nov 1795, Wilberforce Mss c.41 f.67
103 Life II p. 122
104 ibid
105 ibid p. 125
106 ibid p. 127
107 Furneaux p. 138
108 Wilberforce to William Hey, 7 Dec 1795, Furneaux p. 138
109 Life II p. 128
110 W. Cookson to Wilberforce, 3 Dec 1795, Life II p. 130
111 Life II p. 135

ELEVEN: **Consuming Passions**

1 Wilberforce, A Practical View, Chapter III pp. 94–5
2 Journal, 31 Dec 1797, Wilberforce Mss c.41 f.114
3 18 Feb 1796, PH XXXII col. 738
4 ibid col. 739
5 ibid PH XXXII col. 739
6 ibid PH XXXII col. 744
7 Diary, 20 Feb 1796, Wilberforce Mss c.34 f.102
8 Diary, 22 Feb 1796, Wilberforce Mss c.34 f.103
9 Diary, 3 Mar 1796, Wilberforce Mss c.34 f.104
10 15 Mar 1796, PH XXXII col. 874
11 Diary, 15 Mar 1796, Wilberforce Mss c.34 f.106
12 Fuller to Jamaica Committee of Correspondence, 30 Jan 1788, Duke Mss, Fuller Letterbook
13 5 Apr 1796, PH XXXII col. 997
14 Wilberforce to Pretyman, 30 Jun 1796, Stanhope Mss, U1590 S5 04/12
15 Journal, 17 Apr 1796, Wilberforce Mss c.41 f.83
16 Diary, 15 Mar 1796, Wilberforce Mss c.34 f.106
17 Diary, 27 May 1796, Wilberforce Mss c.34 f.114
18 Diary, 7 Jun 1796, Wilberforce Mss c.34 f.117
19 Journal, 15 Jun 1796, Wilberforce Mss c.41 f.88
20 Journal, 3 Jul 1796, Wilberforce Mss c.41 f.89
21 Wilberforce to Muncaster, 18 Aug 1796, Life II p. 167
22 Life V pp. 227–8
23 Journal, 25 Oct 1795, Wilberforce Mss c.41 f.63

24 Newton to Wilberforce, 21 Jul 1796, Wilberforce Mss c.49 f.71

25 Journal, 4 Sep 1796, Wilberforce Mss c.41 f.94

26 Diary, 15 Sep 1796, Wilberforce Mss c.34 f.125

27 Wilberforce to Macaulay, 29 Sep 1796, Life II p. 173

28 2 Nov 1796, PH XXXII col. 1253

29 ibid

30 ibid

31 Life II p. 172

32 Furneaux p. 150

33 Diary, 30 Dec 1796, Wilberforce Mss c.34 f.132

34 Journal, 2 Jan 1797, Furneaux pp. 150–1

35 Diary, 2 Jan 1797, Wilberforce Mss c.34 f.132

36 Diary, Jan 1797, Wilberforce Mss c.34 f.134

37 Anstey, The Atlantic Slave Trade p. 327

38 6 Apr 1797, PH XXXIII col. 277

39 Stephen, Sir J. Vol II p. 164

40 Wilberforce, A Practical View, Introduction p. 1

41 ibid p. 2

42 Stephen, Sir J. Vol II p. 165

43 Life II p. 199

44 Wakefield pp. 3–4, 38–9

45 Belsham p. 3

46 Bishop Porteus to Wilberforce, 10 May 1797, Life II pp. 200–1

47 Newton to Wilberforce, 18 Apr 1797, Wilberforce Mss c.49 f.125

48 Life II pp. 199–200

49 Henry Thornton to Hannah More, 20 Oct 1798, Thornton Mss 7674 1.L.2 f.9

50 Young pp. 287–8

51 Grimshawe p. 27

52 Overton pp. 105–6

53 Wilberforce Mss d.56 f.7

54 Wilberforce, A Practical View, Introduction p. 2

55 ibid Ch VII p. 489

56 ibid Introduction p. 2

57 ibid Ch IV p. 266

58 Pollock p. 146

59 Wilberforce, A Practical View Ch I pp. 7, 12

60 ibid Ch I p. 16

61 ibid Ch II p. 45

62 ibid p. 448

63 Diary, 8 Jan 1797, Wilberforce Mss c.41 f.102

64 Wilberforce, A Practical View Ch IV p. 276

65 ibid Ch III pp. 85–6

66 ibid Ch VII pp. 485–7

67 ibid Ch VI pp. 418–19

68 ibid Introduction p. 3

69 ibid Ch IV pp. 410–11

70 ibid Ch III p. 80

71 ibid Ch III pp. 94–5

72 Life II p. 214

73 ibid

74 Life I p. 304

75 Wilberforce, A Practical View Ch VII pp. 434–5

76 Forster p. 42

77 Diary, 13 Apr 1797, Wilberforce Mss c.34 f.137

78 Forster p. 42

79 Diary, 15 Apr 1797, Wilberforce Mss c.34 f.137

80 Journal, 16 Apr 1797, Wilberforce Mss c.41 f.107

81 Diary, 20 Apr 1797, Wilberforce Mss c.34 f.137

82 Diary, 21 Apr 1797, Wilberforce Mss c.34 f.137

83 Diary, 23 Apr 1797, Wilberforce Mss c.34 f.137

84 Diary, 13 May 1797, Wilberforce Mss c.34 f.138

85 Life II pp. 218–19

86 Diary, 28 May 1797, Wilberforce Mss c.34 f.138

87 Pollock p. 158. Huntingdon Mss, Montagu Papers, W to Montagu, nd

88 Journal, 23 Apr 1797, Wilberforce Mss c.40 f.107

89 Wilberforce Mss d.20 f.34

90 ibid f.36

91 Furneaux p. 165

92 Henry Thornton to his sister, 2 May 1797, Pym pp. 195–6

93 Diary, 28 Oct 1811, Life III p. 555

94 Diary, 24 Apr 1803, Life III p. 95
95 Dorothy Wordsworth to Catherine Clarkson, 18 Sep 1818, Shaver, Moorman and Hill Vol II p. 483
96 Forster p. 43
97 ibid
98 Wilberforce Mss c.41 f.110
99 Diary, 21 Sep 1797, Wilberforce Mss c.34 f.144
100 Life II p. 417
101 Wilberforce to Hannah More, Sep 1797, Correspondence I p. 148
102 Wilberforce to Muncaster, 27 Sep 1797, Life II p. 236
103 10 Nov 1797 PH XXXIII col. 1024
104 Wilberforce to Babington, 6 Nov 1797, Life II p. 241
105 21 Dec 1798, PH XXXIV col. 115
106 ibid
107 ibid col. 122
108 Furneaux p. 191
109 Journal, 23 Dec 1798, Wilberforce Mss c.41 f.124
110 Furneaux pp. 193–4
111 Wilberforce to William Smith, 20 Feb 1798, Life II p. 269
112 Diary, 28 May 1798, Wilberforce Mss c.34 f.153
113 George III to Pitt, 30 May 1798, Stanhope Vol III, Appendix p.xiv
114 Wilberforce, A Practical View, Ch IV p. 219
115 ibid p. 220
116 ibid p. 221
117 Pitt to Wilberforce, 30 May 1798, Duke Mss, Wilberforce letters, Box I, Folder IV
118 Diary, 30 May 1798, Wilberforce Mss c.34 f.153
119 Wilberforce to Pitt, 2 Jun 1798, Life II pp. 283–4
120 Pitt to Wilberforce, 2 Jun 1798, Life II p. 284
121 Life II p. 298
122 Diary, 10 and 11 Jun 1798, Wilberforce Mss c.34 f.154
123 Wilberforce to Barbara, 7 Jul 1798, Life II p. 295
124 Journal, 21 Jul 1798, Wilberforce Mss c.41 f.121
125 Life II pp. 262, 261
126 ibid p. 265
127 ibid
128 The Times, 8 Jul 1799, quoted in The Later Correspondence of George III, Aspinall, III no.1983n
129 Diary, 4 Jun 1799, Wilberforce Mss c.34 f.166
130 Diary, 6 Jul 1799, Wilberforce Mss c.34 f.166

TWELVE: **Darkness Before Dawn**

1 Wilberforce to Muncaster, 6 Jul 1804, Life III p. 182
2 Wilberforce to Babington, 22 Mar 1803, Life III pp. 87–8
3 Thomas pp. 540–1
4 Wilberforce to Hey, 8 Apr 1799, Life II p. 332
5 Diary, 25 Aug 1799, Wilberforce Mss c.34 f.168
6 Diary, 24 Aug 1802, Life III p. 62
7 Life III p. 22
8 Wilberforce to Hannah More, 22 Nov 1804, Correspondence I p. 254
9 Wilberforce to Samuel Wilberforce, 12 Oct 1823, Mss Wilberforce c.1 f.63
10 Diary, 15 Dec 1819, Wilberforce Mss c.37 f.198
11 Warter IV pp. 316–17
12 Teignmouth Vol I p. 3
13 Life III p. 71
14 Wilberforce to Muncaster, 8 Jan 1801, Correspondence I pp. 176–7
15 Henry Thornton to Hannah More, 30 Oct 1799, Life II p. 350
16 Wilberforce to Gisborne, 12 Oct 1801, Life III p. 16
17 Stephen, Sir J. Vol II pp. 143–4
18 Diary, 22 Nov 1803, Life III p. 140
19 Diary, 12 Jan 1800, Furneaux p. 197
20 PR LV p. 397
21 25 Apr 1800, PH XXXV col. 116
22 10 Jun 1800, PH XXXV col. 322
23 24 May 1802, PH XXXVI cols 845, 847
24 Life II pp. 304–5
25 Pollock p. 171

26 ibid p. 170

27 Wilberforce to Muncaster, 6 Dec 1800, Life II p. 384

28 Pollock p. 171

29 ibid

30 Wilberforce to William Hey, 6 Dec 1800, Life II p. 385

31 Wilberforce to Muncaster, 6 Dec 1800, Life II p. 384

32 Pollock p. 171

33 Life II p. 381

34 ibid

35 Wilberforce to William Hey, 20 Oct 1800, Life II p. 382

36 Hague p. 465

37 Earl Camden, Memorandum on Pitt's Retirement, 1803–4, Willis, *Bulletin of the Institute of Historical Research*, XLIV no. 110 p. 252

38 Wilberforce Mss e.11 f.139–40

39 Journal, 8 Feb 1801, Life III p. 3

40 Wilberforce to Muncaster, 7 Feb 1801, Life III p. 2

41 ibid

42 4 Nov 1801, PH XXXVI col. 140

43 Diary, 4 Feb 1802, Life III pp. 37–8

44 Life III pp. 28–34

45 Diary, 27 May 1802, Wilberforce Mss c.35 f.55

46 Wilberforce to William Hey, 14 Apr 1802, Life III p. 51

47 William Gray to Mrs Wilberforce, 14 Jul 1802, Life III p. 52

48 Journal, 17 Aug 1802, Life III p. 60

49 Pollock p. 181

50 23 May 1803, PH XXXVI col. 1400

51 Wilberforce to Muncaster, 14 Jul 1803, Life III p. 107

52 10 Aug 1803, PH XXXVI col. 1702

53 Journal, 4 Sep 1803, Life III p. 122

54 Life III p. 143

55 Wilberforce to Muncaster, 10 Mar 1804, Life III p. 149

56 Owen Vol I p. 62

57 Wilberforce to Muncaster, 10 May 1804, Life III p. 161

58 Diary, 16 May 1804, Life III p. 166

59 ibid

60 Pitt to Wilberforce, 30 May 1804, Life III p. 167

61 Wilberforce to Rev J.J. Plymley, 31 May 1804, Life III p. 169

62 12 Jun 1804, PD II col. 658

63 Diary, 27 Jun 1804, Life III p. 178

64 Wilberforce to Muncaster, 6 Jul 1804, Life III p. 182

65 ibid

66 Diary, 31 Dec 1804, Life III p. 191

67 Wilberforce to Bankes, 4 Oct 1804, Life III p. 207

68 Hague p. 210

69 Journal, 3 Mar 1805, Life III p. 213

70 Diary, 3 Jul 1804, Life III p. 184

71 Life III p. 234

72 ibid p. 218

73 Hathaway Vol IV p. 423

74 Wilberforce Mss d.56 f.171

75 Life III p. 221

76 8 Apr 1805, PD III col. 319

77 Furneaux p. 234

78 8 Apr 1805, PD III col. 320

79 Diary, 8 Apr 1805, Life III p. 222

80 Notebook of Lord Fitzharris, 1806, Malmesbury Vol IV p. 355n

81 Life III p. 241

82 Ashbourne p. 360

83 Diary, 25 Dec 1805, Life III p. 245

84 Harcourt Vol II p. 231

85 Wilberforce to Muncaster, 25 Jan 1806, Life III p. 245

86 Wilberforce to William Hey, 12 Feb 1806, Life III p. 250

THIRTEEN: **Abolition**

1 Porteus Mss 2104 f.91

2 Diary, 5 Apr 1806, Life III p. 260

3 W. Smith to Wilberforce, 17 Nov 1806, Life III p. 259

4 Wilberforce to Gisborne, 11 Feb 1806, Correspondence II p. 330

5 ibid

6 Life III p. 258

7 ibid p. 259

8 Milner to Wilberforce, 7 Feb 1806, Correspondence II p. 327

9 Wilberforce to Grenville, 23 Apr 1806, Dropmore Mss BL Add 58978 f.18

10 Stephen, War in Disguise pp. 74–6

11 Wilberforce to Grenville, 24 Mar 1806, Dropmore Mss BL Add 58978 f.13
12 25 Apr 1806, PD VI col. 919
13 ibid
14 Diary, 5 Apr 1806, Life III p. 260
15 1 May 1806, PD VII col. 1022
16 ibid col. 1023–4
17 7 May 1806, PD VII col. 32–3
18 16 May 1806, PD VII col. 233
19 Life III p. 261
20 6 May 1806, PD VII col. 232
21 Journal, 18 May 1806, Life III p. 261
22 Wilberforce to Grenville, 20 May 1806, Dropmore Mss BL Add 58978 f.31
23 Grenville to Wilberforce, 20 May 1806, Duke Mss, Wilberforce Papers
24 10 Jun 1806, PD VII col. 585
25 ibid col. 580–1
26 ibid col. 593
27 ibid col. 595
28 Wilberforce to Grenville, 5 Jun 1806, Dropmore Mss BL Add 58978 f.37
29 Diary, 28 Jun 1806, Life III p. 271
30 Diary, 10 Jun 1806, Life III p. 263
31 Wilberforce to William Hey, 1 Aug 1806, Life III p. 269
32 Life III p. 273
33 ibid
34 Diary, 15 Oct 1806, Life III p. 275
35 Wilberforce to William Hey, 1 Aug 1806, Life III p. 264
36 Joseph Armytage to Fitzwilliam, 25 Oct 1806, Fitzwilliam (Wentworth Woodhouse) Mss E.209.50
37 Robert Sinclair to Fitzwilliam, 22 Oct 1806, Pollock p. 207
38 Life III p. 278
39 ibid p. 281
40 ibid pp. 281–2
41 Diary, 30 Oct 1806, ibid p. 283
42 Wilberforce to Grenville, 1 Nov 1806, Dropmore Mss BL Add 58978 f.73
43 Wilberforce to Captain Bedford, 7 Dec 1806, Life III p. 286
44 4 Mar 1807, PD VIII col. 1086
45 Grenville to Wilberforce, 5 Nov 1806, Dropmore Mss BL Add 58978 f.78
46 Thomas p. 550
47 Wilberforce, Letter p. 2
48 ibid pp. 4–5

49 ibid p. 6
50 ibid p. 57
51 ibid p. 206
52 ibid pp. 350–1
53 Thornton to Wilberforce, 26 Aug 1806, Life III p. 272
54 Williams p. 152
55 Anstey, The Atlantic Slave Trade p. 387
56 5 Feb 1807, PD VIII col. 664
57 Furneaux p. 250
58 Life III p. 298
59 Porteus Mss 2104 f.91
60 16 Mar 1807, PD IX col. 138
61 ibid col. 139

FOURTEEN: **High Respect; Low Politics**

1 John Hill to Joseph Tarn, Secretary of the British and Foreign Bible Society, 31 May 1808, Bible Society Mss
2 Wilberforce to Bankes, 26 Jul 1809, Life III p. 414
3 Wilberforce to Grenville, 25 Feb 1807, Dropmore Mss Add 58978 f.110
4 Sir James Mackintosh to Wilberforce, 27 Jul 1807, Life III pp. 302–3
5 Life III pp. 270–1
6 Furneaux p. 301
7 Pollock p. 221
8 Wilberforce to Pretyman, 9 Apr 1807, Stanhope MSS, U1590, S5 04/12
9 Wilberforce to Ralph Creyke, 11 Apr 1807, Life III p. 314
10 Life III p. 315
11 A Collection of the Speeches, Addresses, and Squibs p. 100
12 Life III p. 317
13 Gray p.iii
14 Life III p. 315
15 ibid p. 316
16 Furneaux p. 263
17 Pollock p. 216
18 A Collection of the Speeches, Addresses, and Squibs p. 18
19 ibid pp. 18–19
20 ibid p. 19
21 ibid
22 ibid

23 ibid
24 ibid pp. 23–4
25 Furneaux p. 265
26 Gray p. 11
27 ibid p. 13
28 ibid p. 14
29 Life III p. 320
30 ibid p. 322
31 A Collection of the Speeches, Addresses, and Squibs p. 59
32 ibid
33 ibid pp. 60–1
34 Life III p. 324
35 Furneaux pp. 263–4
36 Life III p. 333
37 ibid p. 324
38 A Collection of the Speeches, Addresses, and Squibs p. 61
39 Life III p. 325
40 ibid pp. 335–6
41 Wilberforce to Barbara Wilberforce, 22 May 1807, Life III p. 325
42 Life III p. 329
43 ibid p. 330
44 A Collection of the Speeches, Addresses, and Squibs p. 42
45 Furneaux p. 267
46 Life III pp. 328–9
47 A Collection of the Speeches, Addresses, and Squibs pp. 82–3
48 ibid p. 84
49 Life III p. 331
50 Wilberforce to Barbara Wilberforce, 24 May 1807, Life III p. 326
51 Furneaux p. 270
52 Life III p. 331
53 Pollock p. 217
54 A Collection of the Speeches, Addresses, and Squibs p. 105
55 Wilberforce to Hannah More, 8 Jun 1807, Life III p. 332
56 Life III p. 336
57 ibid pp. 341–2
58 Thornton to Hannah More, 22 Sep 1807, Thornton Mss 7674 1.L.4 f.56–7
59 Wilberforce Mss e.11 f.27–8
60 Life III p. 235
61 ibid
62 Wilberforce to W. Huskinsson, 4 Jul 1810, BM Add Mss 39948 f.25

63 Thornton to Mrs Thornton, 8 Jan 1812, Thornton Mss 7674 1.L.5 f.24
64 Thornton to H. More, 30 Nov 1809, Thornton Mss 7674 1.L.4 f.115–16
65 Wilberforce to Samuel Roberts, 29 Jul 1811, Life III p. 527
66 Life III p. 458
67 Wilberforce to John Jay Esq., 10 Jul 1810, Correspondence II p. 67
68 Life IV p. 208
69 Diary, 15 Jun 1810, Wilberforce Mss d.54 f.60
70 Farington, 19 Jul 1806 Vol VIII p. 2821
71 Harford p. 2
72 ibid p. 8
73 Diary, 5 Jul 1809, Wilberforce Mss d.54 f.35
74 Wilberforce to a friend, Aug 1809, Correspondence II p. 54
75 ibid
76 Wilberforce to Babington, 28 Sep 1808, Life III p. 379
77 Pollock p. 231
78 Furneaux p. 290
79 Wilberforce to R. Creyke, 9 Jan 1811, Wilberforce Mss d.16 f.76
80 Diary, 7 Jun 1811, Wilberforce Mss d.54 f.106
81 Life III p. 521
82 Pollock p. 219
83 Diary, 13 Sep 1807, Furneaux p. 303
84 Life III p. 347
85 29 Mar 1808, PD X col. 1288
86 Furneaux p. 304
87 Diary, 30 Mar 1810, Wilberforce Mss d.54 f.53
88 Wilberforce to Muncaster, 19 Jul 1808, Life III p. 369
89 Wilberforce to Babington, 20 Nov 1809, Life III p. 431
90 ibid
91 Life III p. 432
92 ibid p. 360
93 Furneaux p. 286
94 ibid p. 284
95 Life V p. 241
96 Frothingham, 5 May 1818 p. 50
97 Stephen, G. p. 80
98 Diary, 1 Feb 1809, Wilberforce Mss d.54 f.25

99 Wilberforce to William Hey, 16 Feb
     1809, Life III p. 402
100 Wilberforce to William Hey, 18 Mar
     1809, Life III p. 405
101 Diary, 19 Mar 1809, Wilberforce Mss
     d.54 f.27
102 18 May 1809, PD XIV col. 624
103 Life III p. 487
104 Wilberforce to Lord Grenville, 28 Mar
     1807, Dropmore Mss BL Add 58978
     f.114
105 Thomas p. 562
106 Wilberforce to Macaulay, 19 Oct 1809,
     Mss Wilberforce d.6.66
107 Thomas p. 567
108 Pollock p. 228
109 Life III p. 374
110 ibid
111 ibid p. 518

FIFTEEN: **The Struggle Renewed**

  1 19 Jun 1816, PD XXXIV col. 1166
  2 Freemen of Hull to Wilberforce, 20
     Oct 1812, Wilberforce Mss c.52 f.71
  3 Walpole, S. Vol II p. 193
  4 Diary, 22 Jan 1811, Wilberforce Mss
     d.54 f.81
  5 Diary, 11 May 1812, Wilberforce Mss
     d.54 f.148
  6 ibid f.149
  7 Diary, 14 May 1812, Wilberforce Mss
     d.54 f.149
  8 Journal, 17 May 1812, Wilberforce Mss
     d.54 f.150 and Life IV pp. 26–7
  9 Diary, 16 May 1812, Life IV p. 30
 10 Life IV p. 17
 11 Wilberforce to Hannah More, 5 Nov
     1812, Life IV p. 81
 12 Thomas p. 581
 13 Diary, 30 Nov 1812, Wilberforce Mss
     d.54 f.159–60
 14 Wilberforce to Samuel Roberts, 29 Jul
     1811, Life III pp. 529–30
 15 Diary, 24 Aug 1811, Wilberforce Mss
     d.54 f.114
 16 Life III p. 535
 17 Harford p. 8
 18 Wilberforce to Calthorpe, 23 Oct 1822,
     Calthorpe Mss 26 M62.F.C86
 19 James Stephen to Wilberforce, 26 Jul
     1811, Correspondence II pp. 84–8
 20 Life IV p. 78
 21 Wilberforce to Samuel Roberts, 29 Jul
     1811, Life III p. 531
 22 Life III p. 541
 23 Life IV p. 65
 24 Freemen of Hull to Wilberforce,
     20 Oct 1812, Wilberforce Mss c.52
     f.71–2
 25 Life IV p. 83
 26 Diary, 26 May 1808, Wilberforce Mss
     d.54 f.3
 27 Wilberforce to William Hey, 22 Feb
     1813, Life IV p. 95
 28 ibid p. 96
 29 Diary, 9 Mar 1813, Wilberforce Mss
     d.54 f.171
 30 Barnes p. 71
 31 9 Mar 1813, PD XXIV col. 1239
 32 ibid col. 1239–40
 33 Life IV p. 359
 34 Wilberforce to S. Roberts, 25 Jan 1816,
     Correspondence II p. 168
 35 Wilberforce to Butterworth, 15 Feb
     1812, Life IV pp. 10–11
 36 Life IV p. 112
 37 Pollock p. 237
 38 22 Jun 1813, PD XXVI col. 856
 39 ibid col. 864–5
 40 ibid col. 854–5
 41 Barnes pp. 72–3
 42 1 Jul 1813, PD XXVI col. 1072
 43 Life IV pp. 140–1
 44 Pollock p. 239
 45 Diary, 25 Mar 1814, Wilberforce Mss
     c.37 f.11
 46 Diary, 9 Feb 1814, Wilberforce Mss
     c.37 f.1
 47 Diary, 11 Mar 1814, Wilberforce Mss
     c.37 f.8
 48 Life IV p. 167
 49 ibid p. 373
 50 Diary, 4 Jun 1814, Wilberforce Mss
     c.37 f.23
 51 Life IV p. 188
 52 Thomas p. 580
 53 Life IV pp. 136–7
 54 ibid p. 173
 55 ibid p. 175

56 Diary, 23 Apr 1814, Wilberforce Mss c.37 f.15
57 Wilberforce to Harford, 26 Jul 1814, Duke Mss, Wilberforce Papers, Box III, Folder I
58 Life IV p. 181
59 Wilberforce, Letter to Talleyrand p. 43
60 ibid p. 19
61 Maxwell p. 195
62 Diary, 12Jun 1814 Wilberforce Mss c.37 f.24
63 ibid
64 ibid
65 Petition, agreed at Freemasons' Hall on 17 Jun 1814, Life IV p. 193
66 27 Jun 1814, PD XXVIII col. 278
67 ibid
68 ibid col. 275
69 Duke of Wellington, 29 Jul 1814, Thomas p. 582
70 Wilberforce to Grenville, 21 Dec 1814, Dropmore Mss Add 58978 f.134–5
71 Life IV p. 229
72 Wilberforce to Lady Lieven and Melville, 18 Jan 1815, Melville Mss GD 26.13.873
73 Pollock p. 248
74 Diary, 15 Mar 1815, Life IV p. 249
75 Wilberforce to Lord Liverpool, 17 Mar 1815, Life IV p. 252
76 General Treaty signed in Congress at Vienna, 1816, Thomas p. 584
77 Diary, 8 Mar 1815, Life IV p. 244
78 ibid
79 Wilberforce to his son William, 15 Mar 1815, Life IV pp. 247–8
80 ibid
81 Diary, 10 May 1815, Life IV p. 259
82 Diary, 29 May 1815, Wilberforce Mss c.37 f.41
83 Diary, 18 Jun 1815, Wilberforce Mss c.37 f.43
84 Life IV p. 261
85 ibid p. 262
86 Derry p. 183

SIXTEEN: **Under Attack**

1 Cobbett, *Political Register*, 3 Oct 1818
2 Life IV p. 284

3 Wilberforce to Hannah More, 19 Jul 1815, Correspondence Vol II p. 159
4 ibid
5 Wilberforce to family, 25 Jul 1815, Life IV p. 267
6 Wilberforce to Hannah More, 1 Feb 1816, Correspondence Vol II p. 169
7 Life IV p. 279
8 Wilberforce to Hannah More, 1 Feb 1816, Correspondence Vol II p. 170
9 Life IV p. 281
10 Gurney p. 7
11 ibid
12 ibid p. 8
13 William Wordsworth to Viscount Lowther 14 Oct 1818, Shaver, Moorman and Hill p. 494
14 Gurney p. 9
15 Warter Vol III pp. 99–100
16 Rush, 12 Apr 1818 p. 171
17 Life IV pp. 300–1
18 ibid p. 373
19 Frothingham, 5 May 1818 p. 50
20 Stephen, Sir J. Vol II p. 167
21 Frothingham, 5 May 1818 p. 50
22 22 May 1816, PD XXXIV col. 719–20
23 Life IV p. 305
24 19 Jun 1816, PD XXXIV col. 1158
25 ibid col. 1153
26 ibid
27 ibid col. 1158
28 9 Jul 1817, PD XXXVI col. 1324
29 ibid col. 1323
30 Derry p. 184
31 Diary, 30 Apr 1817, Wilberforce Mss c.37 f.30
32 Wilberforce to Macaulay, 9 Oct 1817, Life IV p. 330
33 Life IV p. 307
34 Belchem p. 64
35 Life IV p. 308
36 Cobbett, *Political Register*, 14 Dec 1816
37 Cobbett, *Political Register*, 3 Oct 1818
38 Ziegler p. 375
39 Life V p. 34
40 23 Nov 1819, PD XXXI col. 135–6
41 Hazlitt p. 219
42 ibid p. 220

43 5 Mar 1818, PD XXXVII col. 852
44 Furneaux p. 365
45 5 Mar 1818, PD XXXVII col. 858
46 27 Jun 1817, PD XXXVI col. 1247
47 Furneaux p. 366
48 Brougham p. 151
49 Life IV p. 315
50 ibid
51 Life V p. 46
52 Life IV p. 308
53 23 Jun 1817, PD XXXVI col. 1120
54 Life IV p. 91
55 Diary, 16 Dec 1819, Wilberforce Mss
    c.37 f.198
56 Wilberforce to S. Roberts, 13 Jul 1820
57 Life IV p. 345
58 ibid p. 355
59 Pollock p. 253
60 ibid p. 254
61 Diary, 30 Jan 1818, Wilberforce Mss
    c.37 f.105
62 Diary, 31 Jan 1818, Wilberforce Mss
    c.37 f.106
63 Diary, 10 May 1818, Wilberforce Mss
    c.37 f.135
64 Life V p. 83

SEVENTEEN: **Trials of Faith**

1 Life V p. 76
2 Bowman p. 180
3 Life IV p. 67
4 Fraser p. 50
5 Castle Vol I p. 75
6 Bury Vol I p. 21
7 Aspinall, Correspondence of George,
   Prince of Wales Vol III p. 379
8 Bowman p. 130
9 Prince to Lord Eldon, 1 Jan 1818,
   Fraser p. 302
10 Bowman p. 180
11 Yonge Vol III p. 17
12 Castlereagh to Lord Stewart, 13 Feb
   1820, Londonderry Vol II p. 211
13 PD, 7 Jun 1820 col. 906
14 ibid col. 982
15 Hobhouse [Broughton] MS diary
   7 June 1820, Add Mss 56541 f.40
16 Diary, 8 Jun 1820, Wilberforce Mss
   c.37 f.234

17 Life V p. 58
18 Pollock p. 273
19 Diary, 21 Jun 1820, Wilberforce Mss
    c.37 f.236
20 Queen Caroline to Wilberforce, 20
    Jun 1820, Wilberforce Mss d.13 f.57
21 PD, 21 Jun 1820 col. 1202
22 Hobhouse [Broughton] MS diary
    21 June 1820, Add Mss 56541 f.43b
23 Fraser p. 393
24 22 Jun 1820, PD col. 1213
25 ibid col. 1223
26 ibid col. 1227
27 Wilberforce to Barbara Wilberforce,
    23 Jun 1820, Life V p. 60
28 Wilberforce to Barbara Wilberforce,
    24 Jun 1820, Life V p. 62
29 Diary, 12 Jul 1820, Wilberforce Mss
    c.37 f.240
30 Life V p. 66
31 Fraser p. 400
32 Smith, A Queen on Trial p. 63
33 Wilberforce to Hannah More, 21 Jul
    1820, Life V pp. 71–2
34 Life V p. 73
35 Cobbett, *Political Register*, 12 Aug 1820
36 Lord Melbourne to Wilberforce, 10
    Aug 1820, Life V p. 76
37 Life V p. 76
38 Wilberforce to Bankes, 19 Sep 1820,
    Life V p. 78
39 Smith, A Queen on Trial, p. 68
40 Barham Vol I p. 199
41 Wilberforce to Barbara Wilberforce,
    22 Jan 1821, Life V p. 84
42 Wilberforce to Robert Wilberforce,
    Jul 1820, Wilberforce Mss d.16
    f.223–4
43 Richardson p. 208
44 Bowman p. 285
45 Diary, 15 Mar 1817, Wilberforce Mss
    c.37 f.63
46 Book of private thoughts, 4 Sep 1816,
    Furneaux p. 352
47 Diary, 8 Jan 1819, Wilberforce Mss c.37
    f.150
48 Pollock p. 265
49 Furneaux p. 352
50 Diary, 14 Mar 1819, Wilberforce Mss
    c.37 f.165

51 Diary, 1 Apr 1820, Wilberforce Mss c.37 f.213
52 William Spooner to Lord Calthorpe, 17 May 1821, Calthorpe Mss 26M62/F/C/273
53 Diary, 21 Feb 1821, Life V p. 95
54 Life V p. 98
55 Wilberforce to Harrison, 16 Jan 1822, Duke Mss, Wilberforce Papers, Box III, Folder IV
56 Pollock p. 280
57 Life V p. 91
58 ibid pp. 112–14
59 26 Jun 1821, PD col. 1327
60 ibid col. 1328
61 26 Jun 1821, PD col. 1329
62 15 Jul 1822, PD col. 1651
63 25 Jul 1822, PD col. 1794
64 Wilberforce to Macaulay, 15 Aug 1821, Life V pp. 105–6
65 Wilberforce to Macaulay, 21 Nov 1821, Life V p. 107
66 Wilberforce to W. Allen, 13 Feb 1822, Life V p. 120
67 Wilberforce to James Stephen, 5 Oct 1820, Life V p. 79
68 Diary, 27 Dec 1822, Wilberforce Mss c.37 f.269–70
69 Diary, 3 Feb 1821, Buxton p. 105
70 Wilberforce to Buxton, 24 May 1821, British Empire Mss s.18 c.106/4–4a
71 Life V p. 136
72 ibid p. 135
73 Wilberforce to Bankes, 4 Nov 1822, Life V p. 143
74 Canning to Wilberforce, 24 Oct 1822, Correspondence II pp. 274–5
75 Wilberforce to Babington, 28 Jan 1823, Life V p. 165
76 Life V p. 170

EIGHTEEN: 'An Increase of Enjoyments'

1 Life V p. 239
2 ibid p. 263
3 Wilberforce, An Appeal p. 3
4 ibid p. 56
5 ibid p. 27
6 Life V p. 171
7 18 Mar 1823, PD XLIX col. 626
8 ibid col. 625
9 Life V p. 171
10 15 May 1823, PD L col. 286
11 Wilberforce to his son, 17 May 1823, Life V p. 178
12 Wilberforce, An Appeal p. 3
13 ibid p. 19
14 ibid
15 Cobbett, Political Register, August 1823
16 ibid p. 352
17 ibid pp. 353–4
18 ibid p. 356
19 Belmonte p. 278
20 ibid
21 Life V p. 202
22 Wilberforce, An Appeal pp. 48–9
23 16 Mar 1824, PD LI col. 1147
24 ibid col. 1148
25 ibid col. 1149
26 Diary, 10 May 1824, Life V p. 221
27 Wilberforce to his son Henry, 5 Jun 1824, Pollock p. 289
28 11 Jun 1824, PD XI col. 1274
29 Life V p. 222
30 15 Jun 1824, PD XI col. 1408
31 ibid col. 1416
32 Forster p. 129
33 Pollock p. 290
34 ibid
35 Clarkson, Diary of Travels, 2 Oct 1824, Clarkson Mss, National Library of Wales, NLW 14984a
36 Heyrick p. 18
37 ibid pp. 3–4
38 Wilberforce to Macaulay, 2 Jul 1824, Huntington Mss, MY 917
39 Life V p. 229
40 ibid pp. 233–4
41 Wilberforce to Babington, 5 Oct 1824, Life V p. 230
42 Buxton to Wilberforce, 6 Feb 1825, Wilberforce Mss d.13 f.67
43 Life V pp. 237–8
44 Newsome p. 37
45 Life V p. 263
46 ibid
47 ibid p. 251
48 ibid p. 247

49 ibid p. 248
50 Diary, 15 June 1826, Life V p. 272
51 Forster p. 136
52 Life V p. 327
53 Sprague p. 46
54 Life V p. 312
55 ibid p. 280
56 ibid pp. 280–1
57 ibid p. 288
58 Wilberforce to Buxton, 23 Mar 1826, Rhodes House Mss c106/7
59 Wilberforce to Buxton, 22 Dec 1832, Rhodes House Mss c106/22
60 Furneaux p. 436
61 Wilberforce to Lady Sparrow, 24 Feb 1830, Life V p. 310
62 Furneaux p. 439
63 Wilberforce to Babington, 14 Mar 1831, Pollock p. 303
64 Life V p. 325
65 Wilberforce to Brougham, 28 Apr 1831, UCL Mss, Brougham Papers 10.439
66 Pollock p. 305
67 Furneaux p. 441
68 Life V p. 332
69 Wrangham pp. 9, 1972
70 Life V p. 332
71 Taylor p. 128
72 Stephen, G. pp. 120–2
73 Wilberforce to Buxton, 23 Nov 1832, Life V p. 351
74 Wilberforce to Macaulay, 1 Jan 1832, Life V p. 352
75 Life V p. 354
76 14 May 1833, PD col. 1229

NINETEEN: **His Feet on the Rock**

1 Life V p. 371
2 Wilberforce to Lord Calthorpe, 27 Jun 1833, Life V p. 356
3 Life V p. 368
4 ibid p. 363
5 ibid p. 365
6 Jay p. 313
7 ibid p. 314
8 Life V p. 368
9 ibid p. 340
10 ibid p. 367
11 Wilberforce to William Smith, 25 Jun 1833, Pollock p. 307
12 Gladstone Vol II p. 51
13 Life V p. 369
14 ibid p. 372
15 J.B. Macaulay to Edward Baines, 30 Jul 1833, Pollock p. 308
16 Life V p. 370
17 ibid p. 373
18 ibid
19 ibid
20 Belmonte, 2007, Appendix p. 344
21 Stephen, Sir J. Vol II pp. 141–2
22 Brougham Vol I pp. 343–4
23 ibid p. 344
24 Lecky Vol VI p. 289
25 Life V p. 241
26 *Gentleman's Magazine*, Sep 1833 p. 274
27 Stephen, G. p. 79
28 ibid
29 Wilberforce Mss e.11 f.20
30 Life V p. 175

BIBLIOGRAPHY

MANUSCRIPTS

Bodleian Library, Oxford

British Empire Mss
Wilberforce Mss

British Library, London

Auckland Papers
Clarkson Mss
Grenville Papers
Hardwicke Papers
Minute Book of the Committee of the Society for Effecting the Abolition of
    the Slave Trade
Wellesley Papers

Cambridge University Library

Bible Society Mss
St John's College, College Examinations Book, 1776–1778
Thornton Mss
Trinity Mss

Duke University, North Carolina

Wilberforce Papers

East Riding of Yorkshire Archives

Wilberforce Papers

HAMPSHIRE RECORD OFFICE
Calthorpe Mss

HUNTINGTON LIBRARY, CALIFORNIA
Wilberforce Papers

KENT RECORD OFFICE
Camden Mss
Stanhope Papers

LAMBETH PALACE LIBRARY
Porteus Mss

LIVERPOOL RECORD OFFICE
Currie Mss

NATIONAL LIBRARY OF WALES
Clarkson Mss

NORTHAMPTONSHIRE RECORD OFFICE
Wentworth Woodhouse Mss

NORTH YORKSHIRE RECORD OFFICE
Wyvill Mss

PRINCETON UNIVERSITY LIBRARY
Hannay Collection

PUBLIC RECORD OFFICE, KEW
Chatham Papers

SHEFFIELD CITY LIBRARY
Wentworth Woodhouse Mss

SUFFOLK RECORD OFFICE

Pretyman Mss

UNIVERSITY OF BIRMINGHAM

Church Society Mss

UNIVERSITY COLLEGE LIBRARY, LONDON

Brougham Papers

WILLIAM L. CLEMENTS LIBRARY, MICHIGAN

Pitt Mss

PARLIAMENTARY PAPERS

Evidence to the Select Committee Appointed to take Examination of
Witnesses on the Slave Trade, 10 May 1790, House of Commons Sessional
Papers of the Eighteenth Century, Vol LXXIII

Extracts from the Evidence delivered before a Select Committee of the
House of Commons, in the Years 1790 and 1791; on the part of the
Petitioners for the Abolition of the Slave Trade

Parliamentary Debates from the Year 1803 to the Present Time. London:
Hansard, 1812 and later years

Parliamentary History of England, from the Earliest Period to the Year 1803.
London: Hansard, 1814

Parliamentary Register: or History of the proceedings and debates of the
House of Commons (and House of Lords) containing the most interesting
speeches, etc., London, 1775–1813

Proclamation for the Encouragement of Piety and Virtue, and for Preventing
and Punishing of Vice, Profaneness and Immorality, George III, June 1787

Report of the Lords of the Committee of the Council appointed for the
Consideration of all Matters relating to Trade and Foreign Plantations;
submitting to His Majesty's consideration the Evidence and Information
they have collected in consequence of his Majesty's Order in Council, 1789

BOOKS AND ARTICLES

A Collection of the Speeches, Addresses, and Squibs, produced by all parties during the late Contested Election for the County of York, Betwixt William Wilberforce, Esq, Lord Viscount Milton, and The Hon Henry Lascelles, which terminated on the fifth of June, 1807, when the two former Gentlemen were declared duly Elected, 1807

An African Merchant, *A Treatise upon the Trade from Great Britain to Africa, humbly recommended to the Attention of Government,* London, 1772

Anonymous, *A Dissertation upon Drunkenness,* 1727

Anonymous, *A Very New Pamphlet Indeed! Being the Truth addressed to the People At Large containing some strictures on the English Jacobins and the evidence of Lord McCartney, and others, before the House of Lords, respecting the Slave Trade,* London, 1792

Anstey, R., *The Atlantic Slave Trade and British Abolition 1760–1810,* Macmillan, 1975

Anstey, R., *Liverpool, the Atlantic Slave Trade and Abolition,* Historic Society of Lancashire and Cheshire, 1976

Aristotle, *Politics,* translated by Jowett, Clarendon Press, Oxford, 1905

Ashbourne Gibson, E., *Pitt: Some Chapters of His Life and Times,* Longmans, London, 1898

Aspinall, A., *Correspondence of George, Prince of Wales,* Vols I–VIII, Cassell, 1963

Aspinall, A., *The Later Correspondence of George III,* Vols I–V, Cambridge University Press, Cambridge, 1962

Baker, T., *History of the College of St. John the Evangelist,* Cambridge University Press, Cambridge, 1869

Barham, R.H.D., *The Life and Remains of Theodore Edward Hook,* Bentley, London, 1849

Baring, H., *The Diary of the Rt Hon William Windham,* London, 1866

Barnes, T., *Parliamentary Portraits,* Baldwin, Craddock and Joy, London, 1815

Bartlett, W., *The History and Antiquities of the Parish of Wimbledon, Surrey,* Simpkin, Marshall, London, 1865

Beckford, W., *Remarks upon the Situation of Negroes in Jamaica, impartially made from a local experience of nearly thirteen years in that island,* Egerton, 1788

Belmonte, K., *Hero for Humanity*, Navpress, Colorado, 2002, and Zondervan, Michigan, 2007

Belsham, T., *A Review of Mr Wilberforce's Treatise, entitled 'A Practical View of the Prevailing Religious System of Professed Christians, &c' in Letters to a Lady*, Johnson, London, 1798

Benezet, A., *A Caution and Warning to Great Britain and her Colonies*, Miller, Philadelphia, 1766

Black, J., *War for America: the Fight for Independence, 1775–1783*, Sutton, Stroud, 1991

Boswell, S., *Life of Johnson*, Constable & Co., London, 1896

Boulton, W., *The Amusements of Old London*, Nimmo, London, 1901

Bowman, W., *The Divorce Case of Queen Caroline*, Routledge & Sons, London, 1830

Brandon, O., *Christianity from Within*, Hodder & Stoughton, London, 1965

Bready, J., *England: Before and After Wesley*, Hodder & Stoughton, London, 1938

Brougham, H., *Historical Sketches of Statesmen Who Flourished in the Time of George III*, Vols I–III, Richard Griffin & Co., London, 1858

Brown, F.K., *Fathers of the Victorians*, Cambridge University Press, 1961

Bruns, R., *Am I Not a Man and a Brother: the Antislavery Crusade of Revolutionary America, 1688–1788*, Chelsea House, New York, 1977

Buckingham, D., *Memoirs of the Court and Cabinet of George III*, Vols I–IV, London, 1853–55

Bullock, *Evangelical Conversion in Great Britain 1696–1845*, Sussex, 1959

Bury, C., *The Court of England Under George IV*, Vols I–II, Macqueen, London, 1896

Buxton, Sir T.F., *Memoirs*, John Murray, London, 1848

Caffrey, K., *The Lion and the Union*, André Deutsch, London, 1978

Carpenter, S.C., *Eighteenth Century Church and People*, Murray, London, 1959

Castle, E., The *Jerningham Letters 1780–1843*, Vols I–II, Bentley, London, 1896

Cecil, R., *The Life of the Rev John Newton*, Religious Tract Society, London, 1843

Clarkson, T., *An Essay on the Slavery and Commerce of the Human Species*, Phillips, London, 1786

Clarkson, T., *The History of the Rise, Progress and Accomplishment of the Abolition of the African Slave-Trade by the British Parliament*, Vols I–II, Longmans, London, 1808

Clarkson, T., *Strictures on a Life of William Wilberforce*, Longmans, London, 1838

Clarkson, T., *An Essay on the Slavery and Commerce of the Human Species, particularly the African*, Cadell, London, 1786

Cobbett, W., *Political Register*, 1802–1835

Cole, W., *The Blecheley Diary*, Constable, London, 1931

Colquhoun, P., *Treatise on the Police of the Metropolis*, Dilly, London, 1796

Corlass, R., *The Hull Grammar School*, H. Bolton, Hull, 1878

Coupland, R., *Wilberforce*, Clarendon Press, Oxford, 1923

Davis, D.B., *The Problem of Slavery in the Age of Revolution, 1770–1823*, Cornell University Press, Ithaca, 1975

Derry, J., *Castlereagh*, Allen Lane, London, 1976

Deverell and Watkins, *Wilberforce and Hull*, Kingston Press, Hull, 2000

Doddridge, P., *The Rise and Progress of Religion in the Soul*, Religious Tract Society, London, 1745

Doddridge, P., *The Life of Colonel James Gardiner*, Edinburgh, 1799

Donnan, E., *Documents Illustrative of the Atlantic Slave Trade*, Vols I–IV, London, 1965

Drescher, S., *Capitalism and Antislavery*, Macmillan, London, 1986

Egan, P., *Life in London*, Book I, London, 1822

Equiano, O., *The Interesting Narrative of the Life of Olaudah Equiano, or Gustavus Vassa, the African*, London, 1789

Falconbridge, A., *An Account of the Slave Trade*, Phillips, London, 1788

Farington, J., *The Diary of Joseph Farington*, Yale University Press, New Haven, 1978

Feiling, K., *The Second Tory Party*, Macmillan, London, 1938

Ferguson, A., *Institutes of Moral Philosophy*, Edinburgh, 1773

Fiennes, C., *Through England on a Side Saddle in the Time of William and Mary*, Field & Tuer, London, 1888

Fitzmaurice, E.G.P., *Life of Shelburne, 1st Marquis of Lansdowne*, Vols I–III, Macmillan & Co., London, 1875

Forster, E.M., *Marianne Thornton*, Edward Arnold, London, 1956

Fortescue, J.B., *The Correspondence of King George III*, Vols I–VI, Macmillan, London, 1928

Fortescue, J.B., *The Manuscripts of J.B Fortescue*, preserved at Dropmore, London, 1892

Fraser, F., *The Unruly Queen*, Macmillan, London, 1996

Fremont-Barnes, G., *The Napoleonic Wars, The Peninsular War 1807–14*, Osprey, Oxford, 2002

Frezier, A., *A Voyage to the South Sea*, London, 1717

Frothingham, P., *Edward Everett Orator and Statesman*, Houghton Mifflin Co., New York, 1925

Furneaux, R., *William Wilberforce*, Hamish Hamilton, London, 1974

Fyfe, C., *A History of Sierra Leone*, Oxford University Press, London, 1962

Gladstone, W.E., *The Gladstone Diaries*, Vols I–II, Clarendon Press, Oxford, 1968

Goldsmith, O., *She Stoops to Conquer*, Belfast, 1773

Gray, J., *An Account of the Manner of Proceeding at the Contested Election, in 1807, Chiefly Relating to the Office of Sheriff*, Wolstenholme, York, 1818

Grimshawe, T., *A Memoir of Rev Leigh Richmond*, London, 1828

Gunning, H., *Reminiscences of the University, Town and County of Cambridge from the Year 1780*, Vols I–II, Bell, London, 1854

Gurney, J., *Familiar Sketch of the Late William Wilberforce*, London, 1838

Hadley, G., *A History of Kingston-upon-Hull*, Briggs, Hull, 1788

Hague, W., *William Pitt the Younger*, HarperCollins, London, 2004

Harcourt, L.V., *The Diaries and Correspondence of the Right Hon George Rose*, Vols I–II, Bentley, London, 1860

Harford, J., *Recollections of William Wilberforce, Esq., M.P. for the County of York During Nearly Thirty Years: with Brief Notices from some of his personal friends and contemporaries*, Longmans, London, 1864

Harris, J., *Diaries and Correspondence of James Harris, First Earl of Malmesbury*, Vols I–IV, Bentley, London, 1845

Harris, R., *Scriptural Researches on the Licitness of the Slave Trade, shewing its conformity with the principles of natural and revealed religion, delineated in the Sacred Writings of the Word of God*, Liverpool, 1788

Hathaway, W.S., *The Speeches of the Right Honourable William Pitt in the House of Commons*, Vols I–IV, Longmans, London, 1806

Hay, D., *Eighteenth Century English Society*, Oxford University Press, Oxford, 1997

Hayward, J. (ed.), *Out of Slavery: Abolition and After*, Cass, London, 1985

Hazlitt, W., *The Spirit of the Age*, Colburn, London, 1825

Heasman, K., *Evangelicals in Action*, Bles, London, 1962

Hempton, D., *Methodism and Politics in British Society 1750–1850*, London, 1984

Hennell, M., *John Venn and the Clapham Sect*, Lutterworth Press, London, 1958

Hennell, M., 'Evangelical Spirituality', *The Westminster Dictionary of Christian Spirituality*, SCM Press, London, 1983

Heyrick, E., *Immediate, not Gradual Abolition: or, an Inquiry into the Shortest, Safest, and Most Effectual Means of Getting Rid of West Indian Slavery*, Hatchard, 1824

Hinde, W., *George Canning*, Collins, London, 1973

Hinde, W., *Castlereagh*, Collins, London, 1981

Hindmarsh, B., *John Newton and the English Evangelical Tradition*, Clarendon Press, Oxford, 1996

Hoare, P., *Memoirs of Granville Sharp*, Vols I–II, Colburn, London, 1828

Hochschild, A., *Bury the Chains*, Macmillan, London, 2005

Holland, Lady, *A Memoir of the Rev. Sydney Smith*, Vols I–II, London, 1855

Howse, E., *Saints in Politics*, Allen & Unwin, London, 1952

Huntington, W., *The Kingdom of Heaven taken by Prayer*, London, 1786

Jackson, G., *Hull in the Eighteenth Century*, Oxford University Press, 1972

Jay, W., *The Autobiography of William Jay, Banner of Truth Trust*, Edinburgh, 1974

Jones, J., *The Mysteries of Opium Reveal'd*, London, 1700

Jupp, P., *Lord Grenville 1759–1834*, Clarendon Press, Oxford, 1985

Katcher, P., *The American War 1812–1814*, Osprey, London, 1990

Klingberg, F., *The Anti-Slavery Movement in England*, Yale University Press, New Haven, 1926

Kolchin, P., *American Slavery 1619–1877*, Penguin, London, 1993

La Trobe, C.I., *Letters to my Children*, London, 1851

Lawson, J., *A Town Grammar School through Six Centuries*, Oxford University Press, 1963

Lecky, W.E.H., *History of England in the Eighteenth Century*, Vols I–VIII, Longmans & Green, London, 1890

Londonderry, R., *Memoirs and Correspondence of Viscount Castlereagh*, Colburn, London, 1850

Lyles, A., *Methodism Mocked*, Epworth Press, London, 1960

Marriott, J., *Castlereagh*, Methuen & Co., London, 1936

Mathieson, W.L., *British Slavery and its Abolition, 1823–1838*, Longmans, London, 1826

Maxwell, H., *The Creevey Papers*, John Murray, London, 1923

Milner, Revd I., *Practical Sermons by the Late Rev. Joseph Milner to which is prefixed An Account of the Life of the Author*, Cambridge, 1801

Milner, Revd I., *The Works of the Late Rev Joseph Milner*, Vol VIII, London, 1812

Milner, M., *Life of Isaac Milner, Dean of Carlisle*, London, 1844

Milward, R., *Wimbledon, Two Hundred Years Ago*, The Milward Press, 1996

Montesquieu, *Esprit des lois*, translated as *The Spirit of the Laws*, by Cohler, Miller & Stone, Cambridge University Press, Cambridge, 1989

More, H., *Thoughts on the Importance of Manners of the Great to General Society*, London, 1788

Morsley, C., *News from the English Countryside 1750–1850*, Harrap, London, 1979

Mullinger, J.B., *St. John's College*, College Histories, Cambridge, 1888

Murray, V., *High Society: A Social History of the Regency Period, 1788–1830*, Viking, London, 1998

Namier, L., *The Structure of Politics at the Accession of George III*, Macmillan, London, 1929

Namier and Brooke, *The House of Commons, 1754–90*, Vols I–IV, London, 1964

Newsome, D., *Parting of Friends*, Murray, London, 1966

Newton, J., *The Journal of a Slave Trader*, Epworth Press, London, 1962

Newton, J., *Memoirs of the Life of Rev William Grimshaw In Six Letters to the Rev Henry Foster*, Greenwood, Haworth, 1865

O'Gorman, F., *Voters, Patrons and Parties: The Unreformed Electoral System of Hanoverian England 1734–1832*, Clarendon Press, Oxford, 1989

Oldfield, J.R., *Popular Politics and British Antislavery: The Mobilisation of Public Opinion Against the Slave Trade, 1787–1807*, Manchester University Press, Manchester, 1995

Overton, J.H., *The Evangelical Revival in the Eighteenth Century*, Longmans, London, 1886

Owen, J., *The History of the Origin and First Ten Years of the British and Foreign Bible Society*, Vols I–II, London, 1816

Paley, W., *The Complete Works of William Paley*, London, 1825

Pereira, J., *The Elements of Materia Medica*, Vol II, London, 1842

Phillips, J., *Electoral Behaviour in Unreformed England*, Princeton University Press, 1982

Picton, J., *Memorials of Liverpool, Historical and Topographical*, Longmans, London, 1873

Pine, L.G., *The Family of Wilberforce or Wilberfoss*, London, 1953

Pollock, Rev J., *Wilberforce*, Constable & Co., London, 1977

Porter, R., *English Society in the Eighteenth Century*, Allen Lane, London, 1982

Porter, D., *The Abolition of the Slave Trade in England, 1784–1807*, Archon, Hamden, 1970

Price, T., *Memoir of William Wilberforce*, 2nd American edition, 1836

Pryme, G., *Autobiographic Recollections of George Pryme*, Cambridge, 1870

Pura, M., *Vital Christianity*, Christian Focus Publications, Toronto, 2003

Pym, D., *Battersea Rise*, Cape, London, 1934

Radzinowicz, L., *A History of English Criminal Law*, Vol III, Steven, London, 1956

Ramsay, J., *An Essay on the Treatment and Conversion of African Slaves in the British Sugar Colonies*, London, 1784

Richardson, J., *The Disastrous Marriage, A Study of George IV and Caroline of Brunswick*, Cape, London, 1960

Rousseau, *Le Contrat social*, translation from Cele, *The Social Contract*, Everyman edition, London, 1968

Rupp, G., *Religion in England 1688–1791*, Clarendon Press, Oxford, 1986

Rush, R., *A Residence at the Court of London*, London, Bentley, 1833

Russell, G.W.E., *The Household of Faith*, Hodder & Stoughton, London, 1902

Russell, Lord J., *Memoirs and Correspondence of Charles J. Fox*, Vols I–II, London, 1853

Russell, Lord J., *Life of Charles J. Fox*, Vols I–III, London, 1859

Sands, P.C., *A History of Pocklington School*, Beverley, Highgate, 1988

Saunders, K.J., *Adventures of the Christian Soul*, Cambridge University Press, Cambridge, 1916

Schama, S., *Rough Crossings*, BBC Books, London, 2005

Scott, J., *A Vindication of the Rev. Joseph Milner*, London, 1834

Selincourt, E., *The Early Letters of William and Dorothy Wordsworth (1787–1805)*, Clarendon Press, Oxford, 1935

Sharp, G., *The Just Limitation of Slavery in the Laws of God*, London, 1776

Shaver, Moorman and Hill, *Letters of William and Dorothy Wordsworth Vol II 1812–1820*, Clarendon Press, Oxford, 1970

Shoemaker, R., *The London Mob*, Hambledon, London, 2004

Sierra Leone Company, *Substance of the Report from the Court of Directors to the General Court of Sierra Leone Company*, J. Phillips, London, 1791

Smith, A., *The Wealth of Nations*, Penguin, London, 1999

Smith, E., *A Queen on Trial*, Sutton, Stroud, 1993

Smith, Revd S., *The Works of The Rev Sydney Smith*, Longmans, London, 1850

Sprague, W.B., *Visits to European Celebrities*, Gould & Lincoln, Boston, 1855

Stanhope, G., *The Life of Charles Third Earl Stanhope*, Longmans, London, 1914

Stanhope, P.H., *Life of the Right Honourable William Pitt*, Vols I–IV, London, 1861

Starbuck, E.D., *The Psychology of Religion*, Scott, London, 1899

Stephen, G., *Anti-Slavery Recollections*, London, 1854

Stephen, J., *The War in Disguise*, Hatchard & Butterworth, London, 1805

Stephen, Sir J., *Essays in Ecclesiastical Biography*, Vols I–II, Longmans, London, 1849

Stirling, A., *Annals of a Yorkshire House*, Vol II, Lane, London, 1911

Taylor and Pringle, *Correspondence of William Pitt, Earl of Chatham*, Vols I–IV, London, 1838–40

Taylor, T., *Biographical Sketch of Thomas Clarkson, M.A. with occasional brief strictures on the misrepresentations of him contained in the Life of William Wilberforce and a concise historical outline of the abolition of slavery*, London, 1839

Teignmouth, Lord C., *Reminiscences of Many Years*, Vols I–II, Edinburgh, 1878

Thomas, H., *The Slave Trade: The Story of the Atlantic Slave Trade, 1440–1870*, Picador, London, 1997

Tickell, J., *The History of the Town and County of Kingston upon Hull*, Lee & Co., Hull, 1798

Timbs, J., *Club Life of London*, Bentley, London, 1866

Tisdall, E., *The Wanton Queen*, Stanley Paul & Co., London, 1939

Townsend, W., *A New History of Methodism*, Hodder & Stoughton, London, 1909

Trevelyan, G., *The Life and Letters of Lord Macaulay*, Vol I, Longmans, London, 1876

Venn, Revd H., *The Life and a Selection from the Letters of the late Rev. Henry Venn MA*, Hatchard, London, 1839

Wade, J., *Extraordinary Black Book*, Effingham Wilson, London, 1831

Wadstrom, C., *Observations on the Slave Trade*, London, 1789

Wakefield, G., *A Letter to W. Wilberforce Esq. on the subject of his late publication [entitled 'a Practical View of the prevailing religious systems,' etc.]*, London, 1797

Walpole, H., *The Letters of Horace Walpole*, Vol VIII, London, 1891

Walpole, S., *The Life of the Rt Hon Spencer Perceval*, Vols I–II, London, 1874

Warter, J., *Selections from the Letters of Robert Southey*, Vol III, Longmans, London, 1856

Warter, J., *Life and Correspondence of Southey*, Vol IV, London, 1849

Watkins and Shoberl, *A Biographical Dictionary of the Living Authors of Great Britain and Ireland*, Colburn, London, 1816

Wearmouth, R., *Methodism and the Common People of the Eighteenth Century*, Epworth Press, London, 1945

Webb, S., *The History of Liquor Licensing in England Principally From 1700 to 1830*, Longmans, London, 1903

Wesley, C., *The Journal of the Rev. Charles Wesley, 1736–1739*, Culley, London, 1909

Wesley, J., *John Wesley's Journal*, Every Age Library, London, 1914

Wesley, J., *Thoughts Upon Slavery*, Hawes, London, 1774

Whiteley, J., *Wesley's England*, Epworth, London, 1938

Wilberforce, A.M., *Private Papers of William Wilberforce*, Fisher Unwin, London, 1897

Wilberforce, R. and S., *Life of Wilberforce*, Vols I–V, John Murray, London, 1838

Wilberforce, R. and S., *Correspondence of William Wilberforce*, Vols I–II, Perkins, Philadelphia, 1841

Wilberforce, W., *A Practical View . . .*, Cadell, London, 1797

Wilberforce, W., *A Letter to His Excellency the Prince of Talleyrand Perigord*, Schulze & Dean, London, 1814

Wilberforce, W., *An Appeal to the Religion, Justice, and Humanity of the Inhabitants of the British Empire, in behalf of the Negro Slaves in the West Indies*, Hatchard's, London, 1823

Wilkinson, T., *Memoirs of His Own Life*, Vol IV, York, 1790

Wilkinson, T., *The Wandering Patentee*, Vol I, York, 1795

Williams, E., *Capitalism and Slavery*, University of North Carolina Press, Chapel Hill, 1944

Willis, T., *Bulletin of the Institute of Historical Research*, no. 44

Winstanley, D.A., *The University of Cambridge in the Eighteenth Century*, Cambridge University Press, Cambridge, 1922

Winstanley, D.A., *Unreformed Cambridge*, Cambridge University Press, Cambridge, 1935

Wrangham, C.E., *East Farleigh and Two Families*, Catterick, 1974

Wraxall, N., *The Historical and the Posthumous Memoirs of Sir Nathaniel William Wraxall 1772–1784*, Vols I–V, Bickers, London, 1884

Wyvill, C., *Political Papers*, Vols I–VI, York, 1794

Yonge, C.D., *The Life and Administration of Robert Bankes, Second Earl of Liverpool*, Vol II, Macmillan & Co., London, 1868

Young, A., *Autobiography*, Smith, Elder & Co., London, 1898

Ziegler, P., *Addington*, Collins, London, 1965

INDEX